An Anthology of Mississippi Writers

AN
ANTHOLOGY OF
MISSISSIPPI
WRITERS

EDITED BY
NOEL E. POLK AND JAMES R. SCAFIDEL

UNIVERSITY PRESS OF MISSISSIPPI
JACKSON · 1979

Copyright © 1979 by the University Press of Mississippi
Manufactured in the United States of America
Designed by James J. Johnson

Library of Congress Cataloging in Publication Data
Main entry under title:
An Anthology of Mississippi Writers.

    Bibliography: p. 529
    1. American literature—Mississippi. I. Polk,
Noel. II. Scafidel, James R.
PS558.M7A5   810'.8'09762   78-14342
ISBN 0-87805-082-5

This volume is sponsored by the
University of Southern Mississippi

Contents

Acknowledgments

It is a pleasure to acknowledge and in this way thank the many people who have contributed their knowledge, time, and interest to the making of this anthology. We are grateful to the following: to Dorothy Twiss, Patty Polk, and Stephanie Rounsaville; to Dr. James Lloyd and the staff of the Mississippi Room at the University of Mississippi; to Dr. Paul Anderson and the staff of the Mississippi Room at the University of Southern Mississippi; to Ron Tomlin and Joanne Bomar and the staff of the Mississippi Department of Archives and History; to Dr. Robert L. Phillips, Jr., and Dr. Hilton Anderson; to Barney McKee of the University Press of Mississippi; to Dr. Charles Moorman of the University of Southern Mississippi; and to Mrs. John Faulkner, Ben Ames Williams, Jr., Leroy Percy, Mrs. Hodding Carter, Elaine Hughes, Dr. John Pilkington, Ruth McDowell Hewlett, and John Schaffner.

A special brand of gratitude is due the following authors who advised us about selections from their work and/or took the time to read, rewrite, revise, or otherwise insure the accuracy of the biographical and bibliographical sketches that accompany the selections: Eudora Welty, Thomas Hal Phillips, Margaret Walker Alexander, Elizabeth Spencer, Shelby Foote, Charles G. Bell, Ellen Douglas, Robert Canzoneri, Charles East, Edgar Simmons, Barry Hannah, Turner Cassity, D. C. Berry, James Whitehead, James Seay, and William Mills. Their contributions to this anthology are inestimable.

In addition, grateful acknowledgments are made to the following:

Margaret Walker Alexander for permission to reprint poems from *Prophets for a New Day*, copyright © 1970 by the Broadside Press.

Charles G. Bell for permission to reprint poems from *Songs for a New America*, © 1953 by the Indiana University Press and 1965 by Norman S. Berg; and from *Delta Return*, © 1956 by Indiana University Press and 1966 by Norman S. Berg.

D. C. Berry for permission to publish "Bass," "Setter" and "Quail" for the first time.

xi

Mrs. Hodding Carter for permission to reprint poems from *The Ballad of Catfoot Grimes*, © 1964 by Doubleday.

Turner Cassity for permission to reprint."The Procurator is Aware That Palms Sweat," "Manchuria 1931," "A Crown for the Kingfish," "Carpenters," "Two Hymns," "In Sydney by the Bridge" from *Steeplejacks in Babel*, published by David R. Godine, © 1973 by Turner Cassity. ·

Mrs. John Faulkner for permission to reprint "Good Neighbors."

Barry Hannah for permission to reprint "Midnight and I'm Not Famous Yet," from *Air Ships*, © 1978 by Alfred A. Knopf.

Harcourt Brace Jovanovich, Inc., for permission to reprint "Journey to the Pyramids," from *Where the Music Was* by Charles East, © 1965.

Harold Matson Company, Inc., for permission to reprint "The Biscuit Eater" by James Street, © 1939.

Harper & Row, Inc., for permission to reprint "The Man Who Was Almost A Man," from *Eight Men* by Richard Wright (World Pub. Co.). Copyright 1940, © 1961 by Richard Wright. Used by Permission of Harper & Row, Publishers, Inc.

Houghton Mifflin Company for permission to reprint "I Just Love Carrie Lee" from *Black Cloud, White Cloud* by Ellen Douglas. Copyright © 1963 by Ellen Douglas; "The Passing" from *The Mystic Adventures of Roxie Stoner* by Berry Morgan. Copyright © 1974 by Berry Morgan; selections from *North Toward Home* by Willie Morris. Copyright © 1967 by Willie Morris.

International Creative Management for permission to reprint "Port of Embarkation" by Elizabeth Spencer, © 1977 by Elizabeth Spencer.

Alfred A. Knopf, Inc. for permission to reprint "Home" from *Lanterns on the Levee* by William Alexander Percy, © 1941 by William Alexander Percy; an excerpt from *The Moviegoer* by Walker Percy, © 1961 by Walker Percy.

Louisiana State University Press for permission to reprint "Watch for the Fox" from *Watch for the Fox* by William Mills, © 1974 by William Mills; "Faulkner," "Bow Down to Stutterers," "Song of the Moth," from *Driving to Biloxi* by J. Edgar Simmons, © 1968; "The Zoo, Jackson, Mississippi, 1960" and "Domains" from *Domains* by James Whitehead, © 1966 by James Whitehead.

New Directions Publishing Corporation for permission to reprint "The Long Stay Cut Short, or, The Unsatisfactory Supper" by Tennessee Williams, from Tennessee Williams, *American Blues*. Copyright, 1946, by Tennessee Williams (Dramatists Play Service, Inc.). Reprinted by permission of New Directions Publishing Corporation. CAUTION: All rights, including professional, amateur, motion picture, recitation, lecturing, public reading, radio and television broadcasting, and the rights of translation into foreign languages, are strictly reserved. Particular emphasis is laid on the question of readings, permission for which must be secured from the author's agent, Bill Barnes, c/o International Creative Management, 40 West 57th Street, New York 10019. All works of Tennessee Williams are subject to royalty, under the laws of the Copyright Union.

Ohio State University Press for permission to publish "To William Faulkner," by Robert Canzoneri, originally published in *Poetry Southeast, 1950–1970*, subsequently included in his collection *Watch Us Pass*; "The Poet Recorded" by Robert Canzoneri, first published in his *Watch Us Pass*, copyright © 1968 by the Ohio State University Press. All rights reserved.

Leroy P. Percy for permission to reprint poems from *Sappho in Levkas, In April Once*, and *The Collected Poems of William Alexander Percy*, © 1915, 1920, and 1943 by William Alexander Percy.

David McKay Company for permission to reprint *Christmas Gift* from the book *Christmas Gift* by Sid Ricketts Sumner. Copyright © 1960 by Sid Ricketts Sumner. Reprinted by permission of the David McKay Company, Inc.

Thomas Hal Phillips for permission to reprint "A Man Named Victor" from his *Search for a Hero*, © 1950. Published by Holt, Rinehart and Winston.

Random House, Inc., for permission to reprint "Mississippi" from *Essays Speeches & Public Letters* by William Faulkner, ed. James B. Meriwether, © 1966. Published by Random House.

R. L. Rosen Associates for permission to reprint "The Sacred Mound" from *Jordan County* by Shelby Foote, © 1953 by Shelby Foote. Originally published by the Dial Press.

Russell & Volkening, Inc., for permission to reprint "Some Notes on River Country" by Eudora Welty, © 1944 by Eudora Welty, and "Women!!! Make Turbans in Own Home!" © 1978 by Random House, Inc.

Mr. John Schaffner for permission to reprint the poems of Hubert Creekmore from *Personal Sun* and *The Long Reprieve* by Hubert Creekmore, © 1940 and 1946.

Charles Scribner's for permission to reprint the excerpt from *The Pavilion* by Stark Young, © 1951.

J. Edgar Simmons for permission to reprint "Osiris and the Sacraments of Erotic Hesitation," first published in *New Directions in Prose and Poetry, No. 20*, James Laughlin, ed. Copyright © 1968 by New Directions Publishing Corporation.

Wesleyan University Press for permission to publish "Let Not Your Hart Be Truble" from *Let Not Your Hart* by James Seay, © 1970; and "Naming the Moon," "It All Comes Together Outside the Restroom in Hogansville," "Natural Growth," and "Patching Up the Past with Water" from *Water Tables* by James Seay, © 1974.

James Whitehead for permission to publish "He Records a Little Song For a Smoking Girl," "About a Year After He Got Married He Would Sit Alone In An Abandoned Shack In a Cotton Field Enjoying Himself," "A Local Man Remembers Betty Fuller," "A Local Contractor Flees His Winter Trouble And Saves Some Lives in a Knoxville Motel Room," and "The Delta Chancery Judge After Reading *Aubrey's Brief Lives*." Copyright 1978 by James Whitehead.

Textual Note

The texts of the selections in this anthology are faithful reproductions of the published text we have determined to be closest to the author's final intentions. Living authors have been queried about these texts, and some have even made revisions and/or corrections to them. Where this has been the case we have made the corrections with no indication save a statement of the fact in the biographical introduction. Otherwise we have made no changes whatsoever, except for clear and undeniable typographical errors, which have been silently emended. There aren't very many of those. A few texts are here published from typescripts furnished to us by the authors.

Preface

"To have even one genius up an anthology's sleeve is very fine," Eudora Welty once wrote.[1] To have more than one would be better. To have several is only a little short of puddle-wonderful. This one, we feel, has more than its share of geniuses because Mississippi, for whatever combination of reasons, has managed to contribute much more than its "share" to the literature of the United States. Indeed, we agree with Robert L. Phillips, Jr.'s, suggestion that Mississippi writers have been so prominent that the state "has played a significant role in shaping the literary imagination of twentieth century America."[2] It is simply incredible to consider even the sheer number of writers that in one way or another are products of this state, not to say the number of really first-rate ones: Nobel Prize winner William Faulkner; Pulitzer Prize winners Eudora Welty, Hodding Carter, and Tennessee Williams; National Book Award winner Walker Percy; as well as a host of established writers of national and international literary significance—Stark Young, Richard Wright, Elizabeth Spencer, Irwin Russell, and Shelby Foote—and younger writers like Barry Hannah, whose work is being widely read and prominently reviewed, looming large on the literary horizon.

Many reasons, naturally, have been advanced for this literary phenomenon. Miss Welty has frequently suggested a number of reasons why so many good writers have come out of the South—the influence of "place," the oral tradition of story-telling, the strength of family and community relationships[3]—and others have been mentioned, variously, the legacy of tragedy left by the Civil War, the effects of fundamentalist religion, the moral sense, and the sense of history. All of these are undeniably related to this remarkable output in ways that seem generally true of *southern* writers; but they do *not* explain why, when the same conditions existed simultaneously and for all practical purposes identically in other southern states, the same outpouring of superior literature did not also occur in Alabama, Louisiana, Georgia, South Carolina, and Tennessee.

xv

Even Shelby Foote's shrewd observation that Greenville became a literary center for no other reason than the example of William Alexander Percy—"If you had a man in the town who had written and published books, writing and publishing books did not seem an impossible thing"[4]—breaks down if one tries to generalize it, extend it beyond Foote's limited application to Greenville: other states have had that example, too. That is, everything we can think of that can be said about Mississippi—its economics, politics, history, religion, education—can generally be said of all other southern states; and yet nowhere else has that combination of elements produced what Mississippi has produced. As Mr. Compson said, of another attempt to understand a very peculiar circumstance, "It just does not explain."[5]

Of course what we hoped to do, when we began planning this anthology, was precisely to explain it, to explain why Mississippi, of all states, should have produced such an unusual number of writers and a body of work unequalled by any other single state (and most countries, too), in either quantity or quality. We began reading with an eye to discovering what, if anything, these writers had in common with each other. What we discovered was, very little save a Mississippi background, and even in that they reflected great diversity—doctors, a governor, Rhodes scholars, the son of a United States senator, a judge, a sharecropper, farmers, professors, housewives, a historian, several editors and journalists, a preacher, a musician, a diplomat—and we found that diversity reflected in a wide variety of subjects, themes, and styles, from the raucous backwoods dialect humor of William C. Hall, Alexander G. McNutt (the "Turkey Runner"), and Henry Clay Lewis to the urban sophistication of Walker Percy, from the romantic poetry of Eliza Jane Poitevent Nicholson to the classical meters of William Alexander Percy, and on to the Whitmanesque verse of J. Edgar Simmons and the terse, laconic poems of D. C. Berry, James Seay, and James Whitehead.

We also expected to find twentieth-century Mississippi authors, like a lot of southern writers, operating under the intoxicating influence, and therefore in the manner, of William Faulkner. What we found was a remarkable independence of him, which suggested to us that Mississippi writers, in their own unique voices, have generally shared Miss Welty's feeling that living in the same state with Faulk-

ner was "like living near a mountain," with her modest but clear im-
plication that mountains live near other mountains too.[6] The best of
Mississippi's writers seem not to have been dominated by anything
save their own particular literary demons, their need to understand
their world in terms of their own, and not somebody else's, experience of it.

In short, we have not been able to discover the perplexing
"why," if indeed there is one, of Mississippi literature; and are now
somewhat inclined to ascribe the phenomenon to the air Mississippians breathe and the water they drink—which is both as facetious
and as serious an answer as we can devise. Clearly, it is in the writers
themselves that any real answer lies, and, clearly, that is what matters. If there is any single common element in their backgrounds,
themes, or styles to explain it, we do not know it. We are content,
finally, merely to be grateful for it.

Impressive as Mississippi's literature is, there has never been
until now any effort to present it as a body. Mississippians have always had a strong sense of place (we memorize the names of the
eighty-two counties in grammar school) and of history (we have a
passion for museums and monuments), but, maybe because our
literary culture hasn't ever been made available to us as an entity, we
have tended to overlook the Harris Dicksons and the Irwin Russells
and many other writers of our literary heritage. It is with great
pleasure that we present selections from thirty-eight of them here.
We acknowledge that we have had to leave out many fine writers,
and we accept beforehand any criticisms of both our exclusions and
inclusions: preliminary work on a biographical dictionary of Mississippi writers, now being compiled under the direction of James
Lloyd at the University of Mississippi, has resulted in an imposing
list of over 1,600 Mississippians who have published a book of one
kind or another—fiction, poetry, history, drama, scholarship—and
it simply was not possible to include everybody. Concentrating on
fiction, poetry, and autobiography, we have selected from this
number what we think are the best and most representative writers
of nearly a century and a half of Mississippi's literary culture. If we
have managed to suggest by this small grouping Mississippi's great
contribution to Southern and to American literature, and if we have

stimulated our readers to go beyond the collection to see for themselves how fruitful the fields are, we are happy. We will have accomplished the chief task of the anthologist, which is to reconnoiter, survey, and describe the terrain so that others may develop it.

NOTES

1. "Ghoulies, Ghosties, and Jumbees," *New York Times Book Review*, September 24, 1944, p. 5.

2. Robert L. Phillips, Jr. (ed.), *A Climate for Genius* (Jackson: Mississippi Library Commission, 1976), i.

3. See William F. Buckley, Jr., "The Southern Imagination: An Interview with Eudora Welty and Walker Percy," *Mississippi Quarterly*, XXVI (Fall, 1973), 493–516, for example.

4. Phillips (ed.), *Climate for Genius*, 18.

5. William Faulkner, *Absalom, Absalom!* (New York: Random House, 1936), 100.

6. Ruth M. Vande Kieft, *Eudora Welty* (New York: Twayne, 1963), 7.

An Anthology of Mississippi Writers

Pseudonymous Fiction

Many sketches belonging to the literary tradition called the Humor of the Old Southwest were pseudonymous. Using pennames typical of this kind of writing ("Ruff Sam," "Delta," "Yazoo," "Obe Oilstone"), Mississippians contributed scores of humorous pieces to such newspapers as the Natchez *Mississippi Free Trader and Natchez Weekly Gazette* and the Natchez *Courier*, the Vicksburg *Whig*, and the New Orleans *Delta*, and published a number of their tales in William T. Porter's New York sporting journal, *The Spirit of the Times*.

The three selections reprinted here are typical examples of the genre, which is said to have developed from A. B. Longstreet's *Georgia Scenes* (1835): Obe Oilstone (identified as P. B. January), "Pulling Teeth in Mississippi," *The Big Bear of Arkansas* (Philadelphia, 1845); "Ruff Sam's Bear Fight," *The Spirit of the Times*, March 4, 1848; and Mike Shouter, "Expedishun to the Lower Rejin of Loozeana," first published in the New Orleans *Delta*, November 23, 1856, is reprinted from Arthur Palmer Hudson's anthology, *Humor of the Old Deep South* (New York: Macmillan, 1936).

Selections by pseudonymous writers in ante-bellum Mississippi appear in Hudson and in Robert L. Phillips (ed.), *Antebellum Mississippi Stories* (Jackson: Mississippi Library Commission, 1976).

2

Pulling Teeth In Mississippi

"Uncle Johnny" [Obe Oilstone]

Election day *is* a day away out here in the woods, and notwithstanding we have precincts scattered throughout the counties, yet the county seat is the place at which most do congregate, for the triple purpose of voting, spreeing, and lastly, for the peculiar pleasure of witnessing the beginning—ay, "the opening of the ball" of the "Fall Fighting Campaign," which interesting event is usually postponed to that exciting period, when party excitement and individual misunderstanding, leave a man very little hesitancy to "pitch" into his neighbour; this comes not oftener than two years—often enough, however, for "regular work."

Having the common anxiety to see the first "regular despatch," I arrived early at Fayette, (our county seat,) on the 4th November last, when and where I had the good luck to see the campaign open; the anxiety, among the numerous spectators, to continue the sport, was really commendable. Both claimed the victory, but the ring declared "a dead match;" another heat was promised by the defendant—I immediately staked a hat on him "what got gouged."

Whilst in the crowd, a well-known voice addressed me, "Hallo, boy! come over here! How are you? I say, it's your treat, now, *certain*. Come in, men."

"Certainly, Uncle Johnny," said I—"pleasure always to treat *you*."

"Me? I'm —— if you don't treat the whole crowd! Rosser, tell *all* them men to come in! *Hyena's breakin' chains and things!* Eh! You thot I'd never see a paper, did you? Well, well, I don't care a cuss about it myself, but the fact is, 'Old Iron's' in town now, and he says when he sees you thar'll be *another* Dog Fite; so if you see him gittin' anyways high, *whar's your hoss?* Well, well, jist keep out'n his way. Is you seen Wills sense them fellers was a pullin' his tooth?"

"What fellows?" was the immediate inquiry.

"Oh, ho! and so, my boy, you aint said nothin' about it, eh! Well that is rich, fond of *ritin'* stories, but never *tells* 'em, eh! Well, I'll"—

"Uncle Johnny, don't tell tales out of school, if you please. Recollect you should do unto others as"—

"I *am* done by,—that's a fact, by gracious, so I'll jist out with it.

"You see, 'twas the night arter the big dinner up here, and Wade got a crowd of youngsters to go home with him for some *fun*. Jist afore they gits to Wade's they overtakes me, and I took him up at his first offer to go by too—he keeps good licker, Wade does. Well, arter supper I seen the boys was in for a frolic. I took two or three hands with 'em at cards, and after punishin' sum of the old stuff, I lays down. Well, I spose it wanted about two hours to day, when I was roused with the wakenest noise I ever riz to. I can't hardly tell how they *was* all fixed in that room, but thar lay Wills flat on his back on the floor, a big nigger a holt of each hand, holdin' him spred out—the doctor settin' straddle of his brest, in his shirt tail, with a pair of bullet moles in his hands, tryin' to pull out one of his teeth! Then thar sat Henry B——nes, from Clairborne county, at his head, a holdin' the candle, and every now and then he would reach one hand over and hyst Wills's upper lip for the doctor to get the moles onto his tooth. Henry had a big pair of goat locks under his chin, and in peepin' over at the operration he'd git 'em right over the candle and they'd *swinge*. I seed him keep turnin' up his nose like he smelt somethin' a burnin', but he never dreamed it was *his* whiskers. Wills was a gruntin' powerful, and what between gruntin' and the hiccups, I thort he'd strangle. Major Bob was thar, too, and he had on a wonderful short shirt for a big fat man. He swore he could beat that doctor a pullin' teeth and he was hollerin for his 'insterments!' (a hammer and nail) to *knock* it out! They got the nail, and as they could'nt find a hammer, in they fetched a pair of shoemaker's pinchers that's got a sort of hammer on one side. The doctor dropt the moles, for he found out that every time he'd *jerk*, they'd *slip*, so he sings out for the pinchers—swore they were his favorite insterments—always used 'em—beat pullicans to h—!

"Well, you never did see a drunken set so busy about a serious job! Every one was in ded ernest tryin' to help Wills, and *he* was a takin' on wonderful, that's a fact! The doctor set to work with the pinchers, and there sot Henry with the pleasinest countenance (and when he gits three sheets spred, and is *tryin'* to unfarl the fourth, he

can jist out-laugh the univarse, or I'll borrow a hat to go home with!)
there sot Henry reddy to hist Wills's upper lip when the doctor
would stagger that way. Well, he got reddy—Henry histed his lip,
and arter two or three false jerks, he found the hammer was on the
wrong side of the pinchers for *that* tooth, so he turns in and asks
Wills on which side the akin tooth *was?* He said he did'nt know!—So
he fastens 'em onto a *sound* tooth on tother side. But the Major had
got impatient, so he riz—pulled his shirt as low as he could git it,
(and then it did'nt hide nothin') picks up the tongs, walks round, and
puts one foot on Wills's brest before the doctor, and says he, 'Doctor, you've been sittin' cross that man for three hours! You can't pull
no tooth, nor never could! Git up, man, git up! I can jist take *these*
tongs, and pull his tooth in half the time.' But he had'nt a chance to
try, for Henry, who had been leanin' over to Wills's lip, puts his chin
right over the candle, and afore he knowed it, his whiskers was in a
big blaze! He drops the candle with a 'hooze' right into Wills's
face—the nigger let go and jumpt—Bob and the doctor fell in a
lump, tongs and all. Wills riz to his all-fours and made for the gallery,
with the stranglinest hiccups I ever heard! I follered the man out—I
rally thort he was stranglin' to deth,—but he had riz up by the gallery post, and was a heavin' and settin'! It beat all tooth pullins I ever
seen. Says I, 'Curnel, what's you doin?' says he, 'tryin' to throw up
(hic) that d— tooth! I think—I must'er *swallered it!'*

"Well, I looks around for *this* boy, and not seein' him, I inquires,
but they had bin so busy they hadn't missed him. Think's I, I'll take a
turn around and see if I can't find him a holdin' up the fence, somewhar! Well, soon as I got out of the noise in the house, I hear somebody hollerin'; and there he was, sure enough, huggin' a red oak,
three feet thru. 'Well,' says I, 'What's you doin here?' 'Uncle
Johnny, come here—for God sake come here,' says he, 'and put a rail
up agin this tree! I'm mighty tired,' says he, 'it's right easy now; but
when the wind blows, O Lord, but its mity heavy—hurrah, here it
comes,' says he, and he spread himself to it as he'd bin holdin' up the
univarse! Ha! ha! 'twas rich, to see him surgin' up agin that tree to
hold it up, and beggin me to prop it up with a rail. I gits a rail, and
leans it agin the tree. 'Uncle Johnny,' says he, 'had'nt you better git
another? It's a mity big tree and ruff at that.' 'Let go,' says I, ''twont

fall—these rails 'll hold it—let go!' Soon as he let go, slam bang he went agin the pickets—knocked some off, and went clean thru!—'G—*durn* them pickets! they bin tryin' to run over me all night,' says he, pickin' himself up mity awkward. I couldn't hold in, he talked so natral. 'Why,' says I, 'you run over *them!*' 'Oh, no,' says he, 'what with holdin' that tree up, and gittin' round on t'other side at the *same* time, to git out in the pickets' way, is nily took all the flesh off 'n my arms—that's proof, aint it?' Well, I could'nt begin to lead him to the house, so jist got behind and pushed him. He's a little man, but you ort'er bin thar if you aint never seen a man walk *tall;* every time he stept, his legs went out to right angles. I say, how's your arms got?"

"That'll do now, Uncle Johnny—treat, won't you?"

"Now you hit me. Come in men, what'll you pull your tooth with?"

Ruff Sam's Bear Fight

MR. PRINTER—I'm rite from the backwoods of Mississippi, and as I told you onct 'bout my fite at Bony Vista, the folks have been pesterin' me to death to tell 'em sumthin' of the bar an' panther hunts I've had, how meny I kilt and wether I was kilt or no, 'twill I've gis' determined to tell 'em of a rale swingin' hunt I had last October.

You see, I left these parts in Ceptember and went strate hum. I arriv thar, and arter shakin' hans with all the wimin folkes and kissin' all the galls, the boys raised a bar hunt, and nuthin' would do but I must go 'long. Thar was Bill Beenyard and Long Jim—but that is no use in givin' names, for you doesn't know 'em—depend on it, thar was a parcel on 'em. We all got reddy at Squire Startises, at the forks of the road, kalkulatin' we'd start out next mornin' by crack of day. Sure nuff next mornin' kum—I shuck myself an' got out in the yard, kommenced blowin' for the dogs. The other boys haint much usen to huntin', so they was a snorin' 'bout that time, I blow'd again and here kum the dogs a howlin' and wagin' thar tales, an' a lookin' so eager—but I hadn't orter sed that Boss was a waggin' his tale, cause he got it bit off onct by a darned old she tiger cat, an' taint never grow'd out yit. The boys kum a stretchin' themselves, and axed me what all fired thunder that was. You see they hearn my horn and took it for thunder—I'm prodeegeous on a wind insterment an' I sorter skeered 'em—but I insured 'em it wouldn't rain nor nuthin', an' everything bein' fixed off we put. They wanted me to go long with the krowd, but I wasn't goin' to do nuthin' of the kind, so I tole 'em they'd fine me at the big bend in the kreek, an' then struck for the kane brake.

Thar haint never been a place yit whar Ruff Sam couldn't git throo. I whistled for Boss and giff him a few injunkshuns, such as, "Look him up, sir-r-r!" "Mine what you 'bout, you bob-taled raskel!"—sorter urgin' of him on—didn't mean to hurt his feelins, an' he noed it. You ort to ha' seen him—Lord, how he riggled himself—a camellin on the groun'—a kockin' his ears up, a histenin his tale, and a whinin' an' cuttin' setch numbersome kapers, that you'd ha' thot he had tread in a wass ness. He seed I wasn't arter no turkeys nor deer, for he never let on he noticed 'em.

We had pushed throo 'bout a mile of kane break when I began to *feel* a varmint of sum sort nigh me, and Boss felt him too. 'Twas powerful dark—the sun wasn't more an up, an' it didn't stan' no chance for the kane, 'twas so 'mazin' thick. "What is ail you, you skoundrel?" sez I, a turnin' roun' to Boss. Thar he stood, his legs spraddled out and his grizzly sides a swellin' in an' out like a pair of bellowses. "What on the airth is the matter?" sez I, agin, a gittin' mad—I patted him on the back an' a coaxed him; 'twant no use—he wouldn't budge. That made me rale feerce, and, rip, rip, diff! I gin it to him in the ribs with my fist shet up. "Now what ails you?" sez I. Boss looked at me an' said, jest as plane as a dog kin say, he was skeered. I knowd sumthin most orful was kummin', or Boss would never ha' been skeered. I stopped an' considered, an' I mout ha' taken a little sumthin' what I have 'long in a goard; but I won't say I did. I studdied on an' speclated, an' I mout ha' taken a nuther drop or so, but I wont swar to it. I looks at Boss, an' sez I, "Boss, is you goin' to foller me, or is you not?" He wanted to sodger out of the skrape, an' I seed it in him; his har was stanin' strate out all over him. Sez I—"If its a whale you shall fite him, you kowardly Mexikin raskil!" You must ha' knowd I was savage, or I never would a called my dog a Mexikin! Suddently I hearn sumthin', an' turnin' I seed one of the most stonishin' big she bars that ever wor'd fur standin' afore me, within ten foot. When she seed me a lookin' at her she grunted, as much as to say—"Who's afeered!" Sez I, "Say your prayers quick; I wants your hide!" and lets drive with my rifle. Jest as I fired she thro'd her head round, an' it took her in the shoulder. That riled her tremendious, and she kum at me afore I kould say who's who. I looked round and seed Boss a watchin' on close by, jest as the kritter klosed in with me. "Charge her in the rair!" I shouted out to Boss. Zip! I kum down with the butt eend of my rifle, smashin' it to pieces. She shuck her head an' grabbed for me; but, feelin' the enimy a worryin' her in the rair, she wheeled. That gin me time to git out my old bowie-knife, and I flanked her with it rale quick. She manoovered an kum to the charge agin in a bilin' swet, bitin' an' showin' fite in dead airnest. I was a fallin' back for a new position as my foot slipped, an ke fetchup! I kum on my back! I thot the thing was out then, an kommenced thinkin' 'bout kingdom kum. She got me in her arms rale sure nuff, and if you say she didn't squeeze me, you dosn't know nuthin' tall 'bout it. I tried to breathe, but the wind in me was so skase I kouldn't. She hugged me so tite that my fingers got as strate as stix; my head begind to swell 'bout the size of a whisky barl, an' I sorter thot I mite bust, or brake, or sumthin', if she presd me much harder. Presently I hearn her a tremblin, an' then she loosend her holt an' rolled over on her side. I laid still 'twill I got to my usual size, and then riz up to look for Boss. I was willin' to quit. Thar was Boss, one of the bisiest dogs you ever seed, a findin' what she was made outen—he naterally had his head clene in the hole I had made in her with "old bowie." The bar was dead, an' me an' Boss had licked her!

I was a skinin' of her when the boys kum up, an' sech a nuther spree we had arter we got to the Squire's I never spects to have agin.

I'm off to-morrow for up the Drink.

Yours 'twill bym-by,   RUFF SAM.

N. O. Picayune.

Expedishun to the Lower Rejin of Loozeana

By Mike Shouter

TICKEER TAVERN, YAZOO CO., MISS., NOV. 18, 1856.

To the Editor of the "Coon Run Banner."

The last time you was down in our range, I happened to let it leak out that I was 'bout gwine on a expedishun to the lower rejin of Loozeana, to that sitty of unhearn-of wikkedness, frogs, katfish and Frenchmen, called Orleans, of which so much has been hearn, spoke, and writ, and the half not told; an' soon as you hearn me say I was gwine thar, up you jumps, an' sez you to me, sez you—Uncle Mike, sez you, do write to us all about what you sees, an' I'll print it in the Banner.

Well, sez I, I will, on one condishin.

What's that, sez you?

It's this here, sez I—that you won't make any mistakes in the spellin', nor put in none of yure commense in 2 the tex'.

Very well, sez you, I won't, by hokey.

Good as tater, then sez I, I'll write—an' if you've a stray quarter 'bout you, we'll take a drink on the stren'th of it. So we adjourned over to the nearest dead-fall, tuck a whoppin' horn of Ball Face, an' you paid for it like a white head. However, this ain't the pint—so we'll jest proseed in the nateral way.

Well, when everything was fixed up, off I started.

When I got down to Satartia, waitin' for the steamboat to come along, sez I to myself, sez I, I ixpect that are tarnation boat will be 'bout a year 'fore she gits here, but I hadn't more'n got the words outen my mouth, when here she come, a snortin' an' a blowin' like a bar an' a whole team of dogs atter him, tearin' threw a cane-brake. Well, toreckly she hauled up to the side of the bank to take on some cotton, an' put off a few bar'ls of whisky, an' I went aboard as sassy as a meat-axe, an' struttin' 'bout dex as large as life. Several fellers from my neck of woods was gwine along with me, an' soon as I got on, they jumps on too, an' thar we was, a whole team of us. In about a minit the boat she put off, an' jest as we was gittin out of site of the town, I don't b'leeve I ever felt so bad in all my born days: For, thar was the tops of the houses—7 or 8 of them in a bunch—fast reseding from the site, an' the pickteresk view of the gable end of Bill Piers's grocery dwindlin' down to a pint—of which, alas! I was about to look on it, prehaps, for the last time! The site was more than I could stand, an' my pheelinx (too deep for expreshun) was about to bust out at my eyes, when a sentiment lower down, in the way of a drought in the stomach, absorbed the moisture in my eyelids,—an' I was dry as a powder-horn! Boys, sez I, look here! We've been on this dug-out 'bout a coon's age, an' I ain't hearn one of you say "treat" yet! With that, Jo Cole sed he had a few bushels of corn left at home yet, and as long as that lasted, he'd be dad burned if Uncle Mike should suffer for a drink. So we walked down to the bar, an' tuk a horn all round. Then we walked out on deck, whar the Cap'n of the boat was standin' (he was one of the nicest fellers you ever see) chawin' backer an' cussin' the deck hands in the most bewtiful style you ever hearn, an' sez I, Cap'n, s'pose we take a drink? An' we tuck it.

Then we went out on the guards, front of the wheel-house, to take a look at the alleygaters an' the cypress trees, an' the long moss, an' the bull-frogs sportin' from bank to bank; an' then we went in agin, an' we all tuck a drink.

In about a minit or 2, a gentlemun with store clothes on, an' a whoppin' site of har under his nose, cum up to our crowd, an' sez he, "gentlemen, 'spose you jine me in a drink?" So we tuck another small horn all round.

Then the gentlemun with the har under his nose an' the store clothes on, sez he to me—as I was the oldest man of the party, an' the cutest lookin' of all of em—sez he to me, "thar's a sight of trees about here, an' cane-breaks, an' a great scarcity of houses; an' sez he, it strikes me this must be a great country for *game?*"

"Yes," sez I, "one of the greatest you ever see; you can have any kind of game you like, from Sunday mornin' to Saturday night."

"You *bag* a great deal then?" sez he.

"Yes," sez I, "all that comes in reach; an' I, for my part, never pretends to quit till my bag is chock full, an' my briches pockets, too, fit to bust," sez I.

"What kind of arms is most in use?" sez he. "Pistols and bowie-knives," sez I!

"The deuce you say," sez he; "whar I cum from they uses mostly rifles and double-barrel fowling pieces!"

"Yes," sez I, "that's the fashion in some places whar they like to take it at long taw, so as to keep out ov danger; but I, for myself, when it comes to close quarters, likes pistols and bowie knives."

"When I was in India," sez he, "whar we amused ourselves in the jungles, an' had sometimes to fight the tiger, pistols was in great demand."

"Yes," sez I, "nothin' like pistols for fightin' the tiger, an' a bowie knife in case of a accident; for then, if he happens to claw you a little too strong, you can jest show him the weapons till he 'turns' to suit you, an' you are bound to win!"

"So you have the tiger, too," sez he, "an' pray what other kind of game have you?"

"Well," sez I, "the 'tiger' * is in genully considered the best, an' then we have poker an' eucre, an' a occasional game of 'seven up' or 'old sledge!' " Moar nex time, an'

Yourn till deth,
MIKE SHOUTER.

*—By the term "Tiger," Mike means "the game of Farro."

(1819–1865)

William C. Hall

William C. Hall, born in Yazoo City in 1819, is said to have attended Transylvania University in Kentucky and to have worked as a newspaper man in New Orleans. Hall's five "Yazoo Sketches," published anonymously in the New Orleans *Delta* 1849–1850, center around one Mike Hooter, a Yazoo City resident whom Hall makes into something of a religious frontier hero. Three of the sketches were reprinted in William T. Porter's *Spirit of the Times*, but it was not until the twentieth century that their author was actually known. Hall may have returned to Yazoo City to live, for he died there in 1865.

The following sketch is reprinted from T. A. Burke (ed.), *Polly Peablossom's Wedding* (1851).

How Sally Hooter Got Snake-Bit

A YAZOO SKETCH.

As our readers will discover, the following mirth-provoking recital is
from the life of our old friend, Mike Hooter, whose bear-hunting
exploits are spoken of in a previous story. Mike is a *team* and no mistake, and we only wish we knew to whom to return our thanks for
the hearty laughs we have enjoyed while reading this account of Sally's adventure with the snake.

OUR OLD ACQUAINTANCE, Mike Hooter, made another visit to
town last week, and being, as he supposed, beyond the hearing of his
brethren in the church, (for be it remembered, that Mike is of pious
inclining, and a ruling elder in the denomination of Methodists,)
concluded that he would go on a 'bust.' Having sold his crop of cotton
and fobbed the 'tin,' forth sallied Mike with a 'pocket full of rocks,'
and bent on a bit of a spree. After patronizing all the groceries, and
getting rather mellow, he grew garrulous in the extreme, and forth-
with began to expatiate on his wonderful exploits. After running
through with a number of 'Pant'er' and 'Bar fights,' and several 'wolf
disputes,' he finally subsided into the recital of events more nearly
appertaining to members of his family. "That Yazoo," said Mike, "is
the durndest hole that ever came along. If it a'n't the next place to no
whar, you can take my head for er drinkin gourd—you can, an' as for
that ar devil's camp ground, what they calls Satartia, if this world was
er kitchen, it would be the slop hole, an 'er mighty stinkin one at
that! I pledge you my word, it comes closer bein' the jumpin off place
than any I ever hearn tell on. Talk about Texas. It an't nothin' to
them Yazoo hills. The etarnalest out-of-the way place for bar, an'
panters, an' wolfs, an' possums, an' coons, an' skeeters, an' nats, an'
hoss flies, an' cheegers, an' lizzards, an' frogs, an' mean fellers, an'
drinkin' whiskey, an' stealin' one-anothers' hogs, an' gittin' corned,
an' swappin' hosses, an' playin' h–ll generally, that ever you did see!
Pledge you my word, 'nuff to sink it. An' as for snakes! whew! don't
talk! I've hearn tell of the Boa Constructor, an' the Annagander, an'
all that kind er ruptile what swollers er he-goat whole, an' don't care
er switch uv his tail for his horns; an' I see the preacher tell 'bout

Aaron's walkin' stick what turned itself into er sarpent, an' swoller'd up ever-so many other sticks, an' rods, an' bean poles, an' chunks o' wood, an' was hungry yet—an' all that kinder hellerbelloo, but that's all moonshine. Jist wait er minit till you've hearn 'bout the snakes what flourishes up 'bout my stompin' ground, an' how one uv um come precious nigh chawin' up my datter Sal, an' if you don't forgit evrything you ever know'd, then Mike Hooter's the durndest liar that ever straddled a fence rail. Jeeminy, criminy! Jest to see him, one uv them ar great big, rusty rattlesnakes, an' hear him shake that ar tale uv hizzen! I tell you what, if you didn't think all the peas in my corn field was er spillin in the floor, thar aint no 'simmons! Talk about the clouds burstin an' the hail rattling down in er tin pan! Why 'taint er patchin to it! Cracky! its worse nor er young earthquake—beats h–ll!

Now, I don't valley er snake no more nor er she bar in suckin time—'specially er rattlesnake, cause you see it's er vurmin what always rattles his tail 'fore he strikes, an' gives you time to scoot out'n the way, but the wimmin folks an' my gal Sally is always, in generally, the skeerdest in the world uv 'em. I never seed but one woman what wouldn't cut up when er snake was 'bout, an' that was ole Misses Lemay, an' she didn't care er dog on bit for all the sarpints that ever cum er 'long. That old gal was er hoss! Pledge you my word I b'leeve she was pizen!—couldn't be no other way. Didn't never hear how that ole petticoat bit the snake? Well, I'll tell you.

She went out one day an' was er squattin' down, pickin' up chips, an' the first thing she know'd she got onto the whappinest, biggest, rustiest yaller moccasin that ever you shuck er stick at, an' bein' as how she was kinder deaf, she didn't hear him when he 'gin to puff an' blow, and hiss like. The fust thing she knowed he bit her, *slap*—the all-firedest, biggest kinder lick! You orter seen that old gal, how she fell down, an' rolled, an' waller'd, an' tumbled 'bout and holler'd nuff, an' screamed, an' prayed, an' tried to sing er sam, and played h–ll generally! You'd er thought the very yearth was er cummin to an eend! Then she begin hollerin' for help. Sez she, Misses Hooter, cum here an' kill this here snake! Well, my wife run out and fotch the old 'oman in the house an' gin her some whiskey, an' she tuk it like milk. Torectly she sorter cum to herself, and sez my wife to her—sez she to Misses Lemay, sez she—"Misses Lemay, what hurts you?"

"Snake-bit!" sez she.

"Whar 'bouts?" sez I.

"Never mind," sez she—"snake bit!"

"But Misses Lemay!" sez I, "tell me whar he bit you, so as we may put somethin' to it."

Sez she, lookin' kinder glum, and turnin' red in the face—sez she to me, "It don't want nuthin' to it: I'm snake-bit, an' taint none er your bizziness whar."

With that I smelt a mice, and commenced larfin. You orter hearn me holler! If I didn't think I'd er bust my biler, I wish I may never see Christmas! I ain't larfed so much since the time John Potter got on the bar's back without no knife, an' rode him 'round, like er hoss, and was skeer'd to get off! I give you my word I farly rolled!

Soon as the ole 'oman 'gin to open her eyes, an' I see thar warnt nuthin' much the matter with her, my wife she grabbed up the tongs an' went out to kill the snake, an' I follered. When I see the reptile, sez I to my wife, jest wait er minit, sez I. 'Taint no use killin' him— he's past prayin' for! I pledge you my word he was as dead as Billy-be-d—d! "What made him die?" sez my wife to me. Don't know, sez I—'spose he couldn't stand it. Torectly Mat Read he cum up, an' when he hearn what had been goin' on, he was so full er larf his face turned wrong side out'ards, and sez he—"Poisoned, by golly!"

That ole 'oman aint been skeer'd uv er snake sense, an' goes out huntin' 'em reglar. I told her one day, sez I, Misses Lemay, sez I, I'll give you the best bunch of hog's bristles I've got to brush your teeth with, if you'll tell me how not to git skeer'd uv er snake! She didn't say nare a word, but she turned 'round an' took me kerbim right 'tween the eyes! I tell you what, it made me see stars. I aint sed snake to her since.

Howsever, that ain't tellin' you how the sarpint kinder chawed up my darter Sal. I'll tell you how 'twas. You see there was gwine to be a mity big camp meetin' down at Hickory Grove, an' we all fixed up to go down an' stay er week, an' my wife, she looked up everything 'bout the house, an' all sorts of good things—bacon, an' possum fat, an' ash cake, an' a great big sausenger, 'bout as big as your arm, an' long enuff to eat er week—'cause, she said Parson Dilly loved sausengers the best in the world. Well, when we got there, I went to the basket what had the vittals in it, to git somethin' to eat, but the sausenger wasn't thar, an' sez I to my darter, sez I, "Sally, gal, what's 'come er that ar sausenger?" Then she turned red in the face, an' sez she, "Never mind—it's all right." I smelt that thar war somethin' gwine on wrong—for you see the wimmin folks 'bout where I lives, is h–ll fur new fashions, an' one day one uv them ar all-fired yankee pedlars come er long with er outlandish kind uv er jigamaree to make the wimmin's coat sorter stick out in the t'other eend, an' the she's, they all put on one, case they 'sposed the he's would love to see it. Well, my Sal, she got monsous stuck up 'bout it, an' axed me to giv her one; but I told her she had no more use for one, nor er sittin' hen had for a midwife, an' I wouldn't do no such er thing, case how she was big enough thar at first.

Well, as I was er sayin', camp meetin' day it came, an' we was all thar, an' the she-folks they was fixed up in er inch uv their lives, an' thar she was er fijjittin, an' er twistin' an' er wriglin about with er new calico coat on, all stuck up at the hind eend, an' as proud as er hee lizzard with two tails! Tell you what—she made more fuss nor er settin' hen with one chicken! I was 'stonished what to make uv that whoppin big lump on behind. Howsever, it was 'simmon time, an' she'd bin eatin er powerful sight uv um, an' I 'sposed she was gittin fat—so I shut up my fly trap, an' lay low an' kep dark! Torectly the preachin' it begin, an' Parson James, he was up on er log er preachin', an' er goin' it "hark from the tomb!" I tell you what Brother James was loud that day! Thar he was, with the Bible on er board—stickin 'twene two saplins, an' he was er cummin' down on it with his two fists worse nor maulin rails; an' er stompin his feet, an' er slobberin' at the mouth, an' er cuttin up shines worse nor er bob-tail bull in fly time! I tell you what, ef he *didn't* go it boots that time, I don't know! Torectly I spy the heatherns they commence takin' on, and the sperit it begin to move um for true—for brother Sturtevant's ole nigger Cain, an' all uv um, they 'gin to kinder groan an' whine, an' feel erbout like er corn stalk in er storm, an brother Gridle, he begin er rubbin his hands an slappin' um together, an' scramblin' about on his knees, an' er cuttin' up like mad! In about er minit, I hearn the all-firedst to do, down 'mongst the wimmin, that ever cum along, and when I kinder cast my eye over that way, I spy my Sal er rarein' and er pitchin', er rippen' an' er tarein' and er shoutin' like flinders! When brother James see that, he thought she'd done got good, an' he cum down off the log, an' sez he, "Pray on sister!"—an' the she's they all got round her, an' cotch hold uv her, and tried to make her hold still. But 'twarnt no use. The more they told her "to don't" the more she hollered. Torecly I diskiver she'd done got 'ligious, an' I was so glad, it kinder lift me off'n the ground—an' sez I, "go it Sal!—them's the licks!—blessed am them what seeks, for them's um what shall find!" Then the wimmin they all cotch holt of her by the har, an' commence wollerin' her 'bout in the straw, an' sez I, "that's right, sisters—beat the Devil out'n her." And they *did* too! I tell you what—the way they did hustle her about mongst the straw and shucks was forked! In about er minit I 'gin to get tired and disgustified, an' tried to make her shet up, but she wouldn't, but kep a hollerin worser and worser, an' she kinder keeled up like a possum when he makes 'ten he's dead! Torecly she sorter cum to herself so she could talk, an' sez I, "Sal, what ails you, gal?" The fust word she sed, sez she, "Snake!"

"Whar 'bouts?" sez I.

"Snake," says she agin—"sarpent! take it off, or he'll chaw me up be g—d!"

"Well!" sez my wife; "that's cussin!"

"Whar's enny snake?" sez I.

"Snake!" sez she; "snake! snake!!" an' then she put her han' on the outside of her coat, an' cotch hold uv somethin, and squeezed it tight as er vice!

When I seed that, I knowed it was er snake sure nuff, what had crawled up under her coat; an' I see she'd put her hand on the outside uv her clothes, an' cotch it by the head. Soon as I see'd that, I knowed he couldn't bite her, for she helt onto him like grim death to a dead nigger; and I 'cluded 'twarn't no use bein' in too big er hurry; so I told John Potter not to be skeer'd, an' go an' grab the sarpent by the tail, and sling him h–llwards! Well, Potter he went and sorter felt uv him on the outside uv her coat, an' I pledge you my word, he was the whappinest biggist reptile that ever scooted across er road!—I tell *you* if he warn't as big as my arm, Mike Hooter is as big er liar as ole Dave Lemay—and you know he's a few in that line! Well, when Potter diskiver that she helt the snake fast, he begin feelin' up for the reptile's tail, sorter like he didn't like to do it at fust, an' then sorter like he did. When it come to that, Sal she kinder turned red in the face and squirmed er bit, but 'twarn' no time for puttin' on quality airs then, and she stood it like er hoss! Well, Potter he kep er feelin' up, an' feelin' an' er feelin' up, sorter easy like, an' torectly he felt somethin' in his han'. "I've got him," sez Potter, "well I have, by jingo!" "Hole on to him, Sal," sez I, "and don't you do nothin, Mr. Potter, till I give the word, and when I say 'go!' then, Sal, you let go uv the varmint's head; and Potter—you give the allfiredest kind on er jerk, and sling him to h–ll and gone!"

I tell you what, them was squally times! and I vise you, the next time you go up to Yazoo, just ax enny body, and if they don't say the snakes up in them parts beats creation, then Mike Hooter'll knock under.

At this point of the narration we ventured to ask Mike what became of the snake?

"As I was er sayin'," continued he, "thar was my Sal er holein the sarpent by the head, and John Potter he had him by the tail, and Sal she was er hollerin' and er screamin', an' the wimmin, they was all stannin' round, skeered into er fit, and the durndest row you ever hearn—"hole on to him, Sal," sez I; "and you, John Potter, don't you move er peg till I give the word; and when I say 'jerk!' then you sling him into the middle of next week." I tell you what, we had the orfullest time that ever I see! Let's liquor!

"That's the best red eye I've swallered in er coon's age," said the speaker, after bolting a caulker. "But, how did you manage at last?" asked a listener.

"Well, you see," said he, "thar was my Sal, an' thar was all the folks, and thar was the snake, an' John Potter holein' him by the tail, skeer'd out'n his senses, and h–ll to pay! I was gettin' sorter weak in the knees, I tell you, an' brother James' eyes looked like they'd pop out'n his head, an' sez I to John Potter, sez I to him, sez I, "John Potter, don't you budge tell I say go! and when I gives the word, then you give him er jerk, and send him kerslap up agin that tree, and perhaps you'll gin him er headache. Now John Potter," sez I, "is you ready?" sez I. "I is," sez he, "Now look at me," sez I, "and when I drap this handkercher," sez I, "then you jerk like flujuns," sez I. "Yes," sez he. Then I turned round to Miss Lester, and sez I, "Miss Lester, bein' as how I haint got no handkercher, 'spose you let me have that koon-skin cape uv yourn." Sez she, "Uncle Mike, you can have enny thing I is got." " 'Bliged to you," sez I, "and now John Potter," sez I, "when I drops this koon-skin cape, then you pull! "Yes," sez he. "Now," sez I, "keep your eye skinned, and look me right plum in the face, and when you see me drap this, then you wallum the sarpent out. Is you ready?" sez I. "Yes," sez he! "Good," sez I, "jerk!" an' when I said jerk, he gin the *whoppinest* pull, and sent him kerwhop! about er mile an er feet! I pledge you my word, I thought he'd er pulled the tail of the varmint clean off!"

Here Mike took a quid of tobacco, and proceeded—"I've bin in er heap er scrapes, and seen some of the allfiredest cantakerous snakes that ever cum erlong, but that time beats all!"

"What kind of a snake was it," asked a listener. "I'll tell you," said he—" 'twarnt nuthin more'n I 'spected. Sal thought she'd look big like, an' when she was shoutin' and dancin' er bout, that sausenger what she'd put on for er bustle, got loose round her ankle, and she thought 'twas er snake crawlin' up her clothes!"

Mike left in a hurry.

(1802?–1848)

Alexander G. McNutt

Alexander Gallatin McNutt, the eleventh governor of Mississippi, was born in Rockbridge County, Virginia, in late 1801 or early 1802. After attending Washington College and studying law in Virginia, he moved to Mississippi, ultimately settling in Vicksburg. While conducting a profitable law practice there he demonstrated a flair for politics and a knack for public oratory. After serving a number of years in the state legislature, he was elected governor in 1837 and reelected in 1839. During his terms (1838–1842), the University of Mississippi was established near Oxford. McNutt ran for a seat in the United States Senate in 1847 but was defeated by Henry S. Foote. He died on October 22, 1848, in DeSoto County, while on a political campaign.

McNutt published his humorous sketches of sporting life in the wilderness from 1844 to 1847 in William Trotter Porter's *Spirit of the Times*. His tales, written under the pseudonym "The Turkey Runner," usually involve two characters, Jim (presumably one James W. Wofford) and Chunky. Both work for the "Captain" (McNutt) on a plantation in Mississippi. McNutt's humorous fiction is no more than a representative of a type; however, Porter wrote in his collection *The Big Bear of Arkansas*

(1845) that "his original sketches of life and manners in the south-west have made him a formidable rival" of Thomas Bangs Thorpe.

"Another Story of Jem and Chunkey," is reprinted from *The Spirit of the Times*, October 18, 1845.

Another Story of Jem and Chunkey

By The Turkey Runner

"SWEET CANAAN," WARREN CO., MISS.,
SEPT. 17th, 1845

My Dear "Spirit"—Now, I wish I may be *eternally*, if this is not the *fourth* time that I have copied the following manuscript. I have been induced to do so, fearing your Compositors would be unable to read it, as they evidently were the last sent you—it is consequently *fourth proof*.

"BOVINA," WARREN CO., MISS. SEPT. 17th, 1845

The high-heeled JIM was sitting in the passage of his wigwam, shielded from an August sun, the rays of which reflected from the surface of the lake and surrounding hills, rendered the heat insupportable. His head was thrown to one side, and his small grey eyes partially hid by their drooping lids. His suspenders were hanging loosely round his waist and his shirt collar thrown back on his shoulders, displaying a chest of herculean dimensions and development, and a neck strong as a ponderous beam. Occasionally a smile would play across his bronzed features, plainly indicating that his mind was on some far off trail, some pleasurable reminiscence connected with the past. At his back, and leaning against the logs of his cabin, rested his yager, from the muzzle of which was suspended his sharp and bright hunting-knife, with which he had fleeced many an old "he." The antlers of the noblest buck of the forest, the jaw-bone of an alligator, the skull of a "catfish," the skin of CHUNKEY'S panther, and the scalp of near every variety of wild-fowl were nailed to the logs of his cabin. Himself and cabin presented a rare picture, and, I question, if in all the romance of backwoods life, there has been conjured into existence a more perfect *beau ideal* of the warm-hearted, careless, reckless and hardy hunter than this self same Jim, the "Yellow Bar of the Sunflower." Uniting with extraordinary physical strength, activity and an elasticity of movement and constitution that sets at defiance fatigue, exposure and dissipation. With a temperament of the most sanguine character, he has blended a mind of singular acuteness and originality—in his action he is governed by impulse and acknowledges no law but his passions. He would be a dangerous man were it not for his great kindness of heart and good nature, which is manifest in the devotion of his friendships. He is as free from care, as careless of consequence as if he had no interest in the affairs of this world—his rifle and knife his only source of solicitude, his only dependence for comfort, sustenance and whiskey. Occasionally he would raise a cup to his lips and a gurgling sound would be followed by a sigh of pure delight, as mouthful after mouthful of the highly concentrated "stranger" would disappear. He had remained in this apparently half-dreaming attitude nearly an hour before he sprung up and said,

"D—n it, Captain, let's wake up and bust about a spell, I reckon I hant never told about them "furrin" varmints what the old man sent down here once to go a huntin with I and Chunkey?"

"Never, Jim, I wish you would do so now."

"Well, come and jine me and ile do so."

"I will listen to you with pleasure, but cannot drink your whiskey, it is so execrably bad."

"Bad! *bad!* you calls this *'bad,'* does you? well, I wish I may be eternally—I thinks as how you are taken on mightly, a rarin powerful high for sich a small hoss! I does, man. Now, I've hearn the old man go on at jest sich licks, acussin and abusin it, but *still a drinkin*—I never does *myself,* I, *I,* likes it, and I *never* abuses *anything* what *I* likes, and, as for it being *bad,* I'm the livin man what hant *never* seen any of that sort, and, I reckon, I've seen *some* about in spots, and I have got to see the first drop yit, that warn't *good.* What you calls bad, Captain, I calls good, what you calls good, I calls better. Now you've got it, I've seen *good* and *better,* but *none* that warn't *good!*"

"Well, Jim, I shall not quarrel with you about taste, but if it will suit you as well, I will listen and you can talk and drink!"

"Oh, good as h–ll; suit yourself and you suits me. A short hoss is soon curried, but it riles me whenever I hears a man abuse a thing to-day what to-morrow he hugs up like kinsfolk,—*in course*, I means rich kinsfolk, poor people hant got no kin, 'thout they's poorer nor—"

"Well, Jim, when did the famous hunt take place?"

"Let me *see*, I reckons it were the year I came back—yes, the very year that lawyer YERGER bot the "Panola" place from the old man; but stop, let me see—"

"Oh! the time is unimportant, go on."

"In course; well, *sir*, one evening we were all sitting in the passage jest as we are now, exceptin we were a leetle of the awfully, d—dest tight; we'd jest got home from a barbecue whar "stranger" and candidates were thick 'till you left—that were a *mighty* year for barbecues, and *that* were the biggest day in that year; maybe as how you recollect it? It were at Cowan's Spring, and COL. HEBRON, DICK SPAUN, and the Clar Creek boys had been spreadin themselves."

"I recollect perfectly well, they give splendid barbecues, but has that anything to do with the hunt?"

"Not the first red, Captain, but I were jest 'gwine to tell you— you see, I were jest in the act of hawlin out a bar skin to lay down on, when *out* busted the dogs like tarin bark from a green tree. 'Hillo,' says Chunkey, poor feller, a snatchin up his gun, 'what *are* bursted;' we all looked expectin to see some varmint, but, in place of that, thar stood, down thar by the draw bars, a couple of fellers, with their hats in thar hands abowin to the dogs—*yes*, d—d if they *warn't*, and the dogs, you see, ya! ya! *whoop!* aseein them throwin thar hats about, thought they were showin *fight*, and were jest in the very act of nailin 'em, and so would you, Captain, I reckon, if you'd been a dog, 'cause, jest edzactly sich a d—d *un*manly lookin couple you never *did* see. We beat the dogs away, and they were in a little of the hottest stew you *ever* seed. You know how a dog will go up and smell a stranger? well, every time a dog would go up and smell 'em, 'Ello Ello!' one feller would say, ajumpin like a turkey-cock and pinchin his hat into all manner of shapes. It had been a long time since we'd had a good frolic and these fellers were jest the sort we were mournin for, and we made it up to give 'em jessy, and maybe we diddent tree 'em! Well, it seems to me we did!

" 'Ow do you do, gentlemen? ow do you do?' said one of 'em, still holdin on to his hat and his little bullet eyes lookin like they'd pop out his head.

" 'How do you do *yourself?*' said Chunkey, in a loud, coarse voice and lookin outen his eyes wus nor a treed wild-cat, makin the feller jump nearly outen his breeches. When we got to the house he pulled out a letter and handed it to Mager, sayin

" 'Eres a letter from the Governor, a letter of introduction to Mager, who will introduce me to the unters of the swamp, Mr. Jim and Mr. Chunkey.' Lord J——s, Captain, if you'd jest been thar *then*, to have seen the boys acomin the extras over him, sich looks, sich a swellin up, and a bustin out and ahemmin!

" 'Hive come hout,' said he, 'like a darn'd *yig*norant Choctaw, what don't know the first principles of the American language, hive come out to ave a nice unt,' and then he commenced bowin to Chunkey, and then Chunkey took a set at him. He sorter put one foot out and jerked it back mighty quick, makin the old puncheons rattle; he'd then take sort of a hop and go over it agin with the yether foot, wus nor an old he bull, all the time lookin mighty serious, like he's aworkin for his life.

" 'Ello! ello!' said he, in a sorter good natured voice, 'veres my man Enry, my servant?' Well, Captain, we looked, and *thar* he stood, *and* if *he* warn't a *white* man, I wish I may be eternally! I'll *swar* to it, and the way he were loaded with clothes and sich like was a caution to all pack hosses!

" 'Chuck your plunder under the bench, thar, stranger,' said Chunkey to the yether feller, 'and come and gine me in a drink.' Mager, you see, were all this time atryin to read the old man's letter, and when he'd come to a word he couldent edzactly make out, he'd twist this way and then that atryin to *acrete* the meanin out it—the old man do rite a mighty mean hand, don't he? The letter said the man were a great man in his own country accordin to *his* sayin, but that lately he'd been hung to a circus company at Jackson, and had piled the agony too high and they'd been compelled to get another feller to attend to their hosses—but he brought all sorts of shootin irons with him, and the letter said he were h–ll at birds on the wing and sich like trash, but that he had never been in a big hunt, and had cum all the way from furrin parts to enjoy one, &c., &c. When Mager had done got through, he turned round to the feller and said,

" 'Stranger, *are* you been in furrin parts?'

" 'Yes, sir,' said he abowin agin, 'hime han Hinglishman—han Hinglishman of fortune, a travellin hin this new country for ha-musement—hime well hedicated, hand hit hamuses me to see the native hignorance of the people!'"

" '*In course* it do,' said Chunkey.

" 'Then *you* are a furriner, *British* furriner, are you?' said Mager, sorter swellin up and aworkin his arms to see if they'd go easy.

" 'Come, come along, stranger,' said Chunkey to the man what he called 'Enry,' 'and take your drink, if you're 'gwine to.'

" 'Eexcuse me, sir! hexcuse me, that is my *servant:* Enry is my servant, sir, you hunderstand me!'

" 'If I do I wish I may be *eternally,*' said Chunkey.

" 'Your servants are black, mine hare vite, we do not heat nor drink with hour servants.'

" '*The* lord J——s,' said Mager, lookin wild as a buck and dartin a regular sockdolager under his linin. 'Look here my friend,' said he, afeelin for the bottle to git another drink, 'do you say that *that* feller *thar* is your servant, that he is your nigger?'

" 'To be sure, Mager, he's my servant, but not my nigger! no! no! he hant no nigger—Enry, *you* Enry?' said he.

" '*Sur*, your honor!' said he, atochin his hat.

" 'Bring hin them ere harticles, hand hundo my straps!'

" 'Yes, *sur*, your honor,' said he agin araisin his hand up to his head sorter.

" 'The *great* Moses,' said Mager in a sorter slow voice, 'the *great moses,*' and I seen h–ll were gettin *in* him, 'cause he commenced warpin hisself up to 'em, his teeth clinched and his face pale as a rag. I sprung up to him—'Hold *hard*,' says I, Mager; 'don't, maybe as how the old man won't like it;' presently he foch a deep sigh and drapt his arms down and said,

" 'Stranger, do you say that feller, what you calls your servant, is a white man, do you say that in this free American Government of the United States whar Gineral Jackson lived, whar,—whar—maybe as how he is sorter *mixed*—I've seen many sich in Georgia.'

" 'Ho no! Mager! ho no! he hant no nigger,' said he, lookin *mighty* wild.

" 'Then, by the eternal,' said Mager, 'he shall drink with *you*— *you*, sir. You are both furriners, and I don't care the fust huckelberry d—n for either of you—every man is a man in this country, if he ain't a nigger, so you are *bound* to drink with each other. But look here, mister, what's *your* name, I couldent make it out in the old man's letter?'

" 'Sir,' said he, abowin *mighty* low, 'my name is Arvey, hat your service, sir, hand hi ham appy to make your acquaintance!'

" 'Then I'm d—d,' said the Mager, 'if the Governor haddent oughter take a few more ritin lessons, for if thar aint an H at the beginnin of your name you can jest take *my* two and a half.'

" 'Ho, hits hall right, Mager,' said he examinin the letter, 'that his han H, hand that is my name—H-a-r-v-e-y—Arvey, Mager, that's hit—Arvey!'

" 'Well, sir, ile jest gin you a little of my level opinion, you infernal Brit——'

" '*Hell*-fire, *camp*-fire and seven yether kinds of fire,' said Chunkey, makin a big spring and lighten on his heels in the middle of the floor, agritten his teeth and bustin about, sometimes agrowlin like a dog, then mewin like a cat, howlin like a wolf, roarin like an alligator, then gittin down on his all fours and bellerin and *pawin* like a bull. 'Seize him,' said Mager, 'he's 'gwine to have another of them spells;' then Chunkey commenced ravin agin, a swarin he smelt blood and *must* chaw *something* up afore he could eat, sleep, or drink. Well, sir, that feller *were* scared and so would most any person have been, 'cause Chunkey played the game mighty fine.

" 'What's the yether feller's name?' said Mager, payin no attention to him.

" 'Enry Ho'Neal, sir!' said he, quick as a flash.

" 'Well, Mr. Ho'Neal,' said Mager, 'I have jest taken a likin to you, I have, so cum up and gine me—go it with a perfect rush—you are at *home*, you are—this is a free country and free doins, so stir the fires. 'Here's to you,' said Mager, atochin his glass, and Squire he did go it, he did stir them fires some, he took drink after drink, gourd full after gourd full, till he nearly emptied the jug. Mager all the time stickin to him close as a brick—and diddent that liquor commence opperatin soon, and diddent that Irishman hump hisself when he got under headway. Speakin about an Irishman's drinkin licker, puts me in mind of what poor Chunkey once said to me about old Mrs. ———. You see the old oman had right smart chance of plunder, and Chunkey wanted me to court her. 'Oh! she is too old to marry, Chunkey,' said I. 'Too old h–ll,' said he, 'they *never* gits too old till they can't feel a live coal of fire on thar foot;' and so it is with an Irishman about drinkin licker, they never gits too old or too sick, whenever thar's life enough in one to feel a live coal of fire on his foot he'll take a drink of whiskey.

"By this time the Irishman had commenced gittin his tail over his back and was givin news like a good one. 'Och! long life to ye, Mager, me jewell, it's you sure that's the jontleman!' You see, Mager had been talkin to him about waiting on the Inglishman, and told him he warn't no better nor a darn'd nigger, and was tryin his darndest to raise a row.

"'You are a free dimmocratic American, Mager, ye are! hurra for liberty and equality!'

"'Them's the licks to count,' whispered Mager to him.

"'By the Howly St. Patrick, I'm a free man in a free country.'

"'You are, by the eternal,' said Mager, 'and I'm your friend,— *roll!*'"

"'Ivery body is free in this country, exceptin the nager, and be J——s I'm nobody's servant—to h—ll wid your servants!'

"'Tell it out to him,' said Mager, 'I begins to love you, let's take something.'

"After takin a drink, Mager took him off and they had a talk together, presently in they come.

"'Mr. Harvey, or Arvey or whatever else yer name, jest be after buyin a d—d nager, will ye, I'm no servant of anybody's; me name is Mr. O'Neal, if you please, *niabocklish.* Whin's the 'lection comin on me Mager, och! hone and it's me that will have a vote! hurra for Daniel O'Connel and repale, be jabbers, Ile jest be after taken another drap of that same for the honor and glory of a free country.'

"The Inglish gentleman, as he called hisself, was perfectly shucked with 'Enry's' takin on, and put me in mind of a big cur in a fence corner with a pack of hounds abeyin him. Mr. Ho'Nale haddent a spec of notion of sarvin anbody, tho 'stranger' had him and he were jest foamin; I knowd as how thar'd be h–ll in the camp afore long, as Mager commenced rollin up his sleeves and undoin his shirt-collar.

" 'Och! Mager, me jewell, it's me that's the rale dimmecrat— Irishman and repaler, and a better man nor any d—d Inglishman, and as good as any mon or man's mon,' then he squar'd hisself at Mager, sorter to show how to work on a man. 'I'm as good as any 'Merican an better nor thim what's born in the counthry, becase they could'ent help themselves, do ye see, and I'm come from me own choice, be jabers—and be this an be that, the counthry of right belongs to the Irish, and we'll have it mon—to h–ll wid ye all,' said he, and by this time he'd got a full head of steam and were aworkin it off with a looseness—'I'm a better 'Merican nor yourself, Mager, me honey, an a better mon ye omadhon, 'ye—'

"*Whah—diff*—and bump went somethin in the middle of the floor. I turned round quick as thought, and thar lay the 'repaler;' Mage were standin over him growlin and snortin and a workin his hind part cat fashion—every time the feller would move, the lord how he'd work on him, sometimes agougin and then a bitin—and he's cience at bitin. He were all the time a gruntin and a cussin; I and Chunkey loped him, and we had it, round and round: the Mage all the time a splungin and surgin like a wild-colt. '*Whar—whar* is that yether feller?' said he, and then he cavorted agin.

" 'Yes! whar *is* that eternal Inglish, British furriner?' said Chunkey, aginin Mage; and sure enough, whar was he, whar did he go to—thar warn't a sign of him to be seen. I knowd he haddent left the house, as the dogs would have made sassage-meat of him. Arter lookin about a spell, I discivered his head a stickin out from under a pile of bar skins; Chunkey seed him, and then *he* commenced, and swore *he'd* have a turn at the furriner—he *must* have a turn at a furriner or *spile*—and then he got on the skins and jumped, and cussed, and tore about till he got tired. It were delightful, it were, jest to behold Mage and Chunkey chargin.

" '*Whar's* my bowyer?' said Mage.

" 'Ile have *his* melt!' said Chunkey.

"Arter a while, Mage got in a good humor, and started down to the lake to cool off, tellin us how to manage the thing. Well, arter a while we commenced pullin the skins off, and out he cum, makin a break to git away, but Chunkey had him.

" 'No harm, stranger! no harm now! Mage has gone and you are safe as an old he in a cane-break—when Mage comes back, he will appolergise.'

" 'Will he hindeed,' said he, a brightenin up.

" 'Sartinly,' said Chunkey, 'he haint got nuthin agin you when he aint mad, and he commenced workin on that sarvant of yourn 'caus he were so alfired sassy to you, you see; and diddent he lumber?'

" 'Hare hit possible, I thought you were hangry with me.'

" 'No sich thing! but the way he used that feller up was curious, it was, I hant never seen it beat, as I knows on, thar warn't scarcely enough left oughten his carkis to make 'sign.' '

" 'What hare become of him, where did Enry go to?'

" 'To h–ll I 'spect, stranger!'

" 'Hare Enry dead!'

" 'Dead, why in course he are.'

" 'Hawful! hawful!' said he, a raisin his hands up and lookin wus nor a *'chicken eater.'*

"Captain, I've seen many a man in a tight place, I've seen an old roarin savage he have his arms round one, and all a tumblin in the cane together, and it a crackin, and the bar a growlin and a smashin his teeth, and the dogs a settin to him and a yellin like so many devils, and then the licks of the rifle and the licks of the bar, until the fight were finished, and when it's all as still as the grave, Captain, a thumpin right here at the heart, and them's the time for a feller to be scar'd very high if he's ever 'gwine to be; at the end of sich a fight, when thar hant no knowin who's whipped, Chunkey or the bar; but, sir, I hant never seen a man scared as bad as he, he couldent speak and could scarcely stand. Chunkey, poor feller, he couldent stand it no longer, so he ups and told him.

" 'Stranger,' said he, 'we are a rough set and carry on a heap of deviltry, but we don't murder people; we's bad enough, God knows at best, but we's jest as free from bein men of that kind as anybody. Henry warn't killed, but he were most *pre*-emptorily chawed up, and had humped hisself for high timber. The reason why Mage jumped him, was 'cause he was so alfired sassy to you, that was all; it's a rule in this country if a man's sarvant cuts up any extras, for us to take him out and thump him, jest to save his master the trouble.'

"Well, sir, when the darned fool found Enry warn't dead he were satisfied in a minit. We soon got him to drinkin agin, and he was jest as easy goin as if he'd been born in the swamp, and a little of *the* perlitest man, oh, hush! Well, sir, we got him to describin his country and his travels—I 'spect the feller had been considerable once—and we all got in a first-rate humour, 'cause he could out talk the Jews, and I had determined to let him alone—the licker, you see, made him feel sorter independent and don't care a d—n-like, until he seed Mage comin back and then the way he looked speckled, the way them little eyes rolled about was a caution. Mage come in and walked straight up to him and held out his hand; at first he diddent know what it meant, but I reckon sorter thought Mage were arter him agin, but when Mage commenced *shakin* his hand, the *lord*, the way he shook back agin, the way he went back at him, was a caution to candidates. Mage asked his pardon for annoyin him, and then they shook hands agin and took a drink—and drink follered drink until both got high.

" 'Hime ighly delighted,' said he.

" 'I'd divide the last bilin of meat with you,' said Mage, and then they bowed and teched each their glasses together, and sich jokes and singin, sich laffin and goin on as they had till night, midnight, you never seed, and when they tumbled in, Mage coulddent have told hisself from the Inglishman, nor the Inglishman from Mage.

"Next mornin they got up mighty early and that Inglishman looked awful, it is perfectly ridiculous to tell; but, sir, he sot to and commenced cleanin his gun. I turned in and made him a big he julep and he swollered it like a nigger do castor oil, with *a rush*. I knowd thar was stranger enough in it to start him to grindin. We had all done got ready to start over to the lake to kill a deer, or maybe as how a bar, when old Diana come bustin in the house.

" 'Massa Mager, I wish you'd let one the boys have the dogs to coch some varmint what's up to the quarter last night, it's done 'stroyed all Big Let's chickens—Nelson say how he 'spect it's a polecat.'

" 'Go long,' said Mage, 'ile tend to it,' then turnin round to the Inglishman, he said 'thar has been some game up at the quarter—how would you like to have a little chase afore we cross the lake?'

" 'Hime hin your ands, gentlemen, hand hit will no doubt be very pleasant to you has hit will be to me.'

"Mage then took down the horn and blowed for the dogs, and in a few minnits we war all ready to start. We haddent reached the 'quarter' afore old Leander opened and all the dogs harked to him in a rush and started off at a smart cry.

" 'Urra! Urra!' said Mr. Arvey, in the tallest kind of joy, a throwin up his cap and a shoutin to the dogs; 'what harn hit, Mager?'

" 'I don't *edzactly* know!' said Mage, a takin a chaw of tobacker, 'but I thinks as how maybe it may be a perfume otter!'

" 'My hies, a perfume hotter, are hit gota perfume?'

" 'Well, it have,' said Chunkey, 'and it arn't none of your common truck perfume at that, but a rale slap, bang, ring tailed he perfume, and supposin as how we can take this feller alive hoss, woulddent you like to have him to take back to Lundon; you'd jest better believe he'd be *some* punkins in a crowd!'

"That notion slayed him, it set him, he were nearly frize at the ide, and went splungin about like he were mad—the jewlep and exercise a makin his face as red as a beet. " 'Hadmirable! hadmirable! glorious! glorious! hant hit.' The thing commenced gettin towards the point, and I couldent help thinkin what a poor *yig*norant set them furriners must be, and the feller, you see, was the tallest kind of a furriner, and set hisself up for somethin, with a *white* man for a *nigger—don't it swinge h–ll Captin.* Well, as I were goin on, as soon as we got thar Chunkey said, 'Mr. Arvey *you* shall have the honor of takin this varmint, you shell; if you shant I wish I may be dod darned to darnation—Ile stick to you tell you git it, I will, if I don't drat my sister's cat, and when you've done coch it you'll be *some*! it will be perfectly mellodious to describe, and if you ever forget *it* or *me* you can jest take my V.'

"The *thing* were in a sassafax stump and we knowd it were open and shut, corn in the hopper, bread in the skillet, meat in the mouth, sugar in the gourd.

" 'Well, what hare hit, gentlemen?' said he, tired nearly to death.

"Why, it *ar* a perfume otter sure as h–ll, and we'll have it *some*,' said Chunkey.

"Mager he went up and looked in mighty cautious. I wish you could have seen him, he stretched that neck longer and higher than the speckled *Gu*raff of the Rocky Mountings; quick as his eye lit on it he give the news, and when Mr. Arvey got a sight, I thought he'd go raven, go stracted—I never *did* see anybody take on so. We commenced talken about who should take him. Mage and Chunkey were for Mr. Arvey, but I opposed it, to give him confidence, you see; diddent I manage it, and thar he stood all the time, lookin fust at one and then at the yether, as if his life depended on which way it went; presently Chunkey turned round and sed, 'I tell you he *shell*, now by the eternal, it's settled,' and then walked up to him said, 'it's settled, sir, you *may* take it!'

" 'Hime a thousand times hobliged to you,' said he.

" 'Go and cut a forked stick,' said Chunkey, 'and Jim, you hold the dogs away.' 'Now, Mr. Arvey,' said he, a pullin a string out of his pocket, 'when Jim gets that stick you must go up to the stump and arter lookin in to see where it ar, run the stick down—you must be *mighty* careful and put the stick across his back quick and hold *hard!*'

" 'Hedzactly, Ile do hedzactly as you tell me, Mager,' said he, a turnin sorter white, but detarmined as the devil.

"I cut the stick and sharpened up the pints fine: when I handed it to him, 'now,' said I, 'Mr. Arvey, you aint to take the buck ager or anything of that sort, you must be careful and not let him git away from you, you'll never have sich another chance.'

"Well, *sir*, he took the stick and started up towards the stump—

" 'Drive away them d—d dogs, will you?' said Chunkey, 'you wants to let them kill it arter he gits it out, don't you, d—n you?'

"I walked back a step or so, sorter to be out the way, and then turned to look at the balance of the boys. Chunkey, he were some distance off, with his arms locked round a saplin, his face jest as red as poke-berries. Mager were holdin the dogs, his back towards the stump and a lookin over his shoulder. I 'spected he'd blow up, he looked swelled out so.

" 'Be careful now, be careful!' said Chunkey. 'You'd better get on the upper side the stump! Thar, now, that's fur enough, *now.*' He run the stick down and made a *powerful* jab. I hearn the thing give one awful scream, and then Lord J——s, what a smell!"

(1825–1850)

Henry Clay Lewis

Henry Clay Lewis, a native of Charleston, South Carolina (born June 26, 1825), was a stowaway on a boat to New Orleans in 1835, then a cabin boy for a year or so. He spent the years 1836–1841 with his brother in Yazoo City and served as an apprentice to a physician there until 1844. After receiving a medical degree from the Louisville Medical Institute in Kentucky, he returned to Yazoo City but was forced to seek a living elsewhere. He chose Madison Parish in northeast Louisiana and became a "swamp doctor." A few years later, after he had managed to establish himself as a competent physician, he drowned in a swamp on August 5, 1850.

Lewis began his writing career with the publication of "Cupping on the Sternum" in the *Spirit of the Times* in August, 1845. His one book, *Odd Leaves from the Life of a Louisiana "Swamp Doctor,"* published in 1850 under the pseudonym "Madison Tensas," is a grim, sometimes surrealistic series of sketches relating to the experiences of a medical student and swamp doctor. The humor of these tales is dark and often violent, but the stories reveal the vitality and youthful spirit of the frontier South.

The following selection is reprinted from *Odd Leaves from the Life of a Louisiana "Swamp Doctor"* (1850).

33

Valerian and the Panther

I HAD JUST RETURNED FROM ATTENDANCE on my first course of medical lectures. Although not a graduate, I had all the pruriency of a young neophyte, and felt very desirous of an occasion wherein my Esculapian acquirements could be exhibited, from call, visit, patient, disease, diagnosis, prognosis, treatment, to cure; or else ominously and sorrowingly murmur to the bereaved friends who are taking the measure—"if he'd only sent for me sooner!" I wanted a case, the management all to myself, from comma to period, white, black, old, young, maid, wife, widow, masculine, feminine, old bachelor, or Indian, I cared not which; a patient was what I wanted, and the shape in which it would come, however questionable, I was indifferent to. The country adjacent to the village where I was studying, is, on two sides, swamp of the vilest, muddiest nature imaginable, with occasional tracts of fine land, generally situated on some bayou or lake; frequently an "island" of tillable land will be found rising out of the muddy swamp, accessible to footmen or horse only, when the river is within its banks, varying in size from fifty to two hundred acres; and, wherever existing, generally occupied by a small *planter*. Every farmer in the South is a planter, from the "thousand baler" to the rough, unshaved, unkempt squatter, who raises just sufficient corn and cotton to furnish a cloak for stealing the year's supply.

A few hours' ride from town was one of these islands, "pre-empted" by a man named Spiffle, whose principal business was to fatigue him devising ways and means to live without work. He would have scorned to hoe an hour in his corn patch, and yet would not have hesitated a moment to pursue a deer or bear for days, with all the indefatigability of a German metaphysical philosopher studying an incomprehensibility. But hunting deer and bear, though it brought more sweat and fatigue in an hour than the hardest day's work, was sport; so was drinking whiskey, and between the two, Jim Spiffle had little time to extend the limits of his demesnes, or multiply the comforts of his household circle, wherein a wife and a dozen children attested Jim's obedience to scripture.

It is a sultry day in June, and I am about describing the external appearance of Jim's pre-emption. A small patch of green and waving corn, surrounded by a brush fence, save where it is eked out, by the side of an antiquated log-cabin, with a dirt chimney, around whose top the smoke is lying in dense heaps, too lazy to curl; one or two bedraggled hens, by noisy cackling, are endeavouring to inform the mistress that their diurnal recumbencies are consummated—whilst the cock of the walk, desirous of egging them on to increased exertions, struts majestically before them, waving one feather, constituting his tail, and seriously meditates a crow; but when he reflects that the exertion of flapping his wings must premise, contents himself with a low chuckle of admiration. An old hound, mangy and bleareyed, is intent upon a deer's leg; and, as he gnaws its tough sinews, tries to delude himself into the belief that it is a delectable morsel from the ham. A boy of some thirteen winters, in full dress swamp costume (a short, well-worn shirt), rifle in hand, at a short distance from the house, is endeavouring to allay the mental and bodily disquietude of a fox-squirrel, so that they both may be on the same side of a chunky gum, up which the aforesaid squirrel, on the approach of the incipient Nimrod, had incontinently retreated. Spiffle, jun., sneaks round to the south side, but "funny" hangs on the north, east, and west—back to the north and south, all in vain! All the points of the mariner's compass are traversed, but still the cunning squirrel evades his foe, who, venting his malediction, finally retires from the pursuit, muttering, "Cuss you! I was only going through the motions; the rifle ain't loaded!" The lord of the soil, extended to his full proportions, is lying on a log, beneath a shady bush; a branch of which is bent down and so ingeniously arranged, that when the breeze moves, it will scratch his head; his mouth is full of tobacco— and as he sleeps, true to his nature, his right hand is busily engaged stealing a couple of dimes and an old jack-knife out of his own pocket; his jaws are relaxed, and the huge, well-chewed quid gleams beautifully dark from the profundity of mouth; a gentle titillation on his lips half arouses him, and, champing his jaws with an emphasis, his waking senses are saluted by the yell of his eldest born, who, on the failure of his squirrel enterprise, finding dad asleep, had made an heroic attempt to hook his sire's quid out of the deep abyss. The poor boy pays dearly for the attempted larceny—three fingers hanging by mere shreds of skin, are the attestations of his dad's strength of jaw.

The scream of the poor devil, and the boisterous grief of the miserable squatter, who, though the "Arab" of the swamp, has still a father's feelings, brings from the cabin a form which, begrimed with dirt, and haggard with premature age, would scarcely be taken for the best of God's works—a woman—but such she was; and her tears and outcries also gave evidence that she, too, amidst the heart-hardenings of poverty, contumely, and lowliness, had still gushing up in her heart the pure waters of love.

"Lordy grashus!" she cried; "you have ruined the child! Oh! how could you do it? You, a man grown, and him, your own son! Oh, Jim!"

" 'Twasn't my fault, Betsy," answered poor Jim; " 'twasn't my fault! Oh! what must I do? He's gwine into 'vulshuns."

"Jump on the critter and git the doctor!" said Betsy. "Quick, Jim! Oh, Lordy! only twelve children—and to lose one of them!" and the poor mother sobbed as if her heart were rending; whilst Jim, jumping on a better horse than befitted his circumstances, made all haste for town, whither he arrived about dinner-time—and dashing up with frantic haste to the office-door, yelled out, "Doctor! oh, doctor! I've bit my son's hand off, and he's dying sarten! Come, quick! dear doctor! that's a good old hoss!—oh, do!"

But the "good old hoss" not responding to his appeal, he dismounted, and rushed in, repeating his cry.

"What's the matter? what's the matter? who's sick?" said I, rushing in from a back room—one book open in my right hand, and a ponderous tome under my left arm.

"Oh! young doctor, where's the old man? I've bit my son's arm off, and he's gone into 'vulshuns, and I want the boss to come right out."

"He's gone into the country, and won't be back before night," replied I. "Did your boy's arm bleed much?"—not reflecting on the absurdity of a man biting a boy's arm off.

"Bleed! Yes, all three stumps bled like a stuck deer."

"Three h–lls! Spiffle, you're drunk! How could you bite off three of his arms?"

"Oh, doctor! I meant his fingers; he put them in my mouth when I war asleep. Sens the old man's out, doctor, you must go. Jes' save his life, doc, and you'll never want vensun or a good trout-hole while I'm in the swamp! Be in a hurry, that's a good fellow."

The chance was too good to be lost—a surgical and medical case combined—amputation and convulsions. What could be more opportune?

Telling Spiffle I would go as soon as I got some medicine suitable to the case, I put near half a peck of valerian in my coat pockets, and an ounce vial of prussic acid in my vest; some calomel, assafoetida, lint, and adhesive plaster, completed my preparations, and I was ready for business. The horse I intended to ride was a favourite one of the old doctor's, but one which, accomplished equestrian as he was, he dare not back, except when the visit lay over some old beaten road; and as for riding him through the devious path of the swamp—one moment on the horse's neck to 'scape an impending limb, the next with the body at a right angle, to avoid a gnarled and thorny tree—now on one side, now on the other, and again on both—wading the backwater, jumping logs, swimming the dark and sullen slough, or with feet raised to the pommel to clear the cypress-knees, which on every side, as the path would cross a brake, obtruded their keen points, ready to impale the luckless wight who there might chance to lose his seat; to ride "Chaos" midst such paths as these, the old doctor, I have said, would never have dreamed of doing, and, most assuredly, had he been at home, would not have allowed me to undertake; but such a ride, with its break-neck peril, chimed well with my youthful feelings, which pursued the same reckless course that the heart's current of the medical student has run in, from the time when "Chiron" was a "grave rat," to the Tyro of yesterday, who is looking in the dictionary for the meaning of "artery."

With all the seriousness naturally to be elicited by a responsible mission, I mounted Chaos, and started at a speed that beplastered the skeleton houses on each side of the way with mud, heaving a delectable morsel, as I passed the "doggery," full in the mouth of a picayune demagogue, who, viewing the political sky with open mouth, was vociferating vehemently on the merits of his side. "Hurrah for——," he had just ejaculated, when the substance, which perhaps assisted in composing an antediluvian megathaslopsyolamagosogiam, or, possibly, "imperial Caesar," hit him "vim" in the patent orifice. Cleaning his throat, he spluttered out, "Cuss the country, when a man can't holler for the feller that he likes best, but the heels of every 'prentice saw-bone's horse must fling clay in his teeth!"

But Chaos heeded him not; imagining I was for a jaunt over his usual road, he gave way to only sufficient movement to indicate his mettle; but when the end of the street was reached, where the roads diverged, one pursuing its upward course over the towering hills— the first from its source that steal down to gaze upon the wavelets of the "dark Yazoo"—the other unobtrusively stealing its way a few hundred yards, and then yielding its being 'neath the placid waters of a bright-eyed lake. Seeing me turn to the latter, the noble horse gave a joyous neigh, and seemed to be imbued with a new life as he viewed the waters stretching far away into the forest, until wave and leaf were melted into one; and as he thought of the wild luxuriance of a hidden dell, gemmed with a glistening spring, the memory of which came floating up, fraught with the enjoyments of a month's pleasure the year gone by, when, disdaining the stable, he had sought the forest, and there, cropping the herbage, and roaming in all the wild luxuriance of freedom, forgot he was a slave, until the insidious wiles of Spiffle restored him to his owner.

Oblivious, apparently, of my weight, he sprung into the waters, and soon—dashing his beautiful head until the spray covered me with delicious coolness—breasted the sleepy lake; and when his feet struck the firm ground, like the fawn from the hunters, away he sprang up the narrow path, which pursued its tortuous way like a monstrous snake, amidst the nodding grass and fragrant spicewood, and old trees, fantastically interweaving their limbs.

But little cared my courser for those old trees, clothed with moss, with the shadows of their arching boughs the pathway thrown across; he heeded not the verdancy beneath the eye displayed, nor the gorgeous summer mingling of the sunshine and the shade; the gentle voice of Eolus, as dallying with the grove, came breathing gentle symphonies, but not on him it wove the spell of soothing, subdued thought, such as the feelings haunt, when its tones renew the memory of a long-forgotten chant. With eye of dazzling brightness, with foam upon the breast, with mane back flaunting on the air, and proud erected crest; with champing bit, and eager bound, and earth-disdaining tread, and air, as if o'er battle-fields victoriously he sped. Soho! Soft, Chaos! Quiet! Soho!

"Which way now, Spiffle?" said I, as the path appeared to cease at a clear, deep, narrow "slough," full of cypress "knees," which did not come to the surface, but seemed some few inches under.

"Right across," was the answer.

"What! through those shoots? Why there's not room enough between them for a dog to swim, let alone a horse," said I.

"You'd be mighty out of breath 'fore you got through with the job, doc, if you tried to swim 'tween them, seein' as thar ten foot under. I war fooled here myself for mor'n a year; I'd take a 'bee' for home, an' come to this slew, an' then have to head it, on 'count of the neas; 'till one day I got on a 'bust' in town, an' my critter got loose and struck for home. I tract him up to whar we is, and here they stopt—the trax and me I mean; but on t'other side I seed them, and I knowed he must have swum. I war clean bothered to know how he got over without leaving some of his innards on the neas,—so I tuck a stick and puncht at one of them that war near outen the water, to see if it war a real cypress nubbin. I missed it clear, and kerchunk I went head foremost 'mongst their sharp points. Oh, my 'viscera!' I yelled; but I'll be cust if I toch a nea; they war ten foot under, and thar they stay, and thar they 'tend stayin', for they ain't grown a lick sens that time, and that war so long ago, that the next day I seed the fust steamboat that kum up the Yazoo skare an old buck to death, makin' him jump so fast that he sprung plum through his skull, and the last I seed of him, as he floated down the river, his head had hung on his lines, and one ear on each horn war fluttering his dying elegy."

By the time this veracious anecdote was over, we had crossed the slough, and a ride of a few miles brought us to the cabin of my patron, who, now elevated with whiskey, had lost his paternal solicitude, and giving way to the garrulity of the drunkard, was making revelations concerning his past history, which, if true, and he had his dues, would have swung him higher than "Barn Poker," of Coahoma, when the regulators were out.

I found my patient doing very well, Mrs. Spiffle having sent, before my arrival, for one of those knowing old dames who match " 'sperience agin book larnin'," and detract so considerably from the physician's income. The old lady, fortunately for the boy, had had sufficient knowledge of surgery to replace the fingers and apply bandages.

Whether it was my naturally prepossessing phiz, or my ready acquiescence in the correctness of her treatment, that softened the old dame, I know not; but she appeared to take to me monstrously; and, after having had her mind satisfied as to my name, natality, and genealogy, she reciprocated intelligence, and, untying the scrap-bag of memory, proceeded to make a patch-quilt for me, of a case that resembled the one we were ministering to.

"Short arter I had kum from Georgy to Mass-ass-sip, a nere nabur—Miss Splicer—had a darter—Miss Spiffle, you had better gin Boney another sup of the sheep safurn—doctor, you said you had no injections to it—what made a slide one day, and 'lowed her dad's axe to fall on her foot, cutting her big toe clean off as sarcumstances would permit. It bled 'mazinly, and the gal hollered out till her mammy, who war splittin'—his throat, Miss Spiffle, a spoonful at a time—rails at the far end of the clearin' (for she was a monstrous 'dustryus woman, Miss Splicer was), heard the rumption and came to the house, lumbrin' over the high logs like a big bull in—a little more whiskey in mine, Miss Spiffle, if you please; what a pity it is that your husband drinks—a small pastur' in the worst of fly-time, as she told me arter, thinking some of the town-boys had got hold of the gal.

"When she got there and seed the blood, and the toe excavated off, a-trying to keep time with the stump which war quiverin' in the air, like the gal had the "skitters," she memorized what a doctor had told her to do in such cases—to displace the parts and heal them up by the fust contention; so she slapt the toe on the foot agin, an' tide a rag on tight, an' put the gal to bed. Well, everything went on monstrous nice—scat! Miss Spiffle, the laws-a'-massy! that cat's tail come mity nigh toching his hand; and 'twould never got well—an' in 'bout two weaks, Miss Splicer axed me to come over and sister her getting the rag off, as she hadn't been informed that far, for her husband had got drunk and run the doctor off jist arter he had showed her how to put the thing up for healin'.

"Well, I went over, and arter soaking her—stumak, Miss Spiffle, put the goose grease on his stumak—foot in hot water, I peeled the rag off; and the Lord be marsyful to a sinful world, fur I seed the toe had grown fust-rate fast but the poor ignerant creetur of a mother had put it on with the *nail turned down,* and the poor gal's dancing were 'ternally spiled."

Telling the people that I would not return unless they sent for me, and the sun being low, I mounted my horse and dashed off for home. Coming to a fork in the path, I took the one I thought I had come in the morning, and gave myself no further concern about the road.

I mentioned that I had filled my pockets with *Valerian* on leaving home, and on this simple thing depended two lives, as the sequel will show.

It is a root, when fresh, of a powerful and penetrating odour peculiar to its species; permeable things, by remaining in contact with it, become imbued with its characteristic odour, which they retain for a considerable length of time. The root possesses great attraction for the cat tribe, who smell it at a great distance, and resort to it eagerly, devouring its fragrant fibres with great apparent relish. The panther of our continent is closely allied to the domestic cat, susceptible, like it, of taming, active, treacherous, and cunning,— only in proportion to its increased size, resembling it in its tastes, and like it, fearless when aroused by appetite or hunger.

I had proceeded some distance, when it began to appear to me that the path I was travelling was not the one by which I had come in the morning, but as it was some miles back to the fork, and as far as I could judge, I seemed to be going in the right direction, I determined to proceed. So, cheering myself with a song, I tried to banish disagreeable reflections, and persuade myself that some recognized object would soon assure me I was in the right track.

It was now near sunset, and, in despite of my endeavours to the contrary, I was becoming somewhat anxious, as a gloom was already settling over the swamp, when, to my joy, I found myself upon the bayou or slough, whose illusory appearance I have noted. Not remarking that the path, instead of crossing, turned up the bank, I gave my horse the rein and he sprang into the stream; but what was my dismay, when I found, by the struggling of my poor steed for releasement, that I was mistaken in the slough, and that in this instance, the proximity of the "knees" to the surface was no illusion. He had fortunately become wedged between two of the largest, which sustained his weight, and saved him from being impaled upon those beneath. I had nothing in the shape of a cutting instrument, except a small penknife, which, under the circumstances, could afford me no aid. Dismounting in the water, by main strength I released my horse, and, as the sun withdrew its last lingering ray from the topmost boughs of the trees—jaded, wet, and exhausted—we stood in the midst of the swamp, on the banks of an unknown slough, without food, fire, or weapon—lost! lost! lost! I could form no idea where I was, and go as I would, it would be hap-hazard if I went right, and the probabilities were that I would have to spend the night in the drearisome place.

I soon discovered that it was losing time and gaining nothing to stand there. So I determined, as I was mightily down in the mouth, my course should accord with my feelings, so down the slough I started.

The land, as far as I could see, was uniform low swamp, subject to the annual inundations of the Mississippi. The height to which the waters usually attained was several feet above my head on horseback, which made it more favourable to me, as the frequent submergings had in a great measure destroyed the undergrowth, and thus facilitated passing between the trees. I would not have cared for the night jaunt, had I only known where I was, and whither I was going; but the uncertainty made my feelings very disagreeable, and I mentally vowed that if I got home that once, Spiffle, Sen., might chaw up Spiffle, Jun., inch by inch, before I would come out to stop it.

I sped on as fast as I dared, the darkness growing profound, and my anxiety—I will not say fear—increasing every moment. An unusual stillness rested over the swamp, unbroken save by the tramp of my horse; not even a frog or chichado was to be heard, and the wind had assumed that low, plaintive wail amidst the leaves, that never fails to cast a melancholy shadow over the heart, and awaken all the superstitions of our minds. I was musing over the sad fate of an intimate friend who had recently come to an untimely death, and reflecting how hard it was that so much youthful ambition should perish, such a glorious sun go down shrouded with darkness whilst it yet was day, when the ominous silence was broken by a sound which, God grant, I may never hear again. Like a woman's shriek, in the damning anguish of desertion and despair—lost and ruined— was the long, piercing scream of the *Panther,* whose awful yell palsied my heart, and curdled the blood within my smallest veins. Again and again it arose, filling the solemn aisles of the darksome swamp, till echo took up the fearful sound, and every tree, bush, and brake, gave back the hellish, agonizing shriek.

It was evidently approaching us; my poor horse trembled like an aspen beneath me, and seemed incapable of moving. Again, still nearer—the fierce and harrowing scream fell on my shrinking ear; and I knew the animal was upon my trail. Shaking off the lethargy into which I was fast sinking, I struck my horse, and, twining my hands in his mane, lay down on his neck, letting him go as he wished, as I did not know which way to guide him. With a snort of terror he sprung off with a speed that seemed miraculous, through the darkness and trees. I flattered myself that the rate at which we went would soon distance the panther; when, God of heaven! it arose more piercing and shrill, still nearer than before. I began to despair, as I had no weapon, save the pen-knife; and the animal, I knew, was one of the fiercest nature—else why did he follow for my blood? (I never thought of the *valerian.*)

The speed of my horse, with the fearfulness of my situation, made me half delirious, and my thoughts began to wander—colours of all hues, shapes, arabesque and fantastical, danced before my eyes. I imagined that I was in the midst of a well-contested battle, and in the wavering fight, and covering smoke, and turmoil of the scene, I caught the emblem emblazoned on the banner of my foe, and it was a panther *couchant.* Making an effort to draw my sword, my hand came in contact with the vial of prussic acid in my vest pocket with considerable force. This aroused me; and, taking it out, I determined to commit suicide, should the panther overtake me— preferring to die thus, to being devoured alive.

Again and again the awful scream of the infuriated animal arose, and fell like the weight of a mountain on my trembling frame. Nobly my gallant horse strove to save me; he required not the whip or spur; I gave him a word of encouragement, and the animal,—which we term a brute,—returned a low, whining neigh, as if he wished me to understand that he knew my danger, and would do all in his power. I looked up as the horse suddenly increased his speed, and found, to my delight, that we were in the right track; I imagined I could almost see the lights in the windows—but this I knew could not be. It was pleasant, however, to think that I was going home, and that if my horse could only keep ahead a few miles further, we would be safe; when—hist!—ha! ha! was it not enough to raise the laugh? I heard the scream of the panther not two hundred yards behind, and could almost hear his feet as they struck the ground after his leaps. He seemed to be rejoicing over his approaching feast—his screams arose fiercer—shriller—more horrid than before. The heavens gave back the sound—it was caught by every breeze—echoed from every dell; a hundred discordant voices joined in the infernal melody, while the loud neigh of my horse, as if for help, framed itself into a panther's shriek. I strove to breathe a prayer; but my parched tongue clove to the roof of my mouth, and what I uttered served but to add to the damning chorus of hellish sounds. I tore the neck of my poor horse with my teeth, to incite him to greater speed; but my time had come. Again I heard the panther's scream, so near that it pierced my brain with its acuteness. I heard his spring, as he threw himself over the lowermost boughs of the trees, and shrank within myself, momentarily expecting him to alight, with his sharp teeth in my heart. The thought occurred to me, as, looking ahead, I really beheld the town lights glimmering—if I kill my horse, may not the panther be satisfied with *his* blood, and allow me to escape? There was reason in it; and, though a pang shot through me as I thought of sacrificing the noble animal who had borne me on thus far, yet the love of life overcame all scruples. With my penknife I felt carefully for the carotid artery, and, when it was found, plunged the blade in, inflicting a small but deadly gash. Giving a terrible spring, the hot blood gushing all over me, he ran as none but a noble horse, in the agonies of death, can run, and then, with a low, reproachful moan, fell dead; whilst I, disengaging myself, at a full run strove to make my escape.

I heard the yell of the panther as he reached the horse, and as he stopped I thought myself safe; but not so long: for again his fierce scream came ringing o'er the air, and I was too well aware of the habits of the animal not to know that when the quarry is being devoured, their voice is still. Suicide by poison, or a more awful death, were all that was now left me. I heard the rapid leap of the panther, yelling at every spring. I uncorked the vial, and was raising it to my lips, when, as if by inspiration, came the blessed thought, that when the panther seized me, to pour the instantaneous poison down his throat. I uttered a low, deep prayer to God, and for one, who, if she had known my peril, would have sought to die with me, and then bracing myself firmly against a tree, with the vial clenched in my right hand, awaited the deadly foe. I heard his shriek, saw a huge form flying through the darkness, felt a keen pang in my shoulder, and then, pouring the acid in the mouth of the panther, fainted.

When I recovered consciousness the moon was shining in my upturned face, and the huge form of the dead panther was lying by my side, *with the pocket holding the valerian firmly clenched in his teeth.*

(1819–1858)

Joseph Beckham Cobb

Joseph Beckham Cobb, born in Lexington, Georgia, on April 11, 1819, lived the life of a rich planter in Noxubee County, Mississippi, from 1838 until his death in 1858. After attending the University of Georgia in 1837, Cobb studied but did not practice law. From 1845 to 1846 he edited the Columbus *Whig* and was involved enough in politics to serve in the Mississippi state legislature. But Cobb's main occupations were to run his plantation near Columbus ("Longwood"), to develop his library, and to pursue a private study of modern and classical literature. His essays and fictional sketches were occasional; he published a few pieces under the pseudonym "Rambler" in Mississippi newspapers, and wrote incidentally for such various journals as *Putnam's National Weekly*, *American Whig Review*, and *The Quarterly Review of the Methodist Episcopal Church, South*. In 1850 he published in Philadelphia a historical romance called *The Creole*, a romantic adventure set in New Orleans 1814–1815. The novel traces the exploits of Henri La Sassauriere, one of Lafitte's pirates who was born a marquis but who nevertheless loses his lover, first to another man, and then to death. Cobb's 1858 collection of literary and historical essays, *Leisure Labors*, has been praised by Jay B. Hubbell and others for its critical sagacity and boldness.

46

It is, however, as the author of *Mississippi Scenes* that J. B. Cobb deserves a unique place in American literary history. Cobb described himself in the Introduction to this collection of sketches and stories as "a journalist or sketcher, not . . . an essayist or politician." And it is with a journalist's detachment that he describes the actions of his characters without a trace of moral judgment. In the manner of a twentieth-century naturalist, he depicts in "The Bride of Lick-the-Skillet" the sexuality and occasional adultery of Sophie Pomroy objectively and with no hint of disapproval. Cobb's aim in this book was to draw his scenes from "real scenes and characters," and to develop them in a language of "everyday thought." He was able to free himself from the moralistic strictures of the fiction of his day by approaching his work more with a desire to amuse than to instruct. As a result, his unmoralistic attitude toward situations which American society generally would regard as immoral (Sophie's adultery, for instance) makes the *Mississippi Scenes* seem much more modern than the work of many later realists, such as William Dean Howells. Although Cobb's poetic descriptions and his preference for narration to dramatic exposition make his fiction appear to be more like the romantic Irving than the realist A. B. Longstreet (to whom Cobb dedicated the book), his journalistic approach to the characters and locale of northeastern Mississippi insures for his book an important place in the realism of the antebellum South.

"The Bride of Lick-the-Skillet" is reprinted from *Mississippi Scenes* (1851).

The Bride of Lick-the-Skillet

THE SOUTH-EASTERN CORNER of N——e county, in Mississippi, is a broken and rugged country, generally poor and unproductive, and peopled by a plain, honest, straightforward sort of folks, who glory more in the simple abundance by which they are surrounded than in any pretensions to high and stylish living. In the midst of this wild and mountainous region, on the head waters of Running Water Creek, which, flowing for some distance through a succession of hills and vales, strikes at last a fruitful land, and empties itself into the principal stream which divides the county— and in a narrow gorge or dell, between two high mountains, dwelt an

honest plain old gentleman who was known as Mr. Peter Pomroy.
The situation was isolated and remarkably picturesque, combining
the quiet prospect of winding valleys, watered by rivulets of the
greenest hue from the reflection of the various trees above and
around, and the more grand and inspiring spectacle of mountains
crowned with verdant shrubbery, from whose lofty summits might
be seen nearly the entire plain of the upper Bigbee. The dwelling
was constructed of hewed logs, like that of all his neighbors (except
that his own was rather more comfortable); and, without claiming
the least pretension even to moderate wealth, Mr. Pomroy was yet
independent in his circumstances, hospitable and open-hearted in
his way of living, and, as the saying is, well to do in the world
every way. The farmers of the country around were not generally so
blessed; they were poor and sometimes dependent—genuine country bumpkins in their manners and customs, careless in dress, rough
in appearance, and, though eminently harmless and good natured,
yet extremely rude and uncouth in their intercourse with strangers,
or with one another. From these facts, as I infer, the name of Lick-
the-skillet was given to their district; and, whether bestowed in de-
rision or waggishness, as it comported with their ways and views to
the very notch, it was readily accepted by the citizens, and the district became so designated throughout all the county. So much,
then, for names!

At the distance of a few paces only from his humble dwelling,
stood Mr. Pomroy's saw and grist-mill, a low one-story building, on
the edge of a steep dam formed of trunks of trees and large rocks,
over which the water roared and dashed like a cataract, filling the
woods around with a continuous sound not unpleasant to the ear on a
still summer evening, and gently relieving the sombre silence of the
scene. The building was the only framed tenement in the country,
and had been erected several years before by an enterprising old
Dutchman, who doubtless would have made his fortune at sawing
and grinding for the people of Lick-the-skillet, if death had not
called for him, and removed him from the scene of his earthly labors,
about a year after he had finished his mill. It now looked quite craggy
and antiquated, and was covered over with a sort of darkish-gray
furze, which gave it an aspect of venerable age. As Mynheer Von

Tromp had died before paying the present owner either for the land or site, or for some two years' bed and board, it fell out, of consequence, that Mr. Peter Pomroy claimed the whole effects of the Dutchman's ingenuity and labor as his own; and, as there was none to dispute either the right or justice of the proceeding, it was whispered that the old architect's death had been, as the neighbors said, a perfect windfall and God-send for his lucky creditor. At all events, it was very well known that the old gentleman had nearly doubled his means since he had been undisputed owner of the mill; and, as the said mill is destined to become quite prominent in the development of this legend, it is thought that a more detailed description of its luckless constructor, and of its own appearance and situation, may be quite necessary.

The old millwright was a stout, chubby, round-bellied Dutchman of the genuine faderland stamp, with a face like the full moon, and eyes so small and smothered up in fat that it was a wonder with many how he managed to squeeze enough sight through this barricade of flesh and blood to carry on his work in a manner so neat and expeditious. He was remarkably industrious and cheerful, sang some old snatch of a German air all the time he labored, though it was seldom he entered into or encouraged lengthened conversation with his numerous and inquisitive visitors. This may have proceeded and doubtless did proceed from two of the very best of causes, viz., he was too frugal and industrious to waste his time in idle talk, and, what was more, he spoke the English language very imperfectly and unintelligibly. The old fellow was wholly absorbed with his plan of turning his time and labor to thrifty account, worked incessantly from sunrise until sunset, never left home during the whole two years that he lived with Mr. Pomroy, except on Sundays, when, instead of going to meeting, he invariably hunted game all day. This gave very considerable offence to the hard-shell people of Lick-the-skillet, many of whom boldly predicted that he would never come to any good or Christian end. Now, whether this sage and charitable prophecy contributed at all towards inducing the melancholy and strange accident which, in the end, brought about the death of Mynheer Von Tromp, it does not avail me to say; but certain it is that it came literally to pass as to the first part, for he surely came to a very bad, though I feel no authority to characterize it as an unchristian, end.

During the time that the mynheer resided in Lick-the-skillet, he showed no especial favor or liking to any persons except the pretty little daughter of his worthy host, and a wild, harum-scarum, rumpusing blade who set up for being a doctor, though more akin, as many said, to old Nick than to Galen, and who was known through the neighborhood by the familiar name of Hop Hubbub. For these two, the old Dutchman always had a kind word and a merry welcome; and Hop and he were wont to smoke many a pipe together in the mill-house, and revel of winter nights over many a steaming and savory whisky stew, for both loved a cup over-well for their good. After the mill-house was covered over, old Von Tromp, with true Dutch providence, fitted off a nice little room at one of the corners, separated from the main room by a substantial sealed and weather-boarded partition, built a genuine broad and capacious Dutch chimney on one side of it, and made the same his sleeping apartment. Here it was that he received and entertained Hop, and being too far away to disturb the quiet of Mr. Pomroy's household, they would spend whole nights singing and drinking, never seeming to care a groat about sleep; for, at the first dawn of light, the clatter of the mill was heard always to break the stillness of the early morning, whilst Hop, at the same time, would mount his steed and scamper off at a reckless gait towards the village in which he dwelt.

Things went on in this way, as I have said, for nearly a twelvemonth, when, one morning in the Christmas holidays, the family waked and dressed without hearing any stir or noise at the millhouse, and when breakfast came in, old Von Tromp was not at his accustomed place. As he was famous for the most rigid regularity and promptness, these two circumstances gave Mr. Pomroy and his family some considerable uneasiness, and the worthy gentleman had scarce swallowed more than half of his usual allowance before he took his hat and cane, and hurried off to find what was the matter with his friend and boarder. Arriving at the mill, he found the door of the honest Dutchman's little apartment wide open, the bed tumbled and pressed as though its occupant had passed the night as usual; but no sign of clothes or of old Von Tromp was to be seen anywhere about. This seriously alarmed him, and the worthy host began to re-trace his steps homeward, with a view to procure aid and institute a more extended search. He had reached the doorway, and was in the act of stepping forth, when his eye fell accidentally upon a dark-looking object underneath the mill, just at the foot of the race. This suggested an alarming idea. Immediately above, a cavity had been left in the floor, of a size fully sufficient for a large man to fall through, which Hans Von Tromp had arranged on purpose that he might al-ways witness the first dash of the waters as they rushed from the gap against the fly-wheel, and set his darling machinery in motion. No one knew better than Mr. Pomroy that the honest Dutchman had his mood of melancholy, or the blues, especially when deep in his cups; and as Hans had indulged more freely than usual in egg-nog and whisky stews the night before, Mr. Pomroy felt a most awful convic-tion run through his brain. He descended, and found the dark object to be what he had already anticipated, the familiar broad-brimmed hat of the hapless Von Tromp. Where now was the owner? Had he drowned himself? These were solemn questions, and the worthy host sadly misgave their answers. He returned, and summoned two negro fellows belonging to his farm. With these he dragged the race, and in the course of fifteen minutes they drew forth the portly car-cass of the old millwright. The neighbors were called together, and among them came Hop Hubbub, the only intimate companion of the deceased. Hop was a sadly wicked fellow, and not a little humorous withal; and when he cast his roguish eyes upon the swelled and dis-torted form of his ancient comrade, so far from showing the least tearful symptom of sorrow, the bystanders were taken all aback to see him curl his lips into a singular sort of smile, peculiar to himself, expressive alike of droll mirth and lurking mischief. Tumbling the body to and fro, pressing the abdomen and bowels, so as to make the water inside roar and gurgle in a manner the most shocking, even to the hardened nerves of the rough sons of Lick-the-skillet, he gave, as his settled opinion, that the fierce old trout (as he called Hans al-ways) had mustered up an extraordinary supply of Dutch courage, whilst drunk the night before, had doubtless raised the d——l in person (which he solemnly averred every German could do when he chose, as they all dealt in the infernal sciences), rashly challenged him to a wrestling match, and that Old Nick had gone off conqueror. In proof of these wise conclusions, Hop pointed mysteriously to a blackened appearance about the throat of the deceased, shook his head ruefully, and, having suddenly exchanged his smile for a look the most portentous and knowing, succeeded in impressing his opinion on the minds of his simple and credulous hearers. The next thing was to bury the dead, and here again Hop interfered. He declared that he had often heard the old Dutchman say, in his lifetime, that, in case he died whilst at Lick-the-skillet, it was his ardent desire to be interred under his mill-house; and as the *Old Boy* had now carried him off before his time, he proposed that the body should be deposited in a shallow grave at the foot of the race, where its hapless soul had been wrested from it, so that, in case Hans should ever get a little respite from his burning resting-place below, he might easily find the way back to his favorite earthly haunts. Hop's opinion was gospel authority on all incidental matters at Lick-the-skillet, and as there was no good reason to the contrary, his suggestions were promptly adopted; and honest Hans Von Tromp was decently buried on the spot where he had yielded up his life, and where his grave might be forever freshened by the spray of that waterfall whose roar had been to him the most delightful sound on earth. His little female favorite reverently cherished the memory of that friendly interest and regard which Hans had ever showed for her during life; and now that he was gone, she visited his grave, over which she strewed the violet and wild rose, to mingle with the moss and grass which carpeted its mound.

Years followed after years, and rolled away, and, in the mean time, whilst Mr. Pomroy was moulding the dollars by old Hans Von Tromp's mill, his daughter Sophronia, or Sophie, as she was called by the neighbors, had shot up into a nice, buxom, blooming girl of seventeen. Confined mostly to her native shaded vale, and fanned only by the cool mountain breeze, her complexion was fairer than the lily, and her cheeks as red as the roses which blushed from amidst her mother's rude, but tasteful trellis-work. She was a wild, wilful romp of a piece, and threaded the winding dells, or scaled the steep mountain crags like any lusty-legged ploughboy or daredevil huntsman. There was no controlling her inclinations. She fished whenever or wherever she pleased, and with anybody, male or female, just as she chose; and it took a strong arm and stout lungs to beat her in a swimming-race up or down the mill-pond. Such were her primitive habits and artless demeanor that she never refused to enter into a contest of this sort with any beau or rustic suitor who might be paying his court at the shrine of her beauty; only she annexed, as an inviolable stipulation, that her competitor should lie concealed and blindfolded until she had covered her charms beneath the surface of the green waves around, and maintain a respectful distance during the race. To violate either of these was to incur Sophie's lasting displeasure, and the prompt dismissal of the offending party. But, unlike the racing damsel mentioned in classic history, she exacted no penalty in case of defeat, and promised no reward to her successful competitor beyond a simple acknowledgment on her part of his superior prowess. In all these wanton sports and wanderings, Sophie was more often accompanied by Dr. Hop Hubbub than any one else, and it was generally whispered, in consequence, that he was to become finally lord of that beauty and those charms which ran half the young sparks in Lick-the-skillet almost distracted whenever they successively engaged with her in the diversion of swimming or muscadine hunting. Whenever she lifted her petticoats to keep from wetting them whilst wading through some shallow mountain brook, in her rambling excursions, she generally gave Hop the preference in carrying over her shoes and stockings, and would only playfully slap at him when he attempted to snatch a kiss from her coral lips, or ventured a sly caress of her plump but soft form. But it was dangerous for another gentleman to hazard a like experiment, for Sophie never hesitated to use her fishing-pole or riding-switch vigorously and effectively, when occasion required. In the merry country reel or exciting jig, in jumping the grape-vine, or playing at prisoner's base of moonlight nights, Hop was always her favorite partner; and whether these manifest and continual preferences for him proceeded from their mutual recollections of friendship with the honest-hearted old Dutchman, or from a softer and more tender feeling, so it was any way; and most of the other sighing swains called off their dogs, to use Lick-the-skillet parlance, and quit the chase in utter despair of ever being in at the death.

But the crisis of Sophie's rustic life was approaching. In the neighborhood of her father's dwelling, lived a singular old bachelor, snug in his means, thrifty and parsimonious in habit, exclusive and retiring in manner, satisfied with himself, and envying nobody. Notwithstanding these habits of life and peculiarities of temperament, so entirely different from his own, Hop Hubbub had caught the blind side of this singular gentleman, and they were regular cronies and comrades. In fact, Captain Lafayette Mantooth had succeeded fully old Hans Von Tromp in Hop's friendship. It was owing entirely to the latter's influence and popularity that the captain had succeeded in being elected over all other candidates to the command of Lick-the-skillet beat company of militia, and, on parade days, he would appear on the field in an old suit of threadbare regimentals, which had belonged to the old corporal, his grandfather, in the war of Independence, with a rusty epaulette stuck on his right shoulder, and an immense dragoon sword swinging at his side. Being at least a foot taller than his worthy ancestor, the captain found it necessary to use straps to keep his breeches down, as well as suspenders to keep them up, and, for this purpose, his friend Hubbub had furnished him with a couple of red morocco strings, which met the hem of his pants just at the top of his boots; whilst the same friendly hand had surmounted the captain's military hat with a bunch of feathers gathered from a cock's tail, and ingeniously tied around a limber whalebone, torn from some cast-away umbrella. Imagine these military appliances attached to a tall, gangling, long-limbed, water-jointed figure of a man, with long bushy red hair and broad projecting teeth, which it was his habit now and then to gnash fiercely and with an air of ludicrous gravity, and you will have a perfect picture of Captain Mantooth, or, as he himself gloried in being called, Captain *Marcus Lafeart* Mantooth. The captain was pertinacious about this first member, and was particularly waspish when corrected either as to that or to the pronunciation of the second part of his beloved name. His grandfather and father had called him thus—the first ought to know, he contended, as he had been under Lafayette—and, so fondly did he cherish these hereditary and ancestral precedents that he actually turned against and helped to defeat a sparkish, school-learned young candidate for the legislature, of his own political party, because he had innocently suggested that the captain had perverted the title of the French Marquis into a Roman name. Now, all of a sudden, it was discovered that the captain's usual quiet of life and equanimity were broken in upon by the ravages of that glowing and exciting passion which so often disturbs the peace of mind of better and wiser men than our captain, and as often changes the whole tenor and habits of life. Captain Mantooth was sorely smitten with love, and his heart ached and thumped whenever he thought of sweet Sophie Pomroy. Not a day-dream floated through his mind but Sophie was the lovely spirit who prompted it; and, at night, he was often heard to glibber and snort while fast asleep, and seen to clasp his long arms convulsively around an extra pillow, as some tempting vision lured him into the joyous belief that the lovely damsel was in his embraces. How this came about, together with all the concomitant circumstances, leaked out in the catastrophe, and it devolves on me now to relate.

It was the custom of Captain Mantooth to carry his own grain to the mill, and at such times he generally went by a path which crossed the stream a short distance below the dam, and which was rarely ever traveled by any one but himself. It was a shady, secluded spot, overhung by intertwining branches, and sheltered all day long from the rays of the sun. The stream spread out into a wide, shallow current, dashing swiftly and noisily over the ledge of rocks which stretched from bank to bank, bubbling with innumerable bright ripples, and dotted here and there, at irregular intervals across, with clusters of green shrubs, which rendered the scene one of almost Arcadian beauty. What wonder, then, that the lovely Sophronia, so fond of such primitive indulgences, should often seek this romantic spot, and, deeming herself safe from prying eyes and unpleasant intrusions, reveal her charms "unadorned" to the mute objects around, and lave her voluptuous figure in the limpid element which flowed so temptingly along!

Now it happened that our friend Captain Mantooth took it into his head to visit the mill just at the same hour, one warm summer day, that the miller's daughter took it into *her* head to go a bathing at the secluded ford. As the captain had his regular days for such visits, the charming little water-nymph was totally unsuspicious, perhaps, of any intention on his part to make an out-of-the-way call at her father's mill. However, she had scarcely disrobed her graceful proportions, on the present occasion, and was seated in an attitude the most inviting and distracting in the world, on a moss-clad rock, about midway the current, preparing to take the water, when our friend, the captain, mounted on his favorite pony, and astride his bag of wheat, rode suddenly and slowly up on the opposite bank. The bubbling waters prevented Sophie from catching any other sound, and she as if totally unconscious that mortal eye was feasting on those charms of person which might have tempted imperial Jove himself; whilst the astonished captain, dumb-stricken and fairly bewitched, let fall his long arms, locked his feet under his pony's belly, drew up his glowering eyes, opened wide his ivory-fenced mouth, and stared at the rapturous vision so long and so delightedly that a cold shiver shook every limb of his lean, lank frame, causing a rattle of dry bones much more definable than that which stirred up the skeletons of old in the vale of Jehoshaphat. The pony went quietly to cropping the herbage on the roadside.

Hitherto the captain had been afforded only a side view, a full-length profile of the unclad damsel; but scarcely had the pony bent his head to enjoy the pasture which tempted him, when, as if tired with one position, Sophie began to face about slowly; a sunbeam, penetrating a chance opening in the thick foliage, lighted up with lustrous and dazzling transparency a neck and bust which Venus might well have envied; and then the whole gorgeous array of beauties, indescribable, unimaginable, burst upon the enraptured vision of the captain, who, with a noise more like the groan of anguish than the sigh of excited love, fell back upon his pony's rump, relaxed and motionless. Never before had woman crossed his path; never had mortal eyes been feasted to the full before with a picture which art vainly endeavored to portray!

No wonder Captain Mantooth was overpowered! No wonder that the blood now hissed and foamed through his veins with a fervor that kindled in his usually languid bosom new, and strange, and delightful emotions! He arose from that posture of prostration an altered man. He looked again with eager and glowing eyes; but the vision had departed; the lovely damsel no longer appeared in sight; a current of blood roared fiercely through his brain and blinded him for an instant, and then all seemed as if he had been in a delightful dream.

But Captain Mantooth never forgot that dream! It had assailed his senses with a reality too overpowering, and opened a train of emotions far too strong for that; and he resolved to devote the balance of his life to the single object of gaining possession of those charms and their fair owner.

Accordingly, the sun was just beginning to sink away over the lofty mountain top on the west, when who should be seen riding up to the gate, in a shambling trot, his long legs dangling about his pony's flanks, and his arms propped akimbo on either side, but the veritable captain of Lick-the-Skillet beat. And who, alighting without ceremony or invitation, walked into the house of the honest old miller, and inquired for Miss Sophie in person, as he was received by Mrs. Pomroy? Sophie, industrious and smart girl that she was, was at her loom, and Captain Mantooth was asked into the weaving-room. As he entered, the captain encountered another familiar face besides that of Miss Pomroy. Hop Hubbub was there, seated on a high warping-stool by the damsel's side, and a look the most meaning dwelt on his features. The namesake of the great marquis was startled and not a little floundered; for he would sooner have fought a battle at the head of his Lick-the-skillet chivalry any day than suffered Hop to get a laugh on him. However, as there was no mending the matter now, the worthy captain stuffed away the dingy ruffles with which he had hoped to captivate the miller's daughter, slipped off nimbly a brass ring which he had put on his right forefinger by way of additional ornament, cleared his throat with a lusty exertion of lungs which jarred the floor under him, and then, catching a skirt of his longtail Sunday coat across each crotch of his elbow, took his seat on another stool opposite to Hop's, first blowing away any dust which might have gathered on it, and running his hand over the whole seat to make sure of a clean sweep. A mischievous, though almost imperceptible, smile lurked on the mouth of the pretty weaver, and she turned her eyes on Hop, now and then, with a glance that plainly betrayed her strong inclination to mirth, and that carried sad misgivings and uneasy thoughts to the breast of Captain

Lafayette Mantooth. He had come to declare his passion and to woo its fair object; but the signs were against him, and his love seemed likely to be lavished where it would meet with no requital. Poor Lafayette sighed deeply and involuntarily, and Hop contracted the muscles of his face still more drolly, and Sophie laughed outright. Neither of the three had yet spoken or made any attempt to speak. Hop sat grave as a judge, and the captain stared at Sophie with open mouth and eye singularly dilated; and Sophie herself kept busily at work with her slaie and treddles. At last, Hop fell, or at least pretended to fall, fast asleep, reclining his head against the wall of the room near which he sat. The captain drew in his breath with a half rattle through the nostrils as the air passed on to the lungs, ventured to display about a third part of his ruffles, and advanced one leg at full length. Hop snored slightly, when on went the brass ring again, and the suitor laid his hand tremblingly on a corner of the loom, at the same time throwing out the other leg, as if to draw the damsel's eye upon his fair proportions of bone and muscle, for of flesh the captain could not lay claim to five pounds from head to foot, through his full stretch of six feet and a half of manhood. Now, he thought, was his opportunity to begin a conversation, and he drew up his mouth as the first necessary step towards preparation.

"You was in a-washing at my ford yesterday, weren't you, Sophie?" he asked in a low tone, blearing his eyes, and leering most hideously at his fair innamorata.

"In a-washing at *your* ford!" repeated Sophie, interrogatively, and turning her face full upon her questioner. "How do you know whether I was or not, Captain Mantooth?"

"Oh! I didn't say I knowed, did I, Sophie?" returned the suitor, throwing his eyes up and down alternately.

"What did you *mean*, then, Captain Mantooth?" asked the maiden, with increased emphasis. "What *can* you mean?"

"Nothing—nothing, Sophie," replied Lafayette, fearing he had made a wrong step; "I jist thought I'd ask you—was you, Sophie?"

"Upon my word, Captain Mantooth, you are a strange sort of creature—very strange!" said Sophie, striving hard to maintain her gravity of demeanor. "One *might* have thought that you *saw* me from the way you talk."

At this, the captain darted bolt upright from his stool with a bound that a person might make who had been jarred by an electric shock. The whole enchanting scene was again before him, and the blood began to burn in his veins and mantle on his cheeks. But, in the midst of this ecstasy of feeling, Hop indulged another snore somewhat louder than the first, and the captain eased himself on the seat again, thoroughly cooled down by this nasal effort of his dreaded friend.

"Sophie, what if I *had* seed you?" asked Lafayette, after he had again composed himself.

"Well, and suppose you had, captain, sure enough, captain," returned Sophie, whilst a smile curled the corner of her mouth next to Hop, "you would only have seen—"

"What Sophie?" ejaculated the excited Lafayette, again half rising, and clapping both hands in his pockets.

"Really, Captain Mantooth, I don't know what's got into you this evening," answered the maiden, coloring slightly.

"It didn't get into me this evening, Sophie," said the captain, with a look half mournful; "it got into me yesterday, about noon, and for the first time in my life, too."

"What?" asked Sophie, now in her turn fairly launched into a mischievous inclination, "*what* got into you, captain?"

"I don't know what to call it, Sophie," answered Lafayette, in the same tone of voice, "but it's the singularest feeling that ever I had in the whole course of my life."

"How, in the world's name, *does* it make you feel, then?" again asked Sophie, stealing a roguish glance towards Hop, who was still nodding and dipping his head from side to side.

"Every which way—a sort o' all-overish—but the best in the whole world at times, Sophie!" answered the captain, with a leer which was intended to convey what he yet scarcely dared to say.

"Why really, captain, I shall begin to think presently that you are in love," said the lady, with a coquettish toss of the head.

"Is that the way love serves a body, Sophie?" asked Lafayette, with a snuffling simper, as he drew a little nearer.

"You'll have to ask them that's felt it," replied Sophie, with an arch, insinuating smile. "But, there! you've made me drop my shuttle with your silly talking!"

The instrument alluded to had only fallen about half way to the floor, and hung suspended by the thread, which had caught in a splinter. The pretty weaver bent over slightly to regain it, and as it had slipped out on the side next to the captain she stooped far enough almost to touch him. The captain's eyes were just in the line of direction with Sophie's stomacher, and he ventured a slight peep at the concealed treasures; the next moment, he dodged back as if he had been suddenly struck at, and brought his teeth in contact with a crash like that of a nut-cracker. Again his blood quickened with a delicious fervor, and, unable longer to resist or subdue the impulse, he had already stretched forth his lank arm, and was just in the act of grasping Sophie's white, bare arm, when a thundering discharge from Hop's nasal artillery arrested his amorous purpose, and sent the blood back again to the heart with a cold, curdling sensation that made his teeth now fairly chatter, as he drew up once more on the stool. The noise seemed also to have aroused the sleeper himself, for Hop now stretched and gave a loud yawn, straightened in his seat, and looked at the captain and Sophie as though he had just awakened from a comfortable and refreshing nap.

"Heigh! thunder and Boston!" he ejaculated, in his sharp, sonorous voice, glancing at the agitated lover, "why, what the deuce is the matter with you, my dear Mantooth?"

"I don't know, unless it be a slight ague," answered the captain, still shaking in every limb. "It'll wear off directly, though."

"I'm not so sure of that," said Hop, rising and approaching his friend.

"I've been thinking that something strange was the matter with Captain Mantooth for this half hour past," now put in Miss Sophie, winking at Hop, slyly.

"I suspect," said this last-named gentleman, assuming a very grave professional look as he pinched the captain's spine and chunked him slightly in the paunch, "I suspect, Mantooth, you've got the *whiffles*."

"The *whiffles!*" repeated Captain Mantooth, inquisitively, as he flinched and slid about under the doctor's rather singular examination, being most sadly alarmed, too, by the grave announcement, "what may them be, Hop?"

"They are the very mischief when they once get a fair hold on a fellow," answered Hop, shifting his point of examination to the groins and kidneys of his shinking friend. "They'll ruin you for life, Mantooth, unless speedily cured."

"How can they be cured, doc?" again asked the captain, for he had the most unshakeable faith in Hop's skill and knowledge, and really felt somewhat uneasy at his symptoms for the last twenty-four hours. "I'll take anthing if you really think they are on me, Hop, for I wouldn't be ruined now for the whole world."

"Oh! as to that," replied Hop, carelessly, "you won't have to TAKE a single thing. The whiffles are cured in quite another way."

The captain's heart fluttered and sank as he heard this; for he had been often enough at his friend's shop in town to hear all about surgery and amputation, and various operations with the knife and tourniquet.

"And how may that be, doc?" asked the quaking lover, feeling his blood congeal at the bare idea of a surgical operation.

"That's a secret for the present," answered the imperturbable Hop, observing that the loom had ceased its motion, and that the merry little weaver was almost smothering with the desire to laugh, which, by the by, as the reader will soon find out, Hop by no means wished her to do for fear of offending the captain. "I'll tell you the whole matter when we get to your house. Come, get your hat and let's be off; you surely didn't intend to stay here all night!"

"Such had been my intention, Hop," answered the precise captain, who was too good a churchman to prevaricate, although he hated badly to confess as much; "but, if you'll go home with me, I shall be more than glad of your company."

This was soon settled, and the two friends proceeded to bid farewell to the charming little weaver, who did not forget to invite Captain Mantooth to repeat his visit, which elicited a low bow and an affirmative answer from that worthy gentleman.

A month had scarcely elapsed from the period of this first visit before the whole neighborhood of Lick-the-skillet was startled with a report that the pretty and admired daughter of Mr. Peter Pomroy was about to contract matrimonial ties with Captain Lafayette Mantooth. What added a great deal to the surprise of everybody, too, was the very curious fact that Hop Hubbub, whom every one had pitched upon for the husband of the fair Sophronia, and who was known to be high in the affections of that little lady, was now openly advocating Captain Mantooth's pretensions, and telling all the neighbors frankly that he had first put the enraptured captain (to use his own expression) on the scent. From this point, matters progressed so rapidly that the wedding day was soon named; the captain and his affianced bride rode always in public together most lovingly and familiarly, and, at last, a runner was sent round to invite the favored neighbors to the hymeneal feast and frolic.

Now, lest the conduct of our friend Hop should be misunderstood about this affair, and undue praise unwittingly lavished upon what may be mistaken for genuine magnanimity, I must here narrate what has been subsequently whispered about among the gossips of Lick-the-skillet, in order to account for this inexplicable interference, on his part, to urge the captain's suit to a successful issue. Hop loved candor in every department of life except one, and now that he is dead and gone, I am sure he will prefer, provided he has any choice in the matter where he now is, that his faithful biographer shall remove the veil even from that. Everybody about Lick-the-skillet knew that Hop was overly fond of the girls, and, as he had a big heart and a general penchant in this respect, he never concealed that he was averse to marriage. In fact, he was often heard to declare, in his own humorous way, that he feared but two things in the world, viz., a hurricane and a mad woman; and gave, among others, as his reason for living a bachelor life, that he dreaded, in case he had a wife, he might meet a girl he could love better, and that he would sooner stir up the d—l, any day, than a jealous woman. Hop, now, had been loving little Sophie Pomroy a long time, ever since old Hans Von Tromp's melancholy decease; and, after she had blossomed into ripe womanhood, and given evidence of those charming rustic accomplishments which soon drew to her general admiration, his passion gave him serious annoyance. Sophie soon showed that he was not disagreeable to her; and when, one day, Hop seized her around the waist just after a swimming race in which she had triumphed, and began to kiss her neck and lips with more than usual ardor, she artlessly indulged a reciprocal tenderness, declaring she loved him better than anything on earth, and dearly enough to become his for life. The first part of this declaration pleased and delighted Hop, but the second did not sound so agreeable. He feared that she might make matrimony indispensable to the fulfilment of his wishes, and in this he was seriously resolved not to engage. A year passed away, and Hop became convinced that Sophie had settled on making this the price of her possession. She would allow him any degree of familiarity, and gratify her own love by taking full liberty with him in turn, yet further than this she would not consent to go, and strenuously repulsed every attempt which Hop ventured to make. She would ride and ramble with him, fish with him, swim with him unreservedly, and go a bathing with him in the same limpid and transparent pools; but there she stopped. She professed to feel, but steadily refused to grant his desires; and Hop at last got to believe her.

This proved a vexatious point, and often disturbed their intimacy for months at a time; but all of a sudden a perfectly agreeable understanding was arranged between them.

Now, whether Sophie's adventure with Captain Mantooth at the secluded ford was the result of pure accident, or of a compact with Hop to that effect, the reader must conjecture from the facts and from the sequel. But certain it is that Hop was soon acquainted with the whole affair, and, truly guessing that the captain had been too deeply smitten to delay making his addresses longer than he could compose himself, had taken up his abode at Mr. Pomroy's to witness the whole future progress of the plan, and was, therefore, fully prepared not only to see his fun, but also to perfect his designs, when his simple-minded friend rode up as described. What these designs were, the courteous reader must divine from what I shall now proceed to relate.

Like most uneducated and secluded people, many of the good citizens about Lick-the-skillet were tinctured with strong tendencies to the marvelous and supernatural. The wild and mountainous character of the country was eminently calculated to beget and nurture superstitious impressions. The dark winding glens, the unfathomed precipices, the unexplored caverns which now and then were discovered in the bed of the mountains, the dashing torrents and unfelled forests around, all contributed to produce such feelings. It will not, therefore, be wondered at that the mysterious and melancholy fate which had overtaken old Hans Von Tromp should have been the source of numerous awful stories in the neighborhood; and that as time wore on these stories had gained firmer hold on the imagination of those who heard or narrated them.

The mill had never been tenanted since the death of its builder, for, as Pomroy had negro fellows to aid him in sawing and grinding, he had no occasion to hire white men, who would, in such a case, have been forced to sleep in Hans Von Tromp's apartment, the owner's dwelling having but two rooms and a garret. The head negro was thoroughly the victim of superstitious fears, and on his authority principally some of the most awful tales were told about, in connection with the mill. It was reported that the black, being detained on a certain night much later than usual at the mill, had been surprised by the sudden entrance of a tall and large man, black like himself, with two small fireballs for eyes, and, instead of teeth of the usual kind, immense fangs of red hot iron supplied their place in his mouth. He proceeded straight to the old Dutchman's sleeping room, and entering without ceremony, his voice and old Von Tromp's were soon heard at a high pitch, and seemingly engaged in a most ferocious quarrel. A noise of scuffling and stamping was heard next, and presently afterward the door of Hans' room flew wide open, whilst he and the black giant, locked in a deadly embrace, came whirling and wrestling through the mill-house, first one falling and then the other. As they approached the cavity near the flywheel, and through which it was the honest old millwright's joy and delight to watch its steady revolutions, Hans began to pull back and struggle more fiercely, and his hair rose erect on his head from excessive fright. The black man, however, urged him vigorously forward with a most unearthly grin; they came to its very edge, and Hans had only time to exclaim, in a voice of despair, "Dish wash no pard of der bargain, goot mynheer teufell!" before both went through together, the black on top, and then nothing more was ever seen of either.

Another version was that an old man who had come to the mill late one evening to get his employer's flour, being rather sleepy-headed, had fallen into a deep slumber in a dark corner of the room; and no one supposing but that he had gone back home, the millers all left for the night, locking him unfortunately in, to take his chances with the goblins and devils who were supposed to infest the house. He slept on very quietly until a little before midnight, when, all of a sidden, he was awakened by the sound of heavy footsteps, sounding over the floor towards the bolting-trough. An immense black figure strode past him, exhaling a strong scent of brimstone, which left no room to doubt that it was the devil. He entered old Von Tromp's room, who greeted him with a scornful guttural grunt as he opened the door. Immediately the noise of a struggle was heard, and fierce imprecations were uttered by both parties; and then a crash followed, which seemed to jar the mill to its deepest foundations, at the same time that a terrible splash was heard in the waters of the race underneath.

These wild stories, and many others of a like marvelous character, were afloat through the whole district of Lick-the-skillet, and no one believed them more devoutly and unqualifiedly, as it happened, than Captain Lafayette Mantooth. Hop Hubbub was well aware of this infirmity of the captain, and he resolved to play off upon his credulous friend, on the night of his marriage, a most cruel and wicked prank.

It has been mentioned that Mr. Pomroy's house afforded not a single spare bed-room, and, as Hop very naturally concluded that they would be compelled to make use of old Hans Von Tromp's snug little apartment in the mill for a nuptial chamber, he determined to oust the unfortunate bridegroom of his promised bridal enjoyments, if personating the devil and the Dutchman could do it. With this view he had to enlist the services of a boon companion in mischief, hardly less known through Lick-the-skillet than himself. But, as Mr. Josiah Morehead was a merchant in full business, besides being a noted sportsman, and, in consequence, often called from home on long journeys, he was not a very frequent visitor at this favorite haunt of his friend Hop, and had not been there for years when called to go down upon this occasion. Joe had a long head and a most inventive genius. He had even been known to outwit Hop himself on several occasions, which caused many to wonder afterwards why the latter should have employed him on that in question. He was handsome and more dressy than Hop, and was always enabled thus to run ahead in the good graces of the tender sex.

The wedding-day came, and the invited guests set busily about preparing to lend their friendly aid in making way with the substantial viands which they knew Mrs. Pomroy had furnished for the occasion. A solemn fast was held during the entire day, that they might not destroy or impair the tone of their eager appetites; and in honor of the event Mr. Pomroy closed his mill until the next morning, which enabled him to devote his whole time in arranging for the festivity. About the middle of the afternoon, Hop Hubbub and his friend Morehead, being both engaged to wait on the impatient bridegroom, rode up to announce the captain's readiness for the event, saying that he had been washed and dressed ever since noon. The fair bride was, however, still engaged at the cake bowls, and received the two groomsmen in the supper room in her ordinary tidy attire, with her sleeves tucked up considerably above the elbow, and her frock and petticoats drawn half way to the knee; whilst her pretty face was all in a flush from excitement and fatigue. Such was the fascination of her looks and manner, such the striking development of her voluptuous figure thus attired, that Joe Morehead, frail creature that he was, fell into ecstasy of admiration at first sight, and as he had known her when a child, and was her father's intimate friend and merchant, the charming Sophie was forced to allow him a hearty salute of her sweet lips; and, it may as well be added, that, improving by the rule of taking an inch where an ell has been granted, Joe could not resist the temptation to press to his bosom her soft and glowing form. Such tokens of warm admiration from this fine and handsome gentleman so pleased the bride elect that she betrayed her joy by a scarlet blush, which, as may be imagined, Joe by no means failed to notice particularly; and when, after a minute or two, Hop stepped out to see the old folks, he availed himself of the opportunity to repeat, far more warmly, the same delightful feats of gallantry and devotion, which thoroughly enraptured the susceptible young creature to whom he had already imparted a share of his glowing passion.

Look out, Hop—that thou hast not a cuckoo's egg in thy nest, and trusted thy secret to wily hands!

The hour approached, and a whole troop of neighbors, all in their Sunday clothes, and rigged out in all the finery they could scrape up by hook or by crook, already filled the parlor of the miller's house, anxiously awaiting the appearance of the wedding folks, as they called the bride and her groom. The parson who was to join them as man and wife had arrived; the old folks had come in and taken their seats; and as, now and then, a fragrant scent from the luscious viands in the next room would flavor the passing breath of wind, and draw the salivary fluids to a hundred craving mouths, the whole company would simultaneously ejaculate a wish that the young people would come along and have it over at once.

At length they were gratified; the bridal party appeared, attended by half a dozen couples of groomsmen and ladies in waiting, and the ceremony was commenced. All eyes were turned to catch a last glimpse of the belle of Lick-the-skillet, ere she changed her lot in life. "Ah, Sophie!" every one thought, "no more wild romping and swimming with thy admirers now!" Sophie never looked prettier in all her life. She was dressed with no pretensions to the fashion of the day; but, if there was none of this, its absence was more than compensated in those round, naked arms, that soft neck, and the glowing bust which was only half concealed by her low stomacher.

But ah! how shall I describe thee, happy, thrice happy Lafayette Mantooth—thou worthy representative of all the pride and chivalry of thy native Lick-the-skillet! Deeply impressed, like a sincere Christian ought to have been, with the importance and solemnity of the occasion, the captain approached to the centre of the room with slow, measured step, eyes half closed, head thrown slightly back, and with a countenance of woe and sanctimony that would have done no discredit to Job in the darkest hour of his affliction. He looked as though he had come to bury Sophie, not to wed her; but the captain had good reason for this unseasonable tristfulness of demeanor. He had pondered the matter well over, and had brought his mind to conclude that, heathen as he was, he was entering into the holy estate of matrimony, not by God's appointment as he should do, but in unworthy obedience to carnal weakness and desires. These, it is true, were uncontrollable and irrepressible, but by way of full penance the captain felt it to be his duty to approach the altar devotionally and meekly; and although he strictly fulfilled this vow in mind and to outward appearance, yet Sophie was, once or twice, in their passage to the wedding apartment, forced to cry out softly for quarter, as the eager groom would involuntarily press and squeeze her tender arm betwixt his sharp, projecting ribs, and the pointed elbow in whose capacious crotch that pretty limb was resting.

The captain's wedding apparel eminently became his lank, ungainly figure. It consisted, first, of a blue broadcloth coat with brass buttons, with an immense collar reaching almost to the crown of his flat head, and falling gradually as it met the lapel; the point of conjunction being marked by two huge intersecting flaps, shaped like dogs' ears, and standing out prominently on either side. The waist of the coat had out-traveled his own by at least half of a foot, and the skirts dangled quite gracefully below the knee as the wearer stalked along; whilst the loose breeches bagged and flapped around his diminutive legs with a motion not unlike that of the elephant's ears as he marches leisurely around the ring. His chin was propped by a high stiff stock, which fitted so closely around his neck that, what with this and the starched shirt collar which covered the whole lower portion of his face, the captain was scarcely enabled to move his head without carrying around his whole body; and to complete the picture, his feet were supplied with a pair of stout-soled high quarter shoes, selected and brought out by Joe Morehead, which creaked forth delightful music by way of heralding his martial steps.

Now, the old preacher, whose jolly, rubicund face had been nothing but a convexity of bland expectant smiles all along (doubtless in anticipation of the good cheer and handsome fee which awaited him), no sooner caught sight of the sanctimonious and rueful expression of the worthy groom, for whose piety and snug property he had all imaginable respect, than he also drew down his features to a genuine religious length, drooped his eyes, and assumed at once a becoming gravity of manner. He began the ceremony in a hoarse, bull-frog sort of drawl, that had nearly discomposed the fair bride and her two mischievous friends at the very outset; whilst it so deeply impressed the captain that he gave a long, deep, penitential sigh by way of response. The answers of the fair bride were made in such subdued whispers that they were scarcely audible to those who stood around, and when interrogated to know whether, forsaking all others, she would cling only to him who was now to become her lord, Sophie responded so indistinctly, and with such an arch expression of eyes and mouth, that none were able to determine clearly whether she had said yes or no. The preacher, however, was not the man to balk at ceremony on this point, and, presuming an affirmative where nothing warranted a negative, he proceeded to put the same question to Captain Mantooth. This time, however, the worthy parson put on rather a more demure face, assumed a more affected and drawling tone of voice, and dwelt tremblingly and lingeringly upon each word as it fell from his lips. The captain all along had attributed Sophie's low, indistinct mutterings to that amiable and becoming diffidence so common and so very natural under the circumstances, and now that his turn had come to promise, solemnly, that he would love, honor, and protect her as his wedded wife, and cling to her only of all women on earth, he resolved, by a master-stroke, to inspire and reassure her with a portion of his own honest confidence and mental tranquillity. To this end he elevated his head an inch or two above the level of his stock, swayed his back slightly, closed his eyes altogether, and responded in the same tone as the preacher's, "I will, Brother Dipwell, the Lord being my helper!"

As the captain uttered these words at full prayer pitch, and just exactly in the attitude which I have described, the effect produced on the auditors was instantaneous, though quite various. The preacher involuntarily opened his eyes, as though taken by surprise; the old Baptist men and women present simultaneously sealed the promise with a fervent amen; some of the young folks tittered, and others giggled outright. But Hop! He would not have taken the profits of a year's practice for the scene—and it would have done one good to have seen how, with a dexterity peculiar to himself, he threw up the corners of his eyes Chinese fashion, and how quizzically he puckered his mouth—though he did not so much as crack a smile.

Not so with the merry-hearted and less stoical bride! She fell, for support, full against the lank, hollow side of her newly-made lord (who could scarcely contain himself for rapture under the sweet burden), and gave vent to her feelings by a flow of uncontainable, though subdued laughter; whilst the muscles of Joe Morehead's mouth and nose began to twitter and jump at a most frolicksome rate, which was a way that worthy had of expressing his diversion and merriment, rather than by the usual vulgar mode.

The ceremony being over, the groom managed, by dint of stretching and propping his sparse allowance of lips, to get a sufficiency of skin over his teeth to give a salute to his shrinking bride; and then her cheeks and mouth were literally stormed with volleys of smacking kisses from those around, male as well as female, whilst many claimed the wedding privilege of hugging and tousing the bride and all her maids. At length a truce was begged and quarter solicited by the weaker party, and then the revels and carousing began. None of your frigid, staid, ceremonious doings! Everybody felt merry, and everybody danced, the preacher himself leading down in the opening reel, and the old miller and his well-worn dame close at his heels. Lafayette capered and shuffled as if he had been born anew in the flesh as well as in the spirit, and if, in crossing over once, his legs had not unfortunately become tangled so as to trip him suddenly over, he would, undoubtedly, have borne off the palm from all competitors, for the captain always danced for the love of the thing, in good, earnest sincerity, not for the purpose of merely showing himself off in certain nimble feats or graceful steps.

How everybody's heart bounded and thumped when the little brass bell rang for supper in Sophie's weaving-room! The dancing ceased in a second, and in the very midst of a merry reel, in which Joe Morehead and the bride were performing cuts and crossings which drew unbounded admiration. Each one seized hold of his partner, and dashed off at a long trot, for the hearty exercise had only served to increase the eagerness of appetites already most severely tested. And then followed such furious assaults upon the carcasses of slaughtered chickens, and ducks, and turkeys, and even of geese, all of whom had yielded up their lives in the cause! The smoke-house had been brought under contribution also, and several greasy, well-smoked, mellow-flavored old hams occupied regular stations along the centre of the table, showing the extent of the innovation; whilst here and there, as if to prove that every species of foray had been put in practice, a haunch of dried venison, and messes of nicely-fried fish, recently drawn from the trap under the mill (a relic of Hans Von Tromp's piscatory achievements and skill), were spread out in tempting array before the delighted guests. A row of side tables groaned beneath the weight of cakes, and puddings, and home-made preserves; and large hampers of apples and peaches were seen planted in every corner of the room; while, to crown all, the jolly old miller would now and then admonish his guests to save themselves as much as possible, as he had in the back entry (to use his own expression and simple language), "a plenty of millions, both water and mush."* Never before had such fine doings been seen in Lick-the-skillet, and several acknowledged frankly that they had set eyes for the first time, that night, on knives and forks. In proof of this, it was remarked that many a forest-born yeoman did not know how to use them, until instructed by some more traveled neighbor, and then they declared, with a grin, "that the things helped a body powerfully in eating."

After supper had been dispatched, and when every one had declared himself fully satisfied, the guests again adjourned to the parlor (or, as the people of Lick-the-skillet would say, the big room), and the dancing was resumed for awhile, that the ample allowance of victuals which had been taken in might be well stowed and settled before bed-time. By way of an agreeable change, dancing was suspended occasionally, and "Sister Phebe," "Grind the Bottle," and "Blind man's buff" were introduced. At length, an hour or so after midnight, the amusements of this pleasant evening, which was marked as having been the brightest in the life of many who were present, were brought to an end by the time-honored custom of selling and redeeming pawns. By three o'clock all the merry guests had departed for their homes, and Lafayette was left, accompanied only

---

*Backwoods people, in the South, invariably pronounce *melon* as if it was *million*, and they conclude that the soft, *mushy* contents of the *musk*melon must, of course, give name to the fruit. [Cobb's note.]

by his two principal attendants, to prepare for the grand finale of all wedding nights.

But a most painful and alarming piece of news was in store for the impatient bridegroom. Hop Hubbub and Joe Morehead, who had just returned from escorting, in company with the maids, the fair bride to her quarters for the night, now entered to inform Captain Mantooth that Sophie was snugly abed in old Von Tromp's room at the mill, and that he might follow as soon as he chose. The captain started, and stared at his attendants with mute incredulity; but when he was seriously assured that such had really been the arrangement, his knees smote together in spite of all efforts to control their motion, and his heart sank within him. The blood which had been coursing through his veins at boiling-point temperature the moment before now dropped to zero in a trice. The captain was actually debating to himself whether he should not fly the track, for his fears of ghosts were too strongly implanted to be shaken from their hold even by his anticipated pleasure.

At this moment, Joe Morehead left the room, and Hop alone undertook the guidance of the now sorely-frightened bridegroom. The captain was ashamed, of course, to explain the cause of his delay and indecision, and Hop was vastly too smart at his business even to hint that he suspected it; so, after the lapse of fifteen or twenty minutes, he at last succeeded in leading the captain out of the house, and, having conducted him to the door of the mill, thrust him forcibly in, and bade him a hasty good night.

The mill room was perfectly dark, and Lafayette, thus suddenly abandoned and left to himself, could perceive only a faint ray of light glimmering through the keyhole of the bridal chamber. Two or three immense strides of his long legs carried him two-thirds of the distance which intervened; and then, collecting his shattered and palsied strength, he succeeded in clearing the remainder by a single leap, striking against the door with a force that actually jarred the whole building. In an instant more he had forced it open, and presented himself before his surprised and laughter-loving spouse an animated mass of shaking terror. But here matters presented to him a worse aspect than ever. There, in its accustomed corner, still stood the rough bedstead of old Von Tromp, and from which he had risen to engage in the unholy strife which ended in his death. Mr. Pomroy had reverentially forbidden all persons under him ever to remove it, and so here it was now just as its occupant had left it six years ago, with his large sea chest, and hat, and boots, all stowed away by its side. Lafayette's teeth chattered, and his long bony limbs shook terribly whilst he undressed and prepared for bed. Not even the sight and presence of that charming little creature who had been the subject of his thoughts by day and of his dreams by night for a month past, added to the consciousness that she was now all his own, could allay or dispel the awful sensations of fright which deprived him of his vigor, and were about to cheat him of his fondest anticipations.

At length, however, he managed to get rid of his outer garments, and then, with quaking heart and fluttering pulse, extinguished the lamp. As the light had been placed on a chair quite near to the bed, it cost the captain but a single exertion to slide in; and, nimbly whisking up the sheets and counterpane, he covered over head and ears before one could have said Jack Robinson, and then tumbled up close to Sophie, who often declared afterwards that his bones felt just like lumps of ice.

All now was quiet for several minutes, and under the soothing influences of Sophie's balmy breath, the captain was beginning to coax and warm himself into comparative forgetfulness and ease of mind, when, suddenly, the large door of the mill-room was heard to swing open with a harsh, reverberating slam. Lafayette jumped as though every nerve in his body had been severed, and shuddered from head to foot with unfeigned alarm. Heavy, clanging footsteps resounded over the floor, and were evidently advancing to the bridal chamber at a regular measured pace. The perspiration gathered in large drops on Lafayette's forehead, and quickly bedewed his whole body; while, at the same time, Sophie's little heart began to beat pitty-pat, in double quick time, though from a very different cause than ghostly fear. Just as the steps paused at the door of the chamber, Lafayette found that sulphurous vapors were penetrating through keyhole, and crevice, and window cranny, and he felt already the symptoms of suffocation. One hope, however, flashed on his mind; he had locked and bolted the door securely, and as old Hans Von Tromp was not there to let the intruder in, he persuaded himself, faintly and partially, that the latter might go away without attempting forcible entrance. But this delusive ray was soon dissipated and obscured. The echo of the last step without had scarcely died away, before Lafayette's sharpened ears caught the sound of a creaking noise in the direction of Von Tromp's bedstead, like that which might proceed from some one moving heavily over in sleep. In a moment, all the wild and awful tales of the strife betwixt the old Dutchman and the black giant, with the whole horrid accompaniments, came to his recollection. He saw already the grim features, the blazing eyeballs, and red hot teeth of the one; the fierce struggles, the harsh imprecations, and frantic appeals of the other, fell next on his ear. Then came the deadly grapple, and the unearthly laughter, and the dying groans, and the splashing uproar of troubled waters.

This ghastly concentration of all that was revolting to mortal man, and appalling to human nature, was more than the weak nerves of Captain Lafayette Mantooth could possibly endure, or have been expected to endure. No wonder he should forget his blooming bride, and forego his eager anticipations!

As things stood, let alone what was expected to ensue, the captain felt that there was no safety for a Christian man but in speedy flight, and for this there was but one only chance. Immediately at the head of his bed was a capacious window, defended only by a stout shutter, which fastened inside by means of an iron hook and staple. The sill was not more than ten feet from the ground, and this to Captain Mantooth's legs was no distance at all. His resolution was formed in a trice of time; and, in momentary dread that he would next hear old Von Tromp's grunt of welcome to his black visitor, without even stopping to catch up a single piece of clothing, and leaving Sophie to take devil's fare with the hindmost, Lafayette opened the window with a nimble, sleight-o'-hand effort, made a swinging leap through the air, with the tail of his long shirt streaming full out behind, and, having reached the ground safely, scampered off towards his own quiet home with the agility and speed of a flying Indian.

The track having thus been cleared, the nocturnal intruder without began to twist and turn softly the knob of the door, and to rap slightly, now and then, on the panels. But all to no purpose; everything was still within. Surely, thought Hop (who, as the reader has doubtless imagined, was personating the black visitor of old Von Tromp) the girl has not followed the groom! Anxious to ascertain this fact and beginning already to distrust his wily confederate, Hop applied his lips to the key-hole, and whispered, in a low tone of voice, "Sophie! Sophie!" No answer came, but a suppressed titter caught his sharpened ear, followed by a smart rustle of shucks and feathers, as if the fair bride had rolled from one side of the bed to the other. Hop waited anxiously one moment to see if his ally would now open the door according to arrangement; but Joe had, apparently, forgotten this part, or, considering that the groom's flight (ere he had even found a chance to grunt for the old Dutchman) was the signal for his own departure, had probably made his escape, as was agreed, through the same aperture. The door remained fast, and Hop, at length, lost all patience. Again, however, he essayed the pronunciation of Sophie's name, and the whispers were sent through the keyhole somewhat louder, but still subdued. His respiration was almost entirely suspended, as he eagerly listened for some answering signal within. Suddenly he started back as if an earwig had leaped into the distended cavity of his ear; a knowing, half-humorous expression flitted over his countenance. He then turned despairingly from the door, and, dismantling himself of the disguise he had adopted, slid quietly back through the window of Sophie's weaving-room, which had been assigned to Joe Morehead and himself for sleeping quarters during the few hours that were yet wanted to bring the daylight.

"The sly old trout!" muttered Hop, as he groped his way cautiously to the pallet, fearing to upset some chair or table, "a nice rare-ripe I have made of myself!"

"Holloh!" exclaimed the voice of Joe Morehead, in a smothered tone, as he turned softly over at hearing Hop, "why, what the deuce brought you back so soon?"

Hop, for the first time in his life, shuddered with sudden apprehension. He was expecting to hear any other voice than that of his friend at that time, and when he called to mind what had transpired scarcely ten minutes since, could not at first believe that it really was the veritable Joe in solid flesh and blood.

"*Here*, are you, curse you!" said Hop, half seriously, as he slipped into the vacant place on the pallet, and chunked Joe's portly side and belly with several vigorous bouts with his fist.

"Here, indeed!" answered the imperturbable Joe. "Why, I've been back these twenty minutes or more! Confess, Hop, didn't I act old Von Tromp's part to the very life?"

"In a horn—" answered Hop mysteriously.

"What do you mean?" asked Joe, quite gravely. "Why, didn't you hear me grunt?"

"Yes did I, by Jucks!" replied Hop, "several times; and much more naturally than ghosts usually grunt. You're a crack grunter, Joe!"

"I thought it was best to give him a *good* scare, you know!" said Joe, archly and dryly.

"It didn't seem to scare *Sophie* much, I thought!" again said Hop, with quizzical emphasis.

"Oh! Sophie understood it all, you know!" answered Joe, in the same artless, indifferent tone.

"I rather think she did!" was Hop's laconic reply.

"What a devilish little hussy she is!" said Joe; laughingly.

"Yes—a *devilish* more so than I *thought!*" replied Hop.

"It's not at all surprising, though!" gaped out Joe; "she's had the best sort of a teacher, you know, Hop!"

"Yes," again answered Hop, chunking Joe stronger than ever, "yes, *the very* best the country affords. I'll knock under after this, old trout!"

"What if Mantooth *should* find it out?" asked Joe, seemingly indifferent.

"I guess Sophie will manage about that for you!" replied Hop.

"For *me!*" said Joe, whistling for surpise. "I suppose *you* had no part in it, then! I thought you were more man than to beat a retreat after the battle's over!"

"Oh! as for *me*," answered Hop, carelessly, "I didn't so much as get a sight of the battle, the escalade, or the escape. The old Dutchman's ghost found better fare, it would seem, than fighting his black visitor, for he did not even think to open the door!"

"Why, I followed Mantooth, you know," said Joe, in a low and lisping sort of tone, "and had no time to open the door; and, besides, I hardly thought it was fair to scare both bride and groom."

"So, it scared Sophie, after all, then!" said Hop. "Why, I thought she understood it all, Joe!"

"Yes," answered Joe, with admirable imperturbability, "but she screamed a *little* when I grunted, in spite of all she could do!"

"No wonder!" said Hop, bluntly.

"And so you came off right away, did you?" asked Joe, again.

"No, I waited a little, just a little while, Joe!" was Hop's answer. "I hardly thought you'd 've beat me back, though."

"Well, I fear it will play the very d—l to-morrow, all through Lick-the-skillet!" said Joe, half seriously.

"No; I think the d—l has played his full part tonight, friend Joe!" answered Hop, in his natural tone. "Come, old trout, no more see-sawing. You've trumped my trick right fairly, and I'm not the man to revoke, you know!"

"Well, well," drawled forth Joe, "you're the strangest fellow I ever saw! Here you go to——"

"True to the last, hey!" said Hop, turning over, laughingly. "Well, there's the roosters—let's go to sleep."

The next morning, soon after sunrise, the worthy and valorous captain, accompanied by one or two of his near neighbors, was seen riding up to Mr. Pomroy's gate. Sophie, already up and dressed, welcomed them at the door, directing towards her husband a look in which disgust was faintly commingled with mischief; whilst Mr. Pomroy and his spouse, totally taken aback by his appearance in such company, and fully believing that he had passed the night with their fair daughter, stared at first one, and then the other, in mutual surprise.

"Good morning, Sophie!" said the captain, approaching his blushing bride, "how did you make out last night after I was forced to leave you?"

"Oh, very well indeed, I thank you, captain!" answered the bride, shrinking back, and curtsying leeringly.

"He didn't get in then?" asked the captain, amazed.

"Who—*who* get in?" asked Sophie, in turn.

"The devil, sure!" answered the captain, with quaking emphasis.

"You must be out of your senses, you old fool!" said the bold Sophie, affecting very considerable pettishness.

"What? and didn't the *inside* one trouble you either?" again asked the puzzled captain, holding up both hands.

"I assure you, my doughty sir, I was never less troubled in my life than last night, especially after *you* left me," answered Sophie, smiling as she again curtsied.

"My God! my God, Sophie!" exclaimed her perplexed lord, in doleful accents, "I made sure, my darling, you'd be ruined forever. Oh, neighbors, and Mr. Pomroy, I was sorely, most sorely beset this overnight."

"Since the world was made," put in old Mrs. Pomroy, casting up her eyebrows, and puckering her mouth, "did ever a man talk before about being *beset* on his wedding night—and Sophie so young, too!"

I do assure you, dear madam," answered the captain, in the same tone, "that I grieve and am ashamed to tell what happened to Sophie and me last night."

"And how do *you* know, sir, *what* happened to me?" asked Sophie, brushing up smartly.

"And I'd make you *know*, if I was Sophie, for blabbing this way before two men neighbors!" again said the now nettled dame.

"Ah, my friends!" sighed the captain appealingly, speaking to Mr. Pomroy and his neighbors, "it was the Dutchman and the Evil One, as sure as earth. It must have been. Nothing else but the fear of the soul's enemy could ever have driven me from my bride's arms."

"Driven you from your bride's arms!" repeated Mr. Pomroy, now joining in also, gravely and sternly. "You surely did not leave Sophronia alone last night, Captain Mantooth; let me hope not, for the sake of all the men in Lick-the-skillet!"

"Not alone, neighbor Pomroy," again sighed the captain, "but worse than alone, I fear—far worse. I fear mightily, dear sir, that the devil was near to her, if not with her, this night last gone."

"The d—l, sure enough!" says Sophie, tossing her head. "I say, too, if the d—l ever goes about in the shape of a flat turnip stuck on two handspikes, with a blown-up eelskin for his body, I surely had him with me last night, but, thank God, not long."

"How strange this all is!" ejaculated Mr. Pomroy.

"Oh, you must know, pa, that Captain Mantooth jumped out of the window and left me, last night, before he ever got cleverly into bed," said Sophie, turning to her father with an air of complaint; "never mind, though, for, as God's my judge, the *creature* never comes a-bed with me again!"

"Oh, don't say that, Sophie; you'll kill me if you do!" said Captain Mantooth, imploringly, and seriously alarmed.

"I *will* say it, and stick to it, too!" answered the offended bride.

"Captain Mantooth, I must say that you've acted the strangest I ever have heard talk of," said Mr. Pomroy.

"Do tell us what's been the cause of all this flare-up."

The captain complied; and, beginning with the time when Hop Hubbub had pushed him into the mill, narrated faithfully the whole scenes that followed—the footsteps, the noise in old Von Tromp's bed, his own fright, and his escape through the window. During this strange recital, the two neighbors, who believed every word of it, as well as the wild tales about the Dutchman and the black giant, listened with staring eyes and open mouths, attesting the same by declaring that they had been aroused soon after midnight by Captain Mantooth, afoot, with nothing on but his shirt, and on his way home, who told them just the same story which he had now told Mr. Pomroy. But this latter sagacious gentleman gave several meaning nods of the head, as though, whilst not doubting his son-in-law's veracity, he was gravely dissenting to his opinions of the supernatural agencies which had been at work, and which showed, moreover, plainly enough, that, with true professional acumen, he could see deeper into the millstone than that. He admitted, very wisely, that somebody had *played* the devil, sure enough, but that he thought that the devil *himself* was free from all guilt in *this* instance; whilst his equally sharp-witted old dame blessed herself that Sophie was married just the same as if she had been the mother of a dozen children.

"And where's Hop Hubbub and Mr. Morehead?" asked one of the neighbors, who had caught an idea from Mr. Pomroy.

"Oh, they left more than an hour ago," answered the miller, as he exchanged a shrewd glance with his brightening neighbor.

"Indeed!" said Sophie, wonderingly and artlessly, "I thought, pa, they went away last night."

"No, child," put in Mrs. Pomroy, regarding Sophie tenderly and pryingly; "we put them in the weaving-room on a pallet after the supper things were moved out; and they must have slept mighty softly and quietly, for we heard nothing of them till just before day."

"Sophie!" said the captain, after he had finished his narration, and sidling up to his bride, whose face was now again bright and beaming as ever, "Sophie, you'll take that back, and go home with me to-night now, won't you, sweet?"

"Yes, Sophie, I think you had best pardon the captain," said her father. "Strange things *will* happen sometimes; and the mill was just the place for them to happen. So, now, neighbors, we'll all agree to say nothing about what's befel the captain here, and Sophie; and you, Sophie, must go home, and behave so prettily for the future that the devil will never get after you again."

To this, the charming bride of Lick-the-skillet found it necessary to assent, and, as a token of her reconciliation with the captain, permitted him to kiss those cherry lips, and embrace that peerless figure, which had so long charmed his imagination, and filled him with fondest love. I have never heard but that they lived most happily together as man and wife, and, though there are some pretty little stories circulated about the night that Sophie spent with the ghost of her old friend, Hans Von Tromp, in the mill-house, and it is whispered that Mr. Joe Morehead is a frequent and favorite visitor at her husband's mansion, yet she has the character of being a pattern of a wife.

Old Peter Pomroy and his wife were still living when I last visited Lick-the-skillet. Hop Hubbub is dead, they say; but when, and how, and where he died, nobody exactly knows. Many believe that he will one day reappear in his old haunts; but it is a thing spoken about as if they thought he might as likely appear in the shape of a ghost as of a man.

I cannot undertake to argue this point, but certain I am, and sadly do I fear that, taking him all in all, we shall never behold Hop's like again.

"But you surely will tell us something more about that wily old mad-cap, Joe Morehead?"

No, kind reader; here must end the Bride of Lick-the-skillet.

(1807–1884)

J. F. H. Claiborne

J[ohn] F[rancis] H[amtramck] Claiborne was born near Natchez on April 24, 1807. He studied law in Virginia, with a cousin, and planned originally to practice there; but delicate health caused him to return to Natchez. There he became active in journalism and politics. He was an active supporter of Andrew Jackson, and himself served in both the Mississippi legislature and the United States Congress. In 1841 Claiborne became editor of the *Mississippi Free Trader,* and in that journal he began his initial work on the history of Mississippi. Following this he edited newspapers in New Orleans before moving to Bay St. Louis, where he engaged in the growing of sea island cotton and in full-scale historical writing. He spent a great deal of time on a history of the Southwest, but lost the completed manuscript in a sunken steamboat on the Mississippi River; from this he salvaged, he claimed, from memory, only a part, published as *The Life and Times of Sam Dale* (1860). In 1870 he returned to Natchez to complete work on his very important magnum opus, *Mississippi As A Province, Territory, and State,* the first volume of which was published in 1881. The manuscript of the second, completed in 1884, was destroyed when his home burned in March of that year; his shock and grief over this loss were so great that he died in Natchez, barely two months later, on May 17.

81

Though he is primarily known to us as a historian, the following selection, first published in *Harper's New Monthly Magazine* of June, 1862, demonstrates not only Claiborne's historian's instinct to record the passing scene, but also his fine sense of humor and, perhaps, his appreciation of the writings of those we now refer to as the "Southwest Humorists." With this sketch, and the better known "A Trip through the Piney Woods," Claiborne proves his right to be counted among them.

Rough Riding Down South

ALONG the Gulf of Mexico, or what the United States Coast Survey styles the Mississippi Sound, extending across the State of Mississippi, with a depth in the interior of about one hundred miles, there lies a region of country usually denominated the Pine Woods. The soil is sandy and thin, producing small crops of rice, potatoes, and corn, a little cotton, indigo, and sugar-cane, for home consumption. But it sustains a magnificent pine forest, capable of supplying for centuries to come the navies of the world. The people are of primitive habits, and are chiefly lumbermen or herdsmen. Exempt from swamps and inundation, from the vegetable decomposition incidental to large agricultural districts, fanned by the sea-breeze and perfumed by the balsamic exhalations of the pine, it is one of the healthiest regions in the world. If the miraculous fountain, in search of which the brave old Ponce de Leon met his death in the lagoons of Florida in 1512, may be found any where, it will be in the district I am now wandering over. I have never seen so happy a people. Not afflicted with sickness or harassed by litigation; not demoralized by vice or tormented with the California fever; living in a state of equality, where none are rich and none in want; where the soil is too thin to accumulate wealth, and yet sufficiently productive to reward industry; manufacturing all that they wear; producing all they consume; and preserving, with primitive simplicity of manners, the domestic virtues of their sires. Early marriages are universal. Fathers yet infants in law, and happy grandams yet in the vigor of womanhood, may be found in every settlement; and numerous are the firesides around which cluster ten or a dozen children, with mothers still lovely and buoyant as in the days of their maiden bloom.

Leaving the Gulf shore at Pascagoula for the interior, in a couple of hours the traveler finds himself on the banks of a broad, deep, beautiful river, the Escatawba, curving gently down to mingle with the ocean. It flows through a forest of colossal growth. Many of these hoary Titans were overthrown by the great hurricane of '52, which began at 10 A.M., August 24, and blew with increasing fury until 12 P.M. next day, raging with undiminished violence until 12 at night, when it began to abate. It tore away whole masses of bluff on the sea-shore, dug up the earth from the roots of trees, blew down the potato hills as it swooped along the surface, and prostrated forests in its mad career.

Here, at what is now called Elder's Ferry, once stood the lodge of the last chieftain of the Pascagoulas. His warriors had all perished in the fatal wars with the Muscogees of Alabama. Sole survivor of the last conflict, the enemy still upon his trail, he led the women and children from the Escatawba to the sea, preferring death in its much loved waters to captivity and slavery. You have heard of the mysterious music which at midnight chimes along these shores; a low, lute-like strain, sometimes a vesper hymn, sometimes like a harp-string breaking. When the winds and surges sleep, in the still hours of night, I have often heard this plaintive anthem; and tradition says it is the death-chant of the Pascagoulas that wails along the sea.

The Indian village stood on a picturesque bluff, the gentle river, flowing through prairies of verdure, margined by aged oaks that lift their heads among the clouds and bathe their mossy beards in the silver spray beneath. the country spreads out into a continuous meadow of boundless extent, on every side dotted with little islets of palm-like trees. At intervals a serpentine line of ravine comes sweeping along, fringed with dwarf laurel, myrtle, jasmine, and other parasites, and the whole plain around is embroidered with flowers of every hue. Ah! it is pleasant to bivouac in these solitary plains, the quiet stars smiling upon you, and the fragrant winds singing in the trees around. There is a charm in these grand old woods— in these laughing waters—in these remote retreats, where only an

echo of the storms of life is heard. No wonder the imaginative an-
cients peopled them with divinities: for here, at every step, one can
but feel the presence of a God; and the feeling chastens and refines
the heart. It is not in your gorgeous temples, with coquettish eyes
and Shylock countenances around, and vanity peeping out even
from the pulpit, that one truly feels the sentiment of religion in its
humanizing and exalting influences.

By the road-side, near the ruins of a rude country meeting-
house, long since deserted, may be seen a solitary grave. Years ago a
wanderer, once favored by fortune, high in the profession of the law,
died near this spot, the wretched victim of a debasing vice. His
body, his bottle, and the last lines he ever penned were found near
where he now sleeps:

> Pilgrim, wheresoe'er thou stray,
> Pause here upon thy weary way.
> Take this relic if thou may,
> And for its thirsty owner pray.
> Fatal gift, when overflowing!
> Oh, that man should ever knowing,
> Servant be to liquor's spell,
> Sorcery from the caves of hell!
>
>> Touch not—'tis poisonous to thee;
>> Taste not—alas, it ruined me!
>> The unclean thing forever shun,
>> Or thou, O pilgrim, art undone!
>> In this silent house of grace
>> Seek thy Maker, face to face;
>> Ask thy conscience, if thou will,
>> Dost thou good, or dost thou ill?
>
> Lonely now my way I go,
> Lingering through my life of woe;
> Stranger, for the lost one pray,
> And God will bless thee every day.
> On thy hearth-stone he will fling
> Countless blessings following,
> In thy spring time, in thy age,

Every day of life's brief page;
In thy health, and in thy store,
Grace and goodness evermore!

Crossing the Chickasawha River I took refuge from the noonday sun in the hospitable dwelling of Mr. R——. It is perched on an elevated bluff. Far down in a field below, on the riverside, his servants had been at work, and might now be seen winding up a zigzag path toward the house, to get the mid-day meal. A group of tiny darkeys were sitting under the trees in the yard awaiting their mothers. Suddenly a little cloud gathered on the horizon—there was a single burst of thunder—a single flash that blinded me for a moment—and then, oh what a shriek of agony from the wretched mothers! Three of the children had been killed by the fatal bolt. Never, ah never shall I forget that sight of sorrow, and the wailings of those broken hearts! I have seen the strong man crushed; the fond mother swooning over the loss of her first-born; the young and beautiful, just stepping into life on a pathway of flowers, stung by the serpent, and snatched away, leaving for the survivors, in the dim future, only a long despair; but never had I witnessed the intense grief of these simple slaves. All that they had to live for was wrapped up in the stricken infants that now, all lifeless, they pressed to their distracted bosoms.

Leaving the scene of sorrow, I entered the great pine forest that leads to the town of Augusta. The woods were on fire. The road lies on a high ridge or backbone, and at short intervals on each side there are lateral ridges running down into deep reed-brakes below. Along one of these vertebrae, on my left, a mighty volume of smoke and flame and eddying leaves came rolling rapidly toward me. The road itself, but rarely traveled at this season of the year, was covered several inches deep with pine straw, which was soon in a blaze. There was literally "a fire in my rear." Dashing forward, I meant to drive down a ridge on my right until the road should be cleared, but the flames, swept by the whirling winds, had by this time burst out there, and came surging into the sea of fire just behind me. I had no choice but to run for it. Though noonday, it was as black as midnight. The smoke of one hundred thousand acres of combustibles was around me. The roar of the devouring element, like the boom of a tremendous surf, was above me. The flames were protruding, like the tongues of boa constrictors, on each side of me, melting the varnish of my buggy and crisping my whiskers; and, ever and anon, the crash of a falling pine, uprooted by the fire, seemed to be discharging minute-guns in token of my distress. On rushed the fiery torrent—flank and rear—up hill and down—and on I drove, at a killing gait, only ten paces in advance; my carpet-bag smoking, my hat and coat singed, my face and hands charred, when suddenly the wind shifted, and the flaming dragon plunged away to the left, hissing through the crackling reed-brakes, and shaking his terrible crest among the lofty trees.

Exhausted by this frightful contention, I was glad to find shelter at the wayside inn of my worthy friend, Mr. Hiram Breeland, of Greene County. He is famous for peach and honey; for river trout, venison steaks, and fried chicken, and indeed for every thing that a weary traveler covets. His wife is a model in her way. They have had eighteen children, and are yet a young and handsome couple. Far and near this is known as "the musical family." Six daughters in the bloom of life, richly dowered with those perfections that men sigh for and never forget, possess rare musical gifts; and their concerts with voice and violins are really enchanting. Excited and nervous after the fiery ordeal I had passed, they soothed my soul with melody, and my slumbers with charming dreams. Long after the witching hour of night, in the delicious delirium between sleeping and waking, the tinkle of the guitar and a sweet voice, softer than a sigh, mingled with the lullaby of the winds in the tops of the aged pines.

Their names are in harmony with their music. What can be more melodious than Elizabeth Amanda, Priscilla Brunetta, Louvena Anneta, Martha Miranda, Zelphi Emmeline, and Sophronie Angelina?

This house has been a favorite stopping-place for candidates for many years, and Breeland is pretty well posted up with anecdotes.

When Harry Cage and Franklin E. Plummer were canvassing for Congress they came here together, and Cage began to joke and sport with the children, much to the mother's delight. But Plummer soon won her heart. He picked up the little wee one, just then toddling about, placed it across his lap, turned up its little petticoats, and began to search for *red bugs!*

Next morning Cage stole out before day, went to the wood-pile, cut a turn of wood, determined to win the "old lady's" favor by making her fire, while Plummer, as he fancied, lay snoring in bed. While toiling up the hill with his load, what was his astonishment to see the old 'un milking her cow, and Plummer *holding off the calf by the tail!*

A day or two after this, said Squire B., Cage made a tip-top speech at Greene Court House. It was hard to beat, and Plummer knew it. So when he got up he said: "Fellow-citizens, I would answer the gentleman's argument if there was any argument to answer. It reminds me of an honest couple down in my county who are troubled with a very small specimen of a child that cries all night. The husband, much tormented, complained that he could not get a moment's sleep. "Spank it, then," says the wife. He fumbled about, but the child continued to cry. "Well, why don't you spank it?" says she. "Because," said he, *"I can't find any thing to spank!"*

It is hardly necessary to say that Cage "incontinently caved in," and refused to travel any farther with the Yankee wagon-boy.

"Plummer was hard pressed sometime after this, being charged with sundry matters affecting his integrity. He deliberately sat down and wrote an account of his visit to my house, charging that he had attempted to swindle me, had behaved with gross indecorum to my family, and had been kicked out of doors. This he contrived to have published, and it went the round of the papers, creating great excitement. He called on me for my certificate, which, of course, was promptly given, for I was surprised and indignant at such a slander. The reaction was tremendous; and after this nobody in this section would believe any thing against Plummer."

When the Hon. Powhatan Ellis, a very finished gentleman, was traveling through this district electioneering for some office, he lost his portmanteau in attempting to ford a creek. Plummer immediately advertised its contents: "6 ruffled shirts, 6 cambric handkerchiefs, 1 hair-brush, 1 tooth-brush, 1 nail-brush, 1 pair curling tongs, 2 sticks pomatum, 1 box pearl-powder, 1 bottle Cologne, 1 do. rose-water, 4 pairs silk stockings, and 2 pairs kid gloves." This defeated the Judge. He was set down as a born aristocrat and "swelled head."

Plummer was a poor young lawyer, boarding, or loafing, at a tavern in Westville, when he announced himself for Congress. He hadn't a single "red" in his pocket. He opened the canvass in Benton, put up at the best hotel, dined a dozen friends every day, and opened a very liberal account at the bar. On the third day, when about to depart, he cried out to the crowd, "Gentlemen, I wish to make my public acknowledgments to our generous landlord. He has treated me like a prince; he has feasted my friends; his tipple has run freely. Sir," said he, turning to the landlord, "if you ever come to my town don't go to a hotel: put up with me; I shall be proud to reciprocate your hospitality!" With these words he vaulted on his horse, and was out of sight before the astonished Boniface could "say turkey" about his bill.

While sojourning at this pleasant retreat it was agreed, one day, that we should go out on a deer-drive. I was wrapping up a lunch to put in my pocket, and said to my boy Tom, "Well, Tom, how about this butter? I can't put it in my pocket." "No, massa," said Tom, "him run away. But you kin *eat him 'fore you go!*"

On a deer-drive in the South one man follows the hounds in the thickets or reed brakes where the herds usually feed, while three or four others take their stands at various points which they are expected to cross in their flight. The dogs soon broke cover; a noble doe came bounding by me. I fired and missed; but passing on, the Squire, who is a noted shot, brought her down. The outcries of the huntsman soon called us down to the brake, and there we saw a most extraordinary spectacle. Two bucks of the largest size in deadly combat, their branching antlers so interlocked that neither could use them against the other. The ground was torn up all around; their sides were dripping blood; and they had evidently fought long before this singular union of their weapons terminated the combat. Their furious struggles at our approach only united them more closely; and thus they would have perished. The hunters shot them, and informed me that they had often found the skeletons of bucks that had thus died, their horns so locked that no ingenuity could undo them.

The buck is a timid animal until wounded. He then stands at bay, and is dangerous to approach. He is the sworn enemy of the rattlesnake. When he perceives one, he walks around it until it throws itself into a coil, and then the buck vaults into the air and comes down upon it with his pointed hoofs. Not content with killing it, he stamps it into shreds. Those noxious reptiles always multiply as the deer diminish.

Speaking of rattlesnakes, my friend Colonel Wilkins, of Green Court House, tells me that he was once rolling logs in a piece of new ground on the Bigbee River, near Bladen Springs, when one of his men cried out, "Here's a rattlesnake!" Presently another sung out; and all round the "clearing" they kept up the cry, until the Colonel, quite angry, cried out, *"Let the logs alone, and all of you go to snaking!"* They piled up fifty-three in the course of the evening.

I once went to purchase a country seat on the bayou of St. John, in the vicinity of New Orleans, belonging to Mr. Michel, who had gone to France. It was occupied by Mr. Creecy, an old Vicksburg editor. Strolling into the garden, I was about to step toward an orange hedge to gather a few leaves, when he said "Look out for snakes!" "What," said I, "have you snakes here?"

"Walk this way," said Creecy. He led me to a point where three or four ditches, communicating with the bayou and with the swamp, intersected, and I counted a dozen dead moccasins lying about, and some twenty navigating the different ditches. "This is our only game," said he. "I shoot moccasins every afternoon!"

Mr. Michel lost an excellent purchaser for his place, and my brother editor held on until the snakes fairly run him out of the house.

There was once a man by the name of Gallendee living in Hancock county, who was, perhaps, rather unjustly suspected of hog stealing. He came running in from the woods one day shouting murder, the shirt fairly whipped off his back. He assured me it had been done by a coach-whip snake that had wrapped itself round his leg and thrashed him over the shoulder; but uncharitable people suspected it had been done by Judge Lynch!

The same man went to the late Judge Daniel to complain of these accusations, and to ask his advice. "Well," said the Judge, "I will tell you what to do. If you feel innocent, face these charges like a man. But if you are guilty, get into Louisiana as soon as you can." That evening his client crossed Pearl River, and became a citizen of our sister State.

Having recruited at this pleasant anchorage, I bid adieu to my friend Breeland, and set out for the village of Augusta, bowling merrily along in my blood-red buggy. The road is beautiful, roofed over with trees and tendrils, and the air fragrant with the breath of flowers. There was, however, one drawback to my comfort—myriads of flies of every species, that swarmed around and ravenously cupped the blood from my horse. It was what is appropriately termed here "fly time"—that is to say, the period when this numerous family of scourges have it all their own way, and neither man nor beast can sojourn in the woods without much suffering. Now the deer plunge into deep pools and lakes, leaving only their heads exposed, and browse only during a portion of the night while these insects sleep. The cattle from a thousand hills seek the abodes of man, and huddle around some smoking pine or in some open field to escape their tormentors.

On a sudden curve of the road I found myself near one of these "stamping grounds," and a simultaneous roar from five hundred infuriated animals gave notice of my danger. It is well known that the Spanish matadores provoke the wounded bulls in the arena by flaunting the *moleta* or blood-red flag in their faces. It was the vermilion of my buggy that excited this bellowing herd. They snuffed the air, planted their heads near the ground, tore it up with their hoofs and horns, and glared at me with savage eyes. The fierce phalanx blocked the road, and it was the "better part of valor" to retreat. The instant I wheeled the pursuit commenced. A cloud of dust enveloped them, and the trampling of their feet was like the roll of thunder. My horse dashed forward frantic with terror, and on they plunged on every side, crushing down the brush-wood in their course, goring and tumbling over each other, filling the forest with their dreadful cries, and gathering nearer and nearer in the fearful chase. The struggle now became desperate. In five minutes we should have been overturned and trampled to death; but at this juncture Tom threw out my overcoat, and with an awful clamor they paused to fight over it, and to tear it into shreds. Driving at full speed, I directed Tom to toss out the cushion. The infuriated devils trampled it into atoms, and came charging on, their horns clashing against the buggy, and ripping up the ribs of my horse. At this fearful moment we were providentially saved. A huge oak, with a forked top, had fallen by the wayside, and into this I plunged my horse breast-high, and he was safe, the back of the buggy being then the only assailable point. At this the whole column made a dash, but I met the foremost with six discharges from my revolver; two bottles of Cognac were shivered on their foreheads; next a cold turkey; and, finally, a bottle of Scotch snuff—the last shot in the locker! This did the business. Such a sneezing and bellowing was never heard before; and the one that got the most of it put out with the whole troop at his heels, circling round, scenting the blood of the wounded, and shaking the earth with their thundering tramp.

I was now fairly in for it, and made up my mind to remain until night, when I knew they would disperse. I was relieved, however, by the approach of some cattle-drivers, who, galloping up on shaggy but muscular horses, with whips twenty feet long, which they manage with surprising dexterity, soon drove the belligerent herd to their cow-pens, for the purpose of marking and branding. This is done every year in "fly time." The cattle ranging over an area of thirty square miles are now easily collected, driven to a common pen or pound, when the respective owners put their mark and brand on the increase of the season. Thus this Egyptian plague is turned to a useful purpose.

I was now approaching the ancient village of Augusta, once the stamping-ground of the famous Coon Morris. Being advised to take a near cut when within three miles, I turned to the right and drove ahead through leafy bypaths and across deserted fields grown over with stunted pines. For three hours I drove about, describing three segments of a circle, and finally got back to the point I started from. [*Nota bene:* Let all travelers stick to the beaten road, for in this country one may travel twenty miles without meeting a traveler or a finger-board.] The country through which I passed was poor, the population sparse, and no indications of the proximity of a town that I had heard of for twenty-five years. I drove on, however, expectation on tip-toe, the sun pouring down vertically, and my flagging steed sinking above his fetlocks in the sand, when, lo! the ancient village stood before me—an extensive parallelogram, garnished round with twelve or fifteen crumbling tenements, the wrecks of by-gone years! Not a tree stood in the gaping square for the eye to rest upon; the grass was all withered up; the burning sun fell on the white and barren sand as on a huge mirror, and was reflected back until your cheeks scorched and your eyes filled with tears. Even of these dilapidated houses several were unoccupied, and we drove round two-thirds of the square before we could find a human being to direct us to the tavern. It was a log-cabin, with one room, a deal table, some benches and cots, and a back shed for kitchen. Stable there was none, nor bar, nor servant, nor landlord visible. I turned my horse on the public square and took peaceable possession of the establishment. Nobody was to be seen. I was hungry and fatigued. The idea of a town once famous, and its hundred-and-one little comforts for the traveler, had buoyed me up during the morning drive, and fancy had diagramed something very different from what I was then realizing. In a few hours, however, the bachelor landlord came in. Not expecting company he had gone out on a foraging expedition. He feasted us on delicious venison, and, being a Virginian, soon concocted an ample julep. The mint grew near the grave of a jolly lawyer, a son of the "Old Dominion," who died there a few years before. No man can live in such a place without losing his energies. The mind stagnates, and in six months one would go completely asleep. I never saw such a picture of desolation. All was silence and solitude. In reply to my inquiry, my old friend, Colonel Mixon, said that times were dull; there was a little activity in one line only; and hobbling off he soon returned with a pair of babies in his arms—twin gems, plump, blue-eyed, rosy-cheeked, hanging around his neck like flowers on the stump of a storm-battered oak. Counselor Barrett, who seemed thoroughly posted in this branch of statistics, informed me that, during the last twelve months, thirteen matrons of that vicinity had produced doublets! The Colonel said that any disconsolate pair who would board with him six months, and drink from a peculiar spring on the premises, without having their expectations realized, should have a free ticket at his table for sixty days to try it again.

These infant phenomena, however, are by no means confined to Perry County. East Mississippi every where is equally prolific. In the *Paulding Clarion* I read the following, from the Rev. Marmaduke Gardiner, of Clarke County:

"FALLING SPRING, *Feb. 2.*

"More than one hundred persons have visited my house since Saturday last, for the purpose of seeing three beautiful boy babies which my wife gave birth to on the 28th ult. One weighs 7½, the others 6½ *each*, and are perfectly formed. We have named them Abraham, Isaac, and Jacob. I married my wife twenty years ago, and she has given me nine sons and nine daughters, but no triplicates until the last."

Married couples in search of heirs often cross the Atlantic, or drug themselves with nostrums and stinking mineral waters, when a single summer in these pine-woods would accomplish what they desire without extraordinary efforts, and at one-twentieth of the expense.

The old town next day presented a more lively scene. That certain premonitory of a piney-woods' gathering, the beer and gingerbread cart, came rumbling into the square.—Rickety vehicles, of odd shapes, laden with melons, trundled along behind. A corner shanty displayed several suspicious-looking jugs and kegs. Buck negroes, dressed in their holiday suits, strode in, looking about for the candidates as one would for the giraffe. No candidate except the Hon. Robert J. Walker had visited the defunct town for years. It was quite an event. Finally, the stout sovereigns from the country came in, and the comedy commenced. The largest portion of the crowd was in the court-house to hear the orators, but a pretty considerable group was posted about the doggery. A number were playing "old sledge" on the heads of empty whisky barrels, and others were discussing the preliminaries of a quarter race.

Three of the candidates had spoken, when the late Judge Mitchell (formerly a well-known Member of Congress from Tennessee) rose. After an elaborate reply to the arguments of two of them, he turned to the third, and laying his hand on his head, said, "I have only one word to say in answer to my young friend. He has a leetle soft spot right here, *and it is mushy all round it.*"

When R. J. Walker was canvassing against George Poindexter for the Senate, he was accompanied, said Colonel Mixon, by a queer fish, one Isaac M'Farren, a fellow of infinite jest, and whose countenance was a comedy of itself. On a certain occasion they put up with a new settler, and had to sleep on the floor, while the man and his wife occupied a bunk in the same room. A very buxom damsel slept in a small kitchen near by. Mac had cast sheep's-eyes at her, and being uncomfortable on the floor, concluded to go and whisper a few soft nothings in her ear. He slipped out very quietly; but it being a crispy and frosty night, the door of the kitchen creaked upon its hinges, and the woman exclaimed, "Husband! husband! one of them men's arter Sally!" He sprang up, seized his rifle, and was rushing out, when Mr. Walker seized his arm. M'Farren hearing the noise, appeared at the other door rather *en déshabillé*. "Je-men-y!" cried the man, and cocked his rifle. Mr. Walker threw it up, and Mac, running forward, seized him by the hand, exclaiming, "Sir, it is only a frolic and an indiscretion; I am a man of honor, incapable of injuring sleeping innocence. Sir, I throw myself on your generosity. I see that you belong to the honorable fraternity of free and accepted masons. Brother, I give you *the right hand of fellowship!*" The man was overwhelmed with this volubility, and flattered at the notion of being mistaken for a mason. He accompanied the party over the county, but finally voted the Poindexter ticket, because Walker would persist in running when M'Farren was the proper man for the place!

"I was in ——," said Counselor Barrett, "when Governor ——, who was a candidate for re-election, came there. The county had been recently organized, and few of the people had been there long enough to vote under the Constitutional provision which requires six months' residence in the county and twelve in the State. They were anxious to vote, and got up a petition to the Board of Police (which has the supervision of elections) to *dispense with the requisitions of the Constitution.*"

"Did the Board comply with the petition?"

"I can't exactly say," said the Counselor; "*but as they all voted*, I presume the order was duly made. The best of the joke was, *the Governor signed the petition!*"

Next day the Counselor accompanied me a few miles on my way. Showing me a road running down toward the swamp, he inquired if I knew how that road came to be made. On replying that I did not, he said: "Some years ago I was down in that swamp with some fellows after wild hogs. I was standing on the edge of it hallooing on the hounds, my gun resting against a tree, when out rushed an enormous boar and charged right at me. I could only straddle my legs to escape his furious onset; but as he passed under, being rather low in the crotch, I found myself astride of him. Almost unconscious from terror, I involuntarily seized his tail, and stuck my heels under his shoulders. At every stride he took my spurs goaded him on. Thus he ran some three miles through the brushwood, making a clean sweep as he went, but finally fell exhausted, when I dispatched the monster with my bowie-knife. The road is now used for hauling timber from Leaf River swamp, and is called Barrett's trail."

The country through which I am journeying is sparsely settled, and is only adapted to grazing. Its surface undulates like the roll of the ocean, and hill and valley are covered with luxuriant grass and with flowers of every hue. Herds of cattle stand in the plashy brooks. Red deer troop along the glades; wild turkeys run before you along your road, and the partridge rises from every thicket. But for these the solitude would be painful. Settlements are often twenty miles apart; the cheering mile-post and gossiping wayfarer are rarely met with. The gaunt pines have a spectral aspect, and their long shadows fall sadly upon the path. At nightfall, when the flowers have faded away, no fire-flies gem the road; one hears no tinkling bell; the robber owl skims lazily by; fantastic shades chase each other into deeper gloom; and instead of "the watch-dog's cheerful cry," the "wolf's long howl" comes from the reed-brakes, and is echoed by its prowling mate on the neighboring hills.

The day was dark and lowering. For weeks nor rain nor gentle dews had refreshed the calcined earth. A heavy cloud hung overhead and its pent-up fury burst upon the forest. The few birds that tenant these silent woods flew screaming to their eyries; some cattle dashed across the hills for shelter. The whole wilderness was in motion. The pines swayed their lofty heads, and the winds shrieked and moaned among the gnarled and aged limbs. A few old ones fell thundering down, casting their broken fragments around; and then the hurricane rushed madly on, tearing up the largest trees, and hurling them like javelins through the air. The sky was covered as with a pall; and lurid flashes, like sepulchral lights, streamed and blazed athwart it. The earthquake voice of nature trembled along the ground, and, ere its running echoes died away, came again, crash after crash thundering forth. But at length, as though weary of the agony, it paused, and the phantom clouds scudded away. The scene around was appalling! Hundreds of trees lay prostrate, while, here and there, others stood shivered by the bolt of heaven and smoking with its fires. God preserve me from another ride through these giant pines in such a tempest!

(1849–1883)

Katherine McDowell
(Sherwood Bonner)

Katherine Sherwood Bonner, born in Holly Springs, Mississippi, on February 26, 1849, published her first story, "Laura Capello, A Leaf From a Traveller's Notebook," at the age of fifteen. In 1871, after publishing three or four more stories, she married Edward McDowell and moved to Texas, where McDowell tried (and failed) to make a fortune collecting bat manure from the caves of the Southwest. Two years later she went to Boston and became an associate to Naham Capen while he was preparing his *History of Democracy.* Later she was secretary to Henry Wadsworth Longfellow, who became her friend and advisor, and godfather to Bonner's daughter Lilian. Bonner dedicated her novel *Like Unto Like* to Longfellow and corresponded with him from 1873 until his death in 1882.

While living in New England, Bonner's literary career acquired momentum. She published several articles in the *Memphis Avalanche* and *Boston Times* in 1875–1876, helped to compile and edit Longfellow's *Poems of Places,* 1876–1879, and placed nearly fifty stories and poems in *Lippincott's Magazine, Harper's Weekly,* and two young peoples' magazines, *Youth's Companion* and *Harper's Young People.* The publica-

97

tion of her novel in 1878 gave her confidence in her work. "I believe now that a great future is possible," she said, and confided to the editor of *Harper's Monthly*, "In ten years I shall be an artist." In three years, however, she discovered that she had breast cancer, and on July 22, 1883, she died in Holly Springs. Her career had come to an end at the age of thirty-four.

Bonner's fiction ranges from local color stories heavy with Negro dialect ("Hieronymous Pop and the Baby") to attempts at near tragedy ("In Aunt Mely's Cabin") to longer, more realistic works such as "The Valcours" and "Two Storms," to which Longfellow is said to have contributed a plot outline. Her novel, *Like Unto Like* (1878) is an effort to dramatize through character relationships the North-South conflict. But in this book, and in "A Volcanic Interlude," another story in the realistic mode, her simple diction and slight characterization make her work seem underdeveloped and consequently superficial. Her forte is clear and accurate description of little known historical events, as in her Reconstruction diary and in "From 60 to 65," and the use of a particular event, such as the yellow fever epidemic of 1878, as an element of short fiction, as in "The Revolution in the Life of Mr. Balingall."

"The Revolution in the Life of Mr. Balingall" is reprinted from *Harper's New Monthly Magazine*, LIX (October, 1879).

The Revolution in the Life of Mr. Balingall

I.

THE AFTERNOON HAD BEEN FINE, but when young Mr. Balingall stepped out of Miss Vancourt's drawing-room, he found that a black drift had blown across the moon, the air had chilled, and drops of rain were falling slow and cold, as if the low-hanging clouds were fringed with melting icicles. He drew on his gloves, buttoned his great-coat over a pink flower, and walked fast, with his head bent slightly to the wind. It was nearing midnight, and the streets were almost deserted. Turning a corner, he came rather suddenly on two people, a man and a woman, who were talking earnestly together.

Barely glancing at them, he gave the inside of the walk, and was about to pass them by, when the woman—a mere girl—raised her hand and stopped him.

"Will you be so kind," said she, with an exquisite gentleness, "as to direct us to a carriage stand? We are strangers in the city, and are somewhat hurried, wishing to take the Southern train."

Her voice shook a little as she ended, and before Mr. Balingall could reply, her companion—a young man with a handsome, irresolute face—burst out in a tone of excessive agitation: "Don't you do it, Sir—don't you do it. She is going to Kilbuck, where the yellow fever is raging. Twenty-five new cases yesterday—frost a month off. I am responsible to her family. She will die; she can't help dying."

"I beg of you not to make a scene," said the girl, sharply. Then, to Mr. Balingall: "Sir, I am compelled to go. It is a matter of life and death. This is entirely my own affair. I am of age. This gentleman promised to take me to the station. We have been walking about for more than an hour. He pretended to lose his way, and I know he has purposely misled me. You are a stranger, but if you have a heart in your bosom"—and she made a passionate gesture—"will you not help me?"

"Her death will be on your head," cried the young man. "Don't dare to give up to her. She is not with her mother, and she is out of her wits with trouble."

To this moment Mr. Balingall had not spoken. He had looked from one to the other of the strange pair. The man, flushed, frightened, with an air of deprecation rather than of authority; the girl, quiet, pale, and cold but for her angrily burning eyes. She was muffled from head to foot in some dark-looking stuff, a veil was wound lightly round her small hat, and pushed up just above square, delicate dark brows. They stood near a gaslight, and these details stamped themselves half unconsciously on Mr. Balingall's mind and memory.

"Oh, my God!" she cried, "while we stand here the time passes, and the Southern train leaves at midnight." She turned her great angry eyes upon her companion. "I will never forgive you while my reason lasts," she said, "if I do not get off. How many times must I tell you that this is no affair of yours? What are you to me?"

"Your brothers will hold me responsible," he said, half sullenly.

"My brothers shall *not* hold you responsible. I made my will this morning, and it exonerates you and every other human being. I act for myself. No one has a right to oppose me, you least of all. I shall kill myself if I do not go. How dare you keep me with your inane talk? You coward! Because you are afraid of fever yourself, you think every one else ought to be. And you tried to deceive me, pretending you could not find a carriage. It is a shame. You may leave me. I will trust myself to this stranger. Will you take me to the station? There is no time to lose."

She poured out the quick sentences in a low but passionately angry voice. It struck Mr. Balingall that the extreme gentleness of her first address to him had been that of a violent repression.

He found his voice, and bowed profoundly. "There is a cab stand not three squares away," he said; "if you will permit me, I will conduct you to it."

Her escort interposed. "Since the young lady will have her way," he said not without dignity, "I will attend her. There is no need of troubling you, Sir."

"I do not trust him," she repeated. "Come with us, if you please."

They started off, the girl almost leading, with quick, long steps. She would not take the arm of either young man, but walked between them in a silence so magnetic that the whole air seemed to vibrate with her pain. The rain was falling faster now. Around the lamp-posts were little circles of light, and each interval of gloom, as they passed from one to another, seemed longer and blacker than the last. Mr. Balingall felt himself in a dream where all is unreal and nothing natural. The only words that would have come to his lips, had he spoken, would have been: "I did not think a woman could take such long steps."

As they neared the cab stand the girl's companion made one more effort. "For God's sake, Miss Idal—" he began, impetuously.

"Do not call out my name on the street, if you please," said she, "and do not speak to me again. I can't bear it."

He shrugged his shoulders and was silent, while she made her own bargain with the cabman, promising him a double fee should he reach the station in time. Mr. Balingall obeyed her motion, and followed her into the carriage. No one spoke during the short drive. The girl leaned back and closed her eyes. It seemed to him almost a dishonorable thing to watch her, but as the carriage rolled in and out of the light he could not for his life restrain an eager glance at the cold young face opposite. Was she always so white? Or was it the effect of all that black about her head and shoulders? And was it the little black hat, tipped low over her brow, that made those deep shadows under her reddened eyelids? The face was clean cut, with a short sensitive nose, and a wide full mouth, now drawn to a straight line of endurance. Her form was of large and noble proportions. Her gloved hands were crossed in front of her, and now and then they trembled slightly.

Arriving at the station, Mr. Balingall stood with the young lady in the waiting-room, while her friend hurried off to buy her ticket.

"He would play me false now if he could," said she, nervously. "He had promised to call for me at ten o'clock, and then he came without a carriage, saying he had hoped to make me change my mind. I insisted on going out with him, and he pretended to be so unfamiliar with the streets that he couldn't find a cab stand. One day's delay might have made me too late. *And the minutes are centuries!*" she cried, in a tone that pierced her hearer's heart.

"I am glad I was able to serve you," he said.

The ticket was secured, and the three hastened to the train. Entering the Southern bound sleeping-car, an oppressive odor of carbolic acid assailed them. To Mr. Balingall the strong sickly smell brought a sudden horror—a realization of poisoned air, and the foulness that disinfectants fight. He looked at the poor young girl so strangely met, and pity, like a wave, surged over his soul. He trembled to think of the result of her wild courage.

Only a few passengers were in the car—a little band of nurses and doctors, a Catholic priest reading his prayers. They all looked curiously at the party who joined them. And the conductor, when he found that only the girl was to go under his guidance into the land of peril, said to her, as a friend might, "Young lady, have you had the fever?"

"No," she said.

"Then I wish I could put you off my train."

"Good-by, Miss Idal," said the young man who had aided her so unwillingly. "You have had your own way all your life, and I might have known you would get the better of me. I know I shall never see you again, and I feel that I am to blame." He broke down, and put his hand to his eyes.

"Good-by," said the girl, her lips parting in a smile. "You meant to take care of me, and so I forgive you for the way you made me walk about the streets this cold evening. Good-by. I am off in spite of you!" And she fairly laughed.

It was Mr. Balingall's turn. But what could he say? Never in all his life had he been agitated by so powerful an emotion. Here was a sweet and strong young life going to face Death in his den as cheerily as ever Sintram rode; and he, staying behind in safety, could only look on dumbly.

The long train of cars quivered with the first throes of its movement. Miss Idal held out her hand.

"Good-by," she said. "I can not tell you how I thank you. I was almost in despair when I met you. As long as I live I shall remember you with gratitude."

Mr. Balingall bowed over her hand. He should have liked to kiss the hem of her dress. Then he passed quickly through the car, catching snatches of conversation that, like the odor of the carbolic acid, brought to him a realization of what all this meant.

"Merely to offer spiritual consolation to the dying," he heard the pale priest say.

And one of the doctors, a gay, boyish-looking fellow, lifted his cap as he caught Mr. Balingall's eye.

"*Morituri te salutamus!*" he said, lightly.

Curiously shaken and bewildered, Mr. Balingall watched the train plunge forward into the darkness.

"It's a bad business," said a gloomy voice at his elbow; and turning, he saw the girl's late companion. "I wish to Heaven that I were not mixed up in it. You see, the way of it was this: her mother and father and all the family are spending the summer up in Minnesota. And when the fever broke out, she insisted on coming here, that she might get news more quickly. She rules the family—you noticed what a temper she had?—so her father brought her here to some friends, and hurried back. The old gentleman wanted to get as far off as possible," said the young man, with a chuckle; "said there were too many refugees here to suit him; and he didn't want Yellow Jack served up as a breakfast, dinner, and supper dish. But Miss Idal, you see, had a lover down there, and he wouldn't run away—got crazy about his duty, staid to help the people. What queer streaks there are in some fellows! Well, he took it at last, of course. Lord bless you! fever doesn't discriminate, you know. It just hits out like a blind man fighting in a crowd—martyr or nigger, it's all the same to Yellow Jack. Soon as ever Miss Idal heard that he had it, she made up her mind to go to him. She has sent a dispatch every hour, and the last one from his doctors said, 'Doing well.' That was enough for her. We've noticed that they always die when the dispatches say, 'Doing well.' Her friends did everything except lock her in her room. So she pounced on me, and forced me to help her. Of course she will die—they all do—and I shall be blamed for it."

Mr. Balingall bit his tongue in the effort to avoid asking a question. He would not take advantage of the strange chance that had led him into this young girl's life. Yet he did not even know her name, except "Miss Idal," which was no name at all. Somebody's "Idol" he could well believe, but not this loquacious young man's, whose chief regret about the whole matter seemed to be that some one might hold him responsible.

They had reached the cab that had brought them to the station, and which Mr. Balingall had ordered to wait.

"Will you get in?" he said to his companion.

"No, thank you. I won't go home just yet; I'm all upset; I must get some beer. Good-night. I hope you won't regret this business."

Mr. Balingall gave the order for home, and soon reached his rooms. As he got out of the cab he noticed a shining something caught in one of the flapping curtains. He was reminded of a gleam of gold he had seen at the young lady's throat, and quickly disengaged it. In his own room he examined it with a singular interest. It was a scarf-pin shaped like a sabre, with the name "Idalia" engraved delicately in the handle.

"Idalia!" he repeated; "and they call her Miss Idal."

II.

Mr. Balingall was an engaged man. He had engaged himself with the deliberateness that up to this time had characterized every action of his life. He was an ambitious young fellow, with a fixed determination to make himself a man of note and position, and while he never demanded help, he was quite as far from disdaining it. He was poor, but had friends of influence. He had graduated at the best medical college in this country, and had practiced two years in the French hospitals. While in Paris he had made the acquaintance of Dr. Vancourt and his daughter. Dr. Vancourt was the leading medical man in the Western city where Mr. Balingall thought his chance was best of making a brilliant name. Miss Fanny Vancourt was pretty, sprightly, winning, kittenish—the adjectives are almost as plentiful as the type. Naturally Mr. Balingall was attracted toward her, and quite as naturally, being a practical man, he understood the advantage that such a marriage might be to him. The result was an engagement pleasing not only to Fanny, but to Fanny's papa. He accepted Mr. Balingall with admirable promptness, and offered to take him into partnership as soon as he should call him son-in-law. From that time the young physician saw his way clear. His future was blocked out as squarely before him as a geometric figure cut into marble. He was accustomed to say that there was no such thing as chance—or fate, as some people named it—that every man was the architect of his own life. For himself he declared that nothing had ever happened to him, but that every effect in his life could be traced directly to its cause, which was always his own deliberate action.

On the night succeeding his adventure, Mr. Balingall went as usual to call on Miss Vancourt. He found her flashing some long needles in and out of a glittering stuff that she called ice wool. She held the sparkling meshes before her face, laughing through them, and her lover was struck anew with her beauty.

"Come, admire me," said she, saucily.

"I am so glad you are pretty, Fanny," he said with a smile; "it does you so much good."

"Don't you like it yourself, George?" she said, with a slight pout.

"Of course, dear. But in the abstract I don't care so much for beauty. I like something grave and noble in a woman's face."

"Something very grave will come into my face if you are not more complimentary. Why, you do not seem to be thinking of me at all."

"I have thought of you all day, Fanny. In fact, I do not believe there has been a time since I have known you that I have thought of you more. I have been wondering if you loved me well enough to die for me."

"What a very queer mood you are in this evening!" said Miss Fanny, slipping her hand into her lover's arm, and looking up into his face with a little coaxing smile.

Her endearments were not to be resisted, and George pressed the yellow head against his heart.

Fanny was never too impassioned to observe details. "What have you in your waistcoat pocket?" she said, rubbing a small pink ear against it.

"Oh, nothing—a little box," said he, reluctantly.

It was Idalia's scarf-pin that he had that evening taken to a jeweller's to have fitted to a box.

"Ah! you have brought me a present," cried Miss Fanny, smiling, and slipping her privileged fingers into his pocket.

"No, dear; do not open it," he exclaimed, impulsively, but too late. She had drawn out the pin.

"Why, George!" she said, in round-eyed surprise.

Mr. Balingall had been the master-spirit through all this courtship; but, for all that, he stood abashed before that innocent "Why, George!" He wondered why he hated to have her hold the little sabre pin, and why he felt like placing his hand over the name she was deciphering slowly, holding it close to her near-sighted eyes.

" 'J'—is it a J or an I?—'I-d-a-l-i-a'—Idalia. What does it all mean, George?"

George felt like a foolish figure in a witness stand. The sensation was not agreeable. Besides, he did not wish to tell Fanny of his adventure.

"Fanny," said he, slowly, "I would rather not tell you—just yet—what it all means. It is another person's secret. Can you not trust me?"

"Trust a man!" said Miss Fanny, with a toss of the head. "I know better."

"Why, I thought you were such a sweet, confiding, innocent little soul."

"I am not so foolish as I look," said Fanny, composedly. "And now I want to hear about Idalia."

"I wonder if I've got to tell it," mused Mr. Balingall. "Is this one of the duties of an engaged man?" Then: "Give me until to-morrow, child, to think it over," he said.

"Indeed I won't. It must be now."

After all, his scruples might be farfetched, thought Mr. Balingall. He would tell, and she would sympathize with that brave girl now at the bedside of her lover. So in a few moments more Miss Fanny was in possession of the facts in the case.

"Was she pretty?" said she, eagerly.

"Not exactly. She had a noble face, but it was too pale and worn for me to judge of its beauty."

"I never heard of anything so queer in all my life," said Mr. Balingall's sweetheart, with stinging emphasis.

"Queer! In what way?"

"Oh, the whole thing: the promenading around the streets at that hour with a man who did not want to go with her, and stopping you, a stranger, and actually making you go to the station with her! Why, she is the sort of girl I should call fast."

"Fast! My God!"

"George, how dare you say such a word in my presence? And how dare you look at me as if I were a little—viper?" Miss Fanny showed symptoms of tears.

"It is only that I was somewhat surprised at your lack of sympathy."

"George dear, to tell the whole truth, I was a little jealous. Now isn't that a confession for me to make? You know it isn't ten minutes since you said that you like something grave and noble in a woman's face, and didn't care for beauty. Then you say that this girl's face was noble and grave. Hateful words! hateful Idalia! George, don't you love me any more?"

"Why, my dear little goose, what are you talking about? Put up your handkerchief now, and show your eyes in their natural color.

What would become of us, Fanny, if we should begin to get jealous of each other?"

"You will never be jealous of me," said Fanny, astutely; "you are too sure of me."

"And are you not quite as sure of me?" asked Mr. Balingall, too indifferently, in Miss Fanny's opinion; so she gave her small head another toss, and said,

"Perhaps so, considering the partnership with papa."

"*Fanny!*"

Mr. Balingall stood up, pale and wrathful. Miss Vancourt was frightened; she flung herself into his arms, but he repulsed her.

"You degrade me," he said, hoarsely.

"George, you are turning into a tragedy hero," cried Fanny, with a stamp of her foot. "You know I didn't mean anything. I only wanted to vex you a little. And you shouldn't be cross with me. Am I not your own, own?"

It was their first quarrel, and they made it up, of course. But when Mr. Balingall stepped out into the night once more, it was with a feeling, new to him, of dissatisfaction with himself. He had never put into words the benefits of his alliance with Miss Vancourt, but now an ugly sense of being self-seeking and mercenary disturbed his composure. The splendid emotion that a fine deed arouses filled his soul, and his personal consciousness became intensified and concentrated, as if he drank a fiery wine. He seemed to be walking in a valley, while clouds rolled away from distant and glorious heights, toward which were climbing others whose ambitions were nobler than his own.

For many days after this, Mr. Balingall found himself reading with avidity the fever reports from the South. Heretofore he had avoided the long columns, vitalized with offensive detail, and had sneered at their sensational headings: "Bronze John still Mowing the Harvest;" "The Breath of the Fiery Dragon;" "No Light in the East;" "The Wrath of God Unbroken." But now the lurid words flickered before his eyes like torches leading to dismal depths, into which he looked, not sparing his sickened sense. But of Idalia he could find nothing. How was it possible? Her very name was unknown to him.

Occasionally there was a brief dispatch from Kilbuck, rendering thanks for aid, or giving a list of dead. Again and again Mr. Balingall, weary of conjecture, tried to shake off the wild, sad impression of the night when he had helped the young girl on her perilous way. He was a man whose thoughts had always been as controlled and methodical as his well-regulated habits; but he found now, as most of us do at one time or another, that there was a rebel in his brain whose wings he could not clip. If he could only know the fate of Idalia, he believed that she would cease to torment his visions; but to a decided nature uncertainty was the most harrowing of feelings. So he reasoned; and at last the time came when he could test this belief.

He was standing one day in the box office of a theatre, buying some tickets for an entertainment to which Miss Vancourt had expressed a wish to go. Among the men awaiting their turn at the ticket stand he saw the young fellow who had been with Idalia. The recognition between them was mutual.

"How do you do?" said the Southerner, with a cordial nod.

"I neglected to exchange cards with you," said Mr. Balingall, after a little talk. "Pray allow me to do so now."

"My name's Ormsby," said his companion; "but it isn't much use to make acquaintance now. I get off to-morrow to a colder country. Yellow Jack is creeping up, and I shouldn't wonder if it got to this very city. Give it time enough before frost, and it will travel to Maine. That's my dead-solemn opinion. It's like a coil of rope that's unwinding."

"May I be allowed to ask after the young lady who went to the South a few weeks ago?" said Mr. Balingall, quietly. "I hope she found her friend recovering."

"She found her friend dying," said Mr. Ormsby, shortly; "and she—she died last week in the Louisville hospital."

Mr. Balingall's heart gave a great sick bound. But he expressed his regrets steadily. Then for a while he walked about the streets, seeing nothing. Dead—that strong, cool face, that smile of heaven's sweetness, that fearless heart—dead! "I had not thought she would die," he muttered; and a fury took possession of him, as of all who suffer and strike with their feeble force against the invisible, invincible monster we call death.

Mr. Balingall did not go to the theatre that evening, but sent an excuse and a substitute to Miss Vancourt. The young lady found neither to her taste, and was as incredulous to the one as indifferent toward the other. Indeed, this was not her lover's first offense; for the past few weeks he had failed to please Miss Fanny entirely. His attentions had been as unremitting as ever, but they lacked flavor. He was sometimes abstracted in her presence; he was less patient than usual with her caprices. Fanny was a born gossip, and a great talker. Mr. Balingall had often laughingly declared that the relation between them was that of fountain pen and diary; and one of the chief joys of her engagement had been the amused interest with which he had listened to her exhaustless detail of the small affairs of her circle. But now he lost the thread occasionally of her long narratives. She had to repeat, which she always did very fully, and with an air of indignant surprise.

"Indeed, he is not the same man," she declared to her intimate friend, to whom she was not too proud to complain of her lover.

The confidante, properly sympathetic, as the maid in white muslin should be, suggested that there must be a reason for such change, which her dear Fanny must find out.

"I believe," said Fanny, thoughtfully, "that I date it all from the night he met that girl."

"The yellow-fever heroine, you mean, with the romantic name?"

"With the very silly name," said Miss Fanny, with an injured look. "*Idalia* indeed! You know we had a little quarrel about her to begin with, and since then I've noticed that he avoids speaking of her, though I've asked him a thousand questions. And it is only since then that he has had that air of being a thousand miles away when I've been talking of the most interesting things."

"Perhaps he is worried about some of his patients? Young doctors sometimes are."

"No; he has no practice apart from papa's, unless it is at the hospitals or among the poor. Of course he wouldn't bother himself about charity patients," said Fanny, with fine indifference.

"So you think it is Idalia?"

"What else can it be? Nothing has happened to him out of the common run of things, except that adventure, as far as I can find out. And I know that he admired her immensely."

"I should not submit to it if I were you."

"Why, what would you do?" cried the helpless Tilburina.

"Oh, I should have all sorts of scenes with him," replied her friend, with pleasing vagueness. "And I should not be too amiable with him, Fanny. You must assert yourself, if you mean that he shall respect your rights."

If it had pleased Heaven to give Miss Vancourt either a little less wit or a little more, the trouble between herself and her lover would have died a natural death. With less quickness of perception, it would have never occurred to her to be jealous of so distant a rival; with more, she would have realized that Idalia was but a shadow on his imagination that she could have effaced by pouring upon him a love that was all sunshine. But when she established a grievance, her good sense failed her; and a grievance in a woman is about as attractive to a man as a scarecrow in a field to a flying bird. She talked "Idalia" with "damnable iteration." She made Mr. Balingall tell over and over again the incidents of his meeting with the poor girl. She repeated the story to all of her intimate friends, and to many who were not intimate. She turned it into ridicule, and being clever with her pencil, drew an absurd caricature of the scene under the street lamp, in which its heroine was represented as tall and gaunt, dragging two young men after her, while tears the size of billiard balls tumbled from her eyes on their heads. To be frank, Miss Fanny revealed herself as a vulgar little soul; and Mr. Balingall had to shut his teeth tight together to keep the very silence that irritated her so much.

"I have thought of something for you to do," said her confidante, one day, with delightful vivacity.

Fanny was in a dejected mood, and looked only a listless interest.

"It is a sure way for you to find out if he really cares anything for Idalia," proceeded her friend, triumphantly.

"What! how is it possible?"

"You say that he still has the scarf-pin that she dropped in the carriage?"

"Yes," said Fanny, with a shrug; "he keeps the tarnished old thing done up in cotton-wool as carefully as if it were a black pearl or a baby."

"Now listen: you are going to the fancy ball for the benefit of the yellow fever sufferers?"

"You know that I am," said Fanny, "and that I am to dress as a vivandière."

"Well, borrow Idalia's scarf-pin to wear in your cap."

Miss Vancourt stared.

"Don't you see," cried her friend, "that if he gives it to you readily, it will prove that he doesn't attach much importance to the whole affair. Once in your possession, you might easily manage to lose it."

"And what good would that do?"

"Oh, it would snap a link, as it were. As long as he has the scarf-pin he will think of the girl who wore it. And it may be in his mind that he ought to look her up to return it. Fancy him running over the South, tracing her by that pretty name of hers, as Becket's sweetheart did, you know, speaking only two English words, 'Gilbert' and 'London.' Really, my dear, if you were not a very, very charming Fanny, and the sweetest thing in the whole world, and Mr. Balingall did not know so well on which side his bread was buttered, I do not see how he could resist the romance of the thing."

If Miss Fanny had been a man she would have slapped her dear friend in the face. As it was, she colored high with resentment, and said, "Very well; if he prefers the romance of the thing, as you call it, to Fanny Vancourt, then he is welcome to his choice, and all it may bring him."

"Keep up that spirit, my dear," said her friend, soothingly, "and you will bring him to terms. You must make him let you have the pin."

Fanny lost not much time in following the advice that had been given her, and, as she had more than half expected, her request met with a decided refusal from Mr. Balingall.

"I will get you any ornament you like for your cap, my dear," he said; "but I can not—I have no right—to give you that scarf-pin."

"Have you any right to keep it yourself?"

"All in the world, until I shall restore it to some member of her family."

"Why do you not say to *her?*" cried Fanny, whose mind in some directions was as acute as a fox's nose. "Have you heard anything from her?"

"Yes, I heard that she had died of the fever."

"Died! Poor girl!" and Fanny was sobered and shocked for a moment. But soon her jealous suspicion was again aroused. "Why did you not tell me sooner, George? You know how interested I have been. How strange to keep it from me!"

"I've only known it myself for a little while. Now do let the subject drop, Fanny."

"Well, I will, since it is too sacred to be talked about, if you will only let me have the pin. I won't wear it to the ball, of course. But just let me keep it for you. I'm sure it will be a great deal safer in my jewel-box than in knocking about among your things."

He moved his head as if a gnat were buzzing about his ears, and began to talk of something else. Fanny brought him back to the subject with an expression of irritation.

To follow a lover's quarrel when it is not meant that the lovers should "kiss again with tears," is a reckless waste of narration. The end of it all was that when Mr. Balingall left Miss Vancourt, he had a sort of feeling that the world had tumbled about his ears, and he rather liked the sensation. In his hand he held the engagement ring that he had fitted to Miss Fanny's finger some months before. Idalia from her grave had parted them.

III.

One never knows what to do just after a great crisis in life. Mr. Balingall found himself thrown into confusion in more ways than one. Dr. Vancourt's dismissal of the young man had followed his daughter's, and a season of involuntary idleness more clearly than anything else marked the change in his affairs. He could not even apply himself to study with the old vigor, and the hours hung as heavy on his hands as if fate had thrust them there as forfeits that no one would redeem.

At this juncture he met one day an old friend of his, who owned and commanded a steamer that plied between Cincinnati and New Orleans. Captain Masterson, who was a man extremely hospitable, and fond of having people about him, had often urged him to make the river trip on the *Lady Gay* to New Orleans and back. It had, in fact, become a matter of habit for the captain to press the invitation on his friend.

"You had better come with us this trip, Balingall," he said. "The *Lady Gay* is in tip-top order—first trip of the season, you know. You'll enjoy New Orleans. It's a city you can do in three days—just the time we stop. There's nothing much to see but the lake and the jolly old houses. It will do you good. You're a little off your color, I can tell you—look as if you've been going through the mill. Haven't killed any of your patients, have you, experimenting on them? I know you doctors. You've lost flesh too. If you could sit on a stump and catch shrimps for a week, it would make a new man of you. Come with us, won't you?"

The invitation was opportune. It chimed with Mr. Balingall's vagrant humor. He felt the need of something vivid and distinct during this pale interlude in his life, and without making any words he gave the captain his hand and an acceptance.

It was a snowy and cold day when the *Lady Gay* left Cincinnati, but soon warm airs blowing from the Gulf met them with a soft welcome. It grew pleasant enough to sit all day on deck, watching with constant interest the woods changing from scarlet and gold to green, the lazy negroes fishing sleepily, the low swamp lands with their clotted growth and serpent-winding vines, the plantations and their tributary fields. The boat moved slowly through the thick waters of the Mississippi. It seemed to drift rather than to be propelled, and each turn of her wheel was like a great sobbing breath. Stoppages were frequent at the plantation landings and small towns along the river, and it was one such chance as this that brought to a climax the revolution in the life of Mr. Balingall.

Early in the afternoon a small town, perched on a bluff, appeared in sight.

"There is the last hill you will see," remarked the captain, who stood on deck near Mr. Balingall. "All low land from this on to Orleans."

"What an air it has of looking down on the river, like a little cock on a fence about to crow!" said Mr. Balingall, with a smile.

"It has had the crow pretty well taken out of it, I guess," replied the captain. "It has gone through devil's days since the *Lady Gay* passed the last time."

"The same old story, I suppose—the fever?"

"Just so. Not a place on the river suffered more. For a while the people were shut in from outside help. And they died like the fellows in the Black Hole; dropped in the streets; and had regular plague-spots on their bodies. It's too bad to think of! And such a clean, healthy place as Kilbuck used to be!"

"Kilbuck! I did not know that was a river town?"

"Oh yes, though it's only five miles from Vicksburg, which makes it easy enough to get there by rail."

"Do you stop here?"

"For a couple of hours. Why don't you go on shore and look around?"

"I will."

As soon as the gang-plank was lowered, Mr. Balingall crossed it, and walked up into the town. With its irregular paths, steep ascents, and many trees, it had a cool air of appearing to hide itself from an obtrusive gaze; but he sought out the houses, trying to fancy in which one of them Idalia had lived. He soon became aware of a confused impression of dead flowers and old clothes. Odd conjunction! In every garden blackened blossoms hung from withering stalks; and along the railings of the verandas, about the houses, on the fences, and on ropes stretched from one tree to another, hung a motley assortment of garments—men's clothes, for the most part—flapping in the wind. There was something ludicrous about the sight, until, with a sudden creeping of the flesh, he understood its dreary significance. These were garments of the dead that living love dared not fold away until air and frost had done their work on the mystery of poison that nothing kills save cold. Doors and windows were open to admit the chill November wind. No sound of laughter was heard. Memories of horror seemed to be in the very air.

Nor was it more cheerful in the business part of the town, though here, at least, there were people to be seen. But everything looked woful and half alive. In front of some of the shops sat old men, their hats pulled down far over their eyes. One could readily imagine that a business transaction would begin with an apology. No one noticed Mr. Balingall. The time had gone by when a trivial interest could move the people of Kilbuck. They had stood too long facing and fighting great terrors. In every face was a look of gloom, whether that of some pale convalescent, or the ruddy countenance of some refugee who had saved himself by flight. The point of interest appeared to be at the door of a small office, over which was written: "Relief Committee Rooms." Here a motley crowd was gathered trying to push a way inside. Through the windows one could see boxes and bales of goods, provisions and half-worn clothing, which some boys and ladies were distributing as fast as possible to the applicants.

After twice making the circuit of the square, Mr. Balingall followed a well-worn path that led him on until he saw stretching before him that sacred expanse of ground where the dead are hidden from the sun. He opened the gate and went in. Ah! sight of thrilling sadness! Filling every glance of the eye as it restlessly sought relief were fresh, thick-planted graves. Red and sinister spots on the green earth, they lay there like bloody swords on a deserted battle-field, each telling its own tale of unimaginable horror.

"And this is the end of every man's desire," he murmured. A profound sense of despair and isolation seized his soul. Twilight was falling, and the mists of the distance seemed like exhalations from the dreadful earth. He turned to leave, when, coming through the gate, he saw a woman's figure. All the glooms of the November day seemed to have gathered about her. Close and black, like a gathered cloud, she came toward him, with a step so gliding that she seemed to float rather than walk. Her hands were slightly extended, to hold a great mass of flowers that trailed to the hem of her dress in falling scarlet. As she passed Mr. Balingall a cluster of blossoms dropped. He stooped to restore it. She bowed mechanically, without looking at him. A thick veil was over her face, but for him only a glance was needed. Through the folds of blinding crape he recognized—Idalia.

The young man could have laughed aloud. "She did not die, then," and "I knew Ormsby was a fool," thought Mr. Balingall in one flash of the mind.

The place was no longer desolate and forbidding. The graves

were no more to him than the leaves that strew the earth after a hurricane. Idalia was alive—that was enough.

He watched her as she went to a distant grave, and laid the flowers upon it in lines and clusters. Then, kneeling, she pressed her face upon the earth, remaining thus so long that Mr. Balingall's professional instincts were aroused, and he wanted to say to her, "Don't you know you will give yourself a dreadful cold?"

"You're a stranger here, Sir, I see," interrupted a voice.

He turned and saw an old negro man, with a spade and a watering-pot in his hand—presumably the sexton.

"Yes," he said; "I've never been to Kilbuck before."

"It's a sorrerful time, marster, for you to see de place for de fust time. I seen all de trouble straight t'rough, an' a powerful misery it was; but dis here tryin' to piece things together agin is de hardest thing yit. 'Tain't no use. De end o' de worl' is at han'. Dey shall see signs an' prophecies. An' de signs an' prophecies is already come to pass."

"You remained through all the epidemic?"

"Yes, marster. Dar warn't no partikeler use in my runnin' off. I've had a misery in my back for so many years dat I'm ready to go whenever de good Lord calls. An' dar was work for me to do. Who'd have buried de po' critters if I hadn't 'a been here? I s'pose dey would have hired some fool nigger, an' he might have made some *holes* to put 'em in. *I* made *graves*—good graves every one of 'em—even in de greatest of de rush."

"Trying work for you."

"Yes, marster, but you know de edge of a thing soon w'ars off. I knowed 'em all, an' loved a many of 'em, and wid de fust dat I put away I shook an' cried like a baby. But pretty soon it got to be business. I was proud o' seein' how many I could git under-groun' in a day. I couldn't eat nor sleep if a corpse was a-waitin' for me. An', Lord! Lord! de very day dat Giueral Cincinnatus Hewett was buried— you've heered of Giueral Cincinnatus Hewett?"

"I think so," said Mr. Balingall, cautiously.

"Oh yes, marster, he was de biggest man in de State—reglar Moses an' Aaron rolled into one! Always on han' at fairs an' barbecues to make de speeches, an' *great* in politics. Take you right off yer feet, he would. An' a good man, ginerous as de flowin' streams. Nobody was too po' or triflin' for him to help. Often an' often have I watched him as he stood on de platform a-talkin' grand talk in dat ringin' voice o' his, an' de boys a-cheerin', an' everybody a-hangin' on his words; an' I've thought to myself, what a funeral he would have! Wid de Masons an' military, an' half de church pews full o' mourners—for de gineral had a great family connection—an' de shops closed, an' de papers wid black around 'em, an' de coffin all a-shinin' wid silver. I used to love to think it over. An', Lord! Lord! de day he was buried, I jes counted him in wid Hinkley's chillen, eight niggers, an' a lot o' po' white-trash emigrants—jes counted him in, you know, *one—Gineral Cincinnatus Hewett!*" and the old sexton shook his head as if scarcely believing now in his insensibility or temerity.

At this moment Idalia passed them.

"Who is that young lady?" asked Mr. Balingall.

"Dat's Miss Ida Carey, po' chile! She was a-gwine to marry young Evans—Fane Evans—a risin' young lawyer here. He'd been a soldier—fought under Morgan when he was a boy. I reckon dat's whar he learnt to be so brave. Den he was good stock, too. No coward's blood in any of 'em. He snapped his fingers at Yellow Jack jes as he'd snapped 'em at de Yankees, an' he played a big part here in Kilbuck. Ever been in a plague city, Sir?"

"No."

"Nor seed a panic?"

"No."

"Den you can't form no imagination, marster, o' dis town. You see, it was on us befo' we knowed it. Twenty cases befo' de doctors would even give up dat it was yellow fever, till de las' day of August. Den ole Dr. Davenport he stood on de street corner wid his han's stretched out as if ter push away de people dat was crowdin' aroun' him, an' his white hair a-blowin' in de wind, an' he said, 'Stan' not on de order of your goin', but go at once!' Lord! to see dat crowd scatter, as if a bum-shell had bust among 'em. An' it was time. Many whose clo's was in deir trunks to go never had need for nothin' more dan a sheet ter wrap 'em in. Dey fell as if fever was a sharp-shooter, an' died—died. Of de fust hundred, jes ten got well. God o' mercy! save dat deir souls ascended to dy throne, how could dy servants bear de burden dat dou hast put upon dem?"

The old man took off his scrap of straw hat and lifted his furrowed face to the sky.

"And Mr. Evans?"

"Yes, marster. He was a public-spirited man. Dar was a little band of 'em—a dozen or mo'—who took it inter deir po' young heads dat dey ought ter stay—hol' de fort, you know. God knows help was needed. Folks was dyin' like pizened dogs in a ditch. An' young Evans he kind o' took de lead. You know niggers is crazy, bad stock, an' in some towns dey carried on like de devil, a-burnin' an' a-robbin'. But dere warn't nothin' like dat in Kilbuck. Mars' Fane let it be known dat he believed in de shot-gun, an' dey was as skeered of him as if he had 'a been de Lord or de devil. He had a mighty great influence wid 'em, keered for 'em, too. Doctors, nusses, an' Champagne jes as plentiful in a nigger's cabin as in de white folks' houses. He'd 'a been as big a man as Gineral Cincinnatus Hewett if he had lived. Dar ain't a nigger in dis county but would 'a voted for him for President, roarin' Democrat dough he was, an' dey straight Republicans."

"But he died?"

"Lord! Lord! yes, marster—dey all died. He was spar'd, an' spar'd, till none of us but t'ought he'd git t'rough. De oders all went, an' dat seemed to make his chance all de better. But he got fuller an' fuller of de pizen, an' weak wid seein' his frien's go, an' tired wid de hard, hard work, an' den, when de cup was full, he was struck down. He made a fight. But pretty soon dem aroun' him saw he was a-goin'. Den Miss Ida come. Dey say she had encouraged him in stayin', an' dat's one reason why she takes it so hard. He was a-lyin' dar, numb an' stupid—for de pizen was a-creepin' t'rough his veins slow an' soft like de smell of an orange bloom—an' he t'ought he was a-gittin' well. De doctors was all aroun'—six of 'em; enough to kill him; but dey was good. Dey was cryin' as if he was deir own flesh an' blood. But Miss Ida didn't cry. An' when one of de doctors, a young, rash sort of fellow—when he said, 'I swear, I would take his place if I could,' she jes said, hard an' scornful, 'Why did you not take his place here, an' send him away?'

"She would not let dem tell him dat he must die, but all night long she stay beside him, a-smilin' an' a-talkin' of de cool air of de mountains. An' at daybreak he started up wild an' mad in convulsions, an' he jumped from de bed, a-strikin' out an' a-callin', 'Water! water!' Den he fell, an' when dey lifted him dere warn't no mo' ter do but ter bury him."

The old sexton's voice sounded hollow and dim. Mr. Balingall put his hand to his head with a confused sense of being some other than himself.

"I'm gwine now to water his grave," said the sexton. "I helps Miss Ida take keer of it."

"Did she have the fever?" asked Mr. Balingall.

"Yes, Sir, up in Louisville. An' we did hear dat she died. But she got well, an' came back here—not de same pretty young lady dough, but a *shadder*, all broke wid grief."

They reached Fane Evans's grave, and Mr. Balingall stooped to read some lines on the rude head-board:

> For their dear country, these, her quenchless glory,
> Won for themselves the dusky shroud of death.
> By that same death they live, whose echoing story
> Rings through the halls Hades inhabiteth.

"One o' de doctors wrote dat on de boa'd," said the sexton. "He said it would do for 'em all. In all dese graves you see aroun' Mr. Evans's is buried de young men who died as he did—for de sake of po' humanity. An' as our blessed Redeemer died," he added, after a pause, again uncovering his head.

Mr. Balingall looked down upon the grave. "And she loved you," he thought—"she loved you, and you could die!"

His name was called. Captain Masterson came hurrying through the gate.

"I've sent all over town after you, Balingall," he cried. "Finally some one directed me here. You've overspent your time. The *Lady Gay* has been waiting for you this last hour."

"Masterson," he replied, earnestly, "do you know, I've taken a fancy to stay a while in this town. You know everybody. Give me an introduction to some of your acquaintances."

"Man, have you lost your wits?"

"Not a bit of it. But it happens that I have a little leisure on my hands. I want a vacation. I may as well spend it here as anywhere."

"All right," said the captain, philosophically. "Haven't time to discuss it. Will give you a line to a preacher here I happen to know. You'll get tired of it soon enough, and the *Lady Gay* will pick you up on her return trip."

Mr. Balingall, however, is still in Kilbuck. He has made friends, and it is intimated that he is building up a practice. Idalia has not recognized him, and he has not yet spoken to her. But in his heart he has vowed to win her back to forgetfulness and a new love. He watches her in her daily pilgrimages to Fane Evans's grave. He sees with sharp pangs that month by month her features are more sharply cut, her form more slight, and her step drags more wearily. But not to himself, in his most fearful dream, does he whisper that she will die. And the future holds her secrets securely.

(1853–1879)

Irwin Russell

Irwin Russell, born in Port Gibson, Mississippi, June 3, 1853, published only a small number of poems and apparently only two short stories by the time of his death in New Orleans on December 23, 1879. Yet the distinction of being the first American writer to make full use of the Negro and his dialect is clearly his. Educated at St. Louis University, Russell returned to Port Gibson in 1869, was admitted to the bar in 1872, and spent some of his time traveling in Tennessee, Texas, and Louisiana. In 1878, encouraged by the publication of his poems in *Scribner's Monthly* and *Puck*, he went to New York to pursue a literary career. He was not successful, however, so he worked his way to New Orleans where, until his death at the age of twenty-six, he worked on the staff of the New Orleans *Times*.

Russell had serious literary aspirations. In 1878 in Port Gibson an acting group performed his "Negro play," "Everybody's Business; or Slightly Mistaken" (now lost), and he once planned a novel—an outline of which survives—which would be, as he put it, "a thing entirely new—nobody has ever tried it. . . . The book I propose making shall be true, if nothing else." But his early death and his inclination to use pseudonyms for his work have left to posterity less than fifty poems and three prose

121

sketches. Other writers have acknowledged their debts to Russell; Thomas Nelson Page and A. C. Gordon dedicated their *Befo' the War— Echoes in Negro Dialect* (1888) to him. Page declared once, "The light of his genius shining through his dialect poems . . . led my feet in the direction I have tried to follow"; and Joel Chandler Harris, in his Introduction to the first edition of the collected poems in 1888, wrote that "Irwin Russell was among the first—if not the very first—of Southern writers to appreciate the literary possibilities of the Negro character, and of the unique relations existing between the two races before the war, and was among the first to develop them." Russell wrote other poems, in Irish dialect ("Larry's on the Force"), on medieval folklore ("The Knight and the Squire"), poems of inspiration ("Hope") and reflection ("Cemetary"), but his genius lay in the vibrant and accurate portrayal of the Mississippi Negro in such works as his best-known "Christmas Night in the Quarters" and in the dramatic monologues "Nebuchadnezzar" and "The Mississippi Witness."

"Nebuchadnezzar" is reprinted from *Scribner's Monthly*, XII (May– October, 1876), 288; "The Mississippi Witness" is based on the text in *Scribner's Monthly*, XIII (November, 1876–April, 1877), 286. "Christmas Night in the Quarters" is based on the original manuscript in the Mississippi Department of Archives and History in Jackson, reproduced in facsimile by Gordon Marks & Company, 1970.

Nebuchadnezzar

YOU, Nebuchadnezzah, whoa, sah!
Whar is you tryin' to go, sah?
I'd hab you for to know, sah,
    I's a-holdin' ob de lines.
You better stop dat prancin';
You's pow'ful fond ob dancin',
But I'll bet my yeah's advancin'
    Dat I'll cure you ob your shines.

Look heah, mule! Better min' out—
Fus' t'ing you know you'll fin' out
How quick I'll wear dis line out
    On your ugly stubbo'n back.

You needn't try to steal up
An' lif' dat precious heel up;
You's got to plow dis fiel' up,
        You has, sah, for a fac'.

Dar, *dat's* de way to do it!
He's comin' right down to it;
Jes' watch him plowin' t'roo it!
        Dis nigger ain't no fool.
Some folks dey would 'a' beat him;
Now, dat would only heat him—
I know jes' how to treat him:
        You mus' *reason* wid a mule.

He minds me like a nigger.
If he was only bigger
He'd fotch a mighty figger,
        He would, I *tell* you! Yes, sah!
See how he keeps a-clickin'!
He's as gentle as a chicken,
An' nebber thinks o' kickin'—
        Whoa dar! Nebuchadnezzah!

Is dis heah me, or not me?
Or is de debbil got me?
Was dat a cannon shot me?
        Hab I laid heah more'n a week?
Dat mule do kick amazin'!
De beast was sp'iled in raisin'—
By now I 'spect he's grazin'
        On de oder side de creek.

The Mississippi Witness

Yoah Honah, an' de jury: Ef you'll listen, now, to me,
I's gwine to straighten up dis case jes like it ought to be:

Dis heah's a case ob stealin' hogs—a mighty ser'ous 'fense—
An' you'll know all about it, when I gibs my ebbydence.

Dis Peter Jones, the plainter, is a member ob de chu'ch,
But Thomas Green, de fender, goodness knows he's nuffin
       much—
A lazy, triflin' nigger is dat berry Thomas Green—
Dese is de dif'rent parties you is called to jedge atween.

Now, gib me stric' contention while I 'lucidates de fac':
Dere's two whole sides to eberyting—de front one an' de back—
What's dat de little lawyer say? To talk about de case?
Dat's jest what I wuz comin' to; you makes me lose de place.

Whar wuz I? Oh! I 'members; I wuz jes about to say,
I heered a disputation 'bout a p'int of law, to-day—
'Bout how to turn State's ebbydence—dat's what dey's dribin
       at—
Now aint it strange some niggers is so ignorant as dat?

Why, when you wants to turn it, you jes has to come to town,
An' fin' de Deestric Turner—he'll be somewhar loafin' 'roun'—
An' den sez you—"Mahs Turner, sah, I zires my compliments;
I's come in town to see you, for to turn State's ebbydence."

As soon's you tells him dat, he knows perzackly what you mean,
An' takes you to his office, whar he's got a big mersheen,
An' dar you cotches hol' de crank, an' den you turns away,
Untell at las' dar's somefin clicks, an' den you's come to A.

"Is dat de letter ob de thing de feller done?" says he—
Ef you says no, you turns ag'in untell you comes to B;
An' so you keeps a-turnin', tell de right one gits aroun',
An' dar de Deestric Turner looks, an' dar de law is foun'.

An' den you gibs de fac's, an' den he reads de law to you,
An' axes you to 'vise him what you think he ought to do;

An' den he say "good-mornin'," an' he gibs you fifty cents,
An' dat's de way you has to do to turn State's ebbydence.

Well, gemmen of de jury, dis heah case is understood,
I doesn't *know* de hog wuz stole, but Peter's word is good—
He up an' sesso manfully, dout makin' any bones;
An' darfore, sahs, ef I wuz you, I think I'd 'cide for Jones.

Christmas Night in the Quarters

When merry Christmas-day is done,
And Christmas-night has just begun;
While clouds in slow procession drift
To wish the moon-man "Christmas gift,"
Yet linger overhead, to know
What causes all the stir below;
At Uncle Johnny Booker's ball
The darkeys hold high carnival.
From all the countryside they throng,
With laughter, shouts, and scraps of song—
Their whole deportment plainly showing
That to THE FROLIC they are going.
Some take the path with shoes in hand,
To traverse muddy bottom-land;
Aristocrats their steeds bestride—
Four on a mule, behold them ride!
And ten great oxen draw apace
The wagon from "de oder place,"
With forty guests, whose conversation
Betokens glad anticipation.
Not so with him who drives: old Jim
Is sagely solemn, hard and grim,
And frolics have no joys for him.
He seldom speaks, but to condemn—
Or utter some wise apothegm—
Or else, some crabbed thought pursuing,
Talk to his team, as now he's doing:

Come up heah, Star! Yee-bawee!
　　You alluz is a-laggin'—
Mus' be you think I's dead,
　　An' dis de hus you's draggin'—
You's mos' too lazy to draw yo' bref,
　　Let 'lone drawin' de waggin.

Dis team—quit bel'rin, sah!
　　De ladies don't submit 'at—
Dis team—you ol' fool ox,
　　You heah me tell you quit 'at?
Dis team's des like de 'Nited States;
　　Dat's whut I's tryin' to git at!

De people rides behind
　　De pollytishners haulin'—
Sh'u'd be a well-bruk ox,
　　To foller dat 'ar callin'—
An' sometimes nuffin won't do dem steers
　　But what dey mus' be stallin'!

Woo bahgh! Buck-Kannon! Yes, sah,
　　Sometimes dey will be stickin';
An' den, fus' thing dey knows,
　　Dey takes a rale good lickin'—
De folks gits down: an' den watch out
　　For hommerin' an' kickin'.

Dey blows upon dey hands,
　　Den flings 'em wid de nails up,
Jumps up an' cracks dey heels,
　　An' pruz'ntly dey sails up,
An' makes dem oxen hump deyse'f,
　　By twistin' all dey tails up!

In this our age of printer's ink,
　　'Tis books that show us how to think—

The rule reversed, and set at naught,
That held that books were born of thought;
We form our minds by pedants' rules;
And all we know, is from the schools;
And when we work, or when we play,
We do it in an ordered way—
And Nature's self pronounce a ban on,
Whene'er she dares transgress a canon.
Untrammeled thus, the simple race is,
That "works the craps" on cotton-places!
Original in act and thought,
Because unlearned and untaught,
Observe them at their Christmas party:
How unrestrained their mirth—how hearty!
How many things they say and do,
That never would occur to you!
See Brudder Brown—whose saving grace
Would sanctify a quarter-race—
Out on the crowded floor advance,
To "beg a blessin' on dis dance":

O Mahs'r, let dis gath'rin' fin' a blessin' in yo' sight!
Don't jedge us hard for what we does—you knows it's Chris'mus
    night;
An' all de balunce ob de yeah, we does as right's we kin—
Ef dancin's wrong—oh! Mahs'r, let de time excuse de sin!

We labors in de vineya'd, workin' hard, an' workin' true—
Now, shorely you won't notus, ef we eats a grape or two,
An' takes a leetle holiday—a leetle restin'-spell—
Bekase, nex' week, we'll start in fresh, an' labor twicet as well.

Remember, Mahs'r—min' dis, now— de sinfulness ob sin
Is 'pendin' 'pon de sperrit what we goes an' does it in:
An' in a righchis frame ob min' we's gwine to dance an' sing;
A-feelin' like King David, when he cut de pigeon-wing.

It seems to me—indeed it do—I mebbe mout be wrong—
That people raly *ought* to dance, when Chrismus comes along;
Des dance bekase dey's happy—like de birds hops in de trees:
De pine-top fiddle soundin' to de bowin' ob de breeze.

We's got no ark to dance afore, like Isrul's prophet King;
We's got no harp to soun' de chords, to help us out to sing;
But 'cordin' to de gif's we has, we'll do de bes' we knows—
An' folks don't 'spise de vi'let-flow'r, bekase it ain't de rose.

You bless us, please sah, eben ef we's doin' wrong to-night;
'Kase den we'll need de blessin' more'n ef we's doin' right;
An' let de blessin' stay wid us, untell we comes to die,
An' goes to keep our Chris'mus wid dem sheriffs in de sky!

Yes, tell dem preshis angels we's a-gwine to jine 'em soon;
Our voices we's a-trainin' for to sing de glory-tune;
We's ready when you wants us, an' it ain't no matter when—
Oh! Mahs'r, call yo' chillen soon, an' take 'em home!—Amen.

————

The rev'rend man is scarcely through,
When all the noise begins anew,
And with such force assaults the ears,
That through the din one scarcely hears
Old Fiddling Josey "sound his A"—
Correct the pitch—begin to play—
Stop, satisfied—then, with the bow,
Rap out the signal dancers know:

————

GIT *yo' pardners, fust kwattilion!*
   Stomp yo' feet, an' raise 'em high;
Tune is: "Oh! dat watermillion!
   Gwine to git to home bime-bye."
S'lute yo' pardners!—scrape perlitely—

Don't be bumpin' gin de res'—
Balance all!—now, step out rightly;
   Alluz dance yo' lebbel bes'.
Fo'wa'd foah!—whoop up, niggers!
   Back agin!—don't be so slow!—
SWING cornahs!—min' de figgers!
   When I hollers, den you go.
Top ladies cross ober!
   Hol' on, tell I takes a dram—
Gemmen solo!—yes, *I's* sober—
   Kain't say how de fiddle am—
Hands around!—hol' up yo' faces,
   Don't be lookin' at yo' feet!
Swing yo' pardners to yo' places!
   Dat's de way—dat's hard to beat.
Sides fo'wa'd!—when you's ready—
   Make a bow as low's you kin!
Swing acrost wid opp'site lady!
   Now we'll let you swap agin—
Ladies change!—shet up dat talkin';
Do yo' talkin' arter while—
   Right an' lef!—don't want no walkin'—
     Make yo' steps, an' show yo' style!

———————

And so the "set" proceeds—its length
Determined by the dancers' strength;
And all agree to yield the palm
For grace and skill, to "Georgy Sam,"
Who stamps so hard, and leaps so high,
"Des watch him!" is the wond'ring cry—
"De nigger mus' be, for a fac',
Own cousin to a jumpin'-jack!"
On, on, the restless fiddle sounds—
Aye chorussed by the curs and hounds—
Dance after dance succeeding fast,
Till SUPPER is announced at last.

That scene—but why attempt to show it?
The most inventive modern poet,
In fine new words whose hope and trust is,
Could form no phrase to do it justice!
When supper ends—that is not soon—
The fiddle strikes the same old tune;
The dancers pound the floor again,
With all they have of might and main;
Old gossips, *almost* turning pale,
Attend Aunt Cassy's gruesome tale
Of conjurors, and ghosts, and devils,
That in the smoke-house hold their revels;
Each drowsy baby droops his head,
Yet scorns the very thought of bed:—
So wears the night; and wears so fast,
All wonder when they find it passed,
And hear the signal sound, to go,
From what few cocks are left to crow.
Then, one and all, you hear them shout:
"Hi! Booker! fotch de banjo out,
An' gib us *one* song 'fore we goes—
One ob de berry bes' you knows!"
Responding to the welcome call,
He takes the banjo from the wall,
And tunes the strings with skill and care—
Then strikes them with a master's air;
And tells, in melody and rhyme,
This legend of the olden time:

———

Go 'way, fiddle!—folks is tired o' hearin' you a-squawkin'.
Keep silence for yo' betters—don't you heah de banjo talkin'?
About de 'possum's tail, she's gwine to lecter—ladies, listen!—
About de ha'r what isn't dar, an' why de ha'r is missin':

"Dar's gwine to be a oberflow," saïd Noah, lookin' solemn—
For Noah tuk the Herald, an' he read de ribber column—

An' so he sot his hands to work a-cl'arin' timber-patches,
An' 'lowed he's gwine to build a boat to beat de steamah
    Natchez.

Ol' Noah kep' a-nailin,' an' a-chippin,' an' a-sawin';
An' all de wicked neighbors kep' a-laughin' an' a-pshawin';
But Noah didn't min' 'em, knowin' whut wuz gwine to happen:
An' forty days an forty nights de rain it kep' a-drappin'.

Now, Noah had done cotched a lot ob eb'ry sort o' beas'es—
Ob all de shows a-trabbelin', it beat 'em all to pieces!
He had a Morgan colt, an' seb'ral head o' Jarsey cattle—
An' druv 'em 'board de Ark as soon's he heered de thunder
    rattle.

Den sech anoder fall ob rain!—it come so awful hebby,
De ribber riz immejitly, an' busted troo de lebbee;
De people all wuz drownded out—'cep' Noah an' de critters,
An' men he'd hired to work de boat—an' one to mix de bitters.

De Ark she kep' a-sailin,' an' a-sailin,' *an'* a-sailin';
De lion got his dander up, an' like to bruk de palin'—
De sarpints hissed— de painters yelled— tell, whut wid all de
    fussin',
You c'u'dn't hardly heah de mate a-bossin' 'roun' an' cussin'!

Now Ham, de only nigger what wuz runnin' on de packet,
Got lonesome in de barber-shop, an' c'u'dn't stan' de racket;
An' so, for to amuse he-se'f, he steamed some wood an' bent it,
An' soon he had a banjo made—de fust dat wuz invented.

He wet de ledder, stretched it on; made bridge an' screws an'
    apron;
An' fitted in a proper neck—'twuz berry long an' tap'rin';
He tuk some tin, an' twisted him a thimble for to ring it;
An' den de mighty question riz: how wuz he gwine to string it?

De 'possum had as fine a tail as dis dat I's a-singin';
De ha'r's so long, an' thick an' strong—des fit fur banjo-stringin':
Dat nigger shaved 'em off as short as wash-day-dinner graces;
An' sorted ob 'em by de size, frum little E's to basses.

He strung her, turned her, struck a jig—'twuz "Nebber min' de
    wedder"—
She soun' like forty-lebben bands, a-playin' all togedder;
Some went to pattin'; some to dancin'; Noah called de figgers—
An' Ham he sot an' knocked de tune, de happiest ob niggers!

Now, sence dat time—it's mighty strange—dar's not de slightes'
    showin'
Ob any ha'r at all upon the 'possum's tail a-growin';
An' curi's, too— dat nigger's ways: his people nebber los' 'em—
For whar you finds de nigger—dar's de banjo an' de 'possum!

—————

The night is spent; and as the day
Throws up the first faint flash of gray,
The guests pursue their homeward way;
And through the field beyond the gin,
Just as the stars are going in,
See Santa Claus departing—grieving—
His own dear Land of Cotton leaving.
His work is done— he fain would rest,
Where people know and love him best—
He pauses— listens— looks about—
But go he must: his pass is out;
So, coughing down his rising tears,
He climbs the fence and disappears.
And thus observes a colored youth—
(The common sentiment, in sooth):
"Oh! what a blessin' 'tw'u'd ha' bin,
Ef Santy had been born a twin!
We'd hab two Chrismuses a yeah—
Or p'r'aps *one* brudder'd *settle* heah!"

(1849–1896)

Eliza Jane Poitevant Nicholson (Pearl Rivers)

Eliza Jane Poitevant, born in Gainesville on March 11, 1849, is known to students of the history of journalism as the dynamic editor of the New Orleans *Picayune*, which flourished under her ownership from 1876 to her death on February 5, 1896. The quality of her poetry, however, which consists of various fugitive pieces in newspapers and magazines and a single volume entitled *Lyrics* (1873) is high enough to make her deserving of a significant place in the history of Southern literature.

After an education in female seminaries in Amite County, Mississippi, and Amite, Louisiana, Poitevant entered the newspaper business through a chance acquaintance with the *Picayune's* owner, Alva Morris Holbrook. She married him in 1872. Her second marriage, on June 28, 1878, to the business manager of the paper, George Nicholson, took place two years after Holbrook's death. Holbrook left his widow in possession of the *Picayune*, and she unhesitatingly took on the traditionally male job of editing a newspaper. She was extraordinarily effective. She introduced the

133

society column to New Orleans, campaigned against cruelty to animals, denounced prize fighting, developed the Sunday edition, emphasized the coverage of sports, and made the *Picayune* into a major metropolitan newspaper. Her working philosophy, she once stated, was that "nobody knows what a woman can do, least of all the woman herself, until she tries."

The poetry of Poitevant, who called herself "Pearl Rivers" after the river she lived near as a child, is crisp, clean, and strong. "I sing only of simple things," she wrote, "In simpler words than all." Though she writes of songs and birds and the death of family pets, her best lyrics turn on the theme of a woman scorned. A woman's heart in a man's world, she writes, is one that can be easily crushed ("Only a Heart"). But a woman can be disciplined. Her passion can, if it is necessary, be shrouded in her lover's cold words, buried beneath the snow, and covered like a corpse with a stone of silence ("Under the Snow"). "Hagar," a dramatic monologue with this theme, was published in *Cosmopolitan* three years before her death. It is Pearl Rivers's finest poem. The narrator, an Egyptian woman being cast into exile by her Hebrew lover Abraham, subtly reveals in her angry words a complex human and religious relationship. Though Hagar, the heathen, loves the man, and Sara, one of the chosen few, loves the man's wealth, it is Hagar and her son who are being pushed aside. She will go, but she coldly vows to her lover that his wrongs someday "Shall waken and uncoil themselves, and hiss/Like adders at the name of Abraham."

Since Rivers's poems are few in number, her contribution to American literature cannot be called great. However, some of her work, notably "Hagar," is of significant literary value.

In the following selections, "Hagar" is reprinted from *The Cosmopolitan*, XVI (November 1893); all others are from *Lyrics* (1873).

Hagar

Go back! How dare you follow me beyond
The door of my poor tent? Are you afraid
That I have stolen something? See! my hands
Are empty, like my heart. I am no thief!
The bracelets and the golden finger rings
And silver anklets that you gave to me,

I cast upon the mat before my door,
And trod upon them. I would scorn to take
One trinket with me in my banishment
That would recall a look or tone of yours.
My lord, my generous lord, who sent me forth,
A loving woman, with a loaf of bread
And jug of water on my shoulder laid,
To thirst and hunger in the wilderness!

Go back! Go back to Sara! See! she stands
Watching us there, behind the flowering date,
With jealous eyes, lest my poor hands should steal
One farewell touch from yours. Go back to her,
And say that Hagar has a heart as proud,
If not so cold, as hers; and, though it break
It breaks without the sound of sobs, without
The balm of tears to ease its pain. It breaks—
It breaks, my lord, like iron; hard, but clean;
And, breaking, asks no pity. If my lips
Should let one plea for mercy slip between
These words that lash you with a woman's scorn,
My teeth should bite them off, and I would spit
Them at you, laughing, though all red and warm with blood.
"Cease!" do you say? No, by the gods
Of Egypt, I do swear that if my eyes
Should let one tear melt through their burning lids,
My hands should pluck them out; and if these hands,
Groping outstretched in blindness, should by chance
Touch yours and cling to them against my will,
My Ishmael should cut them off, and, blind
And maimed, my little son should lead me forth
Into the wilderness to die. Go back!

Does Sara love you as I did, my lord?
Does Sara clasp and kiss your feet, and bend
Her haughty head in worship at your knee?
Ah! Abraham you were a god to me.

If you but touched my hand my foolish heart
Ran down into the palm, and throbbed, and thrilled;
Grew hot and cold, and trembled there; and when
You spoke, though not to me, my heart ran out
To listen through my eager ears and catch
The music of your voice and prison it
In memory's murmuring shell. I saw no fault
Nor blemish in you, and your flesh to me
Was dearer than my own. There is no vein
That branches from your heart, whose azure course
I have not followed with my kissing lips.
I would have bared my bosom like a shield
To any lance of pain that sought your breast.
And once, when you lay ill within your tent,
No taste of water, or of bread or wine
Passed through my lips; and all night long I lay
Upon the mat before your door to catch
The sound of your dear voice, and scarcely dared
To breathe, lest she, thy mistress, should come forth
And drive me angrily away; and when
The stars looked down with eyes that only stared
And hurt me with their lack of sympathy,
Weeping, I threw my longing arms around
Benammi's neck. Your good horse understood,
And gently rubbed his face against my head,
To comfort me. But if you had one kind,
One loving thought of me in all that time,
That long, heart-breaking time, you kept it shut
Close in your bosom as a tender bud
And did not let it blossom into words.
Your tenderness was all for Sara. Through
The door, kept shut against my love, there came
No message to poor Hagar, almost crazed
With grief lest you should die. Ah! you have been
So cruel and so cold to me, my lord;
And now you send me forth with Ishmael.
Not on a journey through a pleasant land

Upon a camel, as my mistress rides,
With kisses, and sweet words, and dates and wine,
But cast me off, and sternly send me forth
Into the wilderness with these poor gifts,
A jug of water, and—a loaf of bread—
That sound was not a sob; I only lost
My breath and caught it hard again. Go back!

Why do you follow me? I am a poor
Bondswoman, but a woman still, and these
Sad memories, so bitter and so sweet,
Weigh heavily upon my breaking heart
And make it hard, my lord—for me to go.
"Your God commands it?" Then my gods, the gods
Of Egypt, are more merciful than yours.
Isis and good Osiris never gave
Command like this, that breaks a woman's heart,
To any prince in Egypt. Come with me
And let us go and worship them, my dear lord.
Leave all your wealth to Sara. Sara loves
The touch of costly linen and the scent
Of precious Chaldean spices, and to bind
Her brow with golden fillets, and perfume
Her hair with ointment. Sara loves the sound
Of many cattle lowing on the hills;
And Sara loves the slow and stealthy tread
Of many camels moving on the plains.
Hagar loves you. Oh! come with me, dear lord.
Take but your staff and come with me. Your mouth
Shall drink my share of water from this jug
And eat my share of bread with Ishmael;
And from your lips I will refresh myself
With love's sweet wine from tender kisses pressed.
Ah! come dear lord. Oh! come, my Abraham.
Nay, do not bend your cold, stern brows on me
So frowningly; it was not Hagar's voice

That spoke from pleading words. Go back! Go back!
And tell your God I hate him, and I hate
The cruel, craven heart that worships him
And dare not disobey. Ha! I believe
'Tis not your far-off, bloodless God you fear,
But Sara. Coward! Cease to follow me!
Go back to Sara. See! she beckons now.
Hagar loves not a coward; you do well
To send me forth into the wilderness,
Where hatred hath no weapon keen enough
That held within a woman's slender hand
Could stab a coward to the heart. I go!
I go, my lord; proud that I take with me
Of your countless herds by Hebron's brook
Of all your Canaan riches, naught but this—
A jug of water and a loaf of bread.
And now, by all of Egypt's gods, I swear
If it were not for Ishmael's dear sake
My feet would tread upon this bitter bread,
My hands would pour this water on the sands;
And leave this jug as empty as my heart
Is empty now of all the reverence
And overflowing love it held for you.
I go! But I will teach my little Ishmael
To hate his father for his mother's sake;
His bow shall be the truest bow that flies
Its arrows through the desert air. His feet,
The fleetest on the desert's sands;
Aye! Hagar's son a desert prince shall be,
Whose hands shall be against all other men;
And he shall rule a fierce and mighty tribe,
Whose fiery hearts and supple limbs will scorn
The chafing curb of bondage, like the fleet
Wild horses of Arabia. I go!
But like this loaf that you have given me,
So shall your bread taste bitter with my hate;

And like the water in this jug, my lord,
So shall the sweetest water that you draw
From Canaan's wells, taste salty with my tears.

Farewell! I go, but Egypt's mighty gods
Will go with me, and my revenge will be,
And in whatever distant land your God,
Your cruel God of Israel, is known,
There, too, the wrongs that you have done this day
To Hagar and your first-born, Ishmael,
Shall waken and uncoil themselves, and hiss
Like adders at the name of Abraham.

Under the Snow

Deep, deep, deep,
    Quickly, so none should know,
I buried my warm love stealthily
    Under the winter snow.

For you had coldly said,
    Coldly and carelessly,
"Bury your love or let it live,
    It is all the same to me."

I tore it out of my heart!
    I crushed it within my hand!
It cried to you in its agony
    For help, but you came not; and

It struggled within my grasp;
    It fought with my woman's will;
It kneeled to my woman's pride with tears;
    Then silent it lay, and still.

I knew that it was not dead,
    But I said: "It soon will die,
Buried under the winter snow,
    Under the winter sky."

I kissed it tenderly,
    Just once, for the long ago;
Then shrouded it with your cold, cold words,
    Colder than all the snow!

Deep, deep, deep,
    Quickly, so none should know,
I buried my warm love stealthily
    Under the winter snow.

Then with my murderous hands
    I raised up the heavy stone
Of SILENCE over my buried love,
    Lest the world should hear it moan.

The Prince of Splendor

Ho, Poet with the harp of Praise,
    And fingers light and slender,
Lo! with a host of shining days
    There comes the Prince of Splendor.

God's chosen month of all the twelve,
    The wise, the good, the sober—
Who ne'er was born to dig and delve,
    The Joseph-like October!

Down in the quiet vales I hear
    This glorious new-comer,
Interpreting unto the Year
    The dreams of Spring and Summer.

And in the busy fields I see
    His golden chariot gliding,
And hear the sheaves cry, "Bow the knee!"
    Where'er the Prince comes riding.

And now upon the hills he stands,
    In colors warm and glowing;
Through all the lands, with willing hands,
    His gathered grain bestowing.

A kinder Hand than Jacob's threw
    That gorgeous robe around him!
A greater King than Egypt knew
    With all this glory crowned him!

Ho, Artist! to the woods away,
    To meet this Prince of Splendor,
And paint his features while you may,
    In colors rich and tender.

(1868–1946)

Harris Dickson

Harris Dickson, born in Yazoo City on July 21, 1868, was by profession a
lawyer and a municipal judge. But before his death in 1946, he had published a total of fifteen books and over a hundred short stories and articles
in the leading magazines of his day. Educated in the public schools of
Vicksburg, at the University of Virginia, and at the law school at Columbia
University, Dickson began publishing his work shortly after he became a
lawyer in Vicksburg in 1896. His early novels, such as *The Black Wolf's
Breed* (1899) and *The Siege of Lady Resolute* (1902), were historical ro-
mances set in Europe, but with the composition of *The Ravanels* (1905), a
post–Civil War story of assassination, revenge, insanity, and love, he
turned his attention to the South for his material.

Dickson's southern stories, most of them virtually unknown today,
depict the customs, manners, and speech of Mississippi blacks, Louisiana
creoles, and lower-class southern whites. Whether his plots revolve
around superstition ("The Ghost and the Gallows Nail"), peculiar racial
abilities ("Cannie the Uncanny"), or one of the sundry crimes he had to
deal with as a judge ("Above Suspicion"), Dickson's intention was usually
to portray for the rest of the country a part of America it was unfamiliar
with. He covers a wide range: light humor in the "Old Reliable" stories of
Uncle Zack, violence in the levee camp tales such as "Man's Love and

142

Woman's," river romance in the Crow series in *The Saturday Evening Post,* and gamboling in New Orleans ("Donna Inez is Indiscreet"). His stories tend to be in the tradition of realistic local color.

Dickson was not a careful writer. His use of Negro dialect is not always correct or consistent, and the facts of history revealed in his novels are sometimes inaccurate. His 1925 biography of John Sharp Williams, *An Old-Fashioned Senator,* is no more than a pleasant run through the senator's life, and the 1917 *The Unpopular History of the United States* is a curiosity piece. But he was always conscientious about what he wrote. His observations on the American scene, in "America by Grace" and "Unbeatable America," his attempts to deal with the social implications of agriculture, in *The Story of King Cotton* (1937), and with what was then called the "Negro Problem," are conceived in what appears to be an honest desire to use for the public good the popularity and influence he had gained as a writer of successful fiction.

Dickson's use of Negro characters and dialects continues the tradition of Irwin Russell and Sherwood Bonner, and some of his local color fiction reminds one of Joel Chandler Harris. But his true place in southern and American literature has not yet been assessed. A wealth of Mississippiana and Americana lies undiscovered, for the most part, in the pages of *Collier's, The Saturday Evening Post, McClure's,* and in the many volumes that bear his name.

"The Striped Man" is reprinted from *The Golden Book Magazine,* III (January, 1926).

The Striped Man

NO CHINK OF LIGHT PEEPED OUT, nor murmur of human voices came from that lone cabin by the forest's edge. Crouching beneath a shrouded water-oak, the funereal mosses drooped above its roof. A black, mysterious density behind pulsated with the crooning life of unseen things. The screech-owl raised his quaver, a tremolo of frozen fear. Half-picked cotton-fields spread before the cabin, in regions of white and patches of brown. Mid-December afternoon had darkened into night.

Within, a negro man rocked to and fro, nodding drowsily at the wide-mouthed chimney. Old Aaron jerked himself awake, then knelt before his burned-down fire. A constellation of sparks glittered amidst the clouds of gray-banked ashes. But a constellation would never roast the yams upon which Aaron depended for his supper. That's why he grumbled, "Dar now! Dis fire is teetotally went out. I jes' *got* to fetch a turn o' wood."

He stood up before the hearth, trying to organize himself for a venture to the woodpile. His monstrous shadow flickered roofward, among the naked joists and rafters. Suddenly the negro threw up his head, listened and shivered at the sinister baying of a solitary hound: "Dat ain't no *bear*-dog; nor yit a 'possum-dog. Dem's *blood*-dogs; dey's chasin' somebody."

The door being stoutly latched, Aaron cautiously opened a shutter, a solid shutter in a window that had no sash. Again he listened. "Sho' *is* blood-dogs. One o' dem convicts got away from de State farm."

With screech-owls, bloodhounds, and fugitives outside, the lonesome negro felt creepy in the dark. He lighted a cheap oil-lamp and set it on the table. "Roarin' fire would make dis cabin look a heap mo' brighter."

While Aaron bent over his hearth and nervously scraped out a place for the backlog, that shutter opened again—noiselessly and warily it opened. A face peered in, a drawn and haggard face. At first it was only the glittering eyes; then a shoulder, a shoulder in stripes, the black-and-white brand of a convict. Those eyes watched Aaron; a striped arm stole through and reached toward the door-latch. The arm was short and the latch was far. Aaron rose. Shoulder and arm drew back. The convict disappeared.

"Huh! Settin' here studyin' 'bout it ain't gwine to roast no taters." Aaron shuffled to his door, and listened before he flung it open. The hound had hushed.

"Huh! Squinch-owl ain't nothin' to be skeered of." Aaron began to whistle, and hustled to the wood-pile.

Immediately a convict's striped garb flitted across the yellow stream that poured from Aaron's doorway. The man dodged inside. He was very young. Swiftly he searched for food, for clothes, and found nothing. At Aaron's returning whistle he melted into formless gloom behind the door. Murky lamp-light glinted upon the long blue barrel of his "navy six."

Aaron stumbled in with an armful of wood, and could see nothing. Cat-like, the convict followed him. At the hearth the negro eased down his load, and rolled a backlog into place. Aaron neither saw nor heard the man behind him; he only felt, and glanced over his shoulder into that surly blue muzzle. His staring white eyes followed the length of a rigid arm, up to a tense and desperate face, whose tight lips opened, "Don't—make—a noise."

Aaron shut his mouth with a gulp.

"Lock that door. No. Stop! You'll run away." Backing to the open door the convict listened, then closed it, and fastened the shutter. Aaron failed to relish these preliminaries. "Mister, what *is* you fixin' to do to me?"

The striped man came at him. "Make up that fire."

Aaron made the fire, promptly. The convict dropped into a chair, faint from hunger and exhaustion. "Have you something to eat?"

"Got taters." Aaron raked a yam from the ashes. The striped man snatched it and ate ravenously. "Give me another."

Aaron had the second yam ready and waiting.

"Anything to drink in the house?" He was wet to the waist, draggled with the blue mud of the swamp.

The negro caught his talking-wind as he found the bottle; "Dis is *good* licker. Cap'n John fotch it hissef, 'cause I had a mizry in my side." Before Aaron could rinse a cup, the convict drank greedily from the bottle, which Aaron frugally removed beyond his reach. Another such drink would empty it.

"Old man, whose plantation is this?"

"B'long to Cap'n Buckner, suh."

"Captain *John* Buckner? The sheriff?"

"Yas, suh; de *High* Sheriff."

"Where is he to-night?"

"At de big house; jes' now glimpsed him ridin' home."

The convict stretched his legs before the fire; steam uprose from drying prison trousers. His eyes closed. Aaron glanced furtively toward the door. If he could only get this man drunk.

"Take another drink, Mister?" pouring wastefully into the cup.

"No! No!" The convict bounded upright. "No! I *mustn't* go to sleep. Here; take off those clothes—quick."

Aaron staggered. "Shuck my clo'es? What fer, Mister?"

"Take—them—off."

Aaron shucked his coat, and looked down.

"Not de breeches, too?"

"Breeches, too—hurry." Off they came.

"Mister, is you gwine to leave me naked as a jaybird?"

"No; put on mine." He flung aside his prison garb, the trousers curling flabbily on the floor, like some huge, distorted serpent. "Get into my breeches—quick."

Aaron wobbled against the table, feeling for the proper place to stick in his trembling leg. The convict put on Aaron's trousers. "Get me some shoes."

"Dese?" Aaron held up a foot.

"No; haven't you a change?"

"Yas, suh; when *I* changes shoes I goes barefooted."

"Then give me those." That "navy six" pointed; had it gone off, Aaron's feet would not have been in the shoes. "Dar dey is."

Kicking out of his rough brogans, the convict slipped into Aaron's ampler footgear, "Now take mine."

"Boss, I can't squeeze my feets into dem shoes."

"Do you want me to slice off your toes?"

"Not ef it's jes' de same to you, suh; thankee, suh." Aaron squeezed, and limped without complaining.

Then the fugitive examined his own shirt, a prison shirt bearing that telltale number, 923. "Old man, have you a clean shirt?"

"Sholy. Jes' washed my udder one dis mornin'. You's more'n welcome to it." Aaron had a hunch that punctuality was the best policy, and grabbed that shirt from the bed-post—a blue-checked gingham, clean, but unstarched and torn.

"Boss, 'tain't much of a shirt. Calf done chawed off one sleeve. It looks all right, ef you roll 'em bofe up."

The convict changed into the blue shirt, then laid his hand upon the door-latch, "Old man, can you run?"

"Dat depends, boss; I runs 'cordin' to what's pushin' me."

"Suppose it's two bloodhounds and four deputies?"

"*Run?* You say *run?* I'd nacherly *fly.*"

"Don't fly. Keep both feet on the ground, and leave a trail."

"Leave a trail? Who? Me?"

"Yes; the dogs are trailing those shoes."

"Dese shoes?" Aaron dropped to the floor and snatched them off. "Dogs ain't gwine to trail *dese* shoes—not wid Aaron in 'em."

"Put those shoes back."

"Boss, lemme git barefooted; I'll show dem dogs *some* runnin'."

"Put—on—those shoes."

Aaron scrouged into the shoes and stood up. "My feets hurts."

"Dogs will make you forget that. Wade in the sloughs, crawl along the fences—break your trail. Keep those dogs away from here as long as you can." Both men stopped, and listened to the deep-mouthed uncertain howling of a beast at fault. The convict smiled. For months he had studied hounds, and knew their baying and barking.

"He's lost my trail—at the slough. I crossed there twice—pulled out by a grapevine, and swung into the cane-brake. It may be an hour before they get here. Hurry, old man."

Aaron didn't hurry. "Boss, my knees is weak. I can't run."

"You've got to run. If the dogs get too close—can you climb?"

"Onpossible to keep a squirrel on de groun'."

"Better climb; the dogs'll eat up those clothes."

"Huh! I'd throw down de clo'es, an' let 'em eat."

"Now start."

Aaron grovelled on the floor, crawled to the convict, and seized his arm. "Boss, I'm teetotally *onqualified* to run."

"Get out and try."

Aaron clung to him, his eyes rolling in terror. Suddenly those eyes snapped into fixed positions. He was staring at the convict's left arm, which showed through the tattered sleeve. The elbow had been broken. An ugly scar, the red scar of a burn, zigzagged from shoulder to wrist. Aaron scrambled to his feet. His eyes bulged wider, searching the face, the figure, every feature of the youth. Slowly dawned the horror; even more slowly came the hesitating words, "Young—Mister—Dancey—MacRae!"

"What?"

"Sho'ly dis is young Mister Dancey MacRae?"

"Shut up! You don't know what you are talking about."

"I *knows* Mister Dancey. Ole Missy's baby boy."

MacRae's face twitched; his eyes drooped, then lifted, "You old black liar; my name is—name is—number nine-twenty-three," emphasized by the "navy six."

"Dat's all right, boss; p'int dat thing t'other way. Thankee, suh." The negro moved closer; his voice lowered.

"Ole Missy had a baby boy what I 'tended to. He warn't no more'n half growed up when he got his arm broke, jes like yourn, fetchin' a crippled nigger ooman outer de fire. Dat's de time our quarters burnt up. You kinder favours him, an—"

"Look at me again, old man. Look hard. Do I favour anybody that you know?" MacRae tried to hold the weapon steady, but it wavered.

Aaron looked closely, and answered positively, "Sho' don't, boss; sho' don't. You don't hardly favor yo' own self."

"Then you never saw me before?"

"Never sot eyes on nobody what look like you."

"Very well; start your running."

From the clearing, closer and closer yet, came one long triumphant howl, rocketting upwards to the stars. The fugitive had heard nothing else for hours. He knew what that meant. They were bounding on, straight on; those grim relentless dogs had struck his trail. They were here.

MacRae slammed the door and gripped his "navy six." "Too late. They've got me."

"No dey ain't, Mister Dancey; no dey ain't. Jes' tie me in dis chair an' put a gag in my mouf. Den you hide. Nigger done dat las' summer, an' *he* got away."

MacRae stood irresolute, hearing the dogs more clearly than he heard the negro. "Aaron, I *must* get away, only for five days. I *must* find somebody; find something. I'm coming back."

"Comin' back?"

"Yes; I couldn't go like this, and stay."

"Den you tie me, an' hide; I'll make 'em think you's gone."

"Hide? Where?"

Something had to be done; the inspiration struck Aaron.

"Hide up dere." He pointed to a couple of planks which rested across the joists, nearly above the hearth. They were wide enough to conceal a man, and except for them the roof was open.

"You lie down flat on dem planks; dey'll never see you. I'll set de lamp right onderneath, and dat'll make a big deep shadder."

It was very dark above those planks, in the peak of the roof. MacRae considered, while Aaron placed the lamp beneath the planks.

"Quick, Mister Dancey. Take dis plowline an' tie bofe o' my hands behind me."

MacRae laid his pistol on the table, and bound the negro to a chair.

"Now put a gag in my mouf, same as dat convict done. Dere's de cotton sack."

Ever nearer came the dogs, nearer, nearer. Hurriedly the boy tore a strip of cloth, tying a knot to fit in Aaron's mouth.

The negro grinned. "Now den, I can't move nary hand, neither foot. Hold on, Mister Dancey, hold on! 'Sposin' dem dogs tuk a notion to eat up dese clo'es." Aaron squirmed and wriggled, while MacRae stopped his mouth with the gag. Now they could hear the gallop of horses; frantic dogs were howling, and trying to scratch beneath the door. MacRae thrust the pistol into his pocket and leaped upon the table.

Bang! Bang! Bang! on the door. MacRae clutched the plank and swung into space.

Bang! Bang! Bill Slaydon's voice outside was shouting, "Aaron! Aaron!"

The young man's dangling body lifted itself convulsively; he threw one leg over a joist. Manifestly his strength was nearly spent.

"Aaron! Aaron, open this door! I see your light."

Aaron's eyes shifted back and forth, from door to writhing man. MacRae hooked an elbow over the joist, and drew himself up just in time. The shutter was snatched open, and Bill Slaydon's bearded face appeared in the window, "Here, nigger; unlatch this door."

MacRae jerked his feet out of the range of light into the realm of shadow. Aaron caught the scintillation of his eyes, the threatening gleam upon his "navy six." Then all had vanished into upper darkness.

Aaron began to scuffle, and make a noise with his feet. The deputy sheriff saw him. Slaydon's face drew back; his voice called out, "Nathan, hold them dogs in leash; that feller's been here."

Then a burly man, booted and spattered, crawled through the narrow window.

"Whicherway did he go? Oh, you're gagged." Bill Slaydon glanced round the room, saw nobody else, and tore away the gag.

"Cut dese ropes, please, suh; dey's hurtin' my legs."

A slash, this way and that, set Aaron free.

"How long has he been gone? Talk sudden!"

Aaron streched himself, and groaned;

" 'Pears like I been tied all night, de way my legs feels."

"No such thing; 'tain't nine o'clock yet."

"Dat man tuk my clo'es; chunky, thickset feller—"

"He's a boy—number nine-twenty-three."

"Mebbe so; mebbe so; he bust in dis house so brief I skacely got a chance to squint at him."

"Did he get anything to eat?"

"Feed dat man? Who? Me? I would give dat man *nothin'*. He ack scandlous."

"Did he rest?"

"Never tarried here no time."

The deputy pulled at his beard. "He can't hold out much longer. Lemme see your foot."

Aaron remembered, and jerked off those prison shoes. "Dogs mought take a notion to eat 'em up."

"Changed with you, did he? He's a slick one." The deputy held a shoe in his hand, and said, "Maybe them dogs won't pick up the new trail."

"Let 'em foller a trail what leads away from *dis* cabin."

Above, in darkness, crouched that tense body, with glistening eyes and ready weapon.

"Which direction did he go?" the deputy demanded.

Aaron grabbed Slaydon's arm, and led him to the door. "Right yonder way, suh. Jes' to de lef' o' dat big oak. Clumb de fence, an' cut across nigh Jim Hering's house."

"How could you see him? With the door shut?"

"Never seed him. I heered Jim Hering's dog abarkin', an' dat's de onliest way he was 'bleeged to travel."

Slaydon strode out into the moonlight. Aaron's heart thumped as he shut the door, and ran to MacRae. "Mister Dancey, lemme fetch you one o' Cap'n John's hosses?"

"Get his *best,* and get it *now.*" MacRae sat up, and swung his legs, preparatory to dropping. The barefoot negro slipped out and dodged back, "Lie down, Mister Dancey, lie down; de sheriff's comin'. Pull in dat foot."

Aaron turned to face Bill Slaydon, who entered, followed by the sheriff, a high-bred old man with keen gray eyes that saw everything—everything except the boy on the plank. Aaron took a sharp breath; no negro had ever succeeded in fooling Cap'n John.

The sheriff glanced around him, then questioned Slaydon. "You say the dogs tracked him here?"

"Yes, sir; they acted fine. He can't travel far. Had no rest, and nothing to eat in two days."

"He swapped his prison clothes and shoes with Aaron?"

"And lit out. We would have caught him right away, but he had a can of powdered pepper and sprinkled it in his tracks. That stopped the dogs for hours. His pepper's gone now. We found the can. Next thing we'll find him—asleep."

"Very well. Be moving."

Slaydon went. Aaron stepped out behind him, hoping that Cap'n John would follow. Instead, the Captain drifted toward the rocking-chair. Aaron darted ahead and placed the rocker, placed it before the fire, with its back turned, so that Cap'n John couldn't see the man above him. "Set here, Cap'n; set here, ef you's jes' *'bleeged* to res' yo'self."

The sheriff sat down. "Shut the door, Aaron; and latch it."

This order made Aaron feel mighty dubious; he fumbled at the latch, fumbled and held back.

"Come here. Stand where I can see you. A convict entered your cabin. You mustn't hide him on the sheriff's plantation."

"How come I want to hide anybody? But he sho' entered. I kin prove dat by dese clo'es."

"What did he look like?"

"Big, fat, red-faced man—wid freckles—"

"What?" Cap'n John turned his head in surprise.

"De bes' I could make out. Dat man behave so rapid he got me flustered."

"Was he young, or old?"

"Kinder 'twixt an' 'tween. Sometimes he 'peared more older dan what he 'peared young. Who dat? Who dat?" Aaron heard a scratching sound upon the plank, and saw a sifting of fine dust. The noise he drowned with a shout. "Who dat?" running to the door, and knocking down a chair. There Aaron stopped and laughed. " 'Twarn't nothin', Cap'n; 'twarn't nothin' 'ceptin' dat ole sow scratchin' herse'f against de house."

Captain Buckner glanced up to see where the falling dust came from. Aaron stood over him and pointed down at the fire. "Cap'n, dem's yaller yams a roastin' in dem ashes."

"Yams?" the sheriff bent forward.

"Keep 'em kivered, Cap'n. Rake up de coals. Taters 'quires steddy watchin'. Now den, I'll fetch some o' yo' own whisky, an' make a hot toddy. Don't let dem taters burn."

Aaron produced the sugar, poured water in the cup of whisky, stirred and gabbled, gabbled and stirred, then set the cup on the fire to heat. "Watch it, Cap'n; don't let dat cup turn over."

The sheriff sat very still, gazing into the fire; presently, without turning his head he inquired, "Aaron, are you sure that wasn't a *young* man? About twenty-four?"

"Lemme ponder, Cap'n; lemme ponder. No, suh, 'peared like more of a settled-looking man; family man." Warily he eyed the sheriff from behind. Cap'n John was examining the prison shirt, which MacRae had left upon the table.

"Aaron, did you observe anything peculiar about his arms?"

"Had two arms, Cap'n; ev'y man nacherly got de same 'mount o' arms, 'ceptin' he gits one cut off."

"Nothing wrong with his—his *left* arm?"

"Nothin' ailed dat arm—not from de way he flung me around."

"He took off this shirt?"

"Yas, suh; shucked it sudden."

"You saw no—no scar—on his left arm?"

"No, suh; jes' clean an' white, like a baby."

Captain John Buckner eased back in his chair and smiled, a smile of intense relief. "Then I must have been misinformed. It was not—it was not—"

"No, suh; 'twarn't him. Didn't favor *him* a bit."

"Didn't favor who?" with a glance of vague suspicion.

"Dunno, suh; jes' didn't favor nobody."

"Didn't favor nobody?" Aaron felt uneasy as the sheriff kept repeating, "Didn't favor nobody." Then a long silence—out of which, "Aaron, by the way, you moved on my place from the old MacRae plantation?"

"Cap'n, you better watch dat toddy." It gave Aaron the fidgets when Cap'n John began putting two and two together.

"You must have known Mr. Dancey MacRae?"

"—Spark's liable to pop in dat toddy, an' spile it."

"You knew Mr. Dancey MacRae?"

Aaron looked mighty solemn, standing behind the sheriff's chair, with one eye cocked upward at the plank. "Cap'n, what you reckon ever 'come o' Mister Dancey?"

Then Aaron's mouth flew open. His eyes widened with horror. Something clicked against the plank; a click, low, but distinct. The muzzle of a pistol crept slowly out of shadow. A hand, and then an arm, followed it. Firelight flickered on a long blue barrel which wavered and trembled, swinging directly downward. The arm behind it hung full length and limp. From where the sheriff sat he could see nothing; but he might turn his head.

Aaron gasped, "Look out, Cap'n; yo' toddy's 'bout to tumble over."

Captain John leaned forward and steadied his cup, while Aaron stood on tiptoe. No other movement came from the plank. Aaron knew that boy, and realized what had happened. In the warmth of the room, from the drink and unconquerable exhaustion, MacRae had fallen asleep.

"Watch yo' toddy, Cap'n." Aaron snatched a stick from the hearth with a fork at the end. Behind the chair he began to shuffle his feet, and sing,

"Ole gray hoss come atearin' out de wilderness"—catching MacRae's arm in the fork of his stick.

"Tearin' out de wilderness; tearin' out de wilderness"—lifting the arm, carefully and slowly.

"Kickin' up dus', an' 'tendin' to his bizziness"—getting the arm safely to its plank again.

"Dar now!" Aaron moved in front of the Captain, and grinned. He dropped his stick and lifted the mellow cup. "Here, take dis, Cap'n. Drink hearty; toddy time is done arrived."

The sheriff nodded, "Thanks. Whew! That's hot. Aaron, won't you have one?"

"No, suh, Cap'n, thankee, suh. Whisky don't he'p me none. An' 'sides dat,"—squinting upward at MacRae—" 'sides dat, I got to keep my head."

The sheriff rocked and sipped, talking half to himself, half to Aaron. "Incomprehensible! Unbelievable, the way that stubborn boy acted at his trial. Refused to defend himself. Told his laywers nothing, except to beg that they get him a five-day parole, so that he might produce certain evidence, the nature of which he refused to divulge. No judge could grant such a request, so Dancey pleaded guilty, and took his sentence. He's protecting somebody, probably a woman. Wouldn't tell his best friends—not even *me*."

"Den you don't believe he done it?" Aaron's black face was very eager.

"Nobody does. We can get him a pardon, but he won't accept it. Wants to clear his name."

"Didn't he come clear at de cote house?"

The sheriff shook his head. "No; and it's my duty to arrest him."

Like an old mud-turtle, Aaron craned his neck around the back of Cap'n John's chair. "Cap'n, what words was dem you spoke?"

"Nothing. Nothing. Never mind." The sheriff checked himself, starting to rise; and as he did, MacRae's arm dropped again. Aaron grabbed his stick and laid a hand upon the sheriff's shoulder. "Set down, Cap'n; set down. You ain't *nigh* finished dat toddy."

"It's too hot."

"Blow on it, Cap'n; blow on it." Aaron hooked MacRae's wrist in the fork of his stick, and began lifting. "Keep ablowin', keep ablowin', keep ablowin'." Having learned the trick he turned it neatly, and let out a deep breath as that betraying arm was hid. But the pistol—MacRae had let go his grip. Aaron saw the weapon toppling from the edge of the plank, and tried to shove it back. He only succeeded in breaking the force of its fall. The forty-four struck Cap'n John's shoulder, and rattled to his feet.

"Hello. What's this?" Aaron was nimble, but Cap'n John got the "navy six." "Hello, what's this?"

"Dat's jes' my pistol. I was fixin' to put it on de shelf."

"*Your* pistol? Navy six, blue barrelled, forty-four. Yes, yes—" looking at the number, and taking out a memorandum. The sheriff was puzzled; then his lips shut a bit tighter, and Aaron got scared.

"Cap'n, yo' toddy's gittin' cold."

"Aaron, is this *your* pistol?" without glancing up.

"Yas, suh—can't you smell dat tater scorchin'?"

"Where did you get it?"

"Traded fer it; I disrecollects perzackly—"

Captain John looked squarely at the negro. "This pistol was taken from the guard by that convict who escaped."

" 'Taint *on*possible. I overspoke myself. You see, Cap'n, when I starts to talkin' my tongue gits in my way."

"Well?" the sheriff continued to look straight through him.

"I 'lowed I done picked up my own pistol, but it mought ha' been de one what dat white man lef'."

"So he left his pistol?"

"Sho'ly done so. Never wanted to tote *nothin'*."

"He didn't need it? Not even for the dogs?"

"No suh; no suh. Dat white man ain't skeered o' dogs. He ain't even *skittish* 'bout dogs. He *loves* dogs."

"Very curious. Very curious." The sheriff's gray eyes snapped; turning the pistol over and over in his hand he kept nodding "That's very curious."

If ever a negro needed wits, Aaron MacRae needed all of his. Aaron realized that fully. He stood like a rabbit, with both ears up.

The shot came, sharply, "Aaron."

"Yas, suh."

"You were *very fond* of Mr. Dancey MacRae?"

"Nowise p'tickler; jes' *knowed* de boy. Who dat? Come right in, Mister Slaydon; Cap'n still here."

Bill Slaydon halted in the doorway; "Cap'n, them dogs won't pick up the new trail. We better start 'em with something of Aaron's."

The sheriff did not want Bill Slaydon to come in; and he wanted to get rid of Aaron. So Captain John rose from the fire, with the lamp, and walked quickly to the door. "Here, Aaron, take this lamp. You and Mr. Slaydon circle round the house; see if you can't find his tracks."

"But, Cap'n, I—"

"Do what I say."

The lamp chimney rattled, and the oil sloshed, as Aaron followed the deputy. Captain Buckner closed the door, looked under the bed, and trampled a pile of seed cotton in the corner—the only possible places of concealment. He glanced upward at the roof—all open, no garret. Then Captain John stood still, very still, hearing the sigh of a sleeper, and seeing an arm that dropped. MacRae had shifted position; it was not his pistol hand, but the left. Captain John kicked the fire into a blaze. Then he heard Aaron at the door, crossed swiftly, and stopped him outside.

"Me an' Mister Slaydon couldn't find nothin'."

"Very well. Give me the lamp. Go with Mr. Slaydon, and show him that little path through the canebrake."

"Wait a minit, Cap'n, wait a minit; lemme—"

The sheriff blocked the door, and called, "Oh, Bill, Aaron will show you where to start the dogs. If they don't strike something in a half hour, bring them up to my house. Needn't come here again."

Again the sheriff shut old Aaron outside of his own cabin. Turning with the lamp he examined MacRae's arm, but did not touch it. He got up on a chair, looked into the boy's face, and stepped down again. He took up the pistol, and hesitated—and hesitated. "Maybe the boy ought to have his chance. Escaping to get that evidence. He'll come back, and give himself up."

When breathless Aaron burst in he found the High Sheriff sitting cozily beside the fire, sipping his toddy. Above his head, hung that accusing arm.

Captain John arose. "Good night, Aaron." Before he could turn, the negro caught his elbow and held the sheriff's face away—away from that arm. Aaron also snatched up the lamp, and held that as if lighting the floor, but always so that his own body cast the arm in shadow. "Walk keerful, Cap'n; dat broken bo'd mought ketch yo' foot."

Blind-bridling him to the door, Aaron pushed out the sheriff. "Now, den, you's all right; got a new moon to light yo' way."

"Oh, Aaron," the sheriff paused; "you've been sick. Bring a basket up to my house, early to morrow morning—very early—and get something to eat. Better come before daylight. Remind me of that suit of clothes I promised you, shirts and shoes and things——"

"Yas, suh; I ain't hankerin' a'ter dese stripety clo'es."

"Those dogs won't bother you again. I'm sending them away."

"Sho' is proud o' dat fack. Good night, Cap'n."

"Good night, Aaron."

Dimly the negro wondered why Captain John Buckner, with a knowing smile upon his lips, and kindness in his eye, should insist upon shaking hands—shaking hands with an old negro, as man to man—"Good night, Aaron."

That was Aaron's chance to shut his own door, from the inside. He leaned against it, and wiped his forehead. The arm swung accusingly.

"Sho' is lucky Cap'n John never seen dat."

Aaron dragged his table beneath the plank, and called, "Mister Dancey! Mister Dancey. Huh! Dat always was de *beatenes'* boy fer gwine to sleep."

In barefoot silence the negro placed a stout chair on the table, and mounted. Strongly, tenderly, he lifted down the lad, started toward his own bed, and halted; "No, suh! *No, suh!* I can't put *dis* boy on nary nigger bed. Ole Missy would turn over in her grave."

Aaron glanced at the fire, and his face lighted. "Dat's it; same as camp huntin'. I'll jes' fix him down a pallet."

Gently he laid MacRae upon the table, with a coat under his head. A sack of cotton from the corner. "Dat makes a nice sof' mattrass." There were no sheets; a blanket served. A log, with another sack, formed the pillow. Aaron tucked the sleeper between his cover. "You sho' needs a good night's res'."

Crooning to himself the negro banked his fire. "Better fix dis tater; he mought git hongry in de night. Lordee, how dat chile used to holler fer 'Aaron! Aaron!' when he woke up hongry."

The negro took his lamp, secured the fastenings of door and windows. Then he filled his old clay pipe. "Reckon dat's 'bout all, 'cept to keep watch."

Puff! The lamp went out. Aaron stooped at the hearth, and picked up a live coal, juggling it in his palm as he walked. At the door, he sat down with his back against it. Then he lighted the pipe. A ruddy glow from the coal, behind his palm, glorified a black and placid face.

"Ole Missy's baby boy! Huh! I reckon nothin' ain't gwine to 'sturb *him*—not *dis* night."

(1881–1963)

Stark Young

Stark Young was one of the most versatile and energetic men of letters
this country has produced. Although he is best known for his best-selling
Civil War novel *So Red the Rose* (1934), during his long and distinguished
career he worked successfully as a poet, painter, novelist, essayist, editor,
translator, playwright, and critic. It is probable, however, that his most
significant contributions to American cultural life were in connection with
his work in and on the theatre: he wrote over thirty plays himself, directed plays at both the Provincetown Playhouse and the Theatre Guild,
and translated plays by Chekhov, Moliere, Regnard, and Machiavelli; but
he was most important to the development of modern American drama in
his editorial work on *Theatre Arts Magazine* and as drama critic for both
the *New Republic* and the *New York Times*.

Young was born in Como on October 11, 1881, and moved with his
family to Oxford in 1895. There he attended the Union Female Academy
and the University of Mississippi, from which he received his B.A. with
honors in 1901. He earned an M.A. in English from Columbia University
in 1902, and returned to Mississippi to teach, first in Water Valley, and
then in the English Department at Ole Miss. From 1907 to 1915 he
taught at the University of Texas, where he first developed his interest in

159

the theatre; he taught at Amherst College from 1915 to 1921, then resigned the academic life in order to move to New York and devote himself full-time to writing and reviewing. He contributed prolifically and regularly to *New Republic, Theatre Arts Magazine, North American Review, Yale Review, Scribner's Magazine,* and *Vanity Fair,* among many others.

Although most of his life after 1915 was spent in the East—out of necessity, for a professional theatre critic—he never abandoned his sense of the South as his home or as the source of his own manners and sensibility. Young regularly spent vacations and holidays with family and friends in Texas and Mississippi, and his contribution to *I'll Take My Stand* (1930), "Not in Memoriam, But in Defense," is a fine discussion of certain southern values and traditions which he felt should not be lost as the South became more and more urban. He died in New York on January 6, 1963.

Our selection is from his book of reminiscences, *The Pavilion* (1951).

The Pavilion, Chapter Five

WE HAD A FAIR NUMBER of books on our shelves, though none too many. The modest libraries that had been in the family had gone when so many of the old places were burnt either during the Civil War or afterwards. I remember that I liked seeing books around, but up to the time I was seven or eight I had never read one at all. There was a small blue book called *Sick Jim* that some cousin had given me, and I read enough in that to see how he got well at last; the rest of the pages seemed useless, though I have come to see that even this sickish juvenilia was no worse than the drivel of the average fiction for adults; they all may well serve to pass the time when people who cannot endure time find that time cannot endure them. As for *Sick Jim,* I had a sense that there were voices stronger than that, and echoes from somewhere in life that made such reading vain. But my father and mother and my two aunts read a good deal aloud to me and my little sister—stories and fairy tales and bits of history.

My father read me always about Napoleon, often later at night than you would think a doctor would commend for a child; and I can see now that woodcut, in whatever book it was, of Napoleon in his sleigh, the galloping, desperate horses, those curved pieces of harness above their necks and bells jangling on them, and always the hint of Russian wolves. I shook with dread lest the wolves might eat Napoleon, but my father said he escaped and was the greatest of all military heroes.

At times my father would be sleepy, and that was natural enough after his trips in the night to the sick and dying; but he let me sit there on his knee with a little finger held up in a way that would poke him in the eye if he nodded. My Aunt Julia said that Dr. Young when he was a bachelor could tell everybody else how children should be disciplined, and now, look, when it came to his!

Auntee, who must at the time have been under thirty, though I naturally thought her a very crone and sibyl, read me the Bible; in all the family she was the Bible student. I liked that best of all, and the precision, color, and glory of the Jacobean prose filled all my heart forever. From the start, however, to her patient regret, I balked at the idea of some infallible rightness there, and said, for example, that Judas could not kill himself in two different ways: one place in the Bible said he hanged himself, and another that he burst his bowels open on the rocks. "Now that's all right, Precious," Auntee would say, "there are some good people who don't read the Bible as much as they should, but God understands that they believe it."

Since there were no learned discussions for me to imitate, I engaged people in arguments as to why they were Episcopalians, Methodists, Baptists, or Presbyterians. On the train from Como to Memphis I used to speak to one passenger or another and ask what church he belonged to and why was that? This, coming from a little boy of five or six, must either have astonished them into orthodoxy or else bored them as some forward precocity. It was about this time that I remember asking Mr. Travis Taylor, a friend of my father's who taught in our Sunday School, when it was that a child was given a soul. He replied that opinions differed as to that; some thought at the moment of conception, some thought the moment we are born

into the world. I understood the implications, thanks to our cook
Frankie and her plain talk; but what I remember especially is that I
thought Mr. Taylor such a dignified and sensible gentleman to give a
little boy like me a direct and honest answer. The last Sunday School
attendance I ever made was about twenty years later, when I es-
corted some tiny cousins to their lesson. The incident turned out to
be an illustration of our general decline in culture. The teacher, a
hollow-chested clerk from one of the stores, told the class that Sol-
omon was the first carpenter, he built the Temple.

Meanwhile, so my old nurse, Aunt Ellen, told me, I used to
scream and kick till they held me up to look at the portraits, most of
all my grandfather's, in the background of which was a small body of
water and some mournful trees. Pictures of any and every kind enchanted me, but I was still more interested in people. I was taken up
with watching people and listening to them talk. You had a good
chance for that in Como those days; nearly everybody was a cousin
and they visited and talked all day long. I listened to them in fact to
such an extent that they used to stop short sometimes and say to my
mother, "Why does that child look at me like that?"

Sometimes it all took a happier turn. "Come here, Honey," Aunt
Sally McGehee would say, lying in her big tester bed with its octag-
onal rosewood posts and overhead the canopy and its red satin
lining—she was kept there flat on her back for eight years by the
threat of hemorrhages, "come here, darlin'; this child understands
me better than anybody in the family does and that's the Lord's
truth. But you mustn't blame good people, darlin', if they hear me
wrong; they just don't know any better—anybody can see I don't
mean half I say. Sit down here by Aunt Sally. Aunt Sally loves you."

Loves you—I have lived long enough to know what that can
mean to a child. If in those days I had no other education of any
worth, I had this: the sense that my own people loved me.

But that, of course, was after I was thirteen and was visiting there
in some style, for I had to myself the south guest room upstairs, as
big as all creation it seemed to me, with doors twelve feet high and a
mahogany Empire bed with eagles' heads at the four corners. Uncle
Abner was dead and Aunt Sally had their vast bedroom on the
ground floor across the hall from the parlor alone to herself. She

slept there with the long French windows on to the porch wide open when the season demanded; on her bed-table a stack of books and a pistol, which for all its mother-of-pearl handle looked ready enough. On summer nights in that upstairs room I had at times been awakened by sounds in the back yard and looked out to see the fragile, white shape of my aunt, walking there in her nightgown, a lamp held high in one hand, her pistol in the other. She had heard noises at the stables and was there to see that some Negro was not stealing the horses out to ride them on the roads all night long.

I used to hear people talk and used to think over whether what they said was gentle, sensible, thoughtlessly cruel, or silly, and whether they were unlike grown people when they talked like that. I used to watch some faces for their sweetness or goodness, or for their beauty and animation, and I would feel them stir in my heart; for it was easy and natural for me as a child that I should worship them. I remember that now and again I would have a dream that some one or other of these persons to whom out of shyness I would never have said more than good morning, had put his hand on my shoulder and said, "This is a fine little boy."

Meantime I used to watch other faces with a sharp sense of comicality, as if life were a circus. It was a strange combination in a child to see that life was all a human comedy—which to me then meant that grown people acted like children—and at the same time to see it all as a dream, full of sad hearts and sighing, and of love and the need for one another that was so kept down within you and so constant.

It was this mingling of traits, no doubt, that made me capable of such extremes. On the one hand, for instance, there was my reply to the old Methodist preacher who had often invited himself to supper and was ready to eat us out of house and home, my stepmother said, for she hated the pill bottle he would put on the table before his plate. He remarked that I would be a good-looking boy when my face grew up to my nose. I said he would be a good preacher when his manners grew up to his profession. My father shook his head sternly at me for that, but did not look me in the eyes.

On the other hand I was led to sit hours with my Uncle Hugh on the porch while he spoke of the books of science that he was reading. I listened with hushed breath while he talked of what science had done to free the mind—that was more than fifty years ago—and even then, I can remember, I had a feeling that the mind was never freed except when it wanted to be. I listened, regarding him the while as a childish old man and at the same time, by some magic not to be explained, understanding that what he knew was both logical and infinite. It may be that I knew this by a kind of physical peace, as it were, within which my uncle thought.

"My God A'mighty," Uncle Hugh would say, "this boy is the only one of father's descendants that's got any brains." That must not have done me much good with my cousins, who very likely detested me for it, however much I may have admired and envied them all and longed for them to feel like that towards me. It was not really fair in general, for I remember well I never thought I was very smart myself, I only marveled that we could all of us be so dull. To this day brains, talent, shine, and perfection seem to me natural and to be expected, judging perhaps by the leaves, the stars, the growth in nature, and the song of our passions. But dullness and vacuity in myself or in another inevitably find me astonished that they could exist thus; or else they invite me to a kind of animal incredulity.

I was also cursed with some gift for mimicry. When I would do Mr. Breckinridge, our postmaster, who had lost one leg in the Civil War, and had a gobble like a turkey cock, my father wrinkled up his eyes with laughter and thought Mr. Breckinridge himself ought to hear that, though I knew better; or when I sang like one of our cousins who had by then reduced whatever voice she had to a mere whooping breath in a determination to outdo every other singer in the congregation. I could belch exactly like Uncle Shelton McGehee, or cough my Aunt Julia's cough when she was justifying herself for an Irish nip of Bourbon from the bottle not supposed to be in the wardrobe.

I did these impersonations out of the sheer joy of life and sharp eyes, as one gathers flowers or sea shells, for the zest of them; but it must have been too much to ask of everybody to take it in the same spirit. They thought me nothing but a bad little boy who ought to be spanked. They said as much at times, and I marveled then how grown people could be so silly and touchy. The really touchy individual in our house was Aunt Julia, who, though she constantly threw herself into the most fantastic angles, could not bear to be thought even slightly comical, not even that summer night on the porch when she presented a Memphis young gentleman to Auntee and got things so turned around: "Mr. Starks, may I present Miss Jones?" We laughed, and she said oh, well, it was so dark she couldn't see. I can still wonder why she could never bring herself to take me into a sort of partnership in these matters, little white lies, whimsical blunders, and the like, and let us two enjoy the gay fraud of them together; for I thought it must certainly be for the fun of it that she acted as she often did. But she never let down those grotesque bars for me; and that kept me from taking her as seriously as I did others in the family.

In those days, at least in Como, we had no terms like high school, grade school, and so on, and I should not know how to say just what the school I went to could have been. There was an old building known as the Lodge, with the Masonic Hall on the upper floor, where we were to suppose took place certain lurid initiative rites about which our curious wives and old maids indulged in many mocking speculations. We had in school only meek, brow-beaten schoolteachers as a rule; the men rough, pious diamonds, the women tinted with a certain dainty education. They were paid little but were assumed to be the patient models of all virtue. One of their chief and evidently gladdest functions was to lecture us with small sermons on piety and moral conduct. I did not know the quotation then, of course, but many of us understood that, as La Rochefoucauld said of old people, most of these teachers of ours liked to give good advice to console themselves for no longer being able to give bad examples.

My career at the school was simple. Various parents said that I was a hard worker, while their children, it was to be inferred, merely tossed things off. I knew that this was not intended for a compliment, but I knew also that I was anything but the laborious creature they spoke of. To judge by my course there the system must have been an odd one. From my seat I used to hear the classes going on, and at such a distance they sounded bright and urgent. The result was that at twelve years I was in nine classes with as many subjects. I cannot

imagine now how all that could have been; but among these subjects
were physics, with water seeking its own level; American history,
with Columbus, Indians, and the Revolution; English history, with
the line of kings; the two kinds of geography; and Latin and English
grammar and what not. As time passed I very likely finished one
study and moved on into others. My custom was as soon as I entered
a class to read the textbook through and after that I rarely opened it
again. It must have served somehow; for nobody in the school, including the teacher, knew how to study, and we all landed together
in the same drifting boat. I see now that, for me, around it all there
was the shining lure of the worlds we live in, and that my child's
mind was drawn toward what was, and is forever, both dim and
startlingly exact, as if from some dream of Elysium one were
awakened by a delicious striking of the hour.

The discipline even of this education was lessened by Uncle
Hugh's practice. He thought that children, if they were such as to be
loved, should do exactly as they wished to do, and nothing they did
not wish; and so whenever Aunt Julia went away to Memphis to visit
her sister we all stopped school and stayed at home with him. Sometimes to keep us nearer him he would pay us for gray hairs that we
found in his head. I do not remember the terms, what sum or the
number of hairs, but I do remember that we sometimes added to
them with hairs plucked from the goatskin seat of his chair.

But in life the books with the balancing columns are sure to be
kept on us, and a curious thing has resulted from that loose and un-
controlled procedure in my early school. It may very well be that
from that slapdash beginning the feeling arises in me of an inade-
quacy in all knowledge. I have, for example, spent days in the Sistine
Chapel, read Vasari's account, read the sonnets, but seem to myself
to have, and probably do have, but a sorry, skimming knowledge of
Michelangelo. I have read often Plato's dialogues on poetic inspiration, something of Plotinus, and all of our Edmund Spenser with his
Neo-Platonism. And I have looked hard at Botticelli in his paintings
of Venus and the rising from the sea, the Becoming as it approaches
the Being, the Corporeal as it shares in the Incorporeal; I perceive
the ardent Neo-Platonism in them, some of it expressed in the
rhythms of the composition, which constantly moves out of the

frame—or into it—as if the idea in the picture were only a part of some ideal Whole. I see there the longing for what has gone before, a sickness for the ideal, and a sense of the passing not so much of life, which is the preacher's theme, but of beauty, which is the poet's. But still, in spite of all, I have behind my conscience the feeling that my knowledge is slight and slipping, a sense of grim ignorance sticks in my craw. I have far too little of that culture which is a heightening of our sense of the antiphonal radiance existing in all things among themselves. If it is possible to have an intuition of knowledge, it should also be possible to have an intuition of ignorance.

Around us meanwhile, of course, were the Negroes in an overwhelming majority, many of whom had once belonged to plantations in our family and still felt a claim on us, as we did on them. Indeed my Cousin Randolph Stewart used to say that every Negro had five white men working for him. This race question has been discussed so much, especially in these latter years, sometimes to good purpose, sometimes in a blind alley, that nothing could be served by my trying, if I were fool enough, to settle it here. As a child I could only sense that my family was forever troubled in their minds about it; and I understood that people like us did not hate the Negroes; the hatred was between them and the lower class of whites. I saw my father going to see Negroes who were sick and had little to offer him but their pain and recklessness. At times late at night one of them would come for him from far out in the country and he would drive all that way to visit some Negro very sick or dying; and now and then he would sit there in the cabin till dawn, and as often as not expect to be paid nothing for it. I never knew, young as I was, what theories he might have advanced on this subject; what he did he thought he must do as a human being, a far lower attitude, no doubt, than sitting at a safe distance and talking in a reforming heat or contributing, variously, sums of money.

I used to go with him to see Aunt Ann Ray, a penniless and very old woman whose small house was in the midst of a ruined garden left over from the time when her husband was alive and a janitor at the university. She would never be out of her bed again, my father told me. He used to wait while I stood at the foot of her bed and she talked to me of her glossy curls when she was a girl, and of how she would never eat any of the chocolates the young gentlemen sent her young mistress, for fear of love potions, wherever she got that idea. Or she would complain of the sermons in church nowadays, which were always scolding about sin and ugly things. In her day, she said, the preacher spoke of heaven and the angels and of the roses kissing in the garden. My father paid some of Aunt Ann's near neighbors to look after her from time to time, but before she was dead they stole her bedcovers and even the funeral clothes from her trunk and the curly black bangs that she was to be buried in. "What can you do, son?" was all my father said. At the same time, for all this kindness and patience and worry, he would have been implacable in the matter of race segregation, though meanwhile, of course, he could have rated higher in some quarters by inviting Aunt Ann to dinner and then after that letting her starve to death. But nothing is as simple as this, and the conclusion remains to be found, when it is found, in an energy of justice, patience, and imagination.

I heard some family talk of giving up cotton because it took so many hands to work it that it could be made to pay only by the system of crediting— "furnishing" —the Negroes against the fall crops, at which time, as was inevitable in the course of things, the good Negroes had to make up for the bad. This practice, however desperate or ruinous it may or may not have been for the South, was one that honorable men saw no easy way to follow.

But for the most part, as a child those many years ago, I knew only Uncle Billy Machedric, of whom I have already told, and Aunt Viney on our nearest plantation and the yellow yams she gave us out of the pot on her hearth. I knew Manny, who lived near her, and Wash, and Shoat, a little runt with a voice like a great bullfrog's, a kind of bull angel, to judge from the way he could sing. His real name was Jezebel, called Jersey Bell and shortened to Shoat, because he was shaped like a fat young pig. These colored playmates gave me early some salty versions of sex and of what in our much widened discussions we now speak of socially as the libido, and to this precocious instruction my nurse Celie added her bit. I knew that Celie was good and gentle, and I thought it odd of my maiden aunts to be outraged when after some months of my mother's care, diets, and dropsy pills, Celie surprised her with a baby, the son, it seemed to me quite naturally, of John Sanford, our man on the place, who did, in fact, marry Celie the next year. I was thus early introduced to a good deal of modernity.

My father had his own way, whatever his success may have been, of trying to educate me, and the years have shown me that his method had at least its points. I remember one scene on Uncle Hugh's porch in the beginning of summer when I had been invited to visit my father's friend, Dr. Yarborough, on his plantation. Dr. Yarborough had long since dropped out of the medical profession and given himself over to the land and the calico ponies he brought out every year from Texas. These he fattened, curry-combed, and sold at a good profit, though it was the oratorical side of the transactions that was most likely to gratify him. He kept the lamp on his bed-table burning all night; I would sleep on the other side of the bed and from time to time wake and see him reading as if he had just discovered the first book ever printed. When he held the book like that I could see high up on his forearm the violent tattoo that in the wildness of his youth he had had done somewhere; it looked, I remember now, as if he had broken out with the Aztec calendar. I cannot recall what the books were that he read by night, there was a great pile of them on the bed-table; but I do know that all day long he was a tremendous talker.

"Now, son, look here," my father said to me when I was about to start off for this visit, "be sure you recollect to ask Dr. Yarborough about the pabula."

I said I already knew that, he had told me twice.

"That has nothing to do with it," my father said. "Dr. Yarborough's told us everything twice, at least twice."

"Great God A'mighty from Hell, Dr. Young," Uncle Hugh said, "you don't care a whoop what a pabulum is, nor do I, why do you pester the life out of that boy with it?"

"I don't care about the pabulum or the pabula," my father said, "any more than I care about the sense of sin his Vermont grandfather talked about, but I do want him to have a sense of deference to others and to try to give them pleasure, and this we are talking about is the kind of thing Dr. Yarborough always likes. So let him tell you about the pabula, son."

He looked at me as if to say that we all knew that this might make no sense, but that it was precisely out of these very things that the integrity of our inheritance might be kept intact and our tradition of decency, in the Latin sense of what is proper and right, might be maintained.

I recalled the summer before, when I was driving somewhere with one of my father's friends, a professor at the university, and we met Dr. Yarborough in the road with two of the calico ponies, frisky still but by now pretty well broken in, hitched up to his buggy. He got out to shake our hands. How we slipped into the matter I never quite knew, but presently he was addressing us about the three kinds of pabula, physical, mental, and spiritual, according to him, standing there in the road, twisting his goatee, flicking the cracker of his whip.

He had developed each of these branches of—if you like—thought, and I watched him standing there against the clouded green of the willows and did not mind at all. Nor really did my companion, the professor of chemistry, who cared nothing about the social implications even of his own science and its responsibility to the future, much less about Dr. Yarborough's pabula.

One summer a number of years after that I came on a passage in Plato's epistles that reminded me of this conversation at Uncle Hugh's about Dr. Yarborough, and read it out to my father, whose only attitude in such matters as this of his friend's pabula was to be civilized and kind. In that epistle Plato says to Dion that he must not forget that the power of accomplishing great things arises from pleasuring mankind, and that moroseness occasions the desertion of associates. My father said the few pieces of Plato that he had been put through at the university had been only vague to him, so far as he remembered, but this remark that I quoted seemed clear enough and he thought the better of Plato for it.

In a way this business of Dr. Yarborough's came to a head some years after I left Como. The Cecil Rhodes Scholarships with their appointments to Oxford University began. At the outset it was all within the province of the governor of each state to make the appointment, and so my father thought that Dr. Yarborough could further my fortunes with his endorsement. Dr. Yarborough wrote our Governor of Mississippi a letter I still have:

Stark Young, son of A. A. Young of Como, Mississippi, wishes to receive the Cecil Rhodes Scholarship to Oxford University. Please appoint him and oblige

Yours truly,

A. S. Yarborough.

My father was the soul of honesty; in fact he often bent over backwards to be so, displeasing people at times by his frankness when there was no real cause either to be frank or not to be; but I remember how once he was anything but truthful and how I understood his intention. He told me how Mrs. William Sledge, one of his patients, lay dying and could get no peace for longing to see her little nephew whom she had loved so much and who had been dead these many years. In her delirium she kept calling him, calling, calling, and my father said I was to go along and let her think it was her nephew. I was five or six at the time. I remember my father's saying, "Here's Charlie to see you, Mrs. Sledge," and how she started up and caught my face in her hands, "Darling! My Darling!" and sank back on the pillow.

We have all our mystery, of course, and it was a part of my father's mystery that he, who was forthrightness itself, should have contrived this scene of make-believe out of the heart of his imagination. With regard to him a curious irony appears in the fact of this dying woman's relation to two people of our nowadays. One is Tallulah Bankhead, the actress, whose great-grandmother she was; the other is William Faulkner, the novelist, who is some lesser cousin of Mrs. Sledge's through the Brown family in Oxford.

Every summer when I went to spend a fortnight with my father in Oxford I would see Phil Stone, a young friend of mine, and a friend of and warm believer in William Faulkner, who was a few years younger than he. It was thus that I first knew Bill Faulkner. At that time he was writing poems and would bring me a notebook of them, I can still see it lying in a parlor table drawer. It is so long ago that I cannot recall the poems now, only that they strove for great intensity of feeling. I would see Bill Faulkner every summer and would at times see things he had written and hear of his life in Oxford. It seemed to me more and more futile that anyone so remarkable as he was should be thus bruised and wasted, and so I proposed that he should come to New York. I promised that my friend Elizabeth Prall, who directed an important bookshop, could give him a job there to tide him over till he could settle into something that suited him better, and meanwhile he was more than welcome to stay with me. Miss Prall not long afterwards married Sherwood Anderson and, through Sherwood Anderson, Bill Faulkner was put in touch with Horace Liveright, who published *Soldier's Pay* and gave him the usual three-book contract, his first contract with a publisher. As to Miss Bankhead and William Faulkner, you could hardly find two people about whom my father would have been more puzzled as to what on earth they are up to.

I profited in those early days by the time in which it all took place. Less than thirty years had passed since the Civil War and the prolonged horrors and wrongs of Reconstruction. From the point of vantage of these recent years of ours it seems now impossible that it could have been so short a time as twelve years, but that was how long the Reconstruction era lasted. Ours, when I was growing up, was a country peopled with ghosts, warm, close, and human; the dead were often as present as the living. Naked chimneys of burnt houses; ruined cemeteries where the dead had sometimes been kicked out of their graves and left lying under the sky overhead; tombstones thrown down, smashed door panels and ripped-up portraits, with often a wretched, proud poverty, were familiar to everyone. I never heard them spoken of save as aspects of war as war is. As for my own people—proud spirits whom history had slapped in the face—no doubt this changed world exaggerated some of their faults and pushed some of their virtues into defects. But I have always chosen to think there was a certain elevation in many older people I knew then that came from suffering and loss, sorrow and humiliation, along with a sense of what had gone before, most of all a way of life now gone forever. In a sense they sought the beautiful, however childish or flamboyant the offshoots of that desire may have sometimes been, and sought what was in its nature grand and spacious of time and place. If there was also the cruel and the unjust in their faces on occasion, I may at the very least say that it was set by convictions that were more determined, mean, or humorless than sour, ignoble, or banal. How much in the midst of a shifting world, more industrial, more restless, and more confused in its aims and standards, how much of that way of life was gone forever, I am not sure they knew; but they felt the sting and blunt edge of the loss of something they had lived by and within which they had thought and had tried to honor themselves. Nearly all of us were poor together. There was a great deal of proper pride and of a kind of civilized style and of a desire for fine manners.

It is curious that though I have been a writer and a painter, professions where self-expression plays the final and largest part, it has taken me many years before I could bring myself to speak even as directly as I am now doing of these things. I have sometimes thought that the measure of our inner intensity is our shyness in revealing it, but such very likely is not true: the very last and ultimate flowering of all human experience is its sharing and revelation.

(1885–1942)

William Alexander Percy

William Alexander Percy, the son of U.S. Senator Leroy Percy, was born May 14, 1885, in Greenville. He received a B.A. from the University of the South at Sewanee, Tennessee, in 1904, and after one year abroad and a year teaching English at Sewanee, he went to Harvard to study law. In 1908, law degree in hand, Percy returned to Greenville and became active as a lawyer and in virtually all phases of the political, cultural, and social life of his city and region. He was instrumental in the creation of the Delta Arts Center and was a leader in the Delta Council, a group formed to help the region's commercial growth. At Herbert Hoover's request, Percy went abroad in 1916 to work with the Committee for Relief for Belgium. During World War I he served with distinction in France, being awarded the Croix de Guerre in 1918. But, aside from his writing, it is perhaps for his leadership at home during the Mississippi River floods that he is best known; his activities as chairman of the Disaster Relief Committee of the Red Cross in Mississippi during the 1927 flood and its aftermath are described, rather modestly, in Chapter XX of *Lanterns on the Levee* (1941), his autobiography. Percy died in Greenville on January 21, 1942.

Reviewing Percy's *In April Once* (1920), William Faulkner wrote that Percy had "suffered the misfortune of being born out of his time." A

174

strong vein of nostalgia does run throughout Percy's work; his tastes for
the classical are reflected both in the diction and in the subject matter of
his poetry, and although he showed himself throughout his life to be perfectly capable of dealing with the modern world, he seems in his work to
express a preference for the past or at least a regret over the passing of
certain characteristics of southern life and manners which he felt were es-
sential to the cultivated person. *Lanterns on the Levee*, which he completed during the last years of his life, when he knew he was dying, is
sometimes criticized as being a defense of the aristocratic way of life. This
it may or may not be; but it certainly is an honest and moving document
that deserves our attention both for the quality of the writing and for its
unique portrait of the world Percy inhabited.

"Chorus" is from *Sappho in Levkas* (1915); "Where Ilium Was Proud,"
"Euripides," "The Squire," and "An Epistle from Corinth" are from *In
April Once* (1920); "Fourteen Sonnets," "Medusa," and "Threnody" are
from *The Collected Poems of William Alexander Percy* (1943); "Home" is
the final chapter of *Lanterns on the Levee* (1941).

Chorus (AFTER THE GREEK)

Surely in no benignant mood
The gods have fashioned us, but craftily
To send us homing to the sod
Wise only in our own futility.

With hyancinthine brows of youth,
We enter life as to a festival;
But, ere the feast is spread, the gods
Snatch back the wine, the song, the coronal.

And, lusterless, we turn, afraid,
Turn to the sole vouchsafèd heritage,
And in the shaken darkness clutch
The disenchanted ledges of old age.

Where Ilium Was Proud

Along the sands where Ilium was proud
A crimson laurel bush, that draws, perhaps,
From Priam's ancient buried house its blood,
Sprinkles with flame the unbeholding waste
In luxury of summer-hearted bliss.
Ah, better so its given years to burn
Unseen of maidens and young warriors
Than, plucked untimely, to have flushed an hour
The white of Helen's bosom on a night
When Paris leaned across the lights and laughter
To drink her up with hot, unmanly eyes.
Its crimson, fading with the dawn, had been
Only a deathless tale in poets' mouths.

Euripides

To him the fate we bear was like a sea
That sweeps above the many ships that sailed,
And waits as home for all that sail again.
Bitter intolerably, and deep as death;
But shining, too, shining and full of spray,
In color stained lovelier than the sky,
Singing a requiem for them that die
Adventuring on its bounds, or, dauntless, sing
When roaring and inevitable wash
Heaves down the prows. . . . His heart was full of stars,
His prayers only to gods that deathlessly
Abide and dream no sin. And Syracuse
That builded on the sea, loved his name most.

The Squire

I have sung me a stave, a stave or two,
    I have drunk me a stoop of wine,
I have roystered across a world that was dew
    And a sea that was sunlight and brine.

And now I'll go down where the need is not
    Of a singing heart, but a sword;
I'll fight where the dead men welter and rot
    With the hard-pressed hosts of the Lord.

And should I come back again, 'twill be
    With accolade and spurs,
And many a tale of chivalry,
    And the deeds of warriors.

And should I not, O break for me
    No buds nor funeral boughs—
I go with the noblest company
    That ever death did house.

An Epistle From Corinth

Paul of Tarsus, I have enquired of Jesus
And meditated much and read your words
Directed to the wise Corinthians
Of whom am I. There is much beauty in
His life and therefore comfort, and there is beauty
In that unreasoning rush of eloquence
Of yours, so much it almost caught me up
And made me Christian. Such is the power of faith
Ablaze in one we know to be no fool!
I watched you as you preached that day in Athens:
You are no fool, nor saint, but one I judge

Of intellect that somehow has caught fire
And so misleads when it is shiningest.

I had hoped to find in you or in your Christ
Some answer to the questions that unanswered
Slay our wills. . . . There's so much lost!
Parnassus there across the turquoise gulf
Still holds its rose and snow to the blown sun,
But no young Phoebus guides the golden car,
Nor will the years' returning loveliness
For all its perfumed broidure bring again
The Twelve to the bright mountain place they loved.
The gods of Greece are dead, forever dead:
The Romans substitute idolatry;
And there's such peace and idleness in the world
As gives the thinking powers full scope to soar,
And soar they do, but in red-beakèd bands
That darken all the sun and nurture find
On the Promethean bare heart of man.
How strange to see the labor of the world
Straining for plenteous food and drink and warmth,
For ease and freedom and the right to choose,
But winning these win only doubt and anguish!
Is this accessory to our coming here?
Is there no answer waiting to be found?

I judge the struggle for perfection if
Engaged in long enough, say thro' the years
Of gorgeous youth, the ashen middle years,
Will end in calm, a kind of stale content—
No gush and quiver in the leafless tree!
But that's the body's dying, not the fight's
Reward, old age not victory!
Yet who, save those few souls and stern
That passionate unto perfection walk
The alien earth scornful and sure,
Would pledge themselves to life-long virtue

Except exchanged for happiness, here
Or hereafter? Who, I ask and hear no answer.
'Twas for the few that Socrates had thought:
Your Jesus had profounder bitterness
And, wroth against a universal woe,
Conceived a universal anodyne—
Heaven, his father's Kingdom, Paradise.

Hence his success with slave and sick and poor—
The solace for their skimped experience
They find in dreams of restitution and
A promised land, whose king will dower and
Reward their loyalty with bliss eternal.
This promise of his kingdom and the immense
Illusion that he had, shared still by you,
Of coming once again and shortly to
Select mankind for punishment or saving
Are above all the concepts that ensure
His following, which when the fact disproves
Will fall away and be forgotten till
His name will vanish and the careless years
Hide with their passing sandals' dust his dream.

Yet in this Jesus I detect always
Something more true and sound and saving than
The postulates of his philosophy.
Compared with Socrates his intellect
Lacked wonder, self-delight, sufficiency.
The Athenian in his noblest eloquence
Assumed himself a son of God, yet him
I understood, somehow: it seemed at least
Poetically true. But when your Jew
Speaks of his father, all that I never learned
Is near, I cannot think, but I can feel,
And 'spite of me, I have the sense of wisdom
Simpler and fruitfuller and wiser than
All wisdom we had hardly learned before,

That turns irrelevant and pitiful
Much we had frayed and tattered our poor souls
In guessing. Yet when I turn to you for counsel—
And who of his untutored band but you
Is qualified in wide and leisured learning
To parley equal-minded with a Greek?—
I find a blur of words, a wall of thought,
That more completely hide the god I sense
Than the fantastic patter of his humble
Ignorant worshipers . . . Paul, Paul, I'd give
My Greek inheritance, my wealth and youth,
To speak one evening with that Christ you love
And never saw and cannot understand!

But he is dead and you alone are left,
Irascible and vehement and sure,
For me to turn to with the bleak bad question—
Do we then die? Or shall we be raised up? . . .
There is the hope always of other life,
After this choking room a width of air,
A star perhaps after this sallow earth,
After this place of prayer, a place of deeds.
No man but in his heart's locked privacy
Dares hope this muffled transiency we hate
For its most bitter and ignoble failure
Ends not with what our ignorance calls death.
A Christ with promise of eternity
And proof could Christianize a hundred hundred worlds!
There are such glimpses of the never-seen,
Such breathings from the outer infinite,
The possible hath such nobility
As makes us suppliants for further chance—
Not repetition, but more scope, O Powers!

Yet better purposeless mortality
Than this mad answer you proclaim to us.
We shall rise up, you say: so far well said.

This essence that disquieteth itself
With less than truth, that will not tolerate
The fare whereon 'tis fed, but sickens so
For immortalities that it doth shape
Of its own yearning — piteously methinks—
Gods and a dwelling place of distant stars,
This surely hath a strength beyond mere days!
But then you add, with equal certainty,
"There's too a resurrection of the flesh."
This is your creed and final comfort, Jew,
That these our gyves and chains are never slipped,
That this captivity we thought a term
Carks to eternity, do what we will!
The impediments to every high resolve,
The traitors to our nascent deity,
The perfumed, warm, corporeal parts of us
That drug to sleep or death the impetuous will,
These are partakers of such after-life
As our fierce souls may grievously attain!
Tarsus, I'll not accept eternal life
Hampered and foiled by this vile thing of flesh!
There is no fire can burn it pure, no rain
Can wash it clean, no death can scourge it slave!
The spirit that is holier than light
Its touch will stain, its vesture will pollute!

You cannot understand, you are a Jew!
Your pores, unsentient, have never drunk
The perfume of a bush that's red by dawn,
And were you here upon this roof tonight
With Corinth at your feet, you'd never know
It was a night of summer, never feel
The straining on the slender leash of will
At all the murmurs and warm silences.
There's a girl's laugh . . . and footsteps loitering.
You'd never guess why they are slow, nor hear
The half-words breathed, nor smile to find yourself

Wondering if the kiss were mouth or throat. . . .
Perfumes! . . .
The night-wind wakes but to caress,
And kissing sleeps . . . the lover's way. . . .
Gods, gods! This fool would have the harlots' mouth
Immortal as the soul of Socrates!
Forgive me, follower of Jesus. I
Am Greek, all Greek; I know the loveliness
Of flesh and its sweet snare, and I am hurt
At finding nothing where I sought for much.
O Paul, had you been more as other men
Your wisdom had been wiser! Christ, perhaps—
But I was born too late and so miss all.
I see no aim nor end. And yet myself
Hopeless of aught of profit from the fight
Fight on. . . . Perhaps there's something truer than
The truth we can deduce. . . . And after all
Our best is but a turning toward the stars,
An upward gaze. . . .

Fourteen Sonnets

Not to be naming you in all my prayers
Has made me prayerless, pagan, atheist;
Not to be knowing I am of your cares
Has loosed a ghost with eyes of amethyst
Into the regal day. The only thread,
Now broke, that bounden me to life was you,
So I am free now to consort with dead
Invisible lovers in their hushed purlieu.
O I am free now to regard the rise
From ocean of the round and rosy moon
Muse on her narrow length of dragon dyes
Like Clytemnestra's carpet—Take the boon!

I saw as much last night, with you away:
The moon was only round, the ocean gray.

Here‘life pays peace and ecstasy for tithe:
The dissonant trumpets of the world are mute
And God is but an old man with a scythe
And love the faltering fancy of a flute.
To lie with kissing lashes and confuse
The silver olives and the golden sun,
To sort the greens and purples from the blues
When the lean racers of the south wind run,
Rounding abreast the bulging Apennine,
And burst upon the clapping bay — ah, these
Are all the drudgeries of this demesne
Whose boundary is music and the sea’s.
Ye starved and hurt, ye hives of busy ghosts,
Would I could lend your ills this sea, these coasts.

Where through the olive trees I see bright shawls
And bathers laughing in the beryl bay,
Lovers more bold for tilted parasols
And waters summery and cerulean, lay
The hoarse and sweating legionnaires of Rome
Breaking their march. When they had marched their last,
Algerian pirates made of this their home
And heckled Genoa from here, and passed.
In some pale after-day of Arctic fear
When all the glittering tribes of us have thinned,
One of our last, perhaps, will wander here
Beneath the sockets of the stars and wind,
And facing seawards in the thickening night
Pray the old prayer to the last god “More light!”

Portofino.

Beloved and alien, gaze with me on the sea:
It kneels before the moon whose crimson blade
Rests on its million shoulders. But for me
The image of that lunar accolade
Is not the one your eyes bring in to you:
It varies by the flinching of a wave,
A widening iris, or a lens more true—
Or, if identical, the fact how prove?
If thus the tangible we may not share,
How hope the gorgeous fabrics of the soul
To spread before each other, or how dare
Another's undecipherable scroll
To con? Even in love we must confess
No understanding and great loneliness.

What disputations doth my spirit hold,
Contending with itself of this and that,
Laggard, alas, in action, but most bold
To storm celestial citadels with chat!
Now will it hale the villain flesh to bar,
Condemning it for all its own transgressions,
Holding itself a virgin winter-star,
Eclipsed but by poor body's vile obsessions.
Now when much weariness hath done it spite
It calleth body as the only leech,
Beggeth of him a music, or a sight
Curative — leaves in rain or thundering beach—
And ever in its loneliness it cries,
"Show me her hands, her mouth, her pitiful eyes."

When I allow my schoolèd eyes to lift
And see the beautiful ones of earth drift past
With parted lips and scooped wings of the swift
Along their temples — each lovelier than the last—

Seeing the wistful hunger in their eyes,
I love those damnèd ladies sweet of heart
Who draw the rippling curtains at sunrise
And watch the stranger, solaced by their art,
Sleeping and warm and childish: I would teach
Their kindness to my heart and solace too,
Like Magdala and Cressid, all and each,
To each unfaithful, but to all most true.
But there are some whose fortune is to be
Lonely: no beautiful one has need of me.

Let me confess I am no Launcelot—
But not to you confess, or you, or you,
The many I have loved, for you have got
What share of me you asked, your every due,
And we are quits. But to my secret soul
I make confession — and absolve as well—
That little parts and never the great rôle
I've played, and often, in love's carnival.
Well cast, no doubt. But I have read, somewhere,
A long time since, and liked, a sadder plot
Of two that wept or kissed on a dark stair
Hearing the winds howl over Camelot. . . .
Thou Maker of hearts flawed and dissonant,
The pain left out of mine — this I resent.

Knowing you give yourself without desire—
No golden turmoil and no fevered shame—
I take you with a four-fold kindled fire,
My salty torment coloring the flame.
Your acquiescence I reward with all
The secret riches only love should see,
Share beauty with you, run before you call,
Make your desires my one idolatry.
O I have made myself so rare a lover

That though I get from you nor praise nor blame
The world applauds, and, seeing but the cover,
Gives to the bawdy thing a sacred name.
But not for you I play this zealous rôle:
From cold-fanged lust somehow it saves the soul.

Though we be breasted shallowly, to hold
Deciduous loves that live their sweetness out,
Impotent by dimension to enfold
One mighty love and single, never doubt
But there are breasts can chalice love's full tide
With all its weight of wind and stars and rain,
Though lodgment for a surge so deep, so wide
Demands the hollow where some sea has lain.
We are but woodland pools whose shallow urns
One summer empties and one April fills,
Doubling a neighborhood of flowers and ferns,
Devout for any star the great dark spills.
We are for wayfarers to drink from and forget,
Parting again the branches low and wet.

All that is lovely is incredible,
No sooner seen or heard or touched than gone
And not believed in by the mind too full
Of mirrors to recall what has withdrawn.
I am so filled with ghosts of loveliness
That I could furbish out and populate
A vacant star, so that the gods would press
To gaze and memorize and duplicate.
But here, alone, with fog about my heart,
Of all the beauty I have seen so plain
I seek to summon up so small a part
Two hands could hold it, and I seek in vain.
I only know your eyes and mouth and hair
Are beauty's own: I cannot see them, dear.

With what unyielding fortitude of heart
We tap the prison walls to find escape,
Measure the thickness, calculate and chart,—
As if mole eyes could read the meagre tape!
Long after our unteemèd brain's forgot
The hope of star or sun or crystal air,
We fumble at the hinges of the plot
And cipher on the whence and how and where.
Our knowledge foots no sum: our seasoned pen
Writes question-marks we dry with our last breath.
Lavish in horror to the race of men,
Thou makest a boon, O God, of horrible death,—
Yet canst not wring this cry from minds mature
"Let us seek anodynes, for there's no cure."

Not the blue flagstones of eternal space,
Sprinkled a little way with frugal fire,
Confound my mind, for there's no mind can pace
Our visible moiety of space entire
From earth to moon, from moon to Formilhaut
And out and out beyond the phosphorent weave
Of nebulae and the last golden tow
Of suns pulsing at anchor, that can conceive
Ending or no beyond. A hope is here,
Ambiguous, obscure, but still a hope:
If mind's machinery, this thinking gear
Boasts the eternal for its mould and scope,
Is he eternal that I thought could die—
This flash of dew, this frosty breath, this I?

I have no patience, no philosophy
To heal at all the wound that we call life:
One after one the anodynes for me
Have failed. Still as of old I see the strife,
Savage and sad, but have forgot its cause

Nor glimpse its outcome any more. The stare
Of truth has not revealed immutable laws
Or far beneficences or the care
Of any intellect, alert, serene.
Instead, these I am sure of as I wait:
Pain, the hot-sanded heart's one evergreen;
Ignorance, rubbing slick the cell of fate.

On, in the dark, then; cloak the decent scars:
The cage of darkness shows, not hides the stars.

Chart back as best he might the way he'd come
And not a turn but still seemed best to choose,
Yet he had reached a wilderness, wherefrom
He must escape or all the struggle lose.
The urgency to act was thick upon him,
But still he paused to place the past mistake:
Inevitable blameless by-gones stun him,
His loyalties to shaping justice break.
At last he saw and took, like one quite tired,
The path ahead, obscure and full of stress:
To see was easy, but to take required
The solemn fortitude of hopelessness.

His clothes are shiny now that once were napped:
The liveliest beast grows somewhat seedy, trapped.

Threnody

All has been said that need be said, all has been done.
Let us return through the fields she loved in the sorrowless sun,
And steady our hearts if we may, our hearts so many, yet one.

Not for forgetting she'd ask, to spare us our brief pain:
She knew the Lethe in all sorrow; she knew the gain,
The flower that blows but by the flower-forgotten rain.

Because of her, life was sweeter: that be the whole of our
    praise—
Tenderness wrought in a few, a few but for all of their days.
Than that is it fairer at last to have honors, anthems, and bays?
Let us touch hands and part. If simple words can bless
May ours through the mothering grass fall softly and caress:
Earth, lie gently on a heart all gentleness.

Medusa

There is a tale of brow and clotted hair
Thrust in the window of a banquet room
Which froze eternally the revellers there,
The lights full on them in their postured doom:
The queen still held the carmine to her lips,
The king's mouth stood wide open for its laugh,
The jester's rigid leer launched silent quips;
Only a blind man moved and tapped his staff.
I cannot guess that physiognomy
The sight of which could curdle into stone
The gazer, though pities, horrors, terrors I
Have made encounter of and sometimes known.
But I knew one who turned to stone with terror
Of facing quietly a flawless mirror.

Home

ONE OF THE PLEASANTEST PLACES near the home town is the
cemetery. It lies along a curve of Rattlesnake Bayou. Across its front
used to run the old dirt road to the riverlanding down which the raiding Yankees would dash on their forays inland while Holt and the
remaining elders of the countryside would snipe them from the
bushes. Now the road is of concrete and its unexpected curve often
sends motorists in their cups or out of their wits headlong into the

well-dredged bayou, which on drainage maps is now called Dredge Ditch No. 4 D. Across the bayou toward the east have grown up new enterprises of which we are proud, a florist's, a nursery, the golf-links, and an exclusive addition full of very old beautiful trees and very new beautiful residences. The cemetery itself was designed during carriage days, with cedar-bordered roads running in parallel semi-circles and too narrow for automobiles. In spite of the neighboring highway with its strident motor-cars it is a quiet spot, eternally green, and from any grave you may look westerly across open fields to the levee and feel the river beyond, deep in its plumy willows. This home of the dead is, quaintly enough, the home of hundreds of mockingbirds, which, mistaking all time for eternal spring, sing the year round. I have heard them append arpeggios and cadenzas to pitiful unreassuring funeral sermons and rain liquid hope while the priest was muttering *in pulverum reverteris*.

Our lot is toward the back and raised a little, as someone hated to think of the river's overflow covering the graves. In the middle of it, backed by a semicircular thicket of evergreens, stands Malvina Hoffman's bronze figure of a brooding knight, sunshine flowing from his body as indicated in low relief on the stone stele behind, and the river at his feet. The one word "Patriot" beneath the statue and Matthew Arnold's "Last Word" on the reverse side of the stele show those who loved him that Father lies near by.

I come here not infrequently because it is restful and comforting. I am with my own people. With them around me I can seem to read the finished manuscripts of their lives, forever unchangeable, and beautiful in the dim way manuscripts have. Here sleep Mother and Father, Mur and Fafar, Mère and Père, the small brother who should be representing and perpetuating the name, Uncle George in one corner, his fishing done, in another under a stone marked "Gentleman" Fafar's brother LeRoy beside Fafar's elder daughter, whose death, caused, he thought, by a quack doctor he himself had chosen, so grieved him he ended his own life. Aunt Fanny is here too, no opiates needed now for her long ills, and close to her her husband, Dr. Walker Percy, who, united and gathered to his own, finds no further need to oppose secession. The latest-comer and the loveliest, Mattie Sue, sleeps to the front, her morning-glory air all gone, but the valor not yet faded from her heart. They are all here, and I am glad there's room to spare. It would be indeed a chilly world without this refuge with its feel of home.

I wish a few others out there, under the cedars, could be in this plot of ours. Miss Carrie's bird-body must by now be a mere pinch of dust and would take no space. Father Koestenbrock, far from his native city and his fathers, might feel less lonely here. Here Judge Griffin might dream of a truer ending for his *Ruin Robed.* And I should like to bring from that far corner where the poor sleep well one brown-eyed lad who sleeps alone there, for he had loved me and gaspingly had told me so while death was choking him and he knew it was death.

I am told that in Arab countries strangers volunteer to carry the coffin of a deceased, and in our cities strangers are hired for this chore. But with us friends are asked to bear their friends to the open grave for the last rites. Far as these white stones reach are graves now closed to which I have carried my friends—poor and well-to-do, obscure and prominent, good and bad, men and women, young and old, Jew and Christian, believer and agnostic. Sometimes with the coffin handle in my grip, staggering heavily toward that angular gash in the curving earth, I forget which one it is this time who is preceding me and wonder absently who will be left to do me a like service. A little while and the living town, this tiny world of mine, will all be here, tucked under the same dark blanket, cosily together. Another little while and the last of us, those I loved and those I disapproved, will be sharing oblivion, for no one will remember any of us. The famous do not share our cedars and our mockingbirds. This is private ground for the lovable obscure. Even Father, who warmed and led and lighted our people—no one will remember him, his name and deeds will be forgotten soon, in another spring, or ten, or a hundred, what matter? Strangers will come and, striving briefly, will join us in our dark, and our mockingbirds, unrecollecting, will sing for them with equal rapture.

While people are still alive we judge them as good or bad, condemn them as failures or praise them as successes, love them or despise them. Only when they are dead do we see them, not with charity, but with understanding. Alive they are remote, even hostile;

dead, they join our circle and you see the family likeness. As I loiter among our graves reading the names on the headstones, names that when they identified live men I sometimes hated or scorned as enemies of me and mine and all that we held good, I find myself smiling. How unreal and accidental seem their defects! I know their stories: this one was a whore and this a thief, here lies the town hypocrite and there one who should have died before he was born. I know their stories, but not their hearts. With a little shifting of qualities, with a setting more to their needs, with merely more luck, this woman could have borne children who would have been proud of her, and this thief might have become the father of the poor. Now death has made them only home-folks and I like the sound of their familiar names. They lie there under the grass in the evening light so helplessly, my townsmen, a tiny outpost of the lost tribe of our star. Understanding breaks over my heart and I know that the wickedness and the failures of men are nothing and their valor and pathos and effort everything. Circumscribed and unendowed, ailing in body, derided and beguiled, how well they have done! They have sipped happiness and gulped pain, they have sought God and never found Him, they have found love and never kept him—yet they kept on, they never gave up, they rarely complained. Among these handfuls of misguided dust I am proud to be a man and assuaged for my own defects. I muse on this one small life that it is all I have to show for, the sum of it, the wrong turnings, the weakness of will, the feebleness of spirit, one tiny life with darkness before and after, and it at best a riddle and a wonder. One by one I count the failures—at law undistinguished, at teaching unprepared, at soldiering average, at citizenship unimportant, at love second-best, at poetry forgotten before remembered—and I acknowledge the deficit. I am not proud, but I am not ashamed. What have defeats and failures to do with the good life? But closer lacks, more troubling doubts assail me. Of all the people I have loved, wisely and unwisely, deeply and passingly, I have loved no one so much as myself. Of all the hours of happiness granted me, none has been so keen and holy as a few unpredictable moments alone. I have never walked with God, but I had rather walk with Him through hell than with my heart's elect through heaven. Of the good life I have learned what it is not and I have loved a few who lived it end to end. I have seen the goodness of men and the beauty of things. I have no regrets. I am not contrite. I am grateful.

Here among the graves in the twilight I see one thing only, but I see that thing clear. I see the long wall of a rampart sombre with sunset, a dusty road at its base. On the tower of the rampart stand the glorious high gods, Death and the rest, insolent and watching. Below on the road stream the tribes of men, tired, bent, hurt, and stumbling, and each man alone. As one comes beneath the tower, the High God descends and faces the wayfarer. He speaks three slow words: "Who are you?" The pilgrim I know should be able to straighten his shoulders, to stand his tallest, and to answer defiantly: "I am your son."

(1897–1962)

William Faulkner

Nobel Prize-winning William Cuthbert Faulkner, by any standard the greatest of Mississippi's writers and in the opinion of many one of the greatest writers of the English language, was born in New Albany on September 25, 1897. Very soon after his birth, however, his family moved to Oxford, where he lived, except for periods in Hollywood and Charlottesville, Virginia, for the rest of his life. What little formal education he received he got in Oxford public schools (though he dropped out during his junior year of high school) and at the University of Mississippi, which he attended as a special student for a little over a year (1919–1920). Faulkner was an omnivorous reader, however, and partly through the friendship of Oxford lawyer Phil Stone, who both encouraged him and supplied him with books, he got a literary education by reading widely in modern literature, especially in the poetry of the French Symbolists, who were an early and profound influence on him. He began writing as a poet—his first published volume, *The Marble Faun* (1924) was a long poem—but he soon found that prose was his true medium, and during his long and truly extraordinary career he produced a large body of fiction which is remarkable for its technical inventiveness, its philosophical scope, its dramatic power, and for its sustained excellence. Few writers—and no other Americans—have produced so many major works of art.

Known throughout his career as a "writer's writer," respected by

194

other writers for his achievements, Faulkner was not the kind of writer to attract a popular audience; and although he did achieve a certain notoriety for *Sanctuary* (1931), he was not able to support himself and his family from the proceeds of his novels until the publication of *Intruder in the Dust* in 1948, and its subsequent sale to the movies. For most of his life he had to eke out a meager living peddling short stories to magazines (not always successfully) and, periodically, hiring out to Hollywood as an underpaid scriptwriter. But his uncompromising high standards and his refusal to write down to a popular audience have made him perhaps the most widely honored of American novelists; his awards include not only the Nobel Prize (1950), but also two Pulitzer Prizes (for *A Fable* in 1954 and for *The Reivers* in 1962), and many other national and international prizes. He died July 6, 1962.

Because so much of his work is set in his own apocryphal city, Jefferson, and county, Yoknapatawpha, and because so much of it draws heavily upon the history of northern Mississippi—including the contributions to that history of his own family—it has been too easily assumed that Faulkner's *subject* was "The South." There is, of course, no denying his concern with and his use of southern materials; but critics who have held this position have usually stopped at this point, and have failed to see that "The South" is rather Faulkner's metaphor for a much larger concern with the human—not just southern—spirit. *The Sound and the Fury* (1929), for example, is not just about a decaying southern family, and *The Hamlet* (1940) is not just about the conflict between greedy commercialism and the agrarian culture in post-Reconstruction Mississippi. The best work on Faulkner has, of course, recognized this, and has also begun to take seriously works set outside Yoknapatawpha County, especially *The Wild Palms* (1939) and *A Fable* (1954).

Faulkner obviously loved Mississippi, but he was not blind to its faults either, and, especially after the Nobel Prize, he became an outspoken analyst of its racial and social problems, deploring all forms of intolerance and violence, advocating moderation and common sense, and believing that blacks and whites could solve their problems without outside interference, by drawing on a large reservoir of shared experiences. But his attitude toward his native state was not, strictly speaking, the bitter ambivalence of Quentin Compson in *Absalom, Absalom!* The semiautobiographical "Mississippi," reprinted here from *Essays Speeches & Public Letters* (1966), though first published in 1954, deals more directly and in some ways more movingly than anything else he ever wrote with his very complex attitudes toward Mississippi: "You dont love because," he concludes, "you love despite; not for the virtues, but despite the faults."

Mississippi

MISSISSIPPI BEGINS IN THE LOBBY of a Memphis, Tennessee hotel and extends south to the Gulf of Mexico. It is dotted with little towns concentric about the ghosts of the horses and mules once tethered to the hitch-rail enclosing the county courthouse and it might almost be said to have only those two directions, north and south, since until a few years ago it was impossible to travel east or west in it unless you walked or rode one of the horses or mules; even in the boy's early manhood, to reach by rail either of the adjacent county towns thirty miles away to the east or west, you had to travel ninety miles in three different directions on three different railroads.

In the beginning it was virgin—to the west, along the Big River, the alluvial swamps threaded by black almost motionless bayous and impenetrable with cane and buckvine and cypress and ash and oak and gum; to the east, the hardwood ridges and the prairies where the Appalachian mountains died and buffalo grazed; to the south, the pine barrens and the moss-hung liveoaks and the greater swamps less of earth than water and lurking with alligators and water moccasins, where Louisiana in its time would begin.

And where in the beginning the predecessors crept with their simple artifacts, and built the mounds and vanished, bequeathing only the mounds in which the succeeding recordable Algonquian stock would leave the skulls of their warriors and chiefs and babies and slain bears, and the shards of pots, and hammer- and arrow-heads and now and then a heavy silver Spanish spur. There were deer to drift in herds alarmless as smoke then, and bear and panther and wolves in the brakes and bottoms, and all the lesser beasts—coon and possum and beaver and mink and mushrat (not muskrat: mushrat); they were still there and some of the land was still virgin in the early nineteen hundreds when the boy himself began to hunt. But except for looking occasionally out from behind the face of a white man or a Negro, the Chickasaws and Choctaws and Natchez and Yazoos were as gone as the predecessors, and the people the boy crept with were the descendants of the Sartorises and De Spains and

Compsons who had commanded the Manassas and Sharpsburg and Shiloh and Chickamauga regiments, and the McCaslins and Ewells and Holstons and Hogganbecks whose fathers and grandfathers had manned them, and now and then a Snopes too because by the beginning of the twentieth century Snopeses were everywhere: not only behind the counters of grubby little side street stores patronised mostly by Negroes, but behind the presidents' desks of banks and the directors' tables of wholesale grocery corporations and in the deaconries of Baptist churches, buying up the decayed Georgian houses and chopping them into apartments and on their death-beds decreeing annexes and baptismal fonts to the churches as mementos to themselves or maybe out of simple terror.

They hunted too. They too were in the camps where the De Spains and Compsons and McCaslins and Ewells were masters in their hierarchial turn, shooting the does not only when law but the Master too said not, shooting them not even because the meat was needed but leaving the meat itself to be eaten by scavengers in the woods, shooting it simply because it was big and moving and alien, of an older time than the little grubby stores and the accumulating and compounding money; the boy a man now and in his hierarchial turn Master of the camp and coping, having to cope, not with the diminishing wilderness where there was less and less game, but with the Snopeses who were destroying that little which did remain.

These elected the Bilboes and voted indefatigably for the Vardamans, naming their sons after both; their origin was in bitter hatred and fear and economic rivalry of the Negroes who farmed little farms no larger than and adjacent to their own, because the Negro, remembering when he had not been free at all, was therefore capable of valuing what he had of it enough to struggle to retain even that little and had taught himself how to do more with less: to raise more cotton with less money to spend and food to eat and fewer or inferior tools to work with: this, until he, the Snopes, could escape from the land into the little grubby side street stores where he could live not beside the Negro but on him by marking up on the inferior meat and meal and molasses the price which he, the Negro, could not even always read.

In the beginning, the obsolescent, dispossessed tomorrow by

the already obsolete: the wild Algonquian—Chickasaw and Choctaw and Natchez and Pascagoula—looking down from the tall Mississippi bluffs at a Chippeway canoe containing three Frenchmen—and had barely time to whirl and look behind him at a thousand Spaniards come overland from the Atlantic Ocean, and for a little while longer had the privilege of watching an ebb-flux-ebb-flux of alien nationalities as rapid as the magician's spill and evanishment of inconstant cards: the Frenchman for a second, then the Spaniard for perhaps two, then the Frenchman for another two and then the Spaniard again and then the Frenchman again for that last half-breath before the Anglo-Saxon, who would come to stay, to endure: the tall man roaring with Protestant scripture and boiled whiskey, Bible and jug in one hand and like as not an Indian tomahawk in the other, brawling, turbulent, uxorious and polygamous: a married invincible bachelor without destination but only motion, advancement, dragging his gravid wife and most of his mother-in-law's kin behind him into the trackless wilderness, to spawn that child behind a logcrotched rifle and then get her with another one before they moved again, and at the same time scattering his inexhaustible other seed in three hundred miles of dusky bellies: without avarice or compassion or forethought either: felling a tree which took two hundred years to grow, to extract from it a bear or a capful of wild honey.

He endured, even after he too was obsolete, the younger sons of Virginia and Carolina planters coming to replace him in wagons laden with slaves and indigo seedlings over the very roads he had hacked out with little else but the tomahawk. Then someone gave a Natchez doctor a Mexican cotton seed (maybe with the bollweevil already in it since, like the Snopes, he too has taken over the southern earth) and changed the whole face of Mississippi, slaves clearing rapidly now the virgin land lurking still (1850) with the ghosts of Murrell and Mason and Hare and the two Harpes, into plantation fields for profit where he, the displaced and obsolete, had wanted only the bear and the deer and the sweetening for his tooth. But he remained, hung on still; he is still there even in the boy's middle-age, living in a log or plank or tin hut on the edge of what remains of the fading wilderness, by and on the tolerance and sometimes even the bounty of the plantation owner to whom, in his intractable way and even with a certain dignity and independence, he is a sycophant, trapping coons and muskrats, now that the bear and the panther are almost gone too, improvident still, felling still the two-hundred-year-old tree even though it has only a coon or a squirrel in it now.

Manning, when that time came, not the Manassas and Shiloh regiments but confederating into irregular bands and gangs owning not much allegiance to anyone or anything, unified instead into the one rite and aim of stealing horses from Federal picket-lines; this in the intervals of rading (or trying to) the plantation house of the very man to whom he had been the independent sycophant and intended to be again, once the war was over and presuming that the man came back from his Sharpsburg or Chickamauga majority or colonelcy or whatever it had been; trying to, that is, until the major's or colonel's wife or aunt or mother-in-law, who had buried the silver in the orchard and still held together a few of the older slaves, fended him off and dispersed him, and when necessary even shot him, with the absent husband's or nephew's or son-in-law's hunting gun or dueling pistols,—the women, the indomitable, the undefeated, who never surrendered, refusing to allow the Yankee *minie* balls to be dug out of portico column or mantelpiece or lintel, who seventy years later would get up and walk out of *Gone with the Wind* as soon as Sherman's name was mentioned; irreconcilable and enraged and still talking about it long after the weary exhausted men who had fought and lost it gave up trying to make them hush: even in the boy's time the boy himself knowing about Vicksburg and Corinth and exactly where his grandfather's regiment had been at First Manassas before he remembered hearing very much about Santa Claus.

In those days (1901 and -2 and -3 and -4) Santa Claus occurred only at Christmas, not like now, and for the rest of the year children played with what they could find or contrive or make, though just as now, in '51 and -2 and -3 and -4, they still played, aped in miniature, what they had been exposed to, heard or seen or been moved by most. Which was true in the child's time and case too: the indomitable unsurrendered old women holding together still, thirty-five and forty years later, a few of the old house slaves: women too who, like the white ones, declined, refused to give up the old ways and forget the old anguishes. The child himself remembered one of them: Caroline: free these many years but who had declined to leave. Nor would she ever accept in full her weekly Saturday wages, the family never knew why unless the true reason was the one which appeared: for the simple pleasure of keeping the entire family reminded constantly that they were in arrears to her, compelling the boy's grandfather then his father and finally himself in his turn to be not only her banker but her bookkeeper too, having got the figure of eighty-nine dollars into her head somehow or for some reason, and though the sum itself altered, sometimes more and sometimes less and sometimes it would be she herself who would be several weeks in arrears, it never changed: one of the children, white or Negro, liable to appear at any time, usually when most of the family would be gathered at a meal, with the message: 'Mammy says to tell you not to forget you owe her eighty-nine dollars.'

To the child, even at that time, she seemed already older than God, calling his grandsire 'colonel' but never the child's father nor the father's brother and sister by anything but their christian names even when they themselves had become grandparents: a matriarch with a score of descendants (and probably half that many more whom she had forgotten or outlived), one of them a boy too, whether a great grandson or merely a grandson even she did not remember, born in the same week with the white child and both bearing the same (the white child's grandsire's) name, suckled at the same black breast and sleeping and eating together and playing together the game which was the most important thing the white child knew at that time since at four and five and six his world was still a female world and he had heard nothing else that he could remember: with empty spools and chips and sticks and a scraped trench filled with well-water for the River, playing over again in miniature the War, the old irremediable battles—Shiloh and Vicksburg, and Brice's Crossroads which was not far from where the child (both of them) had been born, the boy because he was white arrogating to himself the right to be the Confederate General—Pemberton or Johnston or Forrest—twice to the black child's once, else, lacking that once in three, the black one would not play at all.

Not the tall man, he was still the hunter, the man of the woods; and not the slave because he was free now; but that Mexican cotton seed which someone had given the Natchez doctor clearing the land fast now, plowing under the buffalo grass of the eastern prairies and the brier and switch-cane of the creek- and river-bottoms of the central hills and deswamping that whole vast flat alluvial Delta-shaped sweep of land along the Big River, the Old Man: building the levees to hold him off the land long enough to plant and harvest the crop: he taking another foot of scope in his new dimension for every foot man constricted him in the old: so that the steamboats carrying the baled cotton to Memphis or New Orleans seemed to crawl along the sky itself.

And little steamboats on the smaller rivers too, penetrating the Tallahatchie as far up as Wylie's Crossing above Jefferson. Though most of the cotton from that section, and on to the east to that point of no economic return where it was more expedient to continue on east to the Tombigbee and then south to Mobile, went the sixty miles overland to Memphis by mule and wagon; there was a settlement—a tavern of sorts and a smithy and a few gaunt cabins—on the bluff above Wylie's, at the exact distance where a wagon or a train of them loaded with cotton either starting or resuming the journey in the vicinity of Jefferson, would have to halt for the night. Or not even a settlement but rather a den, whose denizens lurked unseen by day in the brakes and thickets of the river bottom, appearing only at night and even then only long enough to enter the tavern kitchen where the driver of the day's cotton wagon sat unsuspecting before the fire, whereupon driver wagon mules and cotton and all would vanish: the body into the river probably and the wagon burned and the mules sold days or weeks later in a Memphis stockyard and the unidentifiable cotton already on its way to the Liverpool mill.

At the same time, sixteen miles away in Jefferson, there was a pre-Snopes, one of the tall men actually, giant of a man in fact: a dedicated lay Bapist preacher but furious not with a furious unsleeping dream of paradise nor even for universal Order with an upper-case O, but for simple civic security. He was warned by everyone not to go in there because not only could he accomplish nothing, he would very likely lose his own life trying it. But he did go, alone, talking not of gospel nor God nor even virtue, but simply selected the biggest and boldest and by appearance anyway the most villainous there and said to him: 'I'll fight you. If you lick me, you take what money I have. If I lick you, I baptise you into my church': and battered and mauled and gouged that one into sanctity and civic virtue then challenged the next biggest and most villainous and then the next; and the following Sunday baptised the entire settlement in the river, the cotton wagons now crossing on Wylie's handpowered ferry and passing peacefully and unchallenged on to Memphis until the railroads came and took the bales away from them.

That was in the seventies. The Negro was a free farmer and a political entity now; one, he could not sign his name, was Federal marshal at Jefferson. Afterward he became the town's official bootlegger (Mississippi was one of the first to essay the noble experiment, along with Maine), resuming—he had never really quitted it—his old allegiance to his old master and gaining his professional name, Mulberry, from the huge old tree behind Doctor Habersham's drugstore, in the gallery-like tunnels among the roots of which he cached the bottled units of his commerce.

Soon he (the Negro) would even forge ahead in that economic rivalry with Snopes which was to send Snopes in droves into the Ku Klux Klan—not the old original one of the war's chaotic and desperate end which, measured against the desperate times, was at least honest and serious in its desperate aim, but into the later base one of the twenties whose only kinship to the old one was the old name. And a little money to build railroads with was in the land now, brought there by the man who in '66 had been a carpet-bagger but who now was a citizen; his children would speak the soft consonantless Negro tongue as the children of parents who had lived below the Potomac and Ohio Rivers since Captain John Smith, and their children would boast of their Southern heritage. In Jefferson his name was Redmond. He had found the money with which Colonel Sartoris had opened the local cottonfields to Europe by building his connecting line up to the main railroad from Memphis to the Atlantic Ocean—narrow gauge, like a toy, with three tiny locomotives like toys too, named after Colonel Sartoris's three daughters, each with its silver-plated oilcan engraved with the daughter's christian name:

like toys, the standard-sized cars jacked up at the junction then lowered onto the narrow trucks, the tiny locomotive now invisible ahead of its charges so that they appeared in process of being snatched headlong among the fields they served by an arrogant plume of smoke and the arrogant shrieking of a whistle—who, after the inevitable quarrel, finally shot Colonel Sartoris dead on a Jefferson street, driven, everyone believed, to the desperate act by the same arrogance and intolerance which had driven Colonel Sartoris's regiment to demote him from its colonelcy in the fall elections after Second Manassas and Sharpsburg.

So there were railroads in the land now; now couples who had used to go overland by carriage to the River landings and the steamboats for the traditional New Orleans honeymoon, could take the train from almost anywhere. And presently pullmans too, all the way from Chicago and the Northern cities where the cash, the money was, so that the rich Northerners could come down in comfort and open the land indeed: setting up with their Yankee dollars the vast lumbering plants and mills in the southern pine section, the little towns which had been hamlets without change or alteration for fifty years, booming and soaring into cities overnight above the stump-pocked barrens which would remain until in simple economic desperation people taught themselves to farm pine trees as in other sections they had already learned to farm corn and cotton.

And Northern lumber mills in the Delta too: the mid-twenties now and the Delta booming with cotton and timber both. But mostly booming with simple money: increment a troglodyte which had fathered twin troglodytes: solvency and bankruptcy, the three of them booming money into the land so fast that the problem was how to get rid of it before it whelmed you into suffocation. Until in something almost resembling self-defense, not only for something to spend it on but to bet the increment from the simple spending on, seven or eight of the bigger Delta towns formed a baseball league, presently raiding as far away—and successfully too—for pitchers and short-stops and slugging outfielders, as the two major leagues, the boy, a young man now, making acquaintance with this league and one of the big Northern lumber companies not only coincidentally with one another but because of one another.

At this time the young man's attitude of mind was that of most of the other young men in the world who had been around twenty-one years of age in April, 1917, even though at times he did admit to himself that he was possibly using the fact that he had been nineteen on that day as an excuse to follow the avocation he was coming more and more to know would be forever his true one: to be a tramp, a harmless possessionless vagabond. In any case, he was quite ripe to make the acquaintance, which began with that of the lumber company which at the moment was taking a leisurely bankruptcy in a town where lived a lawyer who had been appointed the referee in the bankruptcy: a family friend of the young man's family and older than he, yet who had taken a liking to the young man and so invited him to come along for the ride too. His official capacity was that of interpreter, since he had a little French and the defuncting company had European connections. But no interpreting was ever done since the entourage did not go to Europe but moved instead into a single floor of a Memphis hotel, where all—including the interpreter—had the privilege of signing chits for food and theatre tickets and even the bootleg whiskey (Tennessee was in its dry mutation then) which the bellboys would produce, though not of course at the discreet and innocent-looking places clustered a few miles away just below the Mississippi state line, where roulette and dice and blackjack were available.

Then suddenly Mr Sells Wales was in it too, bringing the baseball league with him. The young man never did know what connection (if any) Mr Wales had with the bankruptcy, nor really bothered to wonder, let along care and ask, not only because he had developed already that sense of *noblesse oblige* toward the avocation which he knew was his true one, which would have been reason enough, but because Mr Wales himself was already a legend in the Delta. Owner of a plantation measured not in acres but in miles and reputedly sole owner of one of the league baseball teams or anyway most of its players, certainly of the catcher and the base-stealing shortstop and the .340 hitting outfielder ravished or pirated it was said from the Chicago Cubs, his ordinary costume seven days a week was a two- or three-days' beard and muddy high boots and a corduroy hunting coat, the tale, the legend telling of how he entered a swank St. Louis hotel in that costume late one night and demanded a room of a dinner jacketed clerk, who looked once at the beard and the muddy boots but probably mostly at Mr Wales's face and said they were filled up; whereupon Mr Wales asked how much they wanted for the hotel and was told, superciliously, in tens of thousands, and—so told the legend—drew from his corduroy hip a wad of thousand dollar bills sufficient to have bought the hotel half again at the price stated and told the clerk he wanted every room in the building vacated in ten minutes.

That one of course was apocryphal, but the young man himself saw this one: Mr Wales and himself having a leisurely breakfast one noon in the Memphis hotel when Mr Wales remembered suddenly that his private ball club was playing one of its most important games at a town about sixty miles away at three oclock that afternoon and telephoned to the railroad station to have a special train ready for them in thirty minutes, which it was: an engine and a caboose: reaching Coahoma about three oclock with a mile still to the ball park: a man (there were no taxis at the station at that hour and few in Mississippi anywhere at that time) sitting behind the wheel of a dingy though still sound Cadillac car, and Mr Wales said:

'What do you want for it?'

'What?' the man in the car said.

'Your automobile,' Mr Wales said.

'Twelve fifty,' the man said.

'All right,' Mr Wales said, opening the door.

'I mean twelve hundred and fifty dollars,' the man said.

'All right,' Mr Wales said, then to the young man: 'Jump in.'

'Hold up here, mister,' the man said.

'I've bought it,' Mr Wales said, getting in too. 'The ball park,' he said. 'Hurry.'

The young man never saw the Cadillac again, though he became quite familiar with the engine and caboose during the next succeeding weeks while the league pennant race waxed hotter and hotter, Mr Wales keeping the special train on call in the Memphis yards as twenty-five years earlier a city-dwelling millionaire might have hacked a carriage and pair to his instant nod, so that it seemed to the young man that he would barely get back to Memphis to rest before they would be rushing once more down the Delta to another baseball game.

'I ought to be interpreting, sometime,' he said once.

'Interpret, then,' Mr Wales said. 'Interpret what this goddamn cotton market is going to do tomorrow, and we can both quit chasing this blank blank sandlot ball team.'

The cotton seed and the lumber mills clearing the rest of the Delta too, pushing what remained of the wilderness further and further southward into the V of Big River and hills. When the young man, a youth of sixteen and seventeen then, was first accepted into that hunting club of which he in his hierarchial time would be Master, the hunting grounds, haunt of deer and bear and wild turkey, could be reached in a single day or night in a mule-drawn wagon. Now they were using automobiles: a hundred miles then two hundred southward and still southward as the wilderness dwindled into the confluence of the Yazoo River and the big one, the Old Man.

The Old Man: all his little contributing streams levee-ed too, along with him, and paying none of the dykes any heed at all when it suited his mood and fancy, gathering water all the way from Montana to Pennsylvania every generation or so and rolling it down the artificial gut of his victims' puny and baseless hoping, piling the water up, not fast: just inexorable, giving plenty of time to measure his crest and telegraph ahead, even warning of the exact day almost when he would enter the house and float the piano out of it and the pictures off the walls, and even remove the house itself if it were not securely fastened down.

Inexorable and unhurried, overpassing one by one his little confluent feeders and shoving the water into them until for days their current would flow backward, upstream: as far upstream as Wylie's Crossing above Jefferson. The little rivers were dyked too but back here was the land of individualists: remnants and descendants of the tall men now taken to farming, and of Snopeses who were more than individualists: they were Snopeses, so that where the owners of the thousand-acre plantations along the Big River confederated as one man with sandbags and machines and their Negro tenants and wagehands to hold the sandboils and the cracks, back here the owner of the hundred or two hundred acre farm patrolled his section of levee with a sandbag in one hand and his shotgun in the other, lest his upstream neighbor dynamite it to save his (the upstream neighbor's) own.

Piling up the water while white man and Negro worked side by side in shifts in the mud and the rain, with automobile headlights and gasoline flares and kegs of whiskey and coffee boiling in fifty-gallon batches in scoured and scalded oil-drums; lapping, tentative, almost innocently, merely inexorable (no hurry, his) among and beneath and between and finally over the frantic sandbags, as if his whole purpose had been merely to give man another chance to prove, not to him but to man, just how much the human body could bear, stand, endure; then, having let man prove it, doing what he could have done at any time these past weeks if so minded: removing with no haste nor any particular malice or fury either, a mile or two miles of levee and coffee drums and whiskey kegs and gas flares in one sloughing collapse, gleaming dully for a little while yet among the parallel cotton middles until the fields vanished along with the roads and lanes and at last the towns themselves.

Vanished, gone beneath one vast yellow motionless expanse, out of which projected only the tops of trees and telephone poles and the decapitations of human dwelling-places like enigmatic objects placed by inscrutable and impenetrable design on a dirty mirror; and the mounds of the predecessors on which, among a tangle of moccasins, bear and horses and deer and mules and wild turkeys and cows and domestic chickens waited patient in mutual armistice; and the levees themselves, where among a jumble of uxorious flotsam the young continued to be born and the old to die, not from exposure but from simple and normal time and decay, as if man and his destiny were in the end stronger even than the river which had dispossessed him, inviolable by and invincible to alteration.

Then, having proved that too, he—the Old Man—would withdraw, not retreat: subside, back from the land slowly and inexorably too, emptying the confluent rivers and bayous back into the old vain hopeful gut, but so slowly and gradually that not the waters seemed to fall but the flat earth itself to rise, creep in one plane back into light and air again: one constant stain of yellow-brown at one constant altitude on telephone poles and the walls of gins and houses and stores as though the line had been laid off with a transit and painted in one gigantic unbroken brush-stroke, the earth itself one alluvial inch higher, the rich dirt one inch deeper, drying into long cracks beneath the hot fierce glare of May: but not for long, because almost at once came the plow, the plowing and planting already two months late but that did not matter: the cotton man-tall once more by August and whiter and denser still by picking-time, as if the Old Man said, 'I do what I want to, when I want to. But I pay my way.'

And the boats, of course. They projected above that yellow and liquid plane and even moved upon it: the skiffs and skows of fishermen and trappers, the launches of the United States Engineers who operated the Levee Commission, and one small shallow-draught steamboat steaming in paradox among and across the cotton fields themselves, its pilot not a riverman but a farmer who knew where the submerged fences were, its masthead lookout a mechanic with a pair of pliers to cut the telephone wires to pass the smokestack through: no paradox really, since on the River it had resembled a house to begin with, so that here it looked no different from the baseless houses it steamed among, and on occasion even strained at top boiler pressure to overtake like a mallard drake after a fleeing mallard hen.

But these were not enough, very quickly not near enough; the Old Man meant business indeed this time. So now there began to arrive from the Gulf ports the shrimp trawlers and pleasure cruisers and Coast Guard cutters whose bottoms had known only salt water and the mouths of tidal rivers, to be run still by their salt water crews but conned by the men who knew where the submerged roads and fences were for the good reason that they had been running mule-plow furrows along them or up to them all their lives, sailing among the swollen carcasses of horses and mules and deer and cows and sheep to pluck the Old Man's patient flotsam, black and white, out of trees and the roofs of gins and cotton sheds and floating cabins and the second storey windows of houses and office buildings; then—the salt-water men, to whom land was either a featureless treeless salt-marsh or a snake- and alligator-infested swamp impenetrable with trumpet vine and Spanish moss; some of whom had never even seen the earth into which were driven the spiles supporting the houses they lived in—staying on even after they were no longer needed, as though waiting to see emerge from the water what sort of country it was which bore the economy on which the people—men and women, black and white, more of black than white even, ten to one more—lived whom they had saved; seeing the land for that moment before mule and plow altered it right up to the water's receding edge, then back into the River again before the trawlers and cruisers and cutters became marooned into canted and useless rubble too along with the ruined hencoops and cowsheds and privies; back onto the Old Man, shrunken once more into his normal banks, drowsing and even innocent-looking, as if it were something else beside he who had changed, for a little time anyway, the whole face of the adjacent earth.

They were homeward bound now, passing the river towns, some of which were respectable in age when south Mississippi was a Spanish wilderness: Greenville and Vicksburg, Natchez and Grand-and Petit Gulf (vanished now and even the old site known by a different name) which had known Mason and one at least of the Harpes and from or on which Murrell had based his abortive slave insurrection intended to efface the white people from the land and leave him emperor of it, the land sinking away beyond the levee until presently you could no longer say where water began and earth stopped: only that these lush and verdant sunny savannahs would no longer bear your weight. The rivers flowed no longer west, but south now, no longer yellow or brown, but black, threading the miles of yellow salt marsh from which on an off-shore breeze mosquitoes came in such clouds that in your itching and burning anguish it would seem to you you could actually see them in faint adumbration crossing the earth, and met tide and then the uncorrupted salt: not the Gulf quite yet but at least the Sound behind the long barrier of the islands—Ship and Horn and Petit Bois, the trawler and cruiser bottoms home again now among the lighthouses and channel markers and shipyards and drying nets and processing plants for fish.

The man remembered that from his youth too: one summer spent being blown innocently over in catboats since, born and bred for generations in the north Mississippi hinterland, he did not recognise the edge of a squall until he already had one. The next summer he returned because he found that he liked that much water, this time as a hand in one of the trawlers, remembering: a four-gallon iron pot over a red bed of charcoal on the foredeck, in which decapitated shrimp boiled among handsful of salt and black pepper, never emptied, never washed and constantly renewed, so that you ate them all day long in passing like peanuts; remembering: the predawn, to be broken presently by the violent near-subtropical yellow-and-crimson day almost like an audible explosion, but still dark for a little while yet, the dark ship creeping onto the shrimp grounds in a soundless sternward swirl of phosphorus like a drowning tumble of fireflies, the youth lying face down on the peak staring into the dark water watching the disturbed shrimp burst outward-shooting in fiery and fading fans like the trails of tiny rockets.

He learned the barrier islands too; one of a crew of five amateurs sailing a big sloop in off-shore races, he learned not only how to keep a hull on its keel and moving but how to get it from one place to another and bring it back: so that, a professional now, living in New Orleans he commanded for pay a power launch belonging to a bootlegger (this was the twenties), whose crew consisted of a Negro cook-deckhand-stevedore and the bootlegger's younger brother: a slim twenty-one or -two year old Italian with yellow eyes like a cat and a silk shirt bulged faintly by an armpit-holstered pistol too small in calibre to have done anything but got them all killed, even if the captain or the cook had dreamed of resisting or resenting trouble if and when it came, which the captain or the cook would extract from the holster and hide at the first opportunity (not concealed really: just dropped into the oily bilge under the engine, where, even though Pete soon discovered where it would be, it was safe because he refused to thrust his hand and arm into the oil-fouled water but instead merely lay about the cockpit, sulking); taking the launch across Pontchartrain and down the Rigolets out to the Gulf, the Sound, then lying-to with no lights showing until the Coast Guard cutter (it ran almost on schedule; theirs was a job too even if it was, comparatively speaking, a hopeless one) made its fast haughty eastward rush, going, they always like to believe, to Mobile, to a dance, then by compass on to the island (it was little more than a sandspit bearing a line of ragged and shabby pines thrashing always in the windy crash and roar of the true Gulf on the other side of it) where the Caribbean schooner would bury the casks of green alcohol which the bootlegger's mother back in New Orleans would convert and bottle and label into scotch or bourbon or gin. There were a few wild cattle on the island which they would have to watch for, the Negro digging and Pete still sulking and refusing to help at all because of the pistol, and the captain watching for the charge (they couldn't risk showing a light) which every three or four trips would come—the gaunt wild half-seen shapes charging suddenly and with no warning down at them as they turned and ran through the nightmare sand and hurled themselves into the dinghy, to pull along parallel to the shore, the animals following, until they had tolled them far enough away for the Negro to go back ashore for the remaining casks. Then they would heave-to again and lie until the cutter passed back westward, the dance obviously over now, in the same haughty and imperious rush.

That was Mississippi too, though a different one from where the child had been bred; the people were Catholics, the Spanish and French blood still showed in the names and faces. But it was not a deep one, if you did not count the sea and the boats on it: a curve of beach, a thin unbroken line of estates and apartment hotels owned and inhabited by Chicago millionaires, standing back to back with another thin line, this time of tenements inhabited by Negroes and whites who ran the boats and worked in the fish-processing plants.

Then the Mississippi which the young man knew began: the fading purlieus inhabited by a people whom the young man recognised because their like was in his country too: descendants, heirs at least in spirit, of the tall men, who worked in no factories and farmed no land nor even truck patches, living not out of the earth but on its denizens: fishing guides and individual professional fishermen, trappers of muskrats and alligator hunters and poachers of deer, the land rising now, once more earth instead of half water, vista-ed and arras-ed with the long leaf pines which northern capital would convert into dollars in Ohio and Indiana and Illinois banks. Though not all of it. Some of it would alter hamlets and villages into cities and even build whole new ones almost overnight, cities with Mississippi names but patterned on Ohio and Indiana and Illinois because they were bigger than Mississippi towns, rising, standing today among the tall pines which created them, then tomorrow (that quick, that fast, that rapid) among the stumpy pockage to which they were monuments. Because the land had made its one crop: the soil too fine and light to compete seriously in cotton: until people discovered that it would grow what other soils would not: the tomatoes and strawberries and the fine cane for sugar: not the sorghum of the northern and western counties which people of the true cane country called hog-feed, but the true sweet cane which made the sugar house molasses.

Big towns, for Mississippi: cities, we called them: Hattiesburg, and Laurel, and Meridian, and Canton; and towns deriving by name from further away than Ohio: Kosciusko named after a Polish general who thought that people should be free who wanted to be, and Egypt because there was corn there when it was nowhere else in the bad lean times of the old war which the old women had still never surrendered, and Philadelphia where the Neshoba Indians whose name the county bears still remain for the simple reason that they did not mind living in peace with other people, no matter what their color or politics. This was the hills now: Jones County which old Newt Knight, its principal proprietor and first citizen or denizen, whichever you liked, seceded from the Confederacy in 1862, establishing still a third republic within the boundaries of the United States until a Confederate military force subdued him in his embattled log-castle capital; and Sullivan's Hollow: a long narrow glen where a few clans or families with North Ireland and Highland names feuded and slew one another in the old pre-Culloden fashion yet banding together immediately and always to resist any outsider in the pre-Culloden fashion too: vide the legend of the revenue officer hunting illicit whiskey stills, captured and held prisoner in a stable and worked in traces as the pair to a plow-mule. No Negro ever let darkness catch him in Sullivan's Hollow. In fact, there were few Negroes in this country at all: a narrow strip of which extended up into the young man's own section: a remote district there through which Negroes passed infrequently and rapidly and only by daylight.

It is not very wide, because almost at once there begins to the east of it the prairie country which sheds its water into Alabama and Mobile Bay, with its old tight intermarried towns and plantation houses columned and porticoed in the traditional Georgian manner of Virginia and Carolina in place of the Spanish and French influence of Natchez. These towns are Columbus and Aberdeen and West Point and Shuqualak, where the good quail shooting is and the good bird dogs are bred and trained—horses too: hunters; Dancing Rabbit is here too, where the treaty dispossessing them of Mississippi was made between the Choctaws and the United States; and in one of the towns lived a kinsman of the young man, dead now, rest him: an invincible and incorrigible bachelor, a leader of cotillions and an inveterate diner-out since any time an extra single man was needed, any hostess thought of him first.

But he was a man's man too, and even more: a young man's man, who played poker and matched glasses with the town's young bachelors and the apostates still young enough in time to still resist the wedlock; who walked not only in spats and a stick and yellow gloves and a Homburg hat, but an air of sardonic and inviolable atheism too, until at last he was forced to the final desperate resort of prayer: sitting after supper one night among the drummers in the row of chairs on the sidewalk before the Gilmer Hotel, waiting to see what (if anything) the evening would bring, when two of the young bachelors passing in a Model T Ford stopped and invited him to drive across the line into the Alabama hills for a gallon of moonshine whiskey. Which they did. But the still they sought was not in hills because these were not hills: it was the dying tail of the Appalachian mountain range. But since the Model T's engine had to be running fast anyway for it to have any headlights, going up the mountain was an actual improvement, especially after they had to drop to low gear. And coming from the generation before the motor car, it never occurred to him that coming back down would be any different until they got the gallon and had a drink from it and turned around and started back down. Or maybe it was the whiskey, he said, telling it: the little car rushing faster and faster behind a thin wash of light of about the same volume that two lightning bugs would have made, around the plunging curves which, the faster the car ran, became

only the more frequent and sharp and plunging, whipping around
the nearly right-angle bends with a rock wall on one hand and several hundred feet of vertical and empty night on the other, until at
last he prayed; he said: 'Lord, You know I haven't worried You in
over forty years, and if You'll just get me back to Columbus I promise never to bother You again.'

And now the young man, middleaged now or anyway middleaging, is back home too where they who altered the swamps and forests
of his youth, have now altered the face of the earth itself; what he
remembered as dense river bottom jungle and rich farm land, is now
an artificial lake twenty-five miles long: a flood control project for the
cotton fields below the huge earth dam, with a few more outboard-
powered fishing skiffs on it each year, and at last a sailboat. On his
way in to town from his home the middleaging (now a professional
fiction-writer: who had wanted to remain the tramp and the possessionless vagabond of his young manhood but time and success and
the hardening of his arteries had beaten him) man would pass the
back yard of a doctor friend whose son was an undergraduate at Harvard. One day the undergraduate stopped him and invited him in
and showed him the unfinished hull of a twenty-foot sloop, saying,
'When I get her finished, Mr Bill, I want you to help me sail her.'
And each time he passed after that, the undergraduate would repeat: 'Remember, Mr Bill, I want you to help me sail her as soon as I
get her in the water:' to which the middleaging would answer as always: 'Fine, Arthur. Just let me know.'

Then one day he came out of the postoffice: a voice called him
from a taxicab, which in small Mississippi towns was any motor car
owned by any footloose young man who liked to drive, who decreed
himself a taxicab as Napoleon decreed himself emperor; in the car
with the driver was the undergraduate and a young man whose
father had vanished recently somewhere in the West out of the ruins
of the bank of which he had been president, and a fourth young man
whose type is universal: the town clown, comedian, whose humor is
without viciousness and quite often witty and always funny. 'She's in
the water, Mr Bill,' the undergraduate said. 'Are you ready to go
now?' And he was, and the sloop was too; the undergraduate had
sewn his own sails on his mother's machine; they worked her out into

the lake and got her on course all tight and drawing, when suddenly it seemed to the middleaging that part of him was no longer in the sloop but about ten feet away, looking at what he saw: a Harvard undergraduate, a taxi-driver, the son of an absconded banker and a village clown and a middleaged novelist sailing a home-made boat on an artificial lake in the depths of the north Mississippi hills: and he thought that that was something which did not happen to you more than once in your life.

Home again, his native land; he was born of it and his bones will sleep in it; loving it even while hating some of it: the river jungle and the bordering hills where still a child he had ridden behind his father on the horse after the bobcat or fox or coon or whatever was ahead of the belling hounds and where he had hunted alone when he got big enough to be trusted with a gun, now the bottom of a muddy lake being raised gradually and steadily every year by another layer of beer cans and bottle caps and lost bass plugs—the wilderness, the two weeks in the woods, in camp, the rough food and the rough sleeping, the life of men and horses and hounds among men and horses and hounds, not to slay the game but to pursue it, touch and let go, never satiety—moved now even further away than that down the flat Delta so that the mile-long freight trains, visible for miles across the fields where the cotton is mortgaged in February, planted in May, harvested in September and put into the Farm Loan in October in order to pay off February's mortgage in order to mortgage next year's crop, seem to be passing two or even three of the little Indian-named hamlets at once over the very ground where, a youth now capable of being trusted even with a rifle, he had shared in the yearly ritual of Old Ben: the big old bear with one trap-ruined foot who had earned for himself a name, a designation like a living man through the legend of the deadfalls and traps he had wrecked and the hounds he had slain and the shots he had survived, until Boon Hogganbeck, the youth's father's stable foreman, ran in and killed it with a hunting knife to save a hound which he, Boon Hogganbeck, loved.

But most of all he hated the intolerance and injustice: the lynching of Negroes not for the crimes they committed but because their skins were black (they were becoming fewer and fewer and soon there would be no more of them but the evil would have been done and irrevocable because there should never have been any); the inequality: the poor schools they had then when they had any, the hovels they had to live in unless they wanted to live outdoors: who could worship the white man's God but not in the white man's church; pay taxes in the white man's courthouse but couldn't vote in it or for it; working by the white man's clock but having to take his pay by the white man's counting (Captain Joe Thoms, a Delta planter though not one of the big ones, who after a bad crop year drew a thousand silver dollars from the bank and called his five tenants one by one into the dining room where two hundred of the dollars were spread carelessly out on the table beneath the lamp, saying: 'Well, Jim, that's what we made his year.' Then the Negro: 'Gret God, Cap'n Joe, is all that mine?' And Captain Thoms: 'No no, just half of it is yours. The other half belongs to me, remember.'); the bigotry which could send to Washington some of the senators and congressmen we sent there and which could erect in a town no bigger than Jefferson five separate denominations of churches but set aside not one square foot of ground where children could play and old people could sit and watch them.

But he loves it, it is his, remembering: the trying to, having to, stay in bed until the crack of dawn would bring Christmas and of the other times almost as good as Christmas; of being waked at three oclock to have breakfast by lamplight in order to drive by surrey into town and the depot to take the morning train for the three or four days in Memphis where he would see automobiles, and the day in 1910 when, twelve years old, he watched John Moissant land a bicycle-wheeled aileronless (you warped the whole wing-tip to bank it or hold it level) Bleriot monoplane on the infield of the Memphis race-track and knew forever after that someday he too would have to fly alone; remembering: his first sweetheart, aged eight, plump and honey-haired and demure and named Mary, the two of them sitting side by side on the kitchen steps eating ice cream; and another one, Minnie this time, grand-daughter of the old hillman from whom, a man himself now, he bought moonshine whiskey, come to town at seventeen to take a job behind the soda counter of the drug store, watching her virginal and innocent and without self-consciousness pour Coca-Cola syrup into the lifted glass by hooking her thumb through the ring of the jug and swinging it back and up in one unbroken motion onto her horizontal upper arm exactly as he had seen her grandfather pour whiskey from a jug a thousand times.

Even while hating it, because for every Joe Thoms with two hundred silver dollars and every Snopes in a hooded nightshirt, somewhere in Mississippi there was this too: remembering: Ned, born in a cabin in the back yard in 1865, in the time of the middleaged's great-grandfather and had outlived three generations of them, who had not only walked and talked so constantly for so many years with the three generations that he walked and talked like them, he had two tremendous trunks filled with the clothes which they had worn—not only the blue brass-buttoned frock coat and the plug hat in which he had been the great-grandfather's and the grandfather's coachman, but the broadcloth frock coats which the great-grandfather himself had worn, and the pigeon-tailed ones of the grandfather's time and the short coat of his father's which the middleaged could remember on the backs for which they had been tailored, along with the hats in their eighty years of mutation too: so that, glancing idly up and out the library window, the middleaged would see that back, that stride, that coat and hat going down the drive toward the road, and his heart would stop and even turn over. He (Ned) was eighty-four now and in these last few years he had begun to get a little mixed up, calling the middleaged not only 'Master' but sometimes 'Master Murry', who was the middleaged's father, and 'Colonel' too, coming once a week through the kitchen and in to the parlor or perhaps already found there, saying: 'Here's where I wants to lay, right here where I can be facing out that window. And I wants it to be a sunny day, so the sun can come in on me. And I wants you to preach the sermon. I wants you to take a dram of whiskey for me, and lay yourself back and preach the best sermon you ever preached.'

And Caroline too, whom the middleaged had inherited too in his hierarchial turn, nobody knowing anymore exactly how many more years than a hundred she was but not mixed up, she: who had forgotten nothing, calling the middleaged 'Memmy' still, from fifty-odd years ago when that was as close as his brothers could come to 'William'; his youngest daughter, aged four and five and six, coming in to the house and saying, 'Pappy, Mammy said to tell you not to forget you owe her eighty-nine dollars.'

'I wont,' the middleaged would say. 'What are you all doing now?'

'Piecing a quilt,' the daughter answered. Which they were. There was electricity in her cabin now, but she would not use it, insisting still on the kerosene lamps which she had always known. Nor would she use the spectacles either, wearing them merely as an ornament across the brow of the immaculate white cloth—head-rag—which bound her now hairless head. She did not need them: a smolder of wood ashes on the hearth winter and summer in which sweet potatoes roasted, the five-year-old white child in a miniature rocking chair at one side of it and the aged Negress, not a greal deal larger, in her chair at the other, the basket bright with scraps and fragments of cloth between them and in that dim light in which the middleaged himself could not have read his own name without his glasses, the two of them with infinitesimal and tedious and patient stitches annealing the bright stars and squares and diamonds into another pattern to be folded away among the cedar shavings in the trunk.

Then it was the Fourth of July, the kitchen was closed after breakfast so the cook and houseman could attend a big picnic; in the middle of the hot morning the aged Negress and the white child gathered green tomatoes from the garden and ate them with salt, and that afternoon beneath the mulberry tree in the back yard the two of them ate most of a fifteen-pound chilled watermelon, and that night Caroline had the first stroke. It should have been the last, the doctor thought so too. But by daylight she had rallied, and that morning the generations of her loins began to arrive, from her own seventy and eighty year old children, down through their great- and twice-great-grandchildren—faces which the middleaged had never seen before until the cabin would no longer hold them: the women and girls sleeping on the floor inside and the men and boys sleeping on the ground in front of it, Caroline herself conscious now and presently sitting up in the bed: who had forgotten nothing: matriarchial and imperial, and more: imperious: ten and even eleven oclock at night and the middleaged himself undressed and in bed, reading, when sure enough he would hear the slow quiet stockinged or naked feet mounting the back stairs; presently the strange dark face—never the same one of two nights ago or the two or three nights before that—would look in the door at him, and the quiet, courteous, never servile voice would say: 'She want the ice cream.' And he would rise and dress and drive in to the village; he would even drive through the village although he knew that everything there will have long been closed and he would do what he had done two nights ago: drive thirty miles on to the arterial highway and then up or down it until he found an open drive-in or hot-dog stand to sell him the quart of ice cream.

But that stroke was not the one; she was walking again presently, even, despite the houseman's standing order to forestall her with the automobile, all the way in to town to sit with his, the middleaging's, mother, talking, he liked to think, of the old days of his father and himself and the three younger brothers, the two of them two women who together had never weighed two hundred pounds in a house roaring with five men: though they probably didn't since women, unlike men, have learned how to live uncomplicated by that sort of sentimentality. But it was as if she knew herself that the summer's stroke was like the throat-clearing sound inside the grandfather clock preceding the stroke of midnight or of noon, because she never touched the last unfinished quilt again. Presently it had vanished, no one knew where, and as the cold came and the shortening days she began to spend more and more time in the house, not her cabin but the big house, sitting in a corner of the kitchen while the cook and houseman were about, then in the middleaging's wife's sewing room until the family gathered for the evening meal, the houseman carrying her rocking chair into the dining room to sit there while they ate: until suddenly (it was almost Christmas now) she insisted on sitting in the parlor until the meal was ready, none knew why, until at last she told them, through the wife: 'Miss Hestelle, when them niggers lays me out, I want you to make me a fresh clean cap and apron to lay in.' That was her valedictory; two days after Christmas the stroke came which was the one; two days after that she lay in the parlor in the fresh cap and apron she would not see, and the middleaging did indeed lay back and preach the sermon, the oration, hoping that when his turn came there would be someone in the world to owe him the sermon which all owed to her who had been, as he had been from infancy, within the scope and range of that fidelity and that devotion and that rectitude.

Loving all of it even while he had to hate some of it because he knows now that you dont love because: you love despite; not for the virtues, but despite the faults.

(1909–)

Eudora Welty

The most distinguished of living literary Mississippians, Eudora Welty was born April 13, 1909, in Jackson, and has lived there all her life. She attended Central High School and Mississippi State College for Women before taking her final two years of college, and a B.A., at the University of Wisconsin, and did graduate work in advertising at the Columbia University School of Business. Returning to Jackson in 1931 she went to work part-time for radio station WJDX, and wrote the Jackson Society column for the Memphis *Commercial Appeal.* During the mid-30s she traveled the state for the WPA, taking photographs and writing newspaper copy for local and county weeklies; this job, she has said, "let me get about the State and gave me an honorable reason to talk to people in all sorts of jobs." For a year following the WPA job she worked for the Mississippi Advertising Commission. During all this activity she had been seriously writing fiction; her first published story, "Death of a Travelling Salesman," was published in 1936. In 1941 her first book, *A Curtain of Green,* appeared, to high critical, and some commercial, success, and in the years since she has written, simply, some of the best short stories in the language. She has received numerous awards for her work, including several O. Henry Prizes for her stories, the William Dean Howells award for "the

221

most distinguished work of American fiction" for the period 1950–1955
(for *The Ponder Heart*, 1954), and the Pulitzer Prize, in 1973, for *The Optimist's Daughter* (1972).

Welty is by any standard one of the handful of literary geniuses this country has produced; few American writers have produced work of so consistently high a quality. Her fiction is frequently anthologized, and generally well known; so we have chosen to represent her here by two pieces of nonfiction. The first, "Some Notes on River Country," was originally published in *Harper's Bazaar* in 1944, was slightly revised and collected in Welty's recent *The Eye of the Story* (1978), from which we take our text; the little-known "Women!! Make Turbans in Own Home!" is strictly *sui generis*, a wonderful example of Welty's comic brilliance. It was published in the *Junior League Magazine* in November, 1941.

Some Notes on River Country

A PLACE THAT EVER WAS LIVED IN is like a fire that never goes out. It flares up, it smolders for a time, it is fanned or smothered by circumstance, but its being is intact, forever fluttering within it, the result of some original ignition. Sometimes it gives out glory, sometimes its little light must be sought out to be seen, small and tender as a candle flame, but as certain.

I have never seen, in this small section of old Mississippi River country and its little chain of lost towns between Vicksburg and Natchez, anything so mundane as ghosts, but I have felt many times there a sense of place as powerful as if it were visible and walking and could touch me.

The clatter of hoofs and the bellow of boats have gone, all old communications. The Old Natchez Trace has sunk out of use; it is deep in leaves. The river has gone away and left the landings. Boats from Liverpool do not dock at these empty crags. The old deeds are done, old evil and old good have been made into stories, as plows turn up the river bottom, and the wild birds fly now at the level where people on boat deck once were strolling and talking of great expanding things, and of chance and money. Much beauty has gone, many little things of life. To light up the nights there are no mansions, no celebrations. Just as, when there were mansions and celebrations, there were no more festivals of an Indian tribe there; before the music, there were drums.

But life does not forsake any place. People live still in Rodney's Landing; flood drives them out and they return to it. Children are born there and find the day as inexhaustible and as abundant as they run and wander in their little hills as they, in innocence and rightness, would find it anywhere on earth. The seasons come as truly, and give gratefulness, though they bring little fruit. There is a sense of place there, to keep life from being extinguished, like a cup of the hands to hold a flame.

To go there, you start west from Port Gibson. This was the frontier of the Natchez country. Postmen would arrive here blowing their tin horns like Gabriel where the Old Natchez Trace crosses the Bayou Pierre, after riding three hundred wilderness miles from Tennessee, and would run in where the tavern used to be to deliver their mail, change their ponies, and warm their souls with grog. And up this now sand-barred bayou trading vessels would ply from the river. Port Gibson is on a highway and a railroad today, and lives on without its river life, though it is half diminished. It is still rather smug because General Grant said it was "too pretty to burn." Perhaps it was too pretty for any harsh fate, with its great mossy trees and old camellias, its exquisite little churches, and galleried houses back in the hills overlooking the cotton fields. It has escaped what happened to Grand Gulf and Bruinsburg and Rodney's Landing.

A narrow gravel road goes into the West. You have entered the loess country, and a gate might have been shut behind you for the difference in the world. All about are hills and chasms of cane, forests of cedar trees, and magnolia. Falling away from your road, at times merging with it, an old trail crosses and recrosses, like a tunnel through the dense brakes, under arches of branches, a narrow, cedar-smelling trace the width of a horseman. This road joined the Natchez Trace to the river. It, too, was made by buffaloes, then used by man, trodden lower and lower, a few inches every hundred years.

Loess has the beautiful definition of aeolian—wind-borne. The loess soil is like a mantle; the ridge was laid down here by the wind, the bottom land by the water. Deep under them both is solid blue clay, embalming the fossil horse and the fossil ox and the great mastodon, the same preserving blue clay that was dug up to wrap the head of the Big Harp in bandit days, no less a monstrous thing when it was carried in for reward.

Loess exists also in China, that land whose plants are so congenial to the South; there the bluffs rise vertically for five hundred feet in some places and contain cave dwellings without number. The Mississippi bluffs once served the same purpose; when Vicksburg was being shelled from the river during the year's siege there in the War Between the States, it was the daily habit of the three thousand women, children and old men who made up the wartime population to go on their all-fours into shelters they had tunneled into the loess bluffs. Mark Twain reports how the Federal soldiers would shout from the river in grim humor, "Rats, to your holes!"

Winding through this land unwarned, rounding to a valley, you will come on a startling thing. Set back in an old gray field, with horses grazing like small fairy animals beside it, is a vast ruin—twenty-two Corinthian columns in an empty oblong and an L. Almost seeming to float like lace, bits of wrought-iron balcony connect them here and there. Live cedar trees are growing from the iron black acanthus leaves, high in the empty air. This is the ruin of Windsor, long since burned. It used to have five stories and an observation tower—Mark Twain used the tower as a sight when he was pilot on the river.

Immediately the cane and the cedars become more impenetrable, the road ascends and descends, and rather slowly, because of the trees and shadows, you realize a little village is before you. Grand Gulf today looks like a scene in Haiti. Under enormous dense trees where the moss hangs long as ladders, there are hutlike buildings and pale whitewashed sheds; most of the faces under the straw hats are black, and only narrow jungly paths lead toward the river. Of course this is not Grand Gulf in the original, for the river undermined that and pulled it whole into the river—the opposite of what it did to Rodney's Landing. A little corner was left, which the Federals burned, all but a wall, on their way to Vicksburg. After the war the population built it back—and the river moved away. Grand Gulf was a British settlement before the Revolution and had close connection with England, whose ships traded here. It handled more cotton than any other port in Mississippi for about twenty years. The old cemetery is there still, like a roof of marble and moss overhanging the town and about to tip into it. Many names of British gentry stare out from the stones, and the biggest snakes in the world must have their kingdom in that dark-green tangle.

Two miles beyond, at the end of a dim jungle track where you can walk, is the river, immensely wide and vacant, its bluff occupied sometimes by a casual camp of fishermen under the willow trees, where dirty children playing about and nets drying have a look of timeless roaming and poverty and sameness . . . By boat you can reach a permanent fishing camp, inaccessible now by land. Go till you find the hazy shore where the Bayou Pierre, dividing in two, reaches around the swamp to meet the river. It is a gray-green land, softly flowered, hung with stillness. Houseboats will be tied there among the cypresses under falls of the long moss, all of a color. Aaron Burr's "flotilla" tied up there, too, for this is Bruinsburg Landing, where the boats were seized one wild day of apprehension. Bruinsburg grew to be a rich, gay place in cotton days. It is almost as if a wand had turned a noisy cotton port into a handful of shanty boats. Yet Bruinsburg Landing has not vanished: it is this.

Wonderful things have come down the current of this river, and more spectacular things were on the water than could ever have sprung up on shores then. Every kind of treasure, every kind of bearer of treasure has come down, and armadas and flotillas, and the most frivolous of things, too, and the most pleasure-giving of people.

Natchez, downstream, had a regular season of drama from 1806 on, attended by the countryside—the only one in English in this part of the world. The plays would be given outdoors, on a strip of grass on the edge of the high bluff overlooking the landing. With the backdrop of the river and the endless low marsh of Louisiana beyond, some version of Elizabethan or Restoration comedy or tragedy would be given, followed by a short farcical afterpiece, and the traveling company would run through a little bird mimicry, ventriloquism and magical tricks in-between. Natchez, until lately a bear-baiting crowd, watched eagerly "A Laughable Comedy in 3

Acts written by Shakespeare and Altered by Garrick called Catherine & Petrucio," followed by "A Pantomime Ballet Called a Trip through the Vauxhall Gardens into which is introduced the humorous song of Four and Twenty Fiddlers concluding with a dance by the characters." Or sometimes the troupe would arrive with a program of "divertisements"—recitations of Lochinvar, Alexander's Feast, Cato's Soliloquy of the Soul, and Clarence's Dream, interspersed with Irish songs by the boys sung to popular requests and concluding with "A Laughable Combat between Two Blind Fiddlers."

The Natchez country took all this omnivorously to its heart. There were rousing, splendid seasons, with a critic writing pieces in the newspaper to say that last night's Juliet spoke just a *bit* too loudly for a girl, though Tybalt kept in perfect character to delight all, even after he was dead—signed "X.Y.Z."

But when the natural vigor of the day gave clamorous birth to the minstrel show, the bastard Shakespeare went; and when the showboat really rounded the bend, the theatre of that day, a child of the plantation and the river, came to its own. The next generation heard calliopes filling river and field with their sound, and saw the dazzling showboats come like enormous dreams up the bayous and the little streams at floodtime, with whole French Zouave troops aboard, whole circuses with horses jumping through paper hoops, and all the literal rites of the minstrel show, as ever true to expectations as a miracle play.

Now if you pick up the Rodney Road again, through twenty miles of wooded hills, you wind sharply round, the old sunken road ahead of you and following you. Then from a great height you descend suddenly through a rush of vines, down, down, deep into complete levelness, and there in a strip at the bluff's foot, at the road's end, is Rodney's Landing.

Though you walk through Rodney's Landing, it long remains a landscape, rather than a center of activity, and seems to exist altogether in the sight, like a vision. At first you think there is not even sound. The thick soft morning shadow of the bluff on the valley floor, and the rose-red color of the brick church which rises from this shadow, are its dominant notes—all else seems green. The red of the bricks defies their element; they were made of earth, but they glow as if to remind you that there is fire in earth. No one is in sight.

Eventually you see people, of course. Women have little errands, and the old men play checkers at a table in front of the one open store. And the people's faces are good. Theirs seem *actually* the faces your eyes look for in city streets and never see. There is a middle-aged man who always meets you when you come. He is like an embodiment of the simplicity and friendliness not of the mind— for his could not teach him—but of the open spirit. He never remembers you, but he speaks courteously. "I am Mr. John David's boy—where have you come from, and when will you have to go back?" He has what I have always imagined as a true Saxon face, like a shepherd boy's, light and shy and set in solitude. He carries a staff, too, and stands with it on the hill, where he will lead you—looking with care everywhere and far away, warning you of the steep stile . . . The river is not even in sight here. It is three miles beyond, past the cotton fields of the bottom, through a dense miasma of swamp.

The houses merge into a shaggy fringe at the foot of the bluff. It is like a town some avenging angel has flown over, taking up every second or third house and leaving only this. There are more churches than houses now; the edge of town is marked by a little wooden Catholic church tiny as a matchbox, with twin steeples carved like icing, over a stile in a flowery pasture. The Negro Baptist church, weathered black with a snow-white door, has red hens in the yard. The old galleried stores are boarded up. The missing houses were burned—they were empty, and the little row of Negro inhabitants have carried them off for firewood.

You know instinctively as you stand here that this shelf of forest is the old town site, and you find that here, as in Grand Gulf, the cemetery has remained as the roof of the town. In a mossy wood the graves, gently tended here, send up mossy shafts, with lilies flowering in the gloom. Many of the tombstones are marked "A Native of Ireland," though there are German names and graves neatly bordered with sea shells and planted in spring-flowering bulbs. People in Rodney's Landing won silver prizes in the fairs for their horses; they planted all this land; some of them were killed in battle, some in duels fought on a Grand Gulf sand bar. The girls who died young of the fevers were some of them the famous "Rodney heiresses." All Mississippians know decendants of all the names. I looked for the grave of Dr. Nutt, the man who privately invented and used his cotton gin here, previous to the rest of the world. The Petit Gulf cotton was known in England better than any other as superior to all cotton, and was named for the little gulf in the river at this landing, and Rodney, too, was once called Petit Gulf.

Down below, Mr. John David's boy opens the wrought-iron gate to the churchyard of the rose-red church, and you go up the worn, concave steps. The door is never locked, the old silver knob is always the heat of the hand. It is a church, upon whose calm interior nothing seems to press from the outer world, which, though calm itself here, is still "outer." (Even cannonballs were stopped by its strong walls, and are in them yet.) It is the kind of little church in which you might instinctively say prayers for your friends; how is it that both danger and succor, both need and response, seem intimately near in little country churches?

Something always hangs imminent above all life—usually claims of daily need, daily action, a prescribed course of movement, a schedule of time. In Rodney, the imminent thing is a natural danger—the town may be flooded by the river, and every inhabitant must take to the hills. Every house wears a belt of ineradicable silt around its upper walls. I asked the storekeeper what his store would be like after the river had been over it, and he said, "You know the way a fish is?" Life threatened by nature is simplified, most peaceful in present peace, quiet in seasons of waiting and readiness. There are rowboats under all the houses.

Even the women in sunbonnets disappear and nothing moves at noon but butterflies, little white ones, large black ones, and they are like some flutter of heat, some dervishes of the midday hour, as in pairs they rotate about one another, ascending and descending, appearing to follow each other up and down some swaying spiral staircase invisible in the dense light. The heat moves. Its ripples can be seen, like the ripples in some vertical river running between earth and sky. It is so still at noon. I was never there before the river left, to hear the thousand swirling sounds it made for Rodney's Landing, but could it be that its absence is so much missed in the life of sound here that a stranger would feel it? The stillness seems absolute, as the brightness of noon seems to touch the point of saturation. Here the noon sun does make a trance; here indeed at its same zenith it looked down on life sacrificed to it and was worshipped.

It is not strange to think that a unique nation among Indians lived in this beautiful country. The origin of the Natchez is still in mystery. But their people, five villages in the seventeeth century, were unique in this country and they were envied by the other younger nations—the Choctaws helped the French in their final dissolution. In Mississippi they were remnants surely of medievalism. They were proud and cruel, gentle-mannered and ironic, handsome, extremely tall, intellectual, elegant, pacific and ruthless. Fire, death, sacrifice formed the spirit of the Natchez' worship. They did not now, however, make war.

The women—although all the power was in their blood, and a Sun woman by rigid system married a low-caste Stinkard and bore a Sun child by him—were the nation's laborers still. They planted and they spun, they baked their red jugs for the bear oil, and when the men came from the forests, they would throw at the feet of their wives the tongues of the beasts they had shot from their acacia bows—both as a tribute to womanhood and as a command to the wives to go out and hunt on the ground for what they had killed, and to drag it home.

The town of Natchez was named after this nation, although the French one day, in a massacre for a massacre, slew or sent into slavery at Santo Domingo every one of its namesakes, and the history of the nation was done in 1773. The French amusedly regarded the Natchez as either *"sauvages"* or *"naturels, innocents."* They made many notes of their dress and quaint habits, made engravings of them looking like Cupids and Psyches, and handed down to us their rites and customs with horrified withholdings or fascinated repetitions. The women fastened their knee-length hair in a net of mulberry threads, men singed theirs short into a crown except for a lock over the left ear. They loved vermilion and used it delicately, men and women, the women's breasts decorated in tattooed designs by whose geometrics they strangely match ancient Aztec bowls. *"En été"* male and female wore a draped garment from waist to knee. *"En hyver"* they threw about them swan-feather mantles, made as carefully as wigs. For the monthly festivals the men added bracelets of skin polished like ivory, and thin disks of feathers went in each hand. They were painted fire-color, white puffs of down decorated their shorn heads, the one lock left to support the whitest feathers. As children, the Natchez wore pearls handed down by their ancestors—pearls which they had ruined by piercing them with fire.

The Natchez also laughed gently at the French. (Also they massacred them when they were betrayed by them.) Once a Frenchman asked a Natchez noble why these Indians would laugh at them, and the noble replied that it was only because the French were like geese when they talked—all clamoring at once. The Natchez never spoke except one at a time; no one was ever interrupted or contradicted; a visitor was always allowed the opening speech, and that after a rest in silence of fifteen or twenty minutes, to allow him to get his breath and collect his thoughts. (Women murmured or whispered; their game after labor was a silent little guessing game played with three sticks that could not disturb anyone.) But this same nation, when any Sun died, strangled his wife and a great company of loyal friends and ambitious Stinkards to attend him in death, and walked bearing his body over the bodies of strangled infants laid before him by their parents. A Sun once expressed great though polite astonishment that a certain Frenchman declined the favor of dying with him.

Their own sacrifices were great among them. When Iberville came, the Natchez had diminished to twelve hundred. They laid it to the fact that the fire had once been allowed to go out and that a profane fire burned now in its place. Perhaps they had prescience of their end—the only bit of their history that we really know.

Today Rodney's Landing wears the cloak of vegetation which has caught up this whole land for the third time, or the fourth, or the hundredth. There is something Gothic about the vines, in their structure in the trees—there are arches, flying buttresses, towers of vines, with trumpet flowers swinging in them for bells and staining their walls. And there is something of a warmer grandeur in their very abundance—stairways and terraces and whole hanging gardens of green and flowering vines, with a Babylonian babel of hundreds of creature voices that make up the silence of Rodney's Landing. Here are nests for birds and thrones for owls and trapezes for snakes, every kind of bower in the world. From earliest spring there is something, when garlands of yellow jasmine swing from tree to tree, in the woods aglow with dogwood and redbud, when the green is only a floating veil in the hills.

And the vines make an endless flourish in summer and fall. There are wild vines of the grape family, with their lilac and turquoise fruits and their green, pink and white leaves. Muscadine vines along the stream banks grow a hundred feet high, mixing their dull, musky, delicious grapes among the bronze grapes of the scuppernong. All creepers with trumpets and panicles of scarlet and yellow cling to the treetops. On shady stream banks hang lady's eardrops, fruits and flowers dangling pale jade. The passionflower puts its tendrils where it can, its strange flowers of lilac rays with their little white towers shining out, or its fruit, the maypop, hanging. Wild wistaria hangs its flowers like flower-grapes above reach, and the sweetness of clematis, the virgin's-bower which grows in Rodney, and of honeysuckle, must fill even the highest air. There is a vine that grows to great heights, with heart-shaped leaves as big and soft as summer hats, overlapping and shading everything to deepest jungle blue-green.

Ferns are the hidden floor of the forest, and they grow, too, in the trees, their roots in the deep of mossy branches.

All over the hills the beautiful white Cherokee rose trails its glossy dark-green leaves and its delicate luminous-white flowers. Foliage and flowers alike have a quality of light and dark as well as color in Southern sun, and sometimes a seeming motion like dancing due to the flicker of heat, and are luminous or opaque according to the time of day or the density of summer air. In early morning or in the light of evening they become translucent and ethereal, but at noon they blaze or darken opaquely, and the same flower may seem sultry or delicate in its being all according to when you see it.

It is not hard to follow one of the leapings of old John Law's mind, then, and remember how he displayed diamonds in the shop windows in France—during the organization of his Compagnie d'Occident—saying that they were produced in the cups of the wildflowers along the lower Mississippi. And the closer they grew to the river, the more nearly that might be true.

Deep in the swamps the water hyacinths make solid floors you could walk on over still black water, the Southern blue flag stands thick and sweet in the marsh. Lady's-tresses, greenish-white little orchids with spiral flowers and stems twisted like curls and braids, grow there, and so do nodding lady's-tresses. Water lilies float, and spider lilies rise up like little coral monsters.

The woods on the bluffs are the hardwood trees—dark and berried and flowered. The magnolia is the spectacular one with its heavy cups—they look as heavy as silver—weighing upon its aromatic, elliptical, black-green leaves, or when it bears its dense pink cones. I remember an old botany book, written long ago in England, reporting the magnolia by hearsay, as having blossoms "so large as to be distinctly visible a mile or more—seen in the mass, we presume." But I tested the visibility power of the magnolia, and the single flower can be seen for several miles on a clear day. One magnolia cousin, the cucumber tree, has long sleevelike leaves and pale-green flowers which smell strange and cooler than the grandiflora flower. Set here and there in this country will be a mimosa tree, with its smell in the rain like a cool melon cut, its puffs of pale flowers settled in its sensitive leaves.

Perhaps the live oaks are the most wonderful trees in this land. Their great girth and their great spread give far more feeling of history than any house or ruin left by man. Vast, very dark, proportioned as beautifully as a church, they stand majestically in the wild or line old sites, old academy grounds. The live oaks under which Aaron Burr was tried at Washington, Mississippi, in this section, must have been old and impressive then, to have been chosen for such a drama. Spanish moss invariably hangs from the live oak branches, moving with the wind and swaying its long beards, darkening the forests; it is an aerial plant and strangely enough is really a pineapple, and consists of very, very tiny leaves and flowers, springy and dustily fragrant to the touch; no child who has ever "dressed up" in it can forget the sweet dust of its smell. It would be hard to think of things that happened here without the presence of these live oaks, so old, so expansive, so wonderful, that they might be sentient beings. W. H. Hudson, in his autobiography, *Far Away and Long Ago*, tells of an old man who felt reverentially toward the ancient trees of his great country house, so that each night he walked around his park to visit them one by one, and rest his hand on its bark to bid it goodnight, for he believed in their knowing spirits.

Now and then comes a report that an ivory-billed woodpecker is seen here. Audubon in his diary says the Indians began the slaughter of this bird long before Columbus discovered America, for the Southern Indians would trade them to the Canadian Indians—four buckskins for an ivory bill. Audubon studied the woodpecker here when he was in the Natchez country, where it lived in the deepest mossy swamps along the windings of the river, and he called it "the greatest of all our American woodpeckers and probably the finest in the world." The advance of agriculture rather than slaughter has really driven it to death, for it will not live except in a wild country.

This woodpecker used to cross the river "in deep undulations." Its notes were "clear, loud, and rather plaintive . . . heard at a considerable distance . . . and resemble the false high note of a clarinet." "Pait, pait, pait," Audubon translates it into his French-like sound. It made its nest in a hole dug with the ivory bill in a tree inclined in just a certain way—usually a black cherry. The holes went sometimes three feet deep, and some people thought they went spirally. The bird ate the grapes of the swampland. Audubon says it would hang by its claws like a titmouse on a grapevine and devour grapes by the bunch—which sounds curiously as though it knew it would be extinct before very long. This woodpecker also would destroy any dead tree it saw standing—chipping it away "to an extent of twenty or thirty feet in a few hours, leaping downward with its body . . . tossing its head to the right and left, or leaning it against the bark to ascertain the precise spot where the grubs were concealed, and immediately renewing its blows with fresh vigor, all the while sounding its loud notes, as if highly delighted." The males had beautiful crimson crests, the females were "always the most clamorous and the least shy." When caught, the birds would fight bitterly, and "utter a mournful and very piteous cry." All vanished now from the earth—the piteous cry and all; unless where Rodney's swamps are wild enough still, perhaps it is true, the last of the ivory-billed woodpeckers still exist in the world, in this safe spot, inaccessible to man.

Indians, Mike Fink the flatboatman, Burr, and Blennerhassett, John James Audubon, the bandits of the Trace, planters, and preachers—the horse fairs, the great fires—the battles of war, the arrivals of foreign ships, and the coming of floods: could not all these things still move with their true stature into the mind here, and their beauty still work upon the heart? Perhaps it is the sense of place that gives us the belief that passionate things, in some essence, endure. Whatever is significant and whatever is tragic in its story live as long as the place does, though they are unseen, and the new life will be built upon these things—regardless of commerce and the way of rivers and roads, and other vagrancies.

Women!! Make Turban in Own Home!

I HAVEN'T READ *Popular Mechanics* in years, but when I was a child it was the only magazine I ever would read. I used to keep it in the bottom of my desk, and read it at night.

How I ever got on to the magazine to begin with is a little puzzling. Ours was never a mechanically inclined family. It is more the musical type. Stringed instruments lie around on the sofas, but never tools. The nearest to being handy our men come is in playing golf, although one brother does take a pencil and fix up candidates' campaign photographs in the newspapers—he can make them look like chickens. As for my mother, she would no more have read *Popular Mechanics* than she would *Lady Chatterly's Lover*, and for the same reason. It is safe to say that the knee from which I got my first copy of this magazine was not hers, but our colored cook's. She was a laugher, and probably enjoyed looking at the pictures while she was working. I must have begged the magazine away from her, or even stolen it, because I craved paper-dolls. There are men paper-dolls in

Popular Mechanics. True, they are all busy; many of them are suspended or submerged, or strapped into something with only the eyes showing—hard to fold at the waist and pass for human on a chair. But any child with a shoe-box full of nothing but mothers and children can get desperate. The only men in the mail-order catalogue wore long underwear, smiled, and carried another pair. I think they still do. My choice was the man under water. In *Popular Mechanics,* besides these undersea men at 45-degree angles, and frowning inventors with spangled headlights on their foreheads, you could get standing-up men like Lionel Strongfort and Charles Atlas for fathers of your families. They had their measurements, with fractions, printed on dotted lines across them, I remember. They very nicely matched the mothers with pricemarks on their upper arms.

Once I had found out about *Popular Mechanics,* I went on and read it. I can remember turning the fragmentary pages, where I'd already cut out all the fathers, reading in a tense, disturbed way, generally during a thunderstorm. How well I remember the page, "Once It Was an Old Wash-Stand!!" What was? Don't ask me—but there was a change. Everything either was, or was going to be, something else. That was the thrill and the lure of *Popular Mechanics.* What would be made out of what next month? I couldn't wait. It really was a terrifying, rather Yankee philosophy I was being exposed to, there in secret. Nothing was ever let alone in *Popular Mechanics.* Nothing ever got old in the course of time or fell to pieces. The grim wits were always at work. You waited around with an auger. I read on and on, and acquired *Popular Mechanics* month after month, by whatever means was necessary.

Of course, all that time I never made a thing. As a matter of fact, I am singularly inept at all mechanical tasks. To me, all *things* are motivated and active enemies, and a stuck table drawer will always be more cunning than I am. But throughout my childhood, I was a constant mental handy-man. I could have fixed anything, and if I had ever wanted to, I could have made anything. I could have changed everything in the house hold into something else if I had wanted to, just like a witch. But I never did.

Maybe I had an instinct of what would happen to me, the very first time. If I were to make a ten-passenger pleasure boat out of our old china closet I'd get hell, even today. That word "spare time" (the condition attached to all the stunts) worried me, too. It meant you would have to get busy doing something else first, as a ruse to throw the family off; and I did not think I could fool them.

Maybe, too, I instinctively wondered if I would be happy in the end, after the transformation was all done. At about this same time, my grandfather sent me a very thick book: if I remember correctly the title was *101 Things Any Bright Girl Can Do*. I shied off from it until it was summer and I got poison ivy and was put to bed bandaged from head to toe. Then I told them to bring it to me. I read the book straight through, and mentally accomplished the 101 transformations with both rapidity and distaste. I told them to take it away and bring me *101 Things Any Bright Boy Can Do*, the companion volume, which had come to my brother, and I read that, in a sort of cold horror. That made 202 things done mentally during one day in bed with mittens on.

However, I was definitely haunted by *Popular Mechanics*, and I still am. Only a year ago, when I was ill and in a sulfanilamide dream, I sat up in bed and declared: "Nobody Lifts Anything—Nobody Sweats." That was another legend out of old *Popular Mechanics* —not a set of directions, of course, for, editorially, they wanted you to lift things and sweat, but an advertisement for something. How such a restful message ever crept into the magazine we'll never know: but I caught it. The true message of *Popular Mechanics* is: "You want something? You've got it." And that's like having a finger pointed at you. There's a feeling of guilt there somewhere; I still don't think it's a good idea to read things like that unless you have poison ivy. You haven't got this thing you want, such as a high dive for that home-made pool of yours, in its ultimate form, of course: it's your old fireless cooker. But in its lesser state, that high dive is right there looking at you, staring at you. In one more minute you are going to open a box of as horrible a set of tools as I have ever seen outside "The Return of Frankenstein," and work your head off.

It is to this lifelong haunt of *Popular Mechanics* that I lay my sudden decision of last winter to make a Hedy Lamarr turban. I was going to make it out of something in a trunk, and I was going to make it the hard way.

There was no reason for making a Hedy Lamarr turban, except that my hair had gotten too long and instead of getting it cut I wondered if I couldn't just hide it. As for making it the hard way, that is because I am Southern. We Southern women would not think of having a washing machine installed in the home, but we may at any moment descend (or ascend) to some form of heinous physical drudgery, emerging only to declare our prowess before falling flat. I don't know what causes this. We all do it. We are so proud of being able to do anything you might name. A prominent lifelong resident of my town once papered a room in one of these high-flown moods. It came to me to make a turban, and, because of *Popular Mechanics*, to make it out of something else.

When I opened the first trunk, looking for an old washstand cover or something, there was an old piece of monkey fur. Under that was a band of squirrel on a tunic, that could have been turned into a Daniel Boone hat, but that was too easy. I kept going through Spanish shawls, the saxophone arrangement of "My Sin," Confederate money, and the programs of everything from the "Rabbit's-Foot Minstrel" to "Shan Kar," until I found exactly the right thing, just as is supposed to happen to you in *Popular Mechanics*.

This was the front panel of a dress I bought in Lord & Taylor's Budget Shop. It was a maroon silk panel with a design of little keys. It came off a navy-blue dress—the girls who bought the rest like it on the rack and who read this, will remember. It was about 1932. Everybody who saw you said, "Look at the keys." I wonder if all these girls made turbans. Lord & Taylor had better read no further, but I will say here that the dress did not last through the trip to Mexico for which it was bought; nothing was left but the panel.

I was now ready to make a Hedy Lamarr turban from an old Lord & Taylor Budget Shop dress panel that came out of Mexico whole. But, how?

Talent, of course, is considered purely hereditary in these parts, and it was only too believable that none of my forbears had ever made a turban, or ever worn one except to show off and act funny. Without being a speck of kin to Hedy Lamarr. I therefore saw no use in the method of sitting down and just thinking up how a turban should be made. No telling what would happen. Besides, I wanted to do it the hard way. So the next time I was down town I dashed into a department store and went to the turban department.

I would never have known them. Without heads inside, turbans look utterly unconvincing, rather spurious. The clerk let me handle several, laid them across the palm of my hand, and watched my face, but all to no good. She could see that nothing came to me. The turban, as Hedy Lamarr wore it, remained an abstraction to me. With the clerk's sympathy, I finally had to buy one to take home and study by myself. She explained that she was wrapping up a blouse with the turban, made of the same material and attached to it. I had thought it part of the turban's tail, and that had added to my confusion.

"Comes with it, hon," said the clerk. "It's an inducement." She pointed to where you could break a thread and separate the things: but she said that *I* would have to be the one to do it. It was the religion of the store.

With that complication, a Javanese turban and its Siamese blouse, I almost quit. If only spring would come, I thought, I would call the whole morbid thing off.

Before taking the bought turban to pieces to see how it was made, I wore it awhile. It was not my real turban, of course, but it was a grand concealment for my hair, which was growing longer and longer. I had now, approaching the subject through some other angle, begun the Ogilvie Sisters' Home Treatment, with much brushing, extended through absent-mindedness and brooding, and I daresay the back hair was growing about an inch every other day during all this period.

I would look at the turban each time I put it on or took it off, and all I could safely say about it was that it was made either of two pieces of cloth partly sewed together, or of one piece of cloth partly split. It was completely impossible to tell what made it a turban. Then one day I took the panel and the bought turban and threw them together into a drawer, banged it shut, and left them awhile. Perhaps I thought the panel would turn into a turban by itself.

It was not until the night we had a real snow here, for the first time since I don't know when and everybody was running around outdoors in a kind of madness and exhilaration, that I actually started construction. I had come in from playing in the street, and wanted something to do before I went to bed. I'll make that turban, I thought with flashing eyes. After being out in a ten-inch snowfall, making a turban seemed one of the least far-fetched things I would ever do in my life. I snatched up the bought turban and took one squint at it, holding it up like a dead cat. And it all came to me like a flash. I didn't even have to take it to pieces to see how it was done. Any fool could make a turban, out of anything. I woke my mother up and asked her for the scissors.

"What on earth for, at this time of night?" she asked. "Are you going to cut your hair?" and she pressed them into my hand.

So in one instant, I whacked into the panel and cut out a turban. I must be kin to Lilly Daché. After that, all I had to do was sew on it a little. There was nothing to be dreaded about the process, no soldering or clamping in a vise, or standing and looking out of mounds of sawdust, as there always used to be in *Popular Mechanics*. You didn't even have to make it in a basement; you could make it in bed. I even thought of writing a little article to send *Popular Mechanics* on how to make a turban; but this is it.

Not that I finished the thing that night. It takes a good while to make a turban, at least working under a bed lamp and trying to keep quiet.

My brother noticed me late one night as I was hemming away in my spare time.

"What are you making?" he asked testily.

"Hedy Lamarr turban," I replied.

"Why don't you make a sarong?" he countered.

That could be made out of the bought turban, but I've put it away, in a trunk. I put my handwork away too. When I got through with it, it was tacky. It had ears. When I brushed my hair and put it on, I looked like a lady in *Popular Mechanics*, ready for goggles and a rocket ship. It served me right, I suppose, and all I can say is that I was haunted. But what with the snow melting and all, and the birds singing, I went down the next day and got a haircut and have been taking life easy ever since.

(1903–1954)

James Street

Though his canon consists of seventeen books, over thirty-five short stories, and nearly twenty articles in leading American magazines, James Street, born in Lumberton, Mississippi, on October 15, 1903, is internationally known as the author of the famous boy-and-his-dog story *The Biscuit Eater*. After a number of years spent in southern Mississippi as a hobo, soda jerk, and butcher, Street became the youngest Baptist preacher in the United States, then a reporter for the *Arkansas Gazette* in Little Rock. After working for the Associated Press, he became a reporter for the New York *American* and finally an editor for the the New York *World-Telegram*. In 1937, after acquiring $2500 for the sale of movie rights for his first story, "Nothing Sacred," he launched himself into a career of free-lance writing. He was a successful professional writer until his death of a heart attack in Chapel Hill, North Carolina, in September of 1954.

Street never considered himself a literary artist and did not believe in revising his work; he thought of himself as a professional entertainer with integrity. "No sale," he once wrote, "is worth a lie." He wrote out of his own background and experience, about country boys and dogs (*The Biscuit Eater, Goodbye, My Lady*), preachers (*The Gauntlet, The High Call*

240

ing), and southern Mississippi farmers (*In My Father's House*). But in Street's best work he combined the firsthand knowledge of a particular place, of its people and its legends, with painstaking historical research. Such a combination produced the five historical novels—*Oh, Promised Land, Tap Roots, By Valour and Arms, Tomorrow We Reap,* and *Mingo Dabney*—that depict the saga of the Dabney family in Lebanon, Mississippi, from 1794 to 1896, when Mingo Dabney leaves the state to fight with the insurrectionists in the Cuban Revolution. At the heart of these novels is the Mississippi land itself, which provides the continuity of the past and present. "The ground in which the dead rested," Street (with James Childers) wrote in *Tomorrow We Reap,* "was, in many ways, more important than the ground on which the living walked, for the pattern of yesterday was the covenant of the valley today and the pledge of tomorrow."

"The Biscuit Eater" is based on the text in *Saturday Evening Post,* May 13, 1939.

The Biscuit Eater

LONNIE SET THE GREASY BAG OF TABLE SCRAPS on a hummock of wire grass and leaned over the branch, burying his face in the cool water. He wiped his mouth with the back of his hand. Hundreds of black, frisky water bugs, aroused at his invasion of their playground, scooted to the middle of the stream, swerved as though playing follow-the-leader, and scooted back to the bank.

The boy laughed at their capers. Slowly, he stooped over the water. His hand darted as a cottonmouth strikes and he snatched one of the bugs and smelled it. There was a sharp, sugary odor on the bug.

"A sweet stinker, sure as my name is Lonnie McNeil," the boy muttered. If you caught a sweet stinker among water bugs, it meant good luck, maybe. Everybody knew that. Lonnie held the bug behind him, closed his eyes, tilted his head and whispered, to the pine trees, the branch, the wire grass and anything else in the silence that wanted to hear him and would never tell his wish: "I hope Moreover is always a good dog."

Then Lonnie put the bug back in the branch. It darted in circles for a second and skedaddled across the creek, making a beeline for the other bugs. There were tiny ripples in its wake. The boy grinned. He was in for some good luck. If the sweet stinker had changed its course, it would have broken the charm.

He picked up his bag of scraps, crossed the branch on a log and moseyed to the edge of the woods where the cleared land began. He pursed his lower lip and whistled the call of the catbird, watching the cabin in the field where Text lived with his mother, Aunt Charity, and her brood. Old Charity had a heap of young'uns, but Text was the last. She had listened to her preacher for days during protracted meetings, seeking a fit'n name for her man-child. And because the evangelist took text from this and text from that, she named him Text and reckoned it was a name that God approved. Or else the preacher wouldn't have used it so much.

Lonnie saw Text run to the rickety front gallery of the cabin and listen. He whistled again. Text answered and ran around the house, and a minute later he was racing across the field with a big, brooding dog at his heels. The white boy opened his arms and the dog ran to him and tried to lick his face.

Text said, "Hydee, Lon. Ol' Moreover is glad to see you, Me and him both."

Lonnie said, "Hi, Text. He looks slick as el-lem sap, don't he? Been working him?"

"A heap and whole lot," said Text. "Turned him loose in the wire grass yestiddy and he pointed two coveys 'fore I could say, 'Law 'a' mercy.' He's a prime superfine bird dawg, Lon. He ain't no no-count biscuit eater."

Lonnie, the son of Harve McNeil, and Text had been friends long before they had got the dog on a mine-and-yours basis, but now they were inseparable. Moreover, the dog, was community property between them, and their community was the piney woods of South Alabama, where Lonnie's father trained fine bird dogs for Mr. Ames. The dog had wiped away all class and race barriers between the two.

Moreover's mother had run in the Grand National trials up at Grand Junction, Tennessee—the world series for bird dogs. Then

Mr. Ames had sold her. Moreover's father was a good dog until he killed one of Mr. Eben's sheep, and was shot, according to the code of the piney woods. Harve knew the pup, the outcast of the litter, had a bad streak in him, but had tried to train him only because Lonnie loved the pup. And Lonnie loved him only because nobody else did.

Harve never had been able to get close to the dog's affections. There had been no feeling between them, no understanding. The pup had cowered at Lonnie's feet when Harve had ordered him into the fields to hunt. And when Harve had caught him sucking eggs, he had given him away to a Negro across the ridge.

"He's a suck-egg biscuit eater," Harve had told the Negro. A biscuit eater was an ornery dog. Everybody knew that. A biscuit eater wouldn't hunt anything except his biscuits and wasn't worth the salt in his feed.

The Negro had accepted the dog because he knew he could swap him. That night the dog had stolen eggs from the Negro's henhouse and the Negro had beaten him and called him a low-life biscuit eater. The dog had run under the cabin and sulked.

When Lonnie learned what his father had done with the outcast, he went to Text, and together they went over the ridge to bargain for the dog.

The Negro man was wily. He sensed a good bargain and was trader enough to know that if he low-rated the dog, the boys would want him more than ever. The dog had a cotton rope around his neck and the rope was fastened to a block, and when the dog walked, his head was pulled sideways as he tugged the block. The dog walked to Lonnie and rubbed against his legs. The boy ignored him. He mustn't let the Negro man know he really wanted the dog. The man grabbed the rope and jerked the dog away.

"He's a biscuit eater!" The Negro nudged the dog with his foot. The animal looked sideways at his master and slunk away. "He ain't worth much."

"He's a suck-egg biscuit eater, ain't he?" Lonnie asked. The dog watched him, and when the boy said "biscuit eater," the dog ran under the cabin, pulling the block behind him. "He's scared," Lonnie said. "You been beating him. And ever' time you jump him and you call him 'biscuit eater.' That's how come he's scared. Whatcha take for him?"

The man said, "Whatcha gimme?"

"I'll give you my frog-sticker." Lonnie showed his knife. "And I got a pretty good automobile tire. Ain't but one patch in it. It'd make a prime superfine swing for your young'uns."

The Negro asked Text, "What'll you chip in to boot?"

Text said, "You done cussed out the dawg so far I don't want no share of him. You done low-rated him too much. If he sucks eggs at my house, my maw'll bust me in two halves. Whatcha want to boot?"

"Whatcha got?"

"Nothin'," said Text, "cep'n two big hands what can tote a heap of wood. Tote your shed full of light'r knots for boot."

"What else?"

Text thought for a minute, weighing the deal. "Lon wants that dawg. I know where there's a pas'l of May haws and a honeybee tree."

The Negro man said, "It's a deal, boys, if'n you pick me a lard bucket full of May haws and show me the bee tree."

Lonnie took the block from the dog and led him across the field. Then Text led him awhile. Out of sight of the Negro's shack, the boys stopped and examined their possession.

Text ran his hand over the dog, smoothing the fur. "He's a good dawg, ain't he, Lon? Look at them big ol' eyes, and them big ol' feet, and that big ol' long tail. Bet he can point birds from here to yonder. Betcha if he tries, he can point partridge on light bread. What we gonna name him, Lon?"

Lonnie said, "Dunno, Text. But listen, don't ever call him—" He looked at the dog, then at Text. "You know." He held his fingers in the shape of a biscuit and pantomimed as though he were eating. The dog didn't understand. Neither did Text. So Lonnie whispered, "You know, 'biscuit eater.' Don't ever call him that. That's what's the matter with him. He expects a beating when he hears it."

"It's a go," Text whispered. "Let's name him Moreover. It's in the Bible."

"Where'bouts?"

"I heard the preacher say so. He said, 'Moreover, the dog,' and he was reading from the Bible."

Lonnie held the dog's chin with one hand and stroked his chest with the other. "He's Moreover then. He's a good dog, Text. And he's ours. You keep him and I'll furnish the rations. I can snitch 'em from papa. Will Aunt Charity raise Cain if you keep him?"

"Naw," said Text. "I 'member the time that big ol' brother of mine, ol' First-and-Second-Thessalonians, fetched a goat home, and maw didn't low-rate him. She just said she had so many young'uns, she didn't mind a goat. I spects she feels the same way 'bout a dawg, if'n he's got a Bible name."

"I reckon so too," said Lonnie, and ran home and told his father about the deal.

Harve told his son, "It's all right for you and Text to keep the dog, but keep him away from over here. I don't want him running around my good dogs."

Lonnie said, "He's a good dog, papa. He just ain't had no chance."

Harve looked at his son. The boy was growing, and the man was proud. "I'm going to work Silver Belle in the south forty," he said. "Want to come along?"

Lonnie shook his head. Harve knew then how much the boy loved his new dog; for, ordinarily, Lonnie would have surrendered any pleasure to accompany his father when he worked Silver Belle. She was the finest pointer in the Ames kennels and Harve had trained her since puppyhood. Already, she had won the Grand National twice. A third win would give his employer permanent possession of the Grand National trophy, and Harve wanted to win the prize for Mr. Ames more than he wanted anything in the world. He pampered Silver Belle. She was a small pointer—so small she had to wear a silver bell when hunting in the tall sage.

After his father and Silver Belle were gone, Lonnie collected the table scraps and went across the branch to Text's.

"Let's work him across the ridge today," Lonnie said. "Papa's got Silver Belle in the south forty and he won't want us and Moreover around."

Text said, "It's a go, Lon. I'll snitch ol' First-and-Second-Thessalonians' shotgun and meet you 'cross the ridge. But that there lan' over there is pow'ful close to Mr. Eben's place. I don't want no truck with that man."

"I ain't afraid of Mr. Eben," said Lonnie.

"Well, I am. And so are you! And so is your paw!"

"Papa is not afraid of anything, and I'll bust you in two halves if you say so."

"Then how come he didn't whup Mr. Eben when Mr. Eben kicked his dawg about two years ago?"

Negroes heard everything and forgot nothing. Everybody in the county had wondered why Harve McNeil hadn't thrashed Eben, when the farmer kicked one of the McNeil dogs without cause.

Lonnie was ashamed. He said, "Papa didn't whip Mr. Eben 'cause mother asked him not to, that's why."

"Lady folks sho' are buttinskies," Text said. "All time trying to keep men folks from whupping each other. Lady folks sho are scutters. All 'cept your maw and my maw, huh, Lon?"

Lonnie said, "Mr. Eben is just a crotchety man. Mother said so. He don't mean no harm."

"That's what you say," Text said. "But he's a scutter from way back. Maw says when he kills beeves he drinks the blood, and Ise popeyed scared of him. His lan' say, 'Posted. Keep Off. Law.' And I ain't messin' around over there."

Lonnie often had worked dogs with his father and had seen the best run at field trials. He began training Moreover by inspiring confidence in him. The big dog was clumsy, but Lonnie never upbraided him. When Moreover showed a streak of good traits, Lonnie and Text patted him. When he erred, they simply ignored him. The dog had a marvelous range, and moved through the saw grass at an easy gait, never tiring. He was not spectacular, but constant. He ran with a sort of awkward lope, twisting his head as though he still were tugging a block. But he covered ground. Day after day he trained and worked until the boys panted and stretched on the ground. Then he stood over them.

He had a strange point. He would cock his long head in the air, then turn it slowly toward Lonnie as he came to a point. His tail was like a ramrod. The first time Text shot over him, he cowered. The boys showed their displeasure by ignoring him. He soon was no longer gun-shy and he worked for the sheer joy of working.

"He sho is a good dawg," Text said.

They were working him that day across the ridge near Eben's farm and Moreover, trailing a huge covey, raced through the stubble and disappeared in the sage. When the boys found him he was frozen on a point far inside Farmer Eben's posted land. And watching Moreover from a pine thicket was Eben, a shotgun held loosely in the crook of his arm.

Text was terror-stricken and gaped at Eben as though the stubble-faced man were an ogre. Lonnie took one look at his dog, then at the man, and walked to the thicket. Text was in his shadow. "Please don't shoot him, Mr. Eben," Lonnie said.

The farmer said, "Huh?"

"Naw, suh, please don't shoot him." Text found his courage. "He couldn't read yo' posted sign."

Eben scowled. "I don't aim to shoot him. That is, less'n he gets round my sheep. I was watching his point. Right pretty, ain't it?"

Lonnie said, "Mighty pretty. He's a good dog, Mr. Eben. If ever you want a mess of birds, I'll give you the loan of him."

"Nothing shaking," Eben said. "He's that biscuit eater your paw gave that niggah over the ridge."

Text protested. "Don't go calling him biscuit eater, please, suh. He don't like it."

"He can't read my posted sign, but he can understand English, huh?" Eben laughed. "Well, get him off'n my land or I'll sprinkle him with bird shot."

Lonnie whistled and Moreover broke the point and followed him.

At supper, Lonnie asked his father, "How come you didn't whip Mr. Eben that time he kicked your dog?"

Harve said, "I've had my share of fighting, son. I don't fight for such foolishness any more. How come you ask?"

"Just 'cause," Lonnie said, and Harve knew his son wasn't satisfied with the reply. He frowned and glanced at his wife. He hadn't punished Eben simply because he didn't think the crime of kicking a dog justified a beating. There had been a time when he thought differently. But he was older now, and respected. He wondered if Lonnie thought he was afraid of Eben, and the thought bothered him.

"I wish we had the papers on Moreover," Lonnie changed the subject. "I want to register him."

Harve said. "I've got the papers, son. You can have 'em. What you gonna do, run your dog against my Belle in the county-seat trials?" He was joshing the boy.

"That's what I aim to do," Lonnie said.

The father laughed loudly, and his laughter trailed off into a chuckle. Lonnie enjoyed hearing his father laugh that way. "It's a great idea, son. So you have trained that biscuit eater for the trials! Where you going to get your entry fee?"

"He ain't no biscuit eater!" Lonnie said defiantly.

His mother was startled at his impudence to his father. But Harve shook his head at his wife and said, "'Course he ain't, son. I'm sorry. And just to show that me and Belle ain't scared of you and Moreover, I'll give you and Text the job of painting around the kennels. You can earn your entry fee. Is it a go?"

"Yes-sirree, bob," Lonnie stuffed food in his mouth and hurried through his meal. "I'm going to high-tail it over and tell Text and Moreover."

Harve walked down the front path with his son. The boy reached to his shoulders. It was nice to walk down the path with his son. The father said simply and in man's talk, "Maybe I'm batty to stake you and your dog to your entry fee. You might whip me and Belle, and Mr. Ames might give you my job of training his dogs."

Lonnie didn't reply. But at the gate he paused and faced his father. "Papa, you ain't scared of Mr. Eben, are you?"

The trainer leaned against the gate and lit his pipe. "Son," he said, "I ain't scared of nothing but God. But don't tell your mother."

Mr. Ames, the Philadelphia sportsman, sat on the steps of the gun-club lodge and laughed when he saw his truck coming up the driveway. His cronies, who had come to the county seat for the trials—a sort of a minor-league series—laughed too. Harve was driving. Silver Belle was beside him. Lonnie and Text were on the truck bed with dogs all around them, and behind the truck, tied with a cotton rope, loped Moreover. Mr. Ames shook hands with his trainer and met the boys.

"We got competition," Harve said, and nodded toward Moreover.

Ames studied the big dog. "By Joe, Harve! That used to be my dog. Is that the old bis——"

"Sh-h-h!" Harve commanded. "Don't say it. It hurts the dog's feelings. Or so the boys say."

Ames understood. He had a son at home. He walked around Moreover and looked at him. "Mighty fine dog, boys. . . . If he beats Belle, I might hire you, Lonnie, and fire your father." He winked at Harve, but the boys didn't see him.

They took Moreover to the kennels. They had fetched their own feed. Text ran to the kitchen of the lodge, and soon had a job doing kitchen chores. Moreover's rations were assured, and the best. Lonnie bedded his dog down carefully and combed him and tried to make him look spruce. But Moreover would not be spruce. There was a quizzical look in his eyes. The other dogs took attention as though they expected it, but Moreover rubbed his head along the ground and scratched his ears against the kennel box and mussed himself up as fast as Lonnie cleaned him. But he seemed to know that Lonnie expected something of him. All the other dogs were yelping and were nervous. But Moreover just flopped on his side and licked Lonnie's hands.

Inside the lodge, Ames asked Harve, "How's Belle?"

"Tiptop," said Harve. "She'll win hands down here, and I'm laying that she'll take the Grand National later. I'm gonna keep my boy with me, Mr. Ames. Text can stay with the help."

"What do those kids expect to do with that biscuit eater?" Ames laughed.

"You know how boys are. I'll bet this is the first time in history a colored boy and a white boy ever had a joint entry in a field trial. They get riled if anybody calls him a biscuit eater."

"Can't blame them, Harve," Ames said. "I get mad if anybody makes fun of my dogs. We are all alike, men and boys."

"You said it. Since the first, I reckon, boys have got mad if a fellow said anything against their mothers or dogs."

"Or fathers?" Ames suggested.

"Depends on the father," said Harve. "Wish Lonnie could take his dog to the quarter finals, or thereabouts. Do the boy a heap of good."

They were having a drink by the big fireplace. Ames said, "I hope that big brute is not in a brace with Belle. She's a sensitive dog." Then he laughed. "Be funny, Harve, if that dog whipped us. I'd run you bowlegged."

All the men laughed, but when the waiter told the pantry maid the story, he neglected to say that the threat was a jest. The pantry maid told the barkeeper. The barkeeper told the cook, and by the time the story was circulated around the kitchen, the servants were whispering that rich Mr. Ames had threatened to fire poor Mr. Harve because his son had fetched a biscuit eater to the field trials.

The morning of the first run, Text met Lonnie at the kennels, and together they fed Moreover. "Let's put some good ol' gunpowder in his vittles," Text said. "Make him hunt better."

"Aw, that's superstition," said Lonnie.

"I don't care what it is, it helps," said Text.

Lonnie couldn't see any need of tempting luck, so Moreover was fed a sprinkling of gunpowder.

Text said, "I got my lucky buckeye along. We bound to have luck, Lon."

Lonnie was getting too big for such foolishness, but then he remembered. "I caught a sweet stinker not so long ago," he whispered. "And he swum the right way."

"A good ol' sweet-stinking mellow bug?" asked Text eagerly. "Lon, good luck gonna bust us in two halves."

Harve took Silver Belle out with an early brace and the pointer completely outclassed her rival. Her trainer sent her back to her kennel and went into the fields with Ames to watch Moreover in his first brace. He was braced with a rangy setter. Even the judges smiled at the two boys and their dog. Text, in keeping with rules of the sport, gave not an order. Lonnie put Moreover down on the edge of a clover field and the big dog rolled over, then jumped up and loped around the boy, leaping on him and licking his face. Lonnie and Text walked into the field, and Moreover followed. Lonnie whistled shrilly. The big dog jerked up his head, cocked it and began casting. He ranged to the edge of the field and worked in. He loped past a patch of saw grass, wheeled and pointed, his head cocked toward Lonnie, his right leg poised and his tail stiff as a poker.

Lonnie kept his dog on the point until the judges nodded, then whistled him off of it. He called Moreover to the far edge of the field and set him ranging again. He was on a point in a flash.

Ames looked at Harve. "That's a good dog, McNeil. He's trained beautifully. He'll go to the finals with us, sure as shooting."

Harve was beaming with pride. "It proves what I've always preached," Harve said; "that a bird dog will work for a man, if the man understands him. I couldn't do anything with that dog, but he will go to hell and back for my boy and Text."

Silver Belle and Moreover swept through the quarter and semifinals, and news that father and son would be matched in the finals, with the famous Belle and a biscuit eater, brought sportsmen and sports writers swarming to the county seat. Harve and Lonnie slept and ate together, but the man didn't discuss the contest with his son. He didn't want to make him nervous. He treated Lonnie as he would any other trainer. He knew that boys hate condescension from their fathers. He knew boys could sense condescension if adults eased up in games and that boys never want their fathers to make things too easy for them.

Harve took Silver Belle to the edge of a field of stubble, and she stood motionless as he snapped a tiny silver bell around her neck. He arose from his knees, patted her fondly and whispered, "Go get 'em girl."

The little pointer dashed into the stubble and soon was out of sight. Moreover rubbed against Lonnie's legs and watched her for a minute, then trotted along her path. There was no order between Lonnie and his dog, only understanding.

The men listened for the tingling of the silver bell that told them the champion still was casting. Through the brush the men sauntered, their senses alert. Suddenly the bell hushed.

Belle was on a point. The delicate little animal was rigid. Her trim body was thrown forward a bit, her nose, perfectly tilted, was aimed toward a clump of sage. She didn't fleck a muscle. She might have been made of marble.

The judges nodded approval. Harve motioned to Belle. She took two steps, stopped, then two more. A roar of wings, a whistle of flight, and the covey of partridge was away like feathered lightning. Guns thundered. Belle didn't bat an eye as the salvo cracked over her. When the echoes died, she began fetching, and when the last bird was laid at Harve's feet, she dashed into the sage again, seeking the singles.

Lonnie had held Moreover while Belle worked. Now he turned the big dog loose. Moreover swung along through the sage at an easy gait. He cast a bit to the right, stuck his nose almost to the ground and found the trail Belle had just made. Then he broke into an easy trot. He never depended on ground scents, but on body scents, and kept his nose high enough to catch any smells the wind blew his way.

About a hundred yards back up Belle's trail, Moreover suddenly broke his trot and eased his nose higher in the air. Then he jerked his head toward Lonnie and froze to a point. His right leg came up slowly, deliberately. He cocked his head in that strange fashion, and the quizzical, comical look came in his eyes. Moreover was a still hunter. He never waited for orders. He held the birds until Lonnie clicked the safety off of his gun. When Moreover heard the click, he began creeping toward the covey. He didn't budge as Lonnie began dropping the birds, and then, without orders, he fetched the dead birds and began casting for singles.

The judges whistled softly. "Most beautiful dog work I ever saw," whispered one. Ames' face took on a worried look. So did Harve's. The big dog had picked up a covey right under Belle's nose.

Belle settled down to hunt. She seemed everywhere. She dashed to a point on the fringe of a cornfield, then held another covey while Harve weeded out the first. She raced over the ridge, her nose picking up scents in almost impossible places. Moreover just loped along, but every time Belle got a covey, he would cast for a few minutes, point, fetch and wait for her to set the pace. She was hunting because she was bred to hunt. He was hunting from habit and because Lonnie expected him to.

It was exasperating. Belle tried every trick of her training, but her skill was no match for his stamina. Her heart was pumping rapidly and she was tired when the men knocked off for lunch. Text ran back to the lodge to help fetch food to the field. He strutted into the kitchen and told the servants that Moreover was running Silver Belle ragged.

The servants shook their heads, and one told him that Mr. Ames would fire Harve if Moreover beat Belle. Text couldn't swallow his food. He waited around the fringe of hunters until he caught Lonnie's eye, and motioned to him. "That Mr. Ames sho is a scutter," said Text, after he told his story. "He's worse'n Mr. Eben. What we goin' do, Lon?"

Lonnie said, "He's half your dog, Text. What you say?"

"We can't let yo' paw get in no trouble on account of us, Lon. He got to have a job."

Lonnie nodded and bit his lip. He noticed that his father's face was drawn as the contest was renewed. Ames was nervous. The two men had worked for years to get Belle to perfection, and win the Grand National for the third time. And here an outcast dog was hunting her heart out at a minor meet. Lonnie thought his father was worried about his job and that Ames was angry.

His mind was made up. He watched Moreover leap across a creek, then race into a field of clover. He and Text were right behind him. Moreover came to his point, jerked his head toward his master and waited.

Lonnie cupped his hands and said hoarsely, "Hep!" It was an order Moreover never had heard. He turned and faced Lonnie. The judges gasped when the big dog left his point. Harve was puzzled.

Ames whispered, "He's breaking. That good-for-nothing streak is cropping out."

"Hep!" Lonnie said it again. The judges didn't hear. Moreover deserted the covey and walked to Lonnie and looked up. Lonnie shouted, "Back to your point, you low-life biscuit eater!"

Moreover tucked his tail between his legs and ran to the lodge and hid under it. Lonnie and Text followed him, without a word to the judges.

Ames looked at Harve for an explanation, and Harve said, "I don't get it. My son called his dog off. He quit."

It took Lonnie and Text a long time to coax Moreover from under the lodge. The dog crawled to Lonnie's feet and rolled over. Lonnie patted him, but Moreover didn't lick his face. The boys were with their dog in the kennel when the prize was awarded to Harve and Silver Belle.

"His feelings are hurt," Lonnie told Text as Moreover lay down and thumped his tail. . . . "I'm sorry I said it, Moreover. I had to."

Text said, "We sorry, puppy dawg. But us had to, didn't we, Lon?"

They loaded the truck, and Harve had his boy sit on the front seat by him. They said good-by and rolled away.

Harve said to Lonnie, "How come you did that, son?"

Lonnie didn't reply and the father didn't press the point. Finally, he said, "Don't ever quit, son, if you are winning or losing. It ain't fair to the dog."

"My dog is mad at me," Lonnie said.

"We'll give him a beef heart when we get home. His feelings are hurt because you threw him down. But he'll be all right. Dogs are not like folks. They'll forgive a fellow." He knew Lonnie had a reason for what he had done, and he knew that if his son wanted him to know the reason, he would tell him.

Back home, Lonnie cooked a beef heart for Moreover and took the plate to the back gallery where the dog was tied.

Harve said, "Untie him, son. You can let him run free over here. You don't ever have to keep him over at Text's house, unless you want to."

He untied his dog and put the food before him. Moreover sniffed the food and toyed with it. He never had had such good food before. Lonnie and his father went back into the house.

After supper, Lonnie went to see about his dog. The meat hadn't been touched and Moreover was gone.

Harve said, "He's probably gone back to Text's house."

Lonnie said, "I'm going after him."

"I'll go with you," said Harve, and got a lantern.

Text hadn't seen the dog. He joined the search and the three hunted through the woods for an hour or so, Lonnie whistling for Moreover, and Text calling him, "Heah, heah, fellow. Heah."

Harve sat on a stump, put the lantern down and called the boys to him. He had seen only a few dogs that would refuse to eat beef heart as Moreover had done.

"Text," he said sharply, "did Moreover ever suck eggs at your place?"

Text rolled his eyes and looked at Lonnie. "Yas, suh." He was afraid to lie to Harve. "But I didn't tell Lon. I didn't want to hurt his feelings. Moreover was a suck-egger, good and proper."

Harve said, "Go on, tell us about it."

"Maw put hot pepper in a raw egg, but it didn't break him. My ol' brother, ol' First-and-Second-Thessalonians, reckoned he'd kill Moreover less'n he quit suck-egging. So I got to snitching two eggs ever' night and feeding him with 'em. He sho did like eggs, Mr. Harve, and we had plenty of eggs."

Lonnie said sharply, "You hadn't ought to have done that, Text."

Harve said, "Did you feed him eggs tonight?"

"Naw, suh," said Text. "I reckoned he had vittles at yo' house. We had done gathered all the eggs and maw had counted them by nightfall."

Harve got up. "I'm worried. Let's walk up the branch. . . . Text, you take the left side. . . . Lonnie, you take the right side. I'll walk up the bank."

Lonnie found Moreover's body, still warm, only a few feet from the water. He stooped over his dog, put the lantern by his head, and opened his mouth. The dog had been poisoned. Lonnie straightened. He didn't cry. His emotions welled up within him, and, having no outlet, hurt him.

"I'm sorry I called him a biscuit eater," he said simply.

Text said, "He was trying to get to water. I sho hate to think of him dying, wanting just one swallow of good ol' water."

"Who killed him, papa?" Lonnie turned to his father.

The man picked up the lantern and walked away, the boys at his heels. They walked over the ridge to Eben's house, and Harve pounded on the front gallery until the farmer appeared.

"My boy's dog is dead," Harve said. "Reckoned you might know something about it."

Eben said, "If he was poisoned, I do. He's a suck-egg dog. I put poison in some eggs and left them in the field. Seems he mout have committed suicide, McNeil."

"Seems you made it powerful easy for him to get those poisoned eggs," Harve said.

"Ain't no room round here for suck-egg dogs. His daddy was a sheep killer too. It's good riddance. You ain't got no cause to jump me, Harve McNeil."

Harve said, "He's right, boys. A man's got a right to poison eggs on his own land, and if a dog sucks 'em and dies, the dog's to blame."

Eben said, "Reckon you young'uns want to bury that dog. Buzzards will be thick tomorrow. You can have the loan of my shovel."

Lonnie looked at the man a long time. He bit his lip so he couldn't cry. "Me and Text will dig a hole with a stick," he said, and turned away.

"You boys go bury him," Harve said. "I'll be home in a few minutes."

Lonnie and Text walked silently into the woods. Text said, "He sho was a good dog, huh, Lon? You ain't mad at me 'cause I fed him eggs, are you, Lon?"

"No, Text. Let's wait up here and watch papa. He can't see us."

Back at Eben's gallery, Harve said, "I would have paid you for all the eggs the dog took, Eben. My boy loved that dog a heap."

"Looka heah!" Eben said. "I know my rights."

"I know mine," Harve said. "I always pay my debts, Eben. And I always collect them. I ain't got no cause to get riled because that dog stole poisoned eggs. You were mighty low-life to plant 'em, though. But two years ago you kicked one of my dogs."

"He barked at me and scared my team on the road," Eben said.

"A dog has a right to bark," Harve said, and reached up and grabbed Eben by the collar.

"I'll law you!" Eben shouted.

Harve didn't reply. He slapped the man with his open palm, and when Eben squared off to fight, Harve knocked him down.

In the shadows of the woods, Lonnie whispered to Text, "What did I tell you? My papa ain't scared of nothing cep'n God."

They buried their dog near the branch. Text poured water in the grave. "I can't stand to think of him wanting water when there's a heap of water so close. Reckon if he could have got to the ol' branch he could have washed out that poison? Reckon, Lon?"

"Maybe so."

They were walking to Lonnie's house. "My ol' buckeye and your sweet-stinking mellow bug ain't helped us much, eh, Lon? Luck is plumb mad at us, ain't it, Lon?"

Lonnie waited at the gate until his father arrived. "Me and Text saw the fight," he said. "I won't tell mother. Women are scutters, ain't they, papa? Always trying to keep men folks from fighting."

"I'll give you boys another dog, son," Harve said. He peered into the darkness and saw a car parked behind his house, then hurried inside. Mr. Ames was warming himself by the fire and talking with Mrs. McNeil. She went to the kitchen to brew coffee, and left the men alone, after calling for Lonnie and Text to follow her.

Ames said, "I heard why your boy called his dog off. Call him and that little colored boy in here. I can't go back East with those boys thinking what they do of me."

Lonnie and Text stood by the fire and Ames said, "That story you heard about me isn't so. I wouldn't have fired this man if your dog had won. We were joking about it and the servants got the story all wrong. I just wanted you boys to know that."

Harve said, "Yes. But even if Mr. Ames would have fired me, it wouldn't have made any difference. You did what you thought was right, but you were wrong. Don't ever quit a race, once you start it."

Lonnie told Mr. Ames, "My dog is dead. I'm sorry I called him a biscuit eater. He wasn't. I just want you to know that."

Ames lit his pipe and passed his tobacco pouch to Harve. He saw Harve's bloody hand as the trainer accepted the tobacco.

"Ran into some briers," Harve said.

"Lot of them around here." Ames' eyes twinkled. "Just been thinking, Harve. I got some fine pups coming along. You need help down here. Better hire a couple of good men. Know where you can get two good hands? They got to be men who can lose without grumbling and win without crowing."

Harve looked at Lonnie and Text, and smiled. "I know where I can get a couple of good men."

"All right," said Ames, and shook hands all around. "I've got to be going. Good night, men."

(1908–1960)

Richard Wright

Richard Wright, clearly the greatest of American black writers, was also the first black writer to achieve literary fame and fortune, though his reputation has less to do with his race than with the quality of his work. His first published novel, *Native Son* (1940), is a powerful novel indeed, and his autobiography, *Black Boy* (1945), is a brilliant and moving account of what it was like to grow up black in the South during the first quarter of the twentieth century. Wright was born on a plantation near Natchez on September 4, 1908, the son of an illiterate sharecropper and a school teacher. Beset by extreme poverty, the Wrights moved to Memphis when Richard was six; whereupon his father soon after deserted them and his mother had to find work as a cook. Richard stayed a brief while in a Memphis orphanage; the family's subsequent peregrinations (recounted in *Black Boy*) took them to Jackson, where Wright spent his formative years and first began to write, then to West Helena, Arkansas, and to Greenwood. In December, 1927, he moved to Chicago, where he worked at odd jobs and became involved with the Communist party, writing articles and stories for the *Daily Worker* and the *New Masses*. This era in Wright's life—his membership in and disillusion with the Communist party—is treated in the second half of his autobiography, *American Hunger*, which

258

was written at the same time as *Black Boy*, but not published until 1977. By the time he arrived in Paris in 1946, Wright had become an internationally known writer. He died there on November 28, 1960.

Some have criticized Wright for turning polemical in his later work, citing this fact as among the reasons for a decline in his artistry during the latter years of his career. But few have denied the power and richness of *Native Son*, *Black Boy*, and a handful of short stories, including "The Man Who Was Almost a Man," reprinted here from *Eight Men* (1961).

The Man Who Was Almost A Man

DAVE STRUCK OUT ACROSS THE FIELDS, looking homeward through paling light. Whut's the use talkin wid em niggers in the field? Anyhow, his mother was putting supper on the table. Them niggers can't understan nothing. One of these days he was going to get a gun and practice shooting, then they couldn't talk to him as though he were a little boy. He slowed, looking at the ground. Shucks, Ah ain scareda them even ef they are biggern me! Aw, Ah know whut Ahma do. Ahm going by ol Joe's sto n git that Sears Roebuck catlog n look at them guns. Mebbe Ma will lemme buy one when she gits mah pay from ol man Hawkins. Ahma beg her t gimme some money. Ahm ol ernough to hava gun. Ahm seventeen. Almost a man. He strode, feeling his long loose-jointed limbs. Shucks, a man oughta hava little gun aftah he done worked hard all day.

He came in sight of Joe's store. A yellow lantern glowed on the front porch. He mounted steps and went through the screen door, hearing it bang behind him. There was a strong smell of coal oil and mackerel fish. He felt very confident until he saw fat Joe walk in through the rear door, then his courage began to ooze.

"Howdy, Dave! Whutcha want?"

"How yuh, Mistah Joe? Aw, Ah don wanna buy nothing. Ah jus wanted t see ef yuhd lemme look at the catlog erwhile."

"Sure! You wanna see it here?"

"Nawsuh. Ah wans t take it home wid me. Ah'll bring it back termorrow when Ah come in from the fiels."

"You plannin on buying something?"

"Yessuh."

"Your ma lettin you have your own money now?"

"Shucks. Mistah Joe, Ahm gittin t be a man like anybody else!"

Joe laughed and wiped his greasy white face with a red bandanna.

"Whut you plannin on buyin?"

Dave looked at the floor, scratched his head, scratched his thigh, and smiled. Then he looked up shyly.

"Ah'll tell yuh, Mistah Joe, ef yuh promise yuh won't tell."

"I promise."

"Waal, Ahma buy a gun."

"A gun? Whut you want with a gun?"

"Ah wanna keep it."

"You ain't nothing but a boy. You don't need a gun."

"Aw, lemme have the catlog, Mistah Joe. Ah'll bring it back."

Joe walked through the rear door. Dave was elated. He looked around at barrels of sugar and flour. He heard Joe coming back. He craned his neck to see if he were bringing the book. Yeah, he's got it. Gawddog, he's got it!

"Here, but be sure you bring it back. It's the only one I got."

"Sho, Mistah Joe."

"Say, if you wanna buy a gun, why don't you buy one from me? I gotta gun to sell."

"Will it shoot?"

"Sure it'll shoot."

"Whut kind is it?"

"Oh, it's kinda old . . . a left-hand Wheeler. A pistol. A big one."

"Is it got bullets in it?"

"It's loaded."

"Kin Ah see it?"

"Where's your money?"

"Whut yuh wan fer it?"

"I'll let you have it for two dollars."

"Just two dollahs? Shucks, Ah could buy tha when Ah git mah pay."

"I'll have it here when you want it."

"Awright, suh. Ah be in fer it."

He went through the door, hearing it slam again behind him. Ahma git some money from Ma n buy me a gun! Only two dollahs! He tucked the thick catalogue under his arm and hurried.

"Where yuh been, boy?" His mother held a steaming dish of black-eyed peas.

"Aw, Ma, Ah jus stopped down the road t talk wid the boys."

"Yuh know bettah t keep suppah waitin."

He sat down, resting the catalogue on the edge of the table.

"Yuh git up from there and git to the well n wash yosef! Ah ain feedin no hogs in mah house!"

She grabbed his shoulder and pushed him. He stumbled out of the room, then came back to get the catalogue.

"Whut this?"

"Aw, Ma, it's jusa catlog."

"Who yuh git it from?"

"From Joe, down at the sto."

"Waal, thas good. We kin use it in the outhouse."

"Naw, Ma." He grabbed for it. "Gimme ma catlog, Ma."

She held onto it and glared at him.

"Quit hollerin at me! Whut's wrong wid yuh? Yuh crazy?"

"But Ma, please. It ain mine! It's Joe's! He tol me t bring it back t im termorrow."

She gave up the book. He stumbled down the back steps, hugging the thick book under his arm. When he had splashed water on his face and hands, he groped back to the kitchen and fumbled in a corner for the towel. He bumped into a chair; it clattered to the floor. The catalogue sprawled at his feet. When he had dried his eyes he snatched up the book and held it again under his arm. His mother stood watching him.

"Now, ef yuh gonna act a fool over that ol book, Ah'll take it n burn it up."

"Naw, Ma, please."

"Waal, set down n be still!"

He sat down and drew the oil lamp close. He thumbed page after page, unaware of the food his mother set on the table. His father came in. Then his small brother.

"Whutcha got there, Dave?" his father asked.

"Jusa catlog," he answered, not looking up.

"Yeah, here they is!" His eyes glowed at blue-and-black revolvers. He glanced up, feeling sudden guilt. His father was watching him. He eased the book under the table and rested it on his knees. After the blessing was asked, he ate. He scooped up peas and swallowed fat meat without chewing. Buttermilk helped to wash it down. He did not want to mention money before his father. He would do much better by cornering his mother when she was alone. He looked at his father uneasily out of the edge of his eye.

"Boy, how come yuh don quit foolin wid tha book n eat yo suppah?"

"Yessuh."

"How you n ol man Hawkins gitten erlong?"

"Suh?"

"Can't yuh hear? Why don yuh lissen? Ah ast yu how wuz yuh n ol man Hawkins gittin erlong?"

"Oh, swell, Pa. Ah plows mo lan than anybody over there."

"Waal, yuh oughta keep yo mind on whut yuh doin."

"Yessuh."

He poured his plate full of molasses and sopped it up slowly with a chunk of cornbread. When his father and brother had left the kitchen, he still sat and looked again at the guns in the catalogue, longing to muster courage enough to present his case to his mother. Lawd, ef Ah only had tha pretty one! He could almost feel the slickness of the weapon with his fingers. If he had a gun like that he would polish it and keep it shining so it would never rust. N Ah'd keep it loaded, by Gawd!

"Ma?" His voice was hesitant.

"Hunh?"

"Ol man Hawkins give yuh mah money yit?"

"Yeah, but ain no usa yuh thinking bout throwin nona it erway. Ahm keepin tha money sos yuh kin have cloes t go to school this winter."

He rose and went to her side with the open catalogue in his palms. She was washing dishes, her head bent low over a pan. Shyly he raised the book. When he spoke, his voice was husky, faint.

"Ma, Gawd knows Ah wans one of these."

"One of whut?" she asked, not raising her eyes.

"One of these," he said again, not daring even to point. She glanced up at the page, then at him with wide eyes.

"Nigger, is yuh gone plumb crazy?"

"Aw, Ma—"

"Git outta here! Don yuh talk t me bout no gun! Yuh a fool!"

"Ma, Ah kin buy one fer two dollahs."

"Not ef Ah knows it, yuh ain!"

"But yuh promised me one—"

"Ah don care whut Ah promised! Yuh ain nothing but a boy yit!"

"Ma, ef yuh lemme buy one Ah'll *never* ast yuh fer nothing no mo."

"Ah tol yuh t git outta here! Yuh ain gonna toucha penny of tha money fer no gun! Thas how come Ah has Mistah Hawkins t pay yo wages t me, cause Ah knows yuh ain got no sense."

"But, Ma, we needa gun. Pa ain got no gun. We needa gun in the house. Yuh kin never tell whut might happen."

"Now don yuh try to maka fool outta me, boy! Ef we did hava gun, yuh wouldn't have it!"

He laid the catalogue down and slipped his arm around her waist.

"Aw, Ma, Ah done worked hard alla summer n ain ast yuh fer nothin, is Ah, now?"

"Thas whut yuh spose t do!"

"But Ma, Ah wans a gun. Yuh kin lemme have two dollahs outta mah money. Please, Ma. I kin give it to Pa . . . Please, Ma! Ah loves yuh, Ma."

When she spoke her voice came soft and low.

"Whut yu wan wida gun, Dave? Yuh don need no gun. Yuh'll git in trouble. N ef yo pa jus thought Ah let yuh have money t buy a gun he'd hava fit."

"Ah'll hide it, Ma. It ain but two dollahs."

"Lawd, chil, whut's wrong wid yuh?"

"Ain nothin wrong, Ma. Ahm almos a man now. Ah wans a gun."

"Who gonna sell yuh a gun?"

"Ol Joe at the sto."

"N it don cos but two dollahs?"

"Thas all, Ma. Jus two dollahs. Please, Ma."

She was stacking the plates away; her hands moved slowly, reflectively. Dave kept an anxious silence. Finally, she turned to him.

"Ah'll let yuh git tha gun ef yuh promise me one thing."

"Whut's tha, Ma?"

"Yuh bring it straight back t me, yuh hear? It be fer Pa."

"Yessum! Lemme go now, Ma."

She stooped, turned slightly to one side, raised the hem of her dress, rolled down the top of her stocking, and came up with a slender wad of bills.

"Here," she said. "Lawd knows yuh don need no gun. But yer pa does. Yuh bring it right back t me, yuh hear? Ahma put it up. Now ef yuh don, Ahma have yuh pa lick yuh so hard yuh won fergit it."

"Yessum."

He took the money, ran down the steps, and across the yard.

"Dave! Yuuuuuh Daaaaave!"

He heard, but he was not going to stop now. "Naw, Lawd!"

The first movement he made the following morning was to reach under his pillow for the gun. In the gray light of dawn he held it loosely, feeling a sense of power. Could kill a man with a gun like this. Kill anybody, black or white. And if he were holding his gun in his hand, nobody could run over him; they would have to respect him. It was a big gun, with a long barrel and a heavy handle. He raised and lowered it in his hand, marveling at its weight.

He had not come straight home with it as his mother had asked; instead he had stayed out in the fields, holding the weapon in his hand, aiming it now and then at some imaginary foe. But he had not fired it; he had been afraid that his father might hear. Also he was not sure he knew how to fire it.

To avoid surrendering the pistol he had not come into the house until he knew that they were all asleep. When his mother had tiptoed to his bedside late that night and demanded the gun, he had first played possum; then he had told her that the gun was hidden outdoors, that he would bring it to her in the morning. Now he lay turning it slowly in his hands. He broke it, took out the cartridges, felt them, and then put them back.

He slid out of bed, got a long strip of old flannel from a trunk, wrapped the gun in it, and tied it to his naked thigh while it was still loaded. He did not go in to breakfast. Even though it was not yet daylight, he started for Jim Hawkins' plantation. Just as the sun was rising he reached the barns where the mules and plows were kept.

"Hey! That you, Dave?"

He turned. Jim Hawkins stood eying him suspiciously.

"What're yuh doing here so early?"

"Ah didn't know Ah wuz gittin up so early, Mistah Hawkins. Ah was fixin t hitch up ol Jenny n take her t the fiels."

"Good. Since you're so early, how about plowing that stretch down by the woods?"

"Suits me, Mistah Hawkins."

"O.K. Go to it!"

He hitched Jenny to a plow and started across the fields. Hot dog! This was just what he wanted. If he could get down by the woods, he could shoot his gun and nobody would hear. He walked behind the plow, hearing the traces creaking, feeling the gun tied tight to his thigh.

When he reached the woods, he plowed two whole rows before he decided to take out the gun. Finally, he stopped, looked in all directions, then untied the gun and held it in his hand. He turned to the mule and smiled.

"Know whut this is, Jenny? Naw, yuh wouldn know! Yuhs jusa ol mule! Anyhow, this is a gun, n it kin shoot, by Gawd!"

He held the gun at arm's length. Whut t hell, Ahma shoot this thing! He looked at Jenny again.

"Lissen here, Jenny! When Ah pull this ol trigger, Ah don wan yuh t run n acka fool now!"

Jenny stood with head down, her short ears pricked straight. Dave walked off about twenty feet, held the gun far out from him at arm's length, and turned his head. Hell, he told himself, Ah ain afraid. The gun felt loose in his fingers; he waved it wildly for a moment. Then he shut his eyes and tightened his forefinger. Bloom! A report half deafened him and he thought his right hand was torn from his arm. He heard Jenny whinnying and galloping over the field, and he found himself on his knees, squeezing his fingers hard between his legs. His hand was numb; he jammed it into his mouth, trying to warm it, trying to stop the pain. The gun lay at his feet. He did not quite know what had happened. He stood up and stared at the gun as though it were a living thing. He gritted his teeth and kicked the gun. Yuh almost broke mah arm! He turned to look for Jenny; she was far over the fields, tossing her head and kicking wildly.

"Hol on there, ol mule!"

When he caught up with her she stood trembling, walling her big white eyes at him. The plow was far away; the traces had broken. Then Dave stopped short, looking, not believing. Jenny was bleeding. Her left side was red and wet with blood. He went closer. Lawd, have mercy! Wondah did Ah shoot this mule? He grabbed for Jenny's mane. She flinched, snorted, whirled, tossing her head.

"Hol on now! Hol on."

Then he saw the hole in Jenny's side, right between the ribs. It was round, wet, red. A crimson stream streaked down the front leg, flowing fast. Good Gawd! Ah wuzn't shootin at tha mule. He felt panic. He knew he had to stop that blood, or Jenny would bleed to death. He had never seen so much blood in all his life. He chased the mule for half a mile, trying to catch her. Finally she stopped, breathing hard, stumpy tail half arched. He caught her mane and led her back to where the plow and gun lay. Then he stooped and grabbed handfuls of damp black earth and tried to plug the bullet hole. Jenny shuddered, whinnied, and broke from him.

"Hol on! Hol on now!"

He tried to plug it again, but blood came anyhow. His fingers were hot and sticky. He rubbed dirt into his palms, trying to dry them. Then again he attempted to plug the bullet hole, but Jenny shied away, kicking her heels high. He stood helpless. He had to do something. He ran at Jenny; she dodged him. He watched a red stream of blood flow down Jenny's leg and form a bright pool at her feet.

"Jenny . . . Jenny," he called weakly.

His lips trembled. She's bleeding t death! He looked in the direction of home, wanting to go back, wanting to get help. But he saw the pistol lying in the damp black clay. He had a queer feeling that if he only did something, this would not be; Jenny would not be there bleeding to death.

When he went to her this time, she did not move. She stood with sleepy, dreamy eyes; and when he touched her she gave a low-pitched whinny and knelt to the ground, her front knees slopping in blood.

"Jenny . . . Jenny . . ." he whispered.

For a long time she held her neck erect; then her head sank, slowly. Her ribs swelled with a mighty heave and she went over.

Dave's stomach felt empty, very empty. He picked up the gun and held it gingerly between his thumb and forefinger. He buried it at the foot of a tree. He took a stick and tried to cover the pool of blood with dirt—but what was the use? There was Jenny lying with her mouth open and her eyes walled and glassy. He could not tell Jim Hawkins he had shot his mule. But he had to tell something. Yeah, Ah'll tell em Jenny started gittin wil n fell on the joint of the plow. . . . But that would hardly happen to a mule. He walked across the field slowly, head down.

It was sunset. Two of Jim Hawkins' men were over near the edge of the woods digging a hole in which to bury Jenny. Dave was surrounded by a knot of people, all of whom were looking down at the dead mule.

"I don't see how in the world it happened," said Jim Hawkins for the tenth time.

The crowd parted and Dave's mother, father, and small brother pushed into the center.

"Where Dave?" his mother called.

"There he is," said Jim Hawkins.

His mother grabbed him.

"Whut happened, Dave? Whut yuh done?"

"Nothin."

"C mon, boy, talk," his father said.

Dave took a deep breath and told the story he knew nobody believed.

"Waal," he drawled. "Ah brung ol Jenny down here sos Ah could do mah plowin. Ah plowed bout two rows, just like yuh see." He stopped and pointed at the long rows of upturned earth. "Then somethin musta been wrong wid ol Jenny. She wouldn ack right a-tall. She started snortin n kickin her heels. Ah tried t hol her, but she pulled erway, rearin n goin in. Then when the point of the plow was stickin up in the air, she swung erroun n twisted herself back on it . . . She stuck herself n started t bleed. N fo Ah could do anything, she wuz dead."

"Did you ever hear of anything like that in all your life?" asked Jim Hawkins.

There were white and black standing in the crowd. They murmured. Dave's mother came close to him and looked hard into his face. "Tell the truth, Dave," she said.

"Looks like a bullet hole to me," said one man.

"Dave, whut yuh do wid the gun?" his mother asked.

The crowd surged in, looking at him. He jammed his hands into his pockets, shook his head slowly from left to right, and backed away. His eyes were wide and painful.

"Did he hava gun?" asked Jim Hawkins.

"By Gawd, Ah tol yuh tha wuz a gun wound," said a man, slapping his thigh.

His father caught his shoulders and shook him till his teeth rattled.

"Tell whut happened, yuh rascal! Tell whut . . ."

Dave looked at Jenny's stiff legs and began to cry.

"Whut yuh do wid tha gun?" his mother asked.

"Whut wuz he doin wida gun?" his father asked.

"Come on and tell the truth," said Hawkins. "Ain't nobody going to hurt you . . ."

His mother crowded close to him.

"Did yuh shoot tha mule, Dave?"

Dave cried, seeing blurred white and black faces.

"Ahh ddinn gggo tt sshooot hher . . . Ah ssswear ffo Gawd Ahh ddin. . . . Ah wuz a-tryin t sssee ef the old gggun would sshoot—"

"Where yuh git the gun from?" his father asked.

"Ah got it from Joe, at the sto."

"Where yuh git the money?"

"Ma give it t me."

"He kept worryin me, Bob. Ah had t. Ah tol im t bring the gun right back t me . . . It was fer yuh, the gun."

"But how yuh happen to shoot that mule?" asked Jim Hawkins.

"Ah wuzn shootin at the mule, Mistah Hawkins. The gun jumped when Ah pulled the trigger . . . N fo Ah knowed anythin Jenny was there a-bleedin."

Somebody in the crowd laughed. Jim Hawkins walked close to Dave and looked into his face.

"Well, looks like you have bought you a mule, Dave."

"Ah swear fo Gawd, Ah didn go t kill the mule, Mistah Hawkins!"

"But you killed her!"

All the crowd was laughing now. They stood on tiptoe and poked heads over one another's shoulders.

"Well, boy, looks like yuh done bought a dead mule! Hahaha!"

"Ain tha ershame."

"Hohohohoho."

Dave stood, head down, twisting his feet in the dirt.

"Well, you needn't worry about it, Bob," said Jim Hawkins to Dave's father. "Just let the boy keep on working and pay me two dollars a month."

"Whut yuh wan fer yo mule, Mistah Hawkins?"

Jim Hawkins screwed up his eyes.

"Fifty dollars."

"Whut yuh do wid tha gun?" Dave's father demanded.

Dave said nothing.

"Yuh wan me t take a tree n beat yuh till yuh talk!"

"Nawsuh!"

"Whut yuh do wid it?"

"Ah throwed it erway."

"Where?"

"Ah . . . Ah throwed it in the creek."

"Waal, c mon home. N firs thing in the mawnin git to tha creek n fin tha gun."

"Yessuh."

"Whut yuh pay fer it?"

"Two dollahs."

"Take tha gun n git yo money back n carry it t Mistah Hawkins, yuh hear? N don fergit Ahma lam you black bottom good fer this! Now march yosef on home, suh!"

Dave turned and walked slowly. He heard people laughing.

Dave glared, his eyes welling with tears. Hot anger bubbled in him. Then he swallowed and stumbled on.

That night Dave did not sleep. He was glad that he had gotten out of killing the mule so easily, but he was hurt. Something hot seemed to turn over inside him each time he remembered how they had laughed. He tossed on his bed, feeling his hard pillow. N Pa says he's gonna beat me . . . He remembered other beatings, and his back quivered. Naw, naw, Ah sho don wan im t beat me tha way no mo. Dam em all! Nobody ever gave him anything. All he did was work. They treat me like a mule, n then they beat me. He gritted his teeth. N Ma had t tell on me.

Well, if he had to, he would take old man Hawkins that two dollars. But that meant selling the gun. And he wanted to keep that gun. Fifty dollars for a dead mule.

He turned over, thinking how he had fired the gun. He had an itch to fire it again. Ef other men kin shoota gun, by Gawd, Ah kin! He was still, listening. Mebbe they all sleepin now. The house was still. He heard the soft breathing of his brother. Yes, now! He would go down and get that gun and see if he could fire it! He eased out of bed and slipped into overalls.

The moon was bright. He ran almost all the way to the edge of the woods. He stumbled over the ground, looking for the spot where he had buried the gun. Yeah, here it is. Like a hungry dog scratching for a bone, he pawed it up. He puffed his black cheeks and blew dirt from the trigger and barrel. He broke it and found four cartridges unshot. He looked around; the fields were filled with silence and moonlight. He clutched the gun stiff and hard in his fingers. But, as soon as he wanted to pull the trigger, he shut his eyes and turned his head. Naw, Ah can't shoot wid mah eyes closed n mah head turned. With effort he held his eyes open; then he squeezed. *Blooooom!* He was stiff, not breathing. The gun was still in his hands. Dammit, he'd done it! He fired again. *Blooooom!* He smiled. *Blooooom! Blooooom! Click, click.* There! It was empty. If anybody could shoot a gun, he could. He put the gun into his hip pocket and started across the fields.

When he reached the top of a ridge he stood straight and proud in the moonlight, looking at Jim Hawkins' big white house, feeling the gun sagging in his pocket. Lawd, ef Ah had just one mo bullet Ah'd taka shot at tha house. Ah'd like t scare ol man Hawkins jusa little . . . Jusa enough t let im know Dave Saunders is a man.

To his left the road curved, running to the tracks of the Illinois Central. He jerked his head, listening. From far off came a faint *hoooof-hoooof; hoooof-hoooof; hoooof-hoooof.* . . . He stood rigid. Two dollahs a mont. Les see now . . . Tha means it'll take bout two years. Shucks! Ah'll be dam!

He started down the road, toward the tracks. Yeah, here she comes! He stood beside the track and held himself stiffly. Here she comes, erroun the ben . . . C mon, yuh slow poke! C mon! He had his hand on his gun; something quivered in his stomach. Then the train thundered past, the gray and brown box cars rumbling and clinking. He gripped the gun tightly; then he jerked his hand out of his pocket. Ah betcha Bill wouldn't do it! Ah betcha . . . The cars slid past, steel grinding upon steel. Ahm ridin yuh ternight, so hep me Gawd! He was hot all over. He hesitated just a moment; then he grabbed, pulled atop of a car, and lay flat. He felt his pocket; the gun was still there. Ahead the long rails were glinting in the moonlight, stretching away, away to somewhere, somewhere where he could be a man . . .

(1907–1972)

Hodding Carter

One of the most distinguished journalists of his time, Hodding Carter is best known today for his courageous and outspoken editorials in the *Delta Democrat-Times* advocating racial justice and condemning demagoguery and the militancy of both blacks and whites. These editorials were written at a time when it was dangerous even to hold such positions in Mississippi, much less to proclaim them from the pages of a newspaper. For these editorials Carter gained national acclaim (as well as, for a time, considerable local infamy); he received a Pulitzer Prize in 1946 and, in 1961, the William Allen White citation as the outstanding newspaperman of the year.

He was born February 3, 1907, in Hammond, Louisiana. He attended local schools, and then went north to Bowdoin College in Maine, where he received his B.A. After further study at the Pulitzer School of Journalism at Columbia University, Carter returned to the South, to New Orleans, where he was a teaching fellow for one year at Tulane University. In 1929, he became a reporter for the New Orleans *Item*. In 1930 he served as night manager of the United Press bureau there, and in 1931 and 1932 he managed the Associated Press bureau in Jackson. He then returned home to found and edit the Hammond *Daily Courier*. In 1936, at

272

the invitation of several prominent Greenvillians, William Alexander Percy among them, Carter moved to Greenville and established the *Delta Star*, which two years later took over its chief competitor, the Greenville *Democrat-Times* and became the *Delta Democrat-Times*. Although there were brief stints elsewhere—to Harvard as a Nieman Fellow in 1940; to the U.S. Army during the war (where he helped establish and edit the Middle East editions of *Yank* and *Stars and Stripes*); and to Tulane, as writer-in-residence, toward the end of his life—he lived in Greenville the rest of his life. He died April 4, 1972.

Carter's journalistic work is generally well known. However, he was also a prolific writer of fiction, poetry, history, and biography. The selections here, from his one volume of verse, *The Ballad of Catfoot Grimes* (1964), are intended to recognize the more creative aspects of his literary career.

Flood Song

Lawd, but it's black, with nary star showin',
It's jes' like us was dead.
Light the fire, boys, and keep it going!
But, boss, it turns the river red.

　　　　Ol' Mississip's a-rarin',
　　　　She's growlin' and she's swearin'.
　　　　Ain't that a body floatin' in the light?
　　　　She's reachin' out an' snatchin'
　　　　And she's keepin' what she's catchin'
　　　　Cause she's gonna raise a ruckus tonight.

Jesus Marster, but these bags is heavy,
Cain't stop no river with san'.
Heave up, boys, and pile 'em on the levee.
Us is flirtin' with the Promised Lan'.

　　　　Ol' Mississip's a-rollin',
　　　　Got her spade an' goin' holin'.

Looks mighty like she's spilin' for a fight.
She's traipsin' down a-swingin'
When she rounds the bend she's singin'
That she's gonna raise a ruckus tonight.

Look up yonder, boss, them bags is shakin',
'Taint no use now, that's sho!
God in Heaven, the levee's breaking—
Boss man, let us go.

Ol' Mississip's a-rumblin'
Cain't you see them san' bags tumblin'?
She don't care if you's nigger folks or white.
An' when she starts to spillin'
She's ready for a killin'.
She's raisin' her a ruckus tonight.

Revival Deity

God's in the saddle
And the cinch grips tight.
God is jabbing
With the spurs of fright.
Man is a horse
For God to ride,
Sing out, sister
If you're Jesus' bride.
Walk down, brother
And shout your sin.
But the air might freshen
If Satan danced in.

. . . Voice of God

Morose, unshaved, they hem the sound truck in
To lap metallic promises that roll
From the loud-speaker . . . *starve you with a dole*
While Wall Street steals the flour from your bin.
Harsh fruit from cornucopias of sound
Feeds stagnant, hapless minds and nurtures hate.
The rally ends. They straggle home to prate
Of wealth to come, forgot their unplowed ground.
These stain our world, the vision-lashed and dumb
Who leap to hope at man's voice amplified
To brassy roars that pledge no present crumb
But endless loaves of promise, sweet, untried;
Who surge forever in a chained unrest
While Christ and charlatan pronounce them blessed.

Ashes of Sackcloth

When she was fifteen she last walked the tracks
To town to peer into the Bon-Ton store,
And covet the sheer pink things women wore
Unless their mothers patterned bleached-out sacks
That once held flour and such. The girl was slim
And tawny as a sunset, loving bright
Prohibitives. And so it was to him
An easy lark to coax her in the night.

Her mother found out first, and beat her blue,
And tore away the clinging little bribe.
She crept from home next day. A city's stew
Sucked her into its mess, in friendless gibe
At God the loving whose compassion lacks
Knowledge of flour and fertilizer sacks.

In Depression Time

How many in the family? Five?
Right here is where you sign.
Let's see your work card. Here's your meat—
Back there, don't shove the line.

> *Corn pone and bacon fat*
> *And limp grass for a hoss.*
> *Out yonder runs the river, boys,*
> *Let's beat the Yanks across.*

You need a pair of overalls?
No flour in the bin?
Three days a week will have to do—
Back there, stop pushing in.

> *Mired guns and broken steel,*
> *Old Stonewall, thar he stands.*
> *Hell, we don't need no powder, boys,*
> *Let's lick 'em with our hands.*

The seed won't come until next week,
There's talk of winter fuel;
Don't worry, we'll take care of you—
Back there, you know the rule.

> *Ravaged field and blackened roof,*
> *And faded calico.*
> *We ain't in want of scarecrows, boys,*
> *Let's plough another row.*

Deaths

The morning that my ganddad died
I hid beneath the stairs and cried

Because my father tripped and broke
The gilded saber made of oak

That granddad once had carved for me;
And Father grumbled nervously.

"Go throw those splinters out of here,
God knows today this house is drear

Enough without you underfoot—
Pick up those pieces now, and scoot."

Dad couldn't know the shattered wood
Meant my grandfather's flesh and blood,

And it was all I had to save
Of granddad summoned to his grave.

Circle

Here a valley, here a river,
Woodsman, hew the tall trees down.
Peel the lopped logs bare for chinking,
Mate the tall trees, breed a town.
Townsman, splay the opal valley
Into streets, and conjure this
Coiling smoke of sleeping cabins
To a dazed metropolis.

City eyes, stare at the river
Flowing past your loud unease,
Dream of searching for a valley,
Dream of hewing down tall trees.

(1911–)

Tennessee Williams

Thomas Lanier Williams, born in Columbus on March 26, 1911, is one of America's most important playwrights. After living a number of years in various Mississippi towns, Williams moved with his family to St. Louis in 1918. He went to college at the University of Missouri from 1930 to 1932, worked a while for the International Shoe Company in St. Louis, and then attended Washington University from 1936 to 1937. After having five of his plays produced in St. Louis in 1936 and 1937, he entered the University of Iowa in 1938 and graduated in that year with an A.B. degree.

Until 1944, the year *The Glass Menagerie* was introduced in Cleveland, Williams moved about, working at several jobs in New Orleans and Jacksonville, Florida, writing screenplays at MGM Studios in Hollywood, and composing a number of dramas which were produced in New York City. In that year, however, he decided to devote himself exclusively to writing. He followed *The Glass Menagerie* with two superb plays, *A Streetcar Named Desire* and *Summer and Smoke,* produced in New York in 1947 and 1948, and won both the Pulitzer Prize and the New York Drama Critics Circle Award. The decade that followed the success of these two plays was Williams's most productive period. In those years, from 1949 to 1959, he wrote some of the most effective plays in America's

278

theatrical history, including *Cat on a Hot Tin Roof* and *Sweet Bird of Youth*.

The world Williams has created in his plays is one that has successfully animated both the stage and the movie screen. It is a slightly stylized and sometimes unrealistic world, filled with compelling, emotional characters who may be moving toward insanity like Catherine in *Suddenly Last Summer*, or welling with passion, like Blanche in *A Streetcar Named Desire*, or suffering emotional impotence, like Brick in *Cat on a Hot Tin Roof*. Whatever their physical or spiritual afflictions, his heroes and heroines are usually troubled, lost people who are undergoing terrible crises in their lives. Adding intensity to his plays is the knowledge that somewhere behind the stage or screen, behind the passion and the violence of his tortured characters, is a vision of beauty and peace that is fleeting and illusive, even to the poet-figure who sometimes appears in his plays. Williams's drama is collectively a powerful and poetic evocation of human strife that is unsurpassed in modern drama.

"The Long Stay Cut Short; or The Unsatisfactory Supper," reprinted here from *American Blues: Five Short Plays* (New York: Dramatists Play Service, 1948), was incorporated into the script for the 1955 film *Baby Doll*.

The Long Stay Cut Short,
Or,
The Unsatisfactory Supper

THREE CHARACTERS
BABY DOLL   ARCHIE LEE   AUNT ROSE

THE CURTAIN RISES *on the porch and side yard of a shotgun cottage in Blue Mountain, Mississippi. The frame house is faded and has a greenish-gray cast with dark streaks from the roof, and there are irregularities in the lines of the building. Behind it the dusky cyclorama is stained with the rose of sunset, which is stormy-looking, and the wind has a cat-like whine.*

Upstage from the porch, in the center of the side yard, is a very large rose-bush, the beauty of which is somehow sinister-looking.

A Prokofief sort of music introduces the scene and sets a mood of grotesque lyricism.

The screen door opens with a snarl of rusty springs and latches: this stops the music.

MRS. "BABY DOLL" BOWMAN *appears. She is a large and indolent woman, but her amplitude is not benign, her stupidity is not comfortable. There is a suggestion of Egypt in the arrangement of her glossy black hair and the purple linen dress and heavy brass jewelry that she is wearing.*

ARCHIE LEE BOWMAN *comes out and sucks at his teeth. He is a large man with an unhealthy chalk-white face and slack figure.*

(The evenly cadenced lines of the dialogue between BABY DOLL *and* ARCHIE LEE *may be given a singsong reading, somewhat like a grotesque choral incantation, and passages may be divided as strophe and antistrophe by* BABY DOLL'S *movements back and forth on the porch.)*

ARCHIE LEE. The old lady used to could set a right fair table, but not any more. The food has fallen off bad around here lately.

BABY DOLL. You're right about that, Archie Lee. I can't argue with you.

ARCHIE LEE. A good mess of greens is a satisfactory meal if it's cooked with salt-pork an' left on th' stove till it's tender, but thrown in a platter ha'f cooked an' unflavored, it ain't even fit for hog-slops.

BABY DOLL. It's hard t' spoil greens but the old lady sure did spoil 'em.

ARCHIE LEE. How did she manage t' do it?

BABY DOLL. (*Slowly and contemptuously.*) Well, she had 'em on th' stove for about an hour. Said she thought they wuh boilin'. I went in the kitchen. The stove was stone-cold. The silly old thing had forgotten to build a fire in it. So I called her back. I said, "Aunt Rose, I think I understand why the greens aren't boilin'." "Why aren't they boilin'?" she says. Well, I told her, "it might have something to do with the fack that the stove issen lighted!"

ARCHIE LEE. What did she say about that?

BABY DOLL. Juss threw back her head an' cackled. "Why, I thought my stove was lighted," she said. "I thought my greens wuh boilin'." Everything is *my*. My stove, my greens, my kitchen. She has taken possession of everything on the place.

ARCHIE LEE. She's getting delusions of grandeur. (*A high, thin laugh is heard inside.*) Why does she cackle that way?

BABY DOLL. How should I know why she cackles! I guess it's supposed to show that she's in a good humor.

ARCHIE LEE. A thing like that can become awf 'ly aggravating.

BABY DOLL. It gets on my nerves so bad I could haul off and scream. And obstinate! She's just as obstinate as a mule.

ARCHIE LEE. A person can be obstinate and still cook greens.

BABY DOLL. Not if they're so obstinate they won't even look in a stove t' see if it's lighted.

ARCHIE LEE. Why don't you keep the old lady out of the kitchen?

BABY DOLL. You get me a nigger and I'll keep her out of the kitchen. (*The screen door creaks open and* AUNT ROSE *comes out on the porch. She is breathless with the exertion of moving from the kitchen, and clings to a porch column while she is catching her breath. She is the type of old lady, about eighty-five years old, that resembles a delicate white-headed monkey. She has on a dress of gray calico which has become too large for her shrunken figure. She has a continual fluttering in her chest which makes her laugh in a witless manner. Neither of the pair on the porch pays any apparent attention to her, though she nods and smiles brightly at each.*)

AUNT ROSE. I brought out m' scissors. Tomorrow is Sunday an' I can't stand for my house to be without flowers on Sunday. Besides if we don't cut the roses the wind'll just blow them away.

BABY DOLL. (*Yawns ostentatiously.* ARCHIE LEE *sucks loudly at his teeth.* BABY DOLL, *venting her irritation.*) Will you quit suckin' your teeth?

ARCHIE LEE. I got something stuck in my teeth an' I can't remove it.

BABY DOLL. There's such a thing as a tooth-pick made for that purpose.

ARCHIE LEE. I told you at breakfast we didn't have any toothpicks. I told you the same thing at lunch and the same thing at supper. Does it have to appear in the paper for you to believe it?

BABY DOLL. There's other things with a point besides a toothpick.

AUNT ROSE. (*Excitedly.*) Archie Lee, Son! (*She produces a spool of thread from her bulging skirt-pocket.*) You bite off a piece of this thread and run it between your teeth and if that don't dislodge a morsel nothing else will!

ARCHIE LEE. (*Slamming his feet from porch-rail to floor.*) Now listen, you all, I want you both to get this. If I want to suck at my teeth, I'm going to suck at my teeth!

AUNT ROSE. That's right, Archie Lee, you go on and suck at your teeth as much as you want to. (BABY DOLL *grunts disgustedly.* ARCHIE LEE *throws his feet back on the rail and continues sucking loudly at his teeth.* AUNT ROSE, *hesitantly.*) Archie Lee, son, you weren't satisfied with your supper. I noticed you left a lot of greens on your plate.

ARCHIE LEE. I'm not strong on greens.

AUNT ROSE. I'm surprised to hear you say that.

ARCHIE LEE. I don't see why you should be. As far as I know I never declared any terrible fondness for greens in your presence, Aunt Rose.

AUNT ROSE. Well, somebody did.

ARCHIE LEE. Somebody probably did sometime and somewhere but that don't mean it was me.

AUNT ROSE. (*With a nervous laugh.*) Baby Doll, who is it dotes on greens so much?

BABY DOLL. (*Wearily.*) I don't know who dotes on greens, Aunt Rose.

AUNT ROSE. All these likes and dislikes, it's hard to keep straight in your head. But Archie Lee's easy t' cook for, yes, he is, easy t' cook for! Jim's a complainer, oh, my, what a complainer. And Susie's household! What complainers! Every living one of them's a complainer! They're such complainers I die of nervous prostration when I'm cooking for them. But Archie Lee, here, he takes whatever you give him an' seems to love ev'ry bite of it! (*She touches his head.*) Bless you, honey, for being so easy t' cook for! (ARCHIE LEE *picks up his chair and moves it roughly away from* AUNT ROSE. *She laughs nervously and digs in her capacious pocket for the scissors.*) Now I'm goin' down there an' clip a few roses befo' th' wind blows 'em away 'cause I can't stand my house to be without flowers on Sunday. An' soon as I've finished with that, I'm goin' back in my kichen an' light up my stove an' cook you some eggs Birmingham. I won't have my men-folks unsatisfied with their supper. Won't have it, I won't stand for it! (*She gets to the bottom of the steps and pauses for breath.*)

ARCHIE LEE. What is eggs Birmingham?

AUNT ROSE. Why, eggs Birmingham was Baby Doll's daddy's pet dish.

ARCHIE LEE. That don't answer my question.

AUNT ROSE.(*As though confiding a secret.*) I'll tell you how to prepare them.

ARCHIE LEE. I don't care how you prepare them, I just want to know what they are.

AUNT ROSE. (*Reasonably.*) Well, Son, I can't say what they are without telling how to prepare them. You cut some bread-slices and take the centers out of them. You put the bread-slices in a skillet with butter. Then into each cut-out center you drop one egg and on top of the eggs you put the cut-out centers.

ARCHIE LEE. (*Sarcastically.*) Do you build a fire in th' stove?

BABY DOLL. No, you forget to do that. That's why they call them eggs Birmingham, I suppose. (*She laughs at her wit.*)

AUNT ROSE. (*Vivaciously.*) That's what they call them, they call them eggs Birmingham and Baby Doll's daddy was just insane about them. When Baby Doll's daddy was not satisfied with his supper, he'd call for eggs Birmingham and would stomp his feet on the floor until I'd fixed 'em! (*This recollection seems to amuse her so that she nearly falls over.*) He'd stomp his feet on th' floor!—until I'd fixed 'em. . . . (*Her laughter dies out and she wanders away from the porch, examining the scissors.*)

BABY DOLL. That old woman is going out of her mind.

ARCHIE LEE. How long is she been with us?

BABY DOLL. She come in October.

ARCHIE LEE. No, it was August. She pulled in here last August.

BABY DOLL. Was it in August? Yes, it was, it was August.

ARCHIE LEE. Why don't she go an' cackle at Susie's awhile?

BABY DOLL. Susie don't have a bed for her.

ARCHIE LEE. Then how about Jim?

BABY DOLL. She was at Jim's direckly before she come here and Jim's wife said she stole from her and that's why she left.

ARCHIE LEE. I don't believe she stole from her. Do you believe she stole from her?

BABY DOLL. I don't believe she stole from her. I think it was just an excuse to get rid of her. (AUNT ROSE *has arrived at the rose-bush. The wind comes up and nearly blows her off her feet. She staggers around and laughs at her precarious balance.*)

AUNT ROSE. Oh, my gracious! Ha-ha! Oh! Ha-ha-ha!

BABY DOLL. Why, every time I lay my pocket-book down, the silly old thing picks it up and comes creeping in to me with it, and says, "Count the change."

ARCHIE LEE. What does she do that for?

BABY DOLL. She's afraid I'll accuse her of stealing like Jim's wife did.

AUNT ROSE. (*Singing to herself as she creeps around the rose-bush.*)
Rock of Ages, cleft for me,
Let me hide myself in thee!

ARCHIE LEE. Your buck-toothed cousin named Bunny, didn't he hit on a new way of using oil-waste?

BABY DOLL. He did an' he didn't.

ARCHIE LEE. That statement don't make sense.

BABY DOLL. Well, you know Bunny. He hits on something and ropes in a few stockholders and then it blows up and the stockholders all go to court. And also he says that his wife's got female trouble.

ARCHIE LEE. They've all got something because they're not mental giants but they've got enough sense to know the old lady is going to break down pretty soon and none of 'em wants it to be while she's on their hands.

BABY DOLL. That is about the size of it.

ARCHIE LEE. And I'm stuck with her?

BABY DOLL. Don't holler.

ARCHIE LEE. I'm nominated the goat!

BABY DOLL. Don't holler, don't holler! (AUNT ROSE *sings faintly by rose-bush.*)

ARCHIE LEE. Then pass the old lady on to one of them others.

BABY DOLL. Which one, Archie Lee?

ARCHIE LEE. Eeeny-meeny-miney-mo.—Mo gets her.

BABY DOLL. Which is "Mo"?

ARCHIE LEE. Not me! (*Moving slowly and cautiously around the rose-bush with her scissors,* AUNT ROSE *sings to herself. Intersperses lines of the hymn with dialogue on porch. A blue dusk is gathering in the yard but a pool of clear light remains upon the rose-bush.* ARCHIE LEE, *with religious awe*.) Some of them get these lingering types of diseases and have to be given morphine, and they tell me that morphine is just as high as a cat's back.

BABY DOLL. Some of them hang on forever, taking morphine.

ARCHIE LEE. And quantities of it!

BABY DOLL. Yes, they take quantities of it!

ARCHIE LEE. Suppose the old lady broke a hip-bone or something, something that called for morphine!

BABY DOLL. The rest of the folks would have to pitch in and help us.

ARCHIE LEE. Try and extract a dime from your brother Jim! Or Susie or Tom or Bunny! They're all tight as drums, they squeeze ev'ry nickel until th' buffalo bleeds!

BABY DOLL. They don't have much and what they have they hold onto.

ARCHIE LEE. Well, if she does, if she breaks down an' dies on us here, I'm giving you fair warning —— (*Lurches heavily to his feet and spits over edge of porch*.) I'll have her burned up and her ashes put in an old Coca-cola bottle —— (*Flops down again*.) Unless your folks kick in with the price of a coffin! (AUNT ROSE *has clipped a few roses. Now she wanders toward the front of the cottage with them*.) Here she comes back. Now tell her.

BABY DOLL. Tell her what?

ARCHIE LEE. That she's out-stayed her welcome.

AUNT ROSE. (*Still at some distance*.) I want you children to look.

ARCHIE LEE. You going to tell her?

AUNT ROSE. I want you children to look at these poems of nature!

ARCHIE LEE. Or do I have to tell her?

BABY DOLL. You hush up and I'll tell her.

ARCHIE LEE. Then tell her right now, and no more pussy-footing.

AUNT ROSE. (*Now close to the porch.*) Look at them, look at them, children, they're poems of nature! (*But the "Children" stare unresponsively, not at the flowers but at* AUNT ROSE'S *face with its extravagant brightness. She laughs uncertainly and turns to* ARCHIE LEE *for a more direct appeal.*) Archie Lee, aren't they, aren't they just poems of nature? (*He grunts and gets up, and as he passes* BABY DOLL'S *chair he gives it a kick to remind her.* BABY DOLL *clears her throat.*)

BABY DOLL. (*Uneasily.*) Yes, they are poems of nature, Aunt Rose, there is no doubt about it, they are. And, Aunt Rose—while we are talking—step over here for a minute so I can speak to you. (AUNT ROSE *had started away from the porch, as if with a premonition of danger. She stops, her back to the porch, and the fear is visible in her face. It is a familiar fear, one that is graven into her very bones, but which she has never become inured to.*)

AUNT ROSE. What is it, honey? (*She turns around slowly.*) I know you children are feeling upset about something. It don't take a Gypsy with cards to figure that out. You an' Archie Lee both are upset about something. I think you were both unsatisfied with your supper. Isn't that it, Baby Doll? The greens didn't boil long enough. Don't you think I know that? (*She looks from* BABY DOLL'S *face to* ARCHIE LEE'S *back with a hesitant laugh.*) I played a fool trick with my stove, I thought it was lighted and all that time it was . . .

BABY DOLL. Aunt Rose, won't you set down so we can talk comfortably?

AUNT ROSE. (*With a note of hysteria.*) I don't want to set down, I don't want to set down, I can talk on my feet! I tell you, getting up an' down is more trouble than it's worth! Now what is it, honey? As soon as I've put these in water, I'm going to light up my stove an' cook you two children some Eggs Birmingham. Archie Lee, Son, you hear that?

ARCHIE LEE. (*Roughly, his back still turned.*) I don't want Eggs Birmingham.

BABY DOLL. He don't want Eggs Birmingham and neither do I. But while we are talking, Aunt Rose—well—Archie Lee's wondered and I've been wondering, too . . .

AUNT ROSE. About what, Baby Doll?

BABY DOLL. Well, as to whether or not you've—made any plans.

AUNT ROSE. Plans?

BABY DOLL. Yes, plans.

AUNT ROSE. What kind of plans, Baby Doll?

BABY DOLL. Why, plans for the future, Aunt Rose.

AUNT ROSE. Oh! Future! No—no, when an old maid gets to be nearly a hundred years old, the future don't seem to require much planning for, honey. Many's a time I've wondered but I've never doubted. . . . (*Her voice dies out and there is a strain of music as she faces away from the porch.*) I'm not forgotten by Jesus! No, my Sweet Savior has not forgotten about me! The time isn't known to me or to you, Baby Doll, but it's known by Him and when it comes He will call me. A wind'll come down and lift me an' take me away! The way that it will the roses when they're like I am. . . . (*The music dies out and she turns back to the tribunal on the front porch.*)

BABY DOLL. (*Clearing her throat again.*) That's all very well, Aunt Rose, to trust in Jesus, but we've got to remember that Jesus only helps those that—well—help themselves!

AUNT ROSE. Oh, I know that, Baby Doll! (*She laughs.*) Why, I learned that in my cradle, I reckon I must have learned that before I was born. Now when have I ever been helpless? I could count my sick days, the days that I haven't been up and around, on my fingers! My Sweet Savior has kept me healthy an' active, active an' healthy, yes, I do pride myself on it, my age hasn't made me a burden! And when the time comes that I have to lean on His shoulder, I —— (ARCHIE LEE *turns about roughly.*)

ARCHIE LEE. All this talk about Jesus an' greens didn't boil an' so forth has got nothing at all to do with the situation! Now look here, Aunt Rose—

BABY DOLL. (*Getting up.*) Archie Lee, will you hold your tongue for a minute?

ARCHIE LEE. Then you talk up! And plain! What's there to be so pussy-footing about?

BABY DOLL. There's ways and there's ways of talking anything over!

ARCHIE LEE. Well, talk it over and get off the subject of Jesus! There's Susie, there's Jim, there's Tom and Jane and there's Bunny! And if none of them suits her, there's homes in the county will take her! Just let her decide on which one she is ready to visit. First thing in the morning I'll pile her things in the car and drive her out to whichever one's she's decided! Now ain't that a simple procedure compared to all of this pussy-footing around? Aunt Rose has got sense. She's counted the rooms in this house! She knows that I'm nervous, she knows that I've got work to do and a workingman's got to be fed! And his house is his house and he wants it the way that he wants it! Well, Jesus Almighty, if that's not a plain, fair and square way of settling the matter, I'll wash my hands clean and leave you two women to talk it over yourselves! Yes, I'll—be God damned if—! (*He rushes in and slams the screen door. There is a long pause in which* BABY DOLL *looks uncomfortably at nothing, and* AUNT ROSE *stares at the screen door.*)

AUNT ROSE. (*Finally.*) I thought you children were satisfied with my cooking. (*A blue dusk has gathered in the yard.* AUNT ROSE *moves away from the porch and there is a strain of music. The music is drowned out by the cat-like whine of the wind turning suddenly angry.* BABY DOLL *gets up from her wicker chair.*)

BABY DOLL. Archie Lee, Archie Lee, you help me in with these chairs before they blow over! (*She drags her chair to the screen door.*) It looks and sounds like a twister! Hold that screen open for me! Pull in that chair! Now this one! We better get down in the cellar! (*As an after-thought.*) Aunt Rose, come in here so we can shut this door! (AUNT ROSE *shakes her head slightly. Then she looks toward the sky, above and beyond the proscenium, where something portentous is forming.* BABY DOLL *back in the house.*) Call Aunt Rose in!

ARCHIE LEE. (*Near the door.*) The stubborn old thing won't budge. (*The door slams shut. The whine of the angry cat turns into a distant roar and the roar approaches. But* AUNT ROSE *remains in the yard, her face still somberly but quietly thoughtful. The loose gray calico of her dress begins to whip and tug at the skeleton lines of her figure. She looks wonderingly at the sky, then back at the house beginning to shrink into darkness, then back at the sky from which the darkness is coming, at each with the same unflinching but troubled expression. Nieces and nephews and cousins, like pages of an album, are rapidly turned through her mind, some of them loved as children*

but none of them really her children and all of them curiously un-
needful of the devotion that she had offered so freely, as if she had
always carried an armful of roses that no one had ever offered a vase
to receive. The flimsy gray scarf is whipped away from her shoul-
ders. She makes an awkward gesture and sinks to her knees. Her
arms let go of the roses. She reaches vaguely after them. One or two
she catches. The rest blow away. She struggles back to her feet. The
blue dusk deepens to purple and the purple to black and the roar
comes on with the force of a locomotive as AUNT ROSE's *figure is still*
pushed toward the rose-bush.)

THE CURTAIN FALLS

(1890–1970)

Cid Ricketts Sumner

Cid Ricketts Sumner, born Bertha Ricketts on September 27, 1890, did not publish a book until she was forty-eight. After a number of years spent acquiring academic degrees (B.S., Millsaps College; M.A., Columbia University), attending medical school (Cornell University), and teaching in public schools and at Millsaps College in Jackson, she decided upon a career of writing. Known generally as a writer of "light" fiction, such as the three "Tammy" novels—*Tammy Out of Time* (1948), *Tammy, Tell Me True* (1959), and *Tammy in Rome* (1965)—Sumner wrote a number of other books, thirteen in all, that deal perceptively with important social questions. She was very active in her later years, publishing one-half of her books after the age of sixty-five, going on a donkey ride through the Cevennes Mountains in France, shooting the rapids of the Colorado and Green rivers. "Age," she wrote in *Traveller in the Wilderness* (1957), "should hold not only contemplation but danger, adventure." On October 15, 1970, in her eightieth year, her body was found in her home, wrapped in a curtain; she had been beaten to death with a hammer.

Sumner's most significant work deals with specific social problems. In *Ann Singleton* (1938), a progressive young woman with modern ideas about venereal disease and birth control falls in love with a philanderer; in *But the Morning Will Come* (1949), Bently Churston must tell her son

290

that he has Negro blood. In *Quality* (1946), Pinky Johnson, a Negro, passes for white; in *The Hornbeam Tree* (1953), a middle-aged woman must cope with her love for a young man. But it is in her account of her hike through the Cevennes in *Saddle Your Dreams* (1964), in her descriptions of her boat rides down the Colorado and Green rivers in *Traveller in the Wilderness* (1957), in her tale of a life-saving ghost in *Christmas Gift* (1961), and, of course, in her Tammy books, that one finds the wit, humor, grace, and charm that best distinguish Sumner's literary style. Most of her fiction incorporates the wit and wisdom of a mature woman, the entertainment of a good story, and the light, deft touch of a literary craftsman.

Christmas Gift

ON THE EVENING OF DECEMBER TWENTY-THIRD Miss Fidelia Grey—with an *e*, if you please, as she always said when introduced—sat huddled over a grate fire in the sitting room of a hotel in Fort William, a small town near the west coast of Scotland. The red cotton brocade curtains were drawn but now and then they swayed inward as a gust of cold wind thrust itself through the cracks around the window sash. That Miss Grey should be here at all was due to one of those curious concatenations of circumstance which are sometimes tossed into a well-arranged journey as if Fate, in a mischievous mood, wished to demonstrate the fallibility of mortal planning.

There was nothing wrong with Miss Grey's plans—she had spent all the preceding summer making them. The trouble was that in Glasgow she had picked up a summer bus schedule and the bus which she had expected to take from Fort William on into the Highlands was no longer running. She had picked up an influenza germ too, in that smoky city, and so, aching and sneezing, had been obliged to spend not only one night but a whole week in this small hotel, abed most of the time with a low fever.

Illness had not entered into her calculations. Indeed it was her pride that in all her twenty-two years of teaching history at The Country School for Girls in Hingham, Massachusetts, she had been absent from her classroom only during the week of her father's last illness. The headmistress of that staid, old preparatory school had referred to her admirable record at the last faculty meeting in June. In announcing the establishment of sabbatical leaves, she said, "The first will be granted to our faithful Fidelia."

The announcement had been greeted by a most gratifying round of applause. Miss Grey had her little eccentricities, as they all well knew—for instance, the frequency with which she quoted certain familiar proverbs, always with the explanation that while they might be considered trite by the English Department, they nevertheless contained the wisdom of the ages. New pupils, primed by their seniors, awaited with amused suspense her annual remark on the importance of the study of history. The future was uncertain, she said, the present was chaos. Only the past was sure. And while some of the more disrespectful referred to her as "Old Seeing-is-Believing," faculty and students alike had a genuine appreciation of her sterling qualities, and there was not one of them who had not at some time had cause to be grateful to her, for special tutoring, for taking on extra work in time of illness or for smoothing out some difficulty with an unreasonable parent. Her crisp, matter-of-fact manner often had an almost miraculous effect on emotional situations. Indeed Miss Grey was "New England" from the top of her head—neat gray hair drawn straight back to an uncompromising bun—to the soles of her flat-heeled shoes; she was as humorless and unadorned as boiled cod; yet she was really kind-hearted, and sometimes a bit wistful over people's tendency to take her strictly at face value.

So she was not unmoved by the genuineness of her colleagues' congratulations, and, a bit befogged by this unaccustomed emotion, answered the questions at once put to her with more spontaneity than her usual caution permitted.

"And what will you do with a whole year off?" the young English teacher inquired.

"I shall go to Scotland, of course," Miss Grey replied without hesitation, for the last time she had really wanted to go anywhere had been when she was at work on a master's thesis, her subject, Montrose, to whom she had been attracted not so much by the romance and glamour of the Scottish hero as by the brilliance of his tactical maneuvers.

"But not in winter, surely."

"Certainly," Miss Grey replied. "I prefer to see a country at its most characteristic season. Besides, you will remember, *I* am a New Englander."

The young teacher received this as the delicate rebuke it was doubtless intended to be. She herself had had the misfortune to be born in Virginia and was therefore considered by Miss Grey to be unfamiliar with the Puritan tradition of plain living and high thinking. It was entirely beside the point that Miss Grey's personal contact with plain living or any physical hardship had been limited to nothing more severe than the walk through winter weather across the campus from her snug little Cape Cod cottage. Nor as the only child of a professor of mathematics at the university—"My life has been spent in academic circles," she was wont to say—had she encountered any great rigors in Cambridge where she had been prepared at private schools, educated at Radcliffe. Furthermore, her mother having died many years before, she was now the sole beneficiary of one of those small trust funds for which New England is noted and it was due to this foresight on the part of an ancestor "in wool," as the saying is, that she had been able to build for her father, after his retirement, the comfortable house which she now occupied.

"But won't you freeze in Scotland in the winter?" someone else persisted. "Why not go there this summer and to the Riviera or to one of the Balearic Islands for the winter?"

"It's true I have always loved islands ever since we used to go to Nantucket when I was a child," Miss Grey admitted. "However I would not think of leaving Hingham just now—my garden is all planted. Besides, it is just a matter of woolen underwear and tweeds."

But all the woolens she possessed did not serve to keep Miss Grey warm this December evening as she sat here all alone. She was almost the only guest in the hotel in this off-season period and she supposed that the management was economizing on fuel—an admirable aim in general but in this instance unwelcome. Weak and shaken by her bout with influenza, she felt the cold keenly. She had not planned it so. There was something most disconcerting about this small delay in her schedule, as well as in the unexpected weakness and a sort of light-headedness most unusual with her.

Furthermore, there had been disturbing things of another sort in the course of her two months away from home. Not on the voyage, of course. That she looked back upon with pure pleasure. She had taken a boat from Boston, a small steamer, and in a bad storm off the Grand Banks, had had the satisfaction of being the only passenger not violently seasick. For a moment now she thought with longing of the return passage—the sea air would restore her. Home with all its comforts, called. But to give up was not in her. No, she would go on and finish her study of the Montrose campaigns and write her paper for the historical journal, something on battlefields after three hundred years.

What troubled her about her visits to those scenes was something she had been able to push aside during busy days of catching buses and evenings of writing up notes, but now in this low moment she was defenseless. The truth was that the battlefields had been a great disappointment. On one, a small town of jerry-built houses had sprung up, on another a great forest spoiled the contour of the land. That was bad enough, but worst of all was that the facts of history seemed to blur and withdraw, taking on the illusive quality of fiction or myth, just at the very moment when they should have become most vivid. It was as if facts, reality itself, were but a curtain which had been drawn aside—but what was behind that curtain, she did not know. The stage was dark.

Miss Grey shook her head as if by the gesture she could rid herself of such disturbing notions, for that was all they were. "Don't be notional," her father had often said when she was small and given to rather extravagant fancies. Yet her uneasiness persisted. It was as if she had looked in the looking glass expecting to see her own face and her eyes had met with a total blank. This comparison now impressed itself so strongly upon her that she rose, crossed the room to the small mirror on the wall and stared at herself. Yes, she was there, though she saw that she had lost weight during her illness. Her fine regular features were reduced to something of the delicacy they had possessed in girlhood. "You are like a beautifully carved cameo," George had said.

Miss Grey turned away with a sniff of displeasure. Why on earth should she be thinking of George now? He had been the one small romance in her life, an affair so delicate and tentative that her father's remark that he was not a good student had set him at once out of bounds, turned her from him. She herself had always been a good student—it was the one way of winning her father's approval. She sat down again before the fire and began to poke it in the hope of getting a little warm before going up to her unheated room. The rattle of poker on grate kept her from hearing steps as someone entered the room.

"Ach, and are ye still here?" a voice inquired.

Miss Grey reached for her glasses that hung on a button on the front of her gray tweed jacket and, peering up at the tall lanky figure, recognized him as the young man who had been her companion on the bus and who had carried her suitcase to the hotel for her before going on about his business. "A touch of influenza," she replied. "I thought it wise to wait here till I had quite thrown it off."

"Here, ma'am, just give me that poker." He took it from her, stood it against the chimney and from a woodbox in the shadows brought some small sticks which he thrust between the bars of the grate. At once a bright blaze sprang up. "I thought ye were coming down with something, the way ye were sneezing all that way." He drew up a chair and sat down.

Miss Grey did not care to discuss her symptoms with a stranger, so, remembering he had told her he was an engineer on tour of some of the new power plants of the Highlands, she asked if his visits had been satisfactory.

He gave her a rather sheepish glance. "I haven't made them yet. Truth to tell, when I got to Mallaig, there was the steamer *Lochmor* about to sail for the Outer Isles. And since it was almost Christmas and a wee vacation due me, I took off on sudden impulse to see a young lady friend of mine who is teaching school there. She would be having her holiday and might be lonely, I thought, since it's her first year there."

The mention of school and holidays reminded Miss Grey that it was almost Christmas. She had never paid much attention to Christmas—"a thoroughly commercialized pagan observance suitable only for young children," her father had called it. She listened now to the young man's pleasant Scottish burr rather than to his words as he explained that only the young children of the islands were taught there, the older ones coming to the mainland for schooling. "The islands?" she asked now as he paused.

"The Hebrides, ma'am, off the west coast, and—"

Here Miss Grey interrupted—he need not think her ignorant just because she was an American—"I know exactly where they are and something of their history—occupied by the Norsemen for several hundred years. Lewis, Harris, of tweed fame, Uist where Flora MacDonald was born, Eriskay where Prince Charlie landed in 1745, Barra and certain smaller islands as well. Fishing and weaving are the principal industries of a population greatly decreased by immigration to Canada and America as well as Australia."

She might have continued at greater length had not his rather humorous regard silenced her. "I see, ma'am, that I am in the presence of a scholar. Ye have all the facts at the tip of your tongue, but I doubt if ye've tasted the flavor. It's not in books ye'll be finding the likes of that. Ach, and 'tis the spirit of the place that hits ye."

"Indeed?"

At that he launched into a fairly lyrical description of the Isle of South Uist from which he had just returned. His extravagance was no doubt due in part to his Gaelic temperament, Miss Grey thought, and in part to his feeling for the young lady. In any case it was more poetic an account than she would have expected from one whose profession was engineering. Indeed she was a little annoyed by his fanciful talk—it was too much the sort of inconsequential thing that had plagued her as she stood at the site of the battle of Kilsyth, for instance, thinking not of the strategy of campaign which was her real interest, but of Montrose's "whimsies"—the Blue Ribbon, the wisps of oats in the bonnets of his men, the trumpets sounding.

"It is maybe the light that lends such a strangeness to the atmosphere," the young man continued, "the sun being always low on the horizon, even at noon. The light that never was, I kept thinking all the while. And far off the isles be, for all the actual distance in miles is not so great. A fluid place, too, as if the solid earth had caught some quality of the sea around it. The bracken, now—there it is, brown and wintry, then all at once it is aglowing like the heart of a peat fire. A cliff can look as insubstantial as a cloud, all pink and soft-seeming and a cloud turns out to be a gray solid rock. Times there are when a mountain is no more than a bit of cardboard stuck up against the sky, two-dimensional. And if a mountain can lose a dimension, there be other things that can pick one up, acquiring a fourth. As the poet says, 'Now I a fourfold vision see,' and that's how it is. Ach, and it's an eerie feeling that gives ye, right in the middle of the broad daylight."

It was his tone as much as his words that sent a feeling, new and strange, brushing at the edge of Miss Grey's consciousness, its touch as light and soft as the wing of a moth in the dark. A little shiver ran through her and she bent over, elbows on knees, holding out her hands to the fire.

"Ye wouldn't be huddling over a wee bit of coals like this at Lochboisdale—it's central heating they have at the hotel there."

It was this last remark of his which put the idea into Miss Grey's head. "How long a trip is it, from the mainland out?" Even a few hours at sea might give her a start toward her normal vigor.

"About six hours, it is, ma'am, depending on wind and tide."

Better, even, than the boat trip to Nantucket, she thought, and a queer little nostalgia seized her for those gay childhood summers when she had roamed the shore below high cliffs of sand and had built castles there, collecting odd shells to border the walks and strange bits of seaweed to make gardens such as a mermaid might have planted at the bottom of the sea. Miss Grey brushed aside such memories, even as the tide so long ago had swept away her castles and gardens. Quickly she assembled the facts of the situation in which she found herself—first, she was in no condition to continue her researches at the moment; second, her notes needed to be re-worked and consolidated while fresh in her mind; and last, she did not care to remain longer in this drafty hotel and run the risk of a relapse. She therefore plied the young man with practical questions, and on learning that, tomorrow being Friday, the boat would sail from Mallaig at two-thirty in the afternoon for the Outer Isles she declared her intention of making the journey and spending a week or ten days at the Lochboisdale Hotel on the Isle of South Uist.

When she rose to say good night, the young engineer said, "I'm thinking ye'll never regret it, ma'am. There's something about the place. It leaves its mark. It's out of this world."

Miss Grey had no desire to be out of this world as it was the only one she ever expected to encounter. However, the next morning after a brief visit to a shop where she picked up a copy of Dr. Johnson's *Journey to the Hebrides*, she boarded the train for Mallaig. Activity seemed to improve her vague sense of malaise though her lightheadedness continued, and on arrival at that fishing village on the west coast, she had good appetite for lunch at a small inn not far from the dock. The *Lochmor* was already getting up steam, puffing out smoke as if she alone were charged with the task of clouding over a brilliant blue sky.

On the dock Miss Grey located the old man to whom she had entrusted her suitcase and was following him toward the gangplank when she heard a rustling, rushing sound behind her, a chirping and chattering as if a flock of birds were pursuing her. She turned and saw that it was indeed a flock—but of children just descended from a bus, all of them talking in a language that was indeed as strange and musical to her ears as the song of birds.

As she went on up the gangplank, Miss Grey hoped that they had just come down to see a friend off. Then she remembered what the engineer had told her about the school system in these parts. As this was the day before Christmas, no doubt these boys and girls of high-school age were homeward bound for the holidays. It was going to be as bad as being back at The Country School in Hingham, Miss Grey thought. Not that she did not like young people, it was only that she felt the need of a quiet passage. Still, she might be able to keep apart from them, she decided as she paid the old man, for, once aboard, the children remained milling about the forward deck. She therefore made her way aft, rounded the stern, picking her way among boxes, winches, and coils of rope to reach the starboard side. It was quite deserted, and here was a bench. She sat down, thinking that if it got too cool, she could move into a small empty lounge which she had noted through the windows as she passed. But the air was surprisingly mild. She took her book from the striped bag she carried on her arm, put on her spectacles and began to read. She had always admired Dr. Johnson, a man who knew his own mind.

When she looked up, she saw they were well out in what seemed to be open sea. Land was lost in a mist behind them and the boat was pitching and rolling so that she actually had difficulty keeping her position on the bench. Thankful to seafaring ancestors for the stability of her stomach, she moved to the rail, breathing in the soft air that was far too mild for this latitude, almost contrary to nature. There was a remarkable clarity of atmosphere, too, so that sea gulls swooping and wheeling overhead were incredibly white, the breaking spray of dazzling brilliance. And while the sky was of what Miss Grey considered a normal blue, the sea itself was a vivid blue-green. She had never been one to carry on, as she called it, over the beauties of nature, but for once she was impressed.

As she watched, clouds astern piled high in dark contrast to the rest of the scene and instead of being left behind, they seemed to be following, pursuing, driving the boat to the far ends of the earth. They were a mountain, cutting her off from the known, reasonable, dependable world. No other passengers were within sight, and this added to Miss Grey's uneasy sense of isolation. What am I doing here, she wondered. Who am I? These were queer thoughts indeed for Miss Grey.

At this moment there came from the bow of the boat the sound of young voices singing. The Gaelic words were strange, the airs plaintive, in minor key and, as is the way with all songs that have been handed down from generation to generation, they had a quality that was of no language, of no time, that spoke of the fundamental longings, joys, and despairs of all humanity. Inevitably Miss Grey was reminded of another time when she had experienced this feeling that she was not just herself but a part of something more. So now, clinging to the rail of the *Lochmor*, her black beret snugly down over her hair, gray topcoat fluttering in the wind, she was all at once back in her own library listening to Maria, the young boarding pupil from Caracas, singing a Spanish folk song. Miss Grey had tutored her privately, for she was sadly lacking in preparation, and in a curious way they had come to be friends, almost as if they were contemporaries. It was the girl's Latin temperament, Miss Grey had thought, which allowed her to be so natural, spontaneous, affectionate, and quick to penetrate Miss Grey's reserve, setting aside her seriousness and formality as if she saw at once that it was no more than a mask. She turned it this way and that, holding it up for the amusement of them both. They had talked freely—of religion, of life, even of love, and of death as well.

Now with the sound of the Gaelic songs in her ears Miss Grey was unable to push aside another memory of Maria, one that was bitter to her even after so many years. A slight cold had quickly gone into pneumonia, for this child of the tropics was unaccustomed to the rigors of a New England winter, and Miss Grey, because of a real affection for her as well as to relieve the school nurse, sat beside her bed all that last night before the crisis came, for this was before the days of penicillin.

Toward dawn, rousing from the coma into which she had sunk, Maria turned dark eyes on Miss Grey, eyes wide with an unchildlike awareness of her danger. "So you think—this—is all?" she whispered.

Miss Grey, stricken, torn between honesty and a desire to comfort, was speechless for a long moment. But she could not lie, so she took refuge in quoting a line from Fridtjof Nansen—"The soul is a function of the living brain." That was the best she could do.

The light seemed to go out of Maria's face, she turned away and closed her eyes. The slow minutes passed while Miss Grey sat there thinking, She asked for bread and I gave her a stone. It was all I had— Then a slight movement of the sick child roused her from such bitter thoughts. Maria, her face transfigured, was looking toward the blank white wall of the infirmary room as if she saw something where there was nothing at all. Miss Grey bent over her. "What is it, Maria? What do you see?" and she answered, with a small smile, "I see is I believe"—it was her quaintly foreign version of one of Miss Grey's maxims. Then she closed her eyes and slept.

It was the nurse's touch on Miss Grey's shoulder that made her start up in alarm. "But she is better, the fever is gone, she will be all right," the nurse said, and Miss Grey crept away through the misty dawn. Now, reliving that unforgettable night, a brush against her sleeve startled her so she almost lost her balance and clung to the rail for support. The young boy who, by a sudden rolling of the boat, had swayed against her as he passed murmured an apology. Glad of any interruption to her thoughts, Miss Grey nodded, "That's quite all right." At the same time she noted that he seemed a cut above the others she had observed boarding the boat. He was about thirteen, of grave and thoughtful mien, probably a good student she thought, sturdily built, his features regular without being the least effeminate, his complexion rosy and fair.

He went on a few steps and then, staring off to sea, halted so abruptly that Miss Grey followed his line of vision to discover what had stopped him there, transfixed. It was a sight such as she had never seen before—a complete rainbow, the whole arc like a great many-colored horseshoe stood upright on the water. So brilliant were the colors, so dense its texture that it seemed as if it must continue on down under the sea to form a perfect circle. Porpoises might play at leaping through that lower hoop, or children, lost and drowned, might take it for a slide in their watery playground fathoms deep beneath the waves.

As the colors began to fade, the boy moved on, but slowly, as one under a spell. He mounted one of the great coils of rope that lay in the very stern of the boat and stood there lightly poised with one hand resting on the flagpole. His bare knees were on a level with the top rail, his gaze fastened on the white foam of the wake as if it held some fascination for him. It did not occur to Miss Grey immediately that he was in any danger, she only thought what a fine graceful lad he was, what a picture with his bright plaid kilt fluttering in the wind and the Union Jack flying above his head. But as he leaned farther out over the water, her lips parted to cry out a warning. Yet the fear that this might startle him into losing his balance kept her silent. Could she reach him before a sudden pitch of the boat sent him headlong into the sea?

She was starting toward him when a sudden whirl of damp air struck her, so damp she thought for a second that a wave had crashed over her, and a little girl sped past on light and soundless step. She wore the same tartan as the boy, she was bareheaded, and her two long braids flew out behind her in the swiftness of her going. Laughing to herself, with a step and a leap as light as a dancer's, she sprang up behind her brother—for there was no doubt of their relationship—and with a quick movement reached out, drew him back.

Miss Grey had the impression that she did not actually touch him but perhaps that was due to the angle from which she watched. At all events, much to her relief, the boy regained his balance, leaped down without so much as a glance at his sister and ran off down the deck on the far side, the little girl skipping along behind him with delightfully easy grace.

The incident left Miss Grey shaken. There should be someone aboard in charge of these children, she thought with indignation. She was quite unreasonably upset about it. And chilly, too, for now the clouds had overtaken and enveloped the boat, a mist swirled wraithlike around her, touching her cheek with wet cold fingers. She turned up her coat collar and lingered but a little longer to wonder at the look of the sea. She knew very well that water took its color by reflection from the sky, so how was it now that with so gray a sky it retained that brilliant turquoise? And ahead, low on the horizon, she saw a band of white metallic light as if while night was falling here, a new day might be dawning somewhere in another world. It was very queer.

The small lounge was deserted save for the boy who had given her such a fright. He did not look up as she entered but seemed utterly absorbed in a comic book. Miss Grey sat down across the room from him under a hanging lamp, put on her glasses, and returned to her reading. It was no sound that made her look up after a bit, but a small chill in the air as if someone had opened a window. But the window was fast shut. It was a square of framed black against which, as she watched, a wave struck and washed downward in a brighter darkness, sending small rivulets between sash and sill to lay wet streamers on the back of the cushioned seat opposite her. Miss Grey blinked her eyes. Odd—she had not seen the little girl come in, but there she was, bending over, wringing water from her long chestnut braids. It fell in a small pool at her feet. Straightening up, finding Miss Grey's eyes upon her, a smile lighted her pale little face that was so like her brother's ruddy one. She shook her head faintly, shyly, almost apologetically, as if aware that she should not have brought so much wetness into the lounge, and yet what was she to do about it, she seemed to ask. Evidently a wave had splashed her thoroughly before she took refuge inside.

Miss Grey was quite charmed with her and as she went on with her reading she remained conscious of her two small companions, the boy so absorbed he took no notice of anything, the girl now so restfully quiet as if content just to sit beside her brother. The light was rather dim for the small print of her book so when she finished the chapter, Miss Grey closed her eyes for a little. When she opened them again, she saw that the little girl was untangling a bit of seaweed from her hair. When she got it loose at last, she turned it this way and that in her pale slender hands, studying it with a delightfully serious air of inquiry. Rather stiffly-branched, it was like a miniature gray-green Christmas tree, Miss Grey thought, and as if the idea had occurred to the child at the same moment their eyes met in a flash of understanding. How could it be that this little stranger, half a world and many years away, could bring her that same sense of gay companionship she had once shared so briefly with Maria?

Now with the most delicate movement, the little girl was fastening the seaweed in the long pin that held the skirt of her brother's kilt and so light and airy was her touch that he read on unaware of her prank. When she had finished, she folded her hands in her lap, sitting very straight and proper, nodded and smiled across at Miss Grey as if to say, "Now won't he be surprised when he finds himself all decorated like a Christmas gift!" Miss Grey was quite enchanted with her, all the more so as, when she would have spoken, the child, with a quick glance at her brother, laid one finger to her lips in a little silencing gesture, as if they were fellow conspirators.

At that moment the steward poked his head in the door to say they were entering the harbor, and would dock in a few minutes. By the time Miss Grey had gathered together her things, put away her book, and buttoned her coat, the children were gone. On deck she located her suitcase but lingered amidships, for the boys and girls in eager anticipation were all crowded forward. On her right the black mass of a mountain rising from the water's edge slipped silently by, for here in the harbor there were no waves. The engine's throbbing was subdued. Ahead like a lighted ship at anchor she could make out the shape of a low-lying building, the hotel no doubt. Then, as the boat swung round, she saw the pier, glistening darkly wet under misty lights that were reflected in trembling shafts like spiders' legs spread on the dark surface of the water. There was quite a crowd waiting there—parents come to meet their children, Miss Grey supposed, and she made no effort to hurry ashore, Let them go first. After all, there was no one to meet and welcome her, no one eagerly awaiting her arrival. With a sigh, she leaned on the rail, chin in hand and watched, as the children, chattering and calling back and forth, trooped down the gangplank. She searched the semidarkness for her two, as she thought of them, saw the boy for a second just as he landed. The girl had probably gone on before.

A little later, after she had been shown to a warm comfortable room at the hotel, Miss Grey, having waited only to wash her hands and smooth her hair, went down to dinner which the landlord assured her was always served late on boat nights. There were only a few people in the dining room and Miss Grey was shown to a small table near the window. As she took her place, she saw that there were three other guests at the next table—the boy from the boat and a man and woman whom she knew at once must be his parents. She was disappointed that the sister was not there—she must have gone on home with some other relative, Miss Grey thought, as she gave her attention to the excellent dinner served her.

The tables were so close, however, that she could not help hearing bits of conversation from the adjacent one, and though as a rule she was not sensitive to that sort of thing she gradually became aware of a certain tension among them. The father, as if trying to dispel it, was telling a long story of a shooting expedition. There was mention of the gilly, of the dogs, of a woodcock that got away. The boy laughed at all the proper places. It was the mother who was the uneasy one, Miss Grey decided. Now and then she glanced nervously toward the window, where rain was now beating and wind clawing at the pane. More than once she interrupted the narrative. "I hope there will be no storm when you go back," she said once. Again, addressing the boy in a tone that was almost desperate, "You will be careful, won't you? Stay inside, promise me."

Each time the boy answered with extraordinary patience, "Yes, Mother," or "Oh, rather!" It seemed to Miss Grey that he showed an adult comprehension of her anxiety, a sympathy such as might arise from long tolerance and forbearance. The story was ended at last, coffee had been served, when Miss Grey, looking again toward her neighbors, found the boy's eyes fixed upon her with such questioning interest that she smiled and said, "We crossed together, didn't we? And now I suppose you are all ready for a good holiday."

"Yes, ma'am," he said with a faint smile. The father bowed pleasantly enough, the mother continued to stare straight before her, hands clenched tight in her lap.

Miss Grey might have let the conversation end thus briefly, but something, she did not know quite what, made her add, "Your sister is not with you." Immediately she felt awkward at having made so obvious, indeed so stupid a remark. She was a bit disconcerted, too, by its effect. Even the mother was brought sharply out of her absorption. So she continued, addressing the parents now, "Yes, I noticed her, too, a charming child. I knew at once they were brother and sister—there was the resemblance, and then, too, they wore the same plaid."

The mother was leaning forward now, her eyes widening till they were startlingly large and dark in her pale face. "You—saw—her—" she whispered.

Miss Grey had the feeling that the woman was abnormally interested in what after all was a most commonplace affair, so with an effort at changing the subject somewhat, she said, "Yes, I noticed her first when we were looking at the rainbow. A most remarkable sight. Do you often have such perfect rainbows? I have never seen such a thing in New England."

"A rainbow—too—" the mother breathed rather than spoke the word. The other two were motionless, silent as if transfixed. They made no effort to answer Miss Grey's question. "And she—what did she do?" The mother's voice was hoarse.

Miss Grey wished she had never started the conversation, the woman was so evidently neurotic, if not definitely psychopathic, but having got herself into this she went on to describe the scene on deck. Then, addressing the boy, she added, "You really should not have been standing so close to the rail—discretion is the better part of valor, remember that." The pronouncement of one of her familiar maxims cleared the air, for Miss Grey at least, and she was turning back to her coffee when the mother's voice, insistent, imperative, stopped her.

"And his sister?"

The father spoke for the first time in a low, soothing tone, "Now dear, you know—you know—"

Miss Grey assumed her most matter-of-fact manner, the one which she had always found useful in dealing with unreasonable parents. "Yes, she followed her brother into the lounge where I was reading, she sat there wringing water from her braids—there was quite a high sea you know. We did not talk and yet I felt quite a part of her little joke when she pinned the scrap of seaweed on her brother's kilt—by the way, did you find it? She was so merry about it, I was quite charmed with her." They were all turned from her now, wide eyes fixed on the boy's kilt, the mother half-rising from her chair to snatch the seaweed from his hand as he fumbled at it like one in a daze. But for Miss Grey the scene on the boat had returned with such vividness that she was swept along by her own narrative. "When she had it all fastened there without attracting her brother's attention from his book, she lifted her finger to her lips in a delightful little gesture of silence. And then she lightly touched the seaweed once more, for all the world as if she had done up her Christmas gift and decorated it and was now adding a kiss with her love." There, she had finished, there was nothing more to tell, Miss Grey thought as she turned back to her coffee. Maybe that bit of seaweed would keep the mother quiet, for she was holding it tight in her hand now, turning it this way and that so that it caught the light and glistened as if dipped in liquid silver. The others sat motionless as if hypnotized by the sight of it.

The coffee was cold, and just as well, Miss Grey decided, otherwise she might have drunk it and been kept awake half the night. So she rose, said a brisk good night and was starting toward the door when the mother sprang up and seized both her hands. Her face was transfigured, alight, eyes shining. "Thank you, oh thank you for telling me!" Her clear ringing voice made everyone in the room look around.

Miss Grey, somewhat embarrassed, resorted again to her best schoolmarm manner, remembering that parents were always soothed by a word of praise for their children. "It was nothing. I just happened to be there, that's all, and it was a most delightful little scene—and an enchanting child, so affectionate, so merry." Again she said good night, including the boy and his father in her nod. They had both risen, and, as she crossed to the door, she heard the mother speak again in answer to a murmured word from the father, "But don't you see—she was happy—and she was taking care of him. I shall never be afraid any more. It was her Christmas gift!"

Miss Grey closed the dining-room door behind her and went on, puzzled, yet reminding herself that in her twenty-two years at The Country School in Hingham, Massachusetts, she had encountered some very odd parents, and this one was just a little odder.

Yet she did not forget her conversation and next morning at breakfast was tempted to ask the waitress for some account of the family. But she had never believed in getting information by the back door, so to speak, so she contented herself with remarking on the beauty of the day.

"A fine Christmas day indeed, ma'am. But there's nae wind at all."

"You sound as if you liked the wind," Miss Grey said with some surprise.

"Ah, but it's like the world had stopped breathing when there's nae wind about the place."

A curious point of view, Miss Grey mused. And a little later she set out on an exploratory walk to see for herself how the land lay and what the weather was. She passed the pier and followed the only road there was, enjoying the fresh mild air and a sense of such renewed vigor that she felt very well pleased with herself for having come. She had passed the stone houses that clustered near the water when her landlord overtook her. After an exchange of greetings, she mentioned the family she had encountered in the dining room and asked him if he could tell her anything about them.

"Ah yes," he said, "you must mean the Malcolm MacVees from the far end of the island. Down to meet the boy. A sad case, that. You wouldn't know, of course. The little girl, just a year ago at holiday time, it was. On the *Lochmor*, too, but a rougher passage than you had. The school children were all aboard and they were aft watching the gulls or—no, I believe there was a rainbow that day. At all events, there they were at the rail, lively and jumping about when the boat rolled sharply—and it happened."

"You mean—she—the little girl—overboard—"

"Aye, and never a trace, poor child, though they searched for many a day. The brother took it hard, wee lad that he was, felt he should have saved her, had a mind to drown himself, poor chap. I was glad to see them all so cheerful, quite like themselves again as they left last night after dinner." He tipped his hat and turned off the road by a path that led toward a stone cottage.

Miss Grey walked on, faster and faster. She did not slacken her pace till she had left all the houses far behind and there was only a moor on one side and on the other a loch that lay still as a mirror. There she stood in her black beret and her gray tweed suit, motionless as any stone, her eyes on the ground. "But I saw her," she said aloud. "I saw her with my own eyes. And the seaweed—they all saw that!" It had to be true. To see was to believe, as little Maria had said. With the toe of her sensible flat-heeled shoe she kicked a stone from the road. That was real. But so was all she had seen.

There was a creaking, whirring sound overhead and looking up she saw a great white swan just above her, neck outstretched in the awkward angle of flight, wings moving heavily in the alien air. "She was real as you," she said to the swan as he passed over. "As real as anything in this world." What then, what then? she thought. Why, anything could be! And at that so vast a realm of possibilities opened up before her that she began to tremble. She looked around her and it was as if she saw the world for the first time and found it beautiful and blest—the grasses by the roadside, gray rock that in the sunlight wore a rosy flush, black blocks of peat that were stacked in a field to dry, the swan that floated motionless on the royal-blue loch framed in velvet brown heather. His reflection there was as true as he. Real and unreal, they were all of a piece, they were a part of the whole. The line from Nansen returned to her but reversed, like the image of the swan—"The brain is a function of the living soul." It was equally true right-side up and topsy-turvy. This conviction struck her with all the power of a mystical revelation, and suddenly she felt in her breast a warmth, as if a flame had been lighted there.

At this moment in the village the churchbells began to ring. The sound came clear and sweet through the still air. This was Christmas, Christmas day in the morning. With face aglow, Miss Grey turned, stood motionless for a moment and then set out, walking faster and faster toward the sound of the bells.

(1922–)

Thomas Hal Phillips

Thomas Hal Phillips was born October 11, 1922, on a farm near Corinth, and attended school at Alcorn Agricultural High School in nearby Kossuth. Upon graduation from Mississippi State College in 1943, he went directly into the U.S. Navy and served with distinction with the amphibious forces, as captain of a landing craft, in the invasions of Anzio, Elba, and southern France. After the war Phillips enrolled in the creative writing program at the University of Alabama, and presented his first novel, *The Bitterweed Path*, as his M.A. thesis. From 1948–1950 he taught creative writing at Southern Methodist University, and he spent 1950–1951 in France studying on a Fulbright Fellowship. He then returned to Kossuth, where he has remained, supporting himself as a businessman and farmer, while writing novels. He has worked in various capacities (chiefly production and writing) on a number of movies, such as *Thieves Like Us, Nashville, Miss Jane Pittman, Nightmare in Badham County, Ode to Billy Joe*, and others. Phillips has received numerous awards for his writing, among them a Julius Rosenwald Fellowship and a Saxton Memorial Award for his first novel, the O. Henry award in 1951 for his short story "The Shadow of an Arm," and Guggenheim Fellowships in 1953 and 1955.

"A Man Named Victor" is a self-contained episode from *Search for a Hero*.

310

A Man Named Victor

SOMETHING NEW WAS BORN IN ALL OF US and I don't know what it was, though I have since tried to understand. I think we felt that time itself touched us—all twenty-nine whose names began with M, who lived in a long gray building called Hut M (some of the navy grayness at The Lakes was like Old Shiloh); and we felt ourselves a part of something that would last forever even if we ourselves did not endure—that is the way of uniforms and bands and rules. And that was in the beginning, too, when most of us were nineteen. Later, the feeling changed, perhaps without our knowing; so it didn't matter.

We lived in relative peace, standing in line for everything for which lines could be formed, and learned first of all that navy chiefs are the most efficient devices in the world.

I don't know whether I was homesick or not. I did miss the smell of the store; the sound of the church bell and the sight of Miss Audie clicking along the gravel walk, Sunday-school book and Bible under her arm; the huddle of men before the store on Saturday afternoon, talking about the war as one would talk about a man slowly dying; and the light through the pine trees in late evening.

Nobody seemed like the people back home, but the talk in our hut was sometimes like store-talk. Then I would listen and be glad I was there. Every morning, while we dressed in the cool naked light, we heard a long, thin, black-haired Texan talking to all of us: "I'd love the navy if it didn't have so many goddam buttons." And later, when the hut was warmer, while we waited for something: "You thimble-brain, you think everything you heard in Sunday school is so because you heard it on Sunday. Let me set you straight: It's the love of possessing, not the love of money, that's the root of all evil."

And still later: "Americans were made for war, just like the goddam Germans, and get that through your brain. They love it, and you know why? Because it's the best thing there is for heroes, better than all the home runs and touchdowns and two-under-par's and all the other infantile tricks that have to be concocted for an infantile country where the unweaned reach thirty with a wife and two kids and find out they're too old to swing a bat or kick a field goal . . ."

Then David Mapp, a Pennsylvanian, interrupted him with: "Say just a little more about America, you Texas bastard, and I'm gonna take a swing at your educated face."

But they never fought, for the feel of uniforms and the sound of bugles was still new to us. Usually you could find them, every night after chow, drinking milk shakes together. Often I walked past the small stores and saw them, and while I watched I thought: One of these days I'm going to tell you a big lie. But I preferred to tell it to David Mapp rather than to the Texan, who seemed to see through me.

The afternoon of the twentieth day at The Lakes was set aside for the last of the physical examinations and for some kind of mental examination. While David and the Texan and I waited in our hut I got out Meb's first letter to me and read it again:

Dear Don,

Many things of note and mild fascination have happened since your going away. Miss Audie has been chosen as the candidate for "Saint" next year. Everybody was sure it would be Mrs. Tihliw, but it wasn't. Saint Savanna, a strong erstwhile supporter of Mrs. Tihliw, shifted her weight at the last minute for Miss Audie, and that changed Mrs. Eula Wilkes; from there a whole chain reaction set in, which ended with the holy of holies shifting too. Final votes after eight ballots was 41–9. Some say Mrs. T. could never have got the necessary thirty. (All fifty-one servants were present and voting except Jim Woods. It is rumored that Mr. Wilkes is going to be elected a servant if and when Mr. Jim dies.) As yet, there are no rumors as to why Saint Savanna shifted, but a few days will take care of that. Your mother, bless her, was one of the nine who stuck by Mrs. T.—

The Texan interrupted me. "What's this about Saints and Servants in your neck of the woods?"

For a few seconds I stared at him; I could not remember that I had ever mentioned the Primitive Church to him, or anything from Meb's letter. "Servants are the ruling body of the Church; they're elected by the congregation for life. Once each year they select a woman to be a candidate for Saint. She washes everybody's feet at the ceremonies, and if she serves well she gets sanctified."

The Texan got up and stretched.

"Where you going?" David said.

"Out to worship nature. See you at the quizzing."

We watched until he was outside. Then David said, "Saints and Servants," and grinned as if I had told a weak joke.

I continued the letter:

I know you have heard from home that Wallace graduated after all. It seems that when you dropped out the whole schedule of marching and delivering diplomas and what-not was upset; result was that grades were re-examined at Mr. Little's urgent request and Wallace was inserted in your place.

Graduation—otherwise—was as always. Mr. Walker was there, and of course asked first thing about you. He brought presents for you and me, each a copy of *Poems for Modern Youth*. I have yours. What am I to do with it? He thought it strange that you said nothing of your intentions, having seen him the same day you left. But you are forgiven, if, indeed, any wrong occurred. After graduation, Mr. Walker came to our house and played some Chopin for an hour. Then we all sat quietly on the rug (Nelle and Morris were there) in a circle and held hands and thought of you. Afterward, each had to tell what he thought. Nelle remembered your poem *Beyond the Edge of Time*, and said all of it. Mother remembered the first time she saw you and how you two "amazed" each other. Morris—poor old Morris—he could think of nothing except you in that enormous tuxedo (Who did it belong to?) playing Fidele in *Death Takes a Holiday*. Mr. Walker remembered you as the Unknown Solider that time. And I, well I remembered you in silhouette, far down the road toward the gin, coming toward our house—it was a fall afternoon and everything was covered with blue shadows.

Time stands still here, and some days I stand with it in the doorway of the shop and wonder what all the people passing on the train think of us and our little gray bunch of buildings sitting at the foot of the mountain, and I wonder how they could pass by and not know that you are gone. But all they see here is a difference in the light and shadow of things. Some days I stand in the doorway and know that any minute I am going to see you wave to me through that big glass window—and all the time faces and faces pass along the street, nothing but faces. If it is a dark day, I think of that poem I wrote when we

were juniors (Do you remember it?): "Let me die when rain is falling
. . ." Oh, I know I'm silly. All girls are silly.

I write something from time to time. Worth nothing, but it has
been knitting inside for a wee age, through pain and the frustration
from which The Immense Design spares so few of us.

Ever,
M.

I began to say:

> Let me die when rain is falling,
> Hear the dripping eaves,
> Hear the wind, like children calling,
> Through the autumn leaves.
> Let me lie where snow is heavy,
> Hear the hunters cry,
> Hear the lost . . .

"What's that?"

I turned and saw that David was standing beside his bunk, as if
he were muscle-bound. He was dark brown, heavy, not tall, with
shoulders that would have split his blouse if he ever made a sudden
move. But for all his muscles, shown to advantage by his dark skin,
he had nothing of the athletic appearance of Wallace or even of William. A corner of one front tooth was chipped and filled with gold; it
was very becoming to him.

"What's that?" he said again.

"Ode to a Grecian Yearn."

"You the strangest guy I ever saw. Who wrote it?"

"Longfellow. Henry Wordsworth Longfellow."

He frowned. "I've heard of him."

"He's the greatest American writer that ever lived. He's to
America what Shakespeare is to England."

"I don't want to know nothing about poets. They're not regular
human beings. That was Longfellow, what you was saying a minute
ago?"

"That's right. He first called it *Psalm of Death* to go with *Psalm of
Life*. Later, he changed the title. Wrote it when he was fourteen."

"You don't write poetry, do you?"

"Me? Lord, no. Why?"

"You look like you might."

"What kind of look is that?"

"Strange. Then, you stay in all time, and when you go out, you look like the sun never touched you. I don't mean no harm, you know. Well, I guess I shouldn't of said it, but you know I mean you look like you always studied a lot and me—I never studied nothing. You not huffed at me for what I said?"

"No."

"You know, some of us built for one thing, some for another. You ready to go over for them exams?"

"Sure."

"Which one's first?"

"The physical."

"You have to get used to me, feller. I'm awfully bad to say what I think. I believe in the truth."

"I'm a great believer in the truth myself."

In the sunlight, it looked as if his blouse might split if he so much as turned his head. "I guess they going to ship us out tomorrow."

"That's what I hear," I said.

"This mental test is to see what we fit into. They going to have a hard time getting something to fit me. What you want to strike for?"

"Nothing. I think we're all headed for the amphibious force."

"Think? Don't waste your time thinking. Chief Wheeler already told me so. You'll have to pray to all the saints and light a bushel of candles and it still won't do you any good."

"I'm not Catholic," I said.

"I am," he said.

It was early and there were only a few men in the medical hall. We undressed. David was put into one line and I into another. I was glad, because his body beside mine only made me look hollow, though I was not thin. I was always afraid some examiner would find something wrong with me—except for the dentists, at the end of the line.

Finally I arrived before the dentist and he, as usual, stopped to chat with me. "You've certainly got fine teeth, son. Where you from? Tennessee?"

"Almost. North Mississippi."

"What do you folks eat and drink there?"

"The same as everybody else."

"Lots of minerals in the water there?"

"Yessir."

"You drink lots of milk too?"

"Yessir."

"What kind of paste did you use, when you were little? Salt and soda, and a blackgum toothbrush?"

I thought he was laughing at me, so I said, "Hickory ashes."

I waited for him to trim me down, but he only said, "Hnnn," and looked at my teeth again. "You got any brothers or sisters?"

"Yessir."

"They got the same kind of teeth?"

"I guess so. We've never been to a dentist."

He shook his head. "You don't know what they're worth, son. That's all." I saw that David had come up behind me.

I found my clothes and began to dress. David said, "Lemme see them fine teeth, Mack."

"We've seen your gold," I said.

"You ever work any?"

"That bother you?"

"Plenty."

"That's too bad."

"Rich guy, huh?"

"No," I said. "I haven't got anything, till I'm twenty-one."

"How much you got then?"

"A little."

"You're strowing bull."

"I hope it enriches the land."

"You know, you just crazy enough to have money. You sure as hell never worked none. I can see that."

"I never had a chance. You'd be just like me if you'd been brought up in a family that never let you lift a hand—breakfast in bed, tea at five, never raised my arm to get my coat off a hanger!"

"Take it easy. I didn't mean nothing."

"That's okay. But you don't know the rich—they make me sick.

They're not like ordinary people. Argue over an Indian-head penny, betray a friend for a buffalo nickel. All they want out of anything is more than they ought to have. Don't tell me. I'm talking about the real rich. You ever heard of Wade 55 Motor Oil, Dallas, Texas? My mother owns that. My old man just owns fifty-one per cent of the Trans-Southern Railroad. Started out cutting crossties: you'd think he could remember, but he don't."

"Why didn't he keep you out of this mess?"

"Like all the rich, he had enough sin on his hands already. He kept my brothers out—they're football stars. And besides, I wanted to get away from it; and I didn't bring any of it with me, either. You know what I left with, after my ticket was bought? Two dollars and twenty-five cents. Got ninety cents left. If you think I'm lying, just remember you haven't seen me drinking any milk shakes."

"You're a funny guy. You know, I mean . . . well, I just never knew anybody with a lot of money."

"Money's nothing. Of course, I don't say you can't have some fun making ducks and drakes of it."

We finished dressing. David asked me to pull his blouse down over his shoulders, as if by that gesture he had let me into his world. "I'm going up and see the chief that's giving this exam," he said. "You want to go? He's a good guy."

"Not now. It's too early."

"I'll see you up there then."

"Okay."

I felt purged, but somewhat exhausted, as if I had been swimming a long time. I went to the barracks, wrote four postcards and mailed them. Still, I was early for the exam—eager, I suppose. David came in with the chief and sat behind me. When all twenty-nine of our platoon were there and seated, the chief efficiently distributed the papers, backs up, and gave proper instructions and proper precautions that both speed and accuracy were involved. Then: "Now, men, don't be scared of this thing. Just do the best you can. Remain in your seats when finished. Tomorrow at 0845 grades will be posted, along with your destinations. Ready? On the mark . . . go!"

I was the first to finish—I had not yet learned that one should never be first. But there was nothing to the test if you had read the Blue Jacket's Manual. The chief took my paper and kept eying me, as if he thought I had smuggled in a copy. Occasionally he read a page, and finally called me to the front of the room.

"What kind of mind you got?"

"What kind?"

"Here. Read this." He opened a book—*Dalton's Modern Seamanship.* "Read that page, there."

If the print is not too small I can look at a page and know what's on it—like looking at a face: all at once, not the eyes, then the nose, then the chin. As long as I can remember a part of it, I can remember all of it; when it goes it goes completely.

He closed the book. "What did it say?"

"Word for word?"

"Yeah."

" 'When bearing on points A, B, C are accurate, the fix will be accurate, and all lines will coincide at point F. If a triangle is formed, a less accurate fix will be determined by the center of—' "

"What did the last sentence say?"

" 'Observe the bearing closely; if there is no appreciable change the vessel is steering a collision course.' "

"That's enough. Your paper's all right. I've always wanted to see somebody with a photographic mind. But how's come you ain't got no muscles?"

"Never had to work."

He took hold of my arm. "If you had some meat there, you'd be a whale in this navy. Where you from?"

"Mississippi."

"Oh, hell. Maybe you got hookworm. Course you're not so lean. Hookworm makes you lean, don't it?"

"I wouldn't know."

"You always had enough to eat?"

"Too much."

"Oh . . . You're the kid with dough?"

"Who told you that?"

"I got it straight now. This life's gonna be a little rough on you, but you'll pull through. That's all. List'll be posted outside tomorrow at 0845."

Just as I got outside I heard the chief say, "That kid's got a photographic mind and his old man's a millionaire."

The Texan said, "Yeah, you can tell he's filthy rich—won't spend a quarter for a milk shake."

I thought of the shock the chief would get when he opened my Service Record to record my grade and saw that my father laid ties and drove spikes for a living; then I stopped on the stairs, or the ladder we called it. I remembered the page in my Service Record with *Father's occupation—Trans-Southern Railroad.* Well, the chief could go to hell; everything could go to hell. What did it matter to me? Tomorrow I was going off to the real war, maybe. And maybe I would get killed.

I shrugged and walked on. But that night I avoided the hut. I went to the U.S.O. and read all of the latest *Time* (the Texan quoted frequently from *Time*), and read *Of Mice and Men.* As I walked back to the hut I began to feel that my lie was going to set into motion something inside me, and I would end up like Lennie. But once in my bunk, I satisifed myself that we would be shipping out the next day and that would be the end of every worry I'd ever had or ever would have. I wanted to go overseas, especially to England. (I thought: Now if I were in England I'd never tell a lie like that.) I did not sleep well.

I went early, and the list was there:

Martin, Albert L.	129	Little Creek, Va.
Meadows, Donald D.	136	None
Mills, Robert B.	112	Little Creek, Va.

I hurried to the chief's office. He was drinking coffee, his foot cocked up on the window sill, the saucer resting on his knee, the sunlight on his wide, flush face. In the light, that way, it seemed that he should have been much more than a chief yeoman—a gentleman farmer looking out upon his land, a mill owner, watching his hundreds of workers rush to their jobs.

"Chief, there's no destination listed for me."

He did not move; he was looking out the window. "Maybe you not going nowhere."

"How come?"

"Soft spot in my heart. I got a kid nearly old as you. I'm not gonna feed you to the wolves just because you got dough—had a chance to keep one, and I took you." He put the cup and saucer on the window sill and turned around. The light made his slightly gray hair look thin, made his heavy-set body seem tired; but beyond the tiredness was a kind of vision—all like a schoolteacher just before the end of the term.

"I don't want to stay here. Everybody else is going to the amphibious force. I'd like to go too."

"Kid, you'd be a whale if you had a suntan and a few more pounds up here." He hit his chest. "You gonna stay here with me till you get it. The quickest way is an hour down in Versailles every day, sixteen-thirty to seventeen-thirty. There's a general grudge in this world against rich folks and good minds. I know because I got left out in both cases. When we change you up a little you can take whatever's dished out. Take this back to the galley. You'll have mess-cook duty this week." He handed me the cup and saucer.

I looked at him. "If you're keeping me here because you think I'm rich, maybe you ought to know my daddy is a hand on the railroad. He's not even a section-foreman."

He laughed. "Is that so?"

"Yes, that's so."

"You can't fast-ball me. A mind like you got don't belong to no pore boy."

After a minute I said, "All right, you win. We're rich as hell, if you want it that way, but I want to get away from here."

He laughed again and shook his head. "You can't bribe me. I'm a perfectionist, see? I believe in perfection. I'm gonna make something perfect out of you. That's all I'm interested in in this world—perfection. Now, with a little work in Versailles . . . But trot on to the galley."

He was sometimes called Sergeant Wheeler.

II

VERSAILLES WAS in the basement of building G. It was a long room, rounded at one end, and in the center of the room was a huge square column. On all sides of the column and on the walls of the room were three-by-five-foot mirrors, forty-nine of them. Leading directly away from each mirror, and tacked to the floor, were maroon carpets, six feet long.

The chief, Victor Wheeler, went with me the first day. He assigned me to mirror thirty-three, brought out bar bells, dumbbells, kettle bells, iron boots, and a swing bell, and showed me nine exercises. "On Monday-Wednesday-Friday you do six exercises; Tuesday-Thursday-Saturday three. Heavy day, light day—see?"

I said I understood.

"Do each exercise in three series, fifteen times to each series. You understand?"

"Yes."

"I pick fifteen because that's divisible by five. Now don't count from one to fifteen—that makes it a lot harder. Count: one-two-three-four-five . . . one-two-three-four-five . . . one-two-three-four-five. It adds up to fifteen and it's easier that way; slip up on yourself, that's the idea. Then make like you forgot one, make like you miscounted, and do an extra one. That'll be sixteen. Pretty soon you'll be doing seventeen, eighteen. . . . Got the idea?"

"I think I've got it."

"You know, you're not so bad except, my God, you're wide. And when you get through each time, go out on the back and lay in the sun. But not too long. Did you know you could be court-martialed for getting too much sunburn? Well, you can."

And he left me there, with a half-dozen others, all drawing in air as if to fortify themselves against pain, exhaling like a safety valve on a gin boiler.

When the chief was well out of sight I began to count the mirrors. A big-gutted man, a few mirrors away from me, said, "Used to be fifty of them. One got broke." He sounded as if it were a serious matter, the loss of that mirror, and I stopped counting to look at him. He was past fifty, already gray, slightly bald. His eyes lay deep in a wide, soft face, but he had very good color, well tanned all over. There was no way to tell his rank, for he, like the rest of us, was barefooted and in shorts. I assumed he was an old chief, maybe a quartermaster.

"Who broke it?" I said.

"Some kid, doing squats with a hundred and ten pounds. Too much for him, pitched into the mirror, there beside that leg press. You don't want to work with too much weight; it's no good if you work with too much."

"I don't want to work with any of it. Sergeant Wheeler thought this up."

He began to grin, making tiny furrows in his cheeks, and still grinning he stooped and lifted a sixty-pound bar bell and began an arm exercise. When he had finished eleven lifts he was still grinning and the red from his forehead seemed to run down the furrows on his cheeks, like sweat. His face cleared a little, and while he watched himself in the mirror, he said, "I wasn't here when he broke it. I was in the Pacific. A man could cut the hell out of hisself that way."

"He sure could." I waited for him to go on, but he never said anything else to me that day. A few days later, I asked Chief Wheeler who worked out at mirror thirty-eight.

"That's Commander Rice. Why?"

"I just thought he was starting with weights rather late in life."

"Maybe he's trying to kill himself."

"Couldn't you think of an easier way? He said you got him interested in Versailles."

"I merely made a suggestion."

"Why don't you take some of your own medicine?"

"Huhnnnn!"

The chief never missed a single day checking on me, and he wouldn't let me go near the scales until one month had passed; by then I had gained a few pounds and I was tanned. "See," he said. "Ain't nothing wrong with you but you."

The commander was always at mirror thirty-eight, until the middle of the second month when he missed a day. The following day he said, "You can't make progress if you miss training. I knew a guy in the Coast Guard never missed a day's workout in six years—

he worked three times a week though, not every day. Now yesterday—you'd think it wouldn't matter, but I can tell the difference. Everything feels two or three pounds heavier. But I couldn't get here yesterday. Sometimes it seems like things work exactly contrary to everything you're determined to do. You ever find it so? Or maybe I tend to see it that way. But yesterday, with all that . . . ah, well . . ." He started back to work and never told me what hindered him.

Some days we talked for ten or fifteen minutes; some days he never said a word. I always let him begin the conversation; but with bare feet, shorts, and naked belly rounding out, he never seemed to outrank me.

The whole first week of September passed and I didn't see the commander. I thought perhaps he had gone somewhere to visit his wife and children, until the chief told me he didn't have a wife and children. Then one day I was sitting at the small table, which was my desk, stapling sets of regulations for mess-cooks, when the commander came down the hall and stopped in the doorway. In his neat khaki gabardines he looked quite distinguished, well proportioned, not at all like the man before mirror thirty-eight. I got up quickly, though he made a motion as if I should not be disturbed. The chief had left his desk and was looking out the window at two pet squirrels, romping in the September sun. He whirled and stood at attention.

"Everything all right?" the commander said.

"Yessir," the chief said.

To me the commander said, "How're the workouts?"

"I'm still at it, sir."

"I've changed to the mornings. I believe it's better in the mornings—for me anyway." Then to the chief. "Everything's going all right, you say?"

"Yessir."

The commander left.

"What does he do around here?" I said.

The chief looked hurt at first, then he stared at me. "You lay off him, see? He's a good Joe and don't think he didn't get it poked at him. He's got a right to be a little cuckoo. That man used to have a division of destroyers in the Pacific, an expert in tactics. And something happened: he let some Japs cross the T on him. They finished off four of his six cans. He's now in charge of office equipment here—that's what it really amounts to. You get the idea?"

I nodded.

"He spent the last twenty years on a ship. Now he's here, stuck. They won't let him leave."

"They won't let me leave either—you or somebody."

"You got no reason to go."

"I've got a strong desire; that ought to count something."

"A man's desire leads to nothing but destruction, especially for himself. You hate to go down to Versailles—that means you're building something. The commander wants to go down there—that means he's destroying something or trying to. Do you get the idea?"

"Not very well."

"No? Well, I'm surprised, with the mind you've got. We're keeping you here because of that good mind. We need you."

"For what? I spend half my time with a stapler in my hand."

"But we need you for what might happen. The navy is run on the basis of what might happen; I've had fourteen years at sea—cruisers, cans, one battle wagon, and I know. Always be sharper tomorrow than the day before. That's the road to perfection, and you ought to already know by now I'm a perfectionist; that's the only thing that matters in this world: perfection. Your brain's idle, that's your trouble. Tomorrow I want you to talk to me about books. You ever read *War and Peace*? If you ain't you go read it—because you've got to tell me what it's about. All my life I heard about that book but never had a chance to read it, or was too dumb to. You know how long it takes me to read a hundred pages? I'd hate to tell you. And me married to a schoolteacher, a high-school English teacher. The next time I see her I'm gonna surprise her with some knowledge . . ."

In the afternoons, then, we talked about books, he absorbing what I said as if I knew everything about all books and all authors. We considered *A Farewell to Arms, Look Homeward, Angel* (that took two afternoons), *Grapes of Wrath, Three Soldiers, One of Ours, Tender Is the Night, Sanctuary, Light in August* (He asked me if the title had anything to do with the saying: "Light in August, heavy in December."), and the list went on. I had read Faulkner in high school because Mr. Walker knew him (at least had seen him go by the courthouse in Oxford) and had most of his books; but many of the other books I read for the first time in the U.S.O., where I wrote themes for Wallace.

The first theme was called "A Man Named Victor." I didn't hear right away from Wallace but William wrote. "He got an A– but would have got an A + except he can't even copy, you know that. Why don't you play fair and do me one?" So I sent one for William called "The Art of Being Honest" along with one for Wallace, and Wallace wrote back, "Let's have no more of that old music, brother. We've got the same teacher and he's dumb but not that dumb. He's always talking about current events and one day he cried in class while he was talking about the Armistice and the bells ringing all day in the town where he lived. William don't need no help the way I do and besides if he did you ought to know he's asked Meb down to the first football game. Now are you going to be crazy and write him another theme? I know you like him better than you do me, but I never tried to steal your girl, did I? She's going to stay in one of the sorority houses hot diggity. If this writing looks funny my wrist is about sprained. Our pictures are going to be in a copy of *The Grid-iron* soon."

I didn't write to Meb for a while, and in the meantime I wrote to Bea. I hardly expected her to answer, but she did, saying that her second baby, another boy, had just been born and that Homer, her husband, was being deferred again because he was a farmer now (about a year before, he had quit working in the pants factory in Corinth and gone back to his father's farm). Homer had run away from home at the age of eighteen because his daddy whipped him so much for getting into the cream which his mother carefully skimmed from the milk and sold to the cheese plant each week. When I was working for Uncle Lew, he sent me one day to borrow a grubbing hoe from Homer's daddy. I found Mr. Arcutt planting a small patch of early corn below his orchard. Just as I asked him for the hoe we heard a noise at his house; he dropped the plowlines, let go of the planter, and started running, calling, "Goddam the trifling luck. Homer's in the cream again."

I was not going to think of Meb, and her going down to see William. I would think of everything else first. I wrote Bea another letter, a long one.

About the first of October I had a letter from Mama asking when I would be home (she hoped it would be for Thanksgiving or Christmas); on the back of it Papa wrote his first letter:

Dear son,

Hope you get home soon. Everything is fine here. Jim Woods was buried Saturday. Guess it's for best he suffered so much. Wallace and Wm. both doing fine but Tech's line is about like old man Wilkeses fence, always down. I'm going down for Tech-Ole Miss game. Wallace hurt knee and may not play. But both are doing fine and only freshmen.

Dad

P.S. Enclosing picture of Wallace in *Commercial Appeal* blocking tackle as Wm. scored from four yard line. You can't read number but its Wallace. Tech was hot and would've won even if State had Foster Lloyd back. Played like they did against Alabama. Miss Savanna got word last week he was shot down somewhere over Germany. That don't mean he's killed. You see picture of Wallace and Wm. in the magazine?

The chief let me off one day and I went into Chicago and looked until I found a copy of *The Gridiron*. William and Wallace were on the front cover—Wallace in the foreground leaping, slightly curved, a football at his finger tips; William in the background, fading, completing the motion of a pass. Beneath the picture was a large caption: TWO STARS FELL ON ALABAMA; and beneath that: Mississippi Tech—14, Alabama—0.

There was a glowing story of the nineteen-year-old twin stars, tabbed for greatness; of how they were both good students, even in the dreaded freshman English; of how their father, a hand on the section gang of the Trans-Southern Railroad, had held a dream for them.

I showed the magazine to the chief.

"You can't all be nineteen," he said.

"Somebody made a mistake," I said.

"Any other mistakes in this write-up?"

"I don't reckon. Why?"

"I don't like mistakes. You ought to know by now that I can't afford to allow myself to like mistakes."

That night he took the magazine home with him. From that time on he was very cool to me. He never told jokes in the office; he said, "Take care of that detail," and not, "Will you do so-and-so?"

About a week later he came back from the personnel office one morning and handed me a Manila envelope. "This is it," he said. "What you've been wanting."

"Where to?" I said, without looking at my orders.

"Signalman's school, Little Creek."

"And then?"

"Don't ask me, but I'd bet you won't have Christmas dinner in this country."

"That suits me," I said.

"That's fine. We strive to please."

I didn't think he had a right to treat me so coolly, and I said, "If you ever need a good job on the railroad, just let my daddy know; he carries lots of weight for Trans-Southern."

"You go to hell, sonny." He went to the window and looked out, as if searching for the squirrels he watched so much.

I considered his back a minute, how his size had seemed to change with the coming of fall, how he stood there, bent, like a man who has had a dream shattered. Then I left.

While I was in my berth that night, enroute to Norfolk and Little Creek, I felt that I was about to understand the chief, and this is what I thought: He was a mender of things. I had seen him take Scotch tape and patch a torn sheet of instructions to mess-cooks when there were dozens of extra sheets four steps away. He was much prouder of my tan, and extra pounds, and few new muscles than I was. Still, how account for his unerring habit of shaving every other day, of wearing a clean suit of khakis on the days he did not shave, because, he said, "It sorta balances things, don't you think?" But his dream, for a while, had been shattered; it was finished; and perfection, yet, lay somewhere else, like sunlight on squirrel fur.

I quit thinking about the chief and wrote a letter to Meb, giving her my new address. After all, if I got killed (and I probably would)

she would write a poem about me, and surely the first lines would
have *swift* in them, may be something like:

> Today the sun is overleaping time,
> And swift flames trail . . .

She would do justice by me. The chief—he would come in one day,
drop his paper on his desk, stretch a minute, look out the window,
then begin to write: "Estelle, you remember that funny kid that I
wrote you about who used to talk about books all the time? I heard he
got killed . . ." Or maybe he wouldn't hear, and then it would be
useless: the dying, the talk of the books, the hours in Versailles, everything. I went to sleep. The next morning I awoke in mountain
country, in a vast uninhabited stretch of dark blue that fell almost to
my window. The first look was like cold clippers thrust against the
neck. I pulled the blanket closer around me and stared—cold blue
rock and cold blue woods eternally against the hazy sky. What a fool I
had been to think of dying—I would live to be ninety-two. I remained there at the window for hours.

Often after times like that I say: No, this isn't right for me; I feel
that I was not born to be happy, and this extreme pleasure is like a
mist. Then, I look for something to worry about—that much of me
comes from Mama. She doesn't exactly worry over things in particular; she simply carries enough worry in her mind that delight is
excluded. With the mountain still before me, I was able to think
again of how foolish I was, how (as Mr. Rufe sometimes said, as if he
invented the words on the spur of the moment) I often strained at a
gnat and swallowed a camel. I had not yet learned that there were
other windows than my own, where one looked out onto designs that
were different, and where answers, if at all, were more obscure. But
even then I sensed that I was searching for something, that surely
there was for me a time which would stand sharper than a peak,
longer than a moment, and real enough that no words could hold it.
And it startled me that I was thinking more of Bea than of Meb.

Because of two changes and two delays, I reached Norfolk in the
early morning, and had my first glimpse of the sea while the sun was
rising. A navy ten-wheeler picked me up at the station and trans-
ported me, alone, through the Little Arch of Triumph that leads to

the amphibious base of Little Creek. Many offices were closed for
Sunday, but after two hours I was able to put my sea-bag away safely.
Within another half hour I had met Albert Martin, the Texan, from
my original platoon at The Lakes. I remembered him not only for his
talk, but also because he was tall and lanky, thin and pale enough not
to make me look awful when he stood beside me. He seemed always
to be ambling along, eating an apple, summarizing world situations,
and begging all of us to stop him, some way, from his awful habit of
cussing. When he saw me, his hair, usually uncombed, seemed to fly
against the white brim on the back of his head, and he yelled, "Goddam! There's old rich boy."

First we had a cup of coffee in the Crow's Nest. After one taste,
he puckered his lips and said, "That stuff makes me downright cyni-
cal. The only place in America you can get good coffee is in New Orleans. Why the infernal navy didn't station me there, I don't know.
This Little Creek is a goddam nothing. I've waded ashore from Hig-
gins boats and LCT's and LCI's till there's a water line just under my
armpits; now it's too cold to wade and they shoot me into recognition
school, everything from a Piper Cub to an ME 810. Had so much of it
that a goddam mosquito scares the living hell out of me. They'd better not send me over there and put me in the middle of it—I'll run,
damn, I'll run—but they're going to, all of us. A few weeks from now
we'll be on our way to using *urinoirs* instead of heads: Casablanca,
Oran . . ."

"Do you know French?" I interrupted, but he never really heard
me.

"We'll have our ends shot off before Easter. Thirty per cent
casualties in the amphibs. But hell, what do I care? When it's all
over, the bottom rail will be on top anyway, and come Thanksgiving
the goddam Aggies will probably beat Texas, not that I give two
whispers in hell but my old man will be there and he does. You don't
cuss do you?"

"Wouldn't think of it."

"You're the one I'm looking for—you've got to tame me. Dave
Mapp held me down for a while but they shipped that ignorant bastard out two weeks ago. He failed signalman's school when any peas-

ant with two amps of intelligence could pass it. Listen, when I cuss, I want you to knock the Texas hell out of me. That's the only thing my old man ever whipped me for, but it didn't help. Finally sent me off to military prep school in that God—that bodacious windswept state of Oklahoma, which didn't help. My old aunt still prays for me— she's a Methodist and went to SMU—but she doesn't do any good either. Congress couldn't change me, even. I used to be page boy for Senator Arnoldby, and one night at a reception I let out the ugliest word in the English language. Some old sister Jezebel asked me to leave; but I knew good and damn well you couldn't shock her with direct current—she was just a representative's wife trying to have an affair with a senator—so I looked at her and grinned and it wasn't ten minutes till she was introducing me to people. I even promised her I'd quit cussing. I'll swear to you I'm going to quit. My English teacher used to tell me it showed a lack of vocabulary." He pushed the coffee cup to the far edge of the counter. "Six or eight of our old platoon are still here. Some of them are playing basketball now; you want to go out there?"

We went to the gymnasium. The game stopped immediately, because of the need for two more players. Four or five of them recognized me, while one called: "Come on, Bert. . . you two . . . pull off your shoes." Those not in tennis shoes were in their sock-feet.

Bert said, "Me? I couldn't hit a bull with a bass fiddle."

"It don't matter, come on. One for the skins and one for the shirts."

"Hell, no. Not me," Bert said. "Rich boy can play."

Someone pointed at me. "You come play for the skins. We're losing."

"We can't play four to five," a shirted player said.

Then another, whose name I didn't remember, came to the sideline. "I've got a better idea. Let's make rich boy go buy us all a milk shake."

"Would you, rich boy?"

"He'd be proud to."

"Certainly he'd be proud to. Real thick ones."

"Would you?"

"Of course," I said. So we had milk shakes and they talked.

"What you so quiet about, rich boy?"

"Because he's having to pay, fool."

I was sorry I did not have a chance to play for the skins and show my new tanned muscles. I had worked very hard for them, and now it seemed all for nothing.

(1901–1963)

John Wesley T. Faulkner

John Wesley Thompson Faulkner, III, born in Ripley on September 24, 1901, was a younger brother of William Faulkner. Educated in Oxford, in the public schools and at the University of Mississippi, Faulkner spent most of his life in the town that William was to make famous. He worked with the Mississippi Highway Department and with the Memphis Flying Corps, and as a farmer in Oxford. He married Lucille Ramey in 1922. While he has never received much critical attention as an author, John Faulkner's books, especially the last five novels published as paperback originals, were extremely popular, selling into the hundreds of thousands, possibly the millions, by the time of his death in 1963.

The area Faulkner deals with in most of his novels and his seven short stories is inhabited by the middle-class whites, Negroes, and the poor whites of the hills of northern Mississippi. Their little world, usually Beat Two, is one that is slightly out of time. Its people cannot comprehend the change in America brought about by the Depression. The modern money-oriented society is represented by the outsiders, the government land-buyers and the revenuers, who are beginning to bring to the hills a recognition of a different way of life. Faulkner humorously depicts, with some of the flare of Erskine Caldwell, a world that is in conflict with this change.

332

Faulkner's approach to his material, while it has been correctly likened to that used by the Old Southwest Humorists, is more accurately primitivistic. Unlike his brother, John Faulkner felt no compulsion to imbue his works with "art." He once wrote that "a correct picture of a people and a time is about all that can be put in a book." Hence his method is scenic, rather than thematic. He relates his stories objectively, without much authorial interference, and lets the reader draw whatever conclusions he wishes. He depicts speech and mannerisms accurately and succinctly, but he does not bother to explain the peculiar ways of Jones Peabody, or Ex-Senator and Equator, or Uncle Good, or the phantom preacher who regularly steals into cabins and then leaves the wives with grinning looks of satisfaction and ample rewards of tutti-frutti gum for their trouble. Faulkner's prose is simple and clear, his characters are interesting, and his fiction, while it deals with a relatively small sphere of human existence, is of considerable merit.

The story reprinted here is from *Collier's*, CX (November 7, 1942).

Good Neighbors

UNCLE PETE WAS REALLY TOO OLD for the deputy marshal's job, and the young, hard-boiled prohibition agents resented him because he filled the place that could be given to some younger, more reckless man of their own caliber who would be of use to them in their still raids.

But Uncle Pete's friends were numerous, having been collected from the days when county political campaigning was done on horseback and a man left the county seat on his electioneering tour only to come back to town in time to vote. None of those friends were ever lost to Uncle Pete, and some of them were more than friends now. One of them was a United States senator. And Uncle Pete, though over the age limit for active duty, was still serving as a deputy marshal.

Uncle Pete was set in his ways. It was the well-earned prerogative of seventy-four years of just living and honest independence. He acknowledged none of the weaknesses of his accumulated years and forbade anyone else to mention them. Nor did he ask favors or deference to the indelible marks of time's passing that sat but lightly on his still-erect shoulders.

Through a tacit agreement between the marshal and the prohibition agents, Uncle Pete was never sent out on whisky raids, but was used chiefly to serve summonses and court papers. And also through unspoken agreement between Uncle Pete and his favorite taxi driver, Joe, his trips were always arranged so that he could sleep in his own bed each night.

It became sort of a game with the marshal to try to arrange Uncle Pete's papers so that he would be forced to spend a night away from home, but, somehow, Uncle Pete, tired out but triumphant, would turn up at home by bedtime. That was the only concession he made to old age. He liked his own bed.

When the government started buying up land for the huge reservations and reservoirs in northern Mississippi, the marshal thought the problem of Uncle Pete was settled for good. He put Uncle Pete to posting land.

"By George, I'll bet he has to sleep in a hotel tonight," said the marshal to his office deputy one morning. "I gave him a good two days' work before he left this morning."

"What have you got him doing?" said the office deputy.

"Posting that reservoir land," said the marshal. "I gave him everything north of the Delta Road."

"Why, he won't be back here for a week," said the office deputy.

Uncle Pete phoned the marshal at nine that night.

"Where are you?" said the marshal.

"I'm at home," said Uncle Pete.

"What did you come in for?" said the marshal.

"I finished," said Uncle Pete.

"Finished?" said the marshal. "Why, no one man could post all that land in one day!"

"I made Joe help me," said Uncle Pete.

"Who?" said the marshal.

"Joe. My driver."

"Well, I'll be gosh-darned!" said the marshal.

The next day, Uncle Pete's son stopped by the office at noon to take Uncle Pete to dinner. Uncle Pete greeted him with a bluff, "Hey."

"You 'bout ready to go to dinner?" asked the son.

Uncle Pete pulled a florid gold watch from his pocket and studied it.

"All right," he said. "Let's go."

When they drove up in the driveway at home, Uncle Pete got out of the car and walked across the yard to the porch. As he mounted the steps, the cook, who had just finished placing the last steaming dish on the table and was standing in the back hall door with the bell in her hand waiting the signal of his step on the porch, rang the bell and turned and disappeared into the kitchen.

Uncle Pete hung his hat on the rack, walked into the dining room to his place at the head of the table, and surveyed his layout of special cutlery and utensils and food: his tall, thick, water glass set due south of his plate; his dish of okra to the southeast; the bowl of pot likker to the west; and his gaze came to rest on his knife. He picked it up and sighted down the edge.

"Minnie," he bellowed toward the kitchen.

"Suh?" said Minnie, popping her head in at the door between the dining room and kitchen.

"This is not my knife."

"Oh, Lawd. Oh, Lawd," said Minnie, scurrying back to the sideboard drawer and clattering about among the spare knives and forks and spoons.

"She just does that to aggravate me," said Uncle Pete with a huge frown.

Minnie hurried in with another knife, and Uncle Pete took it and examined it and, satisfied, went to work preparing his food.

The phone bell tinkled while they were still at the table and the son answered it. After a brief conversation, he came into the dining room.

"That was the marshal," he said to Uncle Pete. "He's got two prisoners he wants you to take to Holly Springs this evening. Wants you to catch the one o'clock bus with them."

"By Joe! Won't give a man time to eat," said Uncle Pete.

He finished his dinner and rose and spoke to his son's wife, who kept house for him since his own wife's death. "I may not be back tonight," he said. "I never know how long I might be gone on these trips."

"All right," said the son's wife. Then in a lower voice to the son, "I'll be sure to have a small steak for him at six sharp."

The son took Uncle Pete back to town and the marshal was seated opposite the two prisoners when he entered the office.

"These the prisoners?" said Uncle Pete.

"Hello, Uncle Pete," said one of them, rising and holding out his hand. "Remember me?"

"Well now." Uncle Pete took the hand and peered into the prisoner's face. "Can't rightly say I remember you, boy."

"I'm Luke Jenkins. Remember? You took me to Atlanta seven year ago."

"Well, by Joe!" said Uncle Pete. "How you been getting along, boy?"

"First rate," said Luke.

"How's your paw?" said Uncle Pete.

"Fine," said Luke. "He was talking about you jest the other day."

"I'd like to see old Abe again," said Uncle Pete. "Who's this you got with you?"

"You don't know him," said Luke. "He lives on the place next to us but he ain't been there but about ten year now."

"That's the old Logan place," said Uncle Pete. "I remember—"

"Here, here," said the marshal. "You get on down to the bus station or you'll miss that bus."

Uncle Pete glanced up at the wall clock. "We might at that," he said, then to the two prisoners, "Come on. We better be going."

He walked out the door and down the steps to the sidewalk. The two prisoners rose and followed along in his wake.

"Say, is that the way he carries prisoners around?" asked one of the two prohibition agents who had brought the prisoners in.

"Yes," said the marshal.

"Why, some prisoner is going to knock him in the head one of these days," the agent said.

"There hasn't anyone done it yet," said the marshal dryly.

"That's no sign they won't," said the agent. "That's what I say about keeping an old dodo like him around. Here we've got to go over below Charleston and catch those two Fullers and we need a third man with us. Those boys are dangerous. Got to risk mine and Ed's life just because old man Pete knows some senator. It ain't right."

"You tell that to the senator," said the marshal. "He's the one that appoints us here in the marshal's office. If you find you need reinforcements, I guess you can get them."

"Huh!" snorted the agent.

"When are you leaving for Charleston?" said the marshal.

"Tonight," said the agent. "The Fullers live about twelve miles the other side and we aim to go in on 'em about dawn. Hope to catch 'em at breakfast."

When Uncle Pete got back from his Holly Springs trip that evening, the prohibition agents were gone. The marshal had just entered the office with the evening mail which contained a huge stack of notices for posting the reservoir district. When Uncle Pete left the office at closing time that evening, the marshal watched him going down the steps with the pile of notices in his arms.

"I bet, by George, he won't get home tomorrow night," the marshal said to the office deputy.

"How many did you give him this time?" said the deputy.

"Everything that was left in the reservoir," said the marshal.

"Great day!" said the office deputy. "We won't ever see him again. That stuff runs all the way from Coldwater to way below Charleston."

Uncle Pete and Joe left at daylight next morning. As soon as it got light enough to see, they stopped the car, got out, and spread the notices on the ground. Between them, they knew every path and pig trail in north Mississippi, and they went over the notices and arranged them in a route that swung around in the hills and small creek bottoms, then looped and twisted out into the edge of the Delta. At last, Uncle Pete was satisfied.

"We'll never get back home tonight," said Joe, shaking his head.

"We'll have to do some stepping," said Uncle Pete.

"You don't hope to get all that stuff posted before dark, do you?" said Joe.

"Well, you can't tell," said Uncle Pete.

"Oh, Lord!" said Joe. "Oh, Lord!"

"Huh," said Uncle Pete.

Just about this time, the two prohibition agents were holding a hurried conference behind old man Fuller's barn. They had slipped in as silently as they could with their car, leaving it, they thought, a safe distance down the road. But the keen ears of old Josh Fuller had detected the faint vibrations in the air even before he could hear the sound of the motor. He had risen from the shuck mattress where he slept beside his wife and, slithering across the floor on callused feet, poked his head in the door of the lean-to behind the kitchen where his two sons, Hank and Lon, slept. He brought them upright with a cautious hiss.

"Git into your clothes and come on," he said. "They's some'un a-coming."

The two sons slid from beneath their patchwork quilt and stood like two cranes in their too-short winter underwear. They slid into their overalls and flipped the galluses expertly over their shoulders, then donned their jumpers and placed their wide-brimmed hats on their heads. With shoes in one hand and rifles in the other, they went into the front room where old Josh stood in the open door, listening to the small waking sounds of morning. They crossed the floor to him and he held up his hand for silence.

"They are coming across toward the barn," old Josh said after a long wait.

The two boys placed their shoes noiselessly on the floor and crossed to the side of the room that faced the barn. They slid their rifle barrels through punched-out spaces in the chinking and peered intently into the waking day.

The prohibition agents thought they had used due caution and they breathed triumphantly as they gained the shelter of the barn and still heard no sounds of awakening from the house.

"We got 'em this time," whispered Harry, the senior agent, exultantly. "They ain't even awake yet. All we got to do now is wait till they get up and all get in to breakfast, then move in and taken 'em. Shucks, we don't even need old man Pete."

"It wouldn't hurt to have a couple of men on the other side of the house," said Ed, the other agent. "Just in case they try to run."

"Tell you what we'll do," said Harry. "Let's slip on up to the house and I'll get at one kitchen window and you get at the opposite one, and then when they come in to breakfast, we'll have 'em from both sides."

"You think they won't see us cross the yard?"

"They ain't even awake yet."

So, led by Harry, they eased out from the corner of the barn and started their stooped-over approach toward the house. The first notice they had that they had been detected was a yellow knife of flame from the nearer wall of the house and the unmistakable whip of a high-powered bullet close above their heads. They made a mad dash back to the barn and fell in a panting heap around behind the corner.

"Gosh!" said Ed. "Who done that?"

"The so and sos," said Harry. "They been watching us all the time."

"What we going to do now?" said Ed.

"Call on 'em in the name of the law to surrender," said Harry.

"You reckon that'll do any good?"

"Hello, the house," said Harry in a full-voiced bellow. "Surrender. In the name of the law."

They strained their ears into the silence and Harry tried again.

"Wonder why they don't say something," said Ed.

"They're too smart," said Harry. "As long as they don't say anything, we can't even swear they heard us."

They crouched behind the barn for thirty minutes, but no sound from the house broke the stillness of the morning.

"This ain't getting us nothing, just setting here," said Harry at last. "We'll slip back in that ditch that runs back of the barn and separate, and come in on them from two directions. Maybe we can fool 'em into thinking there are more than two of us. You go up the ditch and I'll go down. When you get to those woods on the other side of the house, crawl out of the ditch and I'll crawl out down here. When I whistle, shoot into the air a couple of times and holler like you're hollering at two or three men. When they run out on my side of the house, I'll catch 'em. You got that? All right. Let's go."

As they wriggled back through the weeds to the ditch and disappeared over the edge, Hank left his hiding place in the corner stall of the barn to which he had slipped in the confusion of the agents' precipitate flight from the first shots and, bending over at the waist, strode rapidly across the yard to the house.

"Two," he reported to old Josh.

"Jest two, huh?" said old Josh. "I knowed they'd be traveling in pairs. They allus travel in pairs."

"You want we should catch 'em while they're separated like?" said Hank, after he had repeated the agents' plan to old Josh.

"Wouldn't know what to do with 'em ifen we had 'em," said old Josh. "Give 'em time to git outen the ditch, then cut loose a few shots through them low branches."

The boys cut loose a few shots even before Ed had time to get out of the ditch or holler, and, with the clipped leaves and branches dropping about him, he made another precipitate flight down the ditch to the rear of the barn. He met Harry there.

"What the dickens do you mean shooting at me?" said Harry before Ed could speak. "And why didn't you holler?"

"You didn't give me time," said Ed. "You started shooting before I could even get out of the ditch."

"Why, I never shot at you," said Harry. "I never even shot at all."

"I didn't neither," said Ed.

They stared at each other, then Harry peered through the weeds toward the house. "They must have found out what we were doing somehow," he said

They crouched in silence for a while.

"We've got to have a third man," said Harry at last.

"We could use two or three more," said Ed.

"One more would have been enough this morning," said Harry. "If we had just had somebody around on the other side when we first surprised 'em—if they would just get rid of old man Pete and give us somebody that could do something—"

"You reckon we had better go back in to Charleston and get some reinforcements?" asked Ed.

"I guess we might as well," said Harry. "This is a lot of expense for the government to just catch two moonshiners. When I get back to headquarters, I'm going to see if I can do something about that old dodo."

They wriggled back down the ditch and made their roundabout way through the cypress and tangled thickets back to their car.

Old man Josh and his two boys listened to the whir of the car starter and the sound of the motor as the agents drove away down the bottom road. The old man nodded his head in grim understanding. "They'll be back," he said.

"How you know they both left?" Hank said.

"They allus travel in pairs," said Josh.

"What did they leave for?" said Lon.

"Gone to get help," said old Josh. "They'll be back, come sundown."

"We going to jest set here and wait fer 'em?" said Hank.

"I been a-setting here waiting fer 'em fer fifty year," said old Josh, standing his rifle in the corner by the fireplace. "You boys go tend the stock and turn 'em out to pasture."

"Had we better take our rifles with us?" said Lon.

"Won't hurt nothing," said old Josh. "But you won't need 'em."

Hank and Lon, with their rifles in the crooks of their arms, walked across the yard to the barn and fed the stock, then turned them out to pasture and returned to the house. Old Josh was seated in the sun on the porch when the two boys came around the corner of the house and dropped to seats on the top step. Mrs. Fuller called them to breakfast, and they ate, and then returned to the porch.

It was almost dinnertime when they heard the car motor returning across the bottom. The two boys looked up quickly at old Josh. Old Josh eased the up-tilted front legs of his chair back to the porch and leaned an ear toward the sound. He listened closely as the sound grew louder and closer, then he rose and, followed by the two boys, entered the door and barred it.

The three of them watched through the holes between the logs, where the chinking had been punched out, with their rifle barrels thrust through the holes to cover the approaching road.

The car drew nearer and broke from cover at the edge of the yard and pulled to a stop in the yard at the front of the house. Three rifles covered Uncle Pete as he clambered from the car and turned to face the house.

"Josh," he bellowed. "Oh, Josh. Got any biting dogs?"

"Well, I swan," said old Josh, lowering his gun. "Hit's old Pete."

He set his gun down by the door and unracked the bar and swung the door open.

"Come in, Pete," he said, stepping out on the porch. "Come right in."

"It's been a long time since I was last here," said Uncle Pete as he mounted the steps and pumped old Josh's hand.

"Yes, hit has," said old Josh; then quickly, "Who's that getting out of your car?"

"That's Joe, my driver," said Uncle Pete.

"Oh," said old Josh. "You in the marshal's office now, ain't you, Pete?"

"Yes. Been there going on seven years now."

"I heared some'un say so a while back."

"Can you give me and my driver some dinner, Josh?"

"Course. Course," said old Josh. "Old woman is just about ready to dish it up. You want to wash first?"

"Wouldn't hurt, I reckon," said Uncle Pete.

"Hank," called old Josh. "Hank. Go git Pete a fresh bucket of water. Come on through to the back porch. The washpan's on the back shelf."

Uncle Pete called to Joe and followed Josh through the house to the back porch, stopping to speak to Mrs. Fuller on the way. Hank came with the fresh bucket of water from the well, and Uncle Pete and Joe washed their faces and hands and combed their hair in front of the cracked mirror nailed to the wall above the shelf.

Mrs. Fuller called them to dinner and the menfolks filed into the dining room in solemn procession and took their seats at the table.

Uncle Pete sat down, then squirmed about, hitching himself forward to the edge of his chair as he reared up on one hip and fumbled at his hip pocket. He finally pulled a pistol and a pair of handcuffs out and looked around for a more comfortable place to keep them through dinner.

"Here," said old Josh. "Give 'em to Lon. You, Lon. Take them things fer Pete and put 'em on the mantel."

Uncle Pete handed the handcuffs and pistol to Lon and turned to his plate of spareribs and turnip greens and pone bread.

After dinner, the men folks retired to the front porch while Mrs. Fuller cleared the table and ate her dinner. After half an hour's reminiscing, Uncle Pete rose and consulted his watch.

"Well, Josh," he said, "I guess we better be going."

"Wait jest a minute, Pete," said old Josh.

He went into the house and called Hank and Lon.

"You boys git your hats and go with Pete," he said. "I never thought about 'em sending him out here fer you. It ain't right to make him git out on them kind of trips. I'm a-going to say something to the senator about hit the very next time I see him. Y'all take keer of Pete now, and don't try to git away. You likely won't git but three or four years, and that ain't wuth gitting Pete hurt over."

Old Josh went back onto the porch. "The boys are going in with you, Pete," he said.

"Well now," said Uncle Pete. "That's going to crowd us a right smart. I don't know whether we got room for them."

"You're jest saying that 'cause you don't want to take 'em," said old Josh. "They ain't going to take up much room an' they might come in handy ifen you git stuck. I'd druther they went in with you than them other fellers."

"Well, if they are going anyhow, I might as well take 'em," said Uncle Pete.

Hank and Lon had returned with their hats on and were standing on the porch waiting. They followed old Josh and Uncle Pete and Joe out to the car and waited again while Uncle Pete and Joe got into the front seat.

"Well, you boys move them suitcases over to the side and get in the back," said Uncle Pete. "It's right crowded."

"That's all right, Uncle Pete," said Hank. "We'll make it all right."

"Well, so long, Josh," said Uncle Pete when they were all seated in the car. "Take care of yourself."

"Same to you, Pete," said old Josh.

Old Josh stood in the front yard and watched the car turn and move off down the rutted bottom road.

They had gone about a hundred yards down the road when Uncle Pete sat up suddenly on his seat and slapped his hip pocket. "Joe. Joe. Stop a minute," he said.

He felt his other pockets. "By thunder, I forgot my pistol and handcuffs."

"Want to turn around and go back for 'em?" said Joe.

"I hate to do that," said Uncle Pete.

"I'll run git 'em, Uncle Pete," said Hank, and he slid over the back door and trotted back down the road to the house and soon returned with the handcuffs and pistol. Uncle Pete took them with a gruff word of thanks and the car got under way once more.

"What's old Josh doing now?" said Uncle Pete, turning to Hank and Lon on the back seat.

"Paw's done got too old and stove up to do anything much," said Hank.

"Jest lays around the house mostly," said Lon.

"I remember one time," began Uncle Pete. "Let me see. It must have been about ninety-eight. Yep. That's when it was. Ninety-eight. I come through here horseback and spent the night with Josh. You boys weren't born then—"

About this time, the two agents were waiting in their car in front of the telephone office in Charleston. When they left Josh's that morning, they had driven straight to the telephone office and Harry had put through a long-distance call to the marshal.

"This the marshal talking? . . . We've got to have help over here . . . Yes. We've got them hemmed up but two men ain't enough to handle 'em. If we had of had one more man this morning, we would have them now. That's all we needed. Just one more man . . . What's that? . . . You're sending a couple of men? . . . Good. Tell 'em we'll be waiting here at the telephone office in Charleston. And tell 'em to make it snappy. Send plenty of ammunition. Those men are killers."

The car with the reinforcements came at last and the two cars roared out to Josh's. The men surrounded the house and wriggled on their bellies through the weeds. When they came to the edge of the clearing in which the house sat and peered through the last weeds, there sat old Josh, tilted back in his chair on the front porch with his hands folded in his lap.

"Surrender. In the name of the law," called Harry from the weeds. "Raise your hands."

Old Josh raised his hands obediently but remained seated in his chair. The four agents, bristling with firearms, rose from the weeds and approached to the edge of the porch, keeping a wary lookout on the house all the while.

"In the name of the law, I command you to produce Henry and Alonzo Fuller," Harry said.

"I cain't," said old Josh. "Pete come by fer 'em about noon and tuck 'em with him."

"Pete? You mean old man Pete from the marshal's office?"

"That's him."

"Good gosh!" said Harry. "Old man Pete and those two killers? Let's go, men. Maybe we can get there in time."

Led by Harry, the men turned and plunged away from the house.

"Well, I swan," old Josh said. "Now what in the world you reckon come over 'em? Revenuers! Pitouey!" And he spat into the front yard.

The agents stopped again in Charleston and Harry jumped to the ground even before his car stopped rolling.

"Keep going. Keep going," he shouted, running up to the other car. "Keep on after 'em. We've got to save that old fool if we can. I'll go in here and call the marshal to send out a car from the office to meet 'em. It'll serve old man Pete right if he does get knocked in the head," he muttered to himself as the other car whirled away in a cloud of dust. "I wonder how he managed to capture 'em. Must have went in on 'em at dinner. And what was he doing messing around in this case anyhow? Must have heard us talking about him being too old the other day and set out to prove he wasn't. I bet the marshal blows up when he hears about it."

The marshal was more indignant than worried when he received the call from Harry that Uncle Pete was on his way in with the two Fuller boys.

"There's no use in him risking himself at something like that," the marshal said to his office deputy after he had talked to Harry. "We've got younger men for those kind of jobs."

"Why in the world do you reckon he did it?" said the office deputy.

"Why, to have an excuse to come in tonight," said the marshal. "I'm going to see that he spends one night away from home if I have to go out with him myself, and arrest him and jail him. But, wherever I arrest him, the jail will probably be full and I'll have to bring him back here to spend the night."

But when the car from the marshal's office met the car from Charleston without having encountered Uncle Pete, and the car containing Harry and Ed drove up to where the first two cars were stopped in the road and they all three returned to the marshal's office empty-handed, the marshal grew worried.

"What if those two men have done away with Uncle Pete and taken his car?" he thought. "I'd better put in a call to the Highway Patrol about him."

So the marshal called the Highway Patrol, and the description of Uncle Pete and Joe and the two Fuller boys, together with the description of the car they were in, went out to all the patrol cars. A state-wide search was under way, but dark came, and there was still no sign of Uncle Pete.

The lights were turned on in the marshal's office and the room gradually filled with Uncle Pete's friends and the idly curious, their attention centered on the marshal hovered over the phone.

"I told you not to let that old dodo handle prisoners," said Harry.

The marshal looked up at him with worried eyes and opened his mouth to speak, but the town clock boomed the first note of nine and the phone bell tinkled at the same time. The marshal grasped the phone quickly to him and placed the receiver against his ear.

"Hello. . . . Yes? . . . Where are you, Pete? . . . At home? . . . Are you all right? . . . I said, Are you all right? . . . Why shouldn't you be all right? And you out all evening and up into the night with

those two killers . . . What killers?—Those *Fullers*. . . . Wouldn't
hurt anybody? . . . Sons of an old friend of yours? Where are they?
. . . Out there at your house? Well, you get 'em right up here. . . .
Yes. Now. . . . Asleep? . . . Worked pretty hard all evening? . . .
Well, I'll be. . . . No. Nothing. I didn't say anything. . . . No. Don't
wake 'em up. Just bring 'em up here in the morning. . . . Good
night."

The marshal placed the receiver slowly back on the hook and
looked up at the crowd about his desk.

"Pete's home," he said. "The Fuller boys are out there asleep.
He'll bring 'em down in the morning when he comes." He turned to
the office deputy: "He says the boys are pretty tired out. They
worked pretty hard all evening helping him finish up posting that
land."

(1907–1966)

Hubert Creekmore

Hubert Creekmore was born January 16, 1907, in Water Valley. He
began writing in grammar school there, but it was not until later, as a student at the University of Mississippi headed for a career in law, that he
decided to be a professional writer. After earning a B.A. at Ole Miss in
1927, he studied drama at the University of Colorado and playwrighting at
Yale under George Pierce Baker. In the early 1930s, to support himself
while writing, Creekmore worked for the Mississippi Highway Department in Jackson and for both the Veteran's Administration and the Social
Security Board in Washington, D.C. He soon returned to graduate
school, however, taking an M.A. at Columbia University in 1940, and at
the same time helping to edit the work done on the Mississippi Writer's
Project. His first volume of poetry, *Personal Sun*, appeared in 1940. He
worked briefly for New Directions Press before entering the U.S. Navy;
his service in the Pacific, especially in New Caledonia, produced his best
volume of poems, *The Long Reprieve*, which was published in 1946. After
the war he again took up fiction, and wrote four novels between 1946 and
1953. Creekmore's final years were devoted to editing and translating. He
died in New York on May 23, 1966.

The eight sonnets reprinted here are from *Personal Sun* (1940); the
other poems are from *The Long Reprieve* (1946).

348

"The Heart's Illusion"

The heart's illusion like a pool reflects
upon its hungry surface all alike
that leans above it. Bravely it elects
some thinnest shape to keep that seems to strike
the very mold of its forecast desire
and reaches hands of skeins of air to hold it.
But those faint fingers cannot grasp a fire:
nor could a pool the clouds that overrolled it.

No image swimming through the mirror stays,
for all, reflecting alien light, erase
their own substance. They are bound with wars,
so strictly orbited that crossing breeds
disaster, so fiercely single each one bleeds.
This must be the loneliness of stars.

"Past Lecheries"

Past lecheries have chewed on innocence:
hungry houndlike tossed it as a bone
and hovered greedy sloppy jaws where once
the delicate taste of youth had somehow been.
It is an arid bone, fleshless, bred
in desert waste, nuzzled by a hound
against a wall, unsatisfying, proud,
and full of tears, and love that never bled.

What years can do! . . . and days; and this one lonely
hour, when skeletons of innocence
hunt with sightless reach the fire that only
in the pure is kindled. Unknown, tense,
and buried ecstasy, revive, and let
me burst with beauty, that I may then forget.

Coincidence of Birds

The chance might not repeat that there be three
and that the sky be sunny empty blue
and that a singing hush imbue the green
of cradling branches with a boundless tune
and that a helpless peace suffuse my brain.
Unlike birds, more like airplanes they dived
triangular in loops and spins, behaved
as aviators in a charted line.
Martins more than three had been too much—
a simple flock at play; and less, a pair
at mating. And if it never more occur,
I shall have seen the three of me to match
a song of motion in the sky. My soul,
my flesh, my brain, that once, were welded whole.

Lullaby

Think not, because I bruise you, I have tired,
or kept too much a tender mind, or hate.
If I flay you, madly tremble, bright
my eyes dance at your tears, and you once dared
defence or slow requital, you would lose
me; lax would fall your fingers from my heart.
The purple on your arms where I have hurt
you, cicatrices on your back that was
a bowl of porcelain beneath my lips,
mean that I am unafraid and risk
the utmost joy to stay my love from husk
and keep it blind ecstatic. From the cups
where pour your wretched tears, deep life I drink
of wounding you and kissing when you shrink.

In Illness

Now let me sever body from my soul
and in their brief divorce forget disease
and pain and final rotting in death throes;
let only my ghost rejoice; my limbs congeal
against one puny effort to exult
in action with my capering thoughts. Then if
my flesh choose not to join the weather's lilt,
the spiritsong, eyesung, will be enough.
The lovely cycle to spring again completes
itself, through beauty more severe and rich
than this faint ferment in the buds. But its
ineffable transport can never reach
as deep as lushing air and leaves that burst
through sickly tissues to a hermit thirst.

By the Window

Reading, I had dropped asleep and stretched
beside the window in the piercing sun.
At length there came a friend who saw me, touched
the window lightly with his knuckles. Then,
as I awoke and threw the window wide,
he came and smiling leaned upon the sill.
So simply done seemed everything I did
that thinking never went beyond the smile.

But it could be that I would fall asleep
and someone knock upon my window pane,
and I'd not hear but lie there mouth agape.
And I'd not lift the window up, nor lean
to talk upon the sill. Then all would say
He's gone. Amen. Yet would I be away?

To the Very Late Mourners of the Old South

Come—decay has crushed your crinolines,
forgetfulness has rusted over the graces
of your courtesy. Too long your faces
now have poured their maudlin might-have-beens
in tears upon the fond remembered scenes
that make the artificial wreath time places
on your tomb of adolescence. Stasis
of perception is all this weeping means.
Come—forget the feudal charm of days
you never can resuscitate, and gaze
upon what breathes in vital beauty here
before your backward turning feet. A near
and burning loveliness you trample down
to hold upon your head this martyr's crown.

Lament

That uniform bed, whereon two bodies lie
in grotesque swooning love, and slay all time
with piercing promises, follows their game
of knitted limbs with vague and slow dismay.
It sees them rising now, and Time, reborn,
in vigor of new youth draw each one taut
with days gone and to come. Another coat
with that one from the needle—(one now torn,
and sewn from a ragged world)—falls over each,
constricts their minds as tailors do their reach.
Hovel of love and tomb of shortdead Now,
the bed may cry *Cannot you choke the doubt
of fawning life and to my beggar mate
my corpse?* But none will hear; none can obey.

Pocket Guide for Service Men

". . .are not molesters of women" the book says,
Balancing in its hopefulness the rape
That spirals in the eye when women pass.

The tower of morale, as plotted in
A filing cabinet, skitters when
The first wind of custom touches it,

And is a sheaf of blowing papers. We,
Who value only sex and money, feed
Our own disaster with decreed pretense.

The sailor, under the feathers and scarlet bloom
Of flamboyants, invites the French girl
To whoredom, if she does not know his tongue.

The soldier thinks all women prey for him,
But prays within himself for one. The game
Has spare reward, win or lose, but shame.

Not hemispheric in its cause, it effects
A geographic contrast. Movie-fostered,
Pulp-fed, dreaming of money and sex,

We live the lives of virile American Men—
An emptiness of mirror-maze reflecting
The wretched ritual of the pool room punk.

Here the pioneering spirit finds
Its last, debased residence, and blind
To honor, honors nothing, so is honored.

It is too late to teach a fighter love
When he must kill. It is too much to build
Respect where none has been, or been owed.

Row Five, Grave Two

Above the mangrove swamp, the cemetery,
Spreading to the hillside's western berm,
Twinkles a sea of flags that would confirm
The clay-bound offered hope of these we bury

In a strange earth, far from home. Screening
Foreign foliage will never shroud
The common sky that floods with sun and cloud
The fighter's final station. But turf is greening

As in their favorite parks and pastures. No burning
Tree will drop a scarlet pall, no vine's
Exotic leaf about each cross entwine:
Sun-glint sod is home's closest returning.

In stony beds on Attu lie their brothers,
In vaults of crowding jungle green are dressed.
Mounds in Africa drift with desert unrest:
The bloody coral crown, Tarawa, smothers

A thousand heroes' heads. From these inventoried
Graves; from those who flag-wound slid beneath
The waves, in blast of science vanished, wreath
Of fire about each cell, in bones ungloried,

Alone, unknown, rest in mystic communion:
From all, earth-girdling as the parallels,
Is no vital knot of purpose to swell,
Triumphant cord of their mortal union

Through a mad geography of divers
Wars? We may have sealed in with these dead
A purpose in their death. It may have fled
Into the tomb, fearful of survivors'

Apathy when peace has come, and guarded
Its memorial against the hold
Of minds that memorize control and gold.
Its home is here, among the graves, greenswarded.

Lacking sounder monuments, caretakers
Will tend our hollow testimony, keep
The grass trim, and let the pilgrim weep
At "Row 5, Grave 2" in acres

Of intentions solemnly entombed. We suffer
No caretaker for our spirit, miss
No money spent on graves and archives. This
Is all that we who bury you can offer:

A sign for country, a sign for love and pain,
A sign for life. And if there be no more
Than a neat plot and record, God rest you, for
This is the ancient deathless tale again:

A million young hearts gone for nothing.

Night Spot

Above them all she sees the languid hand—
The air-shaped hand drooping as if to take
A sweet-meat—idly closing over the instant
Of their years the timeless bones of death.

The young men, laughing one more night, are gods
Around the cocktail bar. To her they gleam
In sentimental lights and music, flame
Like Icarus against the murdering void.

Such radiance the tomb never shed
Around a tenant as now, by its threat,
Aureoles their manhood and the hunger
Of her pantheogonic womb. But sterile

Her conception since her hunger feeds
On symbols: through all the barren nights she winds
Her shroud of thighs about the men who wait
To lie in closer beds with barren Death;

For she is concubine with Death in war's
Debasement. Her hysteric greed blasphemes
The fogy shrine of life; these fighters pour
Their blood libations for so little—so few.

Her arms, that in a calmer day would shame,
Twine about the aviators' throats
Like strangling scarves outblown from Kali's robes;
And she and they forget . . . forget . . . forget.

Ecole Communale—Bourail

Piggy-back, piggy back,
    In the prison yard.
Tag, tag, fierce attack,
    Run behind the guard.

Recessed from class in which their treble monotone
In unison *"les cygnes"* droned, "stretched out their necks
Like serpents. . ." children leap at games, cry in their own
Abandon, still untangled in the incestuous wreck

Of cultures. Where they play, by walls mouldering black,
Sparsely grows the grass—no other thing, nor tree

On hill behind. Here once walked a wretched pack
Of women sent by France to prison across the sea.

> (Back and forth, up and down,
>   In the prison yard . . .
> Wait, weep, days will drown,
>   Eyes and heart be scarred.)

Today they jump, run piggy-back like centaur colts
In capers, on their heads olive soldier caps
To key them to a war whose hidden threat revolts
No more in them than dress. Some far mother, perhaps,

They think not of, paced this paddock while convict eyes,
Drunk with near parole, through a crevice chose
A colonial bride. Straw hats, round and ribboned, cries
Of children, chasing games now fill the prison close.

> *"Reviens! Reviens!"* laugh and call
>   To players galloping by.
> Run, play, the blackened walls
>   Don't yet shut out the sky.

At the bell clang, a last drink from the cistern fed
By rain-spout in the eaves—stooping, spraddled, cup
Of palms—and march to class: to read, with no more dread
Than when they ran from It, "stretched serpent necks
          and *houp!*

Dans le bassin des cygnes," in reedy chant, and dream
Only swans of kindness. The yard is haunted now
By sunshine, steeping from sod of time sorrows that seem
To call "Come back!" as in a desperate game, and vow

The breath of innocence will drown an age of distress.
"Reviens!" the children's cry floods over the walls of time

"Come back, come back!" and washes with their artlessness
The black of ancient wrongs—eternal anodyne:

> Piggy-back, piggy-back,
> In the prison yard.

Outdoor Movie—Noumea

The senile shadow of a vigorous time
  Lurks about the mountain slope.
    Whining for distant days
We crowd the amphitheatre to gaze
  At shadow actors who will mime
    The modern satyr play.

Strophes from the mask of celluloid
  Curl with promise through the tiers.
    Cothurnus in high heels
Tapdances to the cymbals, and ordeals
  Of love drench those lips enjoyed
    But never touched by ours.

Around our emptiness we draw the disguise
  Of movies. Oh, men at Thermopylae,
    This hero is a ghost.
And all are lost upon the hillside, lost
  Beneath the dance of gigantic thighs
    Projected on our will.

Shadows, watching shadows, imitate,
  Drain their dwindling substance through
    Each others' pallid cores.
Beyond the eastern range the great moon pours
  On screen of clouds, then breaks, great
    Cascade of longing, to

The desert of our dreams, breaks that screen
    Hiding the world of man from man,
        And probes the only real
We know within ourselves. Its mirrors steal
    Us from the hypnotist. The lean
        Sinews knot and wake.

Where No Bombs Fell . . .

Where no bombs fell, no conquerors marched,
        No tanks rolled,
      The old folk slept except
For sinking dreams that cried, "My son, my son!"

Where no guns spat at citizens
        Against a wall,
      No laws forbade the mind,
The children slept and dreamed no dreams of pain.

Where airplanes snarled no song of death
        Across the moon
      Young women neither slept
Nor dreamed, but cried to the night, "O lover, husband!"

A kind of peace, a kind of war—
        Anemic balance
      Teetered by the selfish—
Wherein the fear of what may come preserves

Alike the politician and
        The nightmare of
      The village architect.
The trees are spared, but what is cured by war

Remote except in sacrifice?
          No evil dies,
     No good is born—
Folly of monuments intact in stone.

Ave, ad Infinitum

The incidence of heroes has a definite relation to accidents.
The factors are present. Given the quality of men
     The production of heroes would climb to millions
On the assembly line of war—a cumbersome number.

The private in a foxhole, hungry and fevered but constant,
Is not enshrined in publicity especially after
     The enemy's fire has found him. The nearest
Of kin gets a form telegram. Such death has no sales value.

The pilot who downs a covey of airplanes is wined
In Hollywood, displayed at the government's command,
     Paraded to spur the sale of war bonds
To people who cherish heroes ready-made in the gross.

The reference is no longer to the character,
Action's catapult of virtues, but
     To a single temporal point detached
From daily meanness and bloated by the press into a poultice.

The trick is to know how to die—knowledge too often
Put to use. The fertile circumstance
     Allowing distinction is denied
Too many soldiers who got no lauding parade but died.

(1915–)

Margaret Walker Alexander

Novelist and poet Margaret Walker Alexander was born in Birmingham, Alabama, on July 7, 1915, the daughter of a Methodist preacher; she grew up in Alabama, Mississippi, and Louisiana. She received a B.A. from Northwestern University in 1935 and an M.A. in 1940 and Ph.D. in 1965 from the University of Iowa. Before becoming Professor of English at Jackson State University she worked in various capacities as a social worker, newspaper reporter, and magazine editor. Her first book of poems, *For My People* (1942), was a winner of the Yale Series of Younger Poets award, and has been called "probably one of the two or three most important books by a black poet in America since the start of World War II"; and her one novel, *Jubilee* (1966), was a runaway best-seller.

The following poems are from her second collection, *Prophets for a New Day* (1970).

361

Jackson, Mississippi

City of tense and stricken faces
City of closed doors and ketchup splattered floors,
City of barbed wire stockades,
And ranting voices of demagogues,
City of squealers and profane voices;
Hauling my people in garbage trucks,
Fenced in by new white police billies,
Fist cuffs and red-necked brothers of Hate Legions
Straining their leashed and fiercely hungry dogs;
City of tree-lined, wide, white avenues
And black alleys of filthy rendezvous;
City of flowers: of new red zinnias
And oriental poppies and double-ruffled petunias
Ranch styled houses encircled with rose geranium
And scarlet salvia
And trouble-ridden minds of the guilty and the conscienceless;
City of stooges and flunkeys, pimps and prostitutes,
Bar-flies and railroad-station freaks;
City with southern sun beating down raw fire
On heads of blaring jukes,
And light-drenched streets puddled with the promise
Of a brand-new tomorrow
I give you my heart, Southern City
For you are my blood and dust of my flesh,
You are the harbor of my ship of hope,
The dead-end street of my life,
And the long washed down drain of my youth's years of toil,
In the bosom of your families
I have planted my seeds of dreams and visions and prophecies
All my fantasies of freedom and of pride,
Here lie three centuries of my eyes and my brains and my hands,
Of my lips and strident demands,
The graves of my dead,
And the birthing stools of grannies long since fled.
Here are echoes of my laughing children

And hungry minds of pupils to be fed.
I give you my brimming heart, Southern City
For my eyes are full and no tears cry
And my throat is dusty and dry.

Birmingham

I.
With the last whippoorwill call of evening
Settling over mountains
Dusk dropping down shoulders of red hills
And red dust of mines
Sifting across somber sky
Setting the sun to rest in a blue blaze of coal fire
And shivering memories of Spring
With raw wind out of woods
And brown straw of last year's needle-shedding-pines
Cushions of quiet underfoot
Violets pushing through early new spring ground
And my winging heart flying across the world
With one bright bird—
Cardinal flashing through thickets—
Memories of my fancy-ridden life
Come home again.

II.
I died today.
In a new and cruel way.
I came to breakfast in my night-dying clothes
Ate and talked and nobody knew
They had buried me yesterday.
I slept outside city limits
Under a little hill of butterscotch brown
With a dusting of white sugar
Where a whistling ghost kept making a threnody
Out of a naked wind.

III.
Call me home again to my coffin bed of soft warm clay.
I cannot bear to rest in frozen wastes
Of a bitter cold and sleeting northern womb.
My life dies best on a southern cross
Carved out of rock with shooting stars to fire
The forge of bitter hate.

How Many Silent Centuries Sleep in My Sultry Veins?

How many silent centuries sleep in my sultry veins?
The cries of tribal dancers call from far off buried plains;
The plaintive songs of India, the melodies of Spain;
The rhythms of their tom-tom drums;
Of Red men seeking southern lands,
Of Africans in chains.
They call me from their tombs and thrones;
From many distant climes.
They whisper old and sacred names:
Each intonation chimes
An ancient and familiar rite
For primitive and erudite.
I hear them wail loud echoings.
Locked deep inside of me they cry—
And wild their clamorings!
Blood rituals of men and gods
Speak pitiless, and shriek.
And crashing barriers of time
These dark imprisoned sons
Of all my wild ancestral hosts
Break from their time-locked sea
To make these modern, sensate sons
Immortal men, and free.

Sam Tata

(1921–)

Elizabeth Spencer

Elizabeth Spencer was born July 19, 1921, in Carrollton, and grew up there. After receiving a B.A. in English from Belhaven, she went to Vanderbilt for an M.A., also in English. She then taught successively at Northwest Junior College in Senatobia, and at Ward-Belmont in Nashville, before resigning to work as a reporter on the Nashville *Tennessean*. During this time she wrote her first novel, *Fire in the Morning*, published in 1948, while she was on the English faculty at the University of Mississippi. Since then Spencer has been a full-time writer, except for brief teaching stints as writer-in-residence at Bryn Mawr, the University of North Carolina at Chapel Hill, and Hollins College. She has received numerous awards for her work, including a Guggenheim Fellowship in 1953, the Rosenthal Foundation Award of the American Academy of Arts and Letters in 1956, the *Kenyon Review* Fellowship in Fiction in 1957, and the first McGraw-Hill Fiction Award in 1960. She now lives and works in Montreal, Quebec. Since 1976 she has been associated with the creative writing staff of Concordia University in Montreal, where she is now writer-in-residence.

"Port of Embarkation," first published in the *Atlantic* for January, 1977, was one of three stories suggested to us by Spencer, and corrected by her for its appearance here.

365

Port of Embarkation

IT WAS NEARLY NOON OF THE DAY my father went back to his
unit and thence to overseas service in World War II that I saw the
horses. They were coming up the hill from the field, and all I could
see first was the delicately scalloped, chestnut tips of their four ears
all set forward, which showed their effort, one pair lower than the
other. Then their forelocks and long, down-plunging, toiling heads
rose to view, the chins dipped low and lather from the bits splashing
down, to foam across the twinned chests. I saw the black harness,
heard the shout of the driver, and had the impression of a heavily
laden wagon, though who the driver was—somebody working for
us? a stranger?—and what the wagon carried, I did not know.

The team of great strong chestnut horses lingered in my mind's
vision even after I woke on the bed in the far corner of the sleeping
porch where I had gone to cry myself to sleep, not wanting anyone to
see my tears. The hill up from the field was blocked from my view by
the whole of the house which lay between. But caught in the dream,
I lay still in the afternoon July heat, willing for a time for it to extend
its power. There was indeed a moment of further increase when I
knew that the nearer horse had white-stockinged hind legs, and that
the hill, though steep, was nothing to the power of the team which
nobly crested it.

And this was all.

In the center of the house I ran into my mother, who also showed
signs of having been crying, but who at once asked where my
brother was. He had said he was going somewhere, but I had forgotten where. We went into the kitchen together, trying to act as if it
were any other day—we were a reserved kind of family—and found
that my brother had already gotten into the lunch and had eaten
most of it. We would have to scramble eggs, or drive uptown to the
grocery, and we preferred not to have to go out and talk to people.
An alternative was to locate my brother and get him to bring us
something, but this would undoubtedly provoke a quarrel between
him and my mother. My brother was stubborn and seemed to be
unfeeling with us all, but I had caught the worst of his nature, for,
being smaller and younger I was the object of bullying and threats.

In the hallway to which I had returned, to look past the white front porch, across the positive, relentless sun glare of the yard, toward the fall of the hill, to where I had dreamed the horses ascending, I could hear my mother's and brother's voices. Though he had missed my father's departure with us in the car to the airport, he had been somewhere around, it would seem, all the time.

"That food you got into, that was mine and Estelle's lunch. You knew that, didn't you?"

"No, I didn't know it. How would I?"

"You must have heard us say we didn't want to go out, we'd have a cold lunch, I'd make the potato salad and an aspic, then stuff some eggs. You said you wouldn't be here. There's not enough left for one, now, much less both of us."

"Can't you just fix some more?"

"I certainly don't want to, I guess I can . . ." The down-turning of their encounter was like fire in a log smothering down to smoke; then (I knew it would come by the tension in my middle), my mother's voice flared up like flame.

"Why can't you be more considerate! That's all I ever want to know. You're the man of the house now. Your father told you that, last night at dinner. We'd like to count on you, we need to count on you, but you . . . ! What do you care?"

"The way you tell it, I don't care about nothing."

"Do you? I'd dearly love to know."

"What you want me to do? You want me to go uptown and get something for your nourishment?"

My mother started crying. He was that sarcastic. "Oh, we'll manage. We'll manage somehow."

Mother eventually found a can of crabmeat and made another salad and we sat down to a good lunch. Iced tea, crisp and lemony brown, is comforting after you've been crying, especially on a hot day. It soothes out your feelings.

"We're going to be stuck here all summer," I remarked, "with the way he acts. It's all on purpose," I added, which was not a good thought to give her.

She put her hand to her head. "I think he has problems," she said. "I think something worries him deep down."

"Like what?" I asked.

"How do we know each other's problems unless we tell them? How do I know? Maybe there's some girl he likes who doesn't like him, maybe he doesn't know what to do with himself, maybe he hates it about your father and doesn't want to show it."

"Maybe he's just mean and doesn't like us and wants to show that."

"I wish you wouldn't talk like that," Mother said. She looked frail and she was upset, but she could come out with things full force. "It may interest you to know, Missy, that I love you both the same, I've always said that, and it's true. Your brother knows I love him. He'd have to know that."

That afternoon Mother and I went to the picture show in a neighboring town. Our town was too small to have anything but a fleabag for a movie house, so we generally went over to a larger town. The larger towns, having more pavement and less shade, were hotter than our own. We parked between two white slanted lines, each a paintbrush wide, and walked to the movie house. The sidewalk burned through the soles of our shoes.

"If anybody sees us and asks," Mother said, "I'm going to say we went just to get our minds off everything."

"I'll say that too," I said.

Movies in those days were not, I think, air-conditioned, but they were air-cooled, which was not a bad substitute. They had large concealed fans, almost silent, which blew over ice, so that a constant breeze was stirring, moist and pleasant. If something in this apparatus broke, as it sometimes did, you sat there in the dark, sweltering and wondering whether or not the movie was interesting enough to hold you in discomfort.

That day nothing broke and the movie, *Up in Arms*, with Danny Kaye and Dinah Shore, seemed to be making the war a great big joke. We were complete suckers for what they were doing and sat there shaking with laughter.

When we went out together we heard a voice from the lobby where a wave of hot air was coming in through the front door which the matinee crowd was pushing open.

"Hey, wasn't that swell?"

It was my brother, standing in a knot of other boys. He was

laughing and talking out to us. Mother stood stock still when she saw him and I almost laughed out loud, not at the movie, but at them, because she was good and ready in her mind to bless him out for going to a movie the day his father went to port of embarkation, but then, there she was herself. The only difference was that she had her excuse ready and he, undoubtedly, did not.

"Got a ride home now," Brother said to the boys he was with. He came over to us. "Lemme tag a ride," he said. Then he flung an arm around each of us. You could think he was showing off for the benefit of the boys. But, as always with him, you couldn't altogether tell why he was doing anything. He was just doing it, that was all. "I'll buy you girls a coke," he said.

We went next door to a little hamburger shop and sat at a booth. We ordered cokes and glasses of ice, the way we all liked them. Then we went to the car, where hot air had to be let out before we could even get in; and Brother drove us home.

All during the time we had been sitting and drinking the cokes together he had kept laughing and talking about the movie. "It's that scat singing," he said. "I can't see how he does it, 'less they speed up the sound track. I tried it but it didn't work."

"You tried to sing!" my mother exclaimed. "I never knew you to sing a note."

"Oh, I got talents. I got lots of talents." He was laughing at both of us. We might have been people he knew slightly. He was almost sixteen and I was just twelve.

After supper that night my father telephoned to cheer us up. "I been talking to some of the other officers," he said. "They don't see how the war can go on more than another year at the most. I may not even get there."

I was on one phone, Mother on the other, but we couldn't get my brother to hear us as he was moving the furniture in his room, making an awful racket. Wasn't it important that they spoke? No matter what my father said, we all knew the war was reaching its height. He was heading straight to its heart.

"What's going on there?"

"It's Brother," Mother said. "He's started changing his room around. Wait, I'm going to call him again."

"There're a hundred people lined up to use this phone. I've got to get off it in three minutes or my name is mud. Listen, Ginny, you and Estelle both, don't bother that boy."

"We're going to try to do everything right," Mother said. "Don't you worry, not about anything."

"You let him be his own way. Just let him be."

"I promise, Nat. Oh, I do!"

Then we were hollering goodbye, this morning all over again, until the phone clicked off. From my brother's room, immediately after the click, something fell and smashed.

My mother and I rubbed ourselves with 6-12 and went to sit out on the porch in the dark. We hadn't done much of anything, but I felt tired to death.

Neighbors' lights glowed through the trees. Down the hill, the fields slept densely under dewfall. Lightning bugs drifted against a black row of bushes at the field's distant edge. In all that lay out there, I knew the road where I had seen the horses in my dream was rising up as it always did, but I couldn't make it out.

"I had this dream this morning after Daddy left," I said. I told her about the horses, the wagon and driver.

She didn't say anything, and I wondered if I should have mentioned it. I hadn't tried to think what it meant, if anything.

Finally she said, "It's funny what you dream." I wondered whether she would ever think of it again. Maybe she would.

We heard a door slam above us and my brother's heavy steps, coming downstairs. I felt the powerful sway of her promise to my father on the phone, his demand for it all the greater by coming through from afar, as though from an unseeable beyond: *Let him be his own way. Just let him be.*

I heard her talking to herself, whispering that she would try.

(1916–)

Shelby Foote

Now living in Memphis, Tennessee, Shelby Foote was born in Greenville on November 17, 1916. He began reading seriously, he has said, and got his literary education, through his friendship with the Percys, William Alexander and Walker, while growing up there. He was a student at the University of Virginia from 1935 to 1938, and during World War II served as a captain of field artillery in Europe. After the war Foote returned to Greenville and began to write, producing five novels between 1949 and 1954 and establishing his reputation as an author. He is probably best known today, however, for his massive three-volume history *The Civil War: A Narrative*, which he originally undertook as a short history of the war. It took him nearly twenty years to complete and won him, upon publication of the final volume in 1974, a Pulitzer Prize nomination. It is a unique achievement, indeed, for Foote brought to the writing of his heavily researched history not just the historian's reservoir of facts and dates but also the novelist's eye for meaningful detail and the capacity for understanding and depicting character. In addition, his history reflects the novelist's natural way with story-telling and a superb, clear, prose style.

Foote's historical sense, the sense of the relationship between the past

371

and the present, is also very much present in his fiction. "The Sacred Mound," taken from *Jordan County* (1953), deals with an early period in the history of Foote's mythical Jordan County, and the conflict of peoples and cultures that attended its exploration and settlement.

The Sacred Mound
Province of Mississippi, A.D.1797
Number 262: CRIMINAL

Against the Indian, Chisahahoma (John Postoak) *of the Choctaws, self-accused of the grisly murders of* Lancelot Fink *and* ＿＿＿ Tyree (*or* Tyree ＿＿＿) *1796.*

Master Fiscal Judge, Mr John the Baptist of Elquezable, *Lieutenant Colonel and Governor.*

Scrivener,
Andrew Benito Courbiere.

DECLARATION: HEREIN SWORN & SUBSCRIBED. In the town of Natchez and garrison of St Iago, on the 23d day of September, 1797, I, Mr John the Baptist of Elquezable, Lieutenant Colonel of Cavalry and Provisional Governor of this said Province of Mississippi, proceeded to the house Royal of said town (accompanied from the first by Lieutenant Francisco Amangual and Ensign Joseph of Silva, both of the company of my office, as witnesses in the present procedure) where I found the prisoner Chisahahoma, a young man of the color of dusky copper, smallpox pitted, with hair cut straight along his forehead and falling lank to his shoulders at the back, who having been commanded to appear in my presence and in that of the said witnesses, before them had put to him by me the following interrogatories:

Question. What is he called, of what country is he a native, and what religion he professes? Answered that he is called Chisahahoma, that he is native to a region six sleeps north and also on the river, and that he is a Roman Catholic these nine months since the turning of the year. *Q.* Is he sufficiently acquainted with the Spanish language, or if he needs an interpreter to explain his declaration?

Answered that he understood the language after a fashion and that if he doubted any question he would call for the advice of the interpreter. *Q.* If he would promise by our Lord God and the sign of the Cross to speak the truth concerning these interrogations? Answered that he would promise and swear, and did. And spoke as follows, making first the sign of the Cross and kissed his thumbnail:

Lo: truth attend his words, the love of God attend our understanding: all men are brothers. He has long wanted to cleanse his breast of the matter herein related, and has done so twice: first to the priest, as shall be told, then to the sergeant, answering his heart as advised by the priest, and now to myself makes thrice. His people and my people have lived in enmity since the time of the man Soto (so he called him, of glorious memory in the annals of Spain: Hernando de Soto) who came in his forefathers' time, appearing in May two sleeps to the north, he and his men wild-looking and hairy, wearing garments of straw and the skins of animals under their armor; who, having looked on the river, crossed westward and was gone twelve moons, and reappeared (in May again) three sleeps to the south, his face gray and wasted to the bone; and died there, and was buried in the river.

Desecration! his forefathers cried. Pollution!

So they fought: the strangers in armor, man and horse looking out through slits in the steel — of which he says rusty fragments survive in the long-house to commemorate the battle where the Spaniards (he says) wore blisters on their palms with excess of killing — swinging their swords and lances wearily and standing in blood to the rowels of their spurs: and at last retreated, marched away to the south, and were seen no more.

Then all was quiet; the young ones might have believed their fathers dreamed it, except for the rusting bits of armor and the horse skulls raised on poles in the long-house yard. Then came other white men in canoes, wearing not steel but robes of black with ropes about their waists, and bearing their slain god on a cross of sticks, whose blood ran down from a gash in his side: saying, Bow down; worship; your gods are false; This is the true God! and sang strange songs, swinging utensils that sprinkled and smoked, and partook of the wafer and a thin blood-colored liquid hot to the throat; then went away. But the Choctaws kept their gods, saying: How should we forsake the one that made us of spit and straw and a dry handful of dust and sent us here out of Nanih Waiya? How should we exchange Him for one who let himself be stretched on sticks with nails through the palms of his hands and feet, a headdress of thorns, pain in his face, and a spearpoint gash in his side where the life ran out?

Q. Was he here to blaspheme? — for his eyes rolled back showing only the whites and he chanted singsong fashion. Answered nay, he but told it as it was in the dark time; he was the Singer, as all his fathers had been. And continued:

Then came others down the years, also in boats — all came by the river since Soto's time — but bearing neither the arquebus nor the Cross: bringing goods to trade, beads of colored stuff and printed cloth and magic circles no bigger than the inside of a hand, where sunlight flashed and a man could see himself as in unspillable water; for which, all these, the traders sought only the skins of animals in return. Now of all the creatures of the field, only certain ones were worthy of being hunted by a man: the bear, the deer, the broad-wing turkey — the rest were left for boys. Yet the traders prized highest the pelt of a creature not even a boy would hunt: the beaver: and this caused his people to feel a certain contempt. Lo, too, these strangers placed an undue value on women, for they would force or woo a man's wife and lie with her, not asking the husband's permission or agreeing beforehand on a price or an exchange, and though they were liberal with their gifts when the thing was done, there began to be not only contempt but also hard feelings in the breasts of his people.

So much was legend: he but told it as his father before him told it, having it from the father before him, and so on back. Yet what follows, he says, he saw with his own eyes and heard with his ears; God be his witness. And continued, no longer with his eyes rolled, speaking singsong, but as one who saw and heard and now reported (making once more, in attest of truth, the Cross upon his breastbone):

Two summers back, in the late heat of the year, spokesmen arrived from many sleeps to the south, near the great salt river. Three they were, the sons of chiefs, tall men sound of wind and limb, sent

forth by their fathers, saying: We have a thing to impart. Will our
brothers hear? That night they rested and were feasted in the long-
house, and runners went out to bring in the chiefs. Next day as the
sun went bleeding beyond the river all assembled on the sacred
mound, the leaders and the singers (himself being one) and the three
came forward, lean with travel, clean-favored and handsome in
feathers and paint, upright as became the sons of chiefs, and the tallest spoke. It is transcribed.

— Brothers: peace. We bring a message and a warning. May you
hear and heed and so be served. The white ones speak with forked
tongues, no matter what crown they claim their great chief wears
beyond the sea. We bring a warning of calamity. It will be with you
as it was with us, for they will do as they have done. Thus. First they
came boasting of their gods and seeking a yellow metal in their various languages. Or, they call it, or Oro. Then, in guile, they exchanged valuables for the worthless pelts of animals, calling us
Brother, and we believed and answered likewise, Brother. And they
lived among us and shared our pipe and all was well between us. So
we thought.

— Then, lo, they began to ask a strange thing of us, seeking to
buy the land. Sell us the land, they said: Sell us the land. And we told
them, disguising our horror: No man owns the land; take and live on
it; it is lent you for your lifetime; are we not brothers? And they appeared satisfied. They put up houses of plank and iron, like their
ships, and sent back for their women. Soon they were many; the
bear and the deer were gone (— they had seen and known in their
hearts, without words; but we, being men with words, were blind)
and the white men sent forth laws and set up courts, saying This shalt
thou do and This shalt thou not do, and punishment followed hard
upon offense, both the whip and the branding iron and often the
rope. And we said, Can this be? Are we not brothers, to dwell in one
land? And they answered, Yea: but this is Law.

— Nor was it long till the decree came forth, in signs on paper
nailed to the walls of houses and even on trees, and the chiefs were
called into the courts to hear it read. Go forth, the judges read: Go
forth from the land, you and your people, into the north or beyond
the river; for this land now is ours. And our fathers spoke, no longer

trying to disguise the horror: How can this be? Are we not brothers? How can we leave this land, who were sent here out of Nanih Waiya to dwell in it forever down through time? And they answered, Howsomever.

— So it was and is with us, for our people are collecting their goods and preparing for the journey out. So too will it be with you. And soon; for this was all in our own time, and we are young.

I have spoken, the tallest said, and rejoined the circle. The chiefs sat smoking. Then another of the young men spoke, asking permission to retire to the long-house to sleep, for they had far to go tomorrow. And it was granted; they left, all three; and still the chiefs sat smoking.

The moon rose late, red and full to the rear of where the chiefs sat passing the pipe from hand to hand. But no one spoke, neither the chiefs on the mound nor the people below, their faces back-tilted, looking up. Then one did speak — Loshumitubbe, the oldest chief, with the hawk beak and thin gray hair that his ears showed through, a great killer in his day, and lines in his face like earth where rain has run: saying, Yea, the moon be my witness; we have offended, we have strayed. This is not the cunning of the white man. This is anger from the gods. They want it as it was in the old time.

So saying, he made a quick, downward motion with the pipe; it might have been a hatchet or a knife. Some among them understood, the older chiefs and the singers — he being one — and nodded their heads, saying Yea, or smoked in silence. And down at the base of the mound the people waited, faces pale in the moonlight, looking up. After a term the chiefs spoke in turn, grave-faced, drawing out the words, some for and some against. By morning it was decided; they came down off the mound with their minds made up.

Runners were sent one sleep to the north: five they were, strung out along the river bank, a hard run apart. Three weeks the people waited. It was cold and then it faired, the air hazy, leaves bright red and yellow though not yet brown; it was nearing the time of the corn dance, when a man's heart should rejoice for the fruits of the earth. And the people said to one another behind their hands, Can this thing be? (for such had not been done since far before the time of the man Soto; not even in that hard time, he says, was such a thing considered) but others answered, not behind their hands but openly, proud to have gone back: Yea, can and shall: Loshumitubbe says it.

Then came one running, the nearest of the five posted along the river bank, running with his legs unstrung, and knelt before Loshumitubbe, unable to speak but holding up two fingers. Then he could speak, panting the words between breaths: Two come by water. Trappers, O chief. In buckskin.

Here was a halt, the dinner hour being come. Next morning, again at the house Royal, immediately I, the said Governor, together with the aforesaid witnesses of my company, commanded to appear before me Chisahahoma, whom I found a prisoner in the care of the guard as before and still in bonds, who once more subscribed and swore the oath and resumed as follows, confronting the witnesses and Benito Courbiere, scrivener:

That night in the long-house they played the drum and painted, himself among them. Next morning they waited in the willows down at the river bank, again himself among them. For a long time, nothing. The sun went past the overhead; they waited. Then two together pointed, raising each an arm: Lo: for the trappers were rounding the bend in a canoe. Still they waited, knee-deep in the water, screened by willows, watching. The trappers held near to bank, seeking signs of game — one tall and slim; he sat in the stern, and the other short and fat; he was the older. They wondered if they could catch them, for his people had only dugouts: when suddenly the man in the bow stopped paddling. Lance! he shouted, and pointed directly at the willow clump. So he and his people bent their backs to launch out in pursuit. But the one in the stern changed sides with his paddle and the canoe swung crossways to the current, approaching. A sign from the gods, his people thought; their hearts grew big with elation. And when the two were within arm's length they took them so quickly they had not even time to reach for their rifles. Truly a sign from the gods! his people cried, and some began to leap and scream, squeezing their throats with their hands to make it shriller.

So the two were bound at the water's edge and brought up to the town, walking hunched for their wrists were strapped with rawhide at the crotch, one hand coming through from the rear and one from the front so they could not stand upright, though the tall one almost could; his arms were long. They were marched the length of the street, the smell of fear coming strong off the short one. Bent forward — his arms were short, his belly large — he turned his head this way and that, watching the gestures of the women hopping alongside, the potbellied children staring round-eyed, and skipped to save his ankles from the dogs; twice he fell and had to be lifted from the dust. The tall one, however, kept his eyes to the front. The dogs did not snap at him, for even bound he was half a head taller than any Indian.

Hi! the women shouted: Hi! A brave! and made gestures of obscenity, fanning their skirts. Hi! Hi!

The chiefs sat in the council room, wearing feathers and paint in gaudy bars, and the two were brought before them. Now they looked at each other, chiefs and trappers, and no one spoke. Then Loshumitubbe made a gesture, the hand palm down, pushing downward, and they were taken to the pit room at the far end of the long-house. It was dark in there, no fire; the only light was what fell through the paling disk of the smoke hole. The cries of the women came shrill through the roof, mixed with the yapping of dogs. The time wore on. From outside, he says, they began to hear the short one weeping, asking questions in his language, but the tall one only cursed him, once then twice, and then ignored him.

So it was: they on the outside, waiting for the moon to fill, knowing: the trappers on the inside, in the pit, waiting but not knowing. Seven suns they were in there, feeding like hogs on broken bits of food flung through the smole hole — for they remained bound, the rawhide shrinking on their wrists, and had to grovel for it. They fouled themselves and were gutsick on the scraps, he says, and the stench was so great that the women approaching the hole to taunt them held their noses and made squealing sounds. From outside, listening, his people heard words in the strange language: at first only the short one, calling the other Fink or Lance and sometimes Lancelot: then later, toward the close, the tall one too, calling the short one Tyree, though which of his two names this was no man could say, not even now, for they were Americans, a people whose names are sometimes indistinguishable, the last from the first, since they name not necessarily for the saints. At the end, however, they called to one another not by name but by growls, for the food was scant and hard to find on the dark earth floor; they fought for it like dogs, snapping their teeth, still being bound.

Then, lo, the moon would be full that night. Long before sundown the people were painted and ready, dressed as for the corn dance. The young ones wore only breech clouts and feathers, fierce with red and yellow bars of paint, but the older ones brought out blankets rancid with last year's grease and sweat. The cold had returned; the leaves were brown now, falling, and they crackled underfoot. It was yet above freezing, he says, and there was no wind, but the cold was steady and bitter and sharp and a thick mist came rolling off the river.

The trappers were taken from the pit as soon as the sun was gone. Their clothes were cut from their bodies and they were sluiced with hot water to cleanse them of their filth; they stood in only their boots and bonds, their hands purple and puffy because the rawhide had shrunk on their wrists, their skin first pink from the heat of the water, then pale gray, goose-fleshed, and their teeth chattered behind their bluing lips. Then was when they saw that the short one was covered with what appeared to be louse bites, small hard red welts like pimples. The time in the pit had changed them indeed, and not only in appearance. For now it was the tall one who kept glancing about, shifting his eyes this way and that, while the short one stood looking down over his belly at his boots; he did not care. Just as the tall one had used up his courage, so had the short one exhausted his cowardice. Then at a signal the guards took hold of their arms and they went toward the mound, stepping stiff-kneed. The old men with blankets over their shoulders walked alongside. The young men, wearing only feathers and breech clouts, leaped and shouted, their breaths making steam.

Atop the mound the chiefs were waiting, seated in a half circle with a bonfire burning behind them for light. They faced the stakes. One was a single pole with a rawhide thong up high; the other was two low poles with a third lashed as a crosspiece at the height of a man's waist. Then the trappers were brought. From the flat top of the mound, he says, they could see torches burning in the lower darkness, spangling the earth, countless as stars, for the people had come from three sleeps around; they stood holding torches, looking up to where the bonfire burned against the night. The tall trapper was tied to the single stake, arms overhead, hands crossed so high that only the toes of his boots touched the earth — the tallest man they had ever seen, taller than ever, now, with skin as pale in the firelight as the underbark of sycamores in spring. The short trapper stood between the two low stakes, his wrists lashed to the crossbar on each side of his waist. Both were breathing fast little jets of steam, partly from having climbed the mound but mostly from fear; for now, he says, they knew at least a part of what they had been wondering all that long time in the darkness of the pit.

The moon rose, swollen golden red, and now the dancing began, the young men stepping pigeon-toed, shuffling dust, and Otumatomba the rainmaker stood by the fire with his knife. When the dancing was done he came forward, extending the knife flat on the palms of both hands, and Loshumitubbe touched it. The drums began. Then Otumatomba came slowly toward the short one, who was held by four of the dancers, two at the knees and two at the shoulders, bent backward over the crosspole. He did not struggle or cry out; he looked down his chest, past the jut of his belly, watching the knife. What follows happened so fast, he says, that afterwards looking back it seemed to have been done in the flick of an eye.

Otumatomba placed the point of the knife, then suddenly leaned against the handle and drew it swiftly across, a long deep slash just under the last left rib. So quick the eye could barely follow, his hand went in. The knife fell and the hand came out with the heart. It was meaty and red, the size of a fist, with streaks of yellow fat showing through the skin-sack; vessels dangled, collapsed and dripping, except the one at the top, which was dingy white, the thickness of a thumb, leading back through the lips of the gash. Then (there was no signal, he says; they knew what to do, for Otumatomba had taught them) the men at the shoulders pushed forward, bringing the trapper upright off the bar, and for a moment he stood looking down at his heart, which Otumatomba held in front of his chest for him to see. It did not pulse; it flickered, the skin-sack catching highlights from the fire, and it smoked a bit in the night air. That was all. The short one fell, collapsing; he hung with his face just clear of the ground, his wrists still tied to the crosspole.

Hi! a brave, he heard one say among the chiefs.

But that was all; the rest were quiet as the rainmaker took up the knife again and turned toward the tall one, lashed on tiptoe to the stake. As he drew closer the trapper began to swing from side to side, bound overhead at the wrists and down at the ankles. When Otumatomba was very near, the tall white naked man began to shout at him in his language: No! No! swinging from side to side and shouting hoarsely, until the rainmaker, with a sudden, darting motion like the strike of a snake, shot out one hand and caught hold: whereupon the trapper stopped swinging and shouted still more shrilly, like women in the longhouse at the death of a chief, in the final moment before the cutting began. While Otumatomba sawed with the knife, which seemed duller now and slippery with the blood of the other, the tall one was screaming, hysterical like a woman in labor, repeating a rising note: Ee! Eee! Then he stopped. He stopped quite suddenly. Otumatomba stepped back and tossed the trapper's manhood at his feet. The trapper looked down — more than pain, his face showed grief, bereavement — and now he began to whimper. Blood ran down his thighs, curving over the inward bulge of his knees, and filled his boots. He was a long time dying and he died badly, still crying for mercy when he was far beyond it.

Again the young men danced. The moon sailed higher, silver now, flooding the mound. In the distance the river glided slow, bright silver too, making its two great curves. Then it was over; the dead were left to the bone-pickers. The chiefs rose, filing down the mound, and he heard Loshumitubbe say to one beside him:

This will stop them. This will make an end.

Yea, the other told him. This will stop them.

But some there were — himself among them: so he says — who shook their heads, now it was done and they had seen, asking themselves in their hearts: Were they savages, barbarians, to come to this?

Here was a halt, the hour being noon, and after the midday meal and the siesta we returned to the house Royal: I the Governor, together with the aforesaid witnesses and scrivener: before whom the prisoner Chisahahoma, in care of the guard, swore and subscribed and continued, making an end:

Sudden and terrible then came the curse on his people, the wrath of God. The moon was barely on the wane and they felt pain in their heads, their backs, their loins; their skin was hot and dry to the touch; dark spots appeared on their foreheads and scalps, among the roots of hair. The spots became hard-cored blisters; the burning cooled for a day and then returned, far worse, and the blisters (so he called them: meaning *pustules*) softened and there was a terrible itching. Some scratched so hard with their nails and fishbone combs that their faces and bodies were raw. Many died. First went Otumatomba the rainmaker, then Loshumitubbe chief of chiefs, he who had given the signal; men and women and children, so fast they died the bone-pickers had not time to scaffold them. They lay in the houses and in the street, self-mutilated, begging the god for sudden death, release from the fever and itching.

He himself was sick with the sickest, and thought to have died and wished for it; he too lay and hoped for death, but was spared with only this (passing his hand across his face) to show the journey he had gone. Then he lay recovering, the moon swelling once more toward the full. And he remembered the short trapper, the marks on his face and body when they brought him out of the pit, and he knew.

Then he was up, recovered though still weak, and was called before Issatiwamba, chief of chiefs now Loshumitubbe was dead. He too had been the journey; he too remembered the marks on the short trapper. The people still lay dying, the dead unscaffolded.

O chief, he said, and made his bow, and Issatiwamba said:

I have called; are you not the singer? This is the curse of the white man's god, and you must go a journey.

He left next morning, taking the trappers' canoe. Cold it was, approaching the turning of the year, with ice among the willows and overhead a sky the color of a dove's breast. He wore a bearskin and paddled fast to keep from freezing. The second day he reached the Walnut Hills, where the white man had a town, and went ashore. But there was no house for the white man's god; he was in the canoe, continuing downriver, before sunset. The fifth day he reached this place and came ashore, and here was the house of the white man's god and, lo! the God himself as he had heard it told and sung, outstretched and sagging, nailed to the wall and wearing a crown of thorns and the wound in his side and pain in his face that distorted his mouth so you saw the edges of the teeth. And he stood looking, wrapped in the bearskin.

Then came one in a robe of cloth, a man who spoke with words he could not understand. He made a sign to show he would speak, and the priest beckoned: Come, and he followed to the back of the house and through a door, and — lo again, a thing he had never seen before — here was an Indian wearing trousers and a shirt, one of the flatheads of the South, who acted as interpreter.

The priest listened while he told it as Issatiwamba had instructed. The Indians had killed in the Indian way, incurring the wrath of the white man's god; now was he sent for the white men to kill in the white man's way, thus to appease the god and lay the plague. So he told it, as instructed. The flathead interpreted, and when it was done the priest beckoned as before: *Come*, and led the way through another door. He followed, expecting this to be the pit where he would wait. But lo, the priest put food before him: *Eat*, and he ate. Then he followed through yet another door, thinking now surely this would be the pit. But lo again, it was a small room with a cot and blankets, and the priest put his hands together, palm to palm, and laid his cheek against the back of one: *Sleep*. And he slept, still expecting the pit.

When he woke it was morning; he knew not where he was. The pit! he thought. Then he remembered and turned on his side, and the flathead stood in the doorway with a bucket in one hand, steaming, and soap and a cloth in the other. First he declined; it was winter, he said, no time to scrape away the crust. But the other said thus it must be, and when he had washed he led him to the room where he had eaten. He ate again, then followed the other to still a third room where the priest was waiting, and there again on the wall the god was hung, this time in ivory with the blood in bright red droplets like fruit of the holly. The three sat at table; the priest talked and the flathead interpreted, and all this time the god watched from the wall. Here began his conversion, he says, making yet again the sign of the Cross upon his person.

He heard of the Trinity, the creation, the Garden, the loss of innocence, and much else which he could not follow. When the priest later questioned him of what he had heard he found that he had not heard aright, for the priest had said there were three gods and one god; did that not make four? And the priest at first was angry: then he smiled. They had best go slow, he said, and began again, telling now of the Man-God, the redeemer, who died on the cross of sticks but would return. There was where he began to understand, for just as the Garden had been like Nanih Waiya, this was like the Corn God, who laid him down to rise again; perhaps they were cousins, the two gods. But the priest said no, not cousins, not cousins at all; and began again, in soft tones and with patience, not in anger. In time they needed the interpreter no more, for he believed and the words came to him; he understood; Christ Jesus had reached him. Whose strength was in His gentleness, Whose beginning was in His end. Winter was past, and spring came on, and summer, and he was shrived and christened. His name was John; John Postoak, for Postoak was the translation of his name.

Then, being converted, he called to mind the instructions of Issatiwamba; a duty was a duty, whether to tribe or to church. So he asked the priest, kneeling at confession: must he go to the authorities? For a time the priest said nothing, sitting in the box with the odor of incense coming off him, the smell of holiness, and he who now was called Postoak watching through the panel. Then he said, calling him now as always My Son, that was a matter to be decided within himself, between his heart and his head. And he said as before, Bless me, father: knowing. And the priest put forth his hand and blessed him, making the sign of the Cross above his head, for the priest knew well what would follow when he went before the authorities and told what he had told the day when the priest first found him in the bearskin, outside the church where Christ hung on the wall.

He went then to the sergeant of the guard, Delgado, and standing there told it in Spanish, what had been done on the mound and how and his share in the thing, and offered himself this second time, as instructed by Issatiwamba, not to lay the plague, however, but rather to lay the guilt in his own breast. Delgado heard him through, listening with outrage in his face, and when it was done gave orders in a voice that rang like brass. Then was he in the pit indeed, with iron at his wrists and ankles. He dwelt in darkness, how many days he knew not, the year moved into September, the hottest weather; and then came forth under guard to face ourselves, Governor and witnesses, in the formalities which ensued and here have been transcribed even as he spoke, including whatever barbarisms, all his own. So it was and here he stands, having told it this third time: God be his witness.

Q. If he had anything to add or take from this deposition, it having been read to him. Answered that he has nothing to add or take, and that what he has said is the truth under the obligation of the oath he took at the outset, which he affirms and certifies and says he is twenty-four years old, and he subscribes with me and the witnesses over the citation I certify:

Witnessed:	*he signs this*	John the Baptist
Joseph of Silva	Chisa- **X** -hahoma	of Elquezable
Frsco Amangual	HIS MARK	Lt Col Governor

DISPOSITION: BY THE GOVERNOR. In the said Garrison this September 27th 1797 without delay I, Mr John the Baptist of Elquezable, Lieutenant Colonel of Cavalry of the Royal Army, Provisional Governor of the Province of Mississippi, in view of finding the conclusion of the present proceedings, commanded that the original fifteen useful leaves be directed to the Lord Commanding General, Marshal of the Country, Sir Peter de Narva, that they may serve to inform him in reviewing my disposition (tendered subject to his agreeing in the name of His Most Christian Majesty) to wit:

Free him.

First: in that he has renounced his former worship which led him to participate in these atrocities, and intends now therefore (I am assured by the priest, Friar Joseph Manuel Gaetan) to serve as a missionary among his heathen people. Second: in that we are even now preparing to depart this barbarous land, being under orders to leave it to them of the North. And third, lastly: in that the victims were neither of our Nation nor our Faith.

For which I sign with my present scrivener:

J the B	*A Benito*
of El	*Courbiere.*

(1916–)

Charles G. Bell

Charles G. Bell has had a varied career as a novelist, poet, educator, scientist, and humanist. A true renaissance man, with interests covering the complete spectrum of man's activities, Bell has studied nearly all phases of Western culture—math, science, philosophy, literature, music, and the visual arts. He has been at work since the late thirties on a correlated history of culture, which has evolved over the years into thirty-five slide-tape lectures or shows called "Symbolic History: A Dramatic Study of the Western Arts." He sees his entire work as a philosophic articulation; its chief creative fruits to date are two published volumes of poems, *Songs for a New America* (1953) and *Delta Return* (1956), two novels, *The Married Land* (1962) and *The Half-Gods* (1968), and the shows, which he regards as a sound and light reconstitution of poetic tragedy.

Bell was born in Greenville on October 31, 1916, the son of Judge Percy Bell and Nona Oliver Archer. He graduated in 1936 from the University of Virginia with a degree in physics; from there he went to Oxford University on a Rhodes scholarship, taking three degrees in English. He has taught, variously, English, physics, and humanities, at Iowa State College, Princeton University, and the University of Chicago, taking time off during World War II to do research in electronics and to teach Navy engineers in the V-12 program. Since 1948 Bell has held a Fulbright Fellowship and fellowships from the Ford and Rockefeller Foundations,

386

which have allowed him to teach and study in Europe and at the University of Puerto Rico. He now teaches at St. John's College in Santa Fe, New Mexico, and is at work on numerous projects including more poetry, a volume of essays, and a third novel.

"Pioneer Fragments," "Bloodroot," "Fall of Troy," and "Britannic Epistle" are taken from the revised edition of *Songs for a New America;* the others are from *Delta Return.* Bell has made further revisions in these texts, which are recorded here.

Pioneer Fragments

We halted the wagon at the maple grove.
The clear stream choked with leaves. I skimmed them golden
Away. Arm to arm we bent and plunged
Our faces. The brook cold and the air chill.
A good fall. With the tang of smoke in the woods.
Then we pushed on. By afternoon we came
To a fresh water as wide as the sea,
A place of pine and sandy dunes, the clumps
Of yellow spear-grass swaying in the wind.
Russet of autumn. Northward the expanse
Of waves rolling to the smooth hard strand.
We lay in the sun, her head on my arm,
And said: We will build a cabin here
With pines from the farther hill, and raise girls
And boys, a westward race of men. And the wind
Swayed in the spear-grass, yellow against the blue.
And it was good to think of lingering time
And the sunlit wealth of the future years.

*　*　*

My father that last year dreamed hills of the west;
Woke with a smile upon him, kissed
In the night by a goddess. They sold the red earth
Of the gullied farm. Three wagons held
Their promise with their past. Night fires and music

Marked them over the plains.
                              After the desert
And the falling oxen, the last two struggling
To the ridge, just up and over; over
Into evening through the high sweet air,
The Sacramento valley, green with life—
Wading down into that sunshine sea—
They sang a new song, both the hearts and tongues
Singing. And my father said: This is
The promise, dear ones, it is the place of the dream.
I remember the rock hills and the fertile bowl
And teeming ocean of the silent sun—
Like home I have come to, every rock and tree.

*   *   *

Tall, crisp, against the cloud, the swaying pine
On the whistling tuft of the hill. What memories,
My children!

Bloodroot

I walk them in my sleep, those woodland trails
Of the Ragged Mountains. Often when milk-trucks roar
Or garbage cans are gathered in the dusk before
The gray dawn of the city, I stand at the old place
By the tulip tree, where the path bends with the hills,
And a clear spring breaks out cold from the rock face.

It was a long way from the town, a day's tramp
To reach it and return; but the forest there
Was almost virginal, the moss on the ground
Dense as a carpet, and scenting the clean air,
And that was where in the spring I always found
The strange white flower with the bitter stem.

Bitter and dropping blood. It seemed a sign,
That pure loveliness out of the bleeding frond;

And at the same place, in the shelter of the hills,
Brown leather mushrooms grew, the great morels,
That we called devil's fingers, a hideous brood,
Mingling with those flowers as evil with good.

From the tulip tree a trail went up to the ridge,
To a run-down mountain house in an apple grove,
The apples hard and bitter; a wagon groove
Led down the other side to the valley road.
A man lived there of no particular age,
A good-hearted man, but with a rough edge.

I did not like him at first, he had a bride
So beautiful you could only think of her.
Men are slow to learn they must beware
That kind of lonely-eyed excess of beauty.
She left the man one night and their young child
For a boy going in a big car to the city.

The man lived on, nursing his child a year.
He was joined at last by a woman so plain, I thought
Her his sister; but they said otherwise.
I used to camp out overnight quite near.
They would come down with some good surprise;
Sit by the fire while we ate what they had brought.

And something of nature's paradox I learned
That last spring from the man. I had never heard
Such things were edible. He brought them stewed,
Those devil's fingers—"the best food in the wood;
But never you taste," he said, "the bloodroot's blood,
Unless you want your heart and bowels to burn."

So I learned it waking, and afterwards with pain;
But still in sleep I come to the place of the dream,
And trampling the devil's fingers in my old mood,
With the joy of the first sighting, pluck and admire—
The eight long petals yearning like a star—
That pure white beauty from the bine of the bitter blood.

Fall of Troy

The woods are burning. Under mournful light—
Amid long reeds—by the red banks of water—
Stoats and foxes run from slaughter
While a pattering of rabbits fills the night.

And was it all for this, the years of nurture,
Rearing the shoots, and terracing with skill
That downward radiance on the hill,
For this, the sudden suicide of nature?

No sensual trace remains. And yet one ray,
Blood-red of flame, like the last flush of sun,
Caught on the pool the imperilled swan,
Mirrored the pluming breast, and wings that day

Would greet in the new land by the unfired river;
And on that dying world woke such a song
As melodized immortal wrong;
And this has wrung the heart of God forever.

Britannic Epistle

Gaius of Britain to Cinna of Gaul–

Brother:

Here we stand at the northern waste of the world.
Our season's course is gray. It is no place
For leisured living. There is neither wine nor oil.
Most of the country lies in fens and forests,
Savage, inhospitable. Above the lowlands
Shoot bare arms of the moors like land through waters.
Here a little life feeds on the stonecrop acres,

Made almost as savage by the wind and cold.
Our towns are walled with stone, guarding the imperial
Ways; our villas dark, closed to the damp air;
And we conduct hot flues of tile in the walls.
We sit shivering through the long winters. The poems
Of our fathers are without place in this land,
And the women strange fish of the northern seas.
When spring returns I weep for Sirmione,
And the sweet warm days in the wine of Gaul.
Then comes a grunting savage whose wit is alien,
And I must bend to his state our high Roman laws.

Brother, if you may pass a good word to the
Favorite of Caesar in his turn through the province,
Speak of my condition, call me from these shadows.
I have lost enough years holding moorland roads
Over the desert of oak-darkened fens.
I fear that it will never turn to good.
We are building baths west of the central downs,
But never Rome in this sun-forsaken land.
Brother of my youth, let Gaius be enlarged.

I. The Journey Down

A. THE ROAD SOUTH

And in the dusky twilight where I moved, burned
The shadowed woods and the yearning brooks of home.
—HÖLDERLIN, *Patmos*

1. LEAVING CHICAGO

The pole star is high; the others circling
Sweep the cold lake. Dawn spreads across that sky.
The bus takes the parkway from the city of towers.
Wind in the elms quickens the fine lace of spring.
Cars go north where the center wakes into day.

The other motion is ours. It has been long
Since a boy came to conquer that Fair of a World,
The Hall of Science, the Temple of the Arts—
An age of conquering, while the friends at home
Slept at the sun's hearth like peaceful dogs.

South, south by water, heat shimmers on bar sand;
Lazy the land rustling in the bees' drone. . .
To climb is self-possession; to go down
Yields to the homing tide. North, I said,
Is human hope and daring; and so I found.

They say the ice age stirred us to be men;
And I have seen this city when breaking waves
Stretched into crystal on the steel-gray wind;
And I have been one of the muffled faces, leaned
To the blast for the wind-driven prizes.

World-promise melts like cloud when evening brings
Again the low music of the untaut string.
Deeper than the will and before the will was born,
This hunger for night and void where I return
And soft surrender to their welcoming arms.

3. CROSSING THE OHIO

At the day's end of dwindling towns and farms
We are still in Illinois, but as the light goes
We creep on the trestle over the wide Ohio.
The glacial lakes are behind us; down this stream
My grandfather took a proud wife to a Delta home.

If the South is always in my blood, it is not
A life-force only, something as well of the old
Miasma bred in her swamps. Return home.
Full-leafed branches merge on the darkening sky;
We stop in Paducah, Kentucky, first of the South.

Under magnolia trees two waiting rooms,
The black and white, warn of the lingering plague.
Long ago when yellow fever struck in June,
Those grandparents with my father fled past here,
Seeking safety. Where now shall we flee?

The wrecks of southern summers nod, rocked
On the porches still. In the white restaurant
I eat, and the bus is called. We roar to the South.
In the old arms of night protest dissolves.
Sleep sings the remembered beauty daylight mars: —

Walking through the heavy dusk of niggertown,
Past porches of honeysuckle, the swooning smell,
And rich as song those throaty waves of laughter,
Rain-forest rivers deepening under the moon,
Where we paused listening—Listen, drink, be drowned.

D. THE QUEEN CITY

   . . . my most kindly nurse,
That to me gave this life's first native source.
—SPENSER, *Prothalamion*

1. THE TOWER

Nearing the town, first of all I see the tower
That brought the electric lines from Arkansas.
We had climbed trees and hung ropes for the plunge,
One best of all at a blue-hole, where we would swing
And drop to the round water like a stone.

The courthouse was next; we had no peace
Until we had scaled the roof and spire and pole;
But the three-hundred-foot tower was a challenge still.

The pillars were sheer cement; we cut a tree,
Propped it in the mud and worked to the steel.

There the ladders began; I say we climbed
Until the earth was round and the air thin
To reach a platform swaying in the wind.
Current hummed in the wires, incredible power
Of the fire-liquid spilling across the stream.

And we were there at the copper veins of that blood.
It was not the heart leapt only; I climbed the last rail,
Hung by the knees over reeling earth and air,
Daring the comrades, who would not take that dare
From a fool whose eyes loved danger like a girl.

The river coiled beneath its triple coil.
The flat land breeds a hunger for the heights;
And what is climbing and the work to climb
But a moment of vision, at the last verge
Of the wide water, dreaming of the flight down?

3. KNOWN ALL OVER THE WORLD

"Queen City of the Delta" —we slow through the shaded ways.
It was at this corner, sitting on the roots of that tree,
That I passed an old man when I was a boy,
A white-bearded black man who went the rounds
Begging, or working, if work was required.

"Whose boy are you?" he asked as I neared.
"My father's Judge Bell," I answered. He raised his hands:
"Judge Percy Bell, known all over the world!"
When I reached home I found my father there.
It was the climax of his life, that election time;

We had him little then, for always he traveled

In the proud trust that sent him to the masses
With his vision and reliance on their voices.
Now it was over. He was shaving; his face was lathered.
I stood at the mirrored door of the bath; and mother

Came from the telephone bringing the latest
Returns. He had that tragic flush of power
Before our youth is broken. His half-broke then;
His voice was shaken, hearing what pious little
Good effort had garnered. And I a schoolboy, thought

And recall the strangeness of thinking: What else
But failure comes of a temporal undertaking?
At best an old man with eyes to the sky: "Known
All over the world." What worlds to conquer. No cause
To end the search, only the heart's aching.

5. THE COLUMNS

Through trees now gleam white columns; the old South
Beguiled itself in that façade of Greece—
Vision, as always, shadowed by its harm—
These doubly so, built when the First War boom
Launched a lawyer who intended justice and peace.

They were his gesture of Enlightened faith
In a world of human good; their classic form
Clothes the romantic heart; they are Faustian towers,
Crumbling of their own weight, like Beauvais spire,
Flutings of freedom, cloud pillars of our science.

No human condition is more set for sorrow
Than that which asks embodiments to mirror
The hopes of spirit; it was the way of my father.
His failed; and when he died (hard broken death
Of one who dreamed too fondly), I myself

Began to tear pilasters, like limbs of me,
From his library and mine, an apartment now,
Where people come and go; for the great house
Shelters my mother with a tenant crew
Who pay for the blunders of that tragic man.

Promethean father, child of the westward pride,
You beckon from these columns, white on red
Behind the green oak shaodws—you whose end
Was bitterness, beckon and smile. And I climb the wide
Porch stairs under a roof tall and blue like the sky.

E. FABLES OF HOME

2. THE HOUSE PAINTER

He does not know me now, that old deaf man
With the face like Einstein, stumbling as in a daze;
Yet I was formed by him: —Past twelve I was
A hunter. When spring grackles came, gabbling and settling
In all the trees, with a rustle of iridescent

Wings, I dreamed of a bead on the distant shape.
The rifle's crack, black feathers falling limp.
One day I shot two dozen, heaping a pile
On the back porch table by the mackerel pail.
That old deaf German was painting for us then.

As I came in carrying a couple of birds,
He was standing at the table stroking the dead,
Lifting the purple wings and letting them fall,
Saying over and over in his hollow voice:
"Poor things, poor things." I slipped out of the house.

—That sentimental fool!—But the pie I planned
Was never baked; I buried the grackles in mud.
If we relive the race our changes come
No less by revolution; to drown his womanish
Words, I ranged in anger through the woods.

The mother thrasher in a thorn was laying eggs;
I shot into the nest and tore her wide.
As I lifted up those quivering brown dregs,
The old man's spirit caught me in its clutch
Of pain. I did not play with death again.

4. BROTHER

A shade haunts the house, of the father's name
And proud disquiet, the mother's tenderness,
Self-tormenting blend: "Sweetest the fruit
The worm feeds on, the soul preyed on by woe"—
Blake wrote it, brother, and you proved it true.

Gayest born and saddest grown, you took too soon
The vicarious burden of earth's wrong—too gentle
For that weight that falls, falls, like stone.
When I was swimming the river and climbing trees,
You, younger, painted and wrote grieved mysteries.

You were a poet when I studied science.
And spoke the free-verse voice of modern pain,
The broken person, heightening to that harm
By which we lost you and you lost the spring.
Had I been what I am, could my being

Have eased your trial, and both now be singing?
Or is that battle always fought alone?
At your death I was abroad; I crossed
The ocean to a sad home. A grief unhouseled,
As from beyond the tomb, settled upon me.

I found myself, odd times, sketching figures
For poetic lines: "Gray granite faces,
Tight-skinned, brooding, full of silence . . ." So I
Received your spirit. Brother of my blood,
You haunt not this house only, world-wounded shade.

II. The Dialogue of the Mind

B. THE BOOK OF KNOWLEDGE

Still climbing after knowledge infinite.
—MARLOWE, *Tamburlaine*
The eternal silence of those infinite spaces frightens me.
—PASCAL, *Pensees*

1. THE PRISM

Our house was full of books; there was one shelf
This age does not forbid, thought it tempts like fruit:
The Book of Knowledge. When first the wine-ripe skin
Yielded to my young touch, Newton was the man
Who stood at the darkened window prism in hand,

Cleaving white light, which fell in rainbow glowing
Against the farther wall. That thing I desired,
And wrote to Santa Claus, but Christmas morning
Found among toys and marbles no such glass;
Until my father, hearing the tearful case,

Took me down to our reception hall
By the arched door, where the rising winter sun
Struck through leaded windows' bevelled panes,
Painting the walls with rainbows, often seen,
Though not considered. "All these colors," he said,

"Are spectra of such prisms." If they were dim
By the pictured foretaste of the darkened room,
It was enough; I stood in wordless wonder
At the strange aspect of things: white or color?
If both, how much of truth is a metaphor?

From red into violet the patterns played.
I was standing at the fall, where forms go down
In a bright veil of mist, and found myself,
With all I called my own, of such endurance—
Appearance of the moment, mere appearance.

4. THE BOMB

One joined the dark conspiracy, strange son
Of a wandering father, with a stranger name,
Lear Nigssen—where are you now? What flight or ruin
Has drowned you with the monster we made?
We planned to loose the atom and bind the world.

We invented socialism, thought ours the first:
All men to work and share. How ultimate hopes
By promised goods have led us into loss!
That year the Academy failed; it was locked and barred.
We climbed the second story. In the chemistry lab,

With a high-school text we spent our afternoons
Exploding nature, discovering how all things
Are balanced in destruction: hydrogen flamed,
Chlorine coiled its poison, magnesium flared.
Our greatest day we unsettled glycerine

In the nitric bath, heaped up its molecules
At the frightening verge, poised to decompose,
Ten thousand times their bulk; it was our Bomb. . .
Appalling hours nursing the bottled doom,
Frightened of heat and jars. At the cold day's close

We stole to the river, poured the yellow oil
Out in the sluice of nature whence it came.
The pursuit of knowledge had led back to fear.
Over what gulfs we fruit and flower. You moved
From town. Where are you now, strange friend, lost Lear?

E. THE CREED

2. THE ROMAN

We are consumed with a longing beyond the world,
That answers by denial, gives what we are

To the fierce hope of becoming. Gauged by pain
It should be our worst sickness, and yet the cure
Is across that dying to the other shore.

Why not rest easy here? We do not choose.
In the cup of selfhood lies the sensual dreg
That drives us from all calm; the heart's goad
Is the act of satisfaction. Witness in Rome
The pampered patrician, who grew so bored

He turned from the feast of life, trying all creeds
Of painful offering. Stripped to the skin he crawled
In a makeshift grave and was covered with boards;
They slaughtered the bull of Atys over his head.
The god's red rivers brought him from the dead.

He rose incarnadined among the reborn,
But lost, as before. Then a Cynic came,
His hair freaked with knots, a filthy rag
His sole debt to the world, and cried to all men:
"Look at me, look at me; I am your king and lord."

The Roman followed, put off clothes and land,
All but the self. As he turned at last
To the Stoics of death, a Christian caught his hand:
"Take up this Cross." That Easter he was burned
In the Colosseum, a torch that writhed and sang.

III. Perpetual Close

A. THE RIVER

By the rivers of Babylon, there we sat down, yea, we
    wept, when we remembered Zion.
—*Psalm 137*

1. BAPTISM

We drive this Sunday south into the country
Where a white frame Gothic church stands at the levee.
The Negroes, dressed in black, glistening with the heat,
Come early, carrying lunches, and stay late
In the steaming little church where they sing together.

Across the levee at the old landing they still
Hold their baptisms. A live religion deals
In living symbols; so they prefer the river,
Their untamed font of darkness. I recall one evening
When the red sun broke through colonnades of cloud,

And the two tides met, brown and golden, of earth and air—
Light calm and pure, and that violence of water—
How they went down in white and moaning lamentation
To the mud-brown flood and under, then broke up singing,
Rolled on the earth, reborn out of death and nature.

Here at the Christian crossroad we note the cleavage
Between the enlightened few with their stoic wisdom
And the hungry soul of the many whose new Mystery
Is the beat of this spiritual jazz, the loved return
Down to the brown river and wounded Thammuz' blood.

Through all the aseptic channels of the modern
This wild release is pouring; and we who listen,
As the brooding ground and single imploration
Break in waves of answer, group-homing passion,
We whites, who can only listen, are blurred with our tears.

4. HOME-CROSSING

I meet a young fellow on the street, crazy eyed,
Who calls my name. He was at camp, he says,

When I last counselled there. "You did a thing
That struck me more than all the things I've seen.
It was on the ferry that night coming home

Across the river; the current was bad. A stranger
Said he dared anyone to swim. You stripped
And stood at the stern. I thought, 'My God.' Then you
Went in, swam with the ferry, caught it, climbed on
Again. I'll not forget it as long as I live."

For me, I had lived too long. "What? You mean you
don't remember, at all, a thing like that?"
And I: "I've done so many damn fool things
In my time, I can't keep them straight;" and to myself:
"What a stupid act to celebrate so long."

But then like water widening the gap it has made,
All that poured back through the crevice of his words:
I saw the river heaving under the moon
In lighted turbulence and liquid sound;
Once more I took the dare—both boy and man;

For night and water cried to unclothe what we are,
Breathe a time in the moon, then out and down. . .
Mother of waters, may no turn or flinching
Mar the clean line of the plunge, when on
The home-crossing we dive in the deep river of stars.

B. THE FLOOD

4. CRAWDADS

Blind and groping, automatons of life
Begin again in the slime; the strangest birth
Was of crawfish congregations. I had seen
Crawdads enough, by ditches and swamp shores,
Bent claws working in the mud-heaped lairs.

But as the ebbing waters left the town,
Flowing in gutters still or after rains
Rising to fill the streets, those crawdads came
By thousands from the sewers; and what was weird,
They kept their beastly worship. The god they served

Was brazen light; by night arcs' glittering
They flocked like insects in slow clacking swarms,
To the dazzling holiness all waving arms,
While we with buckets and shovels scooped them in.
For days we ate them with every kind of sauce,

Keeping the surplus in the guest-room tub.
Lord, I can see them yet, one on another,
Scrambling, loathsome things, in their own vile water.
We could not eat them all; one night they died.
By morning the stench had crept into every wall.

Clawed and fighting fools, as you abandon
My lord the sun by the waters of earth and air,
And in the town and dark of the moon adore
A guttering lamp, you die in the tile-white pen,
Idolaters of the flickering arc of man.

D. THE DEAD

O here
Will I set up my everlasting rest. . .
   —SHAKESPEARE, *Romeo and Juliet*

1. THE MEMORIAL

At the head of the town by the levee is a new monument
To a free country and to those who died fighting
In its last great war. Above are the stars and stripes
And beneath, a tablet designed for the names of the fallen.
It stands an empty white, the colorless all-color.

Troubled by the incompletion I asked its meaning
And learned the shame of the whiteness: —a cotton broker,
My father's enemy and mine (his ranks are legion),
One who has served our paleness under the hood—
Mark of a cloaked malignance that grows among us,

Accusing by red or brown all uncloaked persons—
This man, I heard, with others of like vision,
Denied the dead black names a place by the white ones;
Therefore the tablet is empty and shall remain so,
The government not permitting a partial monument.

There are times when one doubts the benefits of progress,
Yet serves it still, if only by revulsion
From this wrong. I have not much cared for war either,
And am seldom stirred by battle monuments;
But this featureless sign at the melting river

Moves more than wrath:—Old hater, you have done well.
The god of time is a god too of the whiteness.
You have raised a monument to your own vacancy,
And to all the hearts of the world emptiness,
Nameless names in the masked terror of your voids.

E. TOMORROW

5. IN MY FATHER'S HOUSE

I turn away. In the ultimate shade is a tomb
I played at long ago—a table of stone,
Carved on the top a draughtsman's compass and rule;
Beneath is a name with only this inscription:
"In my Father's house are many mansions."

My own father, whose grave I leave behind,
Told me the story: it was his boyhood friend;

He had set his hopes on being an architect,
Sketched great façades and died in his teens.
I think we are all bearers of such designs,

Getting nowhere with them—architects
Of the unbuilt city, we die more or less as children;
And happy the one who can carve on his coffin
The fable of that hope: In my Father's house
Are many mansions, and go with a good grace.

For my part, I cannot tell. It is strange to think
In the ground of these who have died, something endures;
Yet all things are strange. I suspect indeed
We have died many times, in sleep and dream,
And all our life is a web of dying and return.

Therefore this dark of the water-spilled gray moon
And oaks by the river over the watered plain,
And moon-gray sky and sky's legend of stars,
Are the ebb and flow where we go up and down
In the glimmering swirls of Delta night, our home.

(1921–)

Josephine Ayres Haxton
(Ellen Douglas)

Josephine Ayres was born in Natchez on July 12, 1921, and spent her childhood in Arkansas and Louisiana. She graduated from the University of Mississippi in 1942 and worked afterward for radio stations, bookstores, and the Social Security Board in Alexandria, Louisiana, Natchez, and New York City. She married Kenneth Haxton in 1945, and has since lived in Greenville. Her first novel, *A Family's Affairs* (1962), won the Houghton Mifflin Twenty-fifth Anniversary Fellowship in 1961, and her most recent novel, *Apostles of Light* (1973), was nominated for the National Book Award. She is presently working on another novel, for which she was awarded a grant in 1976 from the National Endowment for the Arts.

"I Just Love Carrie Lee" is one of the stories in *Black Cloud, White Cloud* (1963).

406

I Just Love Carrie Lee

ALL THE TIME WE WERE AWAY FROM HERE, living in Atlanta, I paid Carrie Lee's wages — seven dollars a week for eight years. Of course, part of the time, after Billy married and came back to Homochitto, she was working for him in the country. She rides the bus to Wildwood, seven miles over the river, every day. I don't know why she doesn't move back over there, but she likes to live in town. She owns her own house and she likes to visit around. The truth of the matter is, she thinks she might miss something if she moved over the river; and besides, she never has had any use for "field niggers." (That's Carrie Lee talking, not me.) Anyway, as I was saying, I did pay her wages all those years we were away from here. I knew Mama would have wanted me to, and besides, I feel the same responsibility toward her that Mama did. You understand that, don't you? She was our responsibility. So few poeple think that way nowadays. Nobody has the feeling for Negroes they used to have. People look at me as if they think I'm crazy when I say I paid Carrie Lee all that time.

I remember when I first had an inkling how things were changing. It was during the Depression when the Edwardses moved next door to us. They were Chicago people, and they'd never had any dealings with Negroes. Old Mrs. Edwards expected the baseboards to be scrubbed every week. I suppose she scrubbed them herself in Chicago. Oh, I don't mean there was anything wrong with her. She was a good, hard-working Christian soul; and *he* was a cut above *her*. I've heard he came from an old St. Louis family. But a woman sets the tone of a household, and her tone was middle-western to the marrow. All her children said "come" for "came," and "I want in," and I had a time keeping mine from picking it up.

To make a long story short, she came to me one day in the late fall and asked me what the yardmen in Homochitto did in the winter.

"What do you mean?" I said.

"I mean where do they work?"

"Well," I said, "mine sits around the kitchen and shells pecans and polishes silver all winter."

"You mean you keep him on when there's actually nothing for him to do?" she said.

"He *works* for us," I said. "He's been working for us for years."

"I haven't got that kind of money," she said. "I had to let mine go yesterday, and I was wondering where he would get a job."

I tried to explain to her how things were down here, how you couldn't let a man go in the winter, but she didn't understand. She got huffy as could be.

"I suppose that's what you call *noblesse oblige*," she said.

"You could, if you wanted to be fancy," I said.

And do you know what she said to me? She said, "They're not going to catch me in that trap, the *Nee*-grows. I can do all my own work and like it, if it comes to that. I'm going to stand on my rights."

They didn't stay in Homochitto long.

Wasn't that odd? Everyone is like that nowadays. Maybe not for such a queer reason, but no one feels any responsibility any more. No one cares, white or black.

That's the reason Carrie Lee is so precious to us. She cares about us. She knows from experience what kind of people we are. It's a boon in this day and age just to be recognized.

The truth of the matter is I couldn't tell you what Carrie Lee has meant to us. She's been like a member of the family for almost fifty years. She raised me and she's raised my children. Ask Sarah and Billy, Carrie Lee was more of a mother to them than I was. I was too young when I first married to be saddled with children, and too full of life to stay at home with them. Bill was always on the go, and I wouldn't have let him go without me for anything. It was fortunate I could leave the children with Carrie Lee and never have a moment's worry. She loved them like they were her own, and she could control them without ever laying a hand on them. She has her own philosophy, and while *I* don't always understand it, children do.

Carrie Lee is a bright Negro — both ways, I mean, and both for the same reason, I reckon. I don't know exactly where the white blood came from (it's not the kind of thing they told young ladies in my day), but I can guess. Probably an overseer. Her mama was lighter than she, and married a dark man. The old mammy, Carrie Lee's grandmother, was black as the ace of spades, so Mama said. I judge some overseer on Grandfather's place must have been Carrie

Lee's grandfather. She has always said she has Indian blood, too, said her mama told her so. But how much truth there is in that I don't know. The hawk nose and high cheekbones look Indian, all right, and there is something about her — maybe that she won't make a fool of herself to entertain you. You know she's different. And she could put the fear of God into the children, like a Cherokee chief out after their scalps.

Billy says Carrie Lee taught him his first lesson in getting along with people. He was the youngest boy in the neighborhood, and of course the other children made him run all their errands; they teased and bullied him unmercifully until he was big enough to stand up for himself. This is the kind of thing they'd do. One day in the middle of my mah-jongg club meeting, he came running in the house crying. Some of the children had mixed up a mess of coffee grounds and blackberry jam and tried to make him eat it. It was an initiation. They formed a new club every week or two and Billy was the one they always initiated.

"Mama's busy, honey," I said. "Tell it to Carrie Lee. She'll tend to 'em for you."

Carrie Lee took him on her lap like a baby and rocked him and loved him until he stopped crying, and then he sat up and said, "But Carrie Lee, who am I going to play with? Everybody's in the club but me."

And she said, "Honey, they bigger than you. If you wants to play, you gits on out there and eats they pudding. If you don't like it, you holds it in your mouth and spits it out when they ain't looking."

"But s'pose they feed me more than I can hold in my mouth?" he said.

"Honey, if they does, you got to make your mouth stretch," she said.

Billy has never forgotten that.

Carrie Lee came to work for Mama when she was fourteen years old. She was only a child, it's true, but even then she had more sense than most grown Negroes. Mama had seen her on their place outside Atlanta and taken a fancy to her. *Her* mother (Carrie Lee's, I mean) cooked for the manager's family there, and Carrie Lee was already taking care of five or six younger brothers and sisters while the mother was at work. You can imagine what it meant to her to come to town. Mama clothed her and fed her and made a finished servant of her. Why, she even saw to it that Carrie Lee went to school through the fifth grade; she'd never been able to go more than a couple of terms in the country. Fifty years ago, practically none of the Negroes went more than a year or two, if that long. When they were seven or eight, they either went to the field or stayed at home to nurse the younger ones.

By the time we moved to Homochitto, Mama couldn't have gotten along without Carrie Lee, and so she came with us. At first Mama was miserable here — homesick for Georgia and her own family and the social life of Atlanta. Compared to Atlanta, Homochitto then was nothing but a village. And the weather! We had never been through a Mississippi summer before, or, for that matter, a Georgia summer; we'd always gone to the mountains — Monteagle, or White Sulphur Springs, or some place like that. But that first year in Homochitto Papa couldn't leave, and Mama got in one of her stubborn spells and wouldn't go without him. To tell you the truth, I think she wanted him to see her suffer, so he'd take her back to Atlanta. She used to say then that no one understood how she felt except Carrie Lee. And I suppose it's true that Carrie Lee missed her family too, in spite of the hard life she'd had with them. In the mornings she and Mama would sit in the kitchen peeling figs or pears or peaches, or washing berries, preserving together, and Carrie Lee would tell stories to entertain Mama. I'd hang around and listen. I remember one day Carrie Lee had said something 'specially outrageous, and Mama said, "Carrie Lee, I don't believe half you say. Why do you make up those awful tales?"

Carrie Lee stopped peeling pears and began to eat the peelings. She always did eat the peelings when they were preserving, everything except figs — a hangover from hungry days, I reckon. She hushed talking a minute, eating and thinking, and then she looked at Mama and said:

> "To keep us from the lonely hours,
> And being sad so far from home."

It was just like a poem. I had to get up and run out of the house to keep them from seeing me cry. Do you suppose she understood what she'd said and how beautifully she'd said it? Or is it something about language that comes to them as naturally as sleeping — and music?

When Mama died, I felt as if she had more or less left Carrie Lee to me, and I've been taking care of her ever since. Oh, she's no burden. There's no telling *how* much money she has in the bank. There she is, drawing wages from Billy and from me, owns her own house and rents out a room, nobody to spend it on but herself and one step-daughter, and she never has to spend a dime on herself. Between us, Sarah and I give her everything she wears; and as for her house, every stick she has came out of our old house.

When we sold the house, after Mama died, Carrie Lee took her pick of what was left. Of course, I had gotten all the good pieces — the things that were bought before the war — but she wouldn't have wanted them anyway; nothing I chose would have suited her taste. She has a genius for the hideous. She took the wicker porch chairs — you know, the kind with fan backs and magazine racks in the arms and trays hooked onto the sides for glasses — and painted them blue and put them in her living room; and she took a set of crocheted table mats that Mama made years ago. (They were beautiful things, but if you've ever had a set, you know what a nuisance they are. Not a washwoman in Homochitto does fine laundering any more, and *I* certainly wouldn't wash and starch and stretch them *myself.* And besides, where would anyone in a small apartment like this keep those devilish boards with nails in them, that you have to stretch them on?) Anyway, Carrie Lee took those place mats and put them on the wicker chairs like antimacassars, if you can believe it. But that's just the beginning. All the junk collected by a houseful of pack rats like Bill's family — the monstrosities they acquired between 1890 and 1930 would be something to read about. And Bill and Mama had stored everything in Mama's attic when Bill sold his father's house in 1933. Why, I couldn't say, except that Bill always hated to throw anything away. That's a trait that runs in his family: they hang on to what they have. And if his father hadn't hung on to Wildwood during hard times and good, where would we be now?

Fortunately, he did hang on to it, and to everything else *his* father left him. You know, Bill's family didn't have the hard time most people had after the Civil War. His grandfather started the little railroad line from Homochitto to Jackson that was eventually bought by the Southern. He was a practical businessman and he didn't sit back like so many people, after we were defeated, and let his property get away from him out of sheer outrage. And so, the family was able to travel and to buy whatever was stylish at the time. Carrie Lee loved everything they bought, and she has as much of it as she can squeeze into her house: heavy golden oak sideboard and table, a fine brass bed polished up fit to blind you, a player piano that doesn't work, with a Spanish shawl draped over it, and on the walls souvenir plates from Niagara Falls and the St. Louis Exposition, and pictures of Mama and me and the children, sandwiched in between pictures of all her sisters and brothers and their families. It's too fine.

Actually, there are some people around here who disapprove of Carrie Lee and me; but as far as I'm concerned they can say what they like. I just love Carrie Lee and that's all there is to it. When she comes to call, she sits in the parlor with the white folks. She has good sense about it. If she's in the house on Sunday afternoon visiting with me, and guests come, she goes to the door and lets them in as if she were working that day, and then she goes back to the kichen and fixes coffee and finds an apron and serves us. Everything goes smoothly. She knows how to make things comfortable for everybody. But half the time, whoever it is, I wish they hadn't come. I'd rather visit with Carrie Lee.

And people who talk about it don't know what they're saying. They don't know how I feel. When Bill died (that was only a year after Mama died, and there I was, left alone with a houseful of *babies* to raise and all that property to manage), who do you think walked down the aisle with me and sat with me at the funeral? Carrie Lee. If I hadn't been half crazy with grief, I suppose I might have thought twice before I did a thing like that. But I did it, and I wouldn't have let anyone prevent me.

Weddings are a different matter, of course. If you have them at home, it's no problem; the colored folks are all in the kitchen anyhow, and it's easy enough for them to slip in and see the ceremony. I know Winston and Jimmy and the ones we've known for years who turn up at weddings and big parties would *rather* stay in the kitchen.

Jimmy takes charge of the punch bowl and sees that all the help stay sober enough to serve, at least until the rector goes home.

But it's not customary in Homochitto to include the servants at a church wedding. There's no balcony in the Episcopal church like the slave gallery in the Presbyterian church, and so there's no place to seat them. I couldn't do anything about that at Sarah's wedding; I just had to leave the rest of the servants out, but we did take Carrie Lee to the church.

I'll never forget how she behaved; if she'd been the mama, she couldn't have been more upset.

Sarah was only nineteen, too young, way too young to marry. To tell you the truth I was crushed at the time. I never, *never* thought any good would come of it. Oh, I realize I was even younger when I married. But in my day young ladies were brought up for marriage, and marriages were made on other terms, terms I understood. Bill was nearly thirty when we married, and he had exactly the same ideas Papa had. He simply finished my education. Which proves my contention — that a woman is old enough to marry when she has sense enough to pick the right man. If she doesn't, she isn't ready. That's the way it was with Sarah.

Wesley was just a boy — a selfish, unpredictable boy. He never understood how sheltered Sarah had been, how little she knew of the world, how indulgent we had been with her as a child, how totally unprepared she was for — for him. And afterwards she said it was all my fault. That's children for you. But I hadn't meant to prepare her for *Wesley*. I wouldn't have had him!

To go back to the wedding, Carrie Lee rode to the church with Sarah, and put the finishing touches on her hair and arranged her train. I didn't see this because of course I was sitting in the front of the church, but the people in the back said when Sarah and Brother George started down the aisle, Carrie Lee ran after them, straightening Sarah's train, the tears streaming down her face. I believe she would have followed them to the altar, but Edwin Ware slipped out of his pew and got her to go back. She was crying like a child, saying, "My baby. She's *my baby*."

You'd never have known she had children of her own the way she worshiped mine — still does.

But she had a married interlude. She was too old to carry a child; she had two miscarriages and lost one shortly after it was born. But she raised two or three of her husband's children. Negroes are so funny. Even Carrie Lee, as well as I know her, surprises me sometimes. She turned up at work one morning just as usual. (She never came until ten-thirty, and then stayed to serve supper and wash the dishes at night.) Bertie, who was cooking for me then, had been muttering and snickering to herself in the kitchen all morning, and, when I came in to plan dinner, she acted like she had a cricket down her bosom.

"What in the world are you giggling and wiggling about, Bertie?" I said.

Bertie *fell* out.

Carrie Lee, forty if she was a day, stood there glowering. "You know Bertie, Miss Emma," she said. "Bertie's crazy as a road lizard."

Bertie pointed her finger at Carrie Lee and then she sort of hollered out, "She *ma'ied*, Miss Emma! She ma'ied."

You could have knocked me over with a feather. I didn't even know she was thinking about it. "Are you really, Carrie Lee?" I said.

"Yes'm."

"Well, Carrie Lee!" I said. "My feelings are hurt. Why didn't you tell us ahead of time. We could have had a fine wedding — something special."

I *was* disappointed, too. I've always wanted to put on a colored wedding, and *there*, I'd missed my chance.

Carrie Lee didn't say a word. I never *have* been able to figure out why she didn't tell us beforehand.

And then that nitwit, Bertie, began to laugh and holler again. "She don't need no special wedding, Miss Emma," Bertie said. "Ain't nothing special about getting ma'ied to Carrie Lee."

I was tickled at that, but I was surprised, too. Oh, I'm not so stupid that I don't understand how different Negro morals are from ours. Most of them simply don't have any. And I understand that it all comes from the way things were in slavery times. But our family was different. Grandmother told me many a time that they always went to a lot of trouble with the slave weddings and, after the war, with the tenants'. She kept a wedding dress and veil for the girls to wear, and she made sure everything was done right — license, preacher, reception, and all the trimmings. There was no jumping the broomstick in our family. And Carrie Lee's people had been on our place for generations. I never would have thought she'd carry on with a man.

She seemed devoted to her husband. If she had carried on with one, she must have carried on with others, but I reckon she'd had her fling and was ready to retire. The husband, Henry, was a "settled man," as they say, fifteen years older than Carrie Lee, and had a half-grown son and daughter and two or three younger children. He farmed about thirty acres of Wildwood. I had known the family ever since we moved to Homochitto. (Can you imagine that — my own place, and I didn't know about him and Carrie Lee!)

Later on, shortly before he died, he managed with Carrie Lee's help to buy a little place of his own.

I always let Carrie Lee off at noon on Saturday and gave her all day Sunday, although I hated running after the children. When they got old enough to amuse themselves, it wasn't so bad, but when they were little . . . ! Usually I got Bertie to take over for me. But I never believed in working a servant seven days a week, even when everybody did it, when they were lucky to get Emancipation Day and the Fourth of July. I never treated a servant like that. Bertie had her day off, too.

Henry would be waiting for Carrie Lee in his buggy when she got off on Saturday, and they'd catch the ferry across the river and drive out to Wildwood; and early Monday morning he'd send his son to drive her in to town — it was a couple of hours ride in the buggy. She didn't want to sell her house and move to the country (thank God!) and Henry wouldn't move to town. As Carrie Lee said, he didn't know nothing but farming, and he wasn't fixing to change his ways.

Once in a while she'd take the children to the country with her on Saturday afternoon, and I'd drive over after supper to get them. Every Saturday they begged to go; it was the greatest treat in the world to them to ride to Wildwood in the buggy, and they were crazy about the old man. For a while I kept their horses there, and when Billy was older he used to go over there to hunt. Henry taught him everything he knows about hunting. That was before cotton-dusting killed all the quail in this part of the country.

Well, Carrie Lee lived like that until we moved back to Atlanta, riding to the country every Saturday afternoon and coming in at daybreak on Monday morning. It's hard to understand how anyone could be satisfied with such a life, but Carrie Lee has a happy nature, and of course the fact that she was so much better off financially than most Negroes made a difference. Besides, I wouldn't be surprised if she wasn't glad to have the peace and quiet of a single life during the week. You might say she had her cake and ate it too.

Then I left Homochitto for several years. It's the only time Carrie Lee and I have ever been separated for more than a month or two.

I'd always heard Mama talk about Atlanta; she kept after Papa to go back, right up to his dying day. I'd been too young when we moved to care, but later, after Mama and Bill died, I got the notion that someday I'd go back. So finally, I went. The children were away at school, Billy at Episcopal High and Sarah at Ardsley Hall, and there was no reason for me to stay in Homochitto.

I thought of course Carrie Lee would go with me, but she didn't. For all her talk in Mama's day about how she missed Georgia, she didn't go back. She stayed with Henry. And, as I told you, I paid her wages all the time I was gone. We wrote to each other, and we saw each other when I brought the children to Homochitto for a visit. They never got used to Atlanta and never wanted to stay there in the summer. Then Billy settled in Homochitto and began to farm Wildwood himself, and I came home.

I wish I had kept some of Carrie Lee's letters. She has a beautiful hand. She used to practice copying Mama's script, and finally got so you could hardly tell them apart. It always gives me a turn to get a letter from her, addressed in Mama's hand, and then, inside, what a difference! When she writes something she thinks will amuse me, she puts "smile" after it in parentheses. Did you know that practically all Negroes do that, even the educated ones? I sometimes see pictures of all the ones that are so much in the news nowadays — diplomats and martyrs and so forth, and I wonder if they put (smile) in their letters.

Carrie Lee used to advise me in her letters, where she would never do such a thing face to face. Like one time, I remember, she wrote me, "All the babies is gone, yours and mine. I writes Miss Sarah and Mr. Billy and they don't answer me. True, I got the old man's kids, but you haven't got none. When will you get married again, Miss Emma? Find you a good man to warm your bed." And then she wrote (smile) — to make sure I understood she wasn't being impudent, I reckon.

It was while I was living in Atlanta that Carrie Lee got her picture in the magazine. I never quite understood how it happened, unless through ignorance on all sides—ignorance on the part of the photographer about Carrie Lee's real circumstances, and ignorance on her part about what the photographer wanted. We all laughed about it afterwards, although, of course, I never mentioned it to Carrie Lee.

When we left Homochitto, she had moved over to Wildwood and rented her house in town. That's how they saved enough money for the old man to buy a place of his own. I think she gave him every cent she made. But they had their pictures taken the winter before they bought the place, the last winter they were on Wildwood.

I'll never forget how shocked I was. I had gone out for dinner and bridge one night, and was quietly enjoying a drink when one of the men at the party picked up a copy of *Life* or *Fortune* or one of those magazines.

"By the way," he said to me, "I was reading about your old stamping ground today."

I might have known he was teasing me. None of those magazines ever has anything good to say about Mississippi. But I was interested in news of Homochitto, and never thought of that; and of course *he* didn't know it was Carrie Lee. I sat there while he found the article, and there she was — there they all were, Carrie Lee, Henry, and all the children, staring at me practically life-sized from a full-page picture.

The article was on sharecropping, and *they* were the examples of the downtrodden sharecropper. I must admit they looked seedy. I recognized my dress on Carrie Lee and one of Sarah's on the little girl. They were standing in a row outside the old man's house, grinning as if they knew what it was all about. At least, all of them except Carrie Lee were grinning. She's not much of a grinner.

A November day in the South — the trees bare and black, the stubble still standing in the cotton fields, an unpainted Negro cabin with the porch roof sagging, half a dozen dirty, ragged Negro children, and a bedraggled hound. What more could a Northern editor have asked?

What will these children get for Christmas?

I could have told him what they'd get for Christmas, and who had bought the presents and sent them off just the day before. And I could have told him whose money was accumulating in the teapot on the mantelpiece.

To do them justice, I'll say I don't believe Carrie Lee or Henry had the faintest idea why he'd taken their pictures. They just liked to have their pictures taken. But the very idea of them as poverty-stricken, downtrodden tenants! I couldn't have run them off Wildwood with a posse and a pack of bloodhounds.

We got a big kick out of it. I cut the picture out and sent it to Sarah.

The old man died the year after they began to buy their farm, and then Carrie Lee moved to town, and shortly after that I came back to Homochitto for good. Henry, Jr., took over the payments on the farm and lives on it. He's a sullen Negro — not like his father — but he's good to Carrie Lee. In the summer he keeps her supplied with fresh vegetables; he comes in and makes repairs on her house to save her the price of a carpenter; things like that. But he's sullen. I never have liked these Negroes who're always kowtowing and grinning like idiots — "white folks' niggers," some people down here call them — but it wouldn't hurt that boy to learn some manners. I told Carrie Lee as much one time.

I had gone into the kitchen to see about dinner, and he was sitting at the table with his hat on — this was after we moved back here, and old Henry was dead — eating his breakfast — *my* food, need I add. He didn't even look at me, much less get up.

"Good morning, Henry," I said.

He mumbled something and still didn't get up.

"*Good morning, Henry,*" I said again.

"Morning," he said, just as sullen as he could be.

I went to Carrie Lee later and told her that any man, black, white, blue, or green, could get up and take off his hat when a lady came into the room. That's not prejudice. That's good manners.

"He ain't *bad*, Miss Emma," she said. "Just seems like he always got one misery or another. Born to trouble, as the sparks fly upward, like the Good Book says."

"Well, he'd feel a lot better, if he'd get a smile on that sullen face of his," I said. "Sometimes people bring trouble on themselves just by their dispositions."

"Ah, Miss Emma," she said, "ever since he married, it's been *root, hog, or die* for Henry, Jr. He ain't settled into it yet."

Of course, I didn't know then about the boy's sister, Carrie Lee's stepdaughter. Didn't know she had left Homochitto, much less that she had come back. She apparently married and moved to *"Dee-troit"* while we were living in Atlanta. I didn't see her until some time after she came to live in town with Carrie Lee, just a few years ago. Henry, Jr., finally had to turn her over to Carrie Lee. I can't blame him for *that*, I don't suppose. By then he had five children of his own, and there was scarcely room for them in the house, much less the sister.

I found out about the sister because Sarah left Wesley. That was a hard year. Sarah packed up the children and everything she owned and came home from Cleveland, inconsolable. I suppose I could have said. "I told you so," but I didn't have the heart. She'd married too young, there's no getting around it, and by the time she was old enough to know her own mind, there she was with two children. I tell you, people say to me: "You don't know how lucky you are that Bill left you so well-fixed. Never any money problems." They don't know how wrong they are. Money's a preoccupying worry. It keeps your mind off worse things. If you don't have to work or to worry about money, you're free to worry more about yourself and your children. Believe me, *nobody's* exempt from disappointment. I'm *proud* of the way I've raised my children. I've taught them everything I know about good manners and responsibility and honor, and I've kept their property safe for them. I've tried to give them everything that my family and Bill gave me. But when love fails you, none of it is any use. Your bed is soft and warm, but one dark night you find that sleep won't come.

I was half crazy over Sarah. She slept until noon every day and moped around the house all afternoon. Then she'd start drinking and keep me up till all hours crying and carrying on. "What am I going to do? What am I going to do?"

She still loved that good-for-nothing man.

I borrowed Carrie Lee from Billy to take care of Sarah's babies while she was here. I'm too old to chase a two-year-old child, and Sarah hardly looked at the children. She was too busy grieving over Wesley. So Carrie Lee was a boon; she took over, and we never had a minute's concern for them. Like all children, they adored her.

Billy's wife was furious with me for taking her, but I simply had to. And Carrie Lee was in seventh heaven, back with Sarah and me; she never has gotten along too well with Billy's wife. Oh, she goes out there faithfully, on account of Billy and the children. But Billy's wife is different from us — a different breed of cat, altogether, there's no getting around it. I get along fine with her because I mind my own business, but Carrie Lee considers our business her business. And then too, as I said, Carrie Lee is a *finished* servant. She has run my house for months at a time without a word of direction from me. She can plan and put on a formal dinner for twelve without batting an eye. Billy's wife doesn't know anything about good servants. She tells Carrie Lee every day what she wants done that day; and she insulted her, the first time she had a party, by showing her how to set the table.

No doubt there are two sides to the story. I'm sure Billy's wife gets sick of hearing Carrie Lee say, "But Miss Emma don't do it that way." It must be like having an extra mother-in-law. I won't go into that. I know it's the style nowadays not to get along with your mother-in-law, although I don't see why. I never had a breath of trouble with mine.

But I'm wandering again. I want to tell you the wonderful thing Carrie Lee said when she was telling us about her stepdaughter.

The children were taking their naps one afternoon, and Sarah and I were lying down in my room and Carrie Lee was sitting in there talking to us. Sarah was still thrashing around about Wesley. The truth is she wanted to go back to him. She was hollering to Carrie Lee about how he'd betrayed her and how she could never forgive him — just asking somebody please to find her a good reason why she should forgive him, if the truth be known. But I wasn't going to help her; I knew it would never work.

Carrie Lee listened a while and thought about it a while and then she said, "Miss Sarah, honey, you know I got a crazy child?"

That took the wind out of Sarah's sails, and she sat up and stopped crying and said, "What?"

I was surprised, too. I didn't know a thing about that crazy girl. When I thought about it, I remembered that Carrie Lee had mentioned her to me once or twice, but at the time I hadn't paid any attention.

"I got a crazy child," Carrie Lee says. "Least, she ain't exactly my child, she old Henry's. But she *sho* crazy."

"I didn't know that, Carrie Lee," I said. "Where does she stay?"

"She stay with me," Carrie Lee says. "Right there in the house with me. Neighbors tend to her in the daytime. I ain't had her with me long — no more than a year or two."

"Well, what do I care? What's it got to do with me?" Sarah said, and she began to cry again. She wasn't herself, or she wouldn't have been so mean.

"This what," Carrie Lee says. "You know why she crazy? A man driv her crazy, that's why. You don't watch out, a man gonna drive you crazy."

Sarah lay back on the bed and kicked her feet like a baby.

"Honey, you want me to tell you how to keep a man from driving you crazy? And not only a man. Howsomever it happens, the day comes when one of God's creatures, young or old, is bound to break your heart. I'll tell you how to bear it."

Sarah shook her head.

"I'm gonna tell you anyhow. Look at me. I'm sixty years old. I looks forty-five. No man never driv me crazy, nor nobody else. I tell you how I keep him from it."

Sarah couldn't help it. She sat up and listened.

"See everything, see nothing," says Carrie Lee. "Hear everything, hear nothing. Know everything, know nothing. Trust in the Lord and love little children. That's how to ease your heart."

Did you ever? Well sir, maybe Sarah would have gone anyway,

or maybe she heeded Carrie Lee's advice. Anyway, she took the two children soon afterwards and went back to Wesley, and it wasn't until three years later that they got a divorce.

So here we are, Carrie Lee and I, getting old. You might say we've spent our lives together. I reckon I know her better than I would have known my own sister, if I had had one. As Carrie Lee would say, "We've seen some wonderful distressing times."

On Sundays, when she's off, lots of times she bakes me a cake and brings it around and we sit and talk of the old days when Mama and Bill were alive and when the children were little. We talk about the days of the flood, about this year's crop, about the rains in April, and in August the dry weather, about Billy's wife, and Sarah and Billy's grown-up troubles, about the grandchildren, and "all the days we've seen."

If she comes to see me on Sunday, Carrie Lee will tell me something that amuses me the whole week long. Like a couple of weeks ago we were talking about the crop. I'd been worrying all summer about the drought. It looked for a while as if Billy wouldn't make a bale to the acre. And every time I mentioned it to Carrie Lee, she'd say, "Trust in the Lord, Miss Emma." She's still a great one for leaving things to the Almighty.

Then, bless John, the cotton popped open, and, in spite of everything, it's a good year.

"Well, Carrie Lee," I said, "it looks like you were right and I was wrong. Billy's got a fine crop."

And Carrie Lee says (just listen to this), she says, "Miss Emma, if I say a chicken dips snuff, you look under his bill."

Isn't that killing? When I got by myself, I just hollered.

Looking at it another way, though, it isn't so funny. Billy's a man, and a son is never the companion to his mother that a daughter is. You know the old saying, "A son is a son till he gets him a wife, but a daughter's a daughter all of her life." I think if his father had lived, if there were a man in the house, Billy would come to see me more often. If Sarah were here, we would enjoy each other, I know; but she's married again and lives so far away, they seldom come home, and when they do, it's only for a few days.

I've never been a reader, either. I like to visit, to *talk*. I'm an articulate person. And nowadays, instead of visiting, people sit and stare at a television set. Oh, I still play cards and mah-jongg. I have friends here, but we drifted apart during the years I was in Atlanta, and things have never been quite the same since I came back.

So I'm often alone on Sunday afternoon when Carrie Lee comes to see me. That's how it happens we sit so long together, drinking coffee and talking. Late in the afternoon, Billy sometimes comes and brings the children to call, but they never stay for long. They go home to Wildwood because Billy's wife doesn't like to be there alone after dark. Carrie Lee stays on, and we go in the kitchen and she fixes my supper. As I've told you, I'd rather visit with her than with most white folks. She understands me. When I think about it, it sometimes seems to me, with Bill and Mama dead and the children grown and gone, that Carrie Lee is all I have left of my own.

(1916–)

Walker Percy

Walker Percy, novelist, essayist, and philosopher, was born May 28, 1916, in Birmingham, Alabama, but was reared in Greenville by his uncle, the poet William Alexander Percy. He graduated from the University of North Carolina in 1937, and completed his medical degree at Columbia University in 1941. While an intern at New York City's Bellevue Hospital in 1942, he contracted tuberculosis, retired from medicine, and began writing. His novels, which reflect his philosophical preoccupations, are cast in a satiric mode, often savage, and deal with the more urban southerner's attempts to fight the "malaise" of a modern world which has invaded even the South. *The Moviegoer* (1961), from which the following selection was excerpted, won the National Book Award in 1962.

424

from The Moviegoer

THIS MORNING I GOT A NOTE from my aunt asking me to come for lunch. I know what this means. Since I go there every Sunday for dinner and today is Wednesday, it can mean only one thing: she wants to have one of her serious talks. It will be extremely grave, either a piece of bad news about her stepdaughter Kate or else a serious talk about me, about the future and what I ought to do. It is enough to scare the wits out of anyone, yet I confess I do not find the prospect altogether unpleasant.

I remember when my older brother Scott died of pneumonia. I was eight years old. My aunt had charge of me and she took me for a walk behind the hospital. It was an interesting street. On one side were the power plant and blowers and incinerator of the hospital, all humming and blowing out a hot meaty smell. On the other side was a row of Negro houses. Children and old folks and dogs sat on the porches watching us. I noticed with pleasure that Aunt Emily seemed to have all the time in the world and was willing to talk about anything I wanted to talk about. Something extraordinary had happened all right. We walked slowly in step. "Jack," she said, squeezing me tight and smiling at the Negro shacks, "you and I have always been good buddies, haven't we?" "Yes ma'am." My heart gave a big pump and the back of my neck prickled like a dog's. "I've got bad news for you, son." She squeezed me tighter than ever. "Scotty is dead. Now it's all up to you. It's going to be difficult for you but I know you're going to act like a soldier." This was true. I could easily act like a soldier. Was that all I had to do?

It reminds me of a movie I saw last month out by Lake Pontchartrain. Linda and I went out to a theater in a new suburb. It was evident somebody had miscalculated, for the suburb had quit growing and here was the theater, a pink stucco cube, sitting out in a field all by itself. A strong wind whipped the waves against the seawall; even inside you could hear the racket. The movie was about a man who lost his memory in an accident and as a result lost everything: his family, his friends, his money. He found himself a stranger in a strange city. Here he had to make a fresh start, find a new place to live, a new job, a new girl. It was supposed to be a tragedy, his losing all this, and he seemed to suffer a great deal. On the other hand, things were not so bad after all. In no time he found a very picturesque place to live, a houseboat on the river, and a very handsome girl, the local librarian.

After the movie Linda and I stood under the marquee and talked to the manager, or rather listened to him tell his troubles: the theater was almost empty, which was pleasant for me but not for him. It was a fine night and I felt very good. Overhead was the blackest sky I ever saw; a black wind pushed the lake toward us. The waves jumped over the seawall and spattered the street. The manager had to yell to be heard while from the sidewalk speaker directly over his head came the twittering conversation of the amnesiac and the librarian. It was the part where they are going through the newspaper files in search of some clue to his identity (he has a vague recollection of an accident). Linda stood by unhappily. She was unhappy for the same reason I was happy—because here we were at a neighborhood theater out in the sticks and without a car (I have a car but I prefer to ride buses and streetcars). Her idea of happiness is to drive downtown and have supper at the Blue Room of the Roosevelt Hotel. This I am obliged to do from time to time. It is worth it, however. On these occasions Linda becomes as exalted as I am now. Her eyes glow, her lips become moist, and when we dance she brushes her fine long legs against mine. She actually loves me at these times—and not as a reward for being taken to the Blue Room. She loves me because she feels exalted in this romantic place and not in a movie out in the sticks.

But all this is history. Linda and I have parted company. I have a new secretary, a girl named Sharon Kincaid.

For the past four years now I have been living uneventfully in Gentilly, a middle class suburb of New Orleans. Except for the banana plants in the patios and the curlicues of iron on the Walgreen drugstore one would never guess it was part of New Orleans. Most of the houses are either old-style California bungalows or new-style Daytona cottages. But this is what I like about it. I can't stand the old world atmosphere of the French Quarter or the genteel charm of the Garden District. I lived in the Quarter for two years, but in the end I got tired of Birmingham businessmen smirking around Bourbon Street and the homosexuals and patio connoisseurs on Royal Street.

My uncle and aunt live in a gracious house in the Garden District and are very kind to me. But whenever I try to live there, I find myself first in a rage during which I develop strong opinions on a variety of subjects and write letters to editors, then in a depression during which I lie rigid as a stick for hours staring straight up at the plaster medallion in the ceiling of my bedroom.

Life in Gentilly is very peaceful. I manage a small branch office of my uncle's brokerage firm. My home is the basement apartment of a raised bungalow belonging to Mrs. Schexnaydre, the widow of a fireman. I am a model tenant and a model citizen and take pleasure in doing all that is expected of me. My wallet is full of identity cards, library cards, credit cards. Last year I purchased a flat olive-drab strongbox, very smooth and heavily built with double walls for fire protection, in which I placed my birth certificate, college diploma, honorable discharge, G.I. insurance, a few stock certificates, and my inheritance: a deed to ten acres of a defunct duck club down in St. Bernard Parish, the only relic of my father's many enthusiasms. It is a pleasure to carry out the duties of a citizen and to receive in return a receipt or a neat styrene card with one's name on it certifying, so to speak, one's right to exist. What satisfaction I take in appearing the first day to get my auto tag and brake sticker! I subscribe to *Consumer Reports* and as a consequence I own a first-class television set, an all but silent air conditioner and a very long lasting deodorant. My armpits never stink. I pay attention to all spot announcements on the radio about mental health, the seven signs of cancer, and safe driving—though, as I say, I usually prefer to ride the bus. Yesterday a favorite of mine, William Holden, delivered a radio announcement on litterbugs. "Let's face it," said Holden. "Nobody can do anything about it—but you and me." This is true. I have been careful ever since.

In the evenings I usually watch television or go to the movies. Week-ends I often spend on the Gulf Coast. Our neighborhood theater in Gentilly has permanent lettering on the front of the marquee reading: Where Happiness Costs So Little. The fact is I am quite happy in a movie, even a bad movie. Other people, so I have read, treasure memorable moments in their lives: the time one climbed the Parthenon at sunrise, the summer night one met a lonely girl in Central Park and achieved with her a sweet and natural relationship, as they say in books. I too once met a girl in Central Park, but it is not much to remember. What I remember is the time John Wayne killed three men with a carbine as he was falling to the dusty street in *Stagecoach*, and the time the kitten found Orson Welles in the doorway in *The Third Man*.

My companion on these evening outings and weekend trips is usually my secretary. I have had three secretaries, girls named Marcia, Linda, and now Sharon. Twenty years ago, practically every other girl born in Gentilly must have been named Marcia. A year or so later it was Linda. Then Sharon. In recent years I have noticed that the name Stephanie has come into fashion. Three of my acquaintances in Gentilly have daughters named Stephanie. Last night I saw a TV play about a nuclear test explosion. Keenan Wynn played a troubled physicist who had many a bad moment with his conscience. He took solitary walks in the desert. But you could tell that in his heart of hearts he was having a very good time with his soul-searching. "What right have we to do what we are doing?" he would ask his colleagues in a bitter voice. "It's my four-year-old daughter I'm really thinking of," he told another colleague and took out a snapshot. "What kind of future are we building for her?" "What is your daughter's name?" asked the colleague, looking at the picture. "Stephanie," said Keenan Wynn in a gruff voice. Hearing the name produced a sharp tingling sensation on the back of my neck. Twenty years from now I shall perhaps have a rosy young Stephanie perched at my typewriter.

Naturally I would like to say that I had made conquests of these splendid girls, my secretaries, casting them off one after the other like old gloves, but it would not be strictly true. They could be called love affairs, I suppose. They started off as love affairs anyway, fine careless raptures in which Marcia or Linda (but not yet Sharon) and I would go spinning along the Gulf Coast, lie embracing in a deserted cove of Ship Island, and hardly believe our good fortune, hardly believe that the world could contain such happiness. Yet in the case of Marcia and Linda the affair ended just when I thought our relationship was coming into its best phase. The air in the office would begin to grow thick with silent reproaches. It would become impossible to exchange a single word or glance that was not freighted with a thousand hidden meanings. Telephone conversations would take place at all hours of the night, conversations made up mostly of long silences during which I would rack my brain for something to say while on the other end you could hear little else but breathing and sighs. When these long telephone silences come, it is a sure sign that love is over. No, they were not conquests. For in the end my Lindas and I were so sick of each other that we were delighted to say good-by.

I am a stock and bond broker. It is true that my family was somewhat disappointed in my choice of a profession. Once I thought of going into law or medicine or even pure science. I even dreamed of doing something great. But there is much to be said for giving up such grand ambitions and living the most ordinary life imaginable, a life without the old longings; selling stocks and bonds and mutual funds; quitting work at five o'clock like everyone else; having a girl and perhaps one day settling down and raising a flock of Marcias and Sandras and Lindas of my own. Nor is the brokerage business as uninteresting as you might think. It is not a bad life at all.

We live, Mrs. Schexnaydre and I, on Elysian Fields, the main thoroughfare of Faubourg Marigny. Though it was planned to be, like its namesake, the grandest boulevard of the city, something went amiss, and now it runs an undistinguished course from river to lake through shopping centers and blocks of duplexes and bungalows and raised cottages. But it is very spacious and airy and seems truly to stretch out like a field under the sky. Next door to Mrs. Schexnaydre is a brand new school. It is my custom on summer evenings after work to take a shower, put on shirt and pants and stroll over to the deserted playground and there sit on the ocean wave, spread out the movie page of the *Times-Picayune* on one side, phone book on the other, and a city map in my lap. After I have made my choice, plotted a route—often to some remote neighborhood like Algiers or St Bernard—I stroll around the schoolyard in the last golden light of day and admire the building. Everthing is so spick-and-span: the aluminum sashes fitted into the brick wall and gilded in the sunset, the pretty terrazzo floors and the desks molded like wings. Suspended by wires above the door is a schematic sort of bird, the Holy Ghost I suppose. It gives me a pleasant sense of the goodness of creation to think of the brick and the glass and the aluminum being extracted from common dirt—though no doubt it is less a religious sentiment than a financial one, since I own a few shares of Alcoa. How smooth and well-fitted and thrifty the aluminum feels!

But things have suddenly changed. My peaceful existence in Gentilly has been complicated. This morning, for the first time in years, there occurred to me the possibility of a search. I dreamed of the war, no, not quite dreamed but woke with the taste of it in my mouth, the queasy-quince taste of 1951 and the Orient. I remembered the first time the search occurred to me. I came to myself under a chindolea bush. Everything is upside-down for me, as I shall explain later. What are generally considered to be the best times are for me the worst times, and that worst of times was one of the best. My shoulder didn't hurt but it was pressed hard against the ground as if somebody sat on me. Six inches from my nose a dung beetle was scratching around under the leaves. As I watched, there awoke in me an immense curiosity. I was onto something. I vowed that if I ever got out of this fix, I would pursue the search. Naturally, as soon as I recovered and got home, I forgot all about it. But this morning when I got up, I dressed as usual and began as usual to put my belongings into my pockets: wallet, notebook (for writing down occasional thoughts), pencil, keys, handkerchief, pocket slide rule (for calculating percentage returns on principal). They looked both unfamiliar and at the same time full of clues. I stood in the center of the room and gazed at the little pile, sighting through a hole made by thumb and forefinger. What was unfamiliar about them was that I could see them. They might have belonged to someone else. A man can look at this little pile on his bureau for thirty years and never once see it. It is as invisible as his own hand. Once I saw it, however, the search became possible. I bathed, shaved, dressed carefully, and sat at my desk and poked through the little pile in search of a clue just as the detective on television pokes through the dead man's possessions, using his pencil as a poker.

The idea of a search comes to me again as I am on my way to my aunt's house, riding the Gentilly bus down Elysian Fields. The truth is I dislike cars. Whenever I drive a car, I have the feeling I have become invisible. People on the street cannot see you; they only watch your rear fender until it is out of their way. Elysian Fields is not the shortest route to my aunt's house. But I have my reasons for going through the Quarter. William Holden, I read in the paper this morning, is in New Orleans shooting a few scenes in the Place d'Armes. It would be interesting to catch a glimpse of him.

It is a gloomy March day. The swamps are still burning at Chef Menteur and the sky over Gentilly is the color of ashes. The bus is crowded with shoppers, nearly all women. The windows are steamed. I sit on the lengthwise seat in front. Women sit beside me and stand above me. On the long back seat are five Negresses so black that the whole rear of the bus seems darkened. Directly next to me, on the first cross seat, is a very fine-looking girl. She is a strapping girl but by no means too big, done up head to toe in cellophane, the hood pushed back to show a helmet of glossy black hair. She is magnificent with her split tooth and her Prince Val bangs split on her forehead. Gray eyes and wide black brows, a good arm and a fine swell of calf above her cellophane boot. One of those solitary Amazons one sees on Fifty-seventh Street in New York or in Nieman Marcus in Dallas. Our eyes meet. Am I mistaken or does the corner of her mouth tuck in ever so slightly and the petal of her lower lip curl out ever so richly? She is smiling—at me! My mind hits upon half a dozen schemes to circumvent the terrible moment of separation. No doubt she is a Texan. They are nearly always bad judges of men, these splendid Amazons. Most men are afraid of them and so they fall victim to the first little Mickey Rooney that comes along. In a better world I should be able to speak to her: come, darling, you can see that I love you. If you are planning to meet some little Mickey, think better of it. What a tragedy it is that I do not know her, will probably never see her again. What good times we could have! This very afternoon we could go spinning along the Gulf Coast. What consideration and tenderness I could show her! If it were a movie, I would have only to wait. The bus would get lost or the city would be bombed and she and I would tend the wounded. As it is, I may as well stop thinking about her.

Then it is that the idea of the search occurs to me. I become absorbed and for a minute or so forget about the girl.

What is the nature of the search? you ask.

Really it is very simple, at least for a fellow like me; so simple that it is easily overlooked.

The search is what anyone would undertake if he were not sunk in the everydayness of his own life. This morning, for example, I felt as if I had come to myself on a strange island. And what does such a castaway do? Why, he pokes around the neighborhood and he doesn't miss a trick.

To become aware of the possibility of the search is to be onto something. Not to be onto something is to be in despair.

The movies are onto the search, but they screw it up. The search always ends in despair. They like to show a fellow coming to himself in a strange place—but what does he do? He takes up with the local librarian, sets about proving to the local children what a nice fellow he is, and settles down with a vengeance. In two weeks time he is so sunk in everydayness that he might just as well be dead.

What do you seek—God? you ask with a smile.

I hesitate to answer, since all other Americans have settled the matter for themselves and to give such an answer would amount to setting myself a goal which everyone else has reached—and therefore raising a question in which no one has the slightest interest. Who wants to be dead last among one hundred and eighty million Americans? For, as everyone knows, the polls report that 98% of Americans believe in God and the remaining 2% are atheists and agnostics—which leaves not a single percentage point for a seeker. For myself, I enjoy answering polls as much as anyone and take pleasure in giving intelligent replies to all questions.

Truthfully, it is the fear of exposing my own ignorance which constrains me from mentioning the object of my search. For, to begin with, I cannot even answer this, the simplest and most basic of all questions: Am I, in my search, a hundred miles ahead of my fellow Americans or a hundred miles behind them? That is to say: Have 98% of Americans already found what I seek or are they so sunk in everydayness that not even the possibility of a search has occurred to them?

On my honor, I do not know the answer.

As the bus ascends the overpass, a concrete hill which affords a fine view of New Orleans, I discover that I am frowning and gazing at a noble young calf clad in gunmetal nylon. Now beyond question she is aware of me: she gives her raincoat a sharp tug and gives me a look of annoyance—or do I imagine this? I must make sure, so I lift my hat and smile at her as much as to say that we might still become friends. But it is no use. I have lost her forever. She flounces out of the bus in a loud rustle of cellophane.

I alight at Esplanade in a smell of roasting coffee and creosote and walk up Royal Street. The lower Quarter is the best part. The iron-work on the balconies sags like rotten lace. Little French cottages hide behind high walls. Through deep sweating carriageways one catches glimpses of courtyards gone to jungle.

Today I am in luck. Who should come out of Pirate's Alley half a block ahead of me but William Holden!

Holden crosses Royal and turns toward Canal. As yet he is un-noticed. The tourists are either browsing along antique shops or snapping pictures of balconies. No doubt he is on his way to Galatoire's for lunch. He is an attractive fellow with his ordinary good looks, very suntanned, walking along hands in pockets, rain-coat slung over one shoulder. Presently he passes a young couple, who are now between me and him. Now we go along, the four of us, not twenty feet apart. It takes two seconds to size up the couple. They are twenty, twenty-one, and on their honeymoon. Not Southern. Probably Northeast. He wears a jacket with leather elbow patches, pipestem pants, dirty white shoes, and affects the kind of rolling seafaring gait you see in Northern college boys. Both are plain. He has thick lips, cropped reddish hair and skin to match. She is mousy. They are not really happy. He is afraid their honeymoon is too·conventional, that they are just another honeymoon couple. No doubt he figured it would be fun to drive down the Shenandoah Valley to New Orleans and escape the honeymooners at Niagara Falls and Saratoga. Now fifteen hundred miles from home they find them-selves surrounded by couples from Memphis and Chicago. He is anxious; he is threatened from every side. Each stranger he passes is a reproach to him, every doorway a threat. What is wrong? he wonders. She is unhappy but for a different reason, because he is unhappy and she knows it but doesn't know why.

Now they spot Holden. The girl nudges her companion. The boy perks up for a second, but seeing Holden doesn't really help him. On the contrary. He can only contrast Holden's resplendent reality with his own shadowy and precarious existence. Obviously he is more miserable than ever. What a deal, he must be thinking, trailing along behind a movie star—we might just as well be rubbernecking in Hollywood.

Holden slaps his pockets for a match. He has stopped behind some ladies looking at iron furniture on the sidewalk. They look like housewives from Hattiesburg come down for a day of shopping. He asks for a match; they shake their heads and then recognize him. There follows much blushing and confusion. But nobody can find a match for Holden. By now the couple have caught up with him. The boy holds out a light, nods briefly to Holden's thanks, then passes on without a flicker of recognition. Holden walks along between them for a second; he and the boy talk briefly, look up at the sky, shake their heads. Holden gives them a pat on the shoulder and moves on ahead.

The boy has done it! He has won title to his own existence, as plenary an existence now as Holden's, by refusing to be stampeded like the ladies from Hattiesburg. He is a citizen like Holden; two men of the world they are. All at once the world is open to him. Nobody threatens from patio and alley. His girl is open to him too. He puts his arm around her neck, noodles her head. She feels the difference too. She had not known what was wrong nor how it was righted but she knows now that all is well.

Holden has turned down Toulouse shedding light as he goes. An aura of heightened reality moves with him and all who fall within it feel it. Now everyone is aware of him. He creates a regular eddy among the tourists and barkeeps and B-girls who come running to the doors of the joints.

I am attracted to movie stars but not for the usual reasons. I have no desire to speak to Holden or get his autograph. It is their peculiar reality which astounds me. The Yankee boy is well aware of it, even though he pretends to ignore Holden. Clearly he would like nothing better than to take Holden over to his fraternity house in the most casual way. "Bill, I want you to meet Phil. Phil, Bill Holden," he would say and go sauntering off in the best seafaring style.

It is lunch hour on Canal Street. A parade is passing, but no one pays much attention. It is still a week before Mardi Gras and this is a new parade, a women's krewe from Gentilly. A krewe is a group of people who get together at carnival time and put on a parade and a ball. Anyone can form a krewe. Of course there are the famous old krewes like Comus and Rex and Twelfth Night, but there are also dozens of others. The other day a group of Syrians from Algiers formed a krewe named Isis. This krewe today, this must be Linda's krewe. I promised to come to see her. Red tractors pulled the floats along; scaffoldings creak, paper and canvas tremble. Linda, I think, is one of half a dozen shepherdesses dressed in short pleated skirts and mercury sandals with thongs criss-crossed up bare calves. But they are masked and I can't be sure. If she is, her legs are not so fine after all. All twelve legs are shivery and goosepimpled. A few businessmen stop to watch the girls and catch trinkets.

A warm wind springs up from the south piling up the clouds and bearing with it a far-off rumble, the first thunderstorm of the year. The street looks tremendous. People on the far side seem tiny and archaic, dwarfed by the great sky and the windy clouds like pedestrians in old prints. Am I mistaken or has a fog of uneasiness, a thin gas of malaise, settled on the street? The businessmen hurry back to their offices, the shoppers to their cars, the tourists to their hotels. Ah, William Holden, we already need you again. Already the fabric is wearing thin without you.

The mystery deepens. For ten minutes I stand talking to Eddie Lovell and at the end of it, when we shake hands and part, it seems to me that I cannot answer the simplest question about what has taken place. As I listen to Eddie speak plausibly and at length of one thing and another—business, his wife Nell, the old house they are redecorating—the fabric pulls together into one bright texture of investments, family projects, lovely old houses, little theater readings and such. It comes over me: this is how one lives! My exile in Gentilly has been the worst kind of self-deception.

Yes! Look at him. As he talks, he slaps a folded newspaper against his pants leg and his eye watches me and at the same time sweeps the terrain behind me, taking note of the slightest movement. A green truck turns down Bourbon Street; the eye sizes it up, flags it down, demands credentials, waves it on. A businessman turns in at the Maison Blanche building; the eye knows him, even knows what he is up to. And all the while he talks very well. His lips move muscularly, molding words into pleasing shapes, marshalling arguments, and during the slight pauses are held poised, attractively everted in a Charles-Boyer pout—while a little web of saliva gathers in a corner like the clear oil of a good machine. Now he jingles the coins deep in his pocket. No mystery here!—he is as cogent as a bird dog quartering a field. He understands everything out there and everything out there is something to be understood.

Eddie watches the last float, a doubtful affair with a squashed cornucopia.

"We'd better do better than that."

"We will."

"Are you riding Neptune?"

"No."

I offer Eddie my four call-outs for the Neptune ball. There is always the problem of out-of-town clients, usually Texans, and especially their wives. Eddie thanks me for this and for something else.

"I want to thank you for sending Mr Quieulle to me. I really appreciate it."

"Who?"

"Old man Quieulle."

"Yes, I remember." Eddie has sunk mysteriously into himself, eyes twinkling from the depths. "Don't tell me—"

Eddie nods.

"—that he has already set up his trust and up and died?"

Eddie nods, still sunk into himself. He watches me carefully, hanging fire until I catch up with him.

"In Mrs Quieulle's name?"

Again a nod; his jaw is shot out.

"How big?"

The same dancing look, now almost malignant. "Just short of nine hundred and fifty thou." His tongue curves around and seeks the hollow of his cheek.

"A fine old man," I say absently, noticing that Eddie has become as solemn as a bishop.

"I'll tell you one thing, Binx. I count it a great privilege to have known him. I've never known anyone, young or old, who possessed a greater fund of knowledge. That man spoke to me for two hours about the history of the crystallization of sugar and it was pure romance. I was fascinated."

Eddie tells me how much he admires my aunt and my cousin Kate. Several years ago Kate was engaged to marry Eddie's brother Lyell. On the very eve of the wedding Lyell was killed in an accident, the same accident which Kate survived. Now Eddie comes around to face me, his cottony hair flying up in the breeze. "I have never told anybody what I really think of that woman—" Eddie says "woman" as a deliberate liberty to be set right by the compliment to follow. "I think more of Miss Emily—and Kate—than anyone else in the world except my own mother—and wife. The good that woman has done."

"That's mighty nice, Eddie."

He murmurs something about how beautiful Kate is, that next to Nell etc.—and this is a surprise because my cousin Nell Lovell is a plain horsy old girl. "Will you please give them both my love?"

"I certainly will."

The parade is gone. All that is left is the throb of a drum.

"What do you do with yourself?" asks Eddie and slaps his paper against his pants leg.

"Nothing much," I say, noticing that Eddie is not listening.

"Come see us, fellah! I want you to see what Nell has done." Nell has taste. The two of them are forever buying shotgun cottages in rundown neighborhoods and fixing them up with shutterblinds in the bathroom, saloon doors for the kitchen, old bricks and a sugar kettle for the back yard, and selling in a few months for a big profit.

The cloud is turning blue and pressing down upon us. Now the street seems closeted; the bricks of the buildings glow with a yellow stored-up light. I look at my watch: one is not late at my aunt's house. In an instant Eddie's hand is out.

"Give the bride and groom my best."

"I will."

"Walter is a wonderful fellow."

"He is."

Before letting me go, Eddie comes one inch closer and asks in a special voice about Kate.

"She seems fine now, Eddie. Quite happy and secure."

"I'm so damn glad. Fellah!" A final shake from side to side, like a tiller. "Come see us!"

"I will!"

(1934–   )

Willie Morris

Willie Morris was born in Jackson on November 29, 1934, but he and his family moved to Yazoo City, where he grew up. After high school Morris went to the University of Texas, majored in English, and became the crusading and controversial editor of the student newspaper, *The Daily Texan*. As the first Rhodes Scholar from Texas in ten years, Morris took a degree in history from Oxford University in 1959, then returned to Texas to edit the highly influential *Texas Observer*. In 1963 he joined the staff of *Harper's Magazine*, and in 1966, at the age of thirty-two, became the youngest editor-in-chief in that magazine's long life. Morris has published four books, and has written short stories and articles for such journals as *Harper's*, *The Atlantic Monthly*, *New Yorker*, the *New York Times Magazine*, and the *New Republic*. The following selection is from his first book, an autobiography, *North Toward Home* (1967), for which he received the Houghton Mifflin literary fellowship in nonfiction. He now lives on the eastern end of Long Island and is working on a novel, *Taps*, set in a Mississippi town during the Korean War.

from North Toward Home

TERROR LURKED FOR ME IN THAT SCHOOL. The name *Miss Abbott* brings back long dreary afternoons, weary recitations, secret rage, and wounded bafflement over my own unexpected failure. She was my fourth-grade teacher; I was nine, and for the first time my grades were erratic and my conduct report questionable. My own mother, who had pushed me onward as the nicest and brightest boy in the county, predicted I would never work out, and began blaming the social effects of Radical Reconstruction, always an ominous sign.

Miss Abbott had a pink nose and came from a small town in South Mississippi. She pronounced words like "night," "bright" and "sight" with the "i's" prolonged and nasal, a sure sign of hill-country origins. The only book she read through and through, she told us, was the Bible, and you lived to believe her, and to rue the day she got hold of that book. I myself had my own private relationship with God, which embraced the good old hymns and quiet mumbled prayers and holy vengeance when it was really deserved, and in that town and at that age you took God so much for granted that you knew he was keeping a separate ledger on you simply as a matter of course. But Miss Abbott's religion was Christianity by fear and by rote—so tenacious it got you by the extremities and never let go; it was a thing of interminable monologues, crazed soliloquies; she wanted you to believe she herself was in radio contact with the Deity, and had hung the moon for Him on day number six. When she talked about the time she had been saved, a moist glint began creeping into her eyes, which invariably meant the sermon was on its way. She learned to play a little plastic lute, the kind you could get in Woolworth's for a quarter, and she would play us rousing hymns and Christian marches, heedless of the saliva trickling down that instrument onto the floor. After the music she would preach us on sin and redemption, there being more of the former than the latter, or what the Old Testament said about niggers or Japs, or why we would all end up in hell if God caught us in a backfire. She would not drink Coca-Colas, she said, because of their alcoholic content. Sometimes she would lapse into a sweet, unexpected silence, and gaze out the nearest window for endless minutes. Her features would be bathed in gentle peace. Then I knew Miss Abbott was praying to herself.

Twice a day, in the morning when the class convened, and in the afternoon after lunch, she would call on each of us to pray. We would all begin by blessing our soldiers and then ripping into the Germans and the Japs. Once Bo, from Graball Hill, began his prayer by saying, "Dear Lord, thank you for the bombs that ain't fallin' on us," and then stopped. "What's wrong?" the teacher asked, and Bo said, "I just can't think of nuthin' else to say." The worst tortures were the Bible verses. Two hours each morning she had us recite the verses she had assigned us to learn by heart; when we forgot a verse, she would rap our palm with a twelve-inch ruler. Then out would come that lute again, and if she caught you drowsing, while she piped away on "Onward Christian Soldiers," or scratching at your weary tail, she would go to her "conduct book," and with a slight little flourish, write down a "5."

I made the mistake of correcting her one day, during one of the rare intervals in which we were doing school work. The capital of Missouri, she said, was St. Louis. I held up my hand.

"What is it, Willie?"

"Miss Abbott, the capital of Missouri is Jefferson City."

"No, it's St. Louis."

"I bet it's Jefferson City," and then immediately regretted it, because of the scriptural attitude on gambling.

"Kay King," she snapped, "look in the book and show him it's St. Louis."

The little girl looked in the book and turned red. "Well," she said, "it says here Jefferson City," but obsequiously, like everyone in that ill-fated class, she added, "But Miss Abbott ought to—"

"We'll see," Miss Abbott snapped, and changed the subject. Later, during "silent study," I caught her glowering at me. Why couldn't those people in Missouri have settled on St. Louis?

At noon recess that spring, while the teacher sat on the grass with a group of fawning little girls around her, fetching things for her and scratching her back when it itched, giving her little compliments and practicing their Bible verses, holding her hand and looking for four-leaf clovers to put behind her red ears, we were playing softball nearby. Honest Ed Upton hoisted a lazy foul that went high into the air behind third base; from shortstop I watched its slow descent with interest, with an almost fanatic regard, as it drifted earthward and smacked Miss Abbott on the head. She sprawled on the ground, with a moo like a milk cow's—out cold. *Oh joy of joys!* The other teachers picked her up and carried her away in a car. In our room later, supervised by the principal, all the little girls cried—silent little bawls—and even Honest Ed Upton shed tears. The boys scratched their heads and fiddled with pencils; such was the tyranny in that room, they dared not look into one another's eyes. Except Bo—he caught a glance of mine and puckered his lips, and before long a penciled note came over from him— *"i wich the old bich got hit with a hardbal insted."* I prayed that she would die.

But back she returned, risen on the third day, and on a Friday afternoon, when she had stepped out of the room, I made a spitball and threw it two rows over at Kay King. *"William!"* The sound of Miss Abbott's voice sent terror to my soul. Each afternoon during that incomparable spring I had to "stay in"—two hours a day for six weeks, working long division. Miss Abbott would sit at her desk, reading the Bible or *Reader's Digest*, while the shadows got longer and the sound of boys' voices wafted in through the open window. And when that year ended, with the C on my report card in math, I had crossed, swum, waded the Sea of Galilee, and joyously entered the city limits of old Jerusalem.

The Main Street Elementary School was not all divine retribution. There were trips in the late afternoon to the town library, a cool and private place, where I would sit in a quiet corner and read the latest serials in *Boys' Life* or *Open Road for Boys*, or examine the long rows of books and wonder what was in them and why they were there. On Sundays the town boys would go to the cotton gin, a sprawling tin structure with bales piled almost to the roof, perfect for hiding and climbing. We would take long hikes up the "Bayou," which had been dug deeply into the earth to bring the waters down, two miles or more, from Brickyard Hill and the cemetery, through the white residential section, past the cotton gin and niggertown into the Yazoo River. At some times in the year, when the water was coming out of the hills, the Bayou would be crawling with hundreds of crawfish. Under its bridges it was dark and foul, full of dead fish and bugs. We would walk under one bridge after another, following the source of the water until the Bayou itself ran out, and then on into the hills where the colored shacks were, descending only when the lights of the town twinkled on far below.

In the spring and summer we would go to the political rallies in some vast and dusty clearing in the middle of the woods. The barbecue and yams and corn-on-the-cob and biscuits were stacked on long tables and served up by country Negroes; we would sit on the grass with this steaming feast on our laps, lazily eating and listening to the preachers and politicians. The preachers would bless the barbecue and then bless the politicians. We would sit there and bathe in all that florid rhetoric; you could get a sun-tan just listening to those politicians. At one of these country rallies I first heard Senator Bilbo, a little man with a broad sweaty forehead, as he waved his arms and shouted his wide-ranging denunciations. "It's a miracle," my father said. "He'll carry Yazoo County and get elected, but nobody ever votes for him." After the star attractions, we would hear all the candidates for sheriff and the board of supervisors. Once Pearl Hanna, a shriveled-up old lady who rode in a black carriage and acquired her name from her pearl-handled pistol which she wore at her side, got up to announce her candidacy for sheriff of Yazoo County. She said, "My platform ain't but one thing, and that's to clean up the jail. If you ain't never been in there you should. It's a mess, the floors ain't been swept and the toilets ain't flushed. I intend to get it cleaned out or die tryin'."

We were close to growing plants, to the earth, and to nature's wilder moods. In the Mississippi delta there was nothing gentle about nature—it came at you violently, or in a rush, by turns disordered and oppressively somnolent. In the spring, when the muddy waters overflowed the Yazoo into the town, and the nigger shacks on stilts in the bottoms were sometimes covered over, we would see the open trucks with the Negro convicts crowded up in the back, their black-and-white stripes somber under the ominous gray sky. Or a tornado would twist down and do strange tricks to the things it hit, carrying someone fifty yards and leaving him barely hurt, or driving straws into car tires like needles, or sending our garage across the alley into a field of weeds. One afternoon a tornado hit while we were watching a movie in the Dixie Theater; we heard the hailstones on the roof, hitting in steady torrents. A few minutes later, right on Main Street, I watched a giant rat caught in the water where the gutter was, carried by the strong current closer and closer to the sewer that would transport him into the river, his mouth opening and closing in desperation as three little colored boys pummeled him with rocks and crushed open his head. Then one of them fetched him from the water, held him by the tail in his death throes, and said, "You ain't goin' nowhere, Mr. Rat."

There was something in the very atmosphere of a small town in the Deep South, something spooked-up and romantic, which did extravagant things to the imagination of its bright and resourceful boys. It had something to do with long and heavy afternoons with nothing doing, with rich slow evenings when the crickets and the frogs scratched their legs and made delta music, with plain boredom, perhaps with an inherited tradition of contriving elaborate plots or one-shot practical jokes. I believe this hidden influence, which will explain much that follows, had something to do with the Southern sense of fancy; when one grew up in a place where more specific exercises in intellection—like reading books—were not accepted, one had to work his imagination out on *something*, and the less austere, the better. This quality would stay with one, in only slightly less exaggerated forms, even as a grown man.

So it was, at Christmastime one year, when my feelings against Miss Abbott were running strongest, I went looking for the biggest, darkest, foulest dog turd I could find. I took it home in a paper sack, and when no one was around I put it in a small box and gift-wrapped it in beautiful red paper. I put this box, containing its Christmas cheer, in a larger box and gift-wrapped that one, in fine green and white paper—then a larger box still, then two or three others, each one more elaborately wrapped and ribboned. When I had finshed, I put all six boxes in wrapping paper and, using my left hand, I wrote out Miss Abbott's address. Then I took the parcel to the post office and mailed it. I felt good for days.

When Bubba Barrier and I were ten years old, we found out where the Women's Society of Christian Service was holding its Wednesday afternoon meetings. One morning, following the recipe in a cookbook, we baked two dozen oatmeal cookies, using every ingredient just as directed, and then for good measure we added a mixture of castor-oil, milk of magnesia, and worm medicine for dogs. When the cookies were cool we giftwrapped them and pasted on a card which read, "To the Women's Society of Christian Service from the People of Yazoo City." Then we sneaked through the bushes to Sister Craig's house and deposited the gift inside the screen door. Later we peered through the window off to the side as Sister Craig served the cookies and Coca-Colas. The first guest who bit into our oatmeal cookie chewed on it for a moment, her jaws working politely, but with a purpose, then spit with such exuberance that the crumbs landed at a point six feet away, spraying three other guests with the ruinous matter.

Once I gift-wrapped a dead rat, labeled the package "perfume," and left it in the mailbox belonging to an adult whom we did not admire. At various times I gift-wrapped sheep-droppings, used contraceptives, six-month-old moonpies, live crawfish, grubworms, and hot bacon grease. When we were old enough to learn that in Mississippi, despite its being a dry state, you could order liquor and have it delivered anywhere at any hour of the day, we had a case of Jack Daniels sent to the Tuesday meeting of the Baptist ladies, and watched from the shrubbery while Harry, of the Top-of-the-Hill "Grocery," was berated, stampeded, and torn apart by the ladies when they caught sight of his cargo. "You . . . you . . . Get out of here!" the president cried, and Harry, more frightened of physical injury than fearing a waste of good sour mash, swooped up the case and escaped in fast order.

When we were eleven, Bubba and I started borrowing his family's car. Bubba had learned to drive when he was quite young; early at night we would sneak into the garage where they kept their grand old sedan and drive up Brickyard Hill and through the colored section—up hills and narrow dirt roads, down through the cemetery, anywhere that white adults were not likely to spot us. The Negroes loved the sight of two little boys driving a big Ford. They would shout and wave and come over to look in at the dashboard, and we would sit on the steps of some ragtail Negro grocery store and eat candy bars while they stood around and examined that car right down to the whitewalls. Then back down the hill we would go and sneak the car into the garage, and walk away nonchalantly as if nothing had happened at all.

We took also to spending long hours in the cemetery, the coolest place in town and in some ways the most sensible. Death in a small town is a different proposition from death in a large city; in a small town one associated death with landmarks, with the places people had lived or the places they spent most of their time, so that I connected certain graves with specific houses, or stores. One day when I was ten or eleven, I made a count of all the houses on my street as I walked home, and to my horror discovered that someone I had known or knew about had died at one time or another in more than half of them. Death in a small town deeply affected the whole community. For weeks or even years the physical presence of the dead person would be missed in specific places; his funeral itself would touch closely upon the life of the town. Years later, when I would go to small funerals in non-denominational funeral parlors in New York City, I would be appalled by the cramped impersonality of natural death. The service itself would be hurried, as if they wanted to get it over with as soon as possible; and outside, on the crowded streets, people would never give a thought to the meager little procession. But when I was a boy, and the hearse and dozens of cars weaved slowly through the streets of the town toward the cemetery, people would stop and say: "There goes Mr. Baskin," or "look at that line of cars for Mrs. Scott," or "that Mr. Davis, he sure was popular."

The cemetery itself held no horror for me. It was set on a beautiful wooded hill overlooking the whole town. I loved to walk among the graves and look at the dates and words on the tombstones. I learned more about the town's past here, the migrations, the epidemics, the old forgotten tragedies, than I could ever have learned in the library. My favorites were the graves of two of John Hancock's grandsons, who had died of some colorful disease many years before while passing through Yazoo. They lay here now in the sunshine, side by side and a long way from home. Sometimes we would bring our lunch, ham sandwiches and Nehi strawberry, eating in the shade of a big tree near the Hancock boys. On other days we would come and play until late afternoon, until the lightning-bugs came out and the crickets started making their chirping noises. Or in broad daylight we would wander through the Negro graveyard nearby, a rundown, neglected area, fierce with weeds and insects, joined together by a rutted dirt road that ran interminably up another forlorn hill. Exploring this place one day, we discovered a Negro grave that was badly sunk in because of the heavy rains. Wordlessly we began digging at it with sticks, for thirty minutes or so, until one of us struck something made of hard metal, let up a terrible shriek, and we ran away from there as if Death himself were after us.

We contrived an elaborate hoax that summer against a little boy named John Abner Reeves. We told him we would give him a quarter if he would walk alone, carrying a flashlight, at nine o'clock one night, halfway through the cemetery to the "witch's grave"—the demon who had burned down the town in 1904 and whose resting-place was marked now with a heavy chain, with one link missing where she had escaped. John Abner Reeves consented: two of our conspirators promised to accompany him to the gates at nine and send him alone up the road. At eight-thirty "Strawberry" Alias and I went to the cemetery. It was a still, moonlit night in early June; the light of the sun was just going out on the horizon, giving the evening a wonderful tranquil glow before the coming of the dark. "Strawberry" stationed himself ten yards from the witch's grave in a clump of bushes. He had a long stick, with a white pillowcase attached to the end; I had only my silver trumpet, and I hid behind some trees on the opposite side. As we waited for our victim, I spotted a colored man walking up the road about fifty yards away, taking a shortcut up to Brickyard Hill. I signaled to Strawberry to be still and took out my trumpet. Pressing the valves halfway down, I played a long, ghastly moaning wail, as loud as the horn would go. The man gave a little hop-skip-and-jump, listened again, and then took off at a steady gait up into the woods, while we doubled over and all but rolled on the ground with joy.

Soon we heard the faint sound of footsteps on the gravel, and there was John Abner, a frightened little boy walking stealthily through the trees, looking all around and flashing his light in every direction. When he got within a few steps of the witch's grave, Strawberry all of a sudden stuck the stick out from the bushes, and waved the pillowcase. Then I blew a solemn high note on my trumpet, and descended to the same moan I had used on the Negro. When we looked out, all we could see was a wisp of dust on the road, and we heard the echo of small feet moving fast.

Sometimes these energies were exerted in more constructive causes. Every Saturday morning at ten o'clock there was "the Kiddie Matinee" at the Dixie Theater. On the screen would be the latest chapter of an adventure serial and a full-length western—Roy Rogers or Gene Autry or Lash Larue or Don "Red" Barry. Many of the country people, including the sheriff candidate Pearl Hanna, would bring their lunches in paper sacks and stay all day, right until sunset, watching Roy or Lash over and over again, joining the town children in cheering the scene in which the hero would dash across the range on his horse at the speed of sound to rescue his friends from torture and slow death. The theater would always be crowded, noisy, filthy, full of flying objects; one of the Coleman boys from Eden had his eye put out when somebody threw a BB. In the morning, first thing, there would be a talent hour, where you could save the admission price of ten cents by giving a performance. Almost every Saturday Honest Ed Upton, Bubba Barrier, and I would sing a trio—"The Marines' Hymn," which we dedicated to all the Marines at San Diego; "The Caisson Song," to the Army in North Africa; "Anchors Aweigh," to the sailors in the Pacific; or sometimes, for the hell of it, "Dixie," though that war seemed increasingly remote. We led the drive to collect coathangers and tinfoil for the war effort, and got to see "Spy Smasher" adventures free for our acts of patriotism. Yet we compromised our loyalties by carrying out a lively black-market trade in chocolate bars and bubble gum, the two most flourishing status symbols to my generation in that time of temporary deprivation.

The war itself was a glorious and incomparable thing, a great panorama intended purely for the gratification of one's imagination. I kept a diary on all the crucial battles, which I followed every day in the pages of the *Memphis Commercial Appeal* and the *Jackson Daily*

News, and whenever the Allies won one of them, I would tie tin cans to a string and drag them clattering down the empty sidewalks of Grand Avenue. We never missed the latest war film, and luxuriated in the unrelieved hatred exercised for the Germans and the Japs. How we hated the Japs, those grinning creatures who pried off fingernails, sawed off eyelashes with razors, and bayoneted babies! The Germans we also hated, but slightly less so, because they looked more like us, and because Erich von Stroheim bore an uncomfortably close resemblance to the Methodist preacher. And the English (with whom we shared a "common tongue") and the French and the Russians, they were good fellows, and the Chinese were curious but friendly, and the Italians (the accent on the first "I") were cowards, but in captivity lovable, full of song, and willing to change sides. We worked in victory gardens and looked into the skies for any sign of Junkers or Zeroes, whose shapes I had memorized from twenty-five-cent books on enemy aircraft. Because of the Southland Oil Refinery a few miles from town, and the flow of commerce on the River, Yazoo had been chosen by Berlin as a prime target, and when we noticed a blanket hanging on the clothesline behind a house in niggertown with a swastika emblazoned on the cloth, we sent a letter to the sheriff warning of Nazi agents around the town dump. Only later, and with undisguised disappointment, did I learn that the swastika was an Indian symbol on an old Indian blanket. I resolved to myself that if Yazoo County were ever captured, I would never give in. I would retire to Brickyard Hill and the cemetery as a guerrilla fighter, and if ever caught and put before a firing squad I would yell: "Long live America!"

Bob Edwards had lived in the big white house next door. He had enlisted in the army when he was seventeen. We exchanged V-letters; once he sent me pictures of his tent, full of bullet holes, and told me, "Sometimes I want to stick my leg out of a fox hole and let them shoot it so I can come home." I had no idea what he meant. One day a big package came from France, with a real German helmet, and the name of the soldier—"Willy"—carved inside it, and a German belt, with its engraving "Gott Mit Uns," and an iron cross, and German money, and postcards of SS troops, all wrapped in German newspapers filled with page after page of crosses and death notices.

Tolbert, the Negro man who often did handiwork about our house, was fascinated with that German helmet. Sometimes I let him wear it home, and he would walk off down the alley in an exaggerated goosestep, then turn and wave at me, snapping his heels and giving me the "heil" sign. I wore the helmet, the iron cross, and the belt down Main Street one Saturday afternoon. All the country boys standing on the corners came to look these over.

"Gott Mit Uns," one of them said. "Now what does that suppose to say?"

"God be with us," I replied. "That's a German saying."

"Yeah? Well I'll be damned. Now ain't that sumthin'? 'God be with us.' I'll be damned. You reckon they really mean that?"

One day my mother, my grandmother Mamie, and I were driving to Jackson; there was an army ordnance plant in Flora, and we stopped to pick up two soldiers who were hitchhiking. I was wearing the German helmet and belt. The conversation for a few miles was about the helmet and belt, then about the ordnance plant, and about the Dutch fliers who were stationed in Jackson, and about army life in general. Soon my grandmother asked the boys where they were from.

"I'm from New York," one of them said, "and my buddy here, he's from Massachusetts."

At this point my mother and grandmother exchanged a look and began talking about the Civil War, about how "your people" threw George Harper's printing presses into the well, and about what the Yankees did during Reconstruction. "Oh, you treated us awful," my grandmother said. "You just don't know how awful you treated us, lettin' the niggers run wild, not givin' people enough to eat, stealin' silver, burnin' down houses." The soldiers were silent, looking out the window at the rolling country, and I began to wonder which side they were on after all, and if they bayoneted babies during Reconstruction. Could Yankees be loyal to America during this war? I asked my mother this question. "Oh, we're one country now," she said. "We're united. But it wasn't that way always."

Dominating this good old time was the image of FDR—his voice on the radio, his face with the dark rings under his eyes on the newsreels. FDR was the war itself to me. My father, at the breakfast table reading the *Commercial Appeal,* would whisper, "That damned

Roosevelt!," or, later, taking a ten-cent piece from his pocket with FDR on it, he would say, "Well here's another destroyer dime." Once after having seen FDR on the newsreels in 1945 with his face so gaunt and tired, my father said, "He won't live another month." And when he died, after having heard all the bad things about him, and the neighbors talking about "Eleanor lovin' all the niggers," I came home and said, "I guess it's a good thing old Roosevelt's dead," and my mother told me that wasn't a nice thing to say at all. "He may've done wrong," she said, "but he was our *President.*"

The day the Japs surrendered, I was in the house with Tolbert, who was supposed to be hanging wallpaper. We waited all day for the announcement the radio said was coming. Tolbert was unable to get much work done because of the excitement, so we threw the baseball in the yard for a while, and shelled pecans, and shot a few baskets, while the radio blared out at us from the bedroom window. Then Truman came on and told what had happened, and Tolbert and I shouted and danced around, and hugged each other, and Tolbert said, "That's the end of them old Japs! We whupped them Japs!" and we whacked each other on the back and shouted some more, and got out a whole six-pack of Double-Colas to celebrate.

(1919–)

Berry Morgan

Berry Morgan was born May 20, 1919, in Port Gibson, and grew up there. She attended Loyola University in 1947 and Tulane in 1948–49. Since then she has had a varied life as an executive secretary, as a real estate specialist, as an English instructor at Northeast Louisiana State University, as a free-lance editor, and, most of all, as a writer. She has received two Houghton Mifflin fellowships for her work, one in 1966 and one in 1974, and is now at work on *Fornika Creek*, the third book of a trilogy, of which her other books, *Pursuit* (1966) and *The Mystic Adventures of Roxie Stoner* (1974) are the first two volumes. She is a frequent contributor to the *New Yorker*.

"The Passing" is from *The Mystic Adventures of Roxie Stoner*.

451

The Passing

WHEN MAMA COMES BACK TO ME NOW, it is mostly in some kind of a dream. Reach me that cup, she says, and I see the one she means, but before I can hand it to her, she's left and I know I've been to sleep. Your Mama's on high, Roxie, I tell myself, and I lie there awhile trying not to be ashamed about the passing.

The thing I didn't want to be like it was was that when the Lord sent for Mama I wasn't even home. She'd been down sick so long by that time that people forgot to notice that she was getting lower. Some people—it was the Ingles family on this plantation—sent for me to go to their house and help them. They had sickness and wanted me, and Mama said go on—there's nothing else to do when big people call. Besides, she expected maybe they would give me a little watching over after her day for what I did for them.

Mr. Ned Ingles was back from his good times in New Orleans, but while he had been gone his son had gotten tumors. That was Laurance, the one that played the organ. Well, Mr. Ned had to do right smart drinking to stand up to all of this and he had brought a lady from King's Town, Miss Anna Meredith, to help them get along. It was Miss Anna that said I had to come, that Mama had been sick a long time and now they couldn't wait.

To tell you about Miss Anna Meredith, I would have to go back to olden days when she used to send Mama her overflow sewing work. Miss Anna was a sweet-acting lady and mighty, mighty poor. It could be her poorness made her do what she did, although Mama said to watch out for two kinds of people—those who talk God up to keep their business straight, and those who won't give him any credit at all, even for creation. Miss Anna was this last numbered kind. Until Mr. Ned Ingles brought her out here, she'd been way too hard up to even think of help, and I was the one she lit on right away. Nobody would do but Roxie Stoner to go up to that big house and help them attend to everything.

The first day, I fixed Mama up as good as I could with her Vicks and her new medicines on a chair by her bed and made it across the ridges early. Mr. Ned was already up and sitting on his back steps and it looked like he'd been crying. I was wondering—he used to be a little bit frisky with lady people—but now he stood up just as humble to let me by and told me thanks for coming.

I know that house—the cooks up there used to have me peel and do different things for them—and I walked on through the kitchen and into the hall until I saw Miss Anna. Right away she took her apron off and tied it onto me. Nobody was able to hear, she said—two asleep and one not listening—so she would tell the whole thing now. Laurance was going to die. It might take a month or it might take longer, whichever way, he couldn't stay quiet unless she herself was right with him, waiting on him every minute. I was a special company keeper. I could go on and catch up the housework, she said, that would be all the better, but I was mostly supposed to talk to Laurance's Papa when he jarred up from his whiskey and pay him a lot of notice. He liked to bother Laurance, and Laurance had this ache in his neck that was eventually going to kill him and he didn't want to even see the sight of his Papa much less to start to talk.

I tried to tell Miss Anna that I had sick of my own to tend and I couldn't be gone but a little while from Mama, but she held up her hand again for me to stop. Just listen another minute, she said, before I made my mind up. We had been using this family's tenant house and their land and everything else we could help ourselves to lo these many years and hadn't done a thing to pay it back. If Lilly—that's what she called Mama—saw fit to die right during this jam, there was nothing we could do. She'd made a good thing out of my waiting on her all these years and she didn't believe she would. I've heard people say those Merediths would send a king around to the back, and that's the way she acted.

There was one more reason, Miss Anna said, that I would have to help them. They had this little baby on their hands. His mother had taken about all she could of this kind of life and gone to get some schooling. There isn't any college near to us. She carried me in the front room then, where sure enough there was one, lying in a wicker buggy playing with some dangles. Don't worry about two places at once, Miss Anna said, just be my natural self and help them all I could.

I didn't see how in the world I was going to run this job even by itself without a thought of Mama. And it would be the same as everywhere I go—people get to liking me more than they do each other. Well, I found out I could tote the baby while I did my house-work, and Mr. Ed left us alone to get his drinking done. Then when I'd hear him stirring, I would quick put the baby back in the buggy and push it in a side room with the door shut.

"How do you reckon he is now, Roxie?" was the main thing Mr. Ned wanted to ask me, meaning Laurance, and I'd say about asleep. "Let's us keep quiet now and let him get some rest."

"But I've got to see him, Roxie," and *he'd* commence to cry. "I've got to figure on him while there's time."

I didn't know what he meant by this and I poured him some cof-fee so's to coax him off the whiskey. "Go at him at little at a time," I said. "When once you forget somebody, like you being down in New Orleans so long, it don't do afterwards to celebrate that particular person too fast. Just ease in on him and maybe fix his fire and ease back out." And I told him what Miss Anna said about Laurance not wanting to talk.

He sat straight up then and took the coffee and tried to clear his eyes to see me better. "Anna doesn't know the first thing about him," he said, "any more than I do." And his hands shook so he couldn't hold the coffee and had to lie back down.

Whenever Laurance got to feeling a little better he liked to hold the baby (everybody called him Dana) and make me mirate on him, and watch him at his tricks. It looked to me like the hurting in Laur-ance's neck got better as soon as his Papa went under from the whis-key. The thing Laurance wanted to wonder about was how Dana would turn out when he grew up. Well, I pondered on it for him. Going way back in my head to his grandpa's time—Laurance's grandpa was nice to all the hands. He wouldn't even let the Sheriff know when we would have a killing. Then Mr. Ned was good—he'd just gone down on spirits. Laurance himself was a little bit wrong-headed but he was the same as colored the way he treated people. Taking all of these men and using the schoolhouse way of dividing them up by how they were the same, I'd calculate the baby. He came out fine, as good as any one of them and maybe even better. He wouldn't need whiskey, because days change and confusion's on the wane. He wouldn't be sickly, on account of our lugging him around so much and minding what he needed. He's apt to be a sanctified man, I said, the way he's starting out. This tickled Laurance and he said he hoped he would be. My own grandfather was and I know a good deal about it.

Sometimes people get to liking me so much I have to cure them of it. It got to seeming that way up there—that whole houseful of people hollering Roxie, and Mama across the woods maybe calling too. I could feel it pressing on my mind, trying to suit them all. One evening I made it home just before dark and found Mama out of bed down on the floor. She had eased her feet around the medicine chair until she could touch something else and that way get down to crawl to what she needed. I knew right then I'd have to treat her better. It was when I should of quit.

When I got up to the big house the next morning, I had it in my mind to talk the whole thing out. But Miss Anna was shut up in Laurance's room reading out loud and Mr. Ned was sleeping. The first time I could see Miss Anna it was close to dinner time. When I told her, she let a lot of time pass so I could hear my own self back before she'd say a word. If the worst came to the worst, she said, Mr. Roosevelt would have to bring Mama and slip her in their attic. There was plenty of room up there for her and me too and that way I could stay by them all night. Well, I thanked her, but I knew Mama'd never do it. She was born right in that house we had and took her pills by how the light was changing.

The trouble was my head was getting clogged trying to see which way was which. If I pictured one solvement and felt worse, it must be turning toward sin. About the best in a case like this is to settle on one course and then make up your biscuit. If they turn out light and good, you're on the track of right. The one I picked was Mama— seeing after her. And sure enough, standing right there in the people's kitchen, I made up a pan of the best I'd ever tasted holding to the thought of being home. Mr. Ned himself was the one I'd have to dare up to, because Miss Anna held out she had Laurance and them and I had only one.

In the mornings, Mr. Ned felt bad from the leavings of his whiskey. As a rule, though, he didn't commence drinking it fresh until along this side of evening. There was a little chance in there to catch him in his mind. I watched the hall then until I saw him come out and throw away the paper. That was one sign he was tired of being awake. I started out on Laurance. As long as you said the name of Laurance he would listen good and kind. Then, before he could get started crying, I switched around to Mama. I told him how it was to find her on the floor. And wild as he was with his red hair mussed and his eyes broken into with vein lines, he said go get Miss Anna, that they would have it out.

Well, I tapped real light on Laurance's door and Miss Anna followed me back down the hall. When she got to the kitchen, Mr. Ned told her to pay attention. Did she know that Mama was by herself while I was working here? All right then, he said, we were putting off his rest but arrangements would have to be made so I could go home every now and then to see what all she needed. He wasn't going to have sick neglected on his place as long as he was living.

Miss Anna acted just as meek. She was about afraid I'd let on that I was here to keep him. That would be fine with her, she said, and to take Mama some of whatever was on the stove but hurry back, Laurance was getting tired.

When I started on home this time I found out that as soon as you win over people you go to grieving for them. What would they do in that big house while I was gone? The baby couldn't stay asleep all the time, and Mr. Ned might be needing me to hold him back from Laurance. Here I was able to look after Mama and my mind was back on them. I would have to hunt for something in Scriptures to head up all of this. You can find any kind of trouble there is when you pick up the Bible, people after other people more than they are today.

I had gotten clear through the woods and was close up to our house when I saw a turkey buzzard. It was too high for me to make out its business and then I saw another. All the while more were gathering and wheeling around in a tighter and tighter ring above our chimney. I tried to think it was a whiteface, but when I looked there were all seven, eating by my garden fence.

I could feel something happen then—something like a change *inside* my head. It scared me. I made myself repeat some verses till I could go on in. When I opened the door to Mama's room, she didn't move a bit or tell me what to do. It was like she was watching me though. Sometimes if I haven't been handy when she needs me she teaches me a lesson and won't talk. I kneeled down by her bed and asked her what she wanted, told her all I ever meant to do on this earth was to get her little necessaries for her. I could see the dim spots the birds made when they passed above the hearth light and hear them flapping when they went back up to fly down like they do.

I was crying by now and afraid I'd shake the bed. Dear good sweet Jesus, I said, I've got to have You. I had to keep my feet from heading right back to where the other people were, and I knew good and well they were too laden to even help me wake her. I tried to hear her voice in my remembrance—Mama's I mean—but all I could think was what she said her father said, the Reverend Isaac Stoner: Bless God. Whatever happens, Bless God. Then do your studying out. I took this order then and got down on my knees and blessed Him over and over. This gave me enough space in my head to know that she had risen. Dying means more life (whose voice was telling that?), closer to our Father.

When the bell began to ring out over the woods I knew they wanted me. They would send Mr. Roosevelt though to see why I didn't come. He would start the wake and that was good.

I kept on saying sets of prayers and in between I put on the dress she wanted and found her chinaberry beads. It was hard to get her shoes on, they'd been wrapped up too long. Then while I looked at her, so little lying there but gone, I began to know I'd gotten too interested in the people's troubles when I shouldn't.

I told her I was sorry—still tell her so right on. One of these days she'll excuse me, and she says a lot of things in dreams now when I'm not expecting her to. But she hasn't said that yet.

(1925–   )

Robert Canzoneri

Robert Wilburn Canzoneri has published widely as a poet, playwright, novelist, and short story writer, as an essayist and critic and editor. He was born November 21, 1925, in San Marcos, Texas, the son of a minister who soon after moved to Mississippi, where Canzoneri grew up. After a hitch in the U.S. Navy during World War II, he returned to Mississippi, earning a B.A. from Mississippi College in 1948 and an M.A. from Ole Miss in 1951. He received his Ph.D. from Stanford in 1965; in the intervening years he taught English at Georgetown College, Mississippi College, and Louisiana College. Since 1965 he has been at Ohio State University, where he is professor of English and director of creative writing. His most recent book, *A Highly Ramified Tree* (1976), was awarded the Ohioana award as the best book of the year in the field of autobiography.

The two poems reprinted here are from *Watch Us Pass* (1968).

458

To William Faulkner

Two Weeks After His Death

You stood
(I kept your distance then)
Small and erect, tilting the courthouse square
Into your head,
Pulsing it with your blood.

Even to death
Repulsed,
Today I kept the road despite a grave
Out of the common lot.
No stone yet settled where you lay beneath

Clumps of dry clay,
Shovel carved
Shards of land disturbed; where dust would age
Unmarked,
Your body lay

Biding its decline.
Pulse of your outrage
Blooded my mind.

The Poet Recorded

To Yvor Winters

When you are dead this voice will startle air,
Shake off our nightmare of mortality
One moment of insane belief: you there
Palpable, impassive as reality,
As if the flesh were heavy on the bone,
Mind weighty in the skull, and nothing gone.

How now, old mole, canst work i' the earth so fast?
Stir roots and shift our ground, swear out of time
Progeny you never got? Who guessed
Your seed late scattered should inhabit limb
And lung and blood, reconstitute in essence?
Who dreamed of sonship by your word and presence?

Ingenuity, sending this voice
Unbodied in the world, quibbles with death.
Old use and love, choosing beyond all choice,
Dare to translate sound waves into breath.
But by what subtle rite, past all surprise,
Can words transmute to flesh, insight to eyes?

(1924–)

Charles East

Charles East was born in Shelby on December 11, 1924, and considers himself a Mississippian even though he has spent most of his life in Louisiana. After taking a B.A. at LSU in 1948, he worked for *Collier's Magazine* in New York; the following year he returned to Baton Rouge to work on city newspapers as, successively, reporter, Sunday magazine editor, and assistant city editor. In 1962 he joined the staff of the Louisiana State University Press as editor and in 1970 became director. In 1975 he retired to devote his full energies to writing. He has published fiction in many literary magazines, including the *Virginia Quarterly Review*, the *Red Clay Reader*, *The Southern Review*, *Mademoiselle*, and *The Yale Review*. He currently lives in Baton Rouge, and is working on a novel.

"Journey to the Pyramids" is from East's only collection, *Where the Music Was* (1965).

461

Journey to the Pyramids

THEY HAD BEEN RIDING ALL DAY. They had left Springfield before daylight and by noon had passed Memphis and were headed south and the excitement was beginning to mount in Leggett. "Shit," he said, "I remember these towns." It was all coming back to him, and not only these towns or the camp that he was looking for but a time when he was more alive than he would ever be again. "We finished our basic and we came through here on a troop train," he said, "and all the girls were down to the station to see us." Leggett kept his eyes on the road, but for a moment he was on the troop train again, bare to the waist, leaning out of the door, and the wind was in his face and the smell of train smoke in his nose. Pearson and Federoff and Metcalf were there by him and he could smell their sweat, and Metcalf was singing, *Hidy didy, christamighty, who the hell are we?* Pearson too. *Zim zam, goddam, we're the infantry . . .* And Federoff said, *Knock it off, we're coming into a town.* Then they were passing through the town and the girls were there beside the tracks and the old men who had come out of the pool hall were waving, too, and Leggett thought: There'll never be a time like this. He took the piece of paper out of his pocket and saw it flutter in the wind and swoop almost under the train and out again, and there were other pieces of paper in that wind, and the girls were reaching for them. One of them would sit down and write in a very careful hand, *Dear Pvt. Leggett, I got your name and address you threw off the train . . .* And she would send him a picture, and he would send her a picture, one of those pictures he had taken in Omaha with his cap off, that showed his hair cut short and his sunburnt face, better-looking than he was, and they would write again and maybe never see each other unless he could get there on a weekend pass. Then he would take her a bottle of Channel No. 5 from the PX and she would ask him to her house, and he would meet her folks, and they would sit there in the living room and talk. Later he would take her to the picture show, to the last row in the balcony, or sometimes to a dance, and if he thought she might he would put the make to her, take her outside, out behind the gym or the Legion hall or armory, or to somebody's car, because a girl liked to get laid in the back seat of a car, or on her own front porch, if you talked her into it. Sometimes when Leggett thought about the war he thought about all those soldiers on all those front porches.

"You sure you know where you're going?" Lois said.

"Hell, yes, I know where I'm going," he said.

But toward late afternoon the towns were smaller and farther apart and he stopped and pulled off on the side of the road to look at a map. He had had to detour and he had taken the wrong turn in a town and now he was on the blacktop road that he remembered led up past the camp.

"I don't know what you wanted to come way off down here for," she said, and she reached over the back of the seat into the cooler and opened him another beer.

"You didn't have to come," he said.

"I know I didn't." She drank a swallow of the beer and handed it to him. "Six hundred miles to see a army camp. You must be crazy or something."

Leggett put the can to his mouth and tasted the beer and he thought of the night he and Metcalf chugalugged beer until they staggered out of the beer joint and down the road and into a field, to shake the dew off, and they fell down in the field and laughed, and Metcalf said, *When this is over . . . Christ.* Maybe that was why they laughed. They were there in that field and they could hear the music from the beer joint and the sound of a convoy on the road, and they knew that it would never be over.

Lois said, "What you going to do when you get there? Turn around?"

"For Christ's sake," he said, and he thought: How you going to tell her? She wasn't old enough. She wasn't even on the front porch with one of the others. It was all so long ago, and nothing had happened since. That was the trouble. He had come back from the war to a job he didn't want, to a town he didn't like, to a life like everybody else's. People were born and people died, but nothing happened. So he went back to work at the plant and he joined the VFW and nearly married a girl who had been married to a Marine lieutenant killed on Saipan, but she didn't know what she wanted and he didn't either. Then that summer he met Lois at a skating rink. She was just a kid, not even very pretty, but fun to be with. She reminded him of the girls he had known in the Army. The first thing he knew he was asking her to marry him. Maybe he thought that would change things. It didn't. Once in a while they would go back to the skating rink, or bowl, or he would take her to the picture show and they would sit up in the balcony, but they always came home, and when he tried to tell her he couldn't. If I could tell her, he thought: what it was like. But she wouldn't understand. So he tried not to think about it. Even when he was knocking off a piece he tried not to think about it. *What's the matter?* she'd say. And he'd say, *Nothing,* trying to think of something else.

"I checked the speedometer," Leggett said. "It ought to be right about here."

But when they crossed the hill there was nothing there except the blacktop road and the green fields on either side and a straggly growth of yaupon and briers.

"I would've swore it was right about here," he said. He saw Lois look at him. "It couldn't be much farther."

"I hope you're not getting us lost," she said.

Women, he thought, they can piss you off, and he drove on in silence, faster now, across a hill and another.

"When was that?" she said.

"What you mean?" He turned and looked at her.

"When you were here."

" 'Forty-four," he said.

" 'Forty-four," she said, and laughed.

"What's so funny?"

"Nothing," she said.

"Then what were you laughing at?"

"Oh," she said, "I was just thinking: you should've stayed in the Army."

I sure as hell should have, he thought.

There was a house at the top of the next hill. As they drew nearer Leggett saw that it was one of those big unpainted frame houses that he had seen so often in the South. There was an old man sitting on the porch.

"There's a house," Lois said. "Why don't you ask?"

He began to slow the car and when he reached the turn-off pulled up in the yard and got out.

The old man left his chair and walked to the steps. "Good evening," he said.

"Good evening," Leggett said. "I was looking for the camp . . ."

The old man stared at him.

"I thought the camp was right about here."

"Van Dorn?"

Leggett nodded.

"Back there," the old man said. He pointed. "A couple of miles back. What's left of it."

Leggett looked at him.

"You must've been stationed at Van Dorn."

"In 'forty-four," he said.

"There was many a boy there," the old man said. He said it with a kind of sadness, and Leggett thought: He knows; he wasn't in the war, but he knows. "You might want to go back and have a look. The Government sold the land for pasturage. All the buildings are gone. There's a water tank . . ."

"How long has it been?"

"Oh," the old man said, "not long after the war."

All this time, Leggett thought. He thanked the man and went back to the car.

"Well," Lois said, "what did he say?"

"We passed it."

"Passed it?"

"There's nothing there."

"You mean . . . ?"

"How the hell did I know?" he said.

Leggett turned around and drove back down the blacktop road. He was thinking: I've come all this way and there's nothing there, just a lot of land for pasturage. But he felt it still—the excitement. Like the time he saw Metcalf. He hadn't seen Metcalf since the war and when he sat there in that café in Cleveland, waiting for Metcalf, he kept wondering what it would be like, what they would say. He would say, *You remember the chaplain's wine?* And he did, and Metcalf said, *Boy, you don't forget anything, do you?* Like he was ashamed of stealing that bottle of Communion wine. Only he wasn't ashamed at the time, and over there, in one of those clumps of woods on the side of one of those hills, they drank the wine, he and Metcalf and a boy from Kansas who'd never had his first piece, and broke the bottle on a tree.

"That must be where it was," Lois said.

Leggett slowed the car. Between the trees, half a mile or more away, he could see the water tank. Then he could see, scattered on the ground among the yaupon bushes, the concrete foundations on which the buildings had stood.

"No wonder we missed it," Lois said.

"The main gate used to be here," he said. He pulled off on the shoulder of the road.

"You going to stop?" Lois said. But he was already out of the car. "I'll wait here."

"The hell you will," he said. "You going to come with me . . ."

"Leggett . . ."

"You don't understand, do you?"

"What?" she said.

"What it was like," he said. "I was here, Lois." He remembered how they rode through this gate and how the German POW's looked up from their work to stare at them and how it smelled, the pine trees and the wind up from the Gulf—like it smelled now. "Open me another beer," he said.

She handed it to him through the window.

"Get out," he said. "I want to show you where my barracks was."

"Leggett," she said, "let me wait here in the car. There's briers. They'll tear my stockings."

"Take your goddam stockings off," he said, and he thought: Women, for Christ's sake, they know how to chap your ass.

Lois got out of the car. He helped her under the barbed wire fence and lay on the ground and rolled under himself and came up on the other side.

"There's some cows over there," she said.

"They won't hurt you," he said.

They made their way around a tangle of vines and came to a strip of blacktop almost overgrown with grass. "This used to be one of the streets," Leggett said, the excitement in his voice. "There was a PX down that hill . . ." He pointed. "And over yonder . . . a little to the right of those cows, was the chapel. . . ."

"You mean the church?" she said.

"Yeah," he said, "the church. One time they put Metcalf on the chaplain's work detail. They had caught him answering muster for one of the boys in the company. You know what he did? Slipped the key to the place where the chaplain kept the wine. Stole a bottle, and me and another boy helped him drink it."

"You mean you drank the Communion wine?"

"Hell, yes." Leggett laughed. "Another time," he said, "me and Metcalf figured we had a little leave coming. So we waited until after bed-check and went over the hill. Hitchhiked a ride back into town. There were some girls in town . . ."

"What kind of girls?"

"Aw, some pigs," Leggett said. "But there was a war on. You couldn't afford to be choosy."

"No telling what you did with those girls," Lois said.

Leggett smiled. I sure as hell ain't telling, he thought.

"Well," Lois said, "you've seen what used to be the camp. You ready to go back?"

"Hell, no," he said. "I told you I wanted to show you where our barracks was. First Platoon, Charlie Company."

"How you going to know where your barracks was?"

"You follow me," he said.

They walked up the blacktop street past a herd of grazing cows and crossed the field to another strip of blacktop which ended in a stand of pines. On either side of them, out there in the weeds and briers, were little pyramids of concrete, where the barracks had once stood.

"You see over yonder?" Leggett said. "You see that ditch?"

Lois nodded.

"That used to be the obstacle course. You had to jump the ditch, and there was a wall and some pipe and a lot of other crap. Once they made Metcalf run it three times. They didn't think he could." Leggett remembered Metcalf's face. He had made it around the third time and he was lying on the ground and the sergeant was standing over him, maybe wondering if he'd run his guts out, and Metcalf saw him and kind of smiled, as if to say, *Screw you.* And Leggett remembered how he had waited in that café in Cleveland. He hadn't seen Metcalf since the war and he was passing through and decided to give him a ring. Christ, he thought, it'll be just like the old days. But it wasn't. Metcalf might as well have been a stranger. Oh, they talked about the Army days, but it was Leggett who did most of the talking. Metcalf just sat there, as if it didn't matter. He pulled out pictures of his wife and kids (he had three kids, one of them a sissy-looking boy with glasses Leggett never would have thought was Metcalf's kid) and he asked Leggett how many kids he had and when Leggett told him none, he said, *You ought to.* And Leggett laughed and said, *Yea, I'm trying.* But trying ain't enough, he thought.

"The sun's going to be going down soon," Lois said. "I think we ought to head back." They had crossed one of the hills and the road and the car were out of sight.

"Not until I show you my barracks," Leggett said. "It's over that way . . ."

"I'm going back to the car," she said.

"No, you ain't," he said, and he headed across the field and through a clump of yaupon toward a row of concrete foundations on the other side. He could almost see the barracks and he could smell the barracks smell: sweat and soap and shoe polish and leather and pine lumber, and always the men who had been there earlier. Sometimes, lying awake in his bunk at night, Leggett would wonder who they were, the ones who had been there and moved on and who would follow after him. Jew-boys from the Bronx and Swedes from Minnesota and Texans, mountaineers, men from the plains, plowboys and wanderers.

"Leggett . . ."

He stopped to drink a swallow of the beer and he heard Lois calling him.

"You about to walk me to death."

"Come on over here," he said. He was thinking of Metcalf. I wonder what happened? he thought. Metcalf made it through the war and he went back home to Cleveland and married the most pisspoor girl he could find and got him a job working for the post office and had three sickly-looking kids and all he thought about was showing their pictures. Christ, the post office, Leggett thought.

"Is this it?" she said.

"It's one of these along here," he said. He picked up a stick and beat at a patch of weeds between the rows of concrete pyramids.

"What you doing?" she said.

"Looking," he said.

"What for?"

"I'll show you," he said, and he ran across the field to the next row of foundations, hopping over them.

"You going to fall down and break your crazy neck," she said.

"This must've been the mess hall." Leggett stood among the foundations, looking at the ground.

"You better hurry up," Lois called. "It's going to be dark before long."

He turned and looked across the field toward the road and the sun that was setting in the west. Down the hill the cows were grazing. To his right he could see the water tank—all that was left. A water tank and some blacktop streets that went nowhere and these rows of concrete foundations, like graves. Suddenly he was sad, because time had passed and because Metcalf had changed and because nothing was now this real to him. Not Lois. Not the plant where he worked. Not the bowling alley where he went on Tuesday nights, or anything his television set could bring him. Nothing was this real. He drank the rest of the beer and threw the can—as far as he could; it sailed across the blacktop street where the Old Man used to drive his jeep, out toward the field where the company used to drill.

"I'm going back, Leggett," Lois called.

"No, you ain't," he said. Now, frantically, as if to prove that what he knew was true, he began to run among the concrete pyramids, beating the bushes away, peering at the ground. He was laughing, and when he found what he was looking for he was still laughing. "You see?" he said.

She came across the field toward him, very slowly, and without a word she knelt down and saw in the brown earth in front of four concrete pyramids what two boys, a thousand years before, had written there.

"Me and Metcalf," he said, "we put it there." There in the white shells they had spelled out 1ST PLATOON, C COMPANY. Leggett could read it still. "This was our barracks," he said.

"Now we can go," Lois said. It was almost dark. The sun had dropped behind the trees on the far horizon and the bats had begun to circle in the summer sky.

Leggett sat down on one of the concrete pyramids. "Sit down here," he said.

She sat down there.

"I wish I could tell you," he said. "It was like . . ." He picked up one of the white shells. "Everything that was going to happen happened . . ."

Long after Lois had gotten up and gone down across the field and over the hill to the road and the car, Leggett sat there. He watched the moon come up and he heard a plane pass overhead and once off in the direction of the road he thought he heard Lois calling him. He knew that one minute soon he would get up and go the way that she had gone, back into a life in which nothing happened—and nothing would.

(1921–   )

J. Edgar Simmons

Joseph Edgar Simmons was born in Natchez on May 28, 1921, and educated at Copiah-Lincoln Junior College, Columbia University, and the University of Paris. Over the years he has taught English at Depauw University, the College of William and Mary, Southern Illinois University, Mississippi College, and the University of Texas at El Paso, and has worked as columnist for the *Irish Press* in Dublin, as editorial writer for the New Orleans *Times-Picayune*, and as managing editor of the Natchez *Times*. He has published two volumes of poetry, *Pocahontas* (1957) and *Driving to Biloxi* (1968), which won the Texas Institute of Letters Poetry Award in 1968, and was a finalist for the National Book Award. He has contributed to numerous journals, including *The Nation, Harper's, Chicago Review*, and the *New York Times*. In 1964 he received the Bellamann Literary Award for Poetry. Now living in Jackson, Simmons is at work on a variety of projects, among which is a verse novel.

The following selections were suggested to us by Simmons. "Faulkner," "Bow Down to Stutterers," and "Song of the Moth" are from *Driving to Biloxi;* "Osiris and the Sacraments of Erotic Hesitation" was first published in *New Directions 20* (1968).

471

Faulkner

I

Having often gone privately
through woods and swamp lands near Oxford,
having often trailed in at night through his mother's parlor
in dirty duck pants and muddy sneakers, furtively bobbing
to aunts and spinster librarians lifting in the light
warm muffins —with sweat on him going past
the parlor lamp, going privately and steadily to his room
his heart topsy turvy
with pine pitch & Negroes in the boiling sun—
the shrieking birds, the slick coon hounds
resounding in his blood
inveigling in him a grand privacy

such good hostelry often repeated and privately magnified
the elements breaking and burning
beginning a pattern
the words finally lighting him
like the sun lighting the courthouse in Oxford.

II

—Days and nights of spidery calligraphy, exquisite as a monk's,
jesus corporals gliding from his pen—
Faulkner's private
hot line, his mammy, nanny, his fine rockabye,
his fingers funding the vast rubble of time, the hiss of Controls
working, his face slightly swaying & downed with a lichen that
fringes the slowly turning turret of his face,
the carp-like threads of the thrusting face in a lean to the paper—
he is the ecstatic fox running under the Pleiades,
moustache bristling like a toucan, moist lips making vowels
of agreement—mind, fingers & face dancing so as not to fall,
lips asserting private zonal priorities over the old
irrational cry: Faulkner assimilating Adam and his tree

branching the apples of vision, becoming the grease and shine
of amplitude, providing beneath the jelly
red horns   red cloven feet
                                        wearing finally only the figleaf
of language, knowing that to have moved at all
was to have begun this necessitous rattley dance
this silent private flit through the plot of old thorns:

bard, scop, skald, trouvère
                                this slight Celtic minstrel
—this Falconer—armored—tussling with his bird.

Bow Down to Stutterers

The stutterer's hesitation
Is a procrastinate crackle,
Redress to hot force,
Flight from ancient flame.

The bow, the handclasp, the sign of the cross
Say, "Sh-sh-sheathe the savage sword!"

If there is greatness in sacrifice
Lay on me the blue stigmata of saints;
Let me not fly to kill in unthought.

Prufrock has been maligned.
And Hamlet should have waived revenge,
Walked with Ophelia domestic corridors
Absorbing the tick, the bothersome twitch.

Let me stutter with the non-objective painters
Let my stars cool to bare lighted civilities.

Song of the Moth

it is your sweet propinquity
spins my pinions
to you,
lovely light.
you I prefer
to the black dog scampering in dusk and stubble
bound to ground

for your shapely cone
shines its riddling fugue
of life and death
        —like brass distractions
        at an open grave—
and I touch and let you pander,
be my blending mean

my flaming trope
singeing me
teaching me
fiery hosannahs beyond the mouthing clay.

tell me I reach you to rise
and rise
in your white throb
and tell me
longing was not Faust's ruin
and tell me
in your sacral scathing
the holy ghost is pinched to life.

Osiris and the Sacraments of Erotic Hesitation

I—Osiris Begins the Hestitant Sacraments

Osiris, an infantry GI who went to pieces, later said he came to
know "my mother my terrible mother was in that locked hospital room—a radiator—she exploded at the very thought of
me. My spooky birth flew back on a hinge and slapped my
brain mad as war and hell."

He told the nurse all the power in the world was hisfaulted in the
cold lead nub of the radiator. "I am forced up blow up the
world." In dark he crawled over the floor, a crippled moth
drawing to the fire machine. Later he said, "I lost all my
nouns—I was all verb."

In Craft Therapy men and leather strings weave like snakes in a
fever pile. One spirals beyond keepers. Another mounts the
leather beanstalk crying at ceiling. Down the hall Osiris pees
in the helmet of his hand. Piped news of his execution he
salutes an absolute flag in his dissolving mind. In dog grovel
and bite he eats himself up crying, "The earth is electric—
mother, I am bit all over."

Later, lying on his back he thought he was shaving; in the
ceiling-globes men's bearded faces were pinched in a
plethora of razors crying wretched we cannot stop shaving
until you do but he could not move. He was stuck in drag and
no drag, in beard and no beard, in the hesitant
sacraments that re—define, rari—fy
clarify by blister bath
the shaggy burden.

*II–Osiris Continues the Hesitant Sacraments in the
City of Symbolic Injury*

dear mother, dear unconscious, Hertha my pet: I write you from
Paris. I am out of the Army, my mind still loaded with gre-
nades. I walk around super-aware, seeing many signs of dis-
cord, signs of charm. Often my eyes grow large in freeze, my
fingers rush to my throat to feel the corded rope. Like the
vulture I try to absorb this blackness in order to see. Always I
am arraigned for flight; my mobility begins in a lightest
breeze from a woman's silken pass—my toes tingle against
the ground like ten snakes in a garden. At the Jardin des
Plantes I look at the animals. Blindfolded I try within to
touch them, here, there, everywhere. I name their names
and call myself by them. I study my displacement.

Everywhere in Paris is the sound of Eros—in ornament, fetish,
and gargoyle—even frilly furniture is a pretty consternation
and a girl's rumpled hair—even her curls—are demanding
doomsday—everywhere I see sweet fruits bitten and others
rotten, paining the ground. At my desk I draw an arrow,
careful to join the shaft to the head—I wish no further injury.
In the suburbs I watch the black curls of earth rise from the
plough; in the carpenter's shed blond shavings curve up
from the plane. Nights at L'Opéra I hear the bending reeds,
and in the interval the action shapes of dresses blow me like
storms—all this beauty has a touch of terror that serenely
disdains to destroy me. I believe it desires to fatten me for a
futurity as girls growing into women are balloons dying to be
popped.

Often at night I cry delighted at storms elbowing the chestnut
trees—tramping the woods I see the curled bark in its
beauty cut. In the streets the public is shoved in the windy
lungs of mob. I feel the rub of Paris in the belly gyrations of
dancers in Montmartre and in the chickens rung by the neck
in *Les Halles*—all torsions, dear Hertha, death and delight
abysmally close—even the fiery eyes of the sun and the stars

are wasted to twinkles when they reach me—in the blood
and body of the sacrament, much sundering—as in myths
the gods are cut from the sky—mother I would be mad or
fiercely grabbed but for these sweet thorns of mind. They
give me hints of death which chasten my style . . .

my style, my lip service—not to be despised as many castles
have risen out of the mouth and love children there as well as
arbors planned, boulevards, sewage systems, and cures for
asthma and arthritis—as once, mother, you shaped your
breath that I might sleep in song, as Isaac was once in a war-
ring sham of blood, as I in circumcision fell to appease old
gods,

and now daily I absorb my deaths in the rising, falling implications of oceans, of ravines, mountains, bayous, forests, and
swamps—and I know death in the knobby twists of perser-
vering trees—in the passion mark—in excretion's dark
earths and seas—in my clothes, those bright bandages over
my flesh—and in sleep and dreams and in remembrance of
the catacombs, in the deaths of strangers and in the grindings of my intestines—(as birds stone all but song).

And so I gently go, understanding a skin that comes and goes like
the language and the land. I merely grow old slowly and I
thank you, for you might have burned me on the spot of my
birth, frozen me as a baby hide. But the season of earth is
always fall, the moderate Halloween

where by a careful dilation of my eye I can alter the falling Adam,
Humpty, Judas, Jesus, Icarus, Satan, Cowper, Swift, Smart,
Nietzsche, and Roethke—and all who suffer incubation in
sacrifice—all who are willed by the fuzzed iron of alienation.

It is the task of my life to break down to God, to labor in darkness
as the honeybee, who fits his sweet abstraction to the

dream—as cracks the solid globe to make the organed trees and the flowering nettle garden of men who exist in this fragic show.

Now am I sacred scared, a fireman, in trepidation, raking the enemy fires within.

III—At a Burlesque Osiris Discovers Sacred Eros

Even as Aristotle read the anatomy of the animals, now I, Osiris, slunk in a burlesque seat, would study the powers of Eros. The curtains part. The stage is lit. Now black saxmen slur up natural from flat. The stripper appears in a flood of light. Her jazzy motions, her lines, her mass mount and merge, shine with the secret lights of generics. She moves and burns as virgin queen of cult and metaphysics. She shines her lamps, tends the caves. All is hesitation

even as I in a cave of procrastinate thought shy from assault, desiring only to re-peat the old Eden knowledge, come civil by a complex. As she dances I sing in my limbs of thought.

This stripper's black spike heels speak like an axe and I know myself—a phallus penetrating the matter of self. Myself a phallus arrow splitting space. I am a reed tubing whispers from the mother seas.

Her critical tickle of peelings show me angels do dance upon the pins of my bones. My rib and her thought together become ornament, icon of idea and matter. Now the time is in hot fusion. I breathe the elastic in design. I am a beaked harbinger pecking the walls of form. (Somewhere botanists watch slow motion pictures of the incipient orchid breaking into bloom.)

Now satin lightning damps and creases her body. No tatter without heat. Her swinging fringe and tossing tassels come peripatetic to re-peat, re-collect, ex-tend the action. In flashes she multiplies the show.

Now all is stripped but the sequined G—string—narrow tatter —golden mean—the Lord's reflective body—beneath, like the cone of Dante, is the wounding chasm. Her glittering Gate holds back Time. In mind I see the bending poles of light split to crystal inference. My future nouns I form now in the willed spectrum of intelligence. I feel the golden grindings of her spirit eye—now all dawdle is dead and her pelvic spear thrusts home in seizure of idea.

The house lights go on, the crowd empties the theatre. "A properly studious heart," Osiris says, "takes the agony out of organic—gestures pain away. This Mystery play has calmed the fearful gods in me. I have come clean through my mind. I have learned. The innocent eye sees nothing."

Outside in the night, the town clock in a twig of distance, Osiris laughs. "What a supper! Physics and metaphysics! I believe this holy tart has saved me. What a strange communion—I burst from her divisioning. My eyes are overstuffed—but rather this torment than lust or fear."

In the difficult dusk he polices the area. "I mold in dark the dark to save Illusion, the Lord's only body. Bury now, bright fractions! Bury the devil in God. Always our tragedy was only death to the old, hail to the new. Marry, God and Devil! For the new times! Let God strike Satan as the mother punctures the baby's mouth with the nipple of her breast. Fly Satan to Abraham's bosom! You have suffered too much light. I, Osiris, broken man, son of earth and air, fire and water, close the wounds of my fragic life. By the grace of modulation I am holy fusing. God and devil, in me wedding.

CODA

Even as an occult architect drew Paris, saying the Place de la
   Concord shall join the Arc de Triomphe to L'Opéra and La
   Madeleine, so all Eros is connection. In halls colder than this
   sexual coliseum, Eros cavorts in Rorschach, IBM, teletype,
   player piano, linotype, telegraphy, in the inky engraver's
   dots, in the alphabet of Cadmus—all shard comes mosaic by
   a proper light.

This night in depths of the queen city I have danced my descent,
   twisted in her dusky twist, to softly disconnect. I fell by flesh
   and rose by light to feed the frightened children
   montage,
   the crumbling phonics of design

   From the cave of dark misunderstanding I return to
   work the snows and dreams
   that lash the yellow windows of mind,

   image our mortal fractures
   in
   sac—ral
   de-lights,

   teach the trance
   that cuts the stangers in

   go-ril-la
   je-ho-vah

   im-mac-u-late
   as-tro-naut

(1942–)

Barry Hannah

Barry Hannah was born in Forest on April 23, 1942, but grew up in Clinton. He attended Mississippi College and the University of Arkansas. He has taught at Clemson University and Middlebury College, and now teaches in the Master of Fine Arts program at the University of Alabama. His first novel, *Geronimo Rex* (1972), was nominated for the National Book Award, and in 1977 he was the winner of the Arnold Gingrich Fiction Award from the editors of *Esquire*, in which he has published many stories.

"Midnight and I'm Not Famous Yet" is from *Airships* (1978).

481

Midnight And I'm Not Famous Yet

I WAS WALKING AROUND GON ONE NIGHT, and this C-man—I saw him open the window, and there was a girl in back of him, so I thought it was all right—peeled down on me and shot the back heel off my boot. Nearest I came to getting mailed home when I was there. A jeep came by almost instantly with a thirty cal mounted, couple of allies in it. I pointed over to the window. They shot out about a box and a half on the apartment, just about burned out the dark slot up there. As if the dude was hanging around digging the weather after he shot at me. There were shrieks in the night, etc. But then a man opened the bottom door and started running in the street. This ARVN fellow knocked the shit out of his buddy's head turning the gun to zap the running man. Then I saw something as the dude hit a light: he was fat. I never saw a fat Cong. So I screamed out in Vietnamese. He didn't shoot. I took out my machine pistol and ran after the man, who was up the street by now, and I was hobbling without a heel on my left boot.

Some kind of warm nerve sparklers were getting all over me. I believe in magic, because, million-to-one odds, it was Ike "Tubby" Wooten, from Redwood, a town just north of Vicksburg. He was leaning on a rail, couldn't run anymore. He was wearing the uniform of our Army with a patch on it I didn't even know what was. Old Tubby would remember me. I was the joker at our school. I once pissed in a Dixie cup and eased three drops of it on the library radiator. But Tubby was so serious, reading some photo magazine. He peeped up and saw me do it, then looked down quickly. When the smell came over the place, he asked me, Why? What do you want? What profit is there in that? I guess I just giggled. Sometimes around midnight I'd wake up and think of his questions, and it disturbed me that there was no answer. I giggled my whole youth away. Then I joined the Army. So I thought it was fitting I'd play a Nelda on him now. A Nelda was invented by a corporal when they massacred a patrol up north on a mountain and he was the only one left. The NVA ran all around him and he had this empty rifle hanging on him. They spared him.

"I'm a virgin! Spare me!"

"You, holding the gun? Did you say you were a virgin?" said poor Tubby, trying to get air.

"I am a virgin," I said, which was true, but hoping to get a laugh, anyway.

"And a Southern virgin. A captain. Please to God, don't shoot me," that fat boy said. "I was cheating on my wife for the first time. The penalty shouldn't be death."

"Why'd you run from the house, Tubby?"

"You know me." Up the street they had searchlights moved up all over the apartment house. They shot about fifty rounds into the house. They were shooting tracers now. It must've lit up my face; then a spotlight went by us.

"Bobby Smith," said Tubby. "My God, I thought you were God."

"I'm not. But it seems holy. Here we are looking at each other."

"Aw, Bobby, they were three beautiful girls. I'd never have done the thing with one, but there were *three*." He was a man with a small pretty face laid around by three layers of jowl and chin. "I heard the machine gun and the guilt struck me. I had to get out. So I just ran."

"Why're you in Nam, anyway?"

"I joined. I wasn't getting anything done but being in love with my wife. That wasn't doing America any good."

"What's that patch on you?"

"Photography." He lifted his hands to hold an imaginary camera. "I'm with the Big Red. I've done a few things out of helicopters."

"You want to see a ground unit? With me. Or does Big Red own you?"

"I have no idea. There hasn't been much to shoot. Some smoking villages. A fire in a bamboo forest. I'd like to see a face."

"You got any pictures of Vicksburg?"

"Oh, well, a few I brought over."

The next day I found out he was doing idlework and Big Red didn't care where he was, so I got him over in my unit. I worried about his weight, etc., and the fact he might be killed. But the boys liked a movie-cameraist being along and I wanted to see the pictures from Vicksburg. It was nice to have Tubby alongside. He was hometown, such as he was. Before we flew out north, he showed me what he had. There was a fine touch in his pictures. There was a cute little Negro on roller skates, and an old woman on a porch, a little boy sleeping in a speedboat with the river in the background. Then there was a blurred picture of his wife naked, just moving through the kitchen, nothing sexy. The last picture was the best. It was John Whitelaw about to crack a golf ball. Tubby had taken it at Augusta, at the Masters. I used to live about five houses away from the Whitelaws. John had his mouth open and his arms, the forearm muscles, were bulked up plain as wires.

John was ten years older than me, but I knew about him. John Whitelaw was our only celebrity since the Civil War. In the picture he wore spectacles. It struck me as something deep, brave, mighty, and, well, modern; he had to have the eyeglasses on him to see the mighty thing he was about to do. Maybe I sympathized too much, since I have to wear glasses too, but I thought this picture was worthy of a statue. Tubby had taken it in a striking gray-and-white grain. John seemed to be hitting under a heroic deficiency. You could see the sweat droplets on his neck. His eyes were in an agony. But the thing that got me was that John Whitelaw *cared* so much about what he was doing. It made me love America to know he was in it, and I hadn't loved anything for nigh three years then. Tubby was talking about all this "our country" eagle and stars mooky and had seen all the war movies coming over on the boat. I never saw a higher case of fresh and crazy in my life.

But the picture of John at Augusta, it moved me. It was a man at work and play at the same time, doing his damnedest. And Whitelaw was a beautiful man. They pass that term "beautiful" around like pennies nowadays, but I saw him in the flesh once. It was fall in Baton Rouge, around the campus of LSU. He was getting out of a car with a gypsyish girl on his hand. I was ten, I guess, and he was twenty. We were down for a ball game, Mississippi vs. Louisiana, a classic that makes you goo-goo eyed when you're a full-grown man if your heart's in Dixie, etc. At ten, it's Ozville. So in the middle of it, this feeling, I saw Whitelaw and his woman. My dad stopped the car.

"Wasn't that Johnny Whitelaw?" he asked my grandfather.

"You mean that little peacock who left football for golf? He ought to be quarterbacking Ole Miss right now. It wouldn't be no contest," said my grandfather.

I got my whole idea of what a woman should look like that day . . . and what a man should be. The way John Whitelaw looked, it sort of rebuked yourself ever hoping to call yourself a man. The girl he was with woke up my clammy little dreams about, not even sex, but the perfect thing—it was something like her. As for Whitelaw, his face was curled around by that wild hair the color of beer; his chest was deep, just about to bust out of that collar and bow tie.

"That girl he had, she had a drink in her hand. You could hardly see her for her hair," said my grandfather.

"Johnny got him something Cajun," said my father.

Then my grandfather turned around, looking at me like I was a crab who could say a couple of words. "You look like your mother, but you got gray eyes. What's wrong? You have to take a leak?"

Nothing was wrong with me. I'd just seen John Whitelaw and his girl, that was all.

Tubby had jumped a half-dozen times at Fort Bragg, but he had that heavy box harnessed on him now and I knew he was going down fast and better know how to hit. I explained to him. I went off the plane four behind him, cupping a joint. I didn't want Tubby seeing me smoking grass, but it's just about the only way to get down. If the Cong saw the plane, you'd fall into a barbecue. They've killed a whole unit before, using shotguns and flame bullets, just like your ducks floating in. You hear a lot of noise going in with a whole unit in the air like this. We start shooting about a hundred feet from ground. If you ever hear one bullet pass you, you get sick thinking there might be a lot of them. All you can do is point your gun down and shoot it all out. You can't reload. You never hit anything. There's a sharpshooter, McIntire, who killed a C shooting from his chute, but that's unlikely. They've got you like a gallery of rabbits if they're down there.

I saw Tubby sinking fast over the wrong part of the field. I had two chutes out, so I cut one off and dropped over toward him, pulling on the left lines so hard I almost didn't have a chute at all for a while. I got level with him and he looked over, pointing down. He was doing his arm up and down. Could have been farmers or just curious rubbernecks down in the field, but there were about ten of them grouped up together, holding things. They weren't shooting, though. I was carrying an experimental gun, me and about ten of my boys. It was a big, light thing; really, it was just a launcher. There were five shells in it, bigger than shotgun shells. If you shot one of them, it was supposed to explode on impact and burn out everything in a twenty-five-yard radius. It was a mean little mother of phosphorus, is what it was. I saw the boys shooting them down into the other side of the field. This stuff would take down a whole tree and you'd chute into a quiet smoking bare area.

I don't know. I don't like a group waiting on me when I jump out of a plane. I almost zapped them, but they weren't throwing anything up. Me and Tubby hit the ground about the same time. They were farmers. I talked to them. They said there were three Cong with them until we were about a hundred feet over. The Cong knew we had the phosphorus shotgun and showed ass, loping out to the woods fifty yards to the north when me and Tubby were coming in.

Tubby took some film of the farmers. All of them had thin chin beards and soft hands because their wives did most of the work. They essentially just lay around and were hung with philosophy, and actually were pretty happy. Nothing had happened around here till we jumped in. These were fresh people. I told them to get everybody out of the huts because we were going to have a thing in the field. It was a crisis point. A huge army of NVA was coming down and they just couldn't avoid us if they wanted to have any run of the valley five miles south. We were there to harass the front point of the army, whatever it was like.

"We're here to check their advance," Tubby told the farmers.

Then we all collected in the woods, five hundred and fifty souls, scared out of mind. What we had going was we knew the NVA general bringing them down was not too bright. He went to the Sorbonne and we had this report from his professor: "Li Dap speaks French very well and had studied Napoleon before he got to me. He knows Robert Lee and the strategy of Jeb Stuart, whose daring circles around an immense army captured his mind. Li Dap wants to be Jeb

Stuart. I cannot imagine him in command of more than five hundred troops."

And what we knew stood up. Li Dap had tried to circle left with twenty thousand and got the hell kicked out of him by idle Navy guns sitting outside Gon. He just wasn't very bright. He had half his army climbing around these bluffs, no artillery or air force with them, and it was New Year's Eve for our side.

"So we're here just to kill the edge of their army?" said Tubby.

"That's what I'm here for, why I'm elected. We kill more C's than anybody else in the Army."

"But what if they take a big run at you, all of them?" said Tubby.

"There'll be lots of cooking."

We went out in the edge of the woods and I glassed the field. It was almost night. I saw two tanks come out of the other side and our pickets running back. Pock, pock, pock from the tanks. Then you saw this white glare on one tank where somebody on our team had laid on with one of the phosphorus shotguns. It got white and throbbing, like a little star, and the gun wilted off of it. The other tank ran off a gully into a hell of a cow pond. You wouldn't have known it was that deep. It went underwater over the gun, and they let off the cannon when they went under, raising the water in a spray. It was the silliest-looking thing. Some of them got out and a sergeant yelled for me to come up. It was about a quarter mile out there. Tubby got his camera, and we went out with about fifteen troops.

At the edge of the pond, looking into flashlights, two tankmen sat, one tiny, the other about my size. They were wet, and the big guy was mad. Lot of the troops were chortling, etc. It was awfully damned funny, if you didn't happen to be one of the C-men in the tank.

"Of all the fuck-ups. This is truly saddening." The big guy was saying something like that. I took a flashlight and looked him over. Then I didn't believe it. I told Tubby to get a shot of the big cursing one. Then they brought them on back. I told the boys to tie up the big one and carry him in.

I sat on the ground, talking to Tubby.

"It's so quiet. You'd think they'd be shelling us," he said.

"We're spread out too good. They don't have much ammo now.

They really galloped down here. That's the way Li Dap does it. Their side's got big trouble now. And, Tubby, me and you are famous."

"Me, what?"

"You took his picture. You can get some more, more arty angles on him tomorrow."

"Him?"

"It's Li Dap himself. He was in the tank in the pond."

"No. Their general?"

"You want me to go prove it?"

We walked over. They had him tied around a tree. His hands were above his head and he was sitting down. I smelled some hash in the air. The guy who was blowing it was a boy from Detroit I really liked, and I hated to come down on him, but I really beat him up. He never got a lick in, I kicked his rump when he was crawling away and some friends picked him up. You can't have lighting up that shit at night on the ground. Li Dap was watching the fight, still cursing.

"Asshole of the mountains." He was saying something like that. "Fortune's ninny."

"Hi, General. My French isn't too good. You speak English. Honor us."

He wouldn't say anything.

"You have a lot of courage, running out front with the tanks." There were some snickers in the bush, but I cut them out quick. We had a real romantic here and I didn't want him laughed at. He wasn't hearing much, though. About that time two of their rockets flashed into the woods. They went off in the treetops and scattered.

"It was worthy of Patton," I said. "You had some bad luck. But we're glad you made it alive."

"Kiss my ass."

"You want your hands free? Oliver, get his ropes off the tree." The guy I beat up cut him off the tree.

"You scared us very deeply. How many tanks do you have over there?"

"Nonsense," he said.

"What do you have except for a few rockets?"

"I had no credence in the phosphorus gun."

"Your men saw us use them when we landed."

"I had no credence."

"So you just came out to see."

"I say to them never to fear the machine when the cause is just. To throw oneself past the technology tricks of the monsters and into his soft soul."

"And there you will win, huh?"

"Of course. It is our country." He smiled at me. "It's relative to your war in the nineteenth century. The South had slavery. The North must purge it so that it is a healthy region of our country."

"You were out in the tank as an example to your men?"

"Yes!"

All this hero needed was a plumed hat.

"Sleep well," I said, and told Oliver to get him a blanket and feed him, and feed the tiny gunner with him.

When we got back to my dump, I walked away for a while, not wanting to talk with Tubby. I started crying. It started with these hard sobs coming up like rocks in my throat. I started looking out at forever, across the field. They shot up three more rockets from the woods below the hill. I waited for the things to land on us. They fell on the tops of trees, nothing near me, but there was some howling off to the right. Somebody had got some shrapnel.

I'd killed so many gooks. I'd killed them with machine guns, mortars, howitzers, knives, wire, me and my boys. My boys loved me. They were lying all around me, laying this great cloud of trust on me. The picture of John Whitelaw about to hit that ball at Augusta was jammed in my head. There was such care in his eyes, and it was only a golf ball, a goddamned piece of nothing. But it was wonderful and peaceful. Nobody was being killed. Whitelaw had the right. He had the beloved American right to the pursuit of happiness. The tears were out on my jaws then. Here we shot each other up. All we had going was the pursuit of horror. It seemed to me my life had gone straight from teen-age giggling to horror. I had never had time to be but two things, a giggler and a killer.

Christ, I was crying for myself. I had nothing for the other side, understand that. North Vietnam was a land full of lousy little Commie robots, as far as I knew. A place of the worst propaganda and hypocrisy. You should have read some of their agitprop around Gon, talking about freedom and throwing off the yoke, etc. The gooks went for Communism because they were so ignorant and had nothing to lose. The South Vietnamese, too. I couldn't believe we had them as allies. They were such a pretty and uniformly indecent people. I once saw a little taxi boy, a kid is all, walk into a Medevac with one arm and a hand blown off by a mine he'd picked up. These housewives were walking behind him in the street, right in the middle of Gon. Know what they were doing? They were laughing. They thought it was the most hysterical misadventure they'd ever seen. These people were on our side. These were our friends and lovers. That happened early when I got there. I was a virgin when I got to Nam and stayed a virgin, through a horde of B-girls, the most base and luscious-lipped hustlers. Because I did not want to mingle with this race.

In an ARVN hospital tent you see the hurt officers lined up in front of a private who's holding in his guts with his hands. They'll treat the officer with a bad pimple before they treat the dying private. We're supposed to be shaking hands with these people. Why can't we be fighting for some place like England? When you train yourself to blow gooks away, like I did, something happens, some kind of popping returning dream of murder-with-a-smile.

I needed away. I was sick. In another three months I'd be zapping orphanages.

"Bobby, are you all right?" said Tubby, waddling out to the tree I was hanging on.

"I shouldn't ever've seen that picture of John Whitelaw. I shouldn't'tve."

"Do you really think we'll be famous?" Tubby got an enchanted look on him, sort of a dumb angel look in that small pretty face amid the fat rolls. It was about midnight. There was a fine Southern moon lighting up the field. You could see every piece of straw out there. Tubby, by my ass, had the high daze on him. He'd stepped out here in the boonies and put down his foot in Ozville.

"This'll get me major, anyhow. Sure. Fame. Both of us," I said.

Tubby said: "I tried to get nice touches in with the light coming over his face. These pictures could turn out awfully interesting. I was thinking about the cover of *Time* or *Newsweek*."

"It'll change your whole life, Tubby," I said.

Tubby was just about to die for love of fate. He was shivering.

I started enjoying the field again. This time the straws were waving. It was covered with rushing little triangles, these sort of toiling dots. Our side opened up. All the boys came up to join within a minute and it was a sheet of lightning rolling back and forth along the outside of the woods. I could see it all while I was walking back to the radio. I mean humping, low. Tubby must've been walking straight up. He took something big right in the square of his back. It rolled him up twenty feet in front of me. He was dead and smoking when I made it to him.

"C'mon, I've got to get the pictures," he said.

I think he was already dead.

I got my phosphorus shotgun. Couldn't think of anything but the radio and getting it over how we were being hit, so we could get dragons—helicopters with fifty cals—in quick. The dragons are nice. They've got searchlights, and you put two of them over a field like we were looking at, they'd clean it out in half an hour. So I made it to the radio and the boys had already called the dragons in, everything was fine. Only we had to hold them for an hour and a half until the dragons got there. I humped up front. Every now and then you'd see somebody use one of the experimental guns. The bad thing was that it lit up the gunner too much at night, too much shine out of the muzzle. I took note of that to tell them when we got back. But the gun really smacked the gook assault. It was good for about seventy-five yards and hit with a huge circle burn about the way they said it would. The gooks' first force was knocked off. You could see men who were still burning running back through the straw, hear them screaming.

I don't remember too well. I was just loitering near the radio, a few fires out in the field, everything mainly quiet. Copters on the way. I decided to go take a look at Li Dap. I thought it was our boys around him, though I didn't know why. They were wearing green and standing up plain as day. There was Oliver, smoking a joint. His rifle was on the ground. The NVA were all around him and he hadn't even noticed. There were so many of them—twenty or so—they were clanking rifles against each other. One of them was going up behind Oliver with a bayonet, just about on him. If I'd had a carbine like usual, I could've taken the bayoneteer off and at least five of the others. Oliver and Li Dap might've ducked and survived.

But I couldn't pick and choose. I hardly even thought. The barrel of the shotgun was up and I pulled on the trigger, aiming at the bayoneteer.

I burned them all up.

Nobody even made a squeak.

There was a flare and they were gone.

Some of my boys rushed over with guns. All they were good for was stomping out the little fires on the edges.

When we got back, I handed over Tubby's pictures. The old man was beside himself over my killing a general, a captured general. He couldn't understand what kind of laxity I'd allowed to let twenty gooks come up on us like that. They thought I might have a court-martial, and I was under arrest for a week. The story got out to UPI and they were saying things like "atrocity," with my name spelled all over the column.

But it was dropped and I was pulled out and went home a lieutenant.

That's all right. I've got four hundred and two boys out there—the ones that got back—who love me and know the truth, who love me *because* they know the truth.

It's Tubby's lost fame I dream about.

The Army confiscated the roll and all his pictures. I wrote the Pentagon a letter asking for a print and waited two years here in Vicksburg without even a statement they received the note. I see his wife, who's remarried and is fat herself now, at the discount drugstore every now and then. She has the look of a kind of hopeless cheer. I got a print from the Pentagon when the war was over and it didn't matter. Li Dap looked wonderful—strained, abused and wild, his hair flying over his eyes while he's making a statement full of conviction.

It made me start thinking of faces again.

Since I've been home I've crawled in bed with almost anything that would have me. I've slept with high-school teachers, Negroes and, the other night, my own aunt. It made her smile. All those years of keeping her body in trim came to something, the big naughty surprise that other women look for in religion, God showing up and killing their neighbors, sparing them. But she knows a lot about things and I think I'll be in love with her.

We were at the John Whitelaw vs. Whitney Maxwell play-off together. It was a piece of wonder. I felt thankful to the wind or God or whoever who brought that fine contest near enough by. When they hit the ball, the sound traveled like a rifle snap out over the bluffs. When it was impossible to hit the ball, that is exactly when they hit it.

My aunt grabbed hold of my fingers when the tension was almost up to a roar. The last two holes. Ah, John lost. I looked over the despondency of the home crowd.

Fools! Fools! I thought. Love it! Love the loss as well as the gain. Go home and dig it. Nobody was killed. We saw victory and defeat, and they were both wonderful.

(1929–)

Turner Cassity

Allen Turner Cassity was born in Jackson on January 12, 1929, and graduated from high school there. He attended Millsaps (B.A., 1951), Stanford (M.A., 1952), and Columbia (M.S., 1956). He insists, however, that he received his education in the United States Army and the South African civil service—Cassity began the 1950s in the one and ended them in the other. In between he was at Jackson Municipal Library (1957–1958), and since 1962 he has worked at Emory University Library in Atlanta. In private life the poet is a dedicated traveler and a lifelong Zeppelin buff.

The following selections are from *Steeplejacks in Babel* (1973).

494

The procurator is aware that palms sweat

The hands I wash, I wash advisedly.
The thief I pardon—he is freed to steal,
Theft being, by its nature, rendered thee,
And so the lesser evil. Caesar, Hail!

The vain young man who scourges, who is kissed,
Betrayed, himself is scourged, and all for youth,
May find, in dampened silver, truth I lost
In salvered water. Yes; but what is truth?

Manchuria 1931

Guard duty by the railhead, where the rails
Run into sand, and burlap on high bales

Is ragged in the wind. His angles steep,
The pack-train camel sleeps a shaggy sleep.

He sleeps; I yawn. I settle in my coat;
I feel the dry cold tighten in my throat.

I go on; east or west, I do not know.
Direction, absent in these sands below,

Above is blazoned in the clustered stars,
That chart us, light by light, their blue bazaars,

Their shining trade, their far-flung conquest. Dim,
Descending to the eastern, western rim,

They light, a little, parting caravans
That are their own horizon; or, intense

Among our errant locomotive sparks,
Align the several and smoking darks;

Until—an east of easts and type of types—
The rising sun stands in a sky of stripes;

And I can see, who feel it in my eyes,
A yellow sand that levels out the ties.

A Crown for the Kingfish

(the Huey P. Long Bridge, New Orleans)

Patrol car sirens, anywhere they're bound,
Are, finally, the sine curve done in sound.

In the vicinity of this one bridge,
Though formulary, they are still cortege;

As, underneath that publicizing steel,
The river is an earth and burial:

A redneck mud that past the creole streets
Parades its plethora of old defeats.

The pomps are their reciprocal. Each guard,
Each Buick, each machine-gun late reward

The early want. Innate, it nonetheless
Is colored, channeled, by its time and place.

No empire that the hearth has not rehearsed;
No leader who was not gauleiter first.

Utilitarian, yet arrogant,
A bridge is too exact a monument.

Its profile is the bow cut down and strung.
It is the weapon chosen, challenge flung;

Is hickory turned into metal: all
The taut boy was, and now, all he will be.

Cain precedes Adam, and the central tree,
If knowledge later, first is arsenal.

Carpenters

Forgiven, unforgiven, they who drive the nails
    Know what they do: they hammer.
  If they doubt, if their vocation fails,
    They only swell the number,

Large already, of the mutineers and thieves.
    With only chance and duty
  There to cloak them, they elect and nail.
    The vinegar will pity.

Judas who sops, their silver his accuser, errs
    To blame the unrewarded.
  They guard the branch he hangs from. Guilt occurs
    Where it can be afforded.

Two Hymns

I

THE AFRIKANERS IN THE ARGENTINE
(1902)

You bring us, Lord, from all our loss
To useless hope, beside a second veldt.

Remove and fixative the seas we cross;
No land but home the image held.

The spacious grass, stiff under frost,
Is there as here a planet white on gold.
Such fields, such level sweeps as we have lost,
If space were all, space still might hold.

River nor pampa, silver, mud,
Can now return us, in their tongue of Spain,
The earth-and-silver of the tongue now slain.
And though, raised of our pillared blood,

Arise again the strong, plain church,
It, too, must be a wife to Lot. Look back,
Look forward, there the plain, the cities. Watch:
In static grain, now ends the trek.

II
CONFEDERATES IN BRAZIL
(1866)

Unreconstructed, uncontrite,
We seek the land that we have known by night.
The state of day we can endure to lose.
Never the dark of ancient use.

So long as, on the latticed vine,
The torrid moonlight seeps its gold and brine,
And in the garden pools the flashing carp
Give back its colors, but more sharp,

In that wet tension, haze on water,
Hang yet the motes cast out as of no matter:
Indulgence, common forms, observance, ease;
And, suspended even as these,

Their last illusion: continuity.
Sustain, night, still the same, still other,
Haze and past. By thy filled eye
Make one the mote and beam, the slave and brother.

In Sydney by the bridge

Cruise ships are, for the young, all that which varies.
The aged disembark with dysenteries.
Always, it is middle age that sees the ferries.

They hold no promise. Forward or reverse
Impels them only to where what occurs,
Occurs. Such is, at least, the chance of being terse,

And is their grace. The lengthy liners, fraught
Sublimely, shrill for tugs. If they're distraught,
That is because the thoughts of youth are long, long thoughts—

Save those of gratitude. The slow, massed force
That frees them they will cast off in due course,
To learn, or not to learn, the ferries' sole resource:

How, in the crowding narrows, when the current
Runs in opposition and the torrent
Claws the wheel, to locate in routine, abhorrent

For the storm, the shore that makes it specious;
Where one calls the vicious, curtly, vicious,
And the scheduled ferry, not the cruise ship, precious.

(1942–)

David Chapman Berry

D. C. Berry, presently an associate professor of English at the University
of Southern Mississippi, was born July 23, 1942, in Vicksburg. He grew
up in Greenville, but calls Woodville his home. After taking a B.S. at
Delta State College, and then turning down medical school, he worked a
year for General Motors, then pulled three years as a medical service officer in the United States Army. While in Vietnam Berry wrote his first
volume of poetry, *Saigon Cemetery* (1972). After the service he began
graduate work at the University of Tennessee, and received his Ph.D. in
English in 1973.

The following poems were supplied to us by Berry: "Dusk Between
Vicksburg and Rolling Fork" is slightly revised from its appearance as
"Whitman I Thought of You" in *Snowy Egret*, XXXVI (Autumn, 1973);
"Watermark" first appeared in *Texas Portfolio*, I (1976). "Bass," "Setter,"
and "Quail" are published here for the first time.

Dusk Between Vicksburg and Rolling Fork

The sky's a quail's breast
softly pocked by dark-blue shot,
smoke crawling like fluffy grubs
from the shotgun shacks.
Walt Whitman, I thought of you.

Now at the Bon Ton in Yazoo City,
I can't remember what it was,
something that came when the wind
wrinkled the edge of a cottonfield
as though to blow it off a lap
and a hand quickly pulled it back.

Watermark

You snap your spear when the rain stops
and wade in the creek the last time as a boy. The drop
will come. Not sure just when, you stake your feet
and into a willow drill your eyes
two fingers beneath the brow of the stream
to hook for the drop inside.

Washed out, you'll not be the first. You'll not
be drowned last either, sloshed by current ripples. The drop
in the creek from the mark of its crest to where
your eyes are fastened in the willow will be
the crown which you hereafter wear
when chanting with the chiefs,

your watermark, which allows you only to dance at the feast.
To say your poem you have to go back alone to the creek.

Bass

for Gary Stringer

Stump in the pond, stump in my eye. My fly
pops inches from the stump. Bass, all wrist,
roiling deep in thought, wedge from the bottom
of the headpan, and buckling the surface under
the fly, blur through their tunnel of scales,
shattering the mirrory surface, the fly engorged,
the fly, the fly leading the bass by the lip.

I break their heads with the butt of the Buck knife.
They stiffen shimmering. Scaling rakes the silver
off mirrors—my raw eye a dump of shimmers? I eat fish
to keep my head stocked. Some fellows refinish
mirrors, but I eat fish to restore ponds.
Don't believe it that life's only a matter
of how you look at it. Smell my hands.

Setter

for Arthur

Though barbed wire had cut
an angle in my hip
and up from the ground the air
had blown into buzzing fragments,

though briars had scratched maps
across the back of my hands
and stumps were aimed like mortars
straight up for a last stand,

it was not my war.
The five warm lumps at my back

were quail minus their heads
the setter had swallowed intact,

spoils for having had the nose
that turned to steel before they rose.

Quail

> —for Sunday Stringer, a ritual . . .

The skin over breast and belly is a thin
scrip. Place thumbs together, double-barreled,
and then with trigger fingers pinch
and spread. The Emporium thus revealed.

What looks like a glazed brooch is the breast,
why you cocked. Separate it from the heart
and from the intricate riverbed reds
and purples and feathers that singled it
apart, now chopped hat on the chopping block.

Last, pour yourself a jigger of neat Black Jack,
two-fingers deep (them old double-barrels),
and drink to the hammers cocked back on every flight.
May the hat be knocked-off at least for the feather,
though the rest be carefully tumped in the brown paper sack.

(1939–)

James Seay

James Seay was born on New Year's Day, 1939, in Panola County, and grew up there. He earned a B.A. from Ole Miss in 1964 and an M.A. from the University of Virginia in 1966. He taught English at the Virginia Military Institute, the University of Alabama, and Vanderbilt University before joining the English Department of the University of North Carolina at Chapel Hill. Besides his two collections of poems, *Let Not Your Hart* (1970) and *Water Tables* (1974), he has published widely in periodicals and anthologies, and has received numerous prizes, including a Southern Literary Festival prize in 1964 and an Emily Clark Balch Prize in 1968.

"Let Not Your Hart Be Truble" is from *Let Not Your Hart;* the other poems are from *Water Tables*.

504

Let Not Your Hart Be Truble

For George Garrett

The horn of your silver bus
Sounds in the rocks and trees,
Black Saul of Tarsus turned Paul,
And you come telling
Under what tree and with what light
You were struck blind
And now see.

On faith and a curve, both blind,
You double-clutch and pass my car,
Hoping against the evidence
Of things not seen,
Or, should it appear from around this curve,
You trust the roadside rocks and trees
Will open like the sea. .
That failing, you take the rock and wood
For what it gives.

Your pass is good, and made, I guess,
With the same thick hand that lettered
The words on your rear exit door:
LET NOT YOUR HART BE TRUBLE
You exact too much, black Paul,
My lane, my life on your faith,
My troubled hart.
And yet I do not deny you unlettered
The gift of metaphor, or even parable;
The master himself spoke thus,
Lest the heart of the many be softened.

You talk like you clutch, old black soul,
For you know the troubled hart
Takes the hunt
Into a deeper wood.

Naming the Moon

The moon is in the patch of trees on our hill
and so we go out to name and claim it
for the first time together.
No matter that in the window by your bed alone
it has been *airplane* or *car* or *light;*
tonight it is clearly *moon,*
as big and pale as your mother's belly twenty months ago,
though diminishing as it clears our hill
and pulls toward the Milky Way.   *Moon   Moon*
Your small butt stirs against my chest
and as the word takes hold of you like a possession
I sense tides beginning to draw again over fossil shells
in the limestone wall beneath your boots.
A mist like salt spray finds the light hairs
around my nostrils. I know these stars
were where the seas fell. Sand is running out
from under us.
Trying to hold you from the undertow,
yet steadily giving you to the moon,
I almost call out *airplane airplane car light.*
But then I hear your new word turn to *cold*
and realize it is November, not dead waters,
stirring us. We go inside,
you to your bath, I to a whirlpool of words
that become the whirlpool of draining water
you put your finger in to claim whatever is there.
And whatever it is
now as you come naked into my room bringing back to me
trees hill an airplane cowboy boots limestone dead seas a light
I remember it is out of my hands,
for finally, turning, you give me the moon
before I forget.

It All Comes Together
Outside the Restroom in Hogansville

It was the hole for looking in
only I looked out
in daylight that broadened
as I brought my eye closer.
First there was a '55 Chevy
shaved and decked like old times
but waiting on high-jacker shocks.
Then a sign that said J. D. Hines Garage.
In J. D.'s door was an empty Plymouth
with the windows down and the radio on.
A black woman was singing in Detroit
in a voice that brushed against the face
like the scarf
turning up in the wrong suitcase
long ago after everything came to grief.
What was inside we can only imagine—
men I guess trying to figure what would make it
work again. Beyond them
beyond the cracked engine blocks and thrown pistons
beyond that failed restroom
etched with our acids beyond that American Oil Station
beyond the oil on the ground
the mobile homes all over Hogansville
beyond our longing
all Georgia was green.
I'd had two for the road
a cheap enough thrill
and I wanted to think
I could take only what aroused me.
The interstate to Atlanta was wide open.
I wanted a different life.
So did J. D. Hines. So did the voice on the radio.
So did the man or woman

who made the hole in the window.
The way it works is this:
we devote ourselves to an image
we can't live with and try to kill
anything that suggests it could be otherwise.

Natural Growth

Plant your eyes in the solid bank of trees,
in the room where the pines are counting their long green.
Let your vision grow into the other kingdom.
Look at it this way:
if cows come
grass is happy to be straw
in the mortar that holds the meadow together.
Poppies support their habits
through only the most benevolent of aggressions.
The willow on the river's eroding ledge
says *no money in the bank*
but still it joins its family in green huzzas
for light and space.
That's when you can tell
if your eyes have taken root:
every cheer that reaches you is one
you know by heart.

Patching Up the Past with Water

1.

For a beginning
let yourself be drawn like debris
to all the great bodies of water;
I will be there
asking you to help
lift up a hand of water
and reach into a time
we dream to change.

No matter that even before
your first palm is taken away
the water washes off itself
like quicksilver off a wall of glass
or that your hand becomes a broken colander
wired loosely to the wrist,
sieving whatever drifts by,
no matter—we also want to keep an eye peeled
for anything that might give the past away:
bits and pieces, twigs and such.
We can begin anywhere
you find an entry.

2.

It could be a key
from the Hotel Pemaquid
where the room keys have all been lost
over the years.
For ventilation, the desk clerk will say,
just leave the door ajar
and pull the door curtain for privacy,
nothing has ever been stolen.
Find the room matching your secret key,
lock yourself in and ponder
the clutter of your uninsurable goods,
the fog that curtains
the Maine coast by morning.
Listen as confusion sweeps up the maid service
when they arrive at your door screaming
nothing has ever been stolen, there is someone
needing to trust you
in every room on the hall.
You see your door as *out there*
and fumble to unlock it
through the drape of fog.
The dead air, the foggy misapprehension, the unimaginable
water.

Anything to help you understand
this history better.

3.

A song maybe
but nothing resembling this stone shore.
Someone in lime-green half-sleeves
knows the words. South of here.
The instruments are in fake alligator cases
piled near the lake in the grass,
and he is stretching his arms
toward the one he can chord for this song,
seeing us walk the line
off the interstate.
His band, blowing smoke over the lake
and waiting for the Plymouth to cool down
to their chill lime shirts,
will hear the song come off the water,
blue grass,
and give him the rest of the music
his words need.
They forget the VFW dance three hundred miles away—
these are the old words
they can't leave alone,
broke with love again and singing.
We know now that peace won't come
the whole night through.

4

A dream drifts by, one that recurs:
the bride your wife once was
is the one Mayans dress in precious metals
and stones for the sacrificial lake.
And now a guided tour back by steamer
to the waterfall above her pool:
you, your miserable guide,

the deserted concession stand.
But the dream changes; in this one
you are alone.
In the water the riches you have been coming for
are nothing but silt
except for eyes brighter than any fire,
reaching you like hands.
Whatever the old ritual denied
has been yours for the taking all along.

5.

If the rain comes
let it take you back.
What was it your father brought you
in his voice out of the rain?
You breathed your question alone in the rear seat
that night in the middle of the field
when he came back to the car with your youngest uncle
and the sack of frogs from another man's pond.
The brief interior light
from the opened door in his face
gave you that question and part of its answer;
his changed voice told you more:
the man whose sounds were lost in the dark rain
had caught them at his pond's edge.
That much was available at the border
of their words in the car
as they tried to talk away from you,
but you would never know the secret of their tremor.
Now in the rain
you ask your father to take you back,
show you where the man came out of the trees
down to his pond,
say what was said and done,
not to turn away.

6.

For long spells at a time
any leaf we turn over
turns out to be the chemical paper
where a Polaroid picture cleared
and was torn away.
We trace the shadows of its slate gravestone
as though we were doing a temple rubbing,
and always the ghost of a woman
emerges in silver at the water's edge.
Three frames away, a white heron
in flight, the same day, the same water.
That's when the tracings in our hands
take flight or else become a montage
of all the wrong that lovers always do.
Nothing we can do but return
to where our decoys are waiting in their dream   .
and there resume whittling at the worn reed of desire
that calls up time after time
from its wooden throat
enough down here for us both.

7.

Eventually this intimation:
some matters water won't solve.
Her divorce was four years ago.
Here are new friends, white wine on ice,
and the cigarette coming back around from hand to hand
on this Saturday afternoon where Leaf River eases south
out of a little town in Mississippi called Petal.
She had to get free. You can understand:
he was the one who hung the gaudy dress in her closet.
Leaf and petal, she is thinking,
wash it all away but leaf and petal.

But still his image flashes up
with its one lesson: *root and stalk*.
And water won't tell why.

8.

Children hear what water tells best of all.
It calls up to them from the river
walk out of the empty mansion on the bluff
and find the sundial in the garden.
The line looped around its pedestal
will lead you down the hill to the white boat.
Cut it loose and let it drift away.
Be free of the death they planned for you.
It wasn't malice; they painted the boat each summer
and remembered the customary favors.
Wave your love up the slope to them
and ease into the water.
Follow your death only as far as you have to.

9.

So much in our mothers' eyes
we could not help.
I think of a photograph
of my own mother at seventeen.
She is kneeling beside a lily pond
in someone's yard.
The bathing suit is a one-piece wool jersey
and her body is almost as white as the clouds.
No man has seen it all.
There are goldfish in the water
her hand is in,
but we cannot see them.
Now she has lifted her face to the camera

and I am wishing we could be true—
my father, my sisters,
you and I, all of us
waiting out here in the future
like the stone frog her other hand rests on.

10.

Somewhere your hand or mine
will come to rest
on the water table bearing only itself,
the true food of this dream.
In it we taste fossils, clouds, failure.
For all our palms of water, our sieving,
this is what we come to,
a water that offers nothing
from the private past,
water that down to its last
and smallest particle resists our will.
As it begins to move through us
we feel its secret in each lapse
of our pulse *no one moment separate from another*
no one motion
Never that dreamed absence of succession
in which to reassemble the whole being.
And yet our hands are straining
as though some image, free and alterable,
had dropped from the table
and lay within reach.

(1936–)

James Whitehead

Poet and novelist James Whitehead was born in St. Louis, Missouri, on March 15, 1936, and grew up in Mississippi. He graduated from Jackson Central High in 1954, earned Bachelor's and Master's degrees at Vanderbilt, and in 1965 received an MFA in creative writing from the University of Iowa. Before going to the English Department at the University of Arkansas, where he helped establish a Master of Fine Arts program, he taught at Millsaps and at the University of Iowa. Whitehead's first book of poems, *Domains* (1966), received the Robert Frost Fellowship in Poetry from the Breadloaf Writer's Conference, and he was awarded a Guggenheim Fellowship in fiction for his novel *Joiner* in 1972.

"The Zoo," and "Domains" are from *Domains*; the other poems are from Whitehead's forthcoming book of poems, *Local Men*, to be published later this year, and were supplied to us by the poet.

515

The Zoo, Jackson, Mississippi, 1960

This zoo is a naked place;
Beasts of summer lodge
With habitants from ice;
Here the odd and poor

Of every kingdom come
To sample fear, where bar
And glass protect observer
And observed. The ledge

Of rocks defends their dignity
When lusts are obvious
And the dark throat bawls
For its keeper's pale meat.

Lank giraffes tread
Deliriously through heat—
At the edge of rage and sense
The eagle strains in truss.

Domains

1
Sometimes I find it hard to concentrate
On politics
And the rugged Brotherhood of Man—
I mean to be a Populist
Who goes according to a good reformer's plan
With all the races for a swim . . .
And the local union gets my dues . . .
But still the pamphlets, tracts and speeches bring the blues

And dreams of flight
To Red and Yellow, Black and White
Who tumble on the common beach
And by wild water where
The common terror will be shared.

2.

This is the way a young man has to learn . . .
Making love to economics and the faithless moon.

3.

One great-great-grandfather died
At twenty-seven of rotten meat that carried worms
In the Civil War
For the Union—
But on the other side
Dr. Bourland suffered Vicksburg
Lived to write a book to state the wisdom of his life
And cried when his eyes went out.

4.

I stagger with my banner everywhere
Toward a better state
But always lovely hair
Long limbs negotiate
To turn my mind from taxes
And jack the old reflexes.

5.

It is all death in time I would obliterate
And rigorous confusions of the noble dead—
But be it flesh, or memory,
Or present justice in a rout,
God, give me strength to nervously admit
I am not fit
To serve at once
Two dying bodies with equal wit.

He Records a Little Song
For a Smoking Girl

Smoking all that much has got her eyes
Pinched and a little lined—so the misery
Of cigarettes deserves a song. Prize
For doing anything, catastrophe
In small doses, smoke cuts into a face
Almost as deep as Benzedrine and booze.

Still she's a lovely girl in every place
Because she is so young. O she will lose
Her surfaces of head in love and time
Though all the rest stay smooth and be close-pored.
Her legs would make a blind man smile, and rime—
Her belly and the thing in sweet accord
Years from now will cry, Forgive, forgive
My cigarettes, I swallowed smoke alive.

About a Year After He Got Married
He Would Sit Alone
In An Abandoned Shack In a Cotton
Field Enjoying Himself

I'd sit inside the abandoned shack all morning
Being sensitive, a fair thing to do
At twenty-three, my first son born, and burning
To get my wife again. The world was new
And I was nervous and wonderfully depressed.

The light on the cotton flowers and the child
Asleep at home was marvelous and blessed,
And the dust in the abandoned air was mild

As sentimental poverty. I'd scan
Or draw the ragged wall the morning long.

Newspaper for wallpaper sang but didn't mean.
Hard thoughts of justice were beyond my ken.
Lord, forgive young men their gentle pain,
Then bring them stones. Bring their play to ruin.

A Local Man Remembers Betty Fuller

Betty Fuller cried and said, Hit me.
I did. Which made her good and passionate
But Betty Fuller never came. Fate
Decreed that Betty Fuller would not see
The generosity a lively house
And loyal husband bring. She lost her mind
In Mendenhall. She got herself defined
As absolutely mad. A single mouse
Caused her to run exactly down the line
Of a wide road, running both north and south
With execrations pouring from her mouth.

She's out at Whitfield doing crazy time
And she can't possibly remember me
Among the rest. I'm satisfied she can't.

The Delta Chancery Judge
After Reading *Aubrey's Brief Lives*

1.
I think of shame, embarrassment and crime

Rott with the rotten;
Let the dead bury the dead

And that for William Chillingworth, Divine,
Because he mostly died of siphylis.
I agree with Aubrey—
Dr. Cheynell was unkind to Chillingworth.

Old John Aubrey was a man of parts
And was a sot: *Sot that I am,* he often wrote.

2.
All that rancor, all that plague and fire
And every reputation cheap as lice—
It boggles me the sort of life I know.

"As he laye unravelling in the agonie of death,
the Standers-by could hear him say softly,
I have seen the Glories of the world"—
Isaac Barrow was that decent man.

Moniti meliora We now have better counsel—
How I doubt that sentence!

3.
Last week I fixed divorce for three young men
And each was wrong
Unworldly and unkind to his desperate wife.
Dumb as pig shit, each was terrified
Of anything his mother didn't know.

Our simple education softens teeth
And all their fathers bit their thickened tongues.
Their children never will
Strap on or see the glories of the world.

4.
Who is the King of Chancery today?
Who can personify Sweet Equity
Now everything begins with common law?

My court is for insurance men who lose
And give their money out of policy
Because I contradict my style and rule
Almost exclusively
Against their company.
I will be re-elected.

5.
A year ago there was a funeral,
The mistress to a friend,
And when the graveside nervous prayer was done,
His wife let go a scream:
No one to keep the bastard off of me!

He was gone for fifteen weeks alone
But never more than eighty miles from here
Doing business from his motel rooms.
He got back home and there was no reprieve.

6.
Sometimes my alone.
few good friends with their good wives
And I with mine, we leave
Denying every province of our pain
For days of games and plays.

Sots all, we will maintain some glory for this world.

(b. 1935)

William Mills

William Mills was born in Hattiesburg on June 17, 1935; and though he
has in fact lived most of his life in Louisiana, he maintains family ties in
Mississippi, spends as much time in the state as possible, and considers
himself a Mississippian. He received a B.A. from Louisiana State University in 1959, an M.A. in 1961, and a Ph.D. in 1972 from the same institu-
tion. He has taught English at several schools, including LSU, the
University of New Orleans, and East Carolina University, and he has
served as visiting poet at the University of Arkansas. His poems and
stories have appeared in numerous journals and anthologies. He is at present a full-time writer.

"Our Fathers at Corinth" is taken from his forthcoming book of
poems, *Stained Glass* (1979), and was furnished to us by Mills; the others
are from his first book of poems, *Watch for the Fox* (1974), and were
selected with Mills' advice.

Our Fathers At Corinth

for William J. Mills, Co. A, 24th Mississippi Infantry Regiment. Died
    June 18, 1862. Buried in an unknown soldier's grave, Enterprise,
    Mississippi

"Let the impending battle decide our fate, and add one more illustri-
ous page to the history of our Revolution, one to which our children
will turn with noble pride, saying, 'Our fathers were at the battle of
Corinth.' "

P.G.T. Beauregard, General, Commanding

Winter in Mississippi and your sons stand before you,
All of us together now, here between Chunky River and
Okatibbe Creek. You lie unmarked in these four hundred
Gray stones, still in formation and like enlisted men
Everywhere mostly unknown. It was this
That haunted your children,
That we didn't even know your name,
Only that you never came home.

The specter of our forgetfulness drove us
To front porches of the old of Greene County
Wanting to put a name to your wraith,
An end to our neglect.
As we rocked our way to eighteen hundred and sixty-two,
A hundred year old cousin remembered
You had walked the long way to Corinth.
That your young son got a licking
For trying to follow you.
And, she also said your name, great-grandfather.
With this we followed you.

The records showed it to be
A late spring of blood.
You clustered at the courthouse
With your brash and ruddy cousins

Come to watch the lieutenant in gray
Come to hear him talk about the fight.
He spoke of April at Shiloh and the butcher's bill,
Of General Johnston dying,
Of Mississippians buried there.
He spoke of Halleck with twice our number
Moving on Corinth.
He read a letter from Jeff Davis:
"Beauregard must have reinforcements . . .
    The case of vital importance.
    Send forward to Corinth
    All the armed men you can furnish."
What parts of the late spring day
Warred in your Anglo-Saxon mind
As you moved slowly from the dock
Of rhythmical certainties in Greene County
To the caesura of war, that pause
As the blood boils before its final thickening
Before it is left to cool in Corinth, in Enterprise?
Young yeoman, rude in your blue eyes,
Straw hat cocked in the county's latest style
Was it defense, not wanting to miss the big event,
Or just being shy about staying home?
No matter. You walked to Corinth. You went.

Well, not being cavalry because you had no horse
Means nothing to us now conjuring your ghost.
We have been mostly the infantrymen
Of the country's armies—Hill 209, Hill 800.
Yes sir, they have numbers.
We feel the earth as we walk to the world's wars,
And remembering, we return to care again,
Planting the seeds to tide us till the next
Rearing of the Apocalyptic face.

In the middle of May you found yourself
Not only in Company A, but in Polk's First Corp.
You also found what enlisted men know—

Being scared is only half.
There was typhoid, measles, and dysentery;
Also nothing to eat.
Instead of the clear water of the Chickasawhay
Here muddy, stagnant holes
Held what there was to drink.
How you soldiered and how you died
We don't know. Diaries tell us
What days it rained. We know Polk's Corp
Was beyond the entrenchments skirmishing day and night.
Everyone prepared for the coming fight.

As always the enlisted men were the last to know—
All units would fall back to Tupelo.
Perhaps this was your last bright sight
As the torches were put
To the trunks and tents, the blankets and beds,
As eighteen thousand in hospitals moved
Further south.
No great battle, just plenty dead.

Grandfather, as you leaked away in June
Did you think at all of generation?
Your wife even then carried a son.
Did dreaming take its hands and urge you
Past Corinth to her labor to come,
To us, unnumbered, unknown
But coming, grandfather . . . coming.
Your blood may have thickened in Corinth
Yet your seed twisted to a birthing scream,
Your blood surged to now,
Surges like a sea in my head
Even as it may have spoken to you lying there
In your cocked hat,
Now tipped to shade your eyes, now tipped to die.
What now for the unknown soldier?
Somewhere in this plot of four hundred Confederates
Your bones stopped

But your blood salts leached the ground
On their way to the Chunky and Okatibbe,
On down the Chickasawhay, past the summer corn,
And the homestead you left unfinished,
On to larger holdings. Your salt blood
Moved now down the Pascagoula,
Out to the Gulf of Mexico, out to the salt seas
Embracing the earth, holding us all.
Your home is large now, your wraith has a name.
You rest in your sons
Who must keep you to keep themselves.

Watch for the Fox

He lit it more for the light and
Movement it gave
Than against the cold.
He had felt the old fear
Skulking like a fox
Around a hen house,
Patient,
Time on its side,
People sleep.
But a jerk inside
(something his fathers
had passed on)
Said to get up,
Go deeper in darkness
And get something to burn,
See himself again and
Watch for the fox.
Watching, he knew
The fire
Defines
The fox.

I. Bibliography

Margaret Walker Alexander

1942 *For My People* (poems. With a Foreword by Stephen Vincent Benet). New Haven, Conn.: Yale University Press.
1966 *Jubilee* (novel). Boston: Houghton Mifflin.
1970 *Prophets for a New Day* (poems). Detroit: Broadside Press.
1972 *How I Wrote Jubilee* (essay). Chicago: Third World Press.
1973 *October Journey* (poems). Detroit: Broadside Press.
1974 (with Nikki Giovanni) *A Poetic Equation: Conversations Between Nikki Giovanni and Margaret Walker.* Washington, D.C.: Howard University Press.

Charles G. Bell

1953 *Songs for a New America* (poems). Bloomington: Indiana University Press. Rev. ed. Dunwoody, Ga.: Norman S. Berg, 1966.
1956 *Delta Return* (poems). Bloomington: Indiana University Press. Rev. ed. Dunwoody, Ga.: Norman S. Berg, 1969.
1962 *The Married Land* (novel). Boston: Houghton Mifflin.
1968 *The Half Gods* (novel). Boston: Houghton Mifflin.

D. C. Berry

1972 *Saigon Cemetery* (poems). Athens: University of Georgia Press.
1978 *Jawbone* (poems). Birmingham: Thunder City Press.

Sherwood Bonner. See Katherine McDowell

Robert Canzoneri

1965 *"I Do So Politely": A Voice from the South* (nonfiction). Boston: Houghton Mifflin.
1968 *Watch Us Pass* (poems). Columbus: Ohio State University Press.
1969 *Men with Little Hammers* (novel). New York: Dial Press.
1970 *Barbed Wire, & Other Stories.* New York: Dial Press.
1970 (ed., with Page Stegner) *Fiction and Analysis: Seven Major Themes* (textbook). Glenview, Ill.: Scott, Foresman.
1976 *A Highly Ramified Tree* (autobiography). New York: Viking.

527

Hodding Carter

1942   *Lower Mississippi* (history). New York: Farrar & Rinehart.

1942   (with Richard E. Dupuy) *Civilian Defense of the United States* (nonfiction). New York: Farrar & Rinehart.

1944   *The Winds of Fear* (novel). New York: Farrar & Rinehart.

1946   *Pulitzer Prize Editorials.* Greenville, Miss.: *Delta Democrat-Times.*

1947   *Flood Crest* (novel). New York: Rinehart.

1948   *Jim Crow's Other Side* (pamphlet). Greenville, Miss.: *Delta Democrat-Times.*

1950   *Southern Legacy* (essays and anecdotes). Baton Rouge: Louisiana State University Press.

1952   *John Law Wasn't So Wrong: The Story of Louisiana's Horn of Plenty.* Baton Rouge: Esso Standard Oil Co.

1953   *Where Main Street Meets the River* (nonfiction). New York: Rinehart.

1955   *Robert E. Lee and the Road of Honor* (biography). New York: Random House.

1955   (with Betty Werlein Carter) *So Great a Good: A History of the Episcopal Church in Louisiana and of Christ Church Cathedral, 1805–1955.* Sewanee, Tenn.: Sewanee University Press.

1957   *Faulkner and His Folk* (lecture). Princeton, N.J.: Princeton University Press.

1958   *The Marquis de Lafayette: Bright Sword for Freedom* (biography). New York: Random House.

1959   *The Angry Scar: The Story of Reconstruction.* Garden City, N.Y.: Doubleday.

1959   *The South Strikes Back* (social criticism). Garden City, N.Y.: Doubleday.

1961? *The Editor as Citizen* (lecture?). Lawrence, Kans.: University of Kansas.

1961   (with Anthony Ragusin) *Gulf Coast Country* (history and description). New York: Duell, Sloan & Pearce.

1963   (with Betty Carter) *The Doomed Road of Empire: The Spanish Trail of Conquest.* New York: McGraw-Hill.

1963   *First Person Rural* (nonfiction). Garden City, N.Y.: Doubleday.

1964   *The Ballad of Catfoot Grimes* (verse). Garden City, N.Y.: Doubleday.

1965   *So the Heffners Left McComb* (social criticism). Garden City, N.Y.: Doubleday.

1965   *A Tale of Two Cities* (lecture). Stanford, Calif.: Stanford University Press.

1966   *The Commandoes of World War II* (history). New York: Random House.

1968   (ed., with others) *The Past as Prelude: New Orleans, 1718–1968* (history). New Orleans: Tulane University.

1969   *Their Words Were Bullets: The Southern Press in War, Reconstruction, and Peace.* Athens: University of Georgia Press.

1970   *Man and the River: The Mississippi.* Chicago: Rand McNally.

Secondary

The most complete study of Carter's life is James E. Robinson's "Hodding Carter: Southern Liberal, 1907–1972" (Dissertation, Mississippi State University, 1974). Robinson's bibliography is incomplete, but is still useful as a starting point.

Turner Cassity

1966   *Watchboy, What of the Night?* (poems). Middletown, Conn.: Wesleyan University Press.

1973   *Silver Out of Shanghai; A Scenario for Josef von Sternberg, Featuring Wicked Nobles, a Depraved Religious, Wayfoong, Princess Ida, the China Clipper, and Resurrection Lily, with a Supporting Cast of Old Hands, Merchant Seamen, Sikhs, Imperial Marines, and Persons in Blue* (verse). Atlanta: Planet Mongo Press.

1973   *Steeplejacks in Babel* (poems). Boston: David R. Godine.

1975   *Yellow for Peril, Black for Beautiful: Poems and a Play.* With a note by Richard Howard. New York: G. Braziller.

J. F. H. Claiborne

1830?   *Speech, on the Bill "For the Relief of Jefferson College," Delivered in the House of Representatives, of the State of Mississippi, December, 1830, by . . . a Representative from the County of Adams.* Washington, Miss.: Cadet Office.

1836   *Mississippi Slave Sales.*

1837   *Argument Submitted by Messrs. Claiborne and Gholson, Representatives from the State of Mississippi, to the Committee of Elections.* City of Washington: Blair & Rives.

1843   *Proceedings of the Board of Choctaw Commissioners. Col. Claiborne's Statement.* [Natchez?]: n.p.

1860   *Life and Times of Gen. Sam. Dale, the Mississippi Partisan.* New York: Harper & Brothers.

1860   *Life and Correspondence of John A. Quitman, Major-General, U.S.A., and Governor of the State of Mississippi.* New York: Harper & Brothers.

1876   *Historical Account of Hancock County and the Sea Board of Mississippi. An Address delivered . . . at the Request of the Citizens, and in Compliance with a Resolution of Congress . . . July 4th, 1876.* New Orleans: Hopkins Printing Office.

1880   *Mississippi, as a Province, Territory and State, with Biographical Notices of Eminent Citizens. Vol. I.* Jackson, Miss.: Power & Barksdale.

1885   *A Sketch of Harvey's Scouts, Formerly of Jackson's Cavalry Division, Army of Tennessee . . . Being a Part of the Second Volume of Claiborne's History of Mississippi.* Published for Private Distribution. Starkville, Miss.: Southern Livestock Journal Print.

1927   *A Trip Through the Piney Woods.* New York: Purdy Press.

Joseph Beckham Cobb

1850   *The Creole: or, Siege of New Orleans* (novel). Philadelphia: A. Hart.
1851   *Mississippi Scenes* (stories and sketches). Philadelphia: A. Hart.
1858   *Leisure Labors* (essays). New York: D. Appleton and Co.

Secondary

George T. Buckley's "Joseph B. Cobb: Mississippi Essayist and Critic," *American Literature*, X (May, 1938), 166–78, is the best introduction to Cobb. There is no checklist or bibliography. All essays on Cobb have lacked reference to his classical criticism in Methodist journals.

Hubert Creekmore

1940   *Personal Sun* (poems). Prairie City, Ill.: Village Press.
1940   *Formula* (poems). Norfolk, Conn.:
1943   *The Stone Ants* (poems). Los Angeles: Ward Ritchie.
1943   *Purgative* (story). Corpus Christi, Tex.: privately mimeographed, 100 copies.
1946   *The Long Reprieve and Other Poems from New Caledonia.* New York: New Directions.
1946   *The Fingers of Night* (novel). New York: D. Appleton-Century. Republished, 1950, as *Cotton Country*.
1948   *The Welcome* (novel). New York: Appleton-Century-Crofts.
1950   *Cotton Country* (novel). New York: Bantam. Republication of *The Fingers of Night*.
1950   (trans.) *No Harm to Lovers: the Love of Sulpicia and Cerinthus as Revealed in Six Poems by Sulpicia and six elegies by Albius Tibullus.* Parsippany, N.J.: Blue Ridge Mountain Press.
1952   (ed.) *A Little Treasury of World Poetry.* New York: Scribner.
1953   *The Chain in the Heart* (novel). New York: Random House.
1959   (ed.) *Lyrics of the Middle Ages.* New York: Grove.
1963   (trans.) *The Satires of Juvenal.* New York: New American Library.
1965   (trans.) *The Book of True Love* by Juan Ruiz. New York: Las Americas.
1966   *Daffodils are Dangerous: The Poisonous Plants in your Garden.* New York: Walker.
1966   (trans.) *The Erotic Elegies of Albius Tibullus.* New York: Washington Square.

Harris Dickson

1899   *The Black Wolf's Breed* (novel). Indianapolis: Bowen-Merrill.

1902   *The Siege of Lady Resolute* (novel). New York: Harper & Brothers.
1903   *She That Hesitates* (novel). Indianapolis: Bobbs-Merrill.
1905   *The Ravanels* (novel). Philadelphia: J. B. Lippincott.
1905   *Duke of Devil-May-Care* (novel). New York: D. Appleton.
1906   *Gabrielle, Transgressor* (novel). Philadelphia: J. B. Lippincott.
1911   *Old Reliable* (stories). Indianapolis: Bobbs-Merrill.
1912   *Sunlover Sam Stories.* Boston: Small, Maynard.
1913   *Coffin Club Stories.* Boston: Small, Maynard.
1916   *The House of Luck* (novel). Boston: Small, Maynard.
1917   *The Unpopular History of the United States.* New York: Frederick A. Stokes.
1920   *Old Reliable in Africa* (stories). New York: Frederick A. Stokes.
1925   *An Old-Fashioned Senator* (biography). New York: Frederick A. Stokes.
1928   *Children of the River* (novel). New York: J. H. Sears.
1937   *The Story of King Cotton.* New York: Funk and Wagnalls.

Secondary
No significant work on Dickson has ever been done, but see Charles Kemper's piece in *The Library of Southern Literature,* and L. Moody Simms, Jr., "Harris Dickson and the Post-War South," *Notes on Mississippi Writers,* V (Winter, 1972), 80-83. A list of Dickson's novels and short stories is in Mary Frances Schumpert, "Mississippi Fiction and Verse Since 1900" (M.A. Thesis, University of Mississippi, 1931), 107-13.

Ellen Douglas. See Josephine Ayres Haxton

Charles East

1965   *Where the Music Was* (stories). New York: Harcourt, Brace & World.
1969   *The Face of Louisiana* (photos by Elemore Morgan; text by East). Baton Rouge: Louisiana State University.
1977   *Baton Rouge: A Civil War Album* (photos; text by East). Baton Rouge: limited edition published by the author.

John Faulkner

1941   *Men Working* (novel). New York: Harcourt, Brace.
1942   *Dollar Cotton* (novel). New York: Harcourt, Brace.
1950   *Chooky* (related stories). New York: W. W. Norton.
1951   *Cabin Road* (novel). New York: Fawcett.
1952   *Uncle Good's Girls* (novel). New York: Fawcett.
1955   *The Sin Shouter of Cabin Road* (novel). Greenwich, Conn.: Fawcett.
1959   *Ain't Gonna Rain No More* (novel). Greenwich, Conn.: Fawcett.
1960   *Uncle Good's Week-End Party* (novel). Greenwich, Conn.: Fawcett.

1963   *My Brother Bill* (reminiscence). New York: Trident Press.

Secondary

The most complete bibliographical listing of Faulkner's works is Helen White and Redding S. Sugg, Jr., "John Faulkner: An Annotated Check List of His Published Works and of His Papers," *Studies in Bibliography*, XXIII (1970), 217–29.

William Faulkner

1924   *The Marble Faun* (poem). Boston: Four Seas.
1926   *Soldiers' Pay* (novel). New York: Boni & Liveright.
1927   *Mosquitoes* (novel). New York: Boni & Liveright.
1929   *Sartoris* (novel). New York: Harcourt, Brace. [Note: *Sartoris* is a heavily
          edited and cut version of *Flags in the Dust*, the full text of which was not
          published until 1973.]
1929   *The Sound the the Fury* (novel). New York: Jonathan Cape and Harrison
          Smith.
1930   *As I Lay Dying* (novel). New York: Jonathan Cape and Harrison Smith.
1931   *Sanctuary* (novel). New York: Jonathan Cape and Harrison Smith.
1931   *These 13* (stories). New York: Jonathan Cape & Harrison Smith.
1931   *Idyll in the Desert* (story). New York: Random House. Published in a limited
          edition of 400 copies.
1932   *Miss Zilphia Gant* (story). Dallas: Book Club of Texas. Published in a limited
          edition of 300 copies.
1932   *Light in August* (novel). New York: Harrison Smith & Robert Haas.
1933   *A Green Bough* (poems). New York: Harrison Smith & Robert Haas.
1934   *Doctor Martino and Other Stories.* New York: Harrison Smith and Robert
          Haas.
1935   *Pylon* (novel). New York: Harrison Smith and Robert Haas.
1936   *Absalom, Absalom!* (novel). New York: Random House.
1938   *The Unvanquished* (novel). New York: Random House.
1939   *The Wild Palms* (novel). New York: Random House.
1940   *The Hamlet* (novel; first volume of the Snopes trilogy). New York: Random
          House.
1942   *Go Down, Moses* (novel). New York: Random House.
1948   *Intruder in the Dust* (novel). New York: Random House.
1949   *Knight's Gambit* (stories). New York: Random House.
1950   *Collected Stories.* New York: Random House.
1951   *Notes on a Horsethief* (story). Greenville, Miss.: Levee Press.
1951   *Requiem for a Nun* (novel). New York: Random House.
1954   *A Fable* (novel). New York: Random House.
1955   *Big Woods* (stories). New York: Random House.
1957   *The Town* (novel; second volume of Snopes trilogy). New York: Random
          House.

1959   *The Mansion* (novel; third volume of Snopes trilogy). New York: Random House.

1962   *The Reivers* (novel). New York: Random House.

1967   *The Wishing Tree* (story). New York: Random House. [Note: This story was first written in 1927.]

1973   *Flags in the Dust* (novel). Edited with an introduction, by Douglas Day. New York: Random House. [Note: this is the original version of the novel originally published in 1929, in a heavily edited and cut text, as *Sartoris*.]

1975   *The Marionettes* (play). Charlottesville, Va.: Bibliographical Society of the University of Virginia and the University Press of Virginia. [Note: *The Marionettes* was written in 1920; Faulkner made and bound by hand several copies for distribution to friends. This is, then, a facsimile reproduction of one of the 4 known copies, published in a limited edition of 126 copies, and, in 1978, in a trade issue, with an introduction and textual notes by Noel Polk. Another copy was published in 1975 in Oxford, Miss., by the Yoknapatawpha Press.]

1977   *Mayday* (story). South Bend, Ind.: University of Notre Dame Press. Facsimile reproduction of another of Faulkner's manuscript booklets, first made in 1926. With an introduction by Carvel Collins. Published in a limited edition of 125 copies.

Works by Faulkner collected by others:

1959   *Faulkner in the University* (interviews). Edited by Frederick L. Gwynn and Joseph L. Blotner. Charlottesville: University of Virginia Press.

1962   *Early Prose and Poetry.* Edited by Carvel Collins. Boston: Little, Brown.

1964   *Faulkner at West Point* (interviews). Edited by Joseph L. Fant and Robert Ashley. New York: Random House.

1966   *Essays Speeches & Public Letters.* Edited by James B. Meriwether. New York: Random House.

1968   *Lion in the Garden: Interviews with William Faulkner 1926–1962.* Edited by James B. Meriwether and Michael Millgate. New York: Random House.

1968   *New Orleans Sketches.* Edited by Carvel Collins. New York: Random House.

1977   *Selected Letters of William Faulkner.* Edited by Joseph Blotner. New York: Random House.

Secondary

The most complete listing of Faulkner's work is Carl Petersen's *Each in Its Ordered Place: A Faulkner Collector's Notebook* (Ann Arbor, Mich.: Ardis, 1975), though James B. Meriwether's *The Literary Career of William Faulkner* (Princeton, N.J.: Princeton University Press, 1961; reissue Columbia, S.C.: University of South Carolina Press, 1971) is indispensable for the record of Faulkner's career it provides in, among many other things, its handlist of Faulkner's manuscripts and his description of their relationship to the published works. See also Meriwether's "The Short Fiction of William Faulkner: A Bibliography," *Proof,* I (1971), 293–329. Though not without many problems, Joseph Blotner's massive two-volume *Faulkner: A Biography* (New York: Random House, 1974) is the only, and indispensable, full-scale treatment of Faulkner's life.

The Faulkner field is the largest by far of any American author. The best—that is, the most sensible—general studies of Faulkner are Michael Millgate's *The Achievement of William Faulkner* (New York: Random House, 1966), and two books by Cleanth Brooks: *William Faulkner: The Yoknapatawpha Country* (New Haven, Conn.: Yale University Press, 1963) and *Toward Yoknapatawpha and Beyond* (New Haven: Yale University Press, 1978). These are the best places to begin. The most reliable guide through the tangled thicket of Faulkner criticism is Thomas L. McHaney's *William Faulkner: A Reference Guide* (New York: G. K. Hall, 1976); the annual summer numbers of the *Mississippi Quarterly,* edited by James B. Meriwether, are devoted to Faulkner, and are also worth consulting.

Shelby Foote

1947   *The Merchant of Bristol* (story). Greenville, Miss.: Levee Press.
1949   *Tournament* (novel). New York: Dial.
1950   *Follow Me Down* (novel). New York: Dial.
1951   *Love in a Dry Season* (novel). New York: Dial.
1952   *Shiloh* (novel). New York: Dial.
1953   *Jordan County* (related stories). New York: Dial.
1958   *The Civil War: A Narrative. Volume I: Fort Sumter to Perryville.* New York: Random House.
1963   *The Civil War: A Narrative. Volume II: Fredericksburg to Meridian.* New York: Random House.
1974   *The Civil War: A Narrative. Volume III: Red River to Appomattox.* New York: Random House.
1977   *September, September* (novel). New York: Random House.

Secondary
The most complete bibliographical listing of Foote's work, and of work about Foote, is James E. Kibler's "Shelby Foote: A Bibliography," in the Fall, 1971, number of the *Mississippi Quarterly.* That issue, edited by James B. Meriwether, is a special issue devoted to study of Foote's work, and is the place to start for discussions of Foote's fiction and history.

William C. Hall

Hall published no books during his lifetime.

Secondary
The only article on Hall is John Q. Anderson, "Mike Hooter: The Making of a Myth," *Southern Folklore Quarterly,* XIX (1955), 90–100.

Barry Hannah

1972 *Geronimo Rex* (novel). New York: Viking.

1973 *Nightwatchmen* (novel). New York: Viking.

1978 *Airships* (stories). New York: Knopf.

Josephine Ayres Haxton (*Ellen Douglas*)

1962 *A Family's Affairs* (novel). Boston: Houghton Mifflin.

1963 *Black Cloud, White Cloud* (stories and novellas). Boston: Houghton Mifflin.

1968 *Where the Dreams Cross* (novel). Boston: Houghton Mifflin.

1969 *Walker Percy's "The Last Gentleman"* (criticism). New York: The Seabury Press.

1973 *Apostles of Light* (novel). Boston: Houghton Mifflin.

Joseph Holt Ingraham
(a highly selective list)

1835 *The South West* (sketches). New York: Harper & Brothers.

1836 *Lafitte* (novel). New York: Harper & Brothers.

1838 *Captain Kyd* (novel). London: E. Lloyd.

1839 *The American Lounger* (tales and sketches). Philadelphia: Lea & Blanchard.

1844 *Arnold; or, The British Spy* (novel). Boston: "Yankee" Office.

1845 *The Knights of Seven Lands* (related tales). Boston: F. Gleason.

1845 *Alice May, and Bruising Bill* (two stories). Boston: Gleason's Publishing Hall.

1855 *The Prince of the House of David* (novel). New York: Pudney and Russell.

1859 *The Pillar of Fire* (novel). New York: Pudney & Russell.

1860 *The Sunny South* (novel). Philadelphia: G. G. Evans.

1860 *The Throne of David* (novel). Philadelphia: G. G. Evans.

Secondary
The most important work on Ingraham is Robert W. Weathersby, III, "Joseph Holt Ingraham: A Critical Introduction to the Man and His Work" (Ph.D. dissertation, University of Tennessee, 1974).

Henry Clay Lewis

1850 *Odd Leaves from the Life of a Louisiana "Swamp Doctor." By Madison Tensas.* Philadelphia: A. Hart.

Secondary
The standard reference work on Lewis is John Q. Anderson, *Louisiana Swamp Doctor: The Life of Henry Clay Lewis / Louisiana Swamp Doctor: The Writings of*

Henry Clay Lewis alias "Madison Tensas, M.D." Baton Rouge: Louisiana State University Press, 1962.

Katherine McDowell (*Sherwood Bonner*)

1875 *The Radical Club* (poem). Boston.
1878 *Like Unto Like* (novel). New York: Harper & Brothers.
1883 *Dialect Tales* (stories). New York: Harper & Brothers.
1884 *Suwanee River Tales* (stories). Boston: Roberts Brothers.
1927 *Gran'mammy* (story). New York: Purdy Press.

Secondary

A brief assessment of Bonner's work and a listing of her publications and manuscripts is in Jean Nosser Biglane, "Sherwood Bonner: A Bibliography of Primary and Secondary Materials," *American Literary Realism*, V (Winter, 1972), 39-60. See also William L. Frank, *Sherwood Bonner*. Boston: Twayne, 1976.

Alexander G. McNutt

McNutt published no books in his lifetime.

Secondary

The only article on McNutt is Elmo Howell, "Governor Alexander G. McNutt of Mississippi: Humorist of the Old Southwest," *Journal of Mississippi History*, XXXV (February, 1973), 153–66.

William Mills

1974 *Watch for the Fox* (poems). Baton Rouge: Louisiana State University Press.
1975 *The Stillness in Moving Things: The World of Howard Nemerov* (criticism). Memphis: Memphis State University Press.
1976 *I Know a Place* (stories). Baton Rouge: The Press of the Nightowl.
1977 *Louisiana Cajuns* (photographs; introductory essay by Mills). Baton Rouge: Louisiana State University Press.

Willie Morris

1965 *The South Today, 100 Years after Appomattox.* New York: Harper & Row.
1967 *North Toward Home* (autobiography). Boston: Houghton Mifflin.
1971 *Good Old Boy: A Delta Boyhood* (reminiscences). New York: Harper & Row.
1971 *Yazoo: Integration in a Deep Southern Town* (social criticism). New York: Harper's Magazine Press.
1973 *The Last of the Southern Girls* (novel). New York: Knopf.
1975 *A Southern Album: Recollections of Some People and Places and Times Gone By* (edited by Irwin Glusker; narrative by Morris). Birmingham, Ala.: Oxmoor House.
1978 *James Jones: A Friendship.* New York: Doubleday.

Eliza Jane Poitevant Nicholson (*Pearl Rivers*)

1873 *Lyrics*. Philadelphia: J. B. Lippincott & Co.
1900 *Four Poems*. N.p.
1900 *Two Poems*. N.p.

Secondary

The standard work on Pearl Rivers is a book that is not readily available: J. H. Harrison's *Pearl Rivers, Publisher of the Picayune* (New Orleans: Department of Education, Tulane University, 1932).

Walker Percy

1961 *The Moviegoer* (novel). New York: Knopf.
1966 *The Last Gentleman* (novel). New York: Farrar, Straus and Giroux.
1971 *Love in the Ruins* (novel). New York: Farrar, Straus and Giroux.
1975 *The Message in the Bottle* (essays). New York: Farrar, Straus and Giroux.
1977 *Lancelot* (novel). New York: Farrar, Straus and Giroux.

William Alexander Percy

1915 *Sappho in Levkas and Other Poems*. New Haven, Conn.: Yale University Press.
1920 *In April Once* (poems). New Haven, Conn.: Yale University Press.
1923 (ed.) *The Poems of Arthur O'Shaughnessy*. New Haven, Conn.: Yale University Press.
1924 *Enzio's Kingdom, and Other Poems*. New Haven, Conn.: Yale University Press.
1930 *Selected Poems*. With a Preface by Llewellyn Jones. New Haven, Conn.: Yale University Press.
1941 *Lanterns on the Levee* (autobiography). New York: Knopf.
1943 *The Collected Poems of William Alexander Percy*. New York: Knopf.
1953 *Of Silence and of Stars* (poems). Edited by Anne Stokes, with a Foreword by Hodding Carter. Greenville, Miss.: Levee Press.

Secondary

See the introduction by Walker Percy to LSU Press's 1973 reprint of *Lanterns on the Levee*.

Thomas Hal Phillips

1950 *The Bitterweed Path*. New York: Rinehart.
1951 *The Golden Lie*. New York: Rinehart.

1952 *Search for a Hero.* New York: Rinehart.
1954 *Kangaroo Hollow.* London: W. H. Allen.
1955 *The Loved and the Unloved.* New York: Harper.

Secondary

The most complete biographical and bibliographical guides to Thomas Hal Phillips is Tomma Nan Hill's "Thomas Hal Phillips: A Bio-Bibliography" (M.A. thesis, Florida State University, 1957), which contains a fairly extensive bibliography, some cursory critical comments in the course of a discussion of the critical reception of the novels as they were published; its most important value is in its biographical information, since that information was gleaned largely through interviews and correspondence with Phillips.

Pearl Rivers. See Eliza Jane Poitevant Nicholson

Irwin Russell

1888 *Poems.* New York: Century Co. A second printing, 1889, includes an additional poem.
1917 *Christmas Night in the Quarters, and Other Poems.* New York: Century Co. Includes the text of *Poems,* plus nine additional poems.

Secondary

The best listing of Russell's work is Laura D. S. Harrell, "A Bibliography of Irwin Russell, with a Biographical Sketch," *The Journal of Mississippi History,* VIII (January, 1946), 3–23.

James Seay

1970 *Let Not Your Hart* (poems). Middletown, Conn.: Wesleyan University Press.
1974 *Water Tables* (poems). Middletown, Conn.: Wesleyan University Press.

J. Edgar Simmons

1957 *Pocahontas and Other Poems.* Williamsburg, Va.: Virginia Gazette.
1968 *Driving to Biloxi* (poems). Baton Rouge: Louisiana State University Press.

Elizabeth Spencer

1948 *Fire in the Morning* (novel). New York: Dodd, Mead.
1952 *This Crooked Way* (novel). New York: Dodd, Mead.

1956 *The Voice at the Back Door* (novel). New York: McGraw-Hill.
1960 *The Light in the Piazza* (novel). New York: McGraw-Hill.
1965 *Knights and Dragons* (novella). New York: McGraw-Hill.
1967 *No Place for an Angel* (novel). New York: McGraw-Hill.
1968 *Ship Island and Other Stories.* New York: McGraw-Hill.
1972 *The Snare* (novel). New York: McGraw-Hill.

Secondary

The most complete bibliographical checklist of both primary and secondary materials dealing with Spencer is Laura Barge's "An Elizabeth Spencer Checklist, 1948 to 1976," *Mississippi Quarterly,* XXIX (Fall, 1976), 569–90.

James Howell Street

1936 *Look Away! A Dixie Notebook.* New York: Viking.
1940 *Oh, Promised Land* (novel). New York: Dial.
1941 *The Biscuit Eater* (novella). New York: Dial.
1941 *In My Father's House* (novel). New York: Dial.
1942 *Tap Roots* (novel). New York: Dial.
1944 *By Valour and Arms* (novel). New York: Dial.
1945 *The Gauntlet* (novel). Garden City, N.Y.: Doubleday, Doran.
1945 *Short Stories* by James Street. New York: Dial.
1949 (with James Childers) *Tomorrow We Reap* (novel). New York: Dial.
1950 *Mingo Dabney* (novel). New York: Dial.
1951 *The High Calling* (novel). Garden City, N.Y.: Doubleday.
1953 *The Civil War* (informal history). New York: Dial.
1953 *The Velvet Doublet* (novel). Garden City, N.Y.: Doubleday.
1954 *The Revolutionary War* (informal history). New York: Dial.
1954 *Good-bye, My Lady* (novel). Philadelphia: J. B. Lippincott.
1955 *James Street's South* (essays). Garden City, N.Y.: Doubleday.
1956 *Captain Little Ax* (novel). Philadelphia: J. B. Lippincott.
1960 (with Don Tracy) *Pride of Possession* (novel). New York: J. B. Lippincott.

Secondary

A listing of Street's novels, short stories, and articles appears in Ruth Cooper, "James Street: A Biographical and Bibliographical Study," *Notes on Mississippi Writers,* IX (Spring, 1976), 10–23.

Cid Ricketts Sumner

1938 *Ann Singleton* (novel). New York: D. Appleton-Century.
1946 *Quality* (novel). Indianapolis: Bobbs-Merrill.
1948 *Tammy Out of Time* (novel). Indianapolis: Bobbs-Merrill.
1949 *But the Morning Will Come* (novel). Indianapolis: Bobbs-Merrill.
1951 *Sudden Glory* (novel). Indianapolis: Bobbs-Merrill.

1953   *The Hornbeam Tree* (novel). Indianapolis: Bobbs-Merrill.
1957   *Traveller in the Wilderness* (description). New York: Harper.
1957   *A View from the Hill* (novel). Englewood Cliffs, N.J.: Prentice-Hall.
1959   *Tammy, Tell Me True* (novel). Indianapolis: Bobbs-Merrill.
1961   *Christmas Gift* (story). New York: Longmans, Green.
1964   *Withdraw Thy Foot* (novel). New York: Coward-McCann.
1964   *Saddle Your Dreams* (novel). Indianapolis: Bobbs-Merrill.
1965   *Tammy in Rome* (novel). New York: Coward-McCann.

Secondary
An introduction to Sumner's life and novels is Betty Evans Gurner, "A Bio-Bibliography of Cid Ricketts Sumner and Tom Person" (Library science essay, University of Mississippi, 1971).

Margaret Walker. *See* Margaret Walker Alexander

Eudora Welty

1941   *A Curtain of Green* (stories). Garden City, N.Y.: Doubleday, Doran.
1942   *The Robber Bridegroom* (short novel). Garden City, N.Y.: Doubleday, Doran.
1943   *The Wide Net and Other Stories.* New York: Harcourt, Brace.
1946   *Delta Wedding* (novel). New York: Harcourt, Brace.
1948   *Music From Spain* (story). Greenville, Miss.: Levee Press.
1949   *The Golden Apples* (related stories). New York: Harcourt, Brace.
1950   *Short Stories* (essay). New York: Harcourt, Brace.
1954   *Selected Stories of Eudora Welty.* New York: Modern Library. [Note: Contains all of the stories in *A Curtain of Green* and *The Wide Net.*]
1954   *The Ponder Heart* (short novel). New York: Harcourt, Brace.
1955   *The Bride of the Innisfallen and Other Stories.* New York: Harcourt, Brace.
1957   *Place in Fiction* (essay). New York: House of Books. Limited edition of 300 copies.
1962   *Three Papers on Fiction* (essays). Northampton, Mass.: Smith College.
1964   *The Shoe Bird* (children's story). New York: Harcourt, Brace & World.
1965   *Thirteen Stories.* Selected and edited by Ruth M. Vande Kieft. New York: Harvest Books.
1969   *A Sweet Devouring* (autobiographical essay). New York: Albondocani Press. Limited edition of 176 copies.
1970   *Losing Battles* (novel). New York: Random House.
1970   *A Flock of Guinea Hens Seen from a Car* (poem). New York: Albondocani Press.
1971   *One Time, One Place: Mississippi in the Depression, A Snapshot Album* (photographs). New York: Random House.
1972   *The Optimist's Daughter* (short novel). New York: Random House.
1977   *The Eye of the Story* (essays). New York: Random House.

Secondary

Noel Polk's "A Eudora Welty Checklist," *Mississippi Quarterly*, XXVI (Fall, 1973), 663–93, is the most complete listing of works by Welty, though his listing of secondary material has been largely superseded by Victor Thompson's *Eudora Welty: A Reference Guide*, (New York: G. K. Hall, 1976). The most useful study of Miss Welty's work is still Ruth M. Vande Kieft's *Eudora Welty*, (New York: Twayne, 1963), and there are some fine essays in the Fall, 1973, *Mississippi Quarterly*, which was devoted to Welty, edited by Lewis Simpson.

James Whitehead

1966   *Domains* (poems). Baton Rouge: Louisiana State University Press.
1971   *Joiner* (novel). New York: Knopf.

Secondary

See Marda Burton's "An Interview with James Whitehead," *Notes on Mississippi Writers*, V (Winter, 1972), 71–79.

Tennessee Williams

1944   (with others) *Five Young Poets*. New York: New Directions.
1945   *The Glass Menagerie*. New York: Random House.
1945   *Battle of Angels*. New York: New Directions.
1946   *27 Wagons Full of Cotton and Other One-Act Plays*. Norfolk, Conn.: New Directions.
1947   *A Streetcar Named Desire*. New York: New Directions.
1947   *You Touched Me* (with Donald Windham). New York: S. French.
1948   *American Blues: Five Short Plays*. New York: Dramatists Play Service.
1948   *One Arm and Other Stories*. New York: New Directions.
1948   *Summer and Smoke*. New York: New Directions. Revised as *The Eccentricities of a Nightingale, and Summer and Smoke*. New York: New Directions, 1964.
1950   *The Roman Spring of Mrs. Stone* (novel). New York: New Directions.
1951   *The Rose Tattoo*. New York: New Directions.
1951   *I Rise in Flame, Cried the Phoenix*. New York: New Directions.
1953   *Camino Real*. Norfolk, Conn.: New Directions. Revision of "Ten Blocks on the Camino Real," in *American Blues*.
1954   *Hard Candy: A Book of Stories*. New York: New Directions.
1955   *Cat on a Hot Tin Roof*. New York: New Directions.
1955   *Lord Byron's Love Letter*. New York: Riccordi. Libretto of the play with music by Raffaello de Banfield.
1956   *In the Winter of Cities: Poems*. Norfolk, Conn.: New Directions.

1956 *Baby Doll*. Screenplay incorporating "27 Wagons Full of Cotton" and "The Long Stay Cut Short." New York: New Directions.

1958 *Orpheus Descending, with Battle of Angels*. New York: New Directions. Revision of *Battle of Angels*, produced in Boston in 1940.

1958 *Garden District: Something Unspoken, Suddenly Last Summer*. New York: New Directions. Screenplay, with Gore Vidal, *Suddenly Last Summer*, 1959.

1958 *A Perfect Analysis Given by a Parrot; Comedy in One Act*. New York: Dramatists Play Service.

1959 *Sweet Bird of Youth*. New York: New Directions.

1960 *The Fugitive Kind: Original Play Title: Orpheus Descending* (screenplay). New York: New American Library.

1960 *Three Players of a Summer Game and Other Stories*. London: Secker and Warburg.

1960 *Period of Adjustment: High Point Over a Cavern: A Serious Comedy*. New York: New Directions.

1962 *The Night of the Iguana*. New York: New Directions.

1964 *Grand* (stories). New York: House of Books.

1964 *The Milk Train Doesn't Stop Here Anymore*. Norfolk, Conn.: New Directions.

1966 *The Knightly Quest: A Novella and Four Short Stories*. New York: New Directions. Enlarged edition, *The Knightly Quest: A Novella and Twelve Short Stories*. London: Secker and Warburg, 1968.

1967 *The Mutilated* (play). New York: Dramatists Play Service.

1967 *Slapstick Tragedy (The Mutilated and The Gnädiges Fräulein)*. New York: New Directions.

1968 *Kingdom of Earth: The Seven Descents of Myrtle*. New York: New Directions.

1969 *The Two Character Play*. New York: New Directions. Published as *Out Cry*. New York: New Directions, 1973.

1969 *In the Bar of a Tokyo Hotel*. New York: Dramatists Play Service.

1970 *Dragon Country: A Book of Plays*. New York: New Directions.

1972 *Small Craft Warnings*. New York: New Directions.

1974 *Eight Mortal Ladies Possessed* (stories). New York: New Directions.

1975 *Moise and the World of Reason* (novel). New York: Simon & Schuster.

1975 *Tennessee Williams: Memoirs*. Garden City, N.Y.: Doubleday.

1976 *Tennessee Williams' Letters to Donald Windham*: 1940-1965. Edited by Donald Windham. New York: Holt, Rinehart and Winston.

1977 *Androgyne, Mon Amour* (poems). New York: New Directions.

Secondary

Signi Lenea Falk's *Tennessee Williams* (New Haven: College and University Press, 1961) is a general introduction which contains a bibliography. A list of Williams's books through 1972 appears in James Vinson (ed.), *Contemporary Dramatists* (New York: St. Martin's Press, 1973), 825–28. Secondary bibliographies include Nadine Dony, "Tennessee Williams: A Selected Bibliography," *Modern Drama*, I (1958), 181–91; Charles A. Carpenter, Jr., and Elizabeth Cook, "Addenda to 'Tennessee Williams: A Selected Bibliography,' " *Modern Drama*, II (1959), 220–23; and Delma E. Presley, "Tennessee Williams: 25 Years of Criticism," *Bulletin of Bibliography and Magazine Notes*, XXX (January–March, 1973), 21–29. In the absence of a full biography, see Nancy M. Tischler, *Tennessee Williams: Rebellious Puritan* (New York: Citadel Press, 1961).

Richard Wright

1938   *Uncle Tom's Children: Four Novellas.* New York: Harper.
1938   *Uncle Tom's Children: Five Long Stories.* New York: Harper.
1938   *Bright and Morning Star* (story). New York: International Publishers.
1940   *Native Son* (novel). New York: Harper.
1940   *How "Bigger" Was Born; the Story of Native Son* (nonfiction). New York: Harper.
1941   (with Paul Green) *Native Son (The Biography of a Young American): A Play in Ten Scenes.* New York: Harper.
1941   *12 Million Black Voices: A Folk History of the Negro in the United States.* New York: Viking.
1945   *Black Boy: A Record of Childhood and Youth* (autobiography). New York: Harper.
1953   *The Outsider* (novel). New York: Harper.
1954   *Savage Holiday* (novel). New York: Avon.
1954   *Black Power: A Record of Reactions in a Land of Pathos* (nonfiction). New York: Harper.
1956   *The Color Curtain: A Report on the Bandung Conference* (nonfiction). Cleveland and New York: World.
1957   *Pagan Spain* (reportage). New York: Harper.
1957   *White Man, Listen!* (nonfiction). Garden City, N.Y.: Doubleday.
1958   *The Long Dream* (novel). Garden City, N.Y.: Doubleday.
1961   *Eight Men* (stories). Cleveland and New York: World.
1963   *Lawd Today* (novel). New York: Walker.
1968   *Letters to Joe C. Brown.* Edited by Thomas Knipp. Kent, Ohio: Kent State University Libraries.
1977   *American Hunger* (autobiography; continuation of *Black Boy*). New York: Harper & Row.

Secondary

See Constance Webb's *Richard Wright: A Biography* (New York: Putnam, 1968), and Michel Fabre's *The Unfinished Quest of Richard Wright*, tr. Isabel Barzun (New York: William Morrow, 1973) for biographical information. The bibliographical checklist in Fabre's book is the most comprehensive to date.

Stark Young

1906   *The Blind Man at the Window* (poems). New York: Grafton Press.
1906   *Guenevere: A Play in Five Acts.* New York: Grafton Press.
1911   (ed). *The English Humorists of the Eighteenth Century, by W. M. Thackeray.* Boston, New York: Ginn.
1912   *Addio, Madretta and Other Plays.* Chicago: Charles H. Sergel.
1921   *Three One-Act Plays: Madretta, At the Shrine, Addio.* Cincinnati: Stewart Kidd.
1923   *The Flower in Drama: A Book of Papers on the Theatre.* New York: Scribner's.
1924   *The Colonnade* (play). New York: Theatre Arts, Inc.
1924   *The Three Fountains* (essay). New York: Scribner's.
1924   *The Three Fountains.* New York: Scribner's.
1925   *The Saint: A Play in Four Acts.* New York: Boni and Liveright.
1925   *Glamour: Essays on the Art of the Theatre.* New York and London: Scribner's.
1925   *Sweet Times and the Blue Policeman* (plays for children). New York: Henry Holt.
1926   *Theatre Practice* (essays). New York: Scribner's.
1926   *Encaustics* (essays). New York: New Republic.
1926   *Heaven Trees* (fiction). New York: Scribner's.
1927   (trans) *Mandragola*, by N. Machiavelli. New York: Macauley.
1927   *The Theatre* (essays). New York: George H. Doran.
1928   *The Torches Flare* (fiction). New York: Scribner's.
1929   *River House* (novel). New York: Scribner's.
1930   *The Street of the Islands* (nonfiction). New York: Scribner's.
1934   *So Red the Rose* (novel). New York: Scribner's.
1935   *Feliciana* (sketches). New York: Scribner's.
1937   (ed). *Southern Treasury of Life and Literature.* New York: Scribner's.
1939   (trans) *The Sea-Gull*, by A. Chekhov. New York: Scribner's.
1941   (trans) *The Three Sisters*, by A. Chekhov. New York: S. French.
1942   *Artemise: In Three Acts.* Austin, Tex.: Van Boeckmann-Jones.
1947   (trans) *The Cherry Orchard*, by A. Chekhov. New York: S. French.
1948   *Immortal Shadows: A Book of Dramatic Criticism.* New York: Scribner's.
1951   *The Pavilion: Of People and Times Remembered, of Stories and Places.* New York: Scribner's.

Secondary

The most important source of information about Young's life and work is John Pilkington (ed.), *Stark Young: A Life in the Arts: Letters, 1900–1962*, two volumes, Baton Rouge: Louisiana State University Press, 1975. The most complete bibliographical listing of Young's work, though now badly out of date, is Bedford

Thurman's "Stark Young: A Bibliography of his Writings with A Selective Index to his Criticism of the Arts" (Ph.D. dissertation, Cornell University, 1954).

II. Further Studies

This is a highly selective list of sources for those who wish to pursue the study of Mississippi writing.

A. Bibliographies

Chambers, Moreau Browne Congleton. "A Check List of Mississippi Imprints, 1865–1870." Ph.D. dissertation, Catholic University of America, 1968.

Colliflower, Charles E. "A Check-List of Mississippi Imprints from 1831 through 1840." Ph.D. dissertation, Catholic University of America, 1950.

Lowe, Edna Haley. "Mississippi Bibliography." M.A. thesis, University of Mississippi, 1938.

McMurtrie, Douglas Crawford. *A Bibliography of Mississippi Imprints, 1798–1830.* Beauvoir Community, Miss.: Book Farm, 1945.

Mississippi Library Commission. *Mississippiana: Union Catalog.* Jackson: Mississippi Library Commission, 1971.

Thompson, Louise K. "Mississippi Writers, A Preliminary Hand-List." M.A. thesis, University of Mississippi, 1956.

B. Criticism and Literary History

Rouse, Sarah A. "Literature 1890-1970." *A History of Mississippi*, Vol. II. Edited by Richard Aubrey McLemore. Hattiesburg: University & College Press of Mississippi, 1973, pp. 446–76.

Schumpert, Mary Frances. "Mississippi Fiction and Verse since 1900." M.A. thesis, University of Mississippi, 1931.

Notes on Mississippi Writers, edited by Hilton Anderson, is a journal specializing in Mississippi literature. Readers are advised to consult this journal for information about and studies of Mississippi writers, particularly the minor ones, who don't often get treated in the less specialized journals.

NOTE: See also Section III of this bibliography, and the introductions and editorial apparatus of the books by Hudson, listed in II-C.

C. Other Anthologies of Interest

Deavours, Ernestine Clayton. *The Mississippi Poets.* Memphis: E. H. Clarke & Brother, 1922.

Hudson, Arthur Palmer. *Folksongs of Mississippi and Their Background.* Chapel Hill: University of North Carolina Press, 1936.

———. *Humor of the Old Deep South*. New York: Macmillan, 1936.

James, Alice, ed. *Mississippi Verse*. Chapel Hill: University of North Carolina Press, 1934.

Miller, Russell H., Jr. "Before the White Man Came: A Collection of Indian Legends from the Choctaw Nation." M.A. thesis, University of Mississippi, 1927.

Phillips, Robert L., Jr., ed. *Antebellum Mississippi Stories*. Jackson: Mississippi Library Commission, 1976.

Ruffin, Paul, ed. *Mississippi Poets*. Jackson: Mississippi Library Commission, 1976.

III. Mississippi Writers in Context

From 1975–1977 the Mississippi Library Commission and Mississippi State University, funded by a grant from the National Endowment for the Humanities, sponsored an ambitious project called *Mississippi Writers in Context*, under the general leadership of Professors Robert L. Phillips, Jr., and Joseph E. Stockwell, Jr. The project consisted of six public television programs featuring well-known literary scholars and authors in discussions of Mississippi's literary heritage, and of a series of pamphlets focusing on numerous Mississippi authors and books. The pamphlets, published in Jackson by the Mississippi Library Commission, are listed here for their obvious interest to readers of this anthology.

A. General

Antebellum Mississippi Stories. Edited by Robert L. Phillips, Jr. (1976). An anthology.

A Climate for Genius. Edited by Robert L. Phillips, Jr. (1976). Transcripts of six television programs, featuring discussions by Louis D. Rubin, Jr., Lewis P. Simpson, Shelby Foote, Ellen Douglas, Alice Walworth Graham, Hodding Carter III, T. D. Young, Margaret Walker Alexander, Blyden Jackson, Peggy Prenshaw, and Robert L. Phillips, Jr.

Mississippi Poets. Edited by Paul Ruffin (1976). An anthology.

Mississippi Short Story Writers. Louis E. Dollarhide (1976). Discussions of William Faulkner, Eudora Welty, Ellen Douglas, Charles East, Elizabeth Spencer, Robert Canzoneri, Berry Morgan, and Gordon Weaver.

B. Special Studies

Sherwood Bonner. Betty Hearn (1976).

Borden Deal. James Waddell (1976).

Ellen Douglas. Joe Stockwell (1977).

John Falkner. E. O. Hawkins (1977).

William Faulkner: An Introduction. Daniel G. Hise (1976).

   An Introduction to "Absalom, Absalom!" Walter Everett (1977).

An Introduction to William Faulkner's "Go Down, Moses." Tom Brown (1976).

An Introduction to William Faulkner's "Light in August." Gary Stringer (1976).

An Introduction to William Faulkner's "The Sound and the Fury." William W. Bonney (1976).

Shelby Foote. Robert L. Phillips, Jr. (1977).

Barry Hannah. Jesse McCartney (1977).

Walker Percy. William A. Sullivan, Jr. (1977).

William Alexander Percy: Lanterns on the Levee. Thomas J. Richardson (1977).

Irwin Russell. James W. Webb (1976).

Elizabeth Spencer. Hilton Anderson (1976).

James Street. Frances Tyler (1976).

Eudora Welty. Michael Kreyling (1976).

An Introduction to Eudora Welty's "The Golden Apples." Robert L. Phillips, Jr. (1977).

An Introduction to Eudora Welty's "Losing Battles." Gayle Goodin (1976).

An Introduction to Eudora Welty's "The Optimist's Daughter." Peggy Whitman Prenshaw (1977).

Ben Ames Williams. Brenda S. Stockwell (1977).

Tennessee Williams. Sarah A. Rouse (1976).

Wirt Williams. Gay Chow (1976).

Richard Wright. Roy Hudson (1977).

An Introduction to Richard Wright's "Native Son." Johnny E. Tolliver (1976).

Stark Young. John Pilkington (1976).

Index

Titles

549